Historically Planned Economies

A Guide to the Data

Historically Planned Economies

A Guide to the Data

Paul Marer
Janos Arvay
John O'Connor
Martin Schrenk
Daniel Swanson

The World Bank
Washington, D.C.

This publication has been compiled by the Socio-Economic Data Division of the World Bank's International Economics Department. The World Bank does not accept responsibility for the accuracy or completeness of this publication. The findings, interpretations, and conclusions expressed in this publication are those of the authors and should not be attributed in any manner to the World Bank, to its affiliated organizations, or to the members of its Board of Executive Directors or the countries they represent.

The material in this publication is copyrighted. Requests for permission to reproduce portions of it should be sent to the Office of the Publisher at the address shown in the copyright notice above. The World Bank encourages dissemination of its work and will normally give permission promptly and, when the reproduction is for noncommercial purposes, without asking a fee. Permission to copy portions for classroom use is granted through the Copyright Clearance Center, 27 Congress Street, Salem, Massachusetts 01970, U.S.A.

The complete backlist of publications from the World Bank is shown in the annual *Index of Publications*, which contains an alphabetical title list and indexes of subjects, authors, and countries and regions. The latest edition is available free of charge from Distribution Unit, Office of the Publisher, The World Bank, 1818 H Street, N.W., Washington, D.C. 20433, U.S.A., or from Publications, The World Bank, 66, avenue d'Iéna, 75116 Paris, France.

Library of Congress Cataloging-in-Publication Data

Historically planned economies: a guide to the data / Paul Marer ...
[et al.].
    p. cm.
   ISBN 0-8213-2147-1
   1. Central planning—Communist countries—Statistical methods.
  2. Communist countries—Economic policy—Statistical methods.
  I. Marer, Paul. II. International Bank for Reconstruction and
Development.
HC704.H48 1992
338.9'009'1717—dc20   92-17667
                                     CIP
                                     Rev.

Title HISTORICALLY PLANNED ECONOMIES :
A GUIDE TO THE DATA

Author

Pub./
Prod.   World Bank

Ed.

Series
Ser. St./
#/Date   Yr./Vol. 1992

ISBN/ISSN 0-8213-2147-1

LC Cd#

Cat/Item/Sub.#

Int. Use   FPC PW BUS

Binding/
Mat. Format

SAN:

Ship

SAN:

Bill

SAN
Supl.   Direct
Inst.

Spec.   2/22/93
Inst.

Ord. F23-1064
No.
List $24.95
Pr.
Ext.
Pr.

Order
Date 1/15/93

Order Quantity

1

Contents

Boxes in the Text

Text Tables

Global Tables

Comparator and Basic Tables

Preface

Recent economic policy changes in Eastern Europe and the Soviet Union, and the high-profile efforts of governments around the globe to implement market-oriented reforms, have stimulated worldwide interest in the economic performance of what were once thought of as centrally planned economies. Because of their different economic and statistical systems, efforts to assess the economic performance and financial flows of these countries have been frustrated by the practical problem of finding reliable data and grappling with conceptual problems of converting this information to comparable terms in market economies.

Historically Planned Economies: A Guide to the Data, hereafter referred to as the Guide, is an attempt to address these problems in a rapidly changing environment where new political, economic, and statistical systems are overtaking some of the events and data in this document. Accordingly, most of the Guide will need to be revised; and the Guide can only be a work in progress.

The first part of the document, the Primer, acquaints the newcomer with historically planned economies (HPEs); explores how they differ from market economies; and flags statistical issues that are important to the positioning of HPEs in a global comparison of economic and social conditions. The second part of the document, Global Focus, presents HPE data in tables for comparative analysis, drawing largely from published World Bank and UN sources but with some previously unpublished estimates for HPEs; these data offer, for now, what the authors regard as the best available basis for international comparisons, and a benchmark for comparing and contrasting alternative estimates.

The third part of the document, Country Focus, explores issues common among HPEs but not to market economies. It provides country-specific details on how data are molded during the transition process and cites country examples of basic data problems. It also explains adjustments to the data made by national authorities and external experts, and highlights differing methods used by published data sources to convert national data to dollars. Tables are used to highlight alternative estimates for key concepts and other complete accounts and time series. Part 4, Technical Notes, explains data sources and methods, and deviations from stated expectations. Throughout the Guide, the discussion of common issues makes a dichotomy between the consequences of central planning as a system in which prices have no allocative function, and effects on statistical systems ranging from methodological choices to biases in favor of reporting plan fulfillment.

Although new information on these economies is surfacing daily, many basic data are still difficult to obtain, and for some countries remain largely unavailable. Moreover, a considerable lag in reporting results from the standardization and review processes required by international and local experts to ensure consistency and comparability. The organization of this information in the Guide remains tentative. Thus, the Guide is neither comprehensive nor definitive, nor is it fully up to date. Instead, at this stage, it aims mainly at bringing salient issues to the surface for discussion and at improving the quality and completeness of the database. In this way, it is an evolving working tool, to be strengthened and improved through an interactive process involving feedback between the users and the producers of these statistics.

This document has been prepared at the initiative of the Socialist Economies Reform and Socio-Economic Data Divisions of the World Bank, with the assistance of outside consultants.

A workshop held at the World Bank for the authors and outside experts in February 1991 (see acknowledgment page) initiated a feedback process to address weaknesses and gaps in the document. This exchange resulted in numerous changes and established a channel for many of the experts to continue providing input and guidance for future drafts. Recipients of the current Guide are invited to do the same. Comments may be sent to the Chief, Socio-Economic Data Division, World Bank.

Acknowledgments

The principal authors of this document are Paul Marer, Janos Arvay, John C. O'Connor, Dan Swanson, and Martin Schrenk. Senior contributors included Boris Blazic-Metzner and Jong-goo Park, and other staff of the Socio-Economic Data Division of the International Economics Department and the Socialist Economies Reform Unit of the Country Economics Department of the World Bank. Thomas Kearney and David Stewart drafted text on the environment and debt, respectively. Others provided background texts, notably Anthony Boote, Richard Kaufman, and David Cieslikowski.

The database, tables, and technical notes were produced by Samuel Olayinka, K. Vijayalakshmi, and Cliff Papik, with help from Zlatko Kovach. Computer programming was done by Young Kim and Reza Farivari, with ongoing support from the International Economics Department's Systems Division. Administrative coordination of the project was assured by Estela Zamora. Financial contributions were made by the divisions mentioned above, as well as the World Bank Office of the Publisher.

Many inside and outside the World Bank provided useful comments and helped give shape to the document in its developmental stages, notably, the participants at a workshop held in Washington in February 1991, who included Thad Alton, Abram Bergson, Derek Blades, Josef van Brabant, Patricia Capdevielle, Keith Crane, Bruno Dallago, Edwin Dean, Joseph Duncan, Maurice Ernst, Alan Gelb, Alan Heston, Barry Kostinsky, Gregor Lazarcik, Klaus Loenning, Jacky Sayolle, James Noren, Gur Ofer, John Pitzer, and Leszek Zienkowski.

Most of these workshop participants provided input throughout the life of the project. Valuable comments also came from a number of Bank staff and others, notably Ramesh Chander, John Holsen, D.C. Rao, Claus Wittich, Mario Nuti, Martha de Melo, Stephen Gardner, and David Craig.

The text was edited by Bruce Ross-Larson and Vince McCollough; Joost Polak did the final editing; Elizabeth Crayford and Kenneth Hale coordinated publication; and Oty Harun and Michael W. Rollins provided desktop publishing services.

The cutoff date for all data is April 30, 1992.

This document relies on work done in 1991 and does not take into account information received and significant changes in some of these economies during the first half of 1992.

Initials, Acronyms, and Abbreviations

ACDA	U.S. Arms Control and Disarmament Agency
BLS	U.S. Bureau of Labor Statistics
BoP	Balance of Payments
CIA	Central Intellligence Agency
c.i.f.	Cost, insurance, and freight
CMEA	Council for Mutual Economic Assistance. Member countries included
CPE	Centrally planned economy
CSOs	Central Statistical Offices
DAC	Development Assistance Committee of the Organisation for Economic Co-operation and Development
DM	Deutsche mark
EBRD	European Bank for Reconstruction and Development
EC	European Communities
ECE	Economic Commission for Europe
EEC	European Economic Community
ECEP	Eastern and Central European Program
EIA	Environmental impact assessment
ER	Exchange rate
ERDI	Exchange rate deviation index: the ratio of the exchange rate to purchasing power parity.
ESCAP	Economic and Social Commission for Asia and the Pacific
EUROSTAT	European Statistical Office
f.o.b.	free on board
FSO	Federal Statistical Office
FTO	Foreign Trade Organization
GATT	General Agreement on Tariffs and Trade
GDP	Gross domestic product
GNFS	Goods and Nonfactor Services
GNP	Gross national product
HDR	Human Development Report
HPE	Historically planned economy
HUF	Hungarian forint
IBEC	International Bank for Economic Cooperation (CMEA)
IBRD	International Bank for Reconstruction and Development
ICP	UN International Comparison Program
IDA	International Development Association
IFS	IMF *International Financial Statistics*
ILO	International Labour Organisation
IMF	International Monetary Fund
Kg	Kilogram (2.2 pounds)
LCU	Local currency unit
LRB	Local ruble
LWI	LWI International
ME	Market economies, also referred to as western economies

MPS	Material product system
NBER	U.S. National Bureau of Economic Research
NCUs	National currency units
NMP	Net material product (a socialist concept of national accounts)
NNP	Net national product
OECD	Organisation for Economic Co-operation and Development
OET	Other economies in transition
PIT	Physical indicator tables
PPP	Purchasing power parities. These are the rates of currency conversion that equalize the purchasing power of different currencies.
RB	Ruble
TR	Transferable ruble
SNA	System of national accounts
UN	United Nations
UNCTAD	United Nations Conference on Trade and Development
UNDP	United Nations Development Programme
VAT	Value added tax
WDR	World Development Report
WHO	World Health Organization

Part 1. Primer on Data Issues

Chapter 1. Introduction

Most economies with a legacy of central planning (here called historically planned economies or HPEs) are changing in fundamental ways. They are moving toward market-oriented economic policies and institutions—often in the context of remarkable political liberalization. That transition is generating demand for data on HPEs comparable to those on other economies.

This Guide aims at helping analysts and policymakers understand HPEs in Eastern Europe and elsewhere, as well as their transition to a market economy. It explores basic systemic and statistical issues that impinge on global economic comparisons. It explains divergent methodologies and interpretations of historical and recent data. And it presents alternative sources and methods to those in traditional World Bank statistical publications. However, this Guide and the data in it are necessarily transitional. Since new information about the HPEs is continually emerging, this Guide can only be a work in progress.

The term "historically planned" recognizes the lineage of central planning as it evolved in the Soviet Union. It also recognizes that most HPEs are transforming their economic and statistical systems. HPEs followed a Marxist-Leninist sociopolitical tradition and, with few exceptions, adopted central planning models at some time. Features of this model include public ownership; a system of physical and financial balances; planned allocation, production, and distribution; and noncompetitive trade and industrial organization. A few HPEs began to deviate from this model some time ago—Yugoslavia in the late 1940s and Hungary in the 1960s—but most have experienced change only recently.

In this Guide, HPEs are loosely defined by convention, by self-identification, and by a legacy of central economic planning. They are distinguished from other economies in transition, which include poor countries with only small modern sectors, and from other high-, middle-, and low-income economies. These comparator groups are defined in chapter 5. The term market economies refers here to an alternative model, not to a specific group of countries. The Guide text uses the pre-dissolution country designations for the USSR and the German Democratic Republic, while the tables refer to them as the former USSR and the former German Democratic Republic.

Key statistical issues

There are many statistical problems in comparing HPEs and market economies. A major one stems from the changing role of prices in the economy. In both HPEs and market economies, prices generally clear consumer markets and measure value. But in most HPEs, where until recently prices were administered, their purpose was to meet planned financial balances and to transfer income, and they did not usually reflect resource scarcity. The same is true for measures of value. Analysts and policymakers from market economies often struggle to make sense of administered prices and the value of production and income in the context of a global economy, where markets dominate, and during transition.

Almost as important are the different HPE approaches to economic monitoring and information. For their national accounts, most HPEs adopted the material product system (MPS), which differs in method, coverage, and classification from the UN system of national accounts (SNA) that market economies use. Despite the construction of "fixed" analytical bridges between the two systems (which work mostly in a technical sense), "flexible" bridges are still evolving in areas that address fundamental systemic differences, such as the relative worth of goods and services.

The type and quality of socioeconomic data gathered and disseminated in each system depend on the needs of its economic agents, including government. Information collected by central statistical offices (CSOs) hinges on the flexibility and centrality of decisionmaking and on the tools of economic intervention. On the reporting side, incentives to provide information (truthfully or at all) are determined by whether the authorities reward or penalize, based on the information provided, those who submit the data. In these areas, planned economies and market economies diverged widely and perhaps most in that the reporting of statistics in HPEs and the central control of enterprise performance relied on the same set on primary data. In short, the information system and the system of rewards and penalties are not separated, a precondition for accurate information. Even with the genuine openness now found in many HPEs, it will be some time before the sources and users of the information are free of this legacy.

The economic and statistical systems of HPEs have become unsynchronized during transition. Switching from the Material Product System to the System of National Accounts, gathering basic data from surveys instead of administrative records, adopting price indexes appropriate to market economies—all such statistical changes may occur before or after the adoption of the relevant market mechanisms.

Proper synchronization of economic transition and changing statistical practices in HPEs would relieve some problems of the basic incomparability of data. Even so, new problems, such as statistical inconsistencies with historical data series and new incentives to misreport, may emerge. Because such problems complicate the analysis of structural changes in HPEs and their placement in global comparisons, the statistical systems of HPEs also need monitoring during transition.

The Guide

But no monitoring effort can freeze the rapid changes in HPEs long enough to document and publish them definitively. Thus, the Guide is inevitably to be overtaken by events, which are, at best, reflected here through the end of 1991. With all its caveats, the Guide responds to a demand for comparable data and is intended to promote wider discussion of sources and methods, and to encourage estimates to be updated.

The Guide is divided into four parts. Part 1, the primer, introduces the newcomer to systemic and statistical issues affecting HPE data in global comparisons. It presents a stylized model of the system of traditional central planning (chapter 2) to give the context for the main statistical issues affecting comparisons of historical and recent data (chapters 3 and 4). Part 2, a Global Focus, provides, in a standard format, data tables on social and economic topics. The Global Tables show internationally comparable data by topic for intertemporal (benchmark years only) and cross-country analysis. These data, drawn mostly from published reports of the World Bank and other international agencies, are presented in tables similar to those in the World Bank's annual *World Development Report*. (New York: Oxford University Press).

Part 3, a Country Focus, explains, and documents in detail the differences between the national accounts conventions of the SNA and the MPS and adjustments by recognized experts to national data, including international transactions. It then shows how, and why, different estimates for a statistical indicator can be reported even by experts who seem to agree on broad methodology. These alternative estimates are presented in the Comparator Tables.

For a detailed presentation of the time series (1970–90), by country, the Basic Tables follow.

In Part 4, technical notes cover the basic data presented in Parts 1-3 and explain the standard sources and methods for compiling data, focusing on statistical approaches common to most HPEs. They also include footnotes to tables, which are either general or country-specific: country practices for the MPS and the SNA are discussed in the latter.

The Guide focuses on national accounting and foreign trade indicators, including how administered prices and HPE inflation accounting affect perceptions and comparability of economic structure and growth. It also discusses how to convert key measures of income, such as GNP per capita, to a common numeraire (such as dollars) and the effect of that choice on international comparisons. Another key issue is how to measure the level and direction of foreign trade, given the use of a nonconvertible and accounting currency numeraire (the transferable ruble or TR) among the main HPEs in the Council for Mutual Economic Assistance (CMEA). The transferable ruble was inconsistently valued by the individual HPEs until the entire CMEA apparatus was abandoned at the end of 1990. Until then, a tangle of multiple exchange rates and special trade and settlement arrangements had evolved among CMEA members, which precluded meaningful intra-regional and international comparisons of the prices and values of goods and services exchanged. Uncertainties about how to value much of the trade among CMEA members had much to do with the collapse of this trade and the CMEA in 1991.

The Guide touches lightly on other international transactions statistics (such as foreign debt) and also on domestic financial accounts. International guidelines tend to be less precise in these areas—and significant differences arise even among market economies. A special issue for HPEs concerns the reporting (and valuation) of financial claims among members of the CMEA. Social indicators evidence fewer systematic issues of international comparability between HPEs and other economies. Wages and employment are the main exception and deserve more attention. The one aspect that is taken up is the implication—for comparative analysis—of a relatively narrow wage distribution in HPEs across sectors, despite the relative scarcity of certain skills and variations in productivity.

It is generally recognized that HPEs have addressed environmental issues inadequately because central planners have given little thought to the sustainable use of natural resources. The Guide approaches this issue mainly through the measurement and interpretation of energy consumption in HPEs.

For the near term, meaningful analyses of HPEs will depend heavily on going beyond the generalities in the Primer and will require detailed knowledge of the countries. And comparing their economic and statistical systems will remain as much art as science.

As a starting point for statistical comparisons, a brief overview of the framework of central planning shows the close relationship between the economic systems of HPEs and their statistical conventions and procedures.

Central planning cannot be traced back to a theoretical blueprint; it exists neither in the writings of Marx nor in the Marxist classics. It evolved from a few general principles by trial and error—and successive refinement. This haphazard and empirical approach nevertheless resulted in a workable framework for achieving specific objectives. But its features differed from country to country, since the applicability of the model to actual circumstances was more problematic than its conceptual validity. The model of the traditional centrally planned economy is best illustrated by the Soviet Union through the 1960s, before the first schemes for "perfecting" planning were introduced. The discussion that follows focuses on this model, abstracting from the issues that arose when it was applied in other times and places.

The main economic objective of the centrally planned economy is maximum long-term growth through the highest politically feasible accumulation of capital and the full employment of resources. Social ownership of assets and central control over the "commanding heights" of the economy are both the overriding ideological prerequisites and the administrative means to maximize accumulation and concentrate resources on leading sectors of the economy. The major social aims are full employment, narrow wage differentials, and universal availability of social services, mainly in the form of "collective consumption" (financed from public resources). Low inflation is partly a political objective, partly a means of facilitating central planning. The objectives are implemented by the leading political party through the organs of the state.

The starting point for planning is a set of politically determined economic targets. A central planning office (CPO) guides and organizes planning procedures and sets the plan's targets. But planning is, in fact, a joint task of the government agencies (branch ministries and sub-branch associations) and enterprises that must meet the targets. Planning is iterative, sometimes referred to as "dialogue" or "bargaining" and involves upward flows of microeconomic information on such things as capacities and production processes and downward flows of microeconomic instructions on such things as outputs and inputs. Initial macroeconomic objectives are gradually adjusted for feasibility. Incentives have no role in this framework.

Within the model of centrally planned economies, macromanagement in the conventional sense of the deployment of indirect management tools through monetary, fiscal, and exchange rate policies is redundant. Instead, macroeconomic balances are the aggregate of centrally (and directly) set microbalances. So, if they are correctly planned ex ante and maintained ex post, all macrobalances are met.

Allocation

Allocation of raw materials, intermediate products, and finished goods is the first function of planning. The allocation of producer goods to recipient industries and enterprises is according to technical coefficients that describe the input-output relations of the production processes (see box 2.1). For final demand, the central planning office sets the allocation target (in the aggregate and by sector and enterprise) for household and collective consumption in accord with the plan's feasible objectives. The allocations for investment are according to the investment plan, and net exports according to the trade plan. All allocations are reflected in physical or financial balances.

For each enterprise, at least for those in priority sectors, the final version of the plan determines inputs (by quantity, price, and sources) and outputs (by quantity, price, and recipients). For labor, the aggregate wage sum (a "wage fund") is "allocated" to sectors and enterprises. Along with centrally set wage scales, this aggregate determines roughly the actual allocation of labor. Except for housing, consumer goods and services for fee ("wage goods")

Box 2.1 Input-output analogy

The framework of central planning, its inherent logic, and its limitations are analogous to the familiar input-output table, a double-entry table presenting the deliveries from the sectors and industries listed in the left column to those listed in the top row and to final demand (household and collective consumption, investment, and net exports).

The preparation of the plan is equivalent to computing the vectors of gross output and of primary inputs (labor and capital) for a given vector of deliveries to final demand. Although in some sectors physical balances may underlie the numbers, the input-output table is, for reasons of aggregation, denominated in value terms. This implies that one distinct vector of prices is required for all sectoral inputs and outputs to balance, which is an integral part of the plan. The financial balances of the table, in turn, can serve as a basis for ex ante and ex post national accounts and for the control of plan implementation.

Interindustry deliveries in the cells of the table are on the input side determined by "technical coefficients," whereas the deliveries to final demand, set autonomously, generate "backward" effects throughout the table. The sums of each row and column are the total gross output value of the respective industry, measured horizontally on the output side and vertically on the input side. Many of the models of central planning are applications of the techniques of input-output analysis. The limitations of such analyses—such as fixed technical coefficients, constant returns to scale, and an overly high degree of aggregation dictated by data and computational limitations—are the same as those for central planning.

all levels are also formulated in value terms, involving both quantity and price indicators. This value dimension also establishes a continuum from broad macroeconomic balances to the financial balances of enterprises. Value measures are thus indispensable even to central planners. Aggregate values reflect, on the one hand, physical goals and "norms," such as those for balancing household incomes and the supply of consumer goods and services (at planned quantities and prices) and, on the other, balancing budgetary revenues and expenditures, including total public savings and investment.

Financial balancing is made easier because the money system for transactions between households and enterprises are kept apart from that for transactions between enterprises and state organizations; the exchange of money between the two circuits is strictly controlled by the state bank. The household money circuit is restricted to the use of cash in the narrow sense, and the enterprise circuit to the use of deposit money transactions through accounts with the state bank. Segmenting the household money circuit also helps balance the sums in wage funds with aggregate supply of wage goods, based on expected household savings and administered prices.

Planners have only crude information on future consumer preferences, so shortages and surpluses of consumer goods exist side by side, with involuntary household savings and buildups of "monetary overhang" despite excess inventories of some goods. Moreover, the reliance on material balances brings a strong quantitative bias into planning, and ultimately into statistical reporting. Too much aggregation (lumping together nonsubstituting goods) contributes to simultaneous shortages and excess stocks.

Given that one or a few producers normally supply many customers and has a degree of monopoly power, suppliers typically operate in a sellers' market without competition. Although monopoly rent-seeking is excluded due to central price setting, many subtle aspects of supply elude the rigors of central planning (such as product specification, quality, and delivery schedules). This reinforces the pervasive shortage syndrome in all markets, induces hoarding, and loosens further any connection between prices and scarcity.

Prices and inflation

For central planners, prices enter into ex ante target financial balances and create the conditions for ex post control of plan realization by the state mono-

are allocated not to the final recipients but to trade organizations. Thus, households do have a measure of consumer choice, albeit constrained by their incomes and the amount of goods and services made available to the retail sector according to the output plans, sold at administered retail prices.

For priority sectors with homogenous output such as energy and steel, an important planning tool is "material balances" that compare feasible production levels with tentative requirements. Imbalances are met either by increasing capacity (through investment), or by scaling down (or up) the output targets of receiving sectors, and/or by altering foreign trade targets. The number and coverage of "material balances" varied from country to country and from plan period to plan period.

Because aggregation in physical terms is an impossibility, except for homogeneous products, plans on bank system. Prices are a means of transferring income among enterprises, state organs, and households. Conversely, prices do not affect—nor are they supposed to affect—allocation, which is the function of central planning. Nor are they expected to reflect opportunity costs. For consumer goods, by contrast, prices are supposed to clear specific product markets by balancing financially effective demand and the planned output of supply.

Adjusting prices for changing conditions in centrally planned economies is complex because of the interdependence of all financial balances. Price adjustments can be done only through comprehensive price-resetting exercises. Between these exercises most prices remain fixed. Thus, constant prices are not just a political objective. They are also dictated by the model and by practical constraints. As discussed below, adjusting consistent vectors of relative prices is made easier by using specific taxes and subsidies as "wedges" to "close" financial imbalances.

For homogenous products—such as cement, crude oil, and electricity—prices are set individually. For other products—such as ball-bearings-product variations make detailed price-setting impractical beyond the recognition of average cost of production, sometimes including a planned profit margin, at given input prices. The central planner may then prescribe price indexes for intertemporal changes, assuming a given or specifically shifted output mix of these factors. The financial implications throughout the system are computed, and any imbalances are taken as the basis for iterative adjustments to specific taxes and subsidies.

The banking system automatically finances transactions that are included in the plan or are otherwise authorized. If input prices rise, the funds appropriated to the producer will automatically increase. Thus, trends in costs not in the money supply trigger inflation at the producer and wholesale levels.

Until recently, most statistical offices in HPEs devoted little attention to computing accurate price indexes. Statisticians were required to showcase the advantages of socialism and were discouraged from adjusting for hidden and repressed inflation. Lack of attention was also a reflection of the limited importance of prices. Prices fixed by government agencies—controlled rigidly and revised infrequently—required less monitoring than other indicators of production and trade.

Profits, taxes, and subsidies

In a centrally planned enterprise, profit is a planned or unplanned residual of revenue and costs. Unlike in a market economy, it is based on planned prices and transactions, normally without provisions for capital and land. It internalizes producer taxes and subsidies, so that profits and net taxes are inseparable. In some enterprises, there may be planned profits, which, together with prescribed depreciation, are retained to finance investment (note that the SNA regards exceptional public enterprise profits as indirect taxation). In others, profits may serve as standards for financial control and, in some cases, may even serve as centrally set targets or performance indicators. Whether or not profit is retained, an excess profit tax—which may be negative, implying subsidization, and may vary by enterprise—"closes" any financial imbalance.

Unlike market economies, most of the taxes and subsidies are set separately for each enterprise to maintain its planned cash flow on the basis of planned or unplanned revenues and expenditures. Correspondingly, enterprises surrender "surplus" revenue cash from operations or are reimbursed for "shortfalls." At this point, control over enterprise accounts through the state bank acting for the legal owner, the state, interfaces with the fiscal system. In addition to these discretionary taxes and subsidies, there may be specific excise taxes for basic inputs.

A fundamental financial balance in the planned economy is that between aggregate household incomes and expenditures. At the same time, output prices are to be consistent with the overall price system and prices of basic commodities kept low for equity considerations. How? Through highly differentiated, product-specific—and often producer-specific—turnover taxes (mostly on industrial consumer goods of high price elasticity) and subsidies (mainly on basics). These taxes and subsidies, at least in principle, clear the market for the available supply by driving a wedge between producer (wholesale) and retail prices. In some cases, such as alcohol, the turnover tax is in effect an excise tax.

Investment

At the macroeconomic level, sociopolitical considerations determine the feasible investment rate. At the sectoral level, investment coefficients, equivalent to capital-output ratios, determine the investment required to meet capacity expansion targets. Material balances are the principal tool for discovering supply bottlenecks that require investment. Microeconomic investment decisions are, with the exception of a few large projects, left to subordinate state organs and enterprises. In the absence of prices for inputs and outputs that reflect opportunity costs, planners resort to such criteria as comparisons of investment recovery periods at plan prices. Because the financing of programs and projects supported by the plan is automatic, interest cost has no systemic function on macro or micro investment decisions. Interest rates are normally set at levels far below the marginal product of capital.

Foreign trade and debt

Foreign trade is planned to fill gaps in the material balances that cannot be resolved through investment, and to obtain critical technology embodied in imported capital equipment. From this demand-side perspective, exports are the means to meet import requirements, not a source of growth. But trade with market economies cannot be fixed in a framework of enforceable targets. Nor can it be relied on in an environment of geopolitical confrontations. Central planning has, for these reasons, a systemic preference for autarky and, failing that, for trade with other planned economies. Autarky was impossible, however, even for the Soviet Union, so the HPEs set up a framework for mutual trade through the Council for Mutual Economic Assistance (CMEA).

The CMEA's rules created mutually balanced trade in a bilateral clearing framework, combined with multilateral agreements on specialization. Countries agreed in bilateral "protocols" on the bills of goods to be exchanged and their prices, denominated in transferable rubles, the notional currency for the settlement of trade accounts. This allowed intra-CMEA trade to be integrated into national central planning. Furthermore, as bilateral clearing trade was normally balanced, it did not require currency convertibility or currency reserves. Planned trade and investment credits between CMEA members were relatively small and were granted via physical deliveries of goods at agreed prices. In the absence of both currency and commodity convertibility, the domestic prices and balance of payments from these transactions have none of the analytical meaning that they do in market economies.

For ease of central control, each country had a handful of foreign trade organizations (FTOs) with monopoly/monopsony powers over broad ranges of traded products. To minimize external effects from spilling over into the domestic economy, these organizations dealt with domestic suppliers of exports and domestic users of imports in domestic currency at prescribed domestic prices.

Prices in trade with market economies were generally denominated in foreign currency and roughly in line with international prices. Prices in CMEA trade were notionally taken from international prices, averaged over a moving five-year period, with the formula being periodically revised. The "international prices" so obtained were converted into transferable rubles at the CMEA's exchange rate between the transferable ruble and the international currency. Apart from homogenous products for which this "Bucharest" pricing formula could be applied, CMEA prices were negotiated between the planning offices or the FTOs of the respective countries. The combined effects of international prices and exchange rates were collected in the accounts of the FTOs. While FTOs could be regarded as intermediaries in wholesale-retail trade, implying value added, the actual balances on the FTO accounts also contained a significant element of indirect taxation and subsidization.

Even if trading transactions were fully balanced by currency zone (convertible currencies and transferable ruble), they were balanced in domestic currency only by accident. In other words, international prices were not passed on to domestic end users. The resulting imbalances on the accounts of the FTOs are captured through the institution of "price equalization," with an overall balance between international and domestic values settled with the budget. Unless the effects of different prices are buffered by the application of product-specific coefficients applied to the exchange rates, the disaggregated price equalization flows can become very large, revealing systematic patterns of "taxes and subsidies," by currency zone, by types of exports as well as imports. Aggregate net balances tend to be small and can have either sign. These peculiarities of the price and exchange rate regimes of the CMEA countries make it extremely difficult to assess gains or losses from the terms of trade.

Given a tight trade monopoly/monopsony by a few FTOs under central fiscal, and financial, control, an unplanned accumulation of foreign debt is logically impossible. Historically, debts started to accumulate for some HPEs in the 1960s, initially as part of planned crash modernization programs, on the assumption that improved competitiveness would generate future export earnings to repay the debts. But this assumption proved to be false. Together with the relaxation of strict central planning rules and sharp changes in world prices in the 1970s and 1980s, HPEs began to accumulate sizable foreign debts. Among the HPEs themselves, foreign debt arose as the result of unplanned trade surpluses where the debtor was unwilling or unable to deliver goods according to pre-arranged terms.

Fiscal and monetary balances

Much household consumption takes the form of "common consumption" financed from budgetary resources. The budget is the intermediation device for most enterprise savings and investment. Both producer and consumer taxes and subsidies have large redistributive roles. Traditionally, moderate budget surpluses were targeted to provide room for noninflationary credit expansion. In general, if the discipline of central planning was adhered to and gross planning errors avoided, the fiscal balance could be maintained.

The financial system of the planned economy is passive in the sense that taxation and spending decisions are as planned as other financial balances are—and are not altered to influence the actions of other economic agents. Nevertheless, finance has two important functions. First, it provides liquidity for enterprises to realize output targets. Second, banks are the instruments for the continuous monitoring of financial transactions of enterprises, to make sure that they are in accord with the targets.

The financial system thus performs an auditing function. Auditing is made easier by the "monobank" state bank system. Enterprises and state organs must carry out all current transactions through the state bank, which controls and is supported by few special-purpose banks, such as those for investment, agriculture, foreign trade, and private savings.

National accounts

Since central planning has a coherent financial dimension, there is no logical distinction between plan and national accounts. The HPEs developed their own conventions, codified in the material product system (MPS). Unlike the UN System of National Accounts, the MPS excludes "nonproductive services" (such as administration, the military, education, and health) and depreciation from the measure of aggregate output and income, called net material product (NMP). The gap between them reflects the classical roots of Marxist economics and goes back to Adam Smith's distinction between "productive" and "unproductive" labor. Establishing bridges between the MPS and the SNA has long been a major issue for comparative statistics. This led to different "blind spots" in the two frameworks, with the MPS giving more attention to stock-flow relationships while overlooking much of the services sector. And for some areas, such as depreciation, each framework generates numbers of dubious significance by its own method.

Chapter 3. Statistical Implications of Central Planning

The planning and statistical systems of HPEs are inextricably linked. Reporting by enterprises in HPEs is biased toward showing plan fulfillment because managers are judged and rewarded on that basis. Central statistical offices lack independence, so the bias is reinforced nationally: bureaucratic and political considerations favor reporting improvements in economic performance.

The inconsistency of data can also be a problem. There is often poor coordination between the planning office (responsible for the plan), the national bank (monetary and balance of payments statistics), the ministry of finance (fiscal data), and the CSO (national accounts). Concepts used by each often vary and statistical coordination committees fail to resolve problems of definition and coverage. There is, moreover, a sharp difference between data problems that are systemic (i.e., inherent to the economic system) and those that are statistical (say, differences in definitions and methodology).

National accounting issues

In central planning the objectives (high growth, no inflation, and no unemployment) drive both the reporting system for national accounts and its results, which are difficult to interpret in comparison with economies where markets dominate. Low (or no) inflation, for example, is assured by policy instruments, such as administered prices and wages, which have profound statistical repercussions because they determine relative values.

Administered prices

Payments for production factors in HPEs need not reflect the relative resource costs of producing goods and services. The difference between producer prices and purchaser values (or market prices) is covered by a web of subsidies and so-called turnover taxes, which vary according to where the purchaser is in the production and distribution chain. Moreover, because each enterprise is treated uniquely in the taxes it pays and the grants, loans, and subsidies it receives, assessing

whether a firm is profitable or loss-making is difficult. And reported gross "profit" margins do not reflect actual returns on capital.

In a planned economy, the official price and specifications for a good or service are rigid. There is little scope for manufacturers to vary either in response to changes in costs or demand. So, managers may not perceive or pay attention to these signals. But HPE managers still have constraints, as they face irregular and at times inappropriate supplies of inputs. They must, thus, guard against changes in factor availability by hoarding labor, capital, and material. If they do not, they may fail to reach quantity targets or have to resort to cutting quality.

Cuts in quality may be insidious and symptomatic in a sellers' market. In sectors where confiscatory profit taxes are relaxed but prices remain fixed, enterprises may also reduce quality by introducing pseudo-new products that fetch higher retail prices, part of which may be returned to workers in higher wages.

Administered prices also discourage product innovation and have subtle but profound effects on the range of goods and services produced. For instance, there are few consumer options in goods and services even for colors. These qualitative differences complicate comparisons of quantities between planned and market economies. The implication is that if HPE prices do not reflect underlying costs and buyer preferences, and if quantities carry different qualitative meanings, value (their multiple) in an HPE is not strictly comparable with value in a market economy.

This incomparability carries over to measures of economic structure for the two models and to the corresponding weights used in a variety of their respective aggregate calculations. For example, in an HPE, established prices from price lists for agricultural products and basic consumer necessities tend to be lower than those for industrial products and consumer durables, due to producer or consumer subsidies. Official prices, just as prices in a market economy, include net indirect taxes. HPE national accounts at established prices therefore understate agriculture's share of GDP relative to industry's, which also affects the calculation of aggregate growth rates. See Biased growth rates in this chapter.

The different contextual and quantitative meanings of price and quantity in HPEs usually imply the existence of nonprice mechanisms for allocating scarce goods. These include barter arrangements between enterprises and special stores for privileged consumers.

Under central planning, nonprice trading mechanisms were tolerated periodically to cope with shortages and other problems, but had only limited systematic effects on economic trends. These practices became progressively more important, and accepted in HPEs until they spawned parallel or "secondary" markets. In these markets, monetary values are unmonitored and unrecorded in official statistics and consequently do not enter into measures of price changes.

Measuring inflation only on the basis of administered prices underestimates price level changes. Official sources report quantities sold at official prices, although an increasing share of production is likely to be sold at higher prices in the uncontrolled unofficial economy.

Administered wages

Under central planning, wages and prices are codetermined. Central planners want to ensure that the minimum wage can buy what they consider the minimum socially acceptable basket of goods and services. Changes in the prices of items in that basket require corresponding changes in wages. Central planners often simplify such adjustments by averting price changes through higher consumer subsidies for key items. Nonwage benefits, such as heavily subsidized housing, can be important supplements to wages. Like nonprice mechanisms and administered prices, nonwage forms of benefits have to be considered jointly with administered prices in determining a worker's effective remuneration. By the time a parallel market for goods has emerged in a CPE, there usually is also an equally vibrant "second" market for labor, which distorts aggregate wage data. Permitted wage differences have been too small, and new housing too difficult to obtain, to influence significantly the mobility of labor. And new or expanding enterprises find it difficult to attract labor from other firms.

Wages are set centrally with an emphasis on equality and seniority, which leads to a relative wage structure that has narrow differences and that does not reflect productivity and skills. Moreover, the level of financial remuneration (wages, salaries, and related compensation) is generally low relative to that in comparable economies. Part of the reason is that the state provides large subsidies to the population on housing, utilities, basic foodstuffs, transportation, education, health care, and culture that reflect distributional considerations.

Take, for example, "normalized" indicators of labor productivity in the chemical and pharmaceutical industries for a range of economies (Global Table 13). The indicators are normalized by relating the value of gross output per worker in this sector to the value of gross output across all manufacturing in the same economy. In market economies, workers in the chemical industries appear to be comparatively more productive. But as average income levels rise, the ratio of wages per worker in chemicals to that in total manufacturing declines (note in Global Table 13 the "other middle-income economies" versus "high-income economies"). In the HPEs, these ratios are very low, even more so than in the most highly developed market economies. But this simply reflects the systemic factor of keeping wage differences low, irrespective of differences in productivity among the sector. One further explanation: the value of output in HPEs is exaggerated by chemical product prices that are higher than in market economies. Thus, labor productivity is lower than fixed-price measures suggest. Another explanation: capital-intensive production in HPEs, through subsidized capital inputs, raises labor but not overall productivity.

Input prices

National statistical authorities in HPEs draw basic data from firms where most inputs—raw materials, energy, and working capital—do not reflect their real resource costs. For instance, some cost elements are excluded (interest and rent), and administered input prices deviate from opportunity costs. Although most input costs are subtracted from gross margin, the remaining operating profit (or the return to capital) reflects the underlying cost structure as well as revenues established in nonmarket prices. The net effect of inconsistencies in input prices and cost accounting may be negligible in the aggregate, but for specific sectors such inconsistencies, embedded in output and value added figures, may be significant.

Prices in HPEs deviate from resource costs on domestic and international markets. For example, energy prices are generally underpriced (box 3.1).

Box 3.1 Energy prices and value added

Energy prices set by central planners influence assessments of value added in HPEs. Energy prices (and the enterprises to which they apply) are set in accord with the output goals of the central plan. Technological and allocative efficiency considerations, as well as rates of return to energy producers, are largely ignored in setting planned output targets. Central planners set different prices for wholesale and retail consumers based on production costs reported to the economic planning ministries. Wholesale energy prices are the sum of import or domestic producer prices, marketing cost margins, and net taxes. Retail prices (usually determined by adding turnover taxes to, or subtracting subsidies from, wholesale prices) are charged to particular service industries and individual consumers. In the international context, HPE wholesale energy prices are characteristically underpriced, particularly wholesale electricity prices (see table below).

Wholesale Electricity Prices

(US$/kWh)	1985	1986	1987	1988	1989	1990
Czechoslovakia	0.03	0.03	0.03	0.03	0.03	..
Hungary	0.04	0.05	0.05	0.05	0.06	..
Poland	0.02	0.02	0.02	0.02	0.02	..
Turkey	0.05	0.07	0.07	0.07	0.07	0.08

Source: International Energy Agency, *International Energy Yearbook (1991).*
Note: Prices are based on average market rates (1985 to February 1991) and include taxes.

to state enterprises at low nominal, and in cases at negative real, interest rates.

Nonmaterial service inputs, such as consulting and business travel, used by enterprises and included in NMP as part of value added are a special case of nonmarket input prices. In the MPS, these inputs count as factor payments in material production rather than as intermediate consumption costs. Further, these payments usually include no depreciation, no return on the capital stock, and often no profit markup.

Cost-plus pricing

The CSOs rely on enterprise accounting to determine value added in production. But input costs at administered prices do not reflect scarcity of resources (labor, capital, or technology). And output prices at factor costs reflect cost-plus rather than demand-driven pricing. Firms are able to add costs because of the so-called soft-budget constraint, which insures that enterprises do not become illiquid or bankrupt. Instead, they are automatically reimbursed for excess costs through price increases, subsidies, lowered taxes on profits, or writeoffs of credit. In market economies, costs can be recovered in the long run only if the market "validates" them or if the government absorbs part of the financial risk of some high-risk projects. Central planners tend to set prices on a cost-plus basis, except for goods and services that they deliberately prorate.

Since enterprise residuals—including depreciation and other charge—and profits are submitted to the state budget, their relative importance is indeterminate. Until recently, it did not matter much to firms changing the composition of output and the use of inputs in their range of control whether transfers to the state budget were levies on labor, charges on capital, or taxes on profits. When the principles of pricing, taxation, or subsidization change, there is a shift in relative costs, prices, and profit rates, but most enterprises can recoup costs and make a modest profit with simple cost-plus markups or via reliance on the soft budget constraint to receive greater subsidies. In HPEs the resulting change of added value is not verified by competition because sales are insured by the sellers' market.

Most production in HPEs takes place in monopoly firms with a high degree of vertical integration. Owing to vagaries of supply that prompt resource hoarding, and to insufficient sensitivity to costs in

Energy consumption per capita for the USSR, Czechoslovakia, and the German Democratic Republic were greater than West Germany, despite substantially lower income (Global Table 17). Moreover, because of nonmarket exchange rates and price equalization regimes, prices of imported inputs can similarly deviate from resource costs. Witness oil traded in the CMEA, which until 1991 was priced with a five-year lag on world market prices.

Implicit import price distortions can also arise from central allocation of hard currency and from import licenses that carry an automatic allocation of foreign currency. One result of such implicit trade restrictions is that the low nominal level of import tariffs gives the impression of a liberal trade regime while foreign purchases are controlled through quantitative controls on imports (quotas) or on foreign exchange.

Credit is another usually undervalued input in enterprise production. Credit is normally provided by the national bank or its specialized subsidiaries the competition, managers source work within the firm, foregoing potential economies of scale from specialized supplier firms. This increases value added in the final sector, at the expense of backward-linked more efficient sectors. It also promotes misclassification of activities that add economic value.

As firms in liberalizing HPEs become subject to harder budget constraints, some remuneration in kind—such as housing, medical, and childcare provided previously by firms—may become the responsibility of the individual wage-earner. Higher cash wages may be needed to compensate for the loss of entitlements, effectively shifting a chunk of consumption to the market.

The magnitude of wage increases required could be significant, particularly for housing. In HPEs state- or company-owned housing subsidies can total 3–6 percent of GDP. Rents for state housing averaged 2–5 percent of family income in the 1980s, and rents in the Soviet Union have not changed since the 1920s. Some governments have also subsidized private ownership through low-interest loans, limited to one or two dwellings. A small private rental market existed in Poland and Hungary, but owners' rights were limited. Raising rents (and cutting credit subsidies) is an important, if politically difficult step in reform.

Output measured at factor cost versus market prices

In measuring the returns to capital as a proxy source of value added, three distortions emerge. The first two relate to intertemporal enterprise costs—straight-line depreciation of fixed capital at historical costs, and interest for working capital provided below opportunity costs of capital. The third is in operating income—the difference between operating cost and operating revenue plus net changes in inventory. Operating income is a residual of all prices including subsidies and taxes.

Whether CSOs measure value added before, or after, net indirect taxes is critical to estimating the relative size and growth of sectors. In both the SNA and the MPS, value added at market prices generally refers to the ex-factory value of production less intermediate consumption, including the effects of net indirect taxes (producer taxes less subsidies). Since HPEs have no economy-wide "markets" for most goods or services, the equivalent of "market prices" in the SNA is "established prices" in the MPS, which include net indirect taxes by sector. In measuring value added at factor cost, indirect taxes and subsidies are netted out. This is a way of costing

production at something closer to resource cost than market price, and of eliminating the direct effects of government intervention in production. Estimation of value added at factor cost requires, however, details on taxes and subsidies—a notoriously difficult task when these are discretionary, and essentially a means to balance cash flows. Further complicating comparisons between HPEs and market economies, since central planning did not utilize personal income taxation, indirect taxation in HPEs must be equated with total taxation in a market economy.

In HPEs, counting value added data at established prices is a universal practice. Only Hungary claims to publish such data at "basic prices" (factor costs). The implications are less important for measuring total NMP and GNP than for sectoral shares of income generation, because some sectors benefit from large production subsidies, while others are charged steep sales taxes on outputs and intermediate inputs.

The importance of net indirect taxes as a share of GNP cannot be shown since HPEs rarely produce such data. But net indirect taxes are potentially huge. Countries now publishing SNA data by sector of origin at market prices will need to move to pricing at basic prices, for example, to producer's values.

Evidence for retail prices below producer costs (the opposite of cost-plus pricing) became a sticking point in early attempts to include HPEs in the International Comparison Program (ICP, see chapter 9). Because the state determines prices not only through consumer taxes and subsidies, in most HPEs there are unusually large discrepancies between purchasing power parity (PPP), which compares retail prices—and the exchange rate, which is based on the domestic cost, at producer prices, of earning a unit of foreign currency through exports.

Understated inflation

What types of inflation prevailed in HPEs? What are the common measures in national data? How has the adoption of the SNA affected the practices of CSOs?

Under central planning, the banking system automatically finances transactions that are authorized or included in the national economic plan. If input prices rise, funds made available to the producer will automatically increase. Thus, trends in costs, not in money supply, trigger inflation at the producer and wholesale level.

Until recently, the statistical offices in HPEs devoted little attention to accurate price indexes and were discouraged from improving measures of hidden and repressed inflation. With market reforms and information openness, the role of price statistics has changed dramatically. Vadim Kirichenko, former head of the Soviet State Committee for Statistics (Goskomstat), considers price measurement to be "the principal link in the entire chain of problems" in the statistical system. As central controls are relaxed, it is more important to monitor prices and give greater attention to deflation of income and product statistics. Moreover, as the rate of price inflation increases, it becomes more of a monetary phenomenon.

Because prices in HPEs are frequently below market-clearing levels, unmet demand translates into reduced consumer welfare in ways that are hard to measure statistically. Goods may be "overpriced," given their quality, due to shortages and seller's market conditions; become unavailable; or be replaced by higher priced goods with merely cosmetic improvements. Official measures of living standards and inflation do not usually reflect such changes.

In HPE statistics, inflation is understated in individual price indexes and in the implicit deflator, which reflects price changes in aggregate measures of output. The bias varies greatly among countries and across production sectors and demand categories. It tends to be greatest where nonprice mechanisms attempt to shore up failures in production and distribution. It occurs least where parallel markets are condoned as safety valves to cope with shortages, and where administered prices react to signals from those markets. But the price level (and, perhaps, inflation) on the parallel markets may be artificially high owing to spillover effects, risks, and rent-seeking.

Measures of price changes and basic index issues

The compilation of GDP at current, and constant, prices in market economies provides a measure of overall price changes called the GDP deflator. The deflator reflects the weighted and combined effects of changes in production prices modified by the effect of price changes of intermediate consumption and changes in export and import prices. It is meant to be the current-year quantity-weighted average of the price changes in the economy's producing sectors.

Such a GDP deflator would, in HPEs, yield results for GDP and its components that differ from chain-linked indexes, of the type often used to

evaluate HPEs. For example, HPEs also use constant price compilations that are revised every five to eight years, so volume indexes from the constant price aggregates correspond to Laspeyres-type indexes. In most cases Paasche-type price indexes are used for deflating the individual components of NMP, or other methods applied to the level of the details.

The notion of constant prices, which is the underpinning of conventional growth rates for SNA national accounts, becomes more ambiguous the longer the period covered. There is no satisfactory way to deal with commodities and services that are important at one time but not at another. This is commonly discussed in terms of obsolescence and innovation but applies equally to issues such as fashion and taste. In addition, shifts in relative prices can alter growth rates even when the goods and services appear to be the same. A simple rebasing exercise in a World Bank study (Azam et al, 1958) showed variance in GDP growth rates in excess of a percentage point a year for 22 of 73 countries.

The deflator is implicit in some HPEs. It is derived, for individual products, as the quotient of the current and constant price series where the constant price series has a base year, often the year of the last major price revision at the aggregate level. The fundamental question relating to a deflator's credibility and reliability is whether the individual price indexes used for the compilation of the corresponding components of GDP or NMP are accurate and complete.

Most CPEs modeled cost-of-living indexes on the Soviet "index of state retail prices." This is not a comprehensive consumer price index. Nor does it measure private retail prices or actual transactions. It is based on "list" prices. Moreover, it broadly excludes less homogeneous, less easily controlled products. It takes little account of changes in production quality or mix of the real consumption basket. Products in the price index are unchanged between the base and the current years although the mix, and therefore the weights, can change. Some weights are added with the introduction of new goods, and some are deleted as the production of old goods is discontinued. Thus, new and pseudo-new products absorb most price changes, with little regard to consumer preferences.

Since new products cannot actually be priced in a base year that precedes their existence, the price that is first officially approved may simply be inserted back to the base year, together with some notional weight for the base year, when the goods did not exist. This dampens recorded inflation, since it assigns some weight to an item imputed to have no price increase since the base year. At the same time, the level of such "comparable" prices tends to be overstated, for two reasons. First, they are based on higher than long-term average costs as the productivity effects of "learning" and economies of scale take effect. Second, enterprises are entitled to a surcharge for quality improvement, about which they bargain with the authorities. If improvement can be exaggerated—which is in the producer's interest, because it raises the price and eases the task of plan fulfillment—there will be unmeasured price inflation.

In Hungary in 1968, followed by Czechoslovakia in 1970, and other countries later, more sophisticated price indexes were implemented. In 1989 the USSR introduced a new consumer price index (CPI) based on a wider range of products and outlets. Moreover, Soviet data collectors were required to record a "coefficient of quality." But any single index of quality, say, horsepower for automobiles, was open to distortion and manipulation.

Some countries have begun to construct multivariate indexes that include more goods in the price indexes and take more account of technological improvements. These will require careful interpretation over time. During the planned phase, prices generally reflect costs, including producer subsidies. But since markets do not clear, prices are out of line with user valuations or product quality. Real or pseudo quality changes and forced substitution become instruments of hidden price increases. This may become even more serious in the early transition to a market economy, when enterprises are given more control over the structure of production but are still subject to some central control. But as the transition proceeds and competition increases, producers may begin to deliver more reliable, attractive, and durable goods, with fewer of the tricks used earlier to meet quantity targets and justify price increases. Multivariate equations, estimated on pre- and post-reform data, could imply a deterioration in "quality" (measured in resource cost), while consumer valuations of quality may have improved.

Historic versus current valuation of assets

In all HPEs, there is a widespread distortion in measuring the depreciation of fixed assets and changes in stocks (inventory), exaggerating investment, and overvaluing NMP at current prices. This

is not a system-specific problem, since according to the MPS principle, the distortion should not occur. Indirectly, however, it is closely connected with price increases that are hidden and, therefore, not measured statistically.

For fixed assets, distortions arise from underestimating depreciation. Because depreciation charges were based on the asset's year of acquisition or last revaluation, they tend to fall short of replacement values. For example, in Hungary in 1988, the average price level of depreciation (which represents the mixed values of investment between 1968 and 1989) was about two-thirds the price level of capital goods invested in that year. Since depreciation is underestimated, NMP is overestimated in current prices. This distortion also remains in estimating NMP by industrial origin, because the same undervalued depreciation is deducted from gross output when calculating net value added by the material sphere. When GDP is derived from NMP (by adding back the underestimated value of depreciation), the distortion can automatically be corrected for the GDP figure. But ratios and intertemporal analyses of current price income data, based on national NMP or derived GDP figures, would be affected by the original distortions.

A similar problem of infrequent and inadequate revaluation of inventory can be found in compiling "changes in stocks" within NMP. During strict central planning, enterprises revalue their stocks according to the official price indexes. Additions to stocks are also recorded at the level of increased prices and not at the prices of actual purchase. Because the price level of inputs lags behind the price level of outputs, an increase in stocks occurs irrespective of quantity changes. Hidden price increases or open increases of free prices also have the effect of exaggerating changes in stocks. In valuing material costs of production, the FIFO (first in, first out) principle is followed by enterprises; the costs of materials used from stock in production reflect the prices of an earlier period. On the other hand, additions to stocks are always shown at the price level of the latest purchases. Consequently, the difference between the opening and closing stocks shows not only the physical changes in materials stored, but also the effect of price increases during the year.

In practice, not much information is available on stockbuilding to adjust for these problems. Moreover, national accountants may regard the stockbuilding figures as an adjustment item (errors and omissions) to reconcile the demand and supply sides of the accounts, rather than showing a separate, statistical discrepancy item.

Losses

There is little difference in the treatment of narrowly defined losses between the MPS and the SNA for global NMP or GDP. In both systems, losses, such as unforeseeable damages to fixed assets and stocks, may be included in NMP or in GDP (although they should be regarded as revaluation accounts, intervening between stocks and flows). They are not deducted from total output of the economy (see box 3.2).

There is, however, a big difference in the treatment of other losses. For example, in the MPS, waste and loss during storage of agricultural goods and merchandise in trade are shown and included in aggregate value added as losses. They are not treated as intermediate consumption.

Officially, losses in some countries are relatively low in relation to total NMP. For example, in Bulgaria losses in the 1980s were 1.3–1.4 percent of NMP, and in Czechoslovakia 1.3–1.7 percent. The explicit losses are also small in relation to all losses in HPEs. The most general loss of resources is the value of substandard goods, which are still included in gross output.

There is another, purely mechanical, difference in the treatment of losses between the two systems. In the SNA, gross capital formation is shown as an end-use category of GDP, without mentioning the

size of any type of losses. In the MPS, explicit losses are shown as a separate item of final uses of NMP. So in the MPS, newly produced capital goods are divided into two: one increases the stock of assets, while the other does not since it replaces the capital goods lost due to fire, floods, or other calamities. Disregarding the differences in the treatment of depreciation and inventory replacement, the net increase of the stock of assets (plus the value of losses in the MPS) is equal to the value of capital formation in SNA.

Writing off obsolescent and unwanted goods and inventory is also poorly documented as an adjustment to stockbuilding in NMP. Yugoslavia, like other HPEs, has the framework for such write-offs, but does not follow through in practice. Excessive accumulation (hoarding) results in fixed assets and stocks greater than the technologically required level. Rational reasons why producing units may accumulate excess reserves in production capacity, raw materials, and spare parts include pervasive supply shortages, delivery uncertainties for ordered commodities, and unexpected stops in the flow of imported goods.

Biased growth rates

In measuring growth rates, systemic and statistical biases are introduced in the official estimates. Such biases carry through from NMP to GNP in estimates of growth. The major reason is inadequate accounting for inflation, as discussed in previous sections, including inflation unaccounted for in less homogeneous (and less easily controlled) products, which leads to an understatement of aggregate price deflators (see box 3.3).

Not all production in market economies or HPEs is strictly useful. Some is nonbeneficial, especially where goods are sold or otherwise distributed in a seller's markets. In HPEs there is also a significant amount of waste because of unfinished investment projects, unwanted inventories, and goods sold only because buyers have no alternative choices. These are not treated as losses and not systematically subtracted from GDP or NMP.

Significant distortions may result from the use of established prices to determine weights for aggregating individual volume indexes. In HPEs where the relatively slow-growing agriculture and services sectors were subsidized, use of established market prices for deriving weights for those sectors overstates overall growth because it gives a relatively low weight (owing to low fixed prices) to the slower-growing sectors and a high weight to fast-

---

Box 3.2 Losses in the USSR

Fraud may distort data underlying Goskomstat national income measures. So, too, may insufficient allowance for waste and losses. Official USSR data on the grain harvest, for example, no longer represent the novel concept of "biological yield," which came into use in the 1930s, but they are still believed to incorporate inordinate amounts of waste. Data on other crops, too, are likely to be inflated. Agricultural products may also suffer large losses in transport and storage. And for some industrial products such as coal and cement, there are apparently large losses in transport.

In calculating national income by sector of origin, losses of this sort are supposedly reflected in materials outlays and should not inflate the final aggregate. Among western scholars, it is often assumed that here, too, national income is inflated, though that need not cause any significant distortion in trends over time unless the rate of loss, pilferage, etc., changes.

Box 3.3   Recomputations of growth for the USSR

How much was the Soviet Union's official rate of growth biased upward due to unmeasured price increases? Kushnirsky made calculations for three industries—automotive; electrotechnical; and energy and power machinery. For each, he built an index of average prices adjusted for quality changes. For example, the index for passenger cars included passenger capacity, size, weight, engine volume, horsepower, and fuel efficiency. He found modest to significant hidden inflation in all three.

| Sector | Period | *Average annual real growth* | | |
		Official growth (%)	Hidden inflation (%)	Revised growth (%)
Automotive	1970-82	7.9	1.2	6.6
Electrotechnical	1960-75	10.6	4.4	5.9
Energy and power machinery	1971-85	3.3	2.5	0.8

Source: Kushnirsky 1989.

---

growing industries. The reason is that estimates of GDP/NMP growth rates depend partly on whether they are at market prices or at factor cost: differences in these estimates result from an uneven sectoral distribution of indirect taxes and subsidies. A partial solution would be for HPEs to report at factor cost, before taxes and subsidies. This solution is explained in detail in chapter 9 (alternative computations).

International transactions

Determining levels of foreign trade is bedeviled by statistical problems. Trade with market economies has a margin of error because some transactions are settled through trade (ie, imports for re-export) with unspecified countries in the CMEA. Estimating East-West trade in dollars is difficult too, due to statistical discrepancies revealed in unmatching East and West statistics. And because partner currencies are not convertible, much HPE trade, especially with developing countries, is based on clearing under bilateral trade and financing arrangements where implicit prices often differ from those on the world market.

Vastly more forbidding is the task of interpreting CMEA trade data. Before January 1991, prices in

intra-CMEA trade were averages of past world market prices, converted to transferable rubles (TRs) at the CMEA's official ruble-dollar exchange rate. In practice, bilateral bargaining had yielded TR values and price levels that differed greatly from even past world market prices. In early 1991, the CMEA was terminated and its former members began to move toward current world market prices and settling international transactions in dollars and other convertible currencies. The following generalizations can be made about intra-CMEA prices:

- The principle that intra-CMEA prices should be an average of historical world market prices (the Bucharest formula) was applied with consistency for trade in energy and raw materials. This delayed adjustment meant that when world prices were rising, prices in intra-CMEA trade tended to lag. At official ruble-dollar rates the dollar equivalent of transactions would understate the true value of these commodities for those years and overstate them when world market prices were falling.

- The Bucharest formula provided, at best, an orientation for price negotiations for non-homogeneous products. Often there was no comparable price information because the prices and qualities of supposedly identical export products could differ substantially between destination countries.

- Intra-CMEA prices of "soft" goods tended to be significantly higher than their presumed world market prices. For most of these mainly manufactured products—which could be sold on the world market only at substantial discounts, if at all, owing to generally poorer design and quality—the dollar values obtained from TR transactions via the official ruble-dollar rate were higher than "true" dollar values.

- Domestic USSR prices, which also overvalued manufactures and undervalued primary products, influenced intra-CMEA prices.

- Even if information were available on the quantities and quality of the products traded, there are different ways of estimating the hypothetical dollar values of manufactures. For example, if the focus were on a CMEA country's exports to the USSR, dollar prices could be those that the USSR would presumably pay to import similar commodities from the world market. Under normal conditions in the USSR, those prices may have been higher than the prices at which the identical goods would be exchanged between two market economies. Part of the reason is that East European goods may have been better suited for the Soviet than for Western markets since they were often designed to Soviet specifications. Another set of prices would therefore be West-to-West dollar prices. These, in turn, would likely exceed the prices at which a CMEA country could export those commodities to the West, which is yet a third set.

Such hypothetical dollar prices, however, fail to meet the test of market verification. For most technical manufactures, where imperfect competition dominates, western industrial users and consumers often have doubts about the value of CMEA goods compared with similar goods sold under Western labels. These doubts result in weaker demand and lower prices. Often CMEA exporters could use only the price to compete (versus, for example, brand name, service, advertising, or credits). Moreover, prices may be low in part because of Western discrimination (such as discriminatory quotas or tariffs), whose impact must be absorbed by the sellers.

- Prices in intra-CMEA trade were established annually in bilateral negotiations, more or less simultaneously for all commodities. The price of an item was a function of its price in the base year, changes in world market prices, and the prices (and quantities) of all other commodities traded.

- Terms-of-trade losses vis-à-vis convertible currency countries, and other pressures affecting the supply and demand of foreign exchange in HPEs, were insulated from the official ruble-dollar rate for years. So there is a limited economic basis for determining "the dollar value of the TR." As the UN Economic Commission for Europe says: "Attempts are frequently made ... to estimate the realistic ruble exchange rate against the dollar, but this is probably an inherently impossible task."

The "official" value of the TR, as recorded by the CMEA's International Bank for Economic Cooperation (IBEC), is thus indeterminate against the dollar (see box 3.4). For aggregate trade, but not necessarily for all commodity groups and for all years, the official exchange rate overvalued the TR against the dollar. This is evidenced by CMEA member countries' own valuation of CMEA zone trade, which fell far more during 1986–90 than did the IBEC valuation, though all countries did not discount this trade equally. Intra-CMEA trade thus has different dollar values depending on the point of depar-

ture—the TR or one of the many currencies of the CMEA member countries.

Individual CMEA countries have used different ways to translate TR values to national currency units (NCUs) and these may change as foreign trade and exchange rate systems are reformed. During the central planning phase, the NCU/TR exchange rate was a scaler (as the TR/dollar rate is), so that NCU values of, say, devisa-zloty or devisa-forint are not comparable to domestic zloty or domestic forint values (the "devisa" prefix, used mainly in HPEs in Europe, indicates that the currency is an artificial unit of account). Then, at different times, the CMEA countries introduced the equivalent of commercial NCU/TR exchange rates. These link TR and domestic prices via a complex set of taxes and subsidies that neutralize the difference in relative prices between the domestic market and intra-CMEA trade, and East-West trade. When first introduced, these "commercial" exchange rates aimed at reflecting the average domestic cost (at producer prices) of earning a TR in exports. Interpreting historical table series in light of such changes is discussed in chapter 9.

The national banks of the CMEA countries had various considerations in mind when they established local currency values of the TR and the dollar.

Box 3.4 What is a transferable ruble?

Since 1964, the transferable ruble (TR) has been the bookkeeping currency for intra-CMEA trade—and for bilateral claims settled through the CMEA's International Bank for Economic Cooperation. IBEC acted as a clearinghouse for all intra-CMEA transactions, although no hard cash changed hands. Through IBEC—and under the CMEA's "prompt payment" system—the national bank of the exporting country was automatically credited with a TR claim on its counterpart in the importing country. These claims were neither transferable nor negotiable.

If trade between two CMEA members was not in balance at the end of an accounting period, the claims were settled (at least in principle) by building offsetting imbalances into bilateral trade agreements for the next accounting period. The IBEC rate for the TR against the dollar was more or less the same as that of the Soviet ruble. But the real (purchasing power) dollar value of the TR is impossible to establish because TR prices in intra-CMEA deals were negotiated bilaterally and vary according to the traded goods. So, relative values deviate substantially (by, say, trading partner, commodity, and year) from relative prices in the world market.

As a result, broken ruble-dollar cross-rates emerged, with the transactions value of the TR usually discounted relative to the IBEC rate. Interpretation of these broken cross-rates is not simple, however, because CMEA members used foreign trade coefficients, price equalization funds, and other apparent tax-subsidy mechanisms to neutralize the difference between domestic prices (used for transactions between producers and consumers and the FTOs) and foreign prices (used for transaction between FTOs in different countries). These can alter the effective transactions value of any foreign currency in terms of domestic currency.

Similar to the ways in which soft-currency trade developed in the CMEA, special trade and financing arrangements, called parallel bilateral trade and clearing arrangements, also emerged between HPEs and developing countries. A three-tier system thus arose. Biases were not systematic across commodity groups, nor through time, which makes the TR and dollar segments of exports and imports incomparable and a precise aggregation over all three trade regimes impossible. Thus, official exchange rates have little economic meaning.

Further complication arises in valuing trade for the national accounts and the balance of payments. The system of price equalization insulated domestic price levels and price structures from prices and price changes in external markets (box 3.5). For example, foreign trade participation ratios, conventionally defined as the ratio of exports, imports, or total trade turnover to some measure of national income, supposedly showing the degree of openness of an economy—are problematic in an HPE. The reason is that foreign trade is valued inconsistently at domestic and lagged world prices in official statistics, whereas national income is valued at fixed domestic prices. Both the level and the structure of the two tend to differ substantially.

In all Eastern European countries, the old dollar/ruble exchange rate, based on "devisa" values, grossly overvalued the ruble and thus overstated the relative importance of trade with HPEs as compared with trade with market economies. Some countries introduced more realistic "commercial exchange rates" or their equivalents as early as in the 1960s, others as late as the 1980s or during 1990–91. Although this reduces the bias in an HPE's foreign trade statistics, an economically correct revaluation would require the repricing of all intra-HPE trade to world market prices. Since the Soviets charged relatively low prices for their energy and raw material exports to Eastern Europe and paid

---

Box 3.5 Foreign trade price equalization

In an HPE, the state has a foreign trade monopoly and alone determines the commodity and country composition of exports and imports. Producing enterprises must operate through specialized foreign trade organizations, each with a monopoly in a group of products. The monopoly is reinforced by the inconvertibility of national currency and by prohibitions on organizations or individuals holding or dealing in foreign currencies. Exchange rates do not effectively link foreign and domestic prices and are generally arbitrary. Imports resold by FTOs to domestic users are priced the same as domestically produced goods and are settled in domestic currency; exports delivered by domestic enterprises to FTOs are paid for at the fixed domestic price in domestic currency. In exports, FTOs thus spend domestic currency and earn foreign currency. In imports, they spend foreign currency and earn local currency. Any difference between trade valued in local currency at fixed domestic prices and the arbitrary local-currency equivalent of foreign-currency values is settled automatically with the state budget.

---

relatively high prices for manufactures imported from East Europe, the valuation biases were asymmetrical. Any uniform correction may create new biases, particularly for imports where the inflated value of the TR was at least partly offset by the impact of low import prices from the Soviet Union. Adjusted historical statistics—or the application of commercial exchange rates to all transactions—most likely will yield a picture that is closer to the truth (with lower shares of socialist exports in total exports), but they are likely to understate the share of socialist imports in East Europe's total imports (PlanEcon 1991).

Convertible balance-of-payments data may be distorted by reclassification (to hard currency) of trade negotiated and settled under bilateral agreements and merely denominated in hard currency. For example, exports may be reclassified as convertible exports if payment is in the form of goods that are resold for convertible currencies. Sometimes, with re-exports, only one side of the transaction appears in the trade account. Or they may be entered as exports net of the original imports. Detail on such re-exports can be difficult to obtain as trade in some items, such as transhipments of oil, may have been sensitive. Some triangular trade, such as that in arms, may also be recorded inconsistently, if at all.

External debt and reserves

HPE accounting of external debt, external lending, and reserves has been poor, for several reasons. Although HPE governments control foreign exchange and foreign borrowing, various agencies may contract the external debt. But in some countries (such as Bulgaria and China) there is no central coordination or reporting of the total amounts borrowed. Nor is there much outside discipline. Nonparticipation in international institutions such as the IMF and IBRD, which require accurate and regular reporting of external debt, until recently excluded many HPEs from scrutiny that would have promoted improvement in their statistics. International comparisons are also hampered by differences in definitions. For example, in market economies, short-term debt is normally for maturities under one year, but in HPEs it may include maturities of up to three years. In China, anything under three months is not even classified as debt. Information on types of debtors is also sparse.

By controlling hard-currency debt, the state insulates the domestic economy from the international economy and bears the full exchange rate risk. Usually, external debt is serviced by a national bank or a specialized foreign trade bank, on behalf of the government. With devaluations, servicing this external debt has become increasingly onerous in domestic terms.

Like the balance of payments, external debt is usually reported separately for convertible and nonconvertible currencies. The latter comprises mainly the TR arrangements. Information on nonconvertible debt owed to CMEA partners is particularly hard to verify. Nonconvertible currency balance-of-payments deficits and surpluses are likely to be treated as a change in international liquidity rather than external debt. For example, IBEC maintained swing limits for each country's trade with other CMEA members, and movements within these limits were not reflected in debt statistics.

Moreover, the conversion (for international reporting purposes only) of nonconvertible debt into dollars depends on the TR/$ exchange rate used. Without an economically meaningful basis for the accounting rate, and since HPEs' domestic prices are insulated from CMEA prices (which lag world prices), there is no obvious route for calculating aggregate debt numbers. Moreover, there is no scope for independent verification of nonconvertible currency debt. Even

that part of CMEA lending denominated in convertible currency is difficult to verify.

Intra-CMEA debts normally carried a low (or no) interest rate. Although the amount of interest payments due is known to HPEs, it is capitalized with principal payments, effectively treating interest as part of the debt stock.

In many countries, there are differences between reported and true foreign debt. Under-reporting of debt by HPEs has not been unusual, with revisions always being upward, especially for intra-CMEA loans. There are many incentives to under-report. If fiscal deficits are under-reported to domestic parliaments, so too must external debt be under-reported, partly to be consistent with the understated need for foreign savings to fill the domestic financing gap. Thus, the USSR quietly borrowed from the republics to cover its domestic spending gap in 1989, allowing statistical reporting of surpluses while keeping domestic debt-servicing hidden. Another reason for under-reporting was governmental exclusion from debt figures of certain transactions, such as swaps or movements within IBEC's swing limits.

A wish to project creditworthiness can also play a part. In addition, the general mistrust between East and West precluded accurate reporting of any debt data that might prove useful as a strategic or propaganda issue, especially relating to military expenditure.

For convertible currency assets, HPEs have a particular problem. Under pressure to improve their convertible-currency balance-of-payments positions, exports to developing countries were often promoted by generous export credit. Some of this is unlikely to be repaid. Even so, nonperforming assets probably remain on the books of some official banks. Some HPEs regard short-term loans as part of foreign exchange reserves, although technically the reserves should cover only officially held foreign exchange that is readily marketable and denominated in a major currency or gold. Gold reserves are valued at national prices, which vary greatly from country to country—from substantially below market price to market price.

Government finance and money

State budget and fiscal policy

The state budget collects a portion of the income of

producers (enterprises, collectives, and cooperatives) through discretionary producer taxes, including profits, and of households (through consumer taxes), which planners redistribute to finance investments, to subsidize production and consumption, and to finance social security benefits and public consumption. In general, a larger share of HPE GNP flows through the state budget than in a market economy, for three reasons. Public (collective) consumption is higher. State subsidies generally account for a third of the budget or 15–20 percent of GDP. And the budget and extrabudgetary funds finance most investment. A budget deficit is financed primarily by the national bank. Except for household savings, there are no domestic nonbank sources of finance.

Under central planning, taxes are paid by enterprises. Most producer taxes are set ex post in bargaining between local chambers of the ministry of finance and enterprises—with widespread exemptions—and ad hoc relief is discretionary rather than statutory. This amounts to mandatory submission of much or all of the gross "residual"—that is, the cash-flow surplus after targeted depreciation (to cover replacement), interest on capital, rent on land, turnover tax, and conventional "profit," net of subsidies. And the spending of any "profit" left with an enterprise is regulated. Consumer taxes are captured at the producer or trade level in accord with planned assumptions on product availability and consumer preferences.

Import tariffs are relatively low, and often zero in the case of intra-CMEA trade. While specific price equalization fund transactions (see box 3.5) could be high (positive or negative), the aggregate net balance tends to be insignificant.

In the traditional CPE, where macromanagement is carried out through direct financial control, taxes have no fiscal policy function. In general, there is no treasury function that centralizes the management of government accounts, including cash management and managing domestic and external debt. These operations are shared among the ministry of finance, its (usually subordinated) national bank, and perhaps a specialized foreign trade bank. Easy budgetary access to funds from the national bank, at zero interest cost, obscures the importance of prudent fiscal cash management (see box 3.6 for an example).

State budget and statistics

The budget is only a partial statement of the fiscal impact of the state on the economy. The transactions

---

Box 3.6 Income and expenditure gaps in the USSR

Official publications in the USSR invariably reported a surplus of state revenue over expenditures. In reality, deficits were reaching dangerous proportions in recent years, when strict central control started to lapse.

The most important revenues were declining. In 1987–88, budget receipts from state enterprises based on profits (income) fell by 10 billion rubles, while profits left at the disposal of enterprises increased by nearly 50 billion. Compared with 1985, income from foreign economic activities declined by 8.5 billion rubles.

Each year expenditures increased substantially—by 33.7 billion rubles for the national economy, 25.7 billion rubles for sociocultural projects, and 11 billion for financing foreign economic activities. This was due mainly to increases in the purchase prices of agricultural commodities and supplements to prices.

The income-expenditure gap was filled by transferring general state loan funds to the budget. Only in 1989 did the USSR State Committee on Statistics (Goskomstat) publish figures that showed the growth of this borrowing during the twelfth five-year planning period: from 18 billion rubles in 1985, borrowing rose to 90 billion in 1988. The public was also told that recourse to state loan funds covered nearly 20 percent of budget expenditure, compared with 1 percent in 1970 and 5 percent in 1985. Many problems, including social ones, were being resolved by borrowing against future revenue, which significantly increased domestic and foreign debt.

---

of state-owned enterprises, which are dominant in CPEs, are excluded from the fiscal accounts. In general, expenditures are drawn up on the basis of cash flows rather than commitments. But the budget may be "improved" in any year by a buildup of arrears, often to the national bank. Interest payments from the budget to the national bank are often decided arbitrarily to show profitability of the bank, and in light of budget requirements. The relationship between the budget and the bank can be obscured further by different fiscal years for their accounts. That makes it possible for budgetary transfers to be delayed beyond the fiscal year end without reducing the profits of the bank for its overlapping financial year. There also are often complementary periods at the beginning and end of the fiscal year for the settlement of accounts, with some expenditure items shifted between fiscal years.

The budget is usually drawn up without clear distinction between items recorded above and below the line—those that are deficit-creating and those that are deficit-financing. Payments normally include large financial outflows (for government loans and amortization of government debt). Receipts include large financial inflows (repayments on government loans and new borrowings, including "special" credits from the national bank). A breakdown of budget expenditures by economic category may not be available. Similarly, information on tax revenues cannot be used to deduce meaningful average tax yields, given widespread ad hoc taxes and subsidies. And because of the two-sided nature of foreign trade differentials and turnover taxes, large subsidies may be buried in low net taxes.

In HPEs, as in other economies, money is a unit of account, a means of payment, and a store of value. But money held by enterprises and households is not "integrated." That is, the exchange of money between the two "circuits" is strictly regulated by the state. Moreover, the possession of money by enterprises does not automatically command control of resources in the economy's real sector. Currency circulates exclusively between households and enterprises, whereas enterprises are mandated to deal with each other through transactions between deposit accounts held with the state bank. Bank money is converted to currency when firms draw cash to pay wages, and currency is transformed into bank money when retailers deposit their receipts. Households can have savings accounts, but not checking accounts. So, the total money income of households should be absorbed by retail purchases and voluntary savings. In most cases, however, the value of effective household demand for consumer goods and services exceeds the value of available supply because of disequilibrium in the composition of production, distribution, or in wages. That excess purchasing power causes "repressed" inflation in the controlled sector and "open" inflation in the irregular economy (where activities may be illegal, legal, or illegal but tolerated).

The deposit money of enterprises is not fungible under classical central planning. Some deposits are earmarked for specific uses—such as development projects. Enterprises are generally required to hold funds in particular accounts for, say, working capital, investment, and social development, with transfers from one to another requiring authorization by the controlling bank. Even currency is no more than a conditional means of settlement when shortages are pervasive and privilege as much as money determines command over consumer goods and services.

The main role of national banks and specialized banks is to monitor plan fulfillment. Data of the kind differentiated in Western monetary surveys would not be of analytic interest to central planners and are unlikely to be available. Such indicators —implying, for example, a meaningful relationship between financial and economic aggregates— could be misleading given the segmentation of money in the enterprise and household sectors. Price distortions and excess liquidity foster black markets and currency substitution, making it difficult to obtain reliable measures of the actual money supply and the level of monetary transactions.

Economic reform calls for the provision and interpretation of monetary data. In recent years there has been more interest in HPEs in linking financial and physical aggregates.

Social indicators and employment

Not fully developed in the HPEs are social accounting systems that monitor the gains from development and the vulnerability of certain socioeconomic groups and provide baseline information on social conditions and regular updates for policymakers.

HPEs generally follow international guidelines and classifications set by the UN and its specialized agencies, but these were adapted by the CMEA secretariat to reflect conditions in the HPEs. There still are important questions about data quality and comparability. Little has been done by Western analysts to compensate for possible biases in HPE social indicators. Nor do traditional Western indicators capture social conditions valued highly in HPEs. For example, social indicators in the Global Tables cover none of the following: high job security, low crime, low disparity of income and wealth, and low wage differentials. Other social conditions are more easily measured and compared, such as access to childcare, to maternity and family assistance, to higher education, and to basic health and minimum shelter. But the quality of services is not easily measured.

HPE employment data are also less useful. The emphasis on quantitative plan fulfillment, the tendency by planners to set targets that are difficult to meet, and soft budget constraints on firms led to the hoarding of resources, including labor. As a result, labor shortages coexisted with high underemployment, but little outright unemployment. Moreover there are sectoral and demographic differences in labor statistics owing to rent control and the shortage of adequate housing, both which resulted in labor immobility. Employment data also typically understate the numbers in the irregular economy. For example, in Hungary 45 percent of the value added in agriculture originates from worker and peasant "personal household plots" and 24 percent of construction involves self-employed entrepreneurs seeking a second source of income. In the employment statistics, however, labor is assigned to the sector where these people have their basic first job.

Environment and energy indicators

Standardized reporting on basic environmental conditions and indicators in HPEs lag behind those in developed market economies, where environmental data are gathered mainly through environmental impact assessments (EIAs), which provide information about environmental conditions and the economic factors that influence them. Although many new investments in Eastern Europe and the USSR will include EIAs, the current environmental monitoring is similar to that of Western Europe and North America in the 1970s, before they implemented comprehensive environmental remediation policies. HPEs thus lack extensive and reliable time series of environmental quality, and existing time series have many gaps and extrapolations from under-reported data.

In the mid-1970s, central planners became more open to increasing evidence of declining health, such as the high incidence of respiratory ailments in Polish Silesia, the frequency of birth defects in the central Asian republics of the USSR, and increased environmental degradation. With public pressure, this provoked some governments, notably in Poland, to improve environmental data collection and dissemination.

Because most energy inputs are subsidized in HPEs, prices do not reflect production or replacement costs. Since full energy costs are not internalized in the prices of final products, their valuation does not capture these costs. Individual and household consumption of energy and electricity is even more difficult to measure because of the absence of micro measures of energy, such as home meters. Moreover, statistical responsibility for obtaining this data has been distributed among different planning agencies.

Chapter 4. Statistical Implications of Transition

Given the economic, social, and political changes in HPEs and the avalanche of new information about past and current developments in their economies, it is clear that present data and information systems can not adequately capture what takes place during transition.

The term "transition" encompasses both the introduction of significant market reforms in systems that are centrally planned, and the more fundamental changes that follow as central planning is abandoned. Either type of change has direct and indirect consequences for established statistical systems. For example, enterprises newly freed from ministry tutelage may be unwilling to submit conventional reports. As output becomes more diverse and better suited to the preferences of consumers, these changes may, thus, not be reflected in aggregated production data.

Given the link between reporting and planning under traditional HPE regimes, economic reform will entail new data-reporting systems that should be survey-based and confidential. Promoting new commercial banks and the private sector reinforces the need for such systems. Inevitably, the switch to these systems changes the interpretation of the data produced, and raises the problem of linking data reported under the old and new statistical systems. And, as economic reform reduces price controls on the way to more flexible market-determined prices, measuring prices will have to change from simply consulting price lists to following procedures based on appropriate sampling and weighting.

Costs and prices tend to rise under reform, although much of the rise may be simply recording past events and not indicative of current factors. Costs increase as an economically more meaningful definition of costs is used—including higher depreciation charges and rents and returns on capital—and as subsidies are reduced and input prices increase. Prices rise partly because of shortages, cost increases, and producer monopolies. The resulting large change in price levels and relative prices is likely to cause significant breaks in data series for both nominal and real GDP. More statistical implications follow: definitions of cost improve; hitherto missing cost components, such as rent and interest, are accounted for, and others are being assigned more realistic values, such as higher depreciation rates and exchange rates.

Market forces will move prices up as a wider range of prices is allowed to be set freely. Other prices will be free to move within limits, while in some areas prices remain administratively controlled and price increases by firms need to be justified to the authorities. Whether such reforms move prices closer to market-clearing levels will depend on whether markets prevail. If some prices are freed while others remain controlled, "free" prices will incorporate spillover (substitution) effects from controlled markets. If competition is absent or weak, prices will embody monopoly profits.

Basic data will have to be collected progressively, through sample surveys, since firms will proliferate as new markets are created and enterprises are privatized and broken up to eliminate monopolies. This will require new procedures that will tax the capacities of CSOs (see chapter 7). Concurrently, at the micro level, data provision may be seen less by business as an inherent part of production and more as a necessary step toward a better information base, with enterprises deciding on whether to comply and to what extent the cost of compliance will be charged to overhead. Inducements to report, which emerged gradually and by consensus in market economies, will have to emerge quickly during the transition in HPEs.

In some areas, data quality may deteriorate because of a lag in adjusting to new concepts by those reporting, and because of the greater burdens involved in providing new kinds of data. Moreover, changes in economic policies and the structure of economies will pose problems of data consistency. There may also be new incentives to under-report—for the private sector, to avoid taxes or for large state firms to continue to qualify for subsidies—as long as reported data are not kept confidential and used exclusively for statistical purpose.

Since reform and transformation are usually accompanied by increased openness, improvement is expected in the availability, and in some respects in the quality, of statistical data. The improvement has three overlapping phases. First, the HPEs release previously unpublished data. Second, they shift to international classification and reporting concepts. Third, they improve the reliability, quality, and international comparability of economic aggregates—modifying statistical methods to give more reliable indicators of growth, structure, levels, and conversion to dollar values. Political changes in many HPEs also make possible the retroactive revision of some previously published figures and time series, by their CSOs and by independent experts.

But increased openness may be accompanied by a redrawing of political borders and a redefinition of national economy, as in the USSR. Sorting out the statistical issues for international and intertemporal comparisons and compiling reasonable estimates is thus an iterative process.

Price reform and the private sector

A useful distinction is that between price revision, which adjusts prices without altering the fundamentals of price formation, as done routinely from time to time in CPEs, and price reform, a basic change in how prices are determined and affect resource allocation that devolves price determination from central control to autonomous firms. Price revisions are discussed in chapters 2 and 3; price reform is discussed below.

For goods, services, and factors of production, price reform may entail moving from administered prices to a system of:

- Rule-based prices, in which sellers must follow specific pricing rules or complex formulas to determine allowable increases in the prices of output, in profit markups, in increments in average wages or the total wage bill, in the use of after-tax profits, and so on, or
- Prices freely determined by market forces.

Reforming HPEs may present price statistics that lump together rule-based prices and free prices, as in Hungary during the 1980s. But because some data on free prices are not available from official price lists or not properly weighted by turnover, this may give a misleading indication of how far prices are determined by market forces.

Price reforms may depend on the market served, with output being more or less competitively priced, depending on the degree of liberalization. Take China, which in 1984–85 established a two-tier

price system. One part of a Chinese enterprise's output and corresponding input was planned, subject to administered pricing rules and allocated inputs and outputs while the rest was not. This has created problems for the accurate computation of price indexes.

Normally, HPEs do not move from administered to market prices quickly and across the board because of obstacles. Many economists and decisionmakers do not have a good understanding of the advantages of market pricing, especially during the early stages of reform. Moreover, a rapid across-the-board switch to market prices causes substantial dislocations because many pre-reform prices were far from market-clearing levels and many of the institutional preconditions for a well-functioning market are absent.

Through successive price revisions, measures of total cost and cost structure in HPEs can become economically more meaningful—as interest and capital charges are introduced, wage taxes levied, depreciation rates altered, and retained earnings increased over time. But so long as resources are not allocated through a price mechanism, price revisions do not have the economic effects that similar changes might have in a market economy.

As costs are defined more fully and the prices of imports are neutralized less frequently through price equalization, wholesale prices will increase and be passed on more readily to retail prices. But as more prices become market determined, CSOs may lag in changing the way they construct price indexes. That is, the true weight of goods and services whose prices are market determined may be understated, with a corresponding impact on the price indexes. Thus, inflation may increasingly be understated as price reforms are introduced, or as the authorities ignore the rapid growth of transactions in gray or black markets. Without good price indexes that are sufficiently flexible to follow changes, it will be impossible to construct good volume indexes.

The rapid development of the private sector creates new problems of statistical measurement. One is under-reporting of the level of economic activity by new private owners, essentially for tax reasons. The other is an inability to monitor private-sector activities. HPE statistical offices are geared to deal mainly with a small number of large state-owned firms, each required to complete comprehensive reports. They are not equipped, early in the transition, to switch suddenly to conducting sample surveys based on accurate business registers.

Open inflation and market breakdown

Two things happen as prices are liberalized. First, repressed inflation—expressed as shortages—becomes open inflation. Unless controlled by macroeconomic policies, open inflation will persist or accelerate. Wages in the public sector may keep pace with inflation, or are fed by rising costs in the emerging private sector. Second, as competition increases, arbitrage for inputs and outlets replaces outmoded plans for the allocation and distribution of resources.

Open inflation may emerge and persist for these reasons:

- Price increases not captured previously can now be captured by official statistics.

- Planners continue to push for unsustainably high growth rates, causing the economy to overheat, as happened during the early years of the Gorbachev administration.

- Deficits in the state budget increase and the growth of money and credit becomes excessive.

- Monetary balances held by enterprises and the population—the monetary overhang—increase because price controls do not allow product markets to clear, while tight financial control of enterprises collapses.

- The power of enterprises to make decisions increases without making them subject to the financial discipline of market forces. Receding central control results in excessive growth of wages and investments, which in turn drastically reduces the collection of producer taxes.

- A slow devolution from a mono-bank to a two-tier banking system results in the lack of an independent monetary authority. Enterprises may respond to attempts to tighten monetary policy by granting each other extended—voluntarily or involuntarily—supplier credits.

Reforms typically reduce central control over wages and increase the mobility of labor. In particular, workers can earn higher incomes by leaving the state sector, especially those with scarce skills, driving up labor costs in both markets and increasing moonlighting. Reduced subsidies on consumer goods and services, and therefore higher prices, amplify the pressure for compensating wage increases, which could start a wage-price spiral without hard budget constraints on firms and effective macro policies.

Reporting and measurement issues

The transition from an HPE to a market-based economy involves the gradual substitution of market-tested products and services for those provided in a sellers' market. This move can bring a genuine improvement in economic welfare, which may or may not be recognized in production data, depending on accounting procedures and how well prices reflect quality improvement.

During transition, the amount of nonbeneficial production—substandard goods and projects mothballed without being written off as losses—will increase in the short term, because of a decline in the sellers' market. These changes will result in financial losses, and affect measures of value and growth alike. Declines in growth rates resulting from more accurate reporting must be interpreted as such, and not equated to declines in living standards.

Decentralized decisionmaking by state-owned enterprises may also reduce systemic biases in reporting and growth-rate estimates. If managers are no longer judged on the basis of quantity plan fulfillment, there is no reason to overstate the growth of output. As reforms proceed, truth in reporting at the national level may also improve, as the authorities adequately separate the reporting channels for purposes of measuring activity and for rewarding performance. In any event, as the private sector expands, the authorities will have less and less of a role in directing economic activities at the micro-level.

HPEs will also require improved methods of national inventory accounting. The valuation of changes in stocks and net investment, or net replacement, depend on initial measures of stocks and fixed assets valued at historic (FIFO) cost. When prices are rising, the current price value of net replacement is overstated when there is large increase in prices over a long period, and when revaluation of fixed assets was made a long time ago, as explained in the previous chapter (see *Historic versus current valuation of assets*). The overstatement on current NMP may exceed 10 percent, as for example in Hungary in 1988. These biases in most countries rose in the past 10 years, as open and hidden inflation increased considerably.

New arrangements for foreign trade

Liberalized foreign trade means reducing the isolation of the domestic economy from the global economy by changing the roles of exchange rates and domestic price structures. Combined with privatization, liberalization will increase the number of traders, and compilation of trade data will have to move from state trading firms to customs authorities.

Most of the institutional arrangements for intra-CMEA trade and finance were scrapped in December 1990, when trade between members of the CMEA was changed to current world market prices, settled in convertible currencies. Accumulated TR trade and payment balances were to be settled in several ways, including the delivery of goods and services up to agreed dates on conditions prevailing in 1990. Some balances were to be translated into dollars at a bilaterally negotiated TR/$ rate and settled in cash or converted into bilaterally negotiated loans. In practice, this method of settlement has run into a host of problems, the net effect of which is that it is uncertain when, or even if, the balances will ever be settled.

In 1991 barter trade, arranged by firms in two countries, replaced some trade that was formerly in TRs under intergovernmental agreements. The barter terms negotiated have not necessarily been those that would have prevailed in world markets. The switch to dollar trade brings many practical problems. Most former CMEA exporters to the USSR wanted payment guaranteed by an irrevocable letter of credit drawn on a Soviet bank or on a Western bank. But Soviet banks were willing to open letters of credit only with tight conditions, including a guarantee that the proceeds from matching Soviet export transactions would be allocated on average: 40 percent to the central government, to be used mainly to service debt; 30 percent to the treasury of the republics; 3 percent to the local authority treasury; and only 17 percent to be released to the enterprise. Long administrative delays from the growing use of letters of credit were partly responsible for the drastic fall in Soviet-East European trade in 1991. During the course of 1991–92, economic disruption in the wake of the breakup of the USSR (see box 4.1) became an increasingly important factor.

One aspect of new trade arrangements in HPEs is that exchange rates are expected to perform some of the economic functions they perform in market economies. "Official" and "market" rates are likely to exist side-by-side. Already in some countries, the multiple exchange rate system is being replaced by a unified one, and partial or full currency convertibility has been introduced. But these changes are incomplete; as non-market exchange rates and restrictions on trade (including foreign exchange)

persist, misreporting remains a hazard. Despite the move toward a centralized role for customs authorities in measuring and recording trade, trade data based on customs documents are becoming increasingly difficult to reconcile with actual transaction values and volumes, as revealed, for example, by financial data in the balance of payments.

The exchange rate systems of HPEs pose dilemmas for analyzing historical data. When can HPE exchange rates be used for GNP conversion in the same way that analysts use them in market economies? If a country has multiple exchange rates, which exchange rates should be employed for what kind of conversion to obtain internationally comparable data? Is a market-clearing rate established in a "thin" parallel market appropriate for conversion of all transactions? Can the same approach be used for exchange rates vis-à-vis convertible currencies—the dollar—and nonconvertible currencies—the ruble or the transferable ruble?

Resolving such dilemmas involves judgment. The starting point is to determine how a reforming HPE has established, and uses, its various exchange rates. Once a commercial exchange rate is established that effectively links most domestic and foreign transactions, the official, controlled, exchange rate loses its rationale and can be abolished. Linking means that domestic producers of exports receive, and importers pay, the local currency equivalent of the foreign value of the transaction and that foreign trade price equalization is abandoned. Whether a commercial exchange rate provides the intended incentive to producers to become market-oriented depends on many features of the economic system, especially taxation and subsidization.

Another facet of the new trade arrangements is decreasing the insulation of domestic producers from the rest of the world by allowing them to export/import freely, reducing the quantitative restrictions on trade and abolishing price equalization.

Easing access to foreign exchange for enterprises can be a catalyst for more liberal trade. During the early stage of trade liberalization, exporters in several HPEs were allowed to keep a portion of their export proceeds as "retention quotas" for their own use or to sell through auction markets. This was a step toward making nonconvertible currencies convertible, although this "reform" was not without its problems. For example, under such an arrangement, suppliers of intermediate products often preferred to export them, even at the expense of domestic manufacturers of finished products, whose exports thereby suffered.

Box 4.1 Data issues in the wake of the breakup of the Soviet Union

The *Guide* considers the former Soviet Union (FSU) as it was prior to dissolution in late 1991. Information on the economies emerging from the FSU region are currently being collected and evaluated by the World Bank and others but it will be some months before reasonably complete time series can be presented for each, separately. Hence, this edition of the *Guide* provides only a few key indicators of the relative importance of the 15 former republics, in 1990.

Work is proceeding on recasting the usual FSU measures, like net material product (NMP), into internationally recognized indicators like gross domestic product (GDP). Preliminary estimates show the signi_cant differences in GDP per capita that existed among the republics (see below).

More than reclassification to international standards may be necessary to assess FSU economies. Transactions among the 15 economies should now be regarded as cross-border, or international. For example, the resource balance (exports minus imports) of each economy depends not only on its share in FSU trade with the rest of the world, or what may be called extra-Union trade. It also depends on the movement of goods and services between each FSU economy and the other 14—and how one values such inter-republic exports and imports.

FSU economies traded much more with each other than with the outside world. However, they did so within the context of a central plan and at prices dictated by the plan. It is not clear whether inter-republic trade should be valued at planned internal prices or at average foreign prices suggested by extra-Union trade. The figures in columns 3–6 take the second approach but column 7 indicates the analytical significance of the choice by reporting the impact of such a repricing from internal to foreign prices. For the FSU as a whole there is no difference but the distribution of the gross regional product among the 15 would differ from what is shown in column 2, hypothetically by the percentage shown in column 7 if trade among FSU economies had been at average foreign prices.

Selected Indicators, 1990

	Population (millions) (1)	GDP per capita (rubles) (2)	Exports		Imports		Impact of repricing intra-union trade (percentage of GNP) (7)
			Extra-union (millions of rubles) (3)	Inter-republic (foreign prices) (4)	Extra-union (millions of rubles) (5)	Inter-republic (foreign prices) (6)	
Armenia	3.3	3,050	64	1,989	500	3,155	-8.7
Azerbaidjan	7.1	2,093	423	4,576	826	4,308	-10.6
Belarus	10.3	3,957	2,010	16,043	3,073	17,259	-8.9
Estonia	1.6	5,298	116	1,952	346	3,116	-10.8
Georgia	5.5	2,700	301	2,852	902	4,464	-16.2
Kazakhstan	16.7	3,310	1,039	8,450	1,900	14,550	-0.4
Kyrghyzstan	4.4	2,014	52	1,954	759	2,910	-2.5
Latvia	2.7	4,554	178	3,939	960	4,873	-10.2
Lithuania	3.7	3,757	397	4,155	902	7,169	-16.7
Moldova	4.4	3,035	237	2,705	837	4,947	-23.5
Russia	148.0	4,365	46,468	86,450	46,506	56,583	3.5
Tajikistan	5.2	1,450	356	1,643	383	3,082	-6.0
Turkmenistan	3.6	2,181	114	2,773	306	2,438	10.0
Ukraine	51.8	3,180	7,829	35,969	9,301	42,468	-3.5
Uzbekistan	20.3	1,725	813	6,889	1,296	10,993	-1.2
Former USSR	288.6	3,651	60,397	182,337	68,798	182,313	0.0

Net external debt

The reporting of debt statistics should improve during the transition as more HPEs join international institutions that require proper reporting of external assets and liabilities. Rescheduling with the Paris and London Clubs, as in the cases of Poland, Yugoslavia, and Bulgaria, requires debtors to organize their external debt accounts before negotiating, and thus their debt statistics are likely to improve. For example, the amount of classified information has already been reduced as East-West relations have improved.

Fiscal and monetary policies

Reforms are likely to have a major impact on the interpretation of fiscal and monetary data. In the monetary sphere, with deregulation, higher interest rates, and declining shortages, increases in the holding of money may indicate not involuntary holdings but voluntary savings. Reform is likely to increase state budget expenditures on housing subsidies (because state financial institutions have granted fixed-rate, low-interest mortgages to households) previously covered by low interest rates paid on household deposits. The latter are now rising while mortgage rates have remained unchanged. Social security payments are also likely to increase because of adjustment for inflation and because a new social safety net, including unemployment compensation, also has to be financed by the state budget. Higher interest rates will, as monetary policy becomes a policy instrument, increase internal debt service costs. And devaluation of exchange rates to more realistic levels will raise the domestic costs of external debt servicing. Although price increases for basic goods and services will reduce subsidies, they will increase pressures for wage compensation and higher social security payments for the poor. Greater independence for budgetary institutions may lead to the loss of fully consolidated fiscal accounts, but more local autonomy will also put a strain on budgetary systems. The introduction of new taxes—such as value-added taxes, personal income taxes, and statutory profit taxes—to replace the discretionary turnover taxes will require new data reporting.

Social and employment policies

The transition from an official policy of ensured full employment to the same objectives subject to the conditions of the labor market presents the need for unemployment insurance and the creation of institutions to assist with job placement and retraining. HPEs will have to implement new ways of achieving social goals as they move toward market economies and corresponding new approaches to monitoring conditions. These include:

- Upgrading of training and retraining for the unemployed, and teaching new skills, especially administrative and managerial, to support new institutions and activities.

- Developing unemployment insurance systems and safety nets to protect those worst affected by economic reforms.

- Reforming labor markets to support employment services, increase labor mobility, more market-oriented systems of wage determination, and better means of monitoring employment trends.

- Restructuring health systems to emphasize prevention and to arrest declines in health, with particular attention to environmental and occupational diseases.

Employment studies are biased by counting some employees with full- or part-time jobs in the private sector as employees in the public sector where they may also have a job. A lack of reliable data in base years makes the transition difficult to monitor, especially if unemployment appears in the form of part-time work. One solution is to measure working time spent in the main economic sectors and in auxiliary activities and then translate the hours to full-time equivalents. This is already accepted, as a complementary measure, in several countries, but no international data are as yet available.

Environment and energy policies

The transition to a market economy is likely to improve environmental assessment and energy use in HPEs. As prices are liberalized and firms are forced to pay more for resources, production will have to become more energy efficient and cost-effective. Likewise, as administrative and industrial sectors are decentralized and restructured, and industry opened to foreign trade, environmental concerns and trade liberalization could mutually reinforce efficient energy and natural-resource use. A byproduct of greater market sensitivity by firms and the introduction of effective environmental regulations could be to encourage the public and private sectors to gather more refined and complete data on environmental conditions and energy consumption.

Energy conversion is responsible for much of the air pollution in HPEs; price reforms should force firms to take energy-efficient decisions and rationalize private and government use of environmental goods, such as clean air and water. Emissions taxes, pollution permits, and fines can create incentives for environmental accounting and data-gathering by companies and regulators. Effective enforcement and price reforms compel inefficient firms to make decisions on resource consumption and production on the basis of reliable up-to-date information.

If improved environmental quality is a precondition of membership in regional trading associations, the relaxation of trade barriers and the greater integration of HPEs into the global economy could also motivate energy-efficient production and a demand for better environmental data. In addition, some foreign buyers of HPE industrial sites may have to comply with the environmental standards of their home countries. There is thus the likelihood that higher environmental standards will be "imported" from Western countries. In any event, HPEs will probably require foreigners to meet certain environmental criteria as a prerequisite for transferring ownership to them. International conventions could, also, establish data-gathering bodies to monitor transnational environmental goods, such as international water boundaries, aquifers, and shared air columns. All this will require extensive use of environmental impact assessments and exchanges of information. Unified independent environmental agencies able to levy fines and raise taxes on domestic and foreign-owned firms would greatly help in harmonizing, monitoring, and gathering data in both the private and public sectors.

Part 2. Global Focus

Chapter 5. Framework for Comparing Economies

International comparisons of income and growth are controversial, even where economies share similar features and abide by international standards of macroeconomic accounting. Two fundamental questions of comparative economic theory are how to group countries by significant features, and how to compare the structure and growth of economies with fundamental differences, such as those between countries where governments attempt to exercise pervasive direct control over economic activities and those where market forces largely prevail and governments act mainly through indirect monetary and fiscal means.

For countries relying heavily on direct controls, common problems and rigidities might be expected. But even these countries are quite heterogeneous. In Eastern Europe, the Pacific Basin, Africa, and the Caribbean, they face problems characteristic of their regions. Their economic problems may also relate to relative incomes, historical factors, and resource endowments. The HPEs should be viewed not only for their economic systems but for a variety of other endogenous and exogenous factors.

Most **historically planned economies** that have entered the path of transition are ex-members of the CMEA and relied on the MPS framework of national accounts (see table). Given the large systemic and historical differences among HPEs, they are subdivided into HPEs in Europe and HPEs elsewhere. Ranked by estimated GNP per capita, the HPEs' characteristic institutional features were listed below.

Other Economies in Transition (OET) are those that had dirigiste economic policies, including extensive state ownership of production in the modern sector, but without the full panoply of central planning. In descending order of estimated per capita GNP, these are: Algeria, Angola, Guinea, Myanmar, Madagascar, Afghanistan, Somalia, Tanzania, Ethiopia, and Mozambique. Typically, they had not reached the stage of monetization and information technology where economywide Soviet-style central planning and administration was feasible, even if their political leaders desired to move their

	Member of CMEA	Used or uses MPS accounting framework
HPEs in Europe		
German Dem. Rep.	Yes	Yes
USSR	Yes	Yes
Czechoslovakia	Yes	Yes
Yugoslavia	No	Yes
Hungary	Yes	Yes
Poland	Yes	Yes
Bulgaria	Yes	Yes
Romania	Yes	Yes
Albania	Yes	Yes
HPEs elsewhere		
Cuba	Yes	Yes
Mongolia	Yes	Yes
Nicaragua	No	No
Korea, Dem. Rep.	No	Yes
China	No	Yes
Viet Nam	Yes	Yes
Lao People's Dem. Rep.	No	Yes
Cambodia	No	Yes

countries in that direction. To be sure, today many of these countries are abandoning the limited central planning they had practiced and are moving toward predominantly market systems.

The problems of accurately measuring economic activity in these other economies in transition are numerous. They typically have large "irregular" economies that are poorly measured. Moreover, some countries have produced few statistics, and those they produce seldom meet either SNA or MPS international standards; their data are often simple extensions of previous benchmarks. The problems of weak governments assigning low priority to statistical systems, often compounded by civil strife, further explain why statistical information is meager and not reliable.

The use of data from comparator market economies allows the analyst to consider the effect of system-related, institutional, and statistical features on the economic performance of the planned economies. Even more important, the use of comparators permits an assessment of the effects of system changes on economic structure and outcomes. These comparator countries include a sample of the rich high-income economies, the not-so-rich middle-income economies, and the poor low-income economies. The sample was selected to include at least one market economy that can be approximately matched to each HPE in terms of per capita GNP, country size, and geographic location (see Global Tables).

Framing macroeconomic policies requires statistical data, for example, on real output growth, inflationary pressures, public finance, money, and the balance of payments. These were normally unavailable—or not in accordance with SNA standard—in HPEs. Whether for studies of secular trends or for more near-term needs, the Global Tables provide a convenient starting point for a statistical profile of HPEs.

Data gaps in conventional time series

Weak and missing data result not only from the structures and incentives driving HPE reporting systems, but also from the financial resources spent on statistics, human capital endowments and administrative experience, and the relatively short length of time these statistical systems were operating in some of the countries. Wealthier HPEs could be expected to gather and disseminate more reliable data. Poorer countries have larger informal sectors, fewer resources for statistics, and often other priorities. But measuring an "income effect" on statistics is difficult because the effect of income cannot be easily isolated from the effects of economic and political system differences.

To improve data coverage in the Global Tables, gap-filling is necessary. Gap-filling in this instance generally involves replacing one data series with another where data are judged to be unreliable, rather than substituting single year estimates. Deciding which alternative series are to be used for this purpose is inextricably linked to the definitions and concepts that have been found practical in broad international comparisons. Most studies of HPEs by specialists on those countries tend to compare European HPEs with high-income OECD economies. But World Bank statistical publications must keep a global perspective. Comparing European HPEs with the OECD countries avoids many methodological complications—but at a price, namely, the loss of a global perspective in making inter-country comparisons. The price is particularly high

during transition, because in many respects the most appropriate comparisons for HPEs in transition are with middle-income economies that have been moving up the development scale in recent decades.

In gap-filling, comparability with World Bank data is sought along two planes. First, preference is given to estimates that use methods and converters similar to those used by the World Bank, and are roughly comparable across countries and consistent through time. Generally, these follow the recommendations of the United Nations on national accounting methodology. Second, preference is given to data for which the underlying assumptions and coverage are not in conflict with those of the dominant series.

Next, priority is given to data from official sources, using the closest possible definition to the desired indicator. In some cases, this means substituting MPS measures for SNA measures, such as NMP for GNP, and signalling this with a footnote. In only a few cases are alternative sources used to fill gaps. Differences in NMP estimates from alternative sources are rarely analytically significant, and usually arise from differing vintages of the data. But alternative series built on NMP estimates may embody corrections to reflect perceived or real biases in the official data; such corrections result in analytically significant differences from official data (such as CIA data), documented in chapters 8 and 9, and in the Technical Notes.

Concerns about World Bank GNP per capita methodology

The main issue about international comparisons focuses, not surprisingly, on the most widely recognized measure of development—GNP in U.S. dollars—as the common denominator. The World Bank uses exchange rates as the basis for converting GNP numbers to a common currency. Why? And how does the most widely recognized alternative approach to exchange-rate–based estimates—the purchasing power parity method—work?

All methods of transforming GNP denominated in national currencies to a common basis (see global table 1) suffer from conceptual difficulties. The problem of using official exchange rates is twofold: first, the rates may be very different from hypothetical market-clearing rates that would prevail in the absence of restrictions, and second, abrupt devaluations or revaluations shift countries' relative incomes in a manner inconsistent with any reasonable view of relative changes in real incomes. Nevertheless, use of the official exchange rates has clear advantages, notably in terms of the comprehensiveness of country coverage and timeliness. And the effects of abrupt exchange rate changes can be lessened, as they are in the World Bank's methodology, by such smoothing techniques as employing trade-weighted averaging of multiple exchange rates, etc.

When conditions are substantially different from those prevailing under free trade and currency convertibility, the World Bank resorts to alternative conversion factors to reflect the conditions under which foreign transactions take place. These estimates seek to take into account, among other things, the nature and restrictiveness of the trading regime, information on relative prices, and the evolution of real exchange rates. This is difficult and in part judgmental, and its use has been kept to a minimum.

For reducing numbers to a common base, the World Bank has little choice at present but to use exchange-rate-based measures for international comparisons of per capita GNP and other macroeconomic indicators. But the concept of a market-determined exchange rate for foreign currency is not applicable in HPEs before they entered transition because transactions abroad were handled by centrally guided foreign trading organizations. Nor is it applicable where complex systems of foreign trade "coefficients" or "price equalization" schemes are being used in the absence of market prices and exchange rates. Such mechanisms, developed to keep the domestic economy isolated from external influences, in effect suppress signals that could guide trade choices toward mutual advantage.

One cause of nonmarket trade pricing for tradables is that the structure of relative domestic prices deviates unusually widely from that of relative prices in market economies. So, even if a conversion factor seems economically meaningful in an HPE for the whole economy or for a large basket of goods traded, it may not be a meaningful converter for single products, product groups, or economic activities.

Moreover, the composition of GNP cannot but be affected by systematic differences in relative prices. What would appear as normal responses to price elasticities in market economies may appear in HPEs as distortions in quantities, and hence weights for items priced in the converter basket. This is generally true but particularly significant in both the composition and level of international transactions relative to GNP.

As comprehensive economic reforms progress, the exchange rates of HPEs begin to assume some

of the functions that exchange rates perform in market economies. They thus become more suited to measuring relative prices between traded and nontraded goods and services and to converting GNP into dollars.

It is important to note that the early stage of transition toward a market system may bring about an unusually large real devaluation of the currency of an HPE, for any or all of the following reasons. In most cases, trade can be rapidly reoriented from the CMEA to the world market only by accepting very low prices for HPE manufactures. HPEs compete mainly by varying their prices, whereas market economies rely also on such variables as service, packaging, advertising, and credit. The fact that many enterprises in the HPEs produce goods that do not compete readily with imports from market economies, while there is a pent-up demand for Western imports, may cause policymakers in some HPEs to protect their industries via very large depreciations of their currency. Also, the citizens of countries facing severe economic disruptions and political uncertainties often increase their demand for foreign currency, which is one of the few assets in which they can invest in an attempt to hedge against the large economic and political uncertainties they face. The resulting depreciation of the real exchange rate may well be much greater in the short run than it will be in the long run. Such a depreciation causes a large drop in total dollar and per capita GNP, if the exchange rate is used as the converter.

Alternative approaches to GNP conversion

The main alternative to exchange-rate-based conversions is a multilateral comparison that assigns "prices" to domestic product groupings based on an average of relative price coefficients from countries participating in the exercise. One such approach—the International Comparisons Program (ICP)—is of interest because several HPEs have participated and other HPEs are joining. (For applications of this method, see chapter 9).

The ICP offers conceptually valid expressions of GDP volumes at uniform international or regional prices. It avoids some major problems of exchange-rate comparisons. For GDP and detailed components, the ICP method also yields average international price measures, known mainly as purchasing power parities (PPPs). This provides a basis for analyzing differences in internal relative prices between countries. Theoretically, it also provides alternative quantity weights for constructing price indexes. While the ICP concentrates on expenditure accounts, the time series normally used for estimating growth are available in detail only as production accounts.

Starting with the identity price (P) times quantity (Q) equals value (V), how "true" is the Q obtained from V/P? The answer depends on how closely the P corresponds to the average price used in measuring the V. Despite improvements in recent phases of ICP, it is still difficult to match items because of quality differences, all of which affect P and Q. This problem is especially important for HPEs, where quality is generally lower. For this reason, some analysts argue that early ICP-type comparisons, which do not adequately correct for quality differences, may have overstated the dollar GNP of HPEs.

The choice of prices and linking procedures strongly influences the results. The ICP looks at both tradables and nontradables; an equilibrium exchange rate covers both current-account transactions and capital flows, which are ignored in the ICP. The aggregation procedures employed and the level at which aggregation occurs also influence the measured real economic relationships between two countries. But the ICP does not have near-universal coverage, and data collection is costly. Thus, the results are not timely, even for benchmark years. Methods of consistently extending the ICP benchmarks to other nonbenchmark countries and years are still evolving.

An alternative to exchange rates and purchasing power parities for calculating comparable levels of income is the physical indicators (PI) method. It establishes a relationship between physical outputs and per capita incomes of HPEs and other countries. Using this relationship and data on physical output, it aims to sidestep some problems of exchange rates and the nonparticipation of many HPEs in the ICP.

The PI method is a two-step approach for estimating per capita GDP in dollars. In step one a regression relationship is determined between physical indicators of development—always some type of consumption data—and per capita dollar GNP (GDP) for countries for which reasonably good per capita dollar figures are available. The original dollar per capita GDPs of the comparator

countries could be estimated on the basis of exchange rate conversions or PPPs. Thus, the resulting PI estimates are either exchange rate-based or PPP-based. In step two the statistical relationship obtained is employed to estimate the per capita dollar GDPs of countries for which meaningful dollar exchange rates or PPPs could not be found: that is, HPEs. Some physical indicators, such as consumption volume and stock data for certain products, are generally available for HPEs, and are more reliable than value-based data. PI-based estimates can be made for most HPEs.

The PI method is straightforward. It applies uniform criteria—the same sample of physical indicators—for all countries compared, and its data and computational requirements are not too daunting. It avoids the problem of arbitrary domestic prices and currency converters for countries where such problems are severe, as they are in many HPEs. But quality problems—or associated valuation or pricing issues—re-emerge in the weights assigned to the components of GNP. These quality issues remain a major shortcoming of the PI approach because the high-tech products and services of the high-income countries cannot be compared with those of low-income countries. More generally, insufficient account is taken of the often large differences among countries in the quality of products, services, and stocks of such things as passenger cars, television sets, and the number of hospital beds used as physical indicators. The same is also true for the ICP method. PI results also depend on the choice of indicators and comparator countries.

Applying the PI method to HPEs also engenders system-related problems. Since some physical indicators represent intermediate consumption, the inefficient uses of materials that are characteristic of HPEs will be reflected in relatively high GDP estimates.

In sum, estimating dollar per capita incomes of HPEs is fraught with conceptual difficulties and statistical problems, especially those of conversion. This underscores the importance of carefully documenting and examining any dollar data before relying on them for analysis and cross-country or intertemporal comparisons. For a more detailed discussion of exchange rates and PPPs, see chapter 9. Results of these methods are presented in Table 1 of the Global Tables and in the Comparator Tables.

Chapter 6. Global Tables

Descriptive notes

This section explains the selection and presentation of indicators in the Global Tables; many of them also appear for HPEs later in the Guide and are explained at greater length in chapter 11.

The Global Tables cover per capita income, size, structure and growth of output and demand, inflation, terms of trade, external debt and reserves, fiscal and monetary accounts, human resources, social indicators, and the environment.

Many of the indicators are from data files developed by the World Bank through information obtained directly from national sources, other international and national organizations, and private sources—when they can be fitted to internationally agreed classification schemes. For other data—fiscal, monetary, labor, human resources, world and social indicators—a few of the series made available to the World Bank by other international agencies are recast. Data on the environment and technology are from the World Resource Institute's *World Resources, 1990–91*. Specifics on sources and methods are in the Technical Notes.

Every effort has been made to provide information according to internationally agreed guidelines. But care and caution should be exercised in any comparative analysis of the economic performances of planned economies in the international context. Much is still not known about the methodologies underlying their data, and much remains to be done in improving the comparability of HPE historical data.

The classifications—"HPEs," "OETs," and "Comparator Countries"—are considered analytically useful concepts in this context. Aggregate data for the comparator countries, shown separately for low-, middle-, and high-income economies are not the totals (or averages) of the countries listed, but of a larger universe of countries. For example, totals for the high-income countries also include data for the United Kingdom, which is not shown separately. Dozens of comparator countries are not listed, even though they are accounted for in the aggregate figures. This approach means that the comparator totals and averages are the—unadjusted, for the most part—totals and averages found in standard World Bank publications, except that HPEs and OETs have been excluded where appropriate. Aggregating data for HPEs using the same techniques as for market economies was not possible for this first version of the Guide due to still considerable gaps in time series for some large countries.

Tables 1 and 2. Per capita income

Alternative per capita income measures are especially sensitive to methodological choice. The results have important implications because per capita income is a widely used and recognized indicator of performance.

Legitimate alternatives exist that rank HPEs high or low relative to the per capita GNP of the United States. Table 1 is organized to show this, starting with PPPs and moving toward exchange rates. For example, Yugoslavia's per capita income expressed as a share of U.S. GNP per capita is twice as high using PPPs as using exchange rates: 28 percent versus 14 percent.

This does not by itself point to deficient data. Across income levels and economic systems, the dispersion in total and per capita dollar GNPs between the developed and developing countries is much smaller if the comparisons are based on derived PPPs than on exchange-rate conversions, mainly due to the high value given to nontradables—services—in the former approach. Evidence suggests that there is a systematic relationship between spot exchange rates and PPPs: the ratio of GDP converted at the former to GDP converted at the latter declines with rising income levels (see chapter 9). This relationship, strong in earlier phases (1970, 1975), is less strong in later phases (1980, 1985), especially at the lower end of the income scale.

Data sources for Purchasing Power Parity Indicators in table 1 include the UNDP's *Human Development Report* (HDR), which relies mainly on the Penn World Tables of Summers and Heston; an unpublished study by the CMEA; and World Military Expenditures and Arms Transfers of the Arms Control and Disarmament Agency (ACDA) for HPEs, although Atlas-type conversion is used for other economies. Physical indicators are estimates provided by Hungarian economist Eva Ehrlich (see Bibliography). An interesting alternative set of estimates is provided, based on unpublished work by UN Statistical Office Staff.

To convert local currency GDP data into U.S. dollars, the UNSO uses a price-adjusted rate of exchange (PARE) as the alternative conversion rate. The PARE rate is derived by extrapolating either the exchange rate of a fixed base year or the average exchange rate of a base period, by price changes measured by implicit GDP deflators. The objective is to eliminate the local price fluctuations in the GDP data, and convert it into U.S. dollars at the conversion rate of the base period. There are two kinds of PARE rates developed by UNSO, absolute and relative. The absolute PARE involves adjustments to the exchange rates of all countries including the U.S., whereas relative PARE adjustments are made to the exchange rates of all countries, but not to the U.S. The numbers presented here are the 1989 GDP per capita data converted to U.S dollars at the absolute 1980 to 1989 PARE rate.

Also shown are figures of the OECD's Development Assistance Committee, as reported in its chairman's Annual Report, and those from the World Bank's Atlas (see Bibliography).

Tables 3 to 7. Size, structure, and growth of production and demand

Gross domestic product (GDP), investment, consumption, and savings monitor broad trends in economic performance. The data provide aggregate and sectoral information on production (value added in agriculture, industry, and services), income, expenditure, and international transactions.

Gross national product (GNP) per capita—GDP per capita adjusted for net factor income from abroad—is a widely monitored indicator of economic progress. When expressed in current U.S. dollars, however, the values for these indicators reflect exchange rate fluctuations, as well as underlying economic and demographic changes. These indicators are useful for cross-country comparison in any one year but require special attention when used for trend analysis. An alternative approach uses gross national income at 1987 prices, which holds prices constant except for internationally traded goods, so that terms-of-trade effects are included.

All income is spent on consumption or saved (invested), and each is shown as a share of GDP. Gross domestic investment measures additions to fixed assets of an economy, whether an increment to the stock of capital or replenishing depreciated capital stock, plus net changes in the level of inventories. It is financed through either domestic or foreign savings.

Exports of goods and nonfactor services (GNFS) as a percentage of GDP measures the importance of export trade in each economy and allows comparisons of level of trade across countries. The resource balance is the difference between export and imports of goods and nonfactor services.

The rates of growth of production and demand comprise important indicators of economic progress and are widely monitored. These growth rates, calculated from national data, embody system-specific and country-specific peculiarities. Some may change over time in a given country as a result, say, of changes in the economic system. Thus, cross-country comparisons and trend analyses for individual countries must be made cautiously. Moreover, aggregate values and trends reflect the choice of base year.

A single base year raises problems when there are significant changes in structure—such as in the composition of output—and in relative prices. For instance, values expressed in constant U.S. dollars reflect the exchange rates prevailing during the base year. And a single base year may be the peak, or trough, of a cycle. Where subsequent exchange rate changes have been substantial, as in many HPEs since the late 1980s, comparisons between countries and aggregate trends will be affected. In HPEs the value of the U.S. dollar in domestic currency at official rates was, historically, relatively low in the 1970s and early 1980s. When national economies perform differently, alternative base years or aggregation methods give different, but not necessarily better or worse, results. The Global Tables follow the World Bank's statistical conventions as explained in detail in chapter 11.

The GDP deflator in national currency data shows changes in domestic prices. Overall inflation in GDP, as measured by the implicit deflator, includes all goods and services. The consumer price index measures the change in prices of a unique bundle of consumer goods for each economy.

Table 8. Trade participation and terms of trade

The trade participation ratio is the sum of exports and imports of goods and nonfactor services as a share of GDP. This ratio compares trade with income and is widely used as a measure of openness. These ratios embody for HPEs all the pricing issues discussed in chapter 3, including those affecting foreign trade, and may not be strictly comparable with the ratios in market economies. The terms of trade indicate relative movements of unit values of exports and imports, based on merchandise trade only. If export prices rise and import prices rise more slowly or decline, the same quantity of exports buys more imports. The effect is equivalent to an increase in the real value of output of the export sector. If import prices were to rise more quickly than export prices, the reverse is true. Chapter 11 explains alternative approaches to aggregating ruble and dollar trade price effects. See also the Basic Tables.

Table 9. External debt and international reserves

Stock of external debt shows the gross external obligations of a country to the international community. It is also meaningful for measuring the health of an economy, when, for example, it is compared to GNP or with the country's ability to repay the debt with exports. The gross debt stock, rather than debt service ratios, was chosen as an indicator because no consensus exists as to the value of exports in nonconvertible currency trade in total exports. Even then, debt stock data for such countries is available only for government external debt, potentially understating total external indebtedness. The figures shown for high-income economies under external debt refer to the somewhat different balance of payments measure, of liabilities recorded in the international investment position, excluding equities, trade credits, etc. They are, therefore, not strictly comparable but provide a rough order of magnitude for comparative purposes.

The change in the stock of debt is influenced by rate fluctuations between the dollar and other convertible currencies, as well as by new disbursements and principal payments (net flows). Debt denominated in hard currency usually increases in domestic currency terms from year to year as the fluctuations are upward vis-à-vis the domestic currency. The debt stock for HPEs includes nonconvertible currency amounts for only three countries in table 9 and probably is understated even for those countries. Even for the convertible-currency stock of external debt, the obligations to CMEA partners are assumed to be understated. The debt data ignore outstanding credits, which for some HPEs are substantial.

The source of first choice is the World Bank's

Debtor Reporting System which is a loan by-loan external debt database of information supplied by nations that borrow from the Bank. World Bank members—only seven of the seventeen HPEs-separate the stock into convertible and nonconvertible amounts and CMEA and non-CMEA amounts. The OECD Creditor Reporting System is used as the second database. This contains the external obligations due to OECD members, supplemented by data from the Bank of International Settlements and from the World Bank's Debtor Reporting System for multilateral loans, loans from other non-OECD creditors, and external borrowing with bonds. For the five remaining HPEs, data comes from World Bank country reports (mainly from national sources); the Economic Commission for Europe, which draws on a variety of sources; IMF Occasional Reports; and Joint IBRD/IMF/OECD/EBRD reports. Data for the other low- and middle-income economies come from the Debt Reporting System.

Total reserves in table 9 are the sum of foreign exchange reserves, comprising liquid assets in major currencies in major banks and banking centers and official holdings of gold. Gold is valued at the London gold price. These data are available in the IFS for most countries and in World Bank/IMF/OECD/EBRD publications for the USSR.

Table 10. Fiscal and monetary accounts

The focus here is on the financial transactions of governments—taxing and spending—rather than on production and consumption of goods and services, the use of labor, or other government activities. Government expenditures cover both current and capital transactions. Definitions and concepts generally conform to those in the IMF's *A Manual on Government Finance Statistics.*

HPEs, military expenditures share of GDP is important and is used to estimate value added in certain types of military production. Consult chapter 11, for ACDA and IFS-GFS before comparing HPE data with those of other economies.

Implicit measures of fiscal deficit or surplus—among the most important indicators of government fiscal performance—are usually calculated as the difference between total revenue, including grants, and total expenditure, including lending minus repayments. It shows the government's net financing requirements. However, for most HPEs, data are scarce and unreliable, and are not shown.

Money supply in market economies affects prices and exchange rates. In HPEs, the causality may be reversed with price liberalization, as governments are tempted to create money to keep pace with liberalized prices of imports, domestic goods and services. These data, shown as a percentage of GDP, comprise the monetary and quasi-monetary liabilities of a country's financial institutions to residents other than the central government.

Tables 11 to 13, *Human resources and productivity*

Human resources are an important part of the real capital of a country, along with its land and physical assets. The tables include estimates of population and labor force totals and structures and their changes over time.

Population estimates are made by the World Bank from data provided by the UN Population Division, the UN Statistical Office, and country statistical offices. Estimates take into account the results of the latest population censuses. Note that refugees not permanently settled in the country of asylum are generally considered to be a part of the population of their country of origin. Population growth rates are period averages calculated from midyear populations.

Since urban population estimates are based on different national definitions of what is urban, cross-country comparisons should be made with caution.

Labor force estimates are from the ILO, based on UN population data. The labor force comprises economically active persons aged 10 years and over, including the armed forces and the unemployed, but excluding housewives, students, and other economically inactive groups. The application of the ILO activity rates to the World Bank population estimates may be inappropriate for some economies in which there are important changes in unemployment and underemployment, in international and internal migration, or both. Estimates of the size of armed forces are from the U.S. Arms Control and Disarmament Agency.

For more detailed information on human resources estimates, refer to the World Bank's *Social Indicators of Development.*

Table 13. *Relative wages and output*

Wages for the chemical industry are shown as a ratio of wages for the manufacturing sector in general. Relative output (gross output) is the average of output per chemical worker to the average manufacturing output per worker. Data are from UNIDO. The table suggests that wages tend to be less differentiated in HPEs, at least for the chemical industry.

Table 14. *Health services and vital statistics*

Social and employment conditions. In the long term, changes in the level and distribution of income, shifts in nutritional status and access to health and education, and trends in employment will indicate the success or failure of these policies.

GNP as a broad measure mainly describes production less intermediate consumption and its uses. Per capita GNP does not constitute a complete measure of welfare or success in development. It needs to be complemented by other indicators, such as the quality of life (environment, congestion, infra-structure), the share of GNP that is devoted to consumption versus other final uses, and income distribution. GNP remains, however, the best single indicator of economic capacity and progress.

Relative levels of development may be difficult to link on the basis of relative standards of living. For some countries, the level of development measured by GNP overstates the standard of living for periods of high levels of capital formation. The same bias predominates if resource allocation is less efficient, because more investment is needed per unit of GNP growth.

Tables 15 to 17. *Environment and energy*

Environmental and energy indicators can be useful in measuring the success of related policies. The effects of price reform, privatization of resources, environmental regulation, and trade liberalization should be reflected in improved environmental and energy data. For example, price reform in the energy sector should provide an incentive for conservation. As price hikes reduce net energy demand, CO_2 production, a by-product of energy production, could be expected to decrease. Thus data on CO_2 levels, while not revealing specific economic costs, reflect trends in resource allocation within HPEs and changes in cost-based decisions. Similarly, privatization of agricultural, water, and timber resources can change resource use decisions in favor of conservation, as private owners become responsible for maintaining natural resource stock.

Greenhouse Gases

Carbon dioxide (CO_2), *methane* (CH_4), and CFC constitute the primary greenhouse gases thought to contribute to the phenomenon of global warming. Manmade (anthropogenic) additions of carbon dioxide stem from a number of sources, including fossil fuel burning and cement manufacturing. Methane additions can be traced to the decay of municipal solid waste, hard coal mining, natural gas pipelines, and wet rice farming. CFCs, greenhouse gases that also contribute to stratospheric ozone depletion, are produced in a number of industrial processes.

HPEs in Europe produce sizeable emissions of carbon dioxide and sulfur dioxide due to the widespread use of lignite coal as a source of primary energy and heating. This trend is especially evident in the GDR and Czechoslovakia, and, to a lesser extent, in Poland and Bulgaria. Methane emissions from hard coal mining and natural gas leaks are pervasive in several European HPEs and the USSR. Special note should be made of the methane emission figures for the USSR, as pipeline leakage estimates are thought to be under-reported. Wet rice farming accounts for the majority of methane emissions in Lao PDR.

Other Pollutants

Sulfur dioxide and *oxides of nitrogen* (NOX) are primarily generated in urban areas. Anthropogenic additions of sulfur dioxide (SO_2) are attributed to fossil fuel combustion and industrial activities. SO_2 is a primary precursor to acid rain, a phenomenon conducive to the destructive acidification of soil, lakes, and rivers. Oxides of nitrogen contribute both to acid rain and tropospheric ozone pollution.

Coal dependence and limited pollution controls in HPEs in Europe account for the high level of SO_2 and NOX pollution in most major urban centers in the region.

Population

Population density was derived by using population figures for 1989 published by the UN Population division and 1987 land area data from FAO.

Forest and woodlands

Data for developing countries are contained in *An Interim Report on the State of the Forest Resources in the Developing Countries*, published by the FAO in 1988. Data for developed countries, are based on *The Forest Resources of the ECE Region* published in 1985

by the UN Economic Commission for Europe (ECE). The two reports used different systems of classification and data gathering. Extent of forest and woodlands refers to natural stands of woody vegetation in which trees predominate.

Extent of forest figures for the HPEs in Europe may be seriously overstated, as much the forest land in this region has been degraded due to acid rain and other pollutants. A recent Economic Commission for Europe report cites widespread pollution damage affecting 82 percent of Poland's forests, 78 percent of Bulgaria's, 73 percent of Czechoslovakia's, 57 percent of the GDR's, and 36 percent of Hungary's. The extent of pollution damage to forests in the Soviet Union is just reaching the public domain.

Cultivated areas

The term *nationally protected areas* combines five of the International Union for the Conservation of Nature management categories that were originally developed in 1972. Totally protected areas include strict scientific and nature reserves, national parks, and natural monuments or landmarks. Partially protected areas include managed natural reserves and wildlife sanctuaries and protected landscapes and seascapes. These figures do not include locally or provincially protected sites, privately owned areas, or areas managed primarily for extraction of natural resources.

Cropland refers to land under temporary and permanent crops, temporary meadows, market and kitchen gardens, and temporarily fallow land. *Irrigated land as a percentage of cropland* refers to areas purposely provided with water, including land flooded by river water for crop production or pasture improvement, whether this area is irrigated several times or only once during the year. Much of the land degradation in HPEs in Europe and the Soviet Union is attributed to increased salinization and erosion due to poor drainage from irrigation systems.

Serviceable cropland per capita may be overstated for HPEs in Europe. There are many reports of increasing problems with soil and land degradation that may not be reflected in the current figures. In Bulgaria, for example, 80 percent of cultivable land is affected by soil erosion. In Czechoslovakia, the figure stands at 54 percent. Both Hungary and Romania report erosion levels exceeding 30 percent. A sizable portion of irrigated land in the Central Asian republics of the Soviet Union consists of land irrigated by the Amu Darya and Syr Darya rivers for cotton production. Due to shrinkage of the Aral Sea to 60 percent of its 1960 boundaries, several Central Asian republics have called for a halt to irrigation in the region.

Fertilizer and pesticide use

Average annual fertilizer use refers to the application of nitrogen, phosphate, and potash nutrients. The fertilizer year is July 1 to June 30; data refer to the year beginning in July. The *average annual pesticide use* data were compiled by UNIDO. Data are expressed in net weight of active ingredients in the pesticides consumed.

Fertilizer and pesticide use in HPEs in Europe varies considerably from country to country. Because prices for agricultural inputs such as fertilizer and pesticides were often subsidized, anecdotal evidence and local press reports suggest that application of these inputs usually exceeded standard guidelines. While information on these inputs is lacking, the statistical agency of the Soviet Union reports that large portions of the Transcaucasus and Central Asia are contaminated by overuse of fertilizer and pesticides.

Freshwater

Annual internal renewable water resources refers to the average annual flow of rivers and aquifers generated from endogenous precipitation. Caution should be used when comparing different countries because these estimates are based on differing sources and data. These annual averages also disguise large seasonal, interannual, and long-term variations. *Annual withdrawal as a percentage of water resources* refers to total water withdrawal, not counting evaporative losses from storage basins, as a percentage of internal renewable water resources and river flows from other countries.

Energy consumption

Energy consumption per capita refers to "apparent consumption" and is defined as domestic production plus net imports, minus net stock increases, minus aircraft and marine bunkers. One gigajoule equals one billion joules or 947,800 British Thermal Units (BTUs).

Due to underpricing of energy resources and the use of outdated technology in manufacturing, energy use in HPEs in Europe is substantially higher per unit of output than their market-economy counterparts (see also chapter 3). Unlike many other economies, HPEs evidenced a substantial increase in energy use per capita during the 1970s and 1980s. This increase in use, in part, can be attributed to the Soviet Union's subsidization of energy exports to CMEA countries, which protected HPEs in Europe from global price increases in primary fuels.

Source of electricity

Electricity production data generally refer to gross production. Gross production is the amount of electricity produced by a generating station before consumption by station auxiliaries and transformer losses within the station are deducted.

Energy Reserves

Energy reserve estimates are based on geological, economic, and technical criteria. Resources are first graded according to the degree of confidence in the extent and location of the resource, based on available geological information. Judgments on the technical and economic feasibility of exploiting the resource are then incorporated into the assessment. *Coal reserves* refer to both bituminous and lignite coal deposits. *Crude oil* includes natural gas liquids and reservoir gas recovered in liquid form in surface separators or plant facilities. *Natural gas* represents that calculated in proved recoverable reserves, that is, the fraction of proved reserves in place that can be extracted with existing technology under present and expected economic conditions. *Hydroelectric technical potential* signifies the annual energy potential of all sites where it is physically possible to construct dams. *Hydroelectric installed capacity* represents the combined generating capacity of hydroelectric plants installed in the country as of December 31, 1987.

Table 1. Alternative per capita income measures (as percentage of US)

	Purchasing power parity				Physical indicators		Exchange rates based		World Bank Atlas method	
	UNDP's HDR 1987	CMEA's PPP 1985	US Govt's ACDA /a 1987	WDR's PPP 1990	Linked PPP-Scale 1989	Linked ER-Scale 1989	UN /b 1989	OECD's DAC 1987	1980	1989
HPEs in Europe										
German Dem. Rep.	45	38	64	..	64	48	54	..	37 c	46 c
Former USSR	34	26	47	..	51	34	24	..	23 c	..
Czechoslovakia	44	35	52	..	51	38	18	..	..	17
Yugoslavia	28	..	14	24	29	17	15	13	27	14
Hungary	26	34	45	29	44	30	13	..	16	13
Bulgaria	27	31	39	37	45	29	18	..	..	13
Poland	23	..	37	21	32	20	11	..	..	9
Romania	17	..	34	32	28	16	11	..	..	8
Albania	11	..	5	..	..	..	6	4	..	5 c
HPEs elsewhere										
Cuba	14	16	14	..	..	..	10	6	..	8 c
Mongolia	11	11	..	..	..	..	5	4	4	..
Nicaragua	13	..	6	..	..	..	6	5	5	4
Korea, Dem. People's Rep.	11	..	7	..	..	..	6	5	6 c	4 c
China	12	..	2	9	16 d	6 d	2	2	3	2
Lao PDR	6	..	..	..	..	..	2	1	..	1
Viet Nam	6	..	1	..	..	..	1	1	..	1 c
Cambodia	6	..	..	..	..	..	0	1	..	1 c
Other economies in transition										
Algeria	15	..	15	22	19 d	8 d	13	15	16	11
Angola	6	..	..	..	..	..	3	6	..	3
Guinea	3	..	1	..	..	..	2	2	..	2
Myanmar	4	..	1	..	..	..	1	1	..	..
Madagascar	4	..	1	4	..	..	1	1	4	1
Afghanistan	6	..	1	..	..	..	2	2	2	..
Somalia	6	..	1	3	..	..	2	2	1	1
Tanzania e	2	..	1	3	..	..	1	1	2	1
Ethiopia	3	..	1	2	..	..	1	1	1	1
Mozambique	3	..	0	3	..	..	1	1	..	0
High-income economies										
United States	100	100	100	100	100	100	100	100	100	100
Germany f	84	..	99	76	78	69	85	..	111	98
France	79	..	84	71	72	61	76	..	99	86
Netherlands	82	..	..	68	66	55	69	..	100	77
Austria	70	..	83	69	70	59	71	..	83	83
Italy	61	..	70	68	58	43	61	..	62	73
Spain	51	..	39	51	53	36	38	..	45	45
Other middle-income economies										
Portugal	32	..	18	37	35	19	18	16	20	20
Korea, Rep.	27	..	15	34	43	21	20	14	14	21
Argentina	26	..	13	22	25	15	14	13	16	10
Brazil	24	..	11	22	22	11	12	12	17	12
Malaysia	22	..	10	28	..	..	12	10	14	10
Costa Rica	21	..	8	23	..	..	9	9	16	8
Tunisia	16	..	7	19	..	..	7	7	11	6
Thailand	15	..	5	22	..	..	6	5	6	6
Honduras	6	..	4	8	..	..	4	4	5	4
Morocco	10	..	3	13	..	..	5	3	8	4
Cote d'Ivoire	6	..	5	7	..	..	4	4	10	4
Senegal	6	..	3	6	..	..	3	3	4	3
Other low-income economies										
Indonesia	9	..	2	11	..	..	3	2	4	2
Sri Lanka	12	..	2	11	..	..	2	2	2	2
Kenya	5	..	2	5	..	..	2	2	4	2
India	6	..	2	5	12 d	4 d	2	2	2	2
Nepal	4	..	1	4	..	..	2	1	1	1
Bangladesh	5	..	1	5	..	..	1	1	1	1

Note: Abbreviations in notes column are explained in the General Notes. For sources and methods, see the Technical Notes.
a. ACDA is assumed to use PPPs for HPEs, and exchange rates for converting data for other countries. b. UN's working estimate. c. Authors' estimate.
d. Refers to 1980. e. In all tables GNP and GDP data refers to mainland Tanzania only. f. Data refer to the Federal Republic of Germany before unification.

Table 2. Trends in per capita income

	Gross national product per capita (US dollars, Atlas methodology)						Gross national income per capita (1987 US dollars) a					
	1970	1980	1985	1987	1989	Notes	1970	1980	1985	1987	1989	Notes
HPEs in Europe	..	..	..	..	..		..	..	..	..	..	
German Dem. Rep.	2,110	4,420	..	..	..	DE	..	..	..	..	..	
Former USSR	1,300	2,780	2,520	3,510	..	E	..	2,290	2,660	2,730	..	E
Czechoslovakia	..	..	2,740	3,030	3,460	.	..	3,160	3,240	3,330	3,500	.
Yugoslavia	660	3,250	2,040	2,510	2,940	.	1,780	2,880	2,720	2,780	2,720	.
Hungary	..	1,930	1,930	2,250	2,620	.	..	2,160	2,240	2,360	2,400	.
Bulgaria	..	..	3,380	3,190	2,740	.	..	..	2,770	3,120	3,180	.
Poland	..	..	2,080	1,870	1,890	.	..	1,610	1,530	1,620	1,740	.
Romania	..	..	..	..	1,720	.	..	..	..	..	..	.
Albania	..	..	..	..	..		..	..	..	..	..	
HPEs elsewhere	..	..	..	..	..		..	..	..	..	..	
Cuba	..	..	..	..	..		..	..	..	..	..	
Mongolia	..	..	1,500	1,620	1,820	E	..	..	..	..	..	
Nicaragua	380	650	760	810	..	.	1,440	1,080	940	910	610	.
Korea, Dem. People's Rep.	270	740	..	..	..	E	..	..	..	..	..	
China	130	300	330	300	360	.	110	170	240	280	310	.
Lao PDR	..	..	..	440	220	.	..	..	310	300	310	.
Viet Nam	..	..	..	..	..		..	..	..	..	..	
Cambodia	..	..	..	..	160	E	..	..	..	..	..	
Other economies in transition	90	410	520	540	460	.	570	540	590	520	480	.
Algeria	360	1,940	2,590	2,690	2,280	.	1,750	2,780	3,080	2,730	2,480	.
Angola	..	640	680	610		.	..	..	..	..	..	
Guinea	..	..	..	..	400	.	..	..	..	350	360	.
Myanmar	..	..	..	..	..		..	..	..	..	..	
Madagascar	170	430	310	260	220	.	410	300	240	230	220	.
Afghanistan	..	..	..	..	..		..	..	..	..	..	
Somalia	..	..	..	..	..		130	140	130	140	120	.
Tanzania	..	..	..	..	..		190	170	150	150	..	.
Ethiopia	60	120	110	120	120	.	..	..	..	..	..	
Mozambique	..	..	180	150	80	.	..	130	90	90	100	.
High-income economies	3,060	10,160	11,530	13,990	18,320	.	11,250	13,730	14,890	15,770	16,880	.
United States	4,980	12,000	16,770	18,490	20,930	.	13,930	16,190	17,680	18,430	19,510	.
Germany b	2,230	10,490	8,620	11,220	16,020	.	10,000	12,660	13,340	14,300	15,180	.
France	2,990	11,870	9,750	12,960	17,850	.	11,650	14,330	14,890	15,860	16,920	.
Netherlands	2,560	12,010	9,360	11,660	15,950	.	11,580	13,740	14,240	14,450	15,290	.
Austria	1,960	9,990	9,040	11,870	17,160	.	10,030	13,750	14,620	15,170	16,240	.
Italy	2,000	7,480	7,720	10,410	15,110	.	8,650	11,420	12,100	13,080	13,970	.
Spain	1,110	5,360	4,330	6,090	9,370	.	5,290	6,590	6,690	7,500	8,290	.
Other middle-income economies	490	1,820	1,830	1,820	2,010	.	1,340	1,830	1,930	1,850	1,860	.
Portugal	700	2,370	1,970	2,840	4,260	.	2,250	3,150	3,010	3,490	3,910	.
Korea, Rep.	270	1,620	2,320	2,950	4,400	.	970	1,710	2,400	3,090	3,730	.
Argentina	1,020	1,970	2,130	2,410	2,170	.	2,690	2,990	2,380	2,460	2,160	.
Brazil	450	2,060	1,630	1,910	2,400	.	1,170	2,000	1,830	2,000	1,950	.
Malaysia	390	1,690	1,970	1,830	2,130	.	950	1,740	1,830	1,790	2,070	.
Costa Rica	560	1,960	1,400	1,650	1,750	.	1,380	1,740	1,540	1,620	1,640	.
Tunisia	280	1,280	1,170	1,190	1,290	.	700	1,210	1,250	1,210	1,210	.
Thailand	210	670	800	870	1,230	.	510	700	790	900	1,100	.
Honduras	270	640	740	820	740	.	770	950	810	820	810	.
Morocco	260	930	620	680	890	.	540	720	740	770	820	.
Cote d'Ivoire	270	1,180	670	780	810	.	910	1,130	1,000	900	740	.
Senegal	220	510	380	520	660	.	710	630	620	640	620	.
Other low-income economies	120	330	360	340	360	.	250	300	330	330	360	.
Indonesia	80	470	550	500	510	.	160	340	410	430	460	.
Sri Lanka	180	260	390	410	430	.	250	330	400	410	410	.
Kenya	130	420	310	340	370	.	320	380	330	350	370	.
India	110	240	280	310	350	.	240	260	300	320	350	.
Nepal	80	130	160	150	170	.	..	..	..	..	..	.
Bangladesh	100	150	160	170	190	.	170	150	170	180	170	.

Note: Abbreviations in notes column are explained in the General Notes. For sources and methods, see the Technical Notes.
a. Based on single year convertor. b. Data refer to the Federal Republic of Germany before unification.

Table 3. Size and structure of production

| | GNP (millions of US dollars) a | | | | Distribution of GDP (percent) | | | | | | | |
| | | | | | Agriculture | | | | Industry | | | |
	1970	1980	1989	Notes	1970	1980	1989	Notes	1970	1980	1989	Notes
HPEs in Europe	..	..	..	.	..	..	..	.	..	..	..	.
German Dem. Rep.	36,000	74,000	..	DE	..	8	10	.	..	65	62	.
Former USSR	316,000	737,000	..	DE	22	15	23	Qf	62	62	55	Qf
Czechoslovakia	..	40,690	50,380	.	..	7	8	.	..	60	56	.
Yugoslavia	13,690	72,280	76,820	.	18	12	12	.	41	44	50	.
Hungary	..	21,770	27,900	.	18	17	14	.	45	41	36	.
Bulgaria	..	25,640	21,100	.	..	14	11	.	..	54	59	.
Poland	..	54,430	79,020	.	..	..	12	.	..	..	41	.
Romania	..	..	41,410	.	..	13	14	.	..	60	59	.
Albania	..	..	..	.	35	34	32	Q	53	52	51	Q
HPEs elsewhere	..	..	..	.	..	..	..	.	..	..	..	.
Cuba	..	..	..	.	..	6	..	Qf	..	47	..	Qf
Mongolia	..	2,320	3,560	.	..	..	17	.	..	..	34	.
Nicaragua	760	1,940	..	.	25	23	30	.	26	31	20	.
Korea, Dem. People's Rep.	3,980	13,500	..	DE	..	..	..	.	..	..	..	.
China	93,240	298,400	419,470	.	34	30	27	.	38	45	42	.
Lao PDR	..	..	770	.	..	..	..	.	..	..	..	.
Viet Nam	..	..	9,240	.	..	52	52	Qf	..	24	29	Qf
Cambodia	..	..	1,280	E	..	..	46	E	..	..	17	E
Other economies in transition	14,920	72,970	91,230	.	28	21	27	.	22	34	27	.
Algeria	4,760	41,150	47,300	.	11	10	15	.	41	54	42	.
Angola	..	..	6,030	.	..	18	13	.	..	43	44	.
Guinea	..	..	2,190	.	..	..	24	.	..	..	33	.
Myanmar	..	..	..	.	..	..	..	.	..	..	..	.
Madagascar	1,070	4,000	2,280	.	24	30	34	.	16	16	13	.
Afghanistan	1,780	3,710	..	.	..	..	..	.	..	..	..	.
Somalia	320	600	1,020	.	59	68	64	.	16	8	9	.
Tanzania	1,310	5,120	2,610	.	41	44	59	.	17	17	12	.
Ethiopia	1,780	4,120	5,950	.	56	51	42	.	14	16	16	.
Mozambique	..	2,380	1,080	.	..	54	65	.	..	27	15	.
High-income economies	2,146,820	7,895,680	14,655,230	.	4	3	..	.	40	37	..	.
United States	1,016,470	2,736,060	5,176,400	.	3	3	..	.	35	34	..	.
Germany b	184,620	817,090	1,202,790	.	3	2	..	.	49	43	..	.
France	143,460	667,570	956,270	.	1	4	4	.	61	34	29	.
Netherlands	33,630	169,060	223,040	.	6	4	4	.	37	33	31	.
Austria	14,380	76,240	125,490	.	7	5	3	.	45	40	37	.
Italy	107,980	453,570	858,120	.	8	6	4	.	41	39	34	.
Spain	37,660	212,670	377,050	.	..	..	..	.	..	..	..	.
Other middle-income economies	266,320	1,424,060	1,920,520	.	15	11	11	.	31	40	36	.
Portugal	6,220	24,030	44,150	.	..	10	..	.	..	39	..	.
Korea, Rep.	8,940	60,500	210,090	.	26	15	10	.	29	41	44	.
Argentina	22,890	56,120	54,370	.	13	9	13	.	38	37	42	.
Brazil	41,900	227,230	433,310	.	12	11	9	.	38	44	43	.
Malaysia	4,090	23,610	35,610	.	29	22	..	.	25	38	..	.
Costa Rica	970	4,600	4,850	.	23	18	17	.	24	27	27	.
Tunisia	1,380	8,480	9,700	.	20	16	14	.	24	36	33	.
Thailand	7,100	31,900	68,190	.	26	23	15	.	25	31	38	.
Honduras	700	2,390	3,050	.	32	25	21	.	22	25	25	.
Morocco	3,910	18,220	21,410	.	20	18	17	.	27	31	33	.
Cote d'Ivoire	1,370	9,950	8,320	.	40	33	44	.	23	20	25	.
Senegal	840	2,920	4,430	.	24	19	20	.	20	25	19	.
Other low-income economies	122,710	459,360	548,360	.	39	30	28	.	20	30	27	.
Indonesia	9,700	74,810	90,030	.	45	24	24	.	19	42	37	.
Sri Lanka	2,260	4,000	6,940	.	28	28	26	.	24	30	27	.
Kenya	1,540	7,040	8,020	.	33	33	31	.	20	21	20	.
India	57,310	172,670	262,410	.	45	38	31	.	22	26	29	.
Nepal	870	1,960	3,040	.	67	62	57	.	12	12 .	14	.
Bangladesh	6,720	12,960	20,390	.	55	50	37	.	11	16	15	.

Note: Abbreviations in notes column are explained in the General Notes. For sources and methods, see the Technical Notes.
a. Based on single year convertor. b. Data refer to the Federal Republic of Germany before unification.

Table continues on the following page.

Table 3. Size and structure of output (continued)

	Construction				Services, etc			
	1970	*1980*	*1989*	*Notes*	*1970*	*1980*	*1989*	*Notes*
HPEs in Europe	..	..	..	.	..	..	..	.
German Dem. Rep.	..	5	6	.	..	27	29	.
Former USSR	10	10	13	Qf	17	23	22	.
Czechoslovakia	11	11	..	Q	..	34	36	.
Yugoslavia	12	10	..	.	41	44	39	.
Hungary	8	7	..	.	37	42	50	.
Bulgaria	9	9	9	Q	..	32	29	.
Poland	11	10	10	Qf	..	..	47	.
Romania	..	8	6	.	..	27	27	.
Albania	10	7	7	Q	13	15	16	.
HPEs elsewhere	..	..	..	.	..	..	..	.
Cuba	..	8	..	Qf	..	47	..	.
Mongolia	..	6	7	Qf	..	..	49	.
Nicaragua	3	3	..	.	49	45	51	.
Korea, Dem. People's Rep.	..	..	..	.	..	..	..	.
China	4	5	6	Qf	28	25	32	.
Lao PDR	..	..	..	.	..	..	..	.
Viet Nam	..	3	5	Qf	..	25	20	Qf
Cambodia	..	..	6	E	..	..	36	E
Other economies in transition	..	..	..	.	48	43	44	.
Algeria	..	..	..	.	48	36	43	.
Angola	..	..	..	.	..	39	43	.
Guinea	..	..	6	.	..	..	43	.
Myanmar	..	..	..	.	..	..	..	.
Madagascar	..	..	..	.	59	54	53	.
Afghanistan	..	..	..	.	..	..	..	.
Somalia	5	3	..	.	25	24	28	.
Tanzania	5	4	2	.	42	39	29	.
Ethiopia	5	4	..	.	30	33	42	.
Mozambique	..	..	..	.	..	19	20	.
High-income economies	7	7	..	.	56	60	..	.
United States	5	5	..	.	63	64	..	.
Germany	8	7	..	.	47	55	..	.
France	9	7	5	.	38	62	67	.
Netherlands	8	7	6	.	57	64	65	.
Austria	8	8	7	.	48	56	60	.
Italy	10	7	5	.	51	55	63	.
Spain	..	..	..	.	..	..	..	.
Other middle-income economies	6	7	7	.	52	47	51	.
Portugal	..	7	..	.	..	51	..	.
Korea, Rep.	5	8	10	.	45	44	46	.
Argentina	6	7	..	.	49	55	45	.
Brazil	6	7	9	.	49	45	49	.
Malaysia	4	5	..	.	46	40	..	.
Costa Rica	4	6	3	.	53	55	56	.
Tunisia	6	7	5	.	57	48	54	.
Thailand	5	5	6	.	49	46	47	.
Honduras	5	7	5	.	45	50	55	.
Morocco	4	6	5	.	53	51	50	.
Cote d'Ivoire	9	7	..	.	36	47	30	.
Senegal	4	6	3	.	56	57	62	.
Other low-income economies	4	5	5	.	39	38	43	.
Indonesia	3	5	5	.	36	34	39	.
Sri Lanka	6	9	8	.	48	43	48	.
Kenya	5	6	6	.	47	47	50	.
India	5	5	6	.	33	36	40	.
Nepal	8	7	8	.	21	26	28	.
Bangladesh	2	5	6	.	34	34	47	.

Distribution of GDP (percent)

Table 4. Structure of demand

| | Distribution of GDP (percent) | | | | | | | | | | | | | | | |
| | Total consumption etc. a | | | | Gross domestic investment | | | | Exports of GNFS | | | | Resource balance | | | |
	1970	1980	1989	Notes	1970	1980	1989	Notes	1970	1980	1989	Notes	1970	1980	1989	Notes
HPEs in Europe	..	..	..		..	..	..		..	..	..	.	..	..	..	
German Dem. Rep.	..	73	73	.	..	26	28	.	13	23	40	Lf	..	..	..	.
Former USSR	70	75	76	Qf	29	24	23	Qf	3	8	7	L.	1	2	1	Qf
Czechoslovakia	..	67	71	.	..	33	28	.	..	34	34	.	..	0	1	.
Yugoslavia	73	64	53	.	32	40	44	.	18	19	25	.	-5	-4	3	.
Hungary	69	72	71	.	34	31	26	.	30	39	36	.	-2	-2	3	.
Bulgaria	..	61	67	.	..	34	33	.	..	36	44	.	..	5	0	.
Poland	..	77	57	.	..	26	39	.	..	28	19	.	..	-3	4	.
Romania	..	65	68	.	..	40	27	.	..	35	21	.	..	-5	5	.
Albania	93	70	76	Q	42	30	26	Q	..	23	16	L.	-35	0	-2	Qf
HPEs elsewhere	..	..	..		..	..	..		..	..	..		..	..	..	
Cuba	..	85	..	Qf	..	21	..	Qf	..	..	..		..	-6	..	Qf
Mongolia	..	73	87	.	..	46	46	.	..	19	23	.	..	-20	-33	.
Nicaragua	84	102	107	.	18	17	26	.	26	24	33	.	-2	-19	-33	.
Korea, Dem. People's Rep.	..	..	..		..	..	..		..	..	..		..	..	..	
China	71	68	62	.	29	32	39	.	3	7	13	.	0	0	-1	.
Lao PDR	..	..	101	.	..	..	12	.	..	..	10		..	..	-13	.
Viet Nam	..	104	40	Qf	..	12	10	.	..	..	..	a	..	-16	50	Qf
Cambodia	90	..	..		13	..	..		6	..	..		-2	..	..	
Other economies in transition	76	70	79	.	22	32	24	.	17	28	16	.	2	-1	-3	.
Algeria	71	57	69	.	36	39	31	.	22	34	20	.	-7	4	0	.
Angola	..	..	..		..	..	..		..	..	..		..	..	..	
Guinea	..	..	80	.	..	..	19	.	..	..	30	.	..	..	1	.
Myanmar	..	..	..		..	..	..		..	..	..		..	..	..	
Madagascar	93	101	91	.	10	15	14	.	19	13	18	.	-2	-16	-5	.
Afghanistan	96	..	..		6	..	..		10	..	..		-2	..	..	
Somalia	94	113	107	.	12	42	30	.	12	33	8	.	-5	-55	-37	.
Tanzania	80	90	106	.	23	23	25	.	26	13	18	.	-2	-13	-31	.
Ethiopia	89	95	94	.	12	10	13	.	11	14	13	.	0	-5	-7	.
Mozambique	..	100	117	.	..	19	36	.	..	17	15	.	..	-18	-52	.
High-income economies	76	77	78	.	23	23	22	.	14	21	20	.	1	0	0	.
United States	82	82	85	.	18	19	17	.	6	10	9	.	0	-1	-2	.
Germany b	70	77	73	.	28	24	22	.	21	27	31	.	2	-1	5	.
France	73	77	78	.	27	24	22	.	16	22	23	.	1	-1	0	.
Netherlands	74	79	75	.	28	22	21	.	45	53	58	.	-2	-1	4	.
Austria	69	74	74	.	30	28	26	.	31	37	40	.	1	-2	1	.
Italy	73	76	79	.	27	27	22	.	16	22	21	.	0	-3	0	.
Spain	74	79	78	.	28	24	25	.	13	15	18	.	-1	-2	-3	.
Other middle-income economies	79	73	76	.	22	26	24	.	17	27	26	.	0	1	1	.
Portugal	80	81	79	.	26	34	30	.	24	29	36	.	-7	-15	-10	.
Korea, Rep.	85	76	63	.	25	32	35	.	14	34	34	.	-10	-7	3	.
Argentina	78	80	83	.	22	22	9	.	9	7	19	.	0	-2	8	.
Brazil	80	79	72	.	21	23	25	.	7	9	8	.	0	-2	3	.
Malaysia	73	67	66	.	22	30	30	.	42	58	74	.	4	3	4	.
Costa Rica	86	84	77	.	21	27	26	.	28	27	35	.	-7	-10	-4	.
Tunisia	83	76	81	.	21	29	23	.	22	40	44	.	-5	-5	-4	.
Thailand	79	80	71	.	26	26	32	.	15	24	37	.	-4	-6	-2	.
Honduras	85	83	91	.	21	25	12	.	28	37	33	.	-6	-7	-3	.
Morocco	86	86	82	.	19	24	24	.	18	17	22	.	-4	-11	-6	.
Cote d'Ivoire	71	78	87	.	23	28	10	.	36	34	35	.	7	-6	3	.
Senegal	89	100	95	.	16	15	11	.	27	28	27	.	-5	-16	-5	.
Other low-income economies	86	80	79	.	16	22	23	.	9	18	15	.	-2	-1	-3	.
Indonesia	86	63	62	.	16	24	35	.	13	33	25	.	-2	13	3	.
Sri Lanka	84	89	88	.	19	34	21	.	26	32	27	.	-3	-23	-9	.
Kenya	76	82	81	.	24	29	25	.	30	28	23	.	-1	-11	-6	.
India	84	83	79	.	17	21	24	.	4	7	8	.	-1	-4	-3	.
Nepal	97	89	88	.	6	18	22	.	5	12	13	.	-3	-7	-10	.
Bangladesh	93	98	98	.	11	15	12	.	8	6	8	.	-4	-13	-10	.

Note: Abbreviations in notes column are explained in the General Notes. For sources and methods, see the Technical Notes.
a. Includes statistical discrepancy. b. Data refer to the Federal Republic of Germany before unification.

Table 5. Growth of production

	Agriculture			Total			Construction			Services, etc.		
	1970-80	1980-89	Notes	1970-80	1980-89	Notes	1970-80	1980-89	Notes	1970-80	1980-89	Notes
HPEs in Europe	..	..	.	..	..	.	..	..	.	..	..	.
German Dem. Rep.	..	1.8	.	..	4.7	.	..	4.3	.	..	3.3	.
Former USSR	1.7	1.6	Q	6.2	3.0	Q	4.5	5.1	Q	..	..	.
Czechoslovakia	..	0.3	.	..	2.1	.	..	1.3	Q	..	1.4	.
Yugoslavia	3.1	1.1	.	8.0	1.4	.	5.9	-7.0	.	4.9	1.2	.
Hungary	2.8	2.1	.	6.3	0.1	.	6.5	-0.7	.	5.3	2.7	.
Bulgaria	..	-2.7	.	..	5.8	.	..	4.1	Q	..	1.4	.
Poland	..	..	.	..	..	.	5.2	1.6	Q	..	..	.
Romania	..	2.1	.	..	3.7	.	..	-13.7	.	..	5.2	.
Albania	..	1.3	Q	..	2.2	Q	..	0.3	Q	..	..	.
HPEs elsewhere	..	..	.	..	..	.	..	..	.	..	..	.
Cuba	..	-1.7	Q	..	..	.	..	..	.	..	..	.
Mongolia	..	..	.	..	..	.	..	7.1	Q	..	..	.
Nicaragua	1.9	-2.7	.	1.5	-3.5	.	-3.5	3.1	.	0.5	-0.8	.
Korea, Dem. People's Rep.	..	..	.	..	..	.	..	..	.	..	..	.
China	2.6	6.3	.	7.9	12.6	.	4.8	12.3	Q	4.7	10.6	.
Lao PDR	..	2.9	.	..	3.4	.	..	1.1	.	..	3.0	.
Viet Nam	..	2.3	.	..	3.7	.	..	..	.	..	7.9	.
Cambodia	..	..	.	..	..	.	..	..	.	..	..	.
Other economies in transition	3.9	2.5	.	3.4	3.7	.	..	..	.	4.7	3.0	.
Algeria	7.5	5.3	.	3.5	3.2	.	..	..	.	6.7	3.5	.
Angola	..	-0.5	.	..	12.6	.	..	..	.	..	..	.
Guinea	..	..	.	..	..	.	..	..	.	..	..	.
Myanmar	..	..	.	..	..	.	..	..	.	..	..	.
Madagascar	0.4	2.4	.	0.6	0.8	.	..	..	.	0.6	-0.2	.
Afghanistan	3.2	..	.	5.3	..	.	8.0	..	.	6.0	..	.
Somalia	6.5	3.6	.	-2.8	1.6	.	-5.9	6.8	.	3.7	1.1	.
Tanzania	0.7	4.1	.	2.6	-0.8	.	-0.5	-0.7	.	6.3	1.4	.
Ethiopia	0.7	-0.4	.	1.6	3.3	.	-0.6	2.5	.	4.1	4.1	.
Mozambique	..	0.9	.	..	-4.9	.	..	..	.	..	-4.3	.
High-income economies	0.5	1.6	.	2.6	2.4	.	0.9	1.6	.	3.6	3.1	.
United States	0.6	3.3	.	2.1	3.0	.	0.2	2.3	.	3.2	3.4	.
Germany a	0.9	1.6	.	1.8	0.4	.	0.3	-0.6	.	3.3	2.7	.
France	..	2.0	.	..	0.6	.	..	0.4	.	..	2.9	.
Netherlands	3.9	3.6	.	..	..	.	-1.6	0.5	.	..	..	.
Austria	2.6	1.0	.	3.1	1.7	.	2.3	-0.2	.	3.7	2.1	.
Italy	0.9	0.8	.	3.9	1.9	.	-0.4	-0.8	.	4.0	2.9	.
Spain	..	..	.	..	..	.	..	..	.	..	..	.
Other middle-income economies	3.4	2.9	.	5.6	2.9	.	9.1	-0.3	.	6.5	2.7	.
Portugal	..	-0.9	.	..	1.0	.	..	-2.6	.	..	1.1	.
Korea, Rep.	2.7	3.3	.	15.2	12.4	.	12.7	9.6	.	8.8	9.1	.
Argentina	2.5	1.1	.	2.1	-1.1	.	3.3	-10.0	.	2.7	0.1	.
Brazil	4.2	3.1	.	9.4	2.5	.	9.9	1.0	.	8.0	3.4	.
Malaysia	5.0	3.8	.	8.7	6.5	.	8.6	-0.8	.	9.1	3.9	.
Costa Rica	2.5	2.9	.	8.2	2.7	.	9.9	0.7	.	5.9	2.8	.
Tunisia	4.1	1.6	.	6.8	2.5	.	9.0	-1.8	.	6.7	4.5	.
Thailand	4.4	4.2	.	9.5	8.1	.	6.3	6.6	.	7.2	7.4	.
Honduras	2.6	1.9	.	7.5	2.7	.	10.4	-3.4	.	7.0	2.3	.
Morocco	1.1	6.9	.	6.5	2.6	.	..	-0.3	.	7.0	4.2	.
Cote d'Ivoire	2.7	0.5	.	9.1	1.0	.	9.8	..	.	6.5	-0.9	.
Senegal	1.3	3.0	.	5.3	3.5	.	6.0	-0.7	.	1.6	3.1	.
Other low-income economies	1.9	2.9	.	5.8	5.0	.	4.9	3.1	.	5.9	5.7	.
Indonesia	4.1	3.2	.	9.6	5.3	.	16.3	3.4	.	8.8	6.6	.
Sri Lanka	2.8	2.2	.	3.4	4.4	.	3.2	0.4	.	5.3	4.9	.
Kenya	4.8	3.2	.	8.6	3.7	.	7.7	1.0	.	6.3	4.9	.
India	1.8	2.9	.	4.5	6.6	.	3.3	3.6	.	4.6	6.5	.
Nepal	0.5	4.6	.	..	..	.	..	..	.	..	..	.
Bangladesh	0.6	2.6	.	5.2	4.8	.	5.2	8.1	.	4.3	5.9	.

Note: Abbreviations in notes column are explained in the General Notes. For sources and methods, see the Technical Notes.
a. Data refer to the Federal Republic of Germany before unification.

50

Table 6. Growth of demand

	Total consumption, etc.				Gross domestic investment				Export of GNFS			
	1970-80	1980-89	1985-89	Notes	1970-80	1980-89	1985-89	Notes	1970-80	1980-89	1985-89	Notes
HPEs in Europe	..	..	..	.	..	..	..	.	..	..	..	.
German Dem. Rep.	..	3.2	3.7	.	..	2.2	4.8	.	7.4	14.4	-0.2	Lf
Former USSR	5.0	2.8	3.2	Q	3.2	1.7	0.3	Q	7.3	5.8	-2.5	L.
Czechoslovakia	..	2.0	2.6	.	..	-0.3	1.6	.	..	4.3	1.2	
Yugoslavia	5.7	0.1	-0.7	.	7.2	0.1	1.2	.	3.9	-0.4	-0.7	.
Hungary	3.6	1.4	1.0	.	7.5	-0.4	1.7	.	9.4	4.4	3.3	.
Bulgaria	..	4.1	3.1	.	..	3.3	3.6	.	..	-1.7	-6.2	.
Poland	..	2.2	2.1	.	..	2.1	4.4	.	..	4.6	5.7	.
Romania	..	3.4	1.3	.	..	0.0	-6.4	.	..	-0.5	5.3	.
Albania	..	2.9	3.3	Q	..	-1.2	2.4	Qf	..	..	..	.
HPEs elsewhere	..	..	..	.	..	..	..	.	..	..	..	.
Cuba	..	2.6	0.3	Q	..	-2.1	-19.0	Q	..	..	..	
Mongolia	..	..	12.5	.	..	..	-14.4	.	..	3.7	-0.7	.
Nicaragua	2.6	-0.9	-2.3	.	..	-3.0	-13.2	.	3.3	-6.8	-2.4	.
Korea, Dem. People's Rep.	..	..	..	.	..	..	..	.	..	..	..	.
China	4.4	7.9	8.9	.	7.9	14.6	8.2	.	5.6	13.2	15.7	.
Lao PDR	..	4.3	3.5	.	..	-4.1	-4.1	.	..	6.7	3.7	.
Viet Nam	..	..	4.0	Q	..	8.8	13.1	.	..	..	..	.
Cambodia	..	..	..	.	..	..	..	.	..	..	..	.
Other economies in transition	7.7	2.2	-0.6	.	12.3	-1.2	-3.7	.	1.5	3.2	4.4	.
Algeria	10.2	1.6	-4.0	.	13.6	-1.0	-4.5	.	2.2	4.6	4.1	.
Angola	..	..	..	.	..	..	..	.	..	..	..	.
Guinea	..	..	4.9	.	..	..	-0.2	.	..	..	6.8	.
Myanmar	..	..	..	.	..	..	..	.	..	..	..	.
Madagascar	0.1	-0.8	-0.7	.	0.4	2.7	16.6	.	1.0	0.0	11.3	.
Afghanistan	3.8	..	..	.	12.4	..	..	.	20.1	..	..	.
Somalia	6.7	1.8	7.0	.	18.1	-2.6	-10.0	.	8.2	-12.2	3.4	.
Tanzania	4.3	3.4	5.0	.	3.1	0.3	5.2	.	-4.6	-4.7	1.2	.
Ethiopia	3.1	2.0	..	.	-0.8	2.0	..	.	3.7	-0.6	..	.
Mozambique	..	-0.5	4.0	.	..	0.3	20.5	.	..	-10.8	5.8	.
High-income economies	3.3	3.1	3.3	.	2.0	4.0	6.2	.	5.9	4.8	6.4	.
United States	2.7	3.6	3.1	.	2.4	4.8	3.1	.	7.0	6.1	15.3	.
Germany a	3.3	1.7	2.5	.	0.6	1.9	5.9	.	5.3	3.9	3.6	.
France	3.4	2.4	3.0	.	1.5	1.9	6.7	.	6.8	3.3	5.2	.
Netherlands	3.6	1.4	2.2	.	0.1	2.3	3.2	.	4.5	4.3	5.1	.
Austria	3.8	2.0	2.3	.	2.7	2.4	6.0	.	6.7	4.2	5.0	.
Italy	3.8	2.9	4.1	.	1.6	2.1	5.1	.	6.6	3.8	4.5	.
Spain	4.0	2.8	5.2	.	1.5	4.8	14.6	.	6.5	5.9	4.3	.
Other middle-income economies	6.0	2.3	2.5	.	7.4	-0.6	3.1	.	..	..	..	.
Portugal	5.0	4.0	9.6	.	3.1	-2.7	4.6	.	0.4	9.5	7.9	.
Korea, Rep.	7.4	7.5	9.2	.	14.2	11.6	16.2	.	21.3	12.8	14.2	.
Argentina	2.3	-0.6	-0.8	.	3.1	-8.4	-2.3	.	7.3	4.4	5.4	.
Brazil	7.7	2.5	2.7	.	8.9	0.4	2.6	.	8.5	8.1	8.0	.
Malaysia	7.8	2.8	5.3	.	10.8	1.2	6.8	.	8.4	10.2	13.9	.
Costa Rica	5.3	2.3	3.7	.	9.2	5.0	5.9	.	6.0	5.5	12.5	.
Tunisia	8.1	3.3	1.8	.	6.8	-4.9	-7.1	.	9.6	5.3	12.9	.
Thailand	6.8	5.7	7.6	.	7.2	7.1	16.1	.	8.9	13.4	22.1	.
Honduras	6.1	2.8	5.1	.	9.5	-0.9	-3.6	.	4.2	2.0	2.9	.
Morocco	6.3	4.0	4.8	.	9.9	1.9	3.1	.	2.8	5.0	5.7	.
Cote d'Ivoire	7.8	0.3	-2.6	.	12.6	-11.5	-7.5	.	4.0	3.3	4.7	.
Senegal	3.1	2.6	2.0	.	0.3	2.2	5.8	.	4.6	3.7	5.6	.
Other low-income economies	4.1	4.3	4.5	.	6.8	3.0	3.4	.	5.8	3.2	7.2	.
Indonesia	7.9	4.6	3.6	.	14.1	6.9	2.2	.	8.8	2.2	9.0	.
Sri Lanka	3.7	4.7	2.5	.	13.8	0.3	4.3	.	1.2	3.7	13.8	.
Kenya	6.6	4.0	8.4	.	2.4	0.3	4.7	.	0.9	2.5	2.3	.
India	3.0	5.7	6.0	.	4.5	5.0	6.0	.	7.0	5.8	9.7	.
Nepal	..	..	..	.	..	..	..	.	..	..	..	.
Bangladesh	2.5	4.9	3.4	.	4.8	-0.7	-0.2	.	6.9	5.9	11.6	.

Note: Abbreviations in notes column are explained in the General Notes. For sources and methods, see the Technical Notes.
a. Data refer to the Federal Republic of Germany before unification.

51

Table 7. Overall growth and inflation

	Average annual growth (percent) GDP				Average annual inflation (percent) Overall (GDP deflator)				Consumer prices			
	1970-80	1980-89	1985-89	Notes	1970-80	1980-89	1985-89	Notes	1970-80	1980-89	1985-89	Notes
HPEs in Europe	..	..	..	.	..	..	..	.	..	..	..	.
German Dem. Rep.	..	4.0	3.2	.	..	0.4	0.1	.	-0.1	0.1	0.4	C
Former USSR	..	3.6	3.8	E	-0.3	0.7	0.6	Qf	..	..	3.6	E
Czechoslovakia	..	1.7	1.6	.	..	1.5	1.3	.	1.0	1.3	0.4	.
Yugoslavia	6.2	0.7	0.2	.	18.4	96.4	236.6	.	18.1	96.2	234.8	.
Hungary	5.3	1.6	1.6	.	2.7	7.6	12.3	.	4.9	8.3	11.7	.
Bulgaria	..	3.4	3.4	.	..	1.3	1.6	.	1.7	1.8	2.8	Cf
Poland	..	2.5	2.7	.	..	39.5	71.9	.	4.6	36.6	63.7	.
Romania	..	2.0	-0.6	.	..	1.4	0.4	.	0.9	2.5	0.2	C
Albania	..	1.6	2.6	QI	..	-0.5	-0.6	Q	..	-0.1	0.0	.
HPEs elsewhere	..	..	..	.	..	..	..	.	..	..	..	.
Cuba	..	3.7	-2.2	QI	..	-1.4	-1.2	Qf	..	..	..	.
Mongolia	..	6.1	5.4	.	..	-1.3	-1.5	.	..	0.2	-0.2	E
Nicaragua	1.2	-2.0	-5.6	.	12.6	285.0	2,059.6	.	14.7	236.1	1,778.6	.
Korea, Dem. People's Rep.	..	..	..	E	..	..	..	.	..	..	..	.
China	5.2	10.3	9.0	.	0.9	5.2	7.6	.	..	7.6	13.4	.
Lao PDR	..	2.9	2.6	.	..	37.6	33.0	.	..	32.1	11.5	E
Viet Nam	..	5.0	5.0	.	..	265.2	295.2	.	..	..	..	.
Cambodia	..	..	..	.	..	..	..	.	..	..	..	.
Other economies in transition	5.5	3.0	0.9	.	..	..	..	.	..	..	..	.
Algeria	7.0	3.1	0.1	.	14.1	5.5	5.8	.	8.8	8.8	8.3	.
Angola	..	9.1	10.3	.	..	-3.6	-2.9	.	..	..	..	.
Guinea	..	..	4.6	.	..	..	23.6	.	..	..	..	.
Myanmar	..	..	..	.	..	..	..	.	..	..	..	.
Madagascar	0.6	0.8	2.6	.	9.9	17.5	18.1	.	8.9	17.1	17.1	.
Afghanistan	3.7	..	..	.	5.3	..	..	.	..	21.6	23.8	.
Somalia	4.3	2.3	2.0	.	15.8	42.3	54.9	.	13.8	45.0	44.9	.
Tanzania	3.3	2.5	4.5	.	14.0	26.7	30.9	.	14.0	31.0	30.4	.
Ethiopia	2.4	2.0	5.6	.	4.4	2.0	0.0	.	11.2	3.9	0.8	.
Mozambique	..	-1.5	4.7	.	..	34.9	59.8	.	..	..	..	.
High-income economies	3.1	3.1	3.7	.	..	..	..	.	..	..	..	.
United States	2.8	3.5	3.6	.	7.5	3.7	3.1	.	7.7	4.1	3.7	.
Germany a	2.6	1.9	2.7	.	5.2	2.7	2.2	.	5.1	2.2	1.0	.
France	3.2	2.1	3.1	.	10.2	6.5	3.4	.	9.9	6.2	3.0	.
Netherlands	2.9	1.7	2.3	.	7.9	1.9	0.8	.	7.6	2.1	0.2	.
Austria	3.4	1.9	2.8	.	6.5	3.8	2.6	.	6.6	3.4	1.9	.
Italy	3.8	2.4	3.3	.	15.6	10.3	6.4	.	14.6	9.7	5.4	.
Spain	3.5	2.9	4.8	.	16.1	9.6	7.0	.	15.8	9.5	6.1	.
Other middle-income economies	5.5	2.4	2.8	.	..	..	..	.	..	..	..	.
Portugal	4.4	2.4	4.5	.	16.7	19.2	13.4	.	19.5	18.0	10.5	.
Korea, Rep.	9.4	9.7	10.7	.	20.4	5.0	4.2	.	16.0	4.7	4.7	.
Argentina	2.4	-0.2	0.2	.	133.9	334.8	362.8	.	134.5	328.2	356.5	.
Brazil	8.1	3.0	3.2	.	38.7	225.7	419.8	.	33.8	225.8	436.7	.
Malaysia	7.8	4.9	6.2	.	7.4	1.5	1.8	.	6.3	2.7	1.6	.
Costa Rica	5.8	2.8	4.7	.	15.3	24.9	15.3	.	11.3	24.1	16.9	.
Tunisia	6.9	3.3	2.5	.	8.8	7.6	6.6	.	6.0	8.1	6.7	.
Thailand	7.1	7.0	10.2	.	9.2	3.2	4.8	.	9.8	3.4	3.3	.
Honduras	5.8	2.5	4.1	.	8.1	4.8	4.4	.	7.9	5.5	4.9	.
Morocco	5.5	4.2	4.2	.	8.4	7.4	5.5	.	9.1	7.4	3.9	.
Cote d'Ivoire	6.2	0.3	-0.7	.	13.9	3.7	-1.1	.	13.3	4.9	4.4	.
Senegal	2.1	3.1	3.3	.	8.7	7.2	3.0	.	11.1	7.2	-0.5	.
Other low-income economies	4.1	4.6	5.3	.	..	..	..	.	..	..	..	.
Indonesia	7.7	5.3	5.9	.	21.0	8.3	8.8	.	18.5	8.5	7.6	.
Sri Lanka	4.6	4.1	2.5	.	12.5	10.8	8.8	.	7.7	10.5	10.4	.
Kenya	6.7	4.0	5.9	.	10.2	9.2	7.8	.	13.0	10.0	6.8	.
India	3.3	5.5	6.3	.	8.4	7.8	7.7	.	7.8	8.7	8.4	.
Nepal	2.7	4.8	5.0	.	8.5	9.0	10.1	.	7.8	10.3	11.4	.
Bangladesh	2.6	4.4	3.5	.	20.5	9.8	9.1	.	20.4	10.7	9.9	.

Note: Abbreviations in notes column are explained in the General Notes. For sources and methods, see the Technical Notes.
a. Data refer to the Federal Republic of Germany before unification.

Table 8. Trade participation and terms of trade

	Trade participation rate (exports+imports as percentage of GDP)						Terms of trade index (1980=100)					
	1970	1975	1980	1985	1989	Notes	1970	1975	1980	1985	1989	Notes
HPEs in Europe	..	..	..	..	..	.	..	..	..	..	..	.
German Dem. Rep.	26.8	..	49.1	88.7	80.9	Lf	119.1	101.7	100	100.6	108.8	E
Former USSR	..	..	..	..	..		72.5	74.4	100	115.9	93.6	E
Czechoslovakia	..	..	67.7	69.5	67.0	.	..	..	100	87.8	92.7	.
Yugoslavia	42.0	48.3	41.6	57.9	46.6		102.5	99.5	100	92.9	96.4	.
Hungary	62.6	90.4	80.3	82.3	68.4		134.4	112.3	100	90.6	92.5	.
Bulgaria	..	..	66.4	83.4	87.1		125.8	117.0	100	83.0	83.8	E
Poland	..	..	59.2	35.1	34.0		..	..	100	96.5	117.7	.
Romania	..	..	75.3	41.7	37.8		..	..	100	56.7	110.7	.
Albania	..	..	..	..	..		101.8	..	100	179.5	275.4	Ef
HPEs elsewhere	..	..	..	..	..	.	..	..	..	..	..	.
Cuba	..	..	..	..	..		..	111.9	100	71.0	..	E
Mongolia	..	..	57.6	81.0	79.6		..	..	100	92.7	66.3	.
Nicaragua	55.3	66.0	67.5	36.6	99.5		89.5	65.9	100	123.1	104.1	.
Korea, Dem. People's Rep.	..	..	..	..	..	.	..	..	..	..	..	.
China	5.2	10.2	13.4	24.9	27.4		79.8	71.6	100	76.0	82.1	.
Lao PDR	..	..	..	13.1	32.9		..	..	..	..	..	.
Viet Nam	..	..	..	..	..		..	..	..	100.0	91.9	Ef
Cambodia	13.5	..	..	..	..		..	..	..	..	..	.
Other economies in transition	38.0	56.9	57.1	38.6	34.5	.	97.4	94.2	100	99.0	95.3	.
Algeria	51.2	76.5	64.7	43.9	40.8		27.8	59.9	100	99.0	50.5	.
Angola	..	..	..	..	..		..	..	..	..	..	.
Guinea	..	..	..	..	59.1		..	..	..	..	..	.
Myanmar	..	..	..	..	..		..	..	..	..	..	.
Madagascar	40.7	36.7	43.1	29.2	40.8		187.1	131.6	100	121.7	95.3	.
Afghanistan	21.7	26.9	..	..	..		..	..	..	..	..	.
Somalia	28.3	39.3	121.7	25.6	52.6		84.5	93.3	100	121.0	95.7	.
Tanzania	54.2	52.1	39.5	20.7	67.4		131.3	102.0	100	90.5	..	.
Ethiopia	22.3	27.6	32.9	34.1	32.4		121.3	95.0	100	99.0	..	.
Mozambique	..	..	51.5	18.4	82.9		..	..	100	115.0	113.3	.
High-income economies	27.2	35.6	42.4	37.5	38.8	.	108.3	106.0	100	100.6	103.6	.
United States	11.3	16.1	20.8	17.1	20.6		152.6	126.1	100	109.6	104.2	.
Germany a	40.3	46.9	53.6	61.2	57.3		111.7	106.8	100	96.2	109.4	.
France	31.1	36.9	44.3	47.2	46.3		124.4	112.0	100	99.0	108.9	.
Netherlands	91.4	96.4	105.6	122.2	111.8		107.3	103.6	100	101.6	102.6	.
Austria	61.1	63.1	75.6	81.3	79.5		107.6	106.0	100	99.1	103.6	.
Italy	32.8	41.1	46.5	45.9	41.2		130.6	107.4	100	100.2	115.6	.
Spain	26.8	30.2	33.2	43.5	39.4		114.3	106.4	100	91.4	111.9	.
Other middle-income economies	34.9	47.5	52.2	45.9	50.4	.	102.4	92.4	100	91.3	94.2	.
Portugal	55.3	53.2	72.6	77.9	81.7		111.4	103.0	100	92.4	112.0	.
Korea, Rep.	37.9	64.4	75.5	67.9	65.7		116.7	99.4	100	101.9	119.0	.
Argentina	18.2	16.0	15.9	24.6	29.3		80.1	92.4	100	78.5	61.3	.
Brazil	14.5	19.0	20.4	19.3	13.3		132.3	118.6	100	86.5	87.0	.
Malaysia	79.9	86.8	112.6	104.7	143.4		85.0	74.6	100	94.1	88.1	.
Costa Rica	63.2	68.6	63.3	63.2	73.4		110.8	86.5	100	97.3	96.4	.
Tunisia	48.5	66.9	85.8	71.3	92.3		88.6	96.0	100	94.8	84.6	.
Thailand	34.4	41.3	54.8	51.2	75.6		130.9	112.1	100	82.3	84.9	.
Honduras	62.0	70.4	81.4	56.2	68.7		92.3	78.5	100	86.6	83.9	.
Morocco	39.2	55.9	45.3	58.5	50.2		99.0	122.9	100	93.8	115.2	.
Cote d'Ivoire	64.9	73.3	74.1	78.4	66.7		94.5	79.4	100	101.9	70.3	.
Senegal	59.4	78.4	72.3	70.6	58.9		109.1	105.6	100	105.8	104.4	.
Other low-income economies	20.9	31.0	37.3	29.4	33.7	.	116.9	94.5	100	100.1	89.3	.
Indonesia	28.0	44.2	53.3	42.6	48.3		25.9	56.3	100	114.6	76.1	.
Sri Lanka	54.1	62.4	87.0	62.9	63.0		105.9	73.6	100	108.8	103.1	.
Kenya	60.5	64.3	67.0	51.7	52.1		131.1	99.0	100	76.3	81.4	.
India	8.2	12.8	16.6	15.0	18.3		115.0	106.0	100	114.7	111.2	.
Nepal	13.2	22.3	30.3	31.1	34.9		..	..	..	..	..	.
Bangladesh	20.8	11.0	24.1	25.8	25.8		199.2	85.3	100	130.2	100.9	.

Note: Abbreviations in notes column are explained in the General Notes. For sources and methods, see the Technical Notes.
a. Data refer to the Federal Republic of Germany before unification.

Table 9. External debt and international reserves

Millions of US dollars	Total external debt					Total international reserves (including gold valued at London prices)				
	1970	1975	1980	1985	1990	1970	1975	1980	1985	1990
HPEs in Europe						..	..	..	..	..
German Dem. Rep.	1,100	5,200	13,600	13,600	20,600 a	..	..	..	..	..
Former U.S.S.R.	..	..	..	28,900	54,000 a	..	..	..	12,900	14,700 ab
Czechoslovakia	812	1,922	8,119	5,685	8,959 a	113	459	3,639	2,099	2,060
Yugoslavia	2,053	5,999	18,486	22,278	20,690	143	1,017	2,478	1,704	6,208
Hungary	..	..	9,757	13,955	21,316	..	133	1,220	2,914	1,186
Bulgaria	1,386	3,383	4,387	3,861	9,201 a	..	..	1,396	2,136	1,381 a
Poland	24	698	8,894	33,336	49,386	..	..	574	1,025	4,674
Romania	..	122	9,762	7,008	369	..	904	2,511	1,448	1,374
Albania	..	..	..	..	..	..	..	..	..	..
HPEs ELSEWHERE						..	..	..	..	..
Cuba	..	..	..	7,055	..	..	..	..	..	..
Mongolia	..	..	973	2,800	5,187 a	..	..	23	69	140 a
Nicaragua	155	611	2,170	5,736	10,497	49	124	75	..	..
Korea, Dem. People's Rep.	..	..	..	1,171	..	..	..	..	..	..
China	..	..	4,504	16,722	52,555	..	..	10,091	16,881	34,476
Lao PDR	8	64	293	477	1,064	6	..	13	25	61
Viet Nam	..	..	..	5,428	..	243	..	..	238	..
Cambodia	..	..	..	318	..	..	..	..	..	..
Other economies in transition						695	2,759	8,730	5,661	3,999
Algeria	945	4,633	19,377	18,374	26,806	352	1,896	7,064	4,645	2,704
Angola	..	..	59	2,481	7,710	..	..	..	..	..
Guinea	320	761	1,117	1,438	2,497	..	..	..	..	..
Myanmar	123	328	1,499	3,091	4,675	98	161	409	116	410
Madagascar	90	184	1,257	2,490	3,938	37	36	9	48	245 a
Afghanistan	..	..	..	..	..	50	217	940	611	638
Somalia	77	229	660	1,639	2,350	21	69	26	9	23 a
Tanzania	195	883	2,447	3,577	5,866	65	65	20	16	54 a
Ethiopia	169	344	804	1,869	3,250	72	315	262	216	55
Mozambique	..	..	..	2,714	4,718	..	..	..	..	..
High-income economies						75,420	229,009	721,464	557,823	912,182
United States	8,830	131,370	309,730	683,820	1,350,550	15,237	43,155	171,413	117,982	173,094
Germany c	..	24,658	133,022	158,014	348,514	13,879	42,711	104,702	75,504	104,547
France	609	40,466	121,142	178,260	366,641	5,199	22,613	75,592	53,354	68,291
Netherlands	..	69	8,700	11,654	35,411	3,363	12,504	37,549	25,151	34,401
Austria	841	8,645	33,982	27,900	51,256	1,806	6,511	17,725	11,679	17,228
Italy	0	6,277	85,719	120,796	273,826	5,547	12,874	62,428	37,397	88,595
Spain	0	7,330	22,884	27,573	36,739	1,851	7,507	20,474	15,966	57,238
Other middle-income economies						15,816	83,153	174,078	123,817	175,503
Portugal	1,991	6,489	29,480	47,133	34,014	610	797	3,101	2,972	14,916
Korea, Rep.	782	1,503	9,729	16,633	20,413	1,565	4,285	13,863	8,008	20,579
Argentina	5,128	23,769	70,975	105,966	116,172	1,190	4,167	6,875	11,618	9,200
Brazil	5,171	8,171	27,157	50,945	61,144	682	848	9,297	4,703	6,222
Malaysia	440	1,843	6,611	20,836	19,502	668	1,689	5,755	5,677	10,659
Costa Rica	246	685	2,739	4,399	3,772	16	57	197	525	525
Tunisia	555	1,028	3,527	4,881	7,534	60	398	700	294	867
Thailand	726	1,352	8,297	17,552	23,868	911	2,007	3,026	3,003	14,258
Honduras	109	380	1,470	2,728	3,480	20	97	159	111	47
Morocco	754	1,727	9,707	16,527	23,524	142	438	814	345	2,338
Cote d'Ivoire	267	1,040	5,848	9,745	17,956	119	103	46	19	21
Senegal	145	349	1,473	2,563	3,745	22	31	25	15	22
Other low-income economies						3,207	11,024	37,048	24,383	27,502
Indonesia	3,096	10,372	20,944	36,672	67,908	160	592	6,803	5,989	8,657
Sri Lanka	395	743	1,841	3,538	5,851	43	57	283	472	447
Kenya	406	1,093	3,403	4,186	6,840	220	173	539	417	236
India	7,937	13,234	20,610	41,210	70,115	1,023	2,064	11,924	9,730	5,637
Nepal	3	34	205	590	1,621	94	114	272	106	354
Bangladesh	15	1,812	4,056	6,629	12,245	..	148	331	354	660

Note: Abbreviations in notes column are explained in the General Notes. For sources and methods, see the Technical Notes.
a. 1989 data. b. Reserves excluding gold. c. Data refer to the Federal Republic of Germany before unification.

Table 10. Fiscal and monetary accounts

| | Central government expenditure(as percentage of GDP) | | | | | | | | Current government revenue (percentage of GDP) | | | | Money supply (percentage of GDP) | | | |
| | Total | | | | Military | | | | | | | | | | | |
	1975	1980	1989	Notes	1975	1980	1989	Notes	1975	1980	1989	Notes	1975	1980	1989	Notes
HPEs in Europe																
German Dem. Rep.	..	25.1	26.5	A	..	7.9	8.8	A	..	..	..		..	..	..	
Former USSR	..	24.2	25.5	Af	..	12.9	11.7	A	..	..	..		..	..	..	
Czechoslovakia	..	..	58.8	.	..	..	4.5	.	..	..	56.8	.	..	53.2	73.0	.
Yugoslavia	22.3	8.9	5.1	.	5.6	4.4	2.7	.	22.3	7.8	5.3	.	62.9	68.4	110.0	.
Hungary	..	..	55.4	.	..	..	2.0	.	..	..	53.4	.	..	..	..	.
Bulgaria	..	..	74.8	.	..	..	4.9	.	..	..	76.3	.	..	..	..	.
Poland	..	..	..	.	..	8.9	8.9	A	..	..	..	.	..	61.6	62.9	.
Romania	49.4	44.8	40.2	.	2.2	1.7	3.7	.	49.6	45.3	48.4	.	25.9	35.4	..	.
Albania	..	..	..	A	..	..	4.1	A	..	..	..		..	..	..	
HPEs elsewhere																
Cuba	..	..	38.2	A	..	6.5	3.9	A	..	..	..		..	..	..	
Mongolia	..	..	..		..	..	..		..	..	..		..	..	..	
Nicaragua	17.5	30.4	32.1	.	1.7	3.3	..	.	13.5	23.9	30.1	.	18.5	27.6	..	.
Korea, Dem. People's Rep.	..	..	..	.	..	20.0	20.0	A	..	..	..		..	..	..	
China	..	16.7	11.7	A	..	8.8	3.7	A	..	..	..		..	37.4	71.8	.
Lao PDR	..	..	..	A	..	..	..	A	..	..	..		..	..	9.1	.
Viet Nam	..	..	..	A	..	..	..	A	..	..	..		..	..	..	
Cambodia	..	..	..	A	..	..	..		..	..	..		..	..	..	
Other economies in transition																
Algeria	..	..	..		..	..	..		..	..	..		57.6	63.9	97.8	.
Angola	..	..	..		..	..	..		..	..	..		..	..	..	
Guinea	..	..	22.4	.	..	..	..		..	..	16.3	.	..	..	..	
Myanmar	..	..	..		..	..	..		..	..	..		..	..	..	
Madagascar	..	..	..		..	..	..		..	15.6	..	.	17.7	24.8	24.8	.
Afghanistan	..	..	..		..	..	..		..	..	..		17.0	28.9	..	.
Somalia	15.6	..	..	.	3.2	..	..	.	13.9	..	..	.	22.5	19.5	28.2	.
Tanzania	32.0	28.7	..	.	3.8	2.6	..	.	22.3	20.3	..	.	29.2	41.6	..	.
Ethiopia	17.8	25.4	..	.	..	..	..		14.5	20.7	..	.	22.4	25.8	48.4	.
Mozambique	..	..	..		..	..	..		..	..	..		..	..	..	
High-income economies																
United States	21.1	22.2	23.3	.	5.2	4.7	5.7	.	18.4	20.3	20.4	.	64.7	61.3	68.5	.
Germany a	29.6	30.3	29.2	.	3.2	2.8	..	.	26.6	28.8	29.4	.	61.7	61.8	65.9	.
France	36.6	39.5	42.4	.	2.8	2.9	..	.	35.2	40.0	41.3	.	73.2	72.8	79.1	.
Netherlands	48.4	53.6	54.1	.	3.1	3.0	2.7	.	47.2	50.3	48.6	.	72.5	81.3	..	.
Austria	34.8	37.4	38.7	.	1.1	1.1	1.1	.	31.3	34.9	34.9	.	65.6	76.9	87.8	.
Italy	35.0	41.1	47.5	.	1.7	1.4	..	.	26.5	31.9	38.1	.	97.9	86.8	80.3	.
Spain	20.6	26.4	..	.	1.2	1.1	..	.	20.7	23.9	..	.	86.3	80.1	67.6	.
Other middle-income economies																
Portugal	32.7	38.5	42.5	.	4.3	2.9	..	.	25.4	30.7	38.3	.	102.2	91.2	74.5	.
Korea, Rep.	15.7	17.3	16.7	.	4.5	5.9	4.2	.	15.2	17.7	17.9	.	33.0	35.8	56.7	.
Argentina	..	24.7	..	.	..	3.5	..	.	..	21.2	..	.	25.1	29.0	23.3	.
Brazil	19.9	20.2	34.9	.	..	0.8	1.5	.	19.9	22.6	90.0	.	27.5	23.3	..	.
Malaysia	25.7	28.5	29.1	.	4.5	4.2	2.7	.	21.8	26.3	25.2	.	65.2	77.5	..	.
Costa Rica	19.2	25.0	26.0	.	0.6	0.7	0.4	.	18.0	17.8	24.4	.	29.2	41.6	41.0	.
Tunisia	29.1	31.6	35.5	.	1.3	3.9	2.3	.	29.0	31.9	31.8	.	42.5	45.5	..	.
Thailand	14.6	18.9	15.0	.	2.6	4.1	2.7	.	12.8	14.7	18.2	.	37.8	41.1	73.1	.
Honduras	16.6	..	..	.	1.9	..	..	.	13.7	14.7	..	.	23.7	23.8	35.9	.
Morocco	34.1	33.1	..	.	4.6	5.9	..	.	25.9	23.3	..	.	42.4	44.8	..	.
Cote d'Ivoire	..	30.7	..	.	..	1.2	..	.	..	23.3	..	.	29.3	26.2	29.4	.
Senegal	18.6	23.1	..	.	2.0	3.9	..	.	18.9	24.2	..	.	21.2	27.9	25.0	.
Other low-income economies																
Indonesia	19.4	22.1	19.4	.	3.7	3.0	1.6	.	17.2	21.3	17.4	.	15.2	15.8	34.9	.
Sri Lanka	25.3	41.4	30.3	.	0.7	0.7	1.8	.	19.1	24.1	23.6	.	23.9	39.5	38.8	.
Kenya	21.6	25.3	30.1	.	1.6	4.1	2.3	.	18.9	22.6	24.1	.	33.6	37.9	39.9	.
India	11.8	13.3	18.7	.	3.0	2.6	3.2	.	11.9	12.0	15.3	.	27.7	38.8	48.5	.
Nepal	9.0	14.3	22.2	.	0.6	1.0	1.1	.	7.7	11.2	11.8	.	13.2	23.7	36.5	.
Bangladesh	6.4	10.0	14.9	.	0.5	0.9	1.5	.	9.3	14.0	14.5	.	11.6	16.7	28.9	.

Note: Abbreviations in notes column are explained in the General Notes. For sources and methods, see the Technical Notes.
a. Data refer to the Federal Republic of Germany before unification.

Table 11. Human resources: population

| | Total population | | | | | | | Urban population | | | |
| | (Thousands) | | | | Average annual growth (percent) | | | (percentage of total population) | | | |
	1970	1980	1990	Notes	1970-80	1980-90	Notes	1970	1980	1990	Notes
HPEs in Europe	368,272	399,868	427,207	.	0.8	0.7	.	55	61	65	
German Dem. Rep.	17,068	16,737	15,229	.	-0.2	-0.1	.	74	76	77	
Former USSR	242,757	265,542	288,500	.	0.9	0.9	.	57	63	66	
Czechoslovakia	14,334	15,262	15,662	.	0.7	0.3	.	55	68	78	
Yugoslavia	20,371	22,304	23,809	.	0.9	0.7	.	35	45	56	.
Hungary	10,337	10,710	10,553	.	0.4	-0.2	.	46	54	61	.
Bulgaria	8,490	8,862	8,823	.	0.4	0.0	.	52	61	68	.
Poland	32,526	35,578	38,180	.	0.9	0.7	.	52	58	62	.
Romania	20,253	22,201	23,200	.	0.9	0.4	.	42	49	53	.
Albania	2,136	2,671	3,250	.	2.3	2.0	.	34	34	35	.
HPEs elsewhere	897,173	1,077,074	1,250,779	.	1.8	1.5	.	19	20	54	
Cuba	8,551	9,724	10,617	.	1.4	0.9	.	60	68	75	.
Mongolia	1,256	1,619	2,128	.	2.6	2.8	.	45	51	52	.
Nicaragua	2,053	2,771	3,853	.	3.0	3.4	.	47	53	60	.
Korea, Dem. People's Rep.	14,619	18,260	21,576	.	2.2	1.7	.	53	57	60	.
China	818,315	981,235	1,133,683	.	1.8	1.4	.	18	19	..	
Lao PDR	2,713	3,205	4,140	.	1.6	2.6	.	10	13	19	.
Viet Nam	42,729	53,700	66,312	.	2.3	2.1	.	18	19	22	.
Cambodia	6,938	6,560	8,469	.	-0.8	2.6	.	12	10	12	.
Other economies in transition	125,647	163,002	213,721	.	2.7	2.8	.	16	20	26	
Algeria	13,746	18,669	25,056	.	3.1	3.0	.	40	43	52	.
Angola	5,588	7,723	10,012	.	3.4	2.6	.	15	21	28	.
Guinea	3,851	4,461	5,717	.	1.4	2.5	.	14	19	26	.
Myanmar	27,102	33,821	41,609	.	2.2	2.1	.	23	24	25	.
Madagascar	6,752	8,714	11,673	.	2.6	2.9	.	14	18	25	.
Afghanistan	12,457	15,950	20,445	.	2.5	2.5	.	11	16	18	.
Somalia	4,311	5,746	7,805	.	2.9	3.1	.	23	29	36	.
Tanzania	13,513	18,098	24,517	.	3.0	3.1	.	7	17	33	.
Ethiopia	28,937	37,717	51,180	.	2.7	3.1	.	9	11	13	.
Mozambique	9,390	12,103	15,707	.	2.6	2.6	.	6	13	27	.
High-income economies	705,024	766,080	816,623	.	0.8	0.6	.	74	76	78	
United States	205,052	227,757	249,975	.	1.0	0.9	.	74	74	75	.
Germany a	77,719	78,303	79,479	.	0.0	0.1	.	80	83	84	.
France	50,772	53,880	56,440	.	0.6	0.5	.	71	73	74	.
Netherlands	13,039	14,150	14,943	.	0.8	0.5	.	86	88	89	.
Austria	7,426	7,553	7,712	.	0.1	0.2	.	52	55	58	.
Italy	53,822	56,434	57,663	.	0.5	0.2	.	64	67	69	.
Spain	33,779	37,386	38,959	.	1.0	0.4	.	66	73	78	.
Other middle-income economies	574,676	736,337	925,835	.	2.5	2.3	.	46	53	60	.
Portugal	9,044	9,766	10,354	.	1.3	0.6	.	26	29	34	.
Korea, Rep.	31,923	38,124	42,793	.	1.8	1.2	.	41	57	72	.
Argentina	23,962	28,237	32,293	.	1.7	1.4	.	78	83	86	.
Brazil	95,847	121,286	150,368	.	2.4	2.2	.	56	66	75	.
Malaysia	10,853	13,764	17,861	.	2.4	2.6	.	27	35	43	.
Costa Rica	1,727	2,218	2,807	.	2.5	2.4	.	40	43	47	.
Tunisia	5,127	6,384	8,060	.	2.2	2.4	.	44	52	54	.
Thailand	35,745	46,700	55,801	.	2.7	1.8	.	13	17	23	.
Honduras	2,627	3,662	5,105	.	3.4	3.4	.	29	36	44	.
Morocco	15,310	19,382	25,091	.	2.4	2.6	.	35	41	48	.
Cote d'Ivoire	5,510	8,194	11,902	.	4.1	3.8	.	27	38	40	.
Senegal	4,158	5,538	7,404	.	2.9	2.9	.	33	35	38	.
Other low-income economies	2,014,567	2,500,522	3,058,279	.	2.2	2.0	.	18	21	38	.
Indonesia	117,537	148,303	178,232	.	2.4	1.9	.	17	22	31	.
Sri Lanka	12,516	14,738	17,002	.	1.7	1.4	.	22	22	21	.
Kenya	11,498	16,632	24,160	.	3.8	3.8	.	10	16	24	.
India	547,569	687,332	849,515	.	2.3	2.1	.	20	23	27	.
Nepal	11,350	14,640	18,916	.	2.6	2.6	.	4	6	10	.
Bangladesh	66,671	84,969	106,656	.	2.4	2.3	.	8	11	16	.

Note: Abbreviations in notes column are explained in the General Notes. For sources and methods, see the Technical Notes.
a. Data refer to the Federal Republic of Germany before unification.

Table 12. Human resources: labor force

	Total (thousands)						As a percentage of total population				Annual average growth (percent)		
	1970	1978	1980	1988	1990	Notes	1970	1980	1990	Notes	1970-80	1980-90	Notes
HPEs in Europe	181,568	199,835	204,502	216,334	218,418	.	49	51	51	.	1.2	0.7	.
German Dem. Rep.	8,553	8,960	9,117	9,609	9,670	.	50	55	64	.	0.6	0.6	.
Former USSR	117,276	132,791	136,933	145,296	146,634	.	48	52	51	.	1.6	0.7	.
Czechoslovakia	7,379	7,893	8,025	8,304	8,386	.	52	53	54	.	0.8	0.4	.
Yugoslavia	9,177	9,826	9,958	10,708	10,858	.	45	45	46	.	0.8	0.9	.
Hungary	5,495	5,310	5,220	5,252	5,276	.	53	49	50	.	-0.5	0.1	.
Bulgaria	4,414	4,487	4,480	4,478	4,475	.	52	51	51	.	0.1	0.0	.
Poland	17,336	18,360	18,520	19,511	19,704	.	53	52	52	.	0.7	0.6	.
Romania	11,037	11,066	11,039	11,662	11,825	.	55	50	51	.	0.0	0.7	.
Albania	901	1,144	1,211	1,514	1,591	.	42	45	49	.	3.0	2.8	.
HPEs elsewhere	463,005	562,193	590,130	708,480	735,976	.	52	55	59	.	2.5	2.2	.
Cuba	2,636	3,359	3,567	4,271	4,461	.	31	37	42	.	3.1	2.3	.
Mongolia	582	731	772	975	1,029	.	46	48	48	.	2.9	2.9	.
Nicaragua	619	784	825	1,120	1,204	.	30	30	31	.	2.9	3.9	.
Korea, Dem. People's Rep.	5,908	7,428	7,838	9,916	10,470	.	40	43	49	.	2.9	3.0	.
China	428,309	520,940	547,060	655,102	679,900	.	52	56	60	.	2.5	2.2	.
Lao PDR	1,610	1,808	1,839	2,149	2,239	.	59	57	54	.	1.3	2.0	.
Viet Nam	20,272	23,885	24,930	31,252	32,916	.	47	46	50	.	2.1	2.8	.
Cambodia	3,069	3,262	3,299	3,696	3,758	.	44	50	44	.	0.7	1.4	.
Other economies in transition	54,887	66,695	69,967	83,111	86,956	.	44	43	41	.	2.5	2.2	.
Algeria	2,945	3,813	4,051	5,425	5,819	.	21	22	23	.	3.2	3.7	.
Angola	2,599	3,231	3,414	3,936	4,081	.	47	44	41	.	2.8	1.8	.
Guinea	2,196	2,533	2,626	2,996	3,097	.	57	59	54	.	1.8	1.7	.
Myanmar	12,150	14,526	15,170	17,674	18,324	.	45	45	44	.	2.2	1.9	.
Madagascar	3,303	3,926	4,098	4,806	5,004	.	49	47	43	.	2.2	2.0	.
Afghanistan	4,122	4,706	4,797	5,725	6,229	.	33	30	31	.	1.5	2.4	.
Somalia	1,252	1,691	1,808	2,085	2,143	.	29	32	28	.	3.7	1.8	.
Tanzania	7,176	8,996	9,508	11,924	12,597	.	53	53	51	.	2.9	2.9	.
Ethiopia	14,403	16,921	17,593	20,408	21,225	.	50	47	42	.	2.0	1.9	.
Mozambique	4,742	6,355	6,904	8,131	8,437	.	51	57	54	.	3.9	2.0	.
High-income economies	31,737	353,205	362,776	390,195	395,657	.	45	47	49	.	1.3	0.9	.
United States	87,222	105,064	109,872	119,923	122,005	.	43	48	49	.	2.3	1.1	.
Germany a	44,014	45,899	46,569	48,566	48,651	.	57	60	61	.	0.6	0.5	.
France	21,579	23,182	23,559	25,098	25,404	.	43	44	45	.	0.9	0.8	.
Netherlands	4,718	5,321	5,461	6,036	6,153	.	36	39	41	.	1.5	1.2	.
Austria	3,112	3,297	3,364	3,544	3,570	.	42	45	46	.	0.8	0.6	.
Italy	20,955	21,694	21,936	23,109	23,339	.	39	39	41	.	0.5	0.6	.
Spain	11,956	12,685	12,895	14,163	14,456	.	35	35	37	.	0.8	1.2	.
Other middle-income economies	199,524	249,503	263,017	321,901	337,222	.	35	36	36	.	2.8	2.5	.
Portugal	3,387	4,158	4,347	4,670	4,740	.	37	45	46	.	2.5	0.9	.
Korea, Rep.	11,407	14,059	14,729	17,914	18,664	.	36	39	44	.	2.6	2.4	.
Argentina	9,339	10,139	10,304	11,283	11,548	.	39	37	36	.	1.0	1.1	.
Brazil	31,544	41,541	44,240	52,873	55,026	.	33	37	37	.	3.4	2.2	.
Malaysia	3,694	4,983	5,337	6,711	7,071	.	34	39	40	.	3.7	2.9	.
Costa Rica	531	722	778	976	1,023	.	31	35	37	.	3.9	2.8	.
Tunisia	1,326	1,788	1,908	2,446	2,594	.	26	30	32	.	3.7	3.1	.
Thailand	17,867	22,346	23,582	28,383	29,534	.	50	51	53	.	2.8	2.3	.
Honduras	790	1,011	1,079	1,466	1,576	.	30	30	31	.	3.2	3.9	.
Morocco	4,048	5,275	5,688	7,365	7,825	.	26	29	31	.	3.5	3.3	.
Cote d'Ivoire	2,752	3,389	3,547	4,380	4,599	.	50	43	39	.	2.6	2.6	.
Senegal	1,911	2,482	2,641	3,074	3,192	.	46	48	43	.	3.3	1.9	.
Other low-income economies	916,221	1,094,243	1,144,100	1,358,105	1,413,997	.	45	46	46	.	2.2	2.1	.
Indonesia	45,646	53,962	56,253	68,160	71,314	.	39	38	40	.	2.1	2.4	.
Sri Lanka	4,347	5,183	5,457	6,188	6,367	.	35	37	38	.	2.3	1.6	.
Kenya	4,950	6,599	7,072	9,362	10,011	.	43	43	41	.	3.6	3.5	.
India	223,925	256,584	265,320	311,044	322,944	.	41	39	38	.	1.7	2.0	.
Nepal	5,141	5,919	6,139	7,383	7,725	.	45	42	41	.	1.8	2.3	.
Bangladesh	20,507	24,099	25,133	31,577	33,398	.	31	30	31	.	2.1	2.9	.

Note: Abbreviations in notes column are explained in the General Notes. For sources and methods, see the Technical Notes.
a. Data refer to the Federal Republic of Germany before unification.

Table continues on the following page.

Table 12. Human resources: labor force (continued)

	Agriculture			Industry			Services			Armed forces			
	1970	*1980*	*Notes*	*1970*	*1980*	*Notes*	*1970*	*1980*	*Notes*	*1978*	*1980*	*1988*	*Notes*
HPEs in Europe	29.0	21.4	.	37.7	40.0	.	33.4	38.6	.	..	..	..	.
German Dem. Rep.	12.6	10.6	.	50.2	50.0	.	37.2	39.4	.	2.5	2.5	2.5	.
Former USSR	25.7	20.0	.	37.7	39.0	.	36.7	41.0	.	2.9	2.8	2.7	.
Czechoslovakia	16.9	13.3	.	48.4	49.4	.	34.7	37.4	.	2.3	2.4	2.5	.
Yugoslavia	49.8	32.3	.	29.2	33.3	.	21.0	34.4	.	2.7	2.6	2.1	.
Hungary	25.1	18.2	.	44.8	43.6	.	30.1	38.2	.	2.3	2.3	2.2	.
Bulgaria	34.8	18.1	.	37.8	45.4	.	27.4	36.5	.	4.2	4.2	3.6	.
Poland	38.9	28.5	.	34.2	38.9	.	26.8	32.6	.	2.1	2.2	2.2	.
Romania	48.7	30.5	.	31.1	43.5	.	20.2	26.0	.	1.9	1.9	1.9	.
Albania	66.2	55.9	.	21.2	25.7	.	12.6	18.4	.	3.9	3.8	2.8	.
HPEs elsewhere	77.6	73.2	.	10.2	14.2	.	12.2	12.7	.	..	..	..	.
Cuba	30.2	23.8	.	26.7	28.5	.	43.1	47.7	.	6.3	6.2	7.0	.
Mongolia	47.9	39.8	.	21.0	21.0	.	31.1	39.2	.	4.9	4.7	..	.
Nicaragua	51.5	46.6	.	15.5	15.8	.	33.0	37.6	.	0.8	2.9	6.6	.
Korea, Dem. People's Rep.	52.8	42.8	.	25.7	30.3	.	21.5	26.9	.	8.5	8.9	8.5	.
China	78.3	74.2	.	10.1	14.0	.	11.5	11.8	.	0.9	0.8	0.6	.
Lao PDR	78.9	75.7	.	5.2	7.1	.	15.9	17.2	.	2.6	3.0	2.6	.
Viet Nam	76.6	67.5	.	6.5	11.8	.	16.9	20.7	.	2.8	3.6	3.5	.
Cambodia	78.3	74.4	.	4.2	6.7	.	17.5	19.0	.	2.1	1.1	1.6	.
Other economies in transition	76.1	70.8	.	9.1	11.2	.	14.8	17.9	.	..	..	..	.
Algeria	47.3	31.1	.	21.3	26.9	.	31.4	42.0	.	2.0	2.5	2.3	.
Angola	77.7	73.8	.	8.4	9.6	.	13.8	16.7	.	1.5	1.4	2.7	.
Guinea	85.2	80.7	.	7.0	9.0	.	7.8	10.3	.	0.7	1.1	0.5	.
Myanmar	59.1	53.0	.	15.6	18.6	.	25.3	28.4	.	1.5	1.2	1.1	.
Madagascar	83.7	80.9	.	4.9	6.0	.	11.4	13.2	.	0.5	0.5	0.4	.
Afghanistan	66.1	61.0	.	12.1	14.0	.	21.8	25.0	.	2.3	0.9	1.0	.
Somalia	79.4	75.5	.	7.0	8.4	.	13.6	16.0	.	3.2	3.0	2.3	.
Tanzania	90.4	85.6	.	3.1	4.5	.	6.6	9.9	.	0.7	0.6	0.3	.
Ethiopia	85.0	79.8	.	5.9	7.9	.	9.1	12.3	.	1.4	1.4	1.2	.
Mozambique	86.4	84.5	.	6.1	7.4	.	7.4	8.1	.	0.4	0.4	0.8	.
High-income economies	10.7	7.0	.	38.0	35.1	.	50.4	56.8	.	..	..	..	.
United States	4.3	3.5	.	32.5	31.0	.	63.3	65.5	.	2.0	1.9	1.9	.
Germany a	9.5	7.7	.	48.9	46.3	.	41.7	46.1	.	1.1	1.1	1.0	.
France	13.6	8.6	.	39.3	35.3	.	47.1	56.1	.	2.5	2.4	2.2	.
Netherlands	6.8	5.5	.	39.3	31.5	.	53.9	63.0	.	2.0	2.0	1.8	.
Austria	14.8	9.0	.	43.1	41.1	.	42.1	49.9	.	1.2	1.2	1.6	.
Italy	18.8	12.0	.	43.6	40.5	.	37.6	47.5	.	2.3	2.3	1.9	.
Spain	26.0	17.1	.	37.6	37.1	.	36.4	45.8	.	2.9	2.8	2.1	.
Other middle-income economies	50.7	41.0	.	19.5	23.0	.	29.8	36.0	.	..	..	..	.
Portugal	31.8	25.8	.	31.8	36.7	.	36.4	37.6	.	2.0	2.0	2.2	.
Korea, Rep.	49.1	36.4	.	19.8	26.8	.	31.0	36.8	.	4.3	4.1	3.5	.
Argentina	16.0	13.0	.	34.3	33.8	.	49.7	53.1	.	1.5	1.5	0.8	.
Brazil	44.9	31.2	.	21.8	26.6	.	33.3	42.2	.	1.1	1.0	0.6	.
Malaysia	53.8	41.6	.	14.3	19.1	.	32.0	39.3	.	1.6	1.6	1.6	.
Costa Rica	42.6	30.8	.	20.0	23.1	.	37.5	46.1	.	0.7	0.8	0.8	.
Tunisia	42.2	35.0	.	25.3	36.4	.	32.5	28.6	.	1.2	1.5	1.6	.
Thailand	79.8	70.9	.	6.0	10.3	.	14.2	18.8	.	1.1	1.0	1.0	.
Honduras	64.9	60.5	.	14.1	16.2	.	21.0	23.3	.	1.4	1.3	1.3	.
Morocco	57.6	45.6	.	17.0	25.0	.	25.4	29.4	.	1.6	2.1	2.6	.
Cote d'Ivoire	76.5	65.2	.	5.6	8.3	.	17.9	26.5	.	0.2	0.2	0.2	.
Senegal	82.7	80.6	.	5.7	6.3	.	11.7	13.2	.	0.5	0.3	0.5	.
Other low-income economies	72.0	68.3	.	11.3	12.2	.	16.8	19.6	.	..	..	..	.
Indonesia	66.3	57.2	.	10.3	13.1	.	23.4	29.7	.	0.5	0.4	0.4	.
Sri Lanka	55.3	53.4	.	14.4	13.9	.	30.3	32.7	.	0.3	0.3	0.8	.
Kenya	84.8	81.0	.	5.6	6.8	.	9.6	12.1	.	0.2	0.2	0.2	.
India	71.7	69.7	.	12.6	13.2	.	15.7	17.0	.	0.5	0.4	0.4	.
Nepal	93.6	93.0	.	1.3	0.6	.	5.1	6.5	.	0.5	0.3	0.5	.
Bangladesh	81.4	74.8	.	4.9	6.0	.	13.7	19.2	.	0.3	0.3	0.3	.

Table 13. Relative wages and output: chemicals/total manufacturing

	Ratio of wages per employee				Ratio of gross output per employee			
	1975	1980	1985	1987	1985	1986	1987	1988
HPEs in Europe								
German Dem. Rep.	..	..	..	..	..	..	..	..
Former USSR	106	101	99	..	164	164	175	..
Czechoslovakia	103	103	107	107	103	103	107	107
Yugoslavia	124	113	112	118	162	177	187	183
Hungary	111	114	118	120	183	202	200	200
Bulgaria	102	109	107	115	102	109	107	115
Poland	104	101	102	101	..	..	..	..
Romania	..	..	..	..	..	..	..	..
Albania	..	..	..	..	..	..	..	..
HPEs elsewhere								
Cuba a	..	101	101	103	..	101	101	103
Mongolia								
Nicaragua	104	128	123	..	118	117	130	..
Korea, Dem. People's Rep.	..	..	..	..	..	..	..	..
China	..	97	97	..	..	97	97	..
Lao PDR	..	..	..	..	..	..	..	..
Viet Nam	..	..	..	..	..	..	..	..
Cambodia	..	..	..	..	..	..	..	..
Other economies in transition								
Algeria	125	109	..	..	125	109	..	..
Angola	..	..	..	..	..	..	..	..
Guinea	..	..	..	..	..	..	..	..
Myanmar	..	..	..	..	..	..	..	..
Madagascar	95	85	106	..	158	150	199	..
Afghanistan	88	80	..	..	..	99	..	..
Somalia b	116	..	..	..	241	..	..	..
Tanzania	..	109	149	..	..	125	230	..
Ethiopia	126	109	107	106	213	137	135	129
Mozambique	..	..	..	..	..	..	..	..
High-income economies								
United States	119	122	124	124	171	181	178	180
Germany c	122	121	124	124	138	140	146	140
France	..	129	122	..	132	139	148	140
Netherlands	118	120	121	..	128	145	160	..
Austria	122	125	124	124	122	125	124	124
Italy	130	124	130	129	157	141	171	165
Spain	127	126	132	133	168	157	170	165
Other middle-income economies								
Portugal	138	135	155	..	187	162	228	..
Korea, Rep.	156	141	141	137	182	209	221	210
Argentina	115	118	124	120	115	118	124	120
Brazil	137	143	..	..	137	143	..	..
Malaysia	150	144	172	179	162	141	280	278
Costa Rica	..	..	..	..	..	..	..	..
Tunisia	142	150	..	..	200	245	..	..
Thailand	119	152	154	..	97	126	133	..
Honduras	132	..	..	..	131	..	..	..
Morocco	..	161	168	..	..	192	252	..
Cote d'Ivoire b	153	145	..	..	153	145	..	..
Senegal	..	..	..	..	..	..	..	..
Other low-income economies								
Indonesia	193	201	235	..	129	177	184	..
Sri Lanka	..	121	174	..	..	90	162	..
Kenya	162	143	160	165	208	147	106	110
India	152	154	145	146	217	205	180	191
Nepal	..	..	..	..	..	..	..	..
Bangladesh	112	122	139	139	112	122	139	139

Note: Abbreviations in notes column are explained in the General Notes. For sources and methods, see the Technical Notes.
a. Includes rubber and plastic products. b. Includes plastic products. c. Data refer to the Federal Republic of Germany before unification.

Table 14. Health services and vital statistics

	Population per								
	Physician			Nursing person			Hospital bed		
	1970	1980 a	Notes	1973	1981 a	Notes	1970	1980 a	Notes
HPEs in Europe									
German Dem. Rep.	626	494	.	..	..	.	90	..	.
Former USSR	421	270	.	169		.	91	..	.
Czechoslovakia	471	362	.	167	130	.	98	80	.
Yugoslavia	1,000	679	.	423	300	.	177	167	.
Hungary	507	400	.	214	157	.	123	110	.
Bulgaria	537	407	.	239	190	.	129	90	.
Poland	700	550	.	255	..	.	131	..	.
Romania	844	678	.	430	280	.	121	107	.
Albania	1,068	..	.	232	..	.	141	..	.
HPEs elsewhere									
Cuba	1,222	721	.	..	..	.	217	..	.
Mongolia	578	99	.	248	206	.	105	87	.
Nicaragua	2,136	2,283	.	..	590	.	424	..	.
Korea, Dem. People's Rep.	..		.			.	..		.
China	..	1,100	.	2,500	2,100	.	..	500	.
Lao PDR	15,156	..	.	1,386		.	1,078	..	.
Viet Nam	..	4,151	.	4,305	1,241	.	..	286	.
Cambodia	16,248	..	.	1,376	..	.	925	..	.
Other economies in transition									
Algeria	8,095		.	..	..	.	352		.
Angola	8,597	..	.	1,784	..	.	368	..	.
Guinea	50,013	45,470	.	3,715	5,058	.	562	..	.
Myanmar	8,819	4,949	.	3,056	4,940	.	1,176	1,171	.
Madagascar	10,123	9,891	.	240	1,721	.	353	..	.
Afghanistan	15,417	13,237	.	15,121	8,955	.	5,025	3,699	.
Somalia	27,235	19,217	.	..	2,404	.	883	..	.
Tanzania	22,597	..	.	3,312	..	.	..	697	.
Ethiopia	86,122	88,124	.	..	4,995	.	3,506	3,384	.
Mozambique	18,855	39,168	.	..	5,612	.	851	918	.
High-income economies									
United States	634	549	.	158	180	.	127	171	.
Germany b	583	452	.	288	170	.	73	..	.
France	747	462	.	273	110	.	139	..	.
Netherlands	800	480	.	303	..	.	94	80	.
Austria	543	440	.	303	170	.	92	90	.
Italy	555	750	.	..	250	.	95	..	.
Spain	745	361	.	..	281	.	192	..	.
Other middle-income economies									
Portugal	1,109	494	.	816	..	.	166	..	.
Korea, Rep.	2,216	1,690	.	1,191	..	.	1,930	586	.
Argentina	529	..	.	960		.	179	..	.
Brazil	2,029	1,300	.	4,138	1,141	.	271	..	.
Malaysia	4,310	3,638	.	1,269	1,392	.	288	440	.
Costa Rica	1,619	..	.	460		.	252	293	.
Tunisia	5,934	3,694	.	..	956	.	409	470	.
Thailand	8,288	6,801	.	1,171	2,143	.	879	651	.
Honduras	3,774	3,100	.	1,469	..	.	578	775	.
Morocco	13,086	18,602	.	..	900	.	678	816	.
Cote d'Ivoire	15,521	..	.	1,927	..	.	864	..	.
Senegal	15,810	12,690	.	1,675	1,932	.	770	..	.
Other low-income economies									
Indonesia	26,817	12,458	.	4,805	..	.	1,528	..	.
Sri Lanka	5,904	7,172	.	12,806	1,262	.	332	340	.
Kenya	8,001	10,126	.	2,524	988	.	791	..	.
India	4,889	2,694	.	3,710	4,674	.	1,654	1,299	.
Nepal	51,358	30,062	.	17,700	7,783	.	7,063	5,728	.
Bangladesh	8,447	8,256	.	66,030	14,458	.	6,467	4,608	.

Note: Abbreviations in notes column are explained in the General Notes. For sources and methods, see the Technical Notes.
a. Data refer to 1980 or 1981. b. Data refer to the Federal Republic of Germany before unification. c. Data refer to unified Germany.

Table 14. Health services and vital statistics (continued)

Infant mortality rate (per 1,000 live births)				Life expectancy at birth (years)				
1970	1980	1990	Notes	1970	1980	1990	Notes	
27	23	19		69	69	72		HPEs in Europe
19	12	8	.	70	72	74	.	German Dem. Rep.
24	26	24	.	69	68	71	.	Former USSR
22	18	12	.	70	71	72	.	Czechoslovakia
56	31	23	.	68	69	72	.	Yugoslavia
36	23	16	.	70	70	71	.	Hungary
27	20	13	.	71	71	73	.	Bulgaria
33	21	16	.	70	71	71	.	Poland
49	29	24	.	69	70	71	.	Romania
66	47	24	.	67	70	72	.	Albania
71	43	30		61	67	70		HPEs elsewhere
39	20	12	.	70	74	76	.	Cuba
102	82	62	.	53	58	63	.	Mongolia
106	83	55	.	54	58	65	.	Nicaragua
51	32	26	.	60	67	71	.	Korea, Dem. People's Rep.
69	41	29	.	62	67	70	.	China
146	127	103	.	40	45	50	.	Lao PDR
104	57	42	.	55	63	67	.	Viet Nam
161	201	117	.	42	39	50	.	Cambodia
149	132	112		45	48	52		Other economies in transition
139	98	67	.	53	59	65	.	Algeria
178	153	129	.	37	41	46	.	Angola
181	161	138	.	36	40	43	.	Guinea
104	84	64	.	51	57	61	.	Myanmar
181	138	116	.	45	50	51	.	Madagascar
198	183	169	.	37	40	42	.	Afghanistan
158	145	126	.	40	44	48	.	Somalia
132	122	110	.	45	47	50	.	Tanzania
158	155	131	.	43	44	48	.	Ethiopia
171	156	135	.	40	45	49	.	Mozambique
20	12	8		71	74	77		High-income economies
20	13	10	.	71	74	76	.	United States
23 c	13 c	7 c	.	71 c	73 c	76 c	.	Germany
18	10	7	.	72	74	77	.	France
13	9	7	.	74	76	77	.	Netherlands
26	14	9	.	70	73	76	.	Austria
30	15	9	.	72	75	76	.	Italy
28	12	8	.	72	75	77	.	Spain
90	67	50		58	63	66		Other middle-income economies
56	24	13	.	67	71	75	.	Portugal
51	32	22	.	60	67	70	.	Korea, Rep.
52	38	29	.	67	69	71	.	Argentina
95	74	58	.	59	63	66	.	Brazil
45	30	22	.	62	67	70	.	Malaysia
62	20	17	.	67	72	75	.	Costa Rica
127	72	44	.	54	62	67	.	Tunisia
73	44	27	.	58	62	66	.	Thailand
115	87	64	.	53	60	65	.	Honduras
128	99	67	.	52	57	62	.	Morocco
135	109	91	.	45	50	53	.	Cote d'Ivoire
135	103	80	.	43	45	49	.	Senegal
136	116	91		47	52	57		Other low-income economies
118	99	61	.	47	55	62	.	Indonesia
53	34	19	.	65	68	71	.	Sri Lanka
102	83	66	.	50	55	60	.	Kenya
139	116	93	.	48	54	59	.	India
157	142	122	.	42	47	52	.	Nepal
140	132	105	.	45	48	52	.	Bangladesh

Table 15. Air quality

	Anthropogenic additions of			Net total atmospheric increase (000 tons carbon)	Estimated annual emissions of selected pollutants (thousand of metric tons)			
	Carbon dioxide (tons per capita)	Methane (tons per capita)	CFCs (kilograms per capita)		Sulfur dioxide		Oxides of nitrogen	
	1987	1987	1986	1986	1979-81	1982-84	1979-81	1982-84
HPEs in Europe								
German Dem. Rep.	5.4	0.0	0.7	62	4,000	4,000	..	..
Former USSR	3.7	0.1	0.4	690	..	..	..	..
Czechoslovakia	4.2	0.0	0.1	33	3,100	..	1,200	..
Yugoslavia	1.5	0.0	0.2	26	820	..	..	..
Hungary	2.0	0.1	0.1	13	1,635	1,460	290	300
Bulgaria	3.7	0.0	0.1	17	1,030	1,140	..	150
Poland	3.4	0.1	0.2	76	2,600	3,700	..	1,770
Romania	2.5	0.0	0.0	28	200	..	..	..
Albania	0.9	0.0	..	2	..	..	..	..
HPEs elsewhere								
Cuba	0.9	0.0	0.1	7	..	..	..	..
Mongolia	1.2	0.1	..	2	..	..	..	..
Nicaragua	4.9	0.0	0.1	8	..	..	..	..
Korea, Dem. People's Rep.	1.9	0.0	..	20	..	..	..	..
China	0.6	0.0	0.0	380	14,210	12,920	4,400	4,130
Lao PDR	22.4	0.1	..	38	..	..	..	..
Viet Nam	1.0	0.1	..	38	..	..	..	..
Cambodia	0.6	0.1	..	5	..	..	..	..
Other economies in transition								
Algeria	0.8	0.2	0.1	25	..	..	..	..
Angola	0.7	0.0	..	3	..	..	..	..
Guinea	1.4	0.1	..	5	..	..	..	..
Myanmar	4.0	0.1	0.0	77	..	..	..	..
Madagascar	2.1	0.1	..	13	..	..	..	..
Afghanistan	0.1	0.0	..	2	..	..	..	..
Somalia	0.2	0.1	..	2	..	..	..	..
Tanzania	0.2	0.0	..	5	..	..	..	..
Ethiopia	0.2	0.0	..	8	..	..	..	..
Mozambique	0.5	0.0	..	4	..	..	..	..
High-income economies								
United States	5.0	0.2	0.8	1,000	23,330	21,100	20,670	19,500
Germany a	3.0	0.0	0.9	160	3,300	2,750	3,100	3,000
France	1.7	0.1	0.9	120	3,410	2,305	1,855	1,730
Netherlands	2.5	0.2	0.9	43	390	260	470	450
Austria	2.0	0.0	0.7	17	330	140	200	210
Italy	1.8	0.0	0.9	120	3,210	2,230	1,510	1,530
Spain	1.2	0.0	0.9	73	2,670	..	810	..
Other middle-income economies								
Portugal	0.8	0.0	0.9	17	260	305	210	190
Korea, Rep.	1.1	0.0	0.1	29	..	..	..	..
Argentina	1.0	0.1	0.1	31	..	..	..	..
Brazil	9.1	0.1	0.1	610	..	..	..	..
Malaysia	3.1	0.0	0.1	26	..	..	..	..
Costa Rica	5.7	0.0	0.1	8	..	..	..	..
Tunisia	0.4	0.0	0.1	3	..	..	..	..
Thailand	2.1	0.1	0.0	67	120	310	30	130
Honduras	2.2	0.0	0.0	5	..	..	..	..
Morocco	0.2	0.0	0.0	3	..	..	..	..
Cote d'Ivoire	9.1	0.0	0.1	47	..	..	..	..
Senegal	0.5	0.0	0.1	3	..	..	..	..
Other low-income economies								
Indonesia	1.5	0.0	0.0	140	..	..	..	..
Sri Lanka	0.2	0.0	..	3	..	..	..	..
Kenya	0.1	0.0	0.0	3	..	..	..	..
India	0.4	0.0	0.0	230	..	..	..	..
Nepal	0.4	0.1	..	7	..	..	..	..
Bangladesh	0.1	0.1	0.0	22	..	..	..	..

Note: Abbreviations in notes column are explained in the General Notes. For sources and methods, see the Technical Notes.
a. Data refer to the Federal Republic of Germany before unification.

Table 16. Forest, land, and water resources

	Population density (per 1,000 ha) 1989	Forests & woodlands Extent (percent use of total land) 1980s	Managed (percent use of total land) 1980s	Nationally protected areas (percent of land) 1988	Cultivated areas (MRE) Cropland (hectares per capita) 1989	of which: Irrigated (percent use of cropland) 1985-87	Average annual use of Fertilizers (kilograms per hectare) 1985-87	Pesticides (tons of active ingredient) 1982-84	Fresh water (annual) Internal renewable (cubic meters) 1990	Withdrawals (cubic meters) 1990
HPEs in Europe										
German Dem. Rep.	1,582	28.4	25.6	0.7	0.3	3	333	14,133	1,020	545
Former USSR	128	41.7	35.5	0.9	0.8	9	114	535,400	15,220	1,330
Czechoslovakia	1,247	36.5	35.4	15.8	0.3	4	324	14,970	1,790	379
Yugoslavia	928	41.1	24.7	4.1	0.3	2	131	31,567	6,290	393
Hungary	1,145	17.7	17.5	5.5	0.5	3	258	27,595	570	502
Bulgaria	814	33.7	32.6	1.2	0.5	30	195	32,400	2,000	1,600
Poland	1,255	28.7	26.6	7.2	0.4	1	232	15,277	1,290	472
Romania	1,006	29.0	25.8	0.7	0.5	30	130	17,237	1,590	1,144
Albania	1,164	46.7	..	2.0	0.2	57	133	5,183	3,080	94
HPEs elsewhere										
Cuba	923	13.1	1.8	7.8	0.3	26	192	9,567	3,340	868
Mongolia	14	6.1	..	0.2	0.6	3	16		11,050	272
Nicaragua	315	37.9	2.1	0.4	0.3	7	49	2,003	45,210	370
Korea, Dem. People's Rep.	1,862	39.9	..	0.5	0.1	48	328		2,920	1,649
China	1,201	12.3	..	0.8	0.1	46	195	159,267	2,470	462
Lao PDR	172	59.0	..	0.0	0.2	13	2		66,320	228
Viet Nam	2,019	31.1	..	2.6	0.1	28	61	883	5,600	81
Cambodia	456	71.7	..	0.0	0.4	3	0	833	10,680	69
Other economies in transition										
Algeria	103	0.7	..	0.2	0.3	5	37	21,400	750	161
Angola	78	43.0	..	0.7	0.4		4		15,770	43
Guinea	273	43.3	..	0.1	0.2	4	0		32,870	115
Myanmar	621	48.6	5.2	0.3	0.3	11	18	15,300	25,960	103
Madagascar	200	22.7	..	1.8	0.3	28	4	1,630	3,340	1,675
Afghanistan	241	1.9	0.2	0.2	0.5	33	9	605	3,020	1,436
Somalia	117	14.4	..	0.0	0.1	12	3		1,520	167
Tanzania	297	47.4	..	13.4	0.2	3	9	5,733	2,780	36
Ethiopia	415	24.7	..	6.2	0.3	1	4	993	2,350	48
Mozambique	194	19.7	..	0.0	0.2	3	2		3,700	53
High-income economies										
United States	270	32.3	11.2	8.6	0.8	10	93	373,333	9,940	2,162
Germany a	2,482	29.5	15.9	11.3	0.1	4	425	29,836	1,300	671
France	1,018	27.4	5.4	8.2	0.3	6	301	98,733	3,030	606
Netherlands	4,334	10.5	6.6	4.4	0.1	59	748	9,670	680	1,004
Austria	906	45.4	18.0	19.3	0.2	0	220	4,548	7,510	417
Italy	1,948	27.4	2.4	4.3	0.2	25	178	98,496	3,130	811
Spain	785	21.6	4.0	5.1	0.5	16	92	71,533	2,800	682
Other middle-income economies										
Portugal	1,116	32.4	..	6.8	0.3	23	96	16,016	3,310	1,062
Korea, Rep.	4,366	49.5	..	5.7	0.1	58	395	12,273	1,450	298
Argentina	117	16.3	..	4.0	1.1	5	4	14,313	21,470	1,059
Brazil	174	60.8	..	2.4	0.5	3	49	46,698	34,520	212
Malaysia	516	63.9	7.6	3.4	0.3	8	154	9,730	26,300	765
Costa Rica	576	35.2	..	12.0	0.2	21	166	3,667	31,510	779
Tunisia	514	1.9	1.0	0.3	0.6	5	21	1,330	460	325
Thailand	1,075	30.7	..	9.1	0.4	20	26	22,289	1,970	599
Honduras	445	35.7	0.5	5.2	0.4	5	19	859	19,850	508
Morocco	549	7.3	0.9	0.7	0.3	15	36	3,350	1,190	501
Cote d'Ivoire	380	30.9	0.0	6.2	0.3	2	9		5,870	68
Senegal	372	57.4	..	11.3	0.7	3	4		3,150	201
Other low-income economies										
Indonesia	981	64.5	0.0	7.8	0.1	34	100	16,344	14,020	96
Sri Lanka	2,625	25.6	..	11.4	0.1	30	106	697	2,510	503
Kenya	425	4.2	0.1	5.4	0.1	2	46	1,307	590	48
India	2,811	21.6	10.7	4.4	0.2	25	52	53,087	2,170	612
Nepal	1,366	15.5	..	7.0	0.1	28	20		8,880	155
Bangladesh	8,404	6.9	5.9	0.7	0.1	23	68	234	11,740	211

Note: Abbreviations in notes column are explained in the General Notes. For sources and methods, see the Technical Notes.
a. Data refer to the Federal Republic of Germany before unification.

Table 17. Energy resources and consumption

	Source of electricity (percentage of total production)		Energy reserves (1987)				Hydroelectric power (megawatts)		Energy consumption per capita	
	Fossil fuels 1987	Nuclear power 1987	Coal (millions of tons) Bituminous	Lignite	Crude oil (millions of tons)	Natural gas (millions of tons)	Potential capacity	Installed capacity	Gigajoules 1987	Percent change 1977-87
HPEs in Europe										
German Dem. Rep.	89	10	..	21,000	1	190	..	1,844	231	14
Former USSR	76	11	104,000	137,000	8,000	41,080	766,200	62,695	194	24
Czechoslovakia	68	26	1,870	3,500	4	13	2,165	2,890	185	-1
Yugoslavia	58	6	70	16,500	30	84	13,600	7,000	71	29
Hungary	63	37	596	3,865	39	125	900	46	112	10
Bulgaria	66	29	30	3,700	2	5	5,282	1,975	173	27
Poland	97	0	28,700	11,700	2	130	2,400	1,976	141	5
Romania	83	0	..	..	175	235	7,600	4,640	136	10
Albania	13	0	..	..	27	7	2,800	680	38	31
HPEs elsewhere										
Cuba	100	0	..	..	..	..	..	49	42	11
Mongolia	100	0	..	..	..	..	..	0	53	43
Nicaragua	47	0	..	..	..	..	4,106	103	9	-36
Korea, Dem. People's Rep.	42	0	300	300	..	..	..	4,600	79	3
China	80	0	610,800	120,100	2,451	895	436,197	28,000	22	47
Lao PDR	5	0	..	..	..	..	28,000	200	1	0
Viet Nam	62	0	150	..	..	..	18,000	320	3	0
Cambodia	..	..	..	..	..	..	10,000	10	1	..
Other economies in transition										
Algeria	98	0	43	..	1,593	3,000	287	285	42	110
Angola	26	0	..	..	156	50	17,220	400	3	0
Guinea	67	0	..	..	..	..	5,000	47	2	0
Myanmar	51	0	2	..	8	268	32,000	258	2	0
Madagascar	46	0	..	..	..	..	7,800	45	1	-50
Afghanistan	39	0	66	..	..	64	25,000	281	4	100
Somalia	100	0	..	..	..	6	50	0	2	0
Tanzania	30	0	200	..	..	116	4,000	259	1	-50
Ethiopia	20	0	..	11	..	24	4,000	230	1	..
Mozambique	88	0	240	..	..	65	15,000	1,523	1	-67
High-income economies										
United States	73	17	112,972	102,269	4,385	5,565	183,287	87,192	280	-12
Germany a	64	32	23,919	35,150	36	179	4,200	6,760	165	2
France	10	71	213	45	30	34	20,395	24,100	109	-10
Netherlands	95	5	497	..	26	1,770	100	2	213	22
Austria	29	0	..	65	11	12	11,360	10,575	118	8
Italy	78	0	..	39	91	300	13,000	17,879	105	18
Spain	48	31	379	391	5	14	12,440	14,453	62	-6
Other middle-income economies										
Portugal	54	0	3	33	..	..	7,184	3,173	39	26
Korea, Rep.	44	49	158	..	..	..	2,000	2,236	52	63
Argentina	46	12	..	130	308	670	37,208	6,591	56	12
Brazil	8	0	..	1,245	361	105	150,322	40,106	22	5
Malaysia	72	0	4	..	434	1,462	11,846	1,090	38	90
Costa Rica	2	0	..	..	..	..	9,472	736	15	-17
Tunisia	98	0	..	..	245	85	65	64	19	27
Thailand	86	0	..	914	13	105	3,428	2,256	14	56
Honduras	19	0	..	..	..	..	4,800	130	6	-25
Morocco	91	0	45	..	..	2	2,453	619	10	25
Cote d'Ivoire	41	0	..	..	16	100	3,000	885	6	-14
Senegal	100	0	..	..	..	..	500	0	4	-20
Other low-income economies										
Indonesia	78	0	1,000	2,000	1,142	2,068	141,800	1,600	8	33
Sri Lanka	20	0	..	..	..	..	1,253	801	4	33
Kenya	14	0	..	..	..	..	841	354	3	-25
India	71	2	60,648	1,900	657	500	41,000	17,003	8	33
Nepal	5	0	..	..	..	..	28,800	161	1	..
Bangladesh	91	0	..	..	0	360	800	197	2	100

Note: Abbreviations in notes column are explained in the General Notes. For sources and methods, see the Technical Notes.
a. Data refer to the Federal Republic of Germany before unification.

Part 3. Country Focus

Chapter 7. National Accounts

Introduction

The Country Tables include national and international alternative estimates that show the diverse methods and range of estimates associated with different data sources. Because economic and statistical systems are continuously changing in HPEs and because statistical methods, coverage, practices, and definitions differ widely across countries and time, the data must be interpreted with care. The statistical systems of some HPEs are weak. And economic reforms and especially system transformations imply a break in data comparability that is not always well documented and may be exacerbated by concurrent changes in statistical systems. Moreover, cross-country and cross-time comparisons involve complex technical problems that have no unequivocal solutions. These limitations must be taken into account in using the data and in interpreting the indicators, particularly when making comparisons across economies.

This introduction to the Country Tables covers basic statistical issues involved in comparing national accounts for market economies and HPEs and looks at various ways to make HPE data comparable to international standards. The traditional national accounting framework of HPEs is the material product system. That of Western economies is the system of national accounts, which the HPEs are adopting. The introduction also explains recomputed estimates by research organizations, alternative methods of converting national data to a common unit of account, and alternative estimates of intra-CMEA trade.

National data support most analyses of HPEs and are the building blocks of all alternative estimates. This data, compiled by central statistical offices in local currency on sources and use of resources, are provided in national and foreign-trade accounts. To use national data in an international context, they should be comparable with standard definitions, methods, and units of accounts. But SNA standards are not easily retrofitted to the MPS, especially for periods when central planning, or features of it, prevailed.

There are practical and conceptual issues in comparing MPS accounts and SNA estimates of market economies. Western recomputations from MPS data have yielded GNP or GDP and their components by reworking disaggregated basic data. But a full set of SNA accounts by sector of origin, income, and expenditure is still not available from official sources for any HPE. And since much of the integrity of SNA comes from analytical cross-checks, it is too early to say that an HPE can be studied on a par with, say, OECD countries.

Since World War II, most countries have introduced comprehensive statistical systems for measuring the level, structure, and development of their economies. To ensure international comparability, the United Nations Statistical Commission issued a recommendation on the System of National Accounts (SNA), which most market economies adopted. The central indicator of the SNA is gross domestic product (GDP), which is a basic measure of a country's overall economic performance.

A different approach to national accounts, based on a system introduced in the USSR in the 1920s, was adopted by centrally planned economies. It, too, was harmonized in 1969, by the Statistical Commission of the CMEA in *Basic Principles of the System of Balances of the National Economy.*

There is one fundamental difference between the SNA and the MPS. In the SNA, all sectors of the economy are considered productive; in the MPS, only those that yield "material" goods. This includes "material services" that bring material consumer goods from producers to consumers—transport and trade; and maintaining the capital stock—maintenance and repairs. In the MPS "nonmaterial services" such as health, education, administration, business, and personal services, are not included in productive activities. Thus, the central indicator-national income—encompasses only the total income generated in the material branches. And although both SNA and MPS recognize depreciation, the two systems make different recommendations on the inclusions in national income.

Two systems: MPS and SNA

To avoid confusion with the "national income" of the SNA, international comparisons call the MPS's "national income" net material product. In both accounting systems the main aggregates are calculated by sector of origin and by type of income and expenditure. Since they all supposedly measure the same feature but from different perspectives, they should yield identical estimates. This is rarely the case, owing to differences in data sources and methods.

Both the SNA and the MPS distinguish between "intermediate" and "final" products and between consumption and accumulation.

The three basic accounting identities of the SNA are production, income, and expenditure (table 7.1). The World Bank also makes a terms-of-trade adjustment to arrive at gross national income (GNY), which represents the volume of goods and services that is, or could be, purchased with the total national product. Some economic activities, like small-scale and informal activities, are included in the SNA but are difficult to measure accurately, even through surveys.

Under both the SNA and the MPS, national income excludes intermediate consumption. Under the SNA, the main focus, perhaps for the sake of convenience, is on GDP, which makes no deduction for the "consumption" of productive capital depreciation. "Net national product" or NNP is arrived at when such a deduction is made. Similarly, both the MPS and the SNA distinguish between incomes currently earned by productive activity and incomes originating from secondary redistribution. The latter, including grants (called "transfers" under the SNA), are omitted from national income, which includes only income earned by productive activity of national factors of production.

The treatment of services, sometimes with the confusing labels of "material" and "nonmaterial," originates from a theoretical proposition of Marx. Marx, in the classical tradition of Adam Smith, considered as productive only activities that yield tangible, material goods.

The value of nonmaterial services, such as advertising purchased by the material sector, are treated differently by the SNA and the MPS. In the SNA, for example, costs of advertising services are deducted from the value added of the food processing sector as intermediate consumption, but count as value added in the business service sector. In the MPS, however, these services would count as value added in food processing, on the logic of the contribution to the production of material goods there.

Market economies generally use gross measures of value added that include depreciation, while HPEs prefer net measures. Both indicators are available in both systems, since depreciation is an important cost component in the MPS and the SNA and is shown separately. Certain countries, such as Yugoslavia and Poland, published, as well as NMP, "gross material product" (GMP), which covers the final results of the material branches without deducting depreciation of fixed assets.

Apart from depreciation, many incidental differences exist between GDP and NMP, including the treatment of business travel expenses, which are intermediate consumption in the SNA but labor compensation, and therefore part of sectoral NMP, in the MPS. Cultural and welfare services provided by enterprises to employees are also intermediate consumption in the SNA but final consumption in the MPS. Some losses on fixed capital, the borderline between current and capital repair, and other relatively small items are treated differently.

Another SNA-MPS distinction is in accounting for national versus domestic aggregates. Gross national product differs from GDP by factor income from abroad, mainly workers' remittances, interest received, and returns on foreign securities, net of similar incomes paid to nonresidents. In the MPS there is no "net factor income modified" NMP. When the MPS was adopted in 1969, it was assumed that factor incomes received from or paid abroad were negligible, so no additional income concept was necessary. Where there were such income flows, it could be stated that the NMP was closer to the "national" than to the "domestic" concept of income.

In some HPEs, there are significant differences between GDP and GNP. For the severely indebted countries, such as Poland, Bulgaria, and Hungary, interest payments on outstanding debt are large, reducing GNP below the level of GDP. For Yugoslavia, labor income from abroad partly offsets interest payments, but most repatriated earning is classified as private transfers—workers' remittances—which do not alter GDP or GNP directly.

Both systems expect to show macroeconomic flows in the production process—gross and net of intermediate consumption and, in the MPS, net of depreciation—in the primary incomes generated in production and in the composition of final uses according to main purposes. Owing to the difference in the global value and the difference in classification of the subcategories of GDP and NMP, there may be large discrepancies between the components of each breakdown.

Table 7.1 SNA Concepts, Coverage, and Measurement

I. SNA Concepts

Production (A)	= *Income* (B)	= *Expenditure* (C)
Value added in:		
Agriculture	Compensation of employees	Private consumption
+ Mining		+ General government consumption
+ Manufacturing	+ operating surplus of enterprises	
+ Construction		
+ Utilities	+ Depreciation	+ Gross capital formation
+ Trade and transport		+ Exports of goods and nonfactor services
+ Other services		
+ Government services		- Imports of goods and nonfactor services
= GDP at factor cost		
+ Indirect taxes less subsidies	+ Indirect taxes less subsidies	
GDP at market prices	GDP at market prices	GDP at market prices
	+ Cross-border factor income receipts less payments	+ Cross-border factor income receipts less payments
	= GNP at market prices	= GNP at market prices
	– Depreciation	
	= Net national product (NNP), or national income	

II. World Bank Extension

Additionally, in constant prices, the World Bank measures:

		+ Terms of trade adjustment
		= Gross national income (GNY)

III. Included in SNA, but difficult to measure in HPEs or MEs or in both:

Production	*Income*	*Expenditure*
* Formal private sector (in HPEs)	* Corresponding factor incomes	* Purchases from private sector
* Small-scale activities	* Wages and salaries from informal activities	* Own consumption (subsistence, etc.)
* Informal private sector (moonlighting activities)		* Major repairs and maintenance
	* Corresponding factor incomes	
	* Gratuities for legal, personal services	
	* Tips as a component of compensation of employees	* Addition of tips to consumer prices

Among the components of income in the MPS, wages and salaries paid in the nonmaterial services sectors are considered as secondary incomes and are excluded from NMP, but in the SNA they are part of GDP. This distinction is often overlooked when reference is made to the "blind eye" central planners turned to irregular or private market activities; so long as they were nonmaterial they would not be considered in NMP in any event.

In the MPS the primary income of enterprises comprises social security contributions paid by enterprises, with taxes paid into the state budget and profits retained by the enterprises. Final use of NMP consists of material goods only, since purchases of nonmaterial services are considered redistributive outlays and not final consumption. In NMP, the total value of final consumption covers all material goods used in nonmaterial services. The NMP value of investment is net of depreciation of all fixed assets. Depreciation of fixed assets used in nonmaterial services is included in final consumption of material goods. The weakest component of the MPS, both on the production and the use side, is the measurement of foreign trade transactions—the national value of exports and imports and value added from foreign trade.

Presentational differences exist in the main categories of the SNA and the MPS. Published MPS indicators are typically more aggregated and less transparent basic data. The MPS gives more emphasis to the flows of material goods than to income and financial flows. While the standard "T-account" form will be used in the 1992 version of the SNA, the matrix form is preferred for presenting the economic flows in MPS, with double-entry recording of the components in interrelated accounts.

The MPS was adapted by the CMEA Statistical Commission. But individual countries deviate from the recommendations (see Country Notes). In most countries, more detailed and additional data are compiled for national purposes than is reported, or proposed, by the common MPS system. There is one exception: on financial flows, only limited data are available and even those are not published in full.

Definitions and methodological descriptions of MPS indicators are very general, so that operationally important rules or clarifications are sometimes absent. That makes it difficult to know how similar or dissimilar "nationally defined" indicators are to one another or to the original MPS (see Country Notes). The importance of these vagaries comes to light in international comparisons of GNP to NMP-type ratios, since in most HPEs these SNA-type accounts are constructed from MPS aggregates.

For a summary presentation of SNA and MPS definitions, see the sources and methods in the Technical Notes. For a comparison of the SNA and the MPS, see UN: *Comparison of the System of National Accounts and the System of Balances of the National Economy*, Parts 1 and 2; Series F No. 20; New York 1977 and 1981. Part 1 describes three conversion tables for deriving NMP from GDP according to the production, income, and use components and vice-versa; Part 2 illustrates these conversions with actual data for 10 countries.

Surveying methods

Gathering data from enterprises in HPEs differs from the method in most market economies. The MPS has universal coverage, because the planners need "full" information for control purposes and because the total number of firms is much smaller, and the average size of firms much larger, than in comparable-size market economies. In the HPEs, CSOs require detailed information from all firms on their input and output. In Czechoslovakia, for example, all firms completed long forms that allowed statisticians to derive firm-level gross output and value added, after accounting for intermediate consumption, as part of sectoral value added in final production.

Whereas in the past national statistical offices in HPEs were able to collect data routinely through comprehensive report forms, during transition, privatization, the breakup of large enterprises and the growth of small private enterprises, coupled with the breakdown of reporting arrangements, will require changes in the ways in which data are gathered and reported. Sample surveys of enterprises will need to be launched and this will tax the capacities of CSOs. Two great challenges will need to be met: the preparation and maintenance of registers of businesses and obtaining the cooperation of enterprises in reporting.

In market economies, output is measured regularly by CSOs as part of a broad survey, with a sample of firms volunteering information on inputs/costs and output values that are used to make estimates of value added. These are extrapolated for other firms with similar characteristics to derive sectoral value added. This is complemented by detailed censuses of enterprise activities, preferably every five years.

The current practice of calculating gross output and value added from firm-level data in HPEs with universal coverage and compulsory reporting has three major drawbacks:

- The time and expense needed to gather and compile data are great.
- Because enterprise reports are also used for routine statistical reports, and as success indicators, the likelihood of fraudulent reporting is substantial.

- Enterprise accounting mainly follows concepts of accounting that sometimes are not appropriate for national accounting (as with inventory revaluation, and the depreciation of fixed assets, see chapter 3).

Chapter 8. Moving from NMP to GDP

GDP and NMP are the most highly aggregated indicators used for measuring the economic performance in market economies and HPEs, respectively. Any comparison that aims to measure the different levels, structures, and growth in a market economy and an HPE needs to first identify and then to try to eliminate the definitional differences between these global indicators. These two synthetic aggregates are generally built up from components, using three different ways to arrive at the total: production, income, and expenditure (see table 1).

But global distinctions between GDP and NMP and other components of the two systems are fundamental. These differences have analytical significance for comparing the structure of economies, both in the shares of productive sectors and in the ratios of consumption and investment.

A recent survey showed that, in most European HPEs, estimates of GDP have been compiled, though not always published, for at least a decade. In most HPEs, however, these statistics are available only in current prices. Constant-price estimates of GDP, using reliable measures of inflation, are available for only a few.

While most, if not all, European HPEs are committed to introducing the SNA, many will retain MPS accounting during the transition. In most cases, the GDP of HPEs is derived from earlier compiled official NMP values by the following adjustments:

Starting: NMP

- Add the total value of depreciation of all fixed assets on material production.

Equals: GMP

- Add the gross value added of nonmaterial services.

- Deduct the nonmaterial inputs used for material production.

- Adjust for certain minor differences between the SNA and the MPS (such as travel costs and welfare costs).

Equals: GDP

When a country is introducing SNA principles, basic adjustments should be made to NMP to arrive at GDP, as shown in box 8.1. For a further discussion of the conceptual and practical problems of moving

---

Box 8.1 Components of net material product and gross domestic product on the basis of value added

A MPS concept applies
   BSNA concept applies

A. Net material product (A1+A2)

   A1. Primary income of the population
   +a. Wages and salaries of employees in the nonmaterial sphere
   −b. Income from personal and subsidiary plots of the population
   +c. Employers contributions to social security
       Material sphere
       Nonmaterial sphere
   −d. Business travel expenses
       Material sphere
       Nonmaterial sphere
   =B1.Compensation of Employees
       $(A1 + a − b + c − d)$
   A2. Primary income of enterprises
   +a. Operating surplus and taxes of non-budgetary units in the nonmaterial sphere
   +b. Income from personal and subsidiary plots of the population
   −c. Employers contribution to social security in the material sphere
   −d. Purchase of nonmaterial services in the material sphere
   −e. Expenditure in connection with the provision of cultural, etc.
       Facilities of industries in the material sphere
   −f. Losses in stocks
   =B2.Operating surplus including net indirect taxes
       $(A2 + a + b − c − d − e − f)$
   B3. Consumption of fixed capital, including undepreciated value of scrapped fixed assets

B. Gross domestic product (B1 + B2 + B3)

---

from NMP to GNP, see the World Bank publication *Dollar GNPs of the USSR and Eastern Europe* (Marer 1985).

While some countries issued adjustment items separately, others published only the final results. table 8.1 compares the magnitude of GDP and NMP and their ratio between countries and 1980 and 1988 in current prices.

Aggregate levels

In the European HPEs, except Yugoslavia and Hungary, the value of GDP has been derived by adding to—or, for a few items, deducting from—NMP. Therefore, any distortions in NMP are maintained in the newly published GDP. For example, the prices used to value outputs and inputs, and the classifications of branches and end-use categories are practically the same in both aggregates.

The ratios of GDP to NMP show significant differences among countries and through time; some seem to suggest underlying statistical problems. In general, the GDP/NMP ratios might be expected to be higher in countries with higher per capita incomes than in lower income countries, owing to higher depreciation on a larger capital stock and a larger service sector. But these ratios do not appear closely related to income rankings (see table 8.1). A breakdown of GDP and NMP by main components allows more detailed accounting of material and nonmaterial services and depreciation (table 8.2).

In scaling up from NMP to GDP, the two main

adjustments (depreciation and the addition of nonmaterial services to NMP) account for most of the difference between the two gross aggregates, assuming a consistent methodology across countries. But to determine the relative importance of these two variables, the concepts need further distillation since nonmaterial services include depreciation.

To calculate the relative share of depreciation and nonmaterial services in the GDP-NMP gap (table 8.3), it is necessary to reapportion depreciation from column 2 to column 1, expressing the results in columns 3 and 4 as a share of GDP less NMP. Thus, most of the difference between GDP and NMP (about two-thirds on average) is accounted for by depreciation, the remainder by nonmaterial services. This technique is approximate and may not appropriately reapportion depreciation for all countries.

Methodological issues in estimating the gap between NMP and GDP may account for the differences between the two aggregates across countries and through time. The same issues probably account as well for the differences between GDP estimates of independent Western experts and the newly published "official" GDPs. The main problems of scaling up NMP to GDP are:

The "adding back" of depreciation to NMP, however distorted its original value may be, results in a truer estimated GDP than NMP. NMP is greatly influenced by the arbitrariness of depreciation, which then is reflected in the ratio of GDP to NMP and in their growth. Moreover, the presumably

Table 8.1 Comparison of NMP and GDP for the European HPEs for 1980 and 1988 in current national market prices
(billions of national currency units)

	NMP		GDP		Ratio of GDP to NMP (percentage)	
	1980	*1988*	*1980*	*1988*	*1980*	*1988*
German Dem. Rep. (at 1985 prices)	193.6	268.4	252.7	345.2	130.5	128.6
USSR	462.2	630.8	619.0	875.4	133.9	138.8
Czechoslovakia	486.3	606.4	586.8	740.0	120.7	122.0
Yugoslavia[a]	1,401.0	132,648.0	1,800.7	155,808.0	128.5	117.5
Hungary	582.9	1,152.7	721.0	1,452.2	123.7	126.0
Bulgaria	20.5	29.4	25.8	38.3	125.9	130.3
Poland	1,992.0	24,995.0	2,511.0	29,629.0	126.1	118.5
Romania	513.6	697.4	616.9	857.0	120.1	122.9

a. "Old Dinar."
Sources: These data are official and are either published in the statistical yearbooks of the countries or submitted officially to the World Bank or the IMF. See the Technical Notes.

Table 8.2 Comparison of the differences between NMP, GMP, and GDP (for 1988 in current prices)
(billions of national currency units)

							Percentage share of	
	NMP (1)	Depr. in material sphere (2)	GMP (3)	Gross value added in the nonmaterial sphere (4)	Purchases of nonmaterial services for material & other adjustments (5)	GDP (6)	Depr. in GMP (7)	Gross value added of nonmaterial services in GDP (8)
German Dem. Rep. (1985 prices)	268.4	31.1	299.5	53.2	7.5	345.2	10.3	15.4 [a]
USSR	630.8	114.3 [b]	745.1	175.2	44.9	875.4	15.3 [b]	20.0
Czechoslovakia	606.4	78.4	684.8	116.9	63.6	740.0	11.4	15.8
Yugoslavia	132,648.0	15,912.0	148,560.0	7,248.0	155,808.0	10.7	..	..
Hungary	1,152.7	107.5	1,260.2	255.7	63.7	1,452.2	8.5	17.6 [c]
Bulgaria	29.4	4.9	34.3	5.0	1.0	38.3	14.3	13.0
Poland	24,995.0	1,597.0	26,592.0	3,797.0	760.0	29,629.0	6.0	12.8
Romania	697.4	..	..	87.6	..	857.0	..	10.1

a. This share is lower than that shown in table 2, where the nonmaterial services are compared with an increased GDP (104 percent).
b. Including capital repair.
c. This share is calculated from market price values which is lower than basic values in the case of non-material services.
Sources: For Poland and Yugoslavia GMP is officially published in national statistical yearbook. For the other countries depreciation is published separately for assets used in the material and nonmaterial sphere. In some cases (Bulgaria, the total depreciation and that of the nonmaterial sphere are shown in a separate report sent to the World Bank.
Note: Columns (1) plus (2) equal (3), Plus (4) minus (5) equals (6).

Table 8.3 Relative shares of depreciation and nonmaterial services in the GDP-NMP gap (1988)
(expressed as a share of GDP less NMP)

	Depreciation in the material sphere (1)	Gross value added in the nonmaterial sphere less purchase of nonmaterial services for material production[a] (2)	Share of depreciation [b] (3)	Nonmaterial services [b] (4)
German Dem. Rep.	40	60	55	45
USSR	47	53	60	40
Czechoslovakia	59	40	70	30
Yugoslavia	69	31	77	23
Hungary	42	58	56	44
Bulgaria	55	45	66	34
Poland	34	66	50	50

a. Includes some other minor adjustments
b. Adjusted by 25 percent to reapportion the depreciation component of column 2 to column 1. Adjustment based on actual data for Bulgaria and Czechoslovakia (World Bank).
Source: Basic data from table 3 (same footnotes apply).

large differences in the treatment of capital repairs have a direct effect on the level of GDP. For example, in the USSR, capital repairs are part of fixed capital formation, and their cost is not deducted from gross output. In most other HPEs, they are included in intermediate consumption, reducing the level of GDP. Depreciation rates appear low in HPEs generally, due to insufficient allowance for technological development. There also are conceptual differences in valuing the capital stock, since the established prices of producer durables are often distorted. In some countries they are valued net of taxes, and in others they are taxed. Imported durables are also valued differently, depending on the country and the origin of the durables.

Interest and insurance payments are treated differently by the countries that recently made GDP estimates. Their treatment probably deviates from SNA methods.

Valuing housing services is another problem. Subsidies in most HPEs are large. Thus, in countries where rented apartments are valued at rents actually paid, such as Bulgaria and Hungary, the value added is much lower than that in countries where they are valued at factor costs. Approaches to inputing rent of owner-occupied dwellings are also different.

There is also a lack of reliable data on military production and expenditure, in both content and valuation. There may be differences, too, in the treatment of some items, such as food and clothing, consumed by military personnel (see box 8.2).

Clearly there is a need for more standardization, familiarization, and application of the SNA in many HPEs. But where institutional arrangements in these countries differ from those in market economies, the present SNA does not give appropriate guidelines for adjusting to these special situations. Work is underway to include additional guidelines

in the 1993 version of the SNA for the treatment of special flows in HPEs. Meanwhile, publication of detailed adjustments made in GDP estimates, together with the methodology applied, would help unravel the differences in the measures and statistical systems of market economies and HPEs.

Structure

The introduction of GDP in HPEs implies important modifications to statistical measures that show the structure of the economy in relation to individual producing sectors, and the ratio between consumption and investment. The producing sectors' shares of GDP differ from those in NMP because of the inclusion of nonmaterial branches, which decreases the share of all material branches. Those shares also differ because of the "adding back" of the value of depreciation to the net value added of branches. Since capital intensity and the use of material services differ substantially, the material sectors' shares in GDP do not change proportionally in scaling up from NMP to GDP.

In the sectoral analysis of NMP and GDP (table 8.4), there is no breakdown of the main adjustment items, depreciation, and nonmaterial services. It is thus, not possible to disaggregate their combined effects by sector. Few countries publish such details. In some sectors, such as agriculture, capital has long been substituted for labor. Putting aside differences in depreciation rates owing to valuation of fixed assets, this substitution means that gross value added grows faster than the HPEs' traditional "net" indicators. Depreciation should, therefore, be included in comparisons of the shares of the producing sectors between HPEs and market economies. Value added in the individual sectors should be scaled up separately, since capital intensity and depreciation rates differ across sectors. In particular, the shares of agriculture and transport in the material sphere and of housing in the nonmaterial sphere will have higher shares measured on a gross rather than on a net value added basis, owing simply to depreciation.

Measuring services in HPEs may not be economically meaningful for systemic as well as statistical reasons. Estimates of nonmaterial services reflect the difficulty of quantifying the actual role and level of services in countries without a meaningful recognition of their contribution to national income and without factor cost pricing. For example, the relative importance of labor and capital, especially in health services, differs across the countries. In the health sector low fixed-fee services were typically underval-

---

Box 8.2 The adjusted factor cost and building block method

To reconstruct GNP and value added at established prices by sectors of origin and by end uses, peculiarities of price setting in HPEs, such as large subsidies and taxes on many consumer goods and services and arbitrary profit markups in branches, are corrected. This is done by adding subsidies, subtracting turnover taxes, and imposing an economywide uniform rate of return on fixed and working capital. The AFC valuations of output reveal a different GNP structure, which provides the base-year weights for computing growth of the various branches and sectors.

In the building-block approach, the indexes of growth in the individual producing sectors as well as end-use aggregates are based on sample data in physical units, adjusted when possible for changes in product mix and quality. Where output measures in physical units are unavailable or not applicable, officially published and supposedly constant-value indexes are used. The base year, and hence the weights, are periodically revised.

Table 8.4 Shares of the main producing sectors in NMP and GDP in 1988, based on current (established) market price values
(percentage)

	Agriculture incl. forestry	Industry incl. construction	Services Material	Services Nonmaterial	Services All services	Total
In net material production						
German Dem. Rep. [a]	10.2	74.9	18.6	..	18.6	103.7
USSR	22.7	55.5	21.8	..	21.8	100.0
Czechoslovakia	6.4	70.3	23.3	..	23.3	100.0
Yugoslavia [b]	11.3	57.6	31.1	..	31.1	100.0
Hungary [c]	14.5	58.4	27.1	..	27.1	100.0
Bulgaria	12.9	67.5	19.6	..	19.6	100.0
Poland	14.0	61.1	24.9	..	24.9	100.0
Romania	14.8	67.1	18.1	..	18.1	100.0
In gross domestic product						
German Dem. Rep. [a]	9.5	62.3	16.0	16.2	32.2	104.0
USSR	18.4	43.6	18.0	20.0	38.0	100.0
Czechoslovakia	6.5	59.4	18.3	15.8	34.1	100.0
Yugoslavia	10.1	44.8	..	..	45.1	100.0
Hungary [c]	11.8	45.4	21.0	21.8	42.8	100.0
Bulgaria	11.5	61.0	14.5	13.0	27.5	100.0
Poland	13.1	52.4	21.7	12.8	34.5	100.0
Romania	13.5	60.7	15.6	10.2	25.8	100.0

a. In the German Democratic Republic the total of sectors is more than NMP or GDP. For an explanation, see country practices in the Technical Notes.
b. In Yugoslavia the shares of GMP (and not those of NMP) are shown; the shares of sectors within GMP and NMP are close to each other.
c. In Hungary the shares in both NMP and GDP are calculated from "primary activity" branches measured in basic values.
Sources: Authors' series. See technical notes.

ued, but informal fees and payments in kind were also unrecorded. Owing to undervalued output measured at prevailing prices and the lack of profit in government institutions, or subsidies in some services, the share of nonmaterial services in GDP at current prices is probably understated (table 8.5).

An accurate measurement of the major end-uses aggregates of the final product, consumption and investment is essential for macroeconomic analysis. Consumption measures the level and growth of the goods and services that satisfy the needs of society. Investment indicates sacrifice for future development of the economy (table 8.6).

Shares of investment in GDP relative to GDP growth rates reveal, at least in a long run, the efficiency of investments. That is why the ratio between consumption and investment is regularly measured and analyzed in both HPEs and market economies. Both concepts are defined more narrowly in

NMP than in GDP.

Consumption in NMP covers only material goods consumed and goods, plus a depreciated part of fixed assets, used for providing nonmaterial services. For the full SNA value of consumption, the net value added of nonmaterial services must be included. This will result in:

* A more comparable concept of total final consumption and, within it, of private final consumption, with the similar aggregates of market economies.

* An internationally more comparable structure of final consumption over time, for example, increasing the relative weights of housing, education, health, and general government administration at the expense of food, clothing, and so on.

For internal and international comparisons, the

Table 8.5 Share of nonmaterial services in employment and GDP

	Employment		GDP	
	1980	1988	1980	1988
German Dem. Rep.	19.4	20.8	15.8	16.2
USSR	22.9	24.9	18.0	20.0
Czechoslovakia	20.1	21.8	15.1	15.8
Hungary	19.0	21.6	15.0	21.8
Poland	16.4	19.3	..	12.8
Bulgaria	16.9	18.3	10.6	13.0
Romania	12.4	..	11.2	10.1

Source: For employment: CMEA *Statistical Yearbook 1988*, pp. 566–75.

Table 8.6 Share of consumption and investment in NMP and GDP in selected countries at current prices

	1988 percentage share in			
	Final consumption		Investment	
	NMP	GDP	NMP	GDP
German Dem. Rep.	78	72	22	29
USSR	75	67	25	32
Czechoslovakia	83	69	17	28
Yugoslavia		56		38
Hungary	80	73	20	25
Bulgaria	75	66	25	34
Poland	68	65	32	33
Romania	77	62	23	28

Source: See the Basic Tables. Shares may not sum to 100 because of the resource balance. Consumption in GDP includes statistical discrepancy.

investment component of NMP should also be scaled up to gross capital formation to conform with the GDP concept by:

- Reallocating depreciation from consumption to investment.
- Adding depreciation in material sectors.
- Moving losses to investment.
- Accounting for inventory changes, strategic reserves, and military procurement.

Since the weight of depreciation is high, the relative adjustment for investment is higher than that in final consumption; therefore, as the ratio of consumption decreases, that of investment increases within GDP as compared with ratios in NMP.

Net accumulation and changes in stocks tend to be overstated in the MPS, owing to historical valuation and inadequate accounting for replacement at current prices. Another difference stems from the treatment of capital repairs in HPEs; in the NMP it is counted as depreciation and in SNA as part of gross domestic fixed capital formation.

The SNA concept of investment, by avoiding the estimation of depreciation, alleviates only part of the distortion in investment rates and growth. Several remaining problems hamper the comparability of gross capital formation. These problems are compounded when estimating the constant price value of net or gross investment, since for most investments the "true" changes of prices are almost impossible to measure. So, generally, investment, gross or net, is the least reliable component of NMP or GDP in HPEs.

Growth

Like changes in GDP and NMP at current prices, there are no big differences in the growth rates of these two aggregates in constant prices, except during periods of exceptionally high growth. This is hardly surprising. The material sphere overwhelmingly determines the development of the entire economy. The price indexes used for the deflation of the two current values, whether accurate or not, are basically the same. And the two additional components of GDP—value added by nonmaterial services and depreciation—usually have different growth trends from that of NMP, possibly offsetting one another's effects.

More specifically, the constant price value of depreciation has increased much faster than NMP in all HPEs because the forced pace of investment has resulted in a fast increase of capital stock and rapid depreciation. Although depreciation may still be understated in HPEs (see chapter 3), the growth of depreciation continued to increase despite falling levels of investment during the 1980s. Between 1980 and 1988 the share of depreciation grew in Bulgaria from 13.8 percent to 15.4 percent, in the German Democratic Republic from 12.8 percent to 13.2 percent, in the USSR from 11.7 percent to 14.3 percent, and in Hungary from 14 percent to 16 percent. This growth may reflect an increase in accounting for the deterioration of fixed assets.

For value added of nonmaterial services in real terms, it is assumed that growth is determined by changes in the number of employees, without accounting for increases in productivity, since the majority of these services are not marketed. Only a relatively small part of services—which can be called "modern" services and are marketed—show rapid growth: computer services, banking, insurance, and advertising. But these remained far behind the development of similar services in market economies.

In periods of fast NMP growth, the growth rate of GDP is nearly the same as NMP, or sometimes lower. In periods of stagnation or slow growth of NMP, the GDP growth rate exceeds that of NMP (table 8.7).

The introduction of GDP in HPEs does not automatically improve the reliability and credibility of economic statistics, compared with NMP data. If the same inadequate price indexes are used for deflating GDP as for deflating NMP, the growth rates for the economy remain distorted. And if countries revise the level and growth rates of previously published NMP, the GDP data are modified almost to the same extent as NMP data.

Alternative computations: building block

Some HPEs produce incomparable data using the NMP concept, and officially published growth rates may be biased by such problems as inadequate adjustment for hidden inflation. Western experts and government agencies have constructed independent estimates of the growth and structure of the GNPs of the USSR and 7 countries of Eastern Europe. Comparable estimates have also been made for some non-European HPEs.

The methodology

These recomputations rely on the pioneering work of Abram Bergson, who devised the adjusted factor cost (AFC) method. This method develops a detailed set of GNP accounts for a base year, using each country's official data and then moving the components over time with indexes that reflect changes in real output.

In many cases, the estimates are based on official data relating to the quantities of goods and services produced or consumed, to wages, taxes, the capital stock, and so on. But instead of using established prices for products as a basis for weighting, other weights for aggregations and other deflators are used for calculating growth rates.

The results

The results of factor cost adjustments differ little from official estimates at the aggregate level of GDP or GNP in national currency in the base year. But sectoral shares, which form the basis for weighting estimates of inflation and growth, may differ significantly. Generally, in the building-block approach, individual volume indexes, based on a sample data of physical outputs—or "constant value" indexes—are combined with these newly adjusted sectoral weights, often producing a significantly different aggregate growth rate.

The production volume indexes of many sectors and branches, especially those for industry, are recomputed, based on sample data on physical outputs or some proxy. This requires data on physical quantities that CSOs publish. Where such data are not available, or the products are so diverse that data in physical units would not represent the production volume, as with computers, official production series, denominated in "comparable" prices, or an index number based on constant prices, are used.

In some sectors, notably service employment indexes, typically adjusted for hours worked, are

Table 8.7   Comparison of Volume Indexes for NMP and GDP for 1970–89
(percentage)

	NMP(official)			GDP (official or estimated)		
	1980/70	*1989/80*	*1989/70*	*1980/70*	*1989/80*	*1989/70*
German Dem. Rep.	159	141	225	*159*	140	222
USSR	163	130	212	170	138	235
Czechoslovakia	158	118	187	*158*	*119*	*188*
Hungary	156	110	171	159	115	183
Poland	169	108	183	*167*	112	186
Bulgaria	196	134	262	*193*	*131*	*254*
Romania	245	108	265	*239*	113	270
Yugoslavia	173	104[a]	179[a]	179	105[a]	188[a]

a. 1988 is compared with 1980 and 1970.
Source: The indexes underlined were estimated by the authors, the others represent officially published data.

used as production volume indexes. In the defense sector, military expenditure is used as a proxy for value added (see box 8.3).

Box 8.3 International comparisons of military expenditures

International comparisons of military expenditures—whether the goal is assessment of relative effort or of military strength—often lack credibility and produce distorted results whether the goal is assessment of relative effort or of military strength. Activities covered by military expenditures vary widely among countries; many countries do not provide full accounting of military expenditures, and the index number problem is inherent in all international economic comparisons. Moreover, exchange rate conversions of official statistics from one monetary system to another create distortions, especially for countries with different levels of development or whose currencies are not convertible.

In market economies, the defense sector's portion of GNP or GDP is calculated on the basis of government purchases of goods and services for the military. In addition, defense budget breakdowns are published, permitting cross-checking between planned and actual military expenditures. HPEs typically provided little such information, if any. For example, until 1989 the USSR reported only a single annual figure for military expenditures, that was clearly an understatement of actual amounts. Recently, the USSR increased the official military expenditure figure, in nominal terms, by a factor of about 5, and provided a budget breakdown. Even so, the official figure may still be significantly understated.

Even with comparable coverage, full accounting of military expenditures and budgets, and adjustments for the index number problem and exchange rate conversions, the valuation of military goods and services would remain problematic in relation to assessing the "burden" of defense. If prices do not cover opportunity costs, military expenditure data will be typically understated. Valuation problems also occur where inflation is "hidden" through subsidies to defense manufacturers.

Western governments have used a building block approach to estimate military expenditures in the USSR. The costs of annual production of weapons, operations and maintenance, military pay, military construction, and research and development were estimated on the basis of information collected through intelligence services. This is a time-consuming and expensive process, which has not been applied to other HPEs. Comparisons of military expenditures may become more credible in the future because the Eastern European HPEs have recently been submitting more complete military expenditure data to the United Nations.

The building-block approach will have to rely extensively on official constant price indexes, which tend to be upward-biased, especially for countries where official data on physical quantity series are scant—one reason why no *a priori* judgment can be made about these alternative indexes. They need to be evaluated for each country and period. That requires detailed and transparent documentation on how they were constructed, which may not be available for all countries or periods.

The differences between official and alternatively estimated growth rates are significant. For 1950–88, the GNP volume indexes estimated by Western experts show only a half to a third as rapid a rate of growth as the official volume indexes for NMP. Comparing two kinds of volume indexes for the 1970s and 1980s shows significant differences, but the deviation is smaller than in the two previous decades (table 8.8). Comparisons of end-point years are shown only to give an order of magnitude. Least-squares growth rates are calculated for GDP and components in Global Tables 3–7 (chapter 6) for selected time periods during 1970–90; they can also be calculated for GDP and NMP from time series shown in the Country Tables. Volume indexes for these series, as well as SNA-based GDP, are shown in the Comparator Tables.

Differences in the rate of growth between the official and recomputed indexes can result from differences in coverage (the coverage gap), in weights (the weighting gap), and in the component

Table 8.8 Comparison of official NMP and recomputed GNP volume indexes for European HPEs

	1988 in percentage of 1970	
	NMP official	*GNP recomputed*
German Dem. Rep.	221	153
USSR	207	158
Czechoslovakia	184	146
Yugoslavia	179	180
Hungary	173	140
Bulgaria	276 [a]	146
Poland	183	151
Romania	351 [a]	168

a. Published in 1989. According to the (1990) revised and published data, the corresponding indexes for NMP are for Bulgaria 263, and for Romania 304.
Sources: Officially published indexes for NMP; CIA for GNP of USSR; LWI for other countries. See Technical Notes.

indexes (the index gap). The index gap could result from differences in method, the base and comparator year selected, and the index number formulas employed (whether Paasche, or Laspeyres, or a Fisher ideal index).

The weighting gap

The weights of individual components of NMP or GDP are modified considerably depending on whether value added is aggregated at "established" prices, "adjusted factor cost," or, in a few cases, "factor cost."

To estimate, or adjust, the value of production on a factor cost basis, the global value of GDP (GNP) is divided into returns to labor and to nonlabor—fixed and working capital and agricultural land—factors of production. The returns to labor are roughly equal to the sum of wages, salaries, payments in kind, farm income in kind, and social security contributions paid by employees and employers. It is more difficult to estimate returns to capital. Two basic methods are often used. In calculating factor cost for the USSR (table 8.9), the difference between global GNP and total returns to labor is distributed proportionately according to the stock of fixed and working capital used in each production sector. No separate return is attributed to agricultural land. In calculating factor costs for other European HPEs (table 8.10), the nonlabor portion of GNP is distributed according to the total stock of capital, including agricultural land. For this reason, the shares of agriculture in GNP at factor cost for the USSR in the CIA and U.S. Census Bureau

estimates are almost identical to that figured at established prices (table 8.9). In other HPEs the share of agriculture increases significantly (table 8.10).

The index gap

The results of the building-block approach are shown in the Comparator Tables as a separate series. The data shows the volume indexes of GDP and components calculated by U.S. sources, and the official indexes based primarily on established prices. The differences are substantial.

Growth rates calculated for GNP recomputed through the building-block method have been questioned by some experts. They contend that output indexes measured in physical units, even, say, in West Germany or in the U.S.A., understate real growth rates by accounting insufficiently for improvements in the quality of the goods produced or in changes in product assortment. Some studies suggest that using this building-block approach to national accounts significantly lowers growth rate estimates. A counter argument is that technical progress embodying quality improvements has been slower in HPEs than in market economies, so that the resulting bias for HPEs is less than that of market economies which tend to understate inflation (see chapter 3). Furthermore, for many of the component indices the official "constant price" indices had to be relied on as a default option even in the building-block approach, which causes an overstatement of real growth.

Another deficiency of the building-block ap-

Table 8.9 Gross national product in the USSR by sector of origin in two price systems
(percentage)

	1982 CIA estimates		1985 U.S. Census Bureau estimates	
	Established prices	Factor cost prices	Established prices	Factor cost prices
Industry	50.4	32.0	33.4	30.1
Construction	6.7	7.3	8.0	7.7
Agriculture	15.4	21.1	20.2	18.4
Transportation	8.4	8.7	9.9	8.8
Communication	0.8	0.9	0.9	0.8
Trade	4.7	7.3	6.7	5.8
Services	11.3	20.5	18.5	25.8
Other branches, including military services	0.7	2.2	0.6	2.4
Military personnel	1.6	2.0	..	..
Total	100.0[a]	100.0	100.0	100.0 [a]

a. Because of rounding, components may not add to 100.
Sources: Belkindas, Diamond, and Tretyakova 1985 "USSR: Gross National Product Accounts," U.S. Bureau of the Census, Washington, D.C.

Table 8.10 Net material product at established prices and at adjusted factor cost
(percentage of total)

	Industry	Agriculture	Other	Total
German Dem. Rep., 1975				
At established prices	59.1	10.3	30.6	100.0
At adjusted factor cost	52.7	16.8	30.5	100.0
Czechoslovakia, 1977				
At established prices	67.1	10.8	22.2	100.0
At adjusted factor cost	47.6	19.5	32.9	100.0
Yugoslavia, 1976				
At established prices	35.1	16.8	48.2	100.0
At adjusted factor cost	37.7	22.7	39.6	100.0
Hungary, 1976				
At established prices	47.7	16.0	36.3	100.0
At adjusted factor cost	40.0	28.8	31.2	100.0
Bulgaria, 1975				
At established prices	51.0	21.4	27.5	100.0
At adjusted factor cost	41.2	32.0	26.8	100.0
Poland, 1977				
At established prices	52.5	14.7	32.8	100.0
At adjusted factor cost	40.2	30.4	29.4	100.0
Romania, 1977				
At established prices	57.0	15.8	27.2	100.0
At adjusted factor cost	43.5	31.4	25.1	100.0

Note: Percentages at established prices are calculated from values for net material product given directly in official yearbooks. Percentages at adjusted factor cost are calculated from project weights as follows: LWI occasional paper #100 shows adjusted factor cost weights for GNP. NMP weights are estimated by excluding nonmaterial service sectors and then recomputing the weights in the adjusted total.

proach is its lack of accounting for changes in production technologies in recent years, especially after the energy crises of 1973–75 and 1979–81, which altered the input-output relationships. This change is not reflected in the building-block type index, which tends to be a gross output measure. If individual volume indexes of physical output quantities are weighted with actual value added or adjusted factor costs of a single year, it is not clear

that the resulting global index will correctly express the change in volume of value added. In some industries, where the trend between gross output and intermediate consumption diverges considerably, as in agriculture, the double-deflation method—a deflation of the gross value of output and inputs—provides theoretically more plausible results than the building-block approach with fixed weights.

Chapter 9. Converting National Data to Dollars

Estimating the size of a country's economy and income for comparative purposes requires a common definition, such as per capita GNP or GDP, expressed in a common currency or unit of account. Because no single method is perfect, the methods are often subject to controversy, especially when the comparisons involve countries at different levels of per capita income. (See chapter 5 for a general discussion and Global Table 1 for the main results.) Alternative estimates for the HPEs are more questionable than those for other countries, partly because analysts face serious difficulties in interpreting statistics and obtaining evaluations of product quality and availability and partly because their "convertors" (e.g., exchange rates) have more than the usual degree of uncertainty.

National income

There are two problems in computing dollar estimates of GNP or GDP for the HPEs: obtaining estimates in national currency units (NCUs), and converting these to dollars.

Many analysts have confidence in current-value estimates of GNP in NCUs because, for most HPEs, the error margins are within 10–20 percent, even when the problems in scaling up NMP to GNP are taken into account. Problems are much greater, however, in converting GNP to dollars. Estimations for dollar valuations of HPE GNP differ by 300–500 percent, a range much wider than the variability typically found in the developed market economies. This was one of the main findings of a project sponsored by the World Bank (Marer 1985).

Leaving aside the physical indicators method (see Part 2, Global Focus), there are two main approaches to estimating the *level* of a country's GNP or GDP in dollars:

- An exchange-rate based conversion.
- A purchasing-power-parity (PPP) type conversion.

Exchange-rate-based conversion

Exchange rates are almost always available, for almost all countries of the world, but comparability does not rest on whether the prevailing exchange rate of a country is at or close to its equilibrium level, however defined. It rests on whether the exchange rate used performs the basic economic role that such converters are supposed to perform in a market economy. When domestic prices are set with little heed to market forces, as in the HPEs, no conversion factor can be considered an equilibrium rate. What is needed, in such cases, is a price for foreign currency that is consistent with the prices for goods and services whose national currency values are to be converted—which is as much a matter of tracing bookkeeping procedures as economics (see box 9.1).

One universal problem with exchange rate conversions, in times of floating exchange rates, is that real exchange rates—nominal exchange rates adjusted for inflation differentials—may change by as much as 50–100 percent or more within relatively short periods. The reasons have little to do with the country's volume of production, consumption or, by extension, the size of its economy. In market economies, exchange rates also reflect financial capital flows not measured in GDP or NMP. Another problem relates to the size of the tradable versus nontradable sector and the relative purchasing power of each.

Many HPEs have the added problem of multiple exchange rates, an indication of large degree of government intervention in the operation of market forces and the absence of full currency convertibility. Where available, multiple exchange rates governing diverse transactions in HPEs are shown in the Country Tables.

Finding an appropriate converter for countries that have multiple exchange rate regimes poses another set of difficulties. For example, consider the range of Poland's average zloty per dollar exchange

---

Box 9.1 Problems of using exchange rates as converters

The use of exchange rates as converters presents a number of difficulties. To compare the total (or per capita) dollar GNP or GDP of an HPE with those of market economies, it is best to use a converter that is similar to those used for comparator market economies. In most cases, the unified exchange rate that effectively governs the market economies' international transactions serves as a convertor.

For countries that do not have unified exchange rates, but may have multiple (including black market) rates, or pervasive governmental controls over economic activity, weighted average effective exchange rates serve as useful converters. Using a country's official exchange rate as the sole conversion factor to express its international transactions in dollars or convert its GNP or GDP from local currency to dollars, is not applicable to countries that:

- Have dual or multiple exchange rates.
- Have active parallel or black markets.
- Maintain extensive price controls and trade-related restrictions.

Countries that show large deviations between official exchange rates and the actual transaction rates include HPEs and most economies in transition, as well as many other countries (see the IMF's *Annual Report on Exchange Arrangements and Exchange Restrictions*).

Multiple exchange rates are manifested directly when certain international transactions are conducted at different exchange rates and indirectly when, say, taxes, subsidies, and surcharges are applied to international transactions. A preferential rate for essential imports, and in some cases, for debt service payments, is a common feature of multiple currency regimes. Separate exchange rates based on distinctions between capital- and current-account transactions and for important current invisible payments is another.

If the official exchange rate is overvalued, an opportunity arises for the existence of a parallel or black market for foreign currency. A formal parallel market exists where authorities maintain an official multiple exchange rate system; an informal parallel market exists when international exchange transactions occur beyond the bounds of legal channels.

Although many countries have illegal or black markets that operate as important and integral parts of their trade and exchange systems, it is rarely possible to assign or agree on a weight for the parallel markets because their very nature makes them difficult to assess. Therefore, computing and using weighted average effective exchange rate converter is particularly difficult.

---

rates and PPPs in 1988. Poland introduced a unified zloty-dollar rate in January 1990.

Exchange rates
    Commercial exchange rate   431
    Parallel (black) market rate   900
    Auction (sanctioned inter-enterprise rate)   1,950
PPPs
    PPP (CIA estimate)   109
    PPP (PlanEcon estimate)   146
Source: PlanEcon Report, VI, 3–4, January 24, 1990.

Because the range of zlotys per dollar (109–1,950) is so wide, it is difficult to select the rate at which zloty GNP data should be converted to dollars. In the Guide, the conversion factor shown in the comparator pages implicitly reflects a combination of the multiple rates shown in the basic table.

Exchange rates during transition

Under central planning, there is no sanctioned market for foreign currency and international transac-

tions are tightly controlled; exchange rates are not determined by the market. The authorities establish a set of exchange rates for the inconvertible local currency that does not directly link domestic and foreign prices. A system of price equalization aims to insulate the domestic economy from the rest of the world, even if the HPE has a significant volume of exports and imports.

To determine whether exchange rates can be employed to convert statistics in local currency, such as those for trade flows, debt, wage rates, incomes, and GNP into values expressed in foreign currencies and compare the resulting values with similar data from other countries, a distinction must be made between the rates governing transactions of specific goods and services and the average, or unified rate. Owing to the large differences between HPEs and market economies in the structure of relative prices, lack of wage differentials, and the systematic undervaluation of basic goods in HPEs, *average* exchange rates, or PPPs, that could be meaningful for converting national income aggregates to dollars may be inappropriate for converting partial or microeconomic data.

Until 1990 the currencies of HPEs were not convertible because these countries maintained de facto multiple exchange-rate systems. Exchange-rate-based estimates of dollar per capita GNPs were usually based on commercial exchange rates or their equivalents (see chapter 11).

Because commercial rates approximate the average, rather than the marginal, cost of earning a unit of foreign currency through exports, the rates may be *overvalued* relative to the hypothetical values that would prevail if rates were determined by market forces. Black-market rates substantially lower than commercial exchange rates suggest that most HPE currencies are overvalued. Evidence for this is implied by large export subsidies in HPEs. But, considering that the "market" for foreign currency is likely to incorporate large spillover effects from controlled markets for goods or services, the meaning of a "market-determined" exchange rate is at best ambiguous.

An exception is when prices or values, initially expressed in a foreign currency and then transformed into local currency via a prevailing exchange rate, are converted back into foreign-currency prices or values at the same exchange rate. This implies that only international transactions, such as trade flows or foreign borrowing and lending, are convertible. Trade originally denominated in transferable rubles (TRs), however, cannot be easily transformed into dollars. These calculations are expressed "meaningfully" only in TRs.

As HPEs open to unfettered international trade, exchange rates will start to play the role they do in market economies. At some point, large deviations between multiple exchange rates will decrease. Ultimately, multiple exchange rate systems may be replaced by unified exchange rates and the introduction of a partially or fully convertible currency.

Purchasing power parities

Cross-country comparisons of output of goods and services based on purchasing power parity ratios fall into two categories: bilateral and multilateral.

Bilateral comparisons

In the bilateral approach, the GNPs of two countries are compared first in terms of one country's currency and prices and then in the other country's currency and prices. Average ratios of prices in the two countries for a great many end-use categories of GNP are derived and then used to convert the expenditures of one country in a given category, e.g., household consumption of meat and dairy products, into the prices of the other country, and vice versa. In each case, these ratios, known as PPPs, will be a weighted average of individual price ratios, with the weights reflecting the relative importance of the item in the expenditures of the country whose expenditures are being revalued in the prices of the other country. Where these conversions are carried out for all categories of expediture, country *A*'s GNP is revalued in terms of its own quantity weights and country *B*'s prices, and country *B*'s GNP is revalued at its own quantity weights and in country *A*'s prices. The GNPs of the two countries can then be compared in either country's prices (see box 9.2).

The CIA's estimate of the relative size of the U.S. and Soviet economies is an example of a PPP-based bilateral comparison involving an HPE. (The USSR's Central Statistical Administration published its own estimates of the relative size of the two economies for many years, but its estimates were based only on a comparison in U.S. prices.) When measured in dollars, at U.S. prices, the USSR had an economy roughly 66 percent as large as that of the United States in 1989 according to the CIA estimates (table 9.1). In the comparison in rubles, at Soviet prices, the USSR's GNP is 39 percent of U.S. GNP. The geometric mean of these two comparisons places Soviet GNP at 51 percent of the U.S. level. In per capita terms, the USSR/U.S. ratio is 44 percent—much higher than an exchange-rate-based conversion would yield.

Two size comparisons—one in rubles, one in dollars—yield different answers because of differences in the relative price and quantity structures in the two countries: the "index number problem". Goods produced in relatively large quantities in either country tend to sell at relatively low prices in that country. Soviet GNP is, therefore, a larger share of U.S. GNP when the comparisons are made in dollars (66 percent) than in rubles (39 percent), because dollar prices place a greater weight on investment and defense goods, which account for larger shares of output in the Soviet Union than in the United States. Valuations can be expressed either in rubles or dollars. When a single comparison of U.S. and Soviet GNP is sought, the geometric mean of the ruble and dollar comparisons is a reasonable compromise that falls between the two estimates, but is not necessarily better than either.

Considerable uncertainty surrounds comparisons of this kind, however. When binary or multilateral PPP-based comparisons involve countries at

---

Box 9.2   Problems of estimating PPPs in HPEs

PPP-based estimates of HPE dollar per capita GNPs tend to be upward biased because the usual methods of computation do not sufficiently account for:

- Differences in the quality of goods and services whose prices are being compared, even when the countries are at roughly similar income levels. In HPEs, standard durable consumer goods and machinery have lower use values. As they require more energy and repairs—which are difficult to secure—maintenance costs are unusually high. The computation of PPP requires establishing equivalent production or consumption. In successive phases, the Austria-based part of the ICP has tried to use quality differences to take this into account, and considerable documentation is expected to emerge on the subject when 1990 results became available.

- Shortages of many goods and services that reduce the true value of those available, owing to costs incurred waiting in lines, and untimely purchases.

- Actual prices on the various parallel gray and black markets are higher than official prices used in computing PPPs. Whether this causes a bias depends on whether the quantities produced in the parallel market are recorded in official statistics in the first place.

- Distortions in wages and salaries, perceived through official exchange rates, may be equal or greater than those perceived in purchasers' prices.

If each of these systemic factors were incorporated into ICP assessments, PPPs in HPEs would be lower, and increase the NCU/$ ratios. Therefore, using PPPs as converters will bias resulting dollar figures upward (see Penn World Tables and CIA in the Comparator Tables). Estimating the extent of the bias or devising methods to correct for it is fraught with difficulty.

PPP represents the weighted average ratio of representative prices for identical goods and services in two or more countries in a given period. Suggestions for which appropriate price indexes should be used in computing PPP time series have ranged from measuring unit labor costs for nontraded goods, the broadest domestic index available, to an index comprised only of traded goods, to individual prices of traded commodities.

There are also several practical problems in computing accurate price indexes. Even apparently identical goods and services can be produced differently in the same country. Differences in circumstances of sale—such as location, credit terms, packaging, convenience of access, service, delivery time after purchase, brand name, performance guarantees, availability and cost of spare parts and repair services, and the availability and cost of substitutes—account for some price discrepancies between apparently similar goods and services. Such differences are magnified when comparisons are made across countries. Thus, it is not possible to obtain accurate and fully representative prices of identical baskets of goods and services that accurately represent production or consumption in the compared countries, and it is impossible to obtain absolutely accurate PPPs.

---

very different levels of development, the comparisons are likely to be biased in favor of the less developed country. These countries generally produce a narrower range of goods and services of lower quality than more developed countries. PPP comparisons do not account for the welfare implications of limited assortment, the PPP price ratios do not reflect fully differences in product quality, and the samples of goods and services from which the price ratios are drawn are almost always more representative of the output of the developed country. All of these considerations tend to lead to an overstatement of the size of a lesser developed country's GNP relative to that of a more developed country. In addition, HPEs have frequently set prices at less than market-clearing levels. The resulting shortages have reduced consumer utility by increasing time spent searching for goods and services or in queuing for them, but these costs are not captured in international comparisons of GNP

(National Research Council, 1991) (GAD, 1991).

Some alternative estimates of the relative size of Soviet and U.S. GNPs have attempted to correct for what is believed to be an insufficient allowance for quality differences in the CIA price ratios. For example, an experimental comparison by the USSR's State Committee for Statistics puts Soviet GNP at 43 percent of the U.S. level in 1985 compared with the CIA's estimate at 54 percent. Abram Bergson, reviewing the attempts to measure the size of Soviet GNP, criticized many of the alternative estimates but concluded that the CIA's ratio for 1985 should be lowered only modestly, not by a hundred or more percent, as some critics allege (Bergson, 1991). With the disintegration of the Soviet Union, the question of the size of its economy is likely to remain controversial because a new comparison of sufficient scope cannot be carried out. Instead, attention will turn to the levels of development of the new states that have emerged from what was the USSR.

Multilateral comparisons: the ICP

Because exchange rates often do not reflect the purchasing power of currencies, there are sizable errors in comparisons based on them. The United Nations International Comparison Program, begun by Gilbert and Kravis in post-war Europe and long associated with Kravis, Summers, and Heston at the University of Pennsylvania, tries to fill this gap by providing detailed, intercountry comparisons of GDP and purchasing power of currencies.

The ICP approach developed a system of converting different countries' national account aggregates to a common numeraire currency on the basis of the PPPs of the currencies in the different domestic markets. It sought to establish a method that could be applied to all countries, regardless of economic system or geographic location. To date, the ICP has completed five phases, each including the participation of several HPEs; the sixth phase (1990) includes reports from the Soviet Union and Czechoslovakia and partial reports from China as well as from previous HPE participants (Hungary, Poland, Yugoslavia, and sometimes Romania). These are actually bilateral exercises each performs with Austria. Preliminary results from the 1990 exercise may be available by late 1992.

In ICP comparisons, the GDP of each participating country is disaggregated into approximately 150 expenditure categories, termed "basic headings". Quantities are derived implicitly from expenditures and observed prices in each country. These quantities are then expressed in average international prices (AIPs), which are estimated as a globally weighted averages of prices for individual items under the basic heading. The derived measure (Quantity x AIP) represents an internationally comparable real economic value or "volume," because quantities of all countries are valued at a single set of prices. The ICP thus provides an expenditure view of GDP. Different results might be obtained applying the same basic method using an industrial origin approach. Given sufficient detail, essentially an input-output table with price details, a bridge could be built between the two approaches.

The relationship between exchange rates and PPPs that has developed during these phases appears to be primarily a function of per capita GDP (GNP) levels of countries. This relationship, clearly apparent in earlier phases (1970, 1975), is not as visible in later phases (1980, 1985), especially toward the lower end of the income scale.

The vertical axis in the charts in box 9.3 is the price level index (the ratio of the PPP to the exchange rate). A price level index lower than one signifies that the PPP is lower than the exchange rate, so that the real value of the country's currency is higher in terms of its PPP than in terms of its exchange rate and a PPP-based conversion of GNP will yield a higher dollar figure than if the exchange rate were used. Lower income countries have, on average, lower price level indexes. Thus, PPP-based conversions will yield both absolutely and relatively higher dollar GNPs for low-income countries than in conversions based on exchange rates. But the price level index can change and vary significantly between ICP phases.

Foreign trade

Monitoring trade flows for international comparisons and for direction of trade statistics and settlements is particularly challenging. Distinct problems arise in East-West and intra-CMEA trade. While only the sum of the two is comparable in coverage to the trade data of market economies, the range of estimates for this total is wide because of complexities in each subset. Hence, a mosaic of sources and methods must be constructed. To the extent that trade and balance-of-payments items were initially denominated in dollars or other convertible currencies, they can be reconverted into their original currencies at the accounting rate initially used to convert them into local currency, provided one can identify this accounting rate. That, however, is difficult, given the role of foreign trade organizations, price equalization funds, etc. With regard to types of accounting rates, HPEs have not followed uniform procedures. And for any given country, there will have been changes over time in the types of accounting rates used.

Further complicating matters, the coverage of convertible-currency trade or payments is not the same as trade and payments with Western countries, as some transactions between CMEA countries were settled in convertible currencies. Inferences about accounting rates used vary, depending on which series is taken as a starting point.

Total trade

In the Basic Tables, trade figures are expressed in national currencies, disaggregated by major directions of trade. Socialist trade with market economies was originally conducted at world market prices and settled in convertible currencies. Most intrasocialist trade—among HPEs but including a number of OETS—was conducted at negotiated, or lagged world

Box 9.3   Ratio of PPP to exchange rate related to per capita GDP

ICP Phase III, 1975

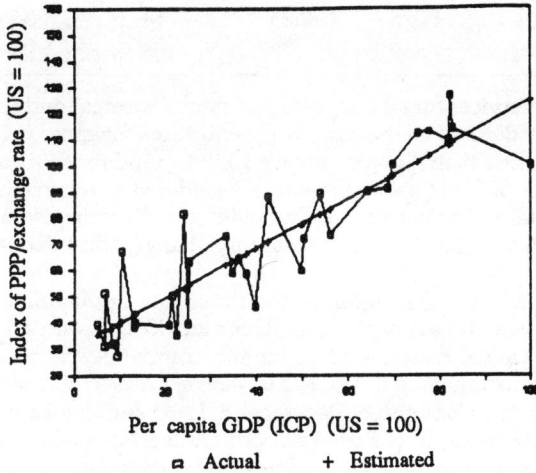

Per capita GDP (ICP) (US = 100)

□ Actual   + Estimated

ICP Phase IV, 1980

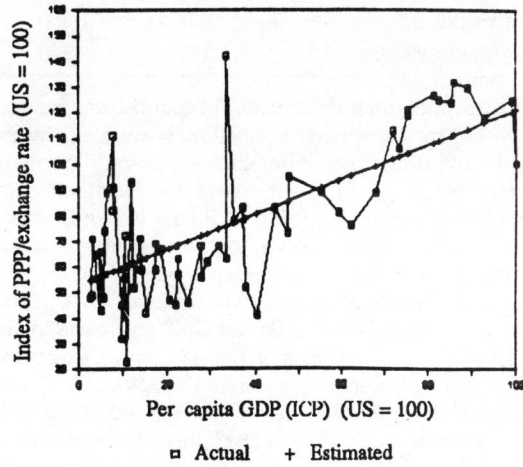

Per capita GDP (ICP) (US = 100)

□ Actual   + Estimated

ICP Phase V, 1985

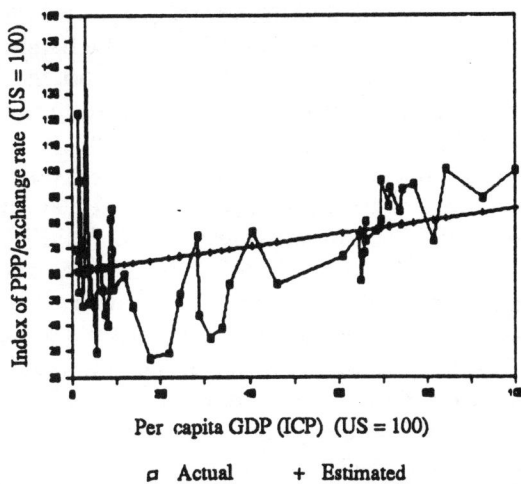

Per capita GDP (ICP) (US = 100)

□ Actual   + Estimated

Regression Lines: 1975, 1980 & 1985

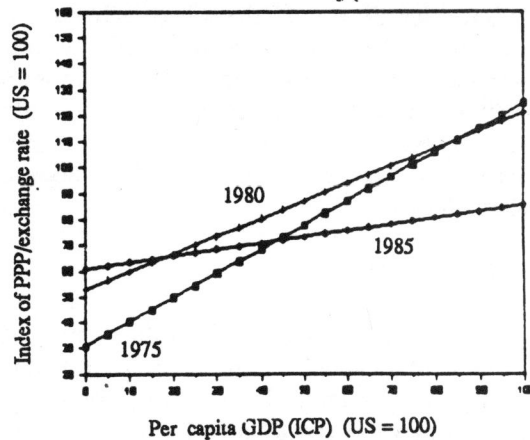

Per capita GDP (ICP) (US = 100)

Table 9.1 USSR and U.S. GNPs in 1989: estimates of relative size

	Billion 1982 rubles			Billion 1982 U.S. dollars			Geometric mean of the comparisons in dollars and rubles
	USSR	U.S.	USSR as a percentage of U.S.	USSR	U.S.	USSR as a percentage of U.S.	
GNP, of which:	796	2,042	39	2,753	4,144	66	51
Consumption [a]	437	1,656	26	1,375	2,837	48	36
New fixed investment [a]	199	240	83	859	797	108	95

a. Consumption includes personal expenditures for goods and services for all purposes and noninvestment outlays by government for health and education. New fixed investment is defined as the sum of expenditures for gross private domestic investment net of inventories; for public construction other than that for military facilities; and for equipment purchased by the government except that for defense. (Since part of Soviet capital repair is considered new investment in the Western sense, a portion of Soviet expenditures on capital repair is included in Soviet new fixed investment.) Other uses of GNP, not shown, include defense, space, research and development, inventory change, administration, net exports, and a statistical discrepancy.

Source: CIA, *Handbook of Economic Statistics, 1990*, Table 8. (A detailed discussion of the procedure of obtaining the geometric mean of U.S. and Soviet GNP comparisons in rubles and dollars is given in "U.S. and USSR: Comparisons of GNP," in *Soviet Economy in a Time of Change*. Congress of the United States, Joint Economic Committee, October 10, 1979, pp. 369–401. Reconstruction of the Soviet GNP accounts is documented in *USSR: Measures of Economic Growth and Development, 1950–80*. Congress of the United States, Joint Economic Committee, December 8, 1982) and in *Measures of Soviet Gross National Product in 1982 prices*. Congress of the United States, Joint Economic Committee, November 1990). Special problem of GNP computations are discussed in CIA, *Measuring Soviet GNP: Problems and Solutions* (A Conference Report) (September 1990).

prices and settled via transferable rubles. Most UN documents publish trade data from national sources, with the ECE filling gaps from mirror statistics of trade partner countries, and convert these series into dollars via the nationally reported local currency/dollar exchange rates used to convert the initial convertible transactions. However, the ECE also publishes an alternative dollar series (as shown in the Comparator Tables) using a uniform ruble/dollar cross rate, which differs somewhat from the uniform cross rate used by the authors. This difference is described in chapter 11.

The Basic Tables show series on trade in goods and services that appear in each CMEA member's convertible-currency balance of payments. But only a country-specific reconciliation of these series can fully explain the discrepancies among them (see the Technical Notes).

Intra-CMEA trade

The internationally comparable dollar-value of trade, payments, and debt denominated in transferable rubles cannot be reliably determined owing to the uncertainty about the dollar value of the TR (see the Primer). For example, Hungary's trade with the USSR in 1988 (table 9.2) shows that estimated dollar values may differ by as much as 300 percent, depending on the approach selected.

After selecting representative products of Hungary's exports to and imports from the USSR in 1988, objective data for homogeneous primary products and expert opinions of those directly engaged in trade with the Soviet Union and with the West for manufactures served as the basis for estimating the dollar prices on goods traded with the USSR, based on the 1990 TR-dollar conversion rate. These estimates took into account prices and trading conditions in the Soviet, Hungarian, and World markets, and yielded the values shown in column 2, the 1.17 average implicit TR-dollar exchange rate in Hungary's exports to the USSR, and the 0.90 average implicit TR-dollar rate in its imports from the USSR.

Another estimate of dollar values was obtained by converting the actual TR values to dollars at the official IBEC TR-dollar rate for 1988: 0.6315 TR = $1.00. A third estimate of dollar value of exports and imports is based on conversion of TR data at the 1.94 TR-dollar cross rate implicit in Hungary's commercial exchange rates for both currencies in 1988. This is computed from TR values converted to forints at the forint-TR rate and then to dollars at the forint-dollar rate.

The difference between the high and low estimates is 300 percent. Accordingly, the value of Hungarian products exported to the Soviet Union could total $7.6 billion or $2.5 billion, depending on the exchange rate, because each approach assumes an unchanged level and composition of trade after the switch to dollars, which is certainly not realistic. And an apparent surplus of Hungarian exports to the USSR in TR terms may instead be a bilateral deficit, expressed in dollar terms.

In effect, this procedure yields implicit TR-dollar exchange rates in Hungarian-Soviet export and import trade in 1988 (table 9.3).

Expressing TR trade in dollars for Hungary illustrates the range of estimates, depending on the source and exchange rate used, for valuing the trade of former CMEA countries. As a recent ECE publication points out: "Beginning with Hungary in the mid-1970s, all East European countries ... have by now introduced their own 'realistic' ruble/dollar exchange rates, which differ from those used by the Soviet Union and the CMEA, and from each other... Consequently, the national ruble/dollar cross rates varied in the first half of 1990 from about 0.60 rubles per dollar in Bulgaria and the Soviet Union to as much as 4.50 per dollar in Poland."

Alternative dollar estimates of intra-CMEA trade

Differences in the official, the implicit, and the implied TR/$ ratios by year, for exports and imports, for total trade and by commodity categories, illustrate the point emphasized in chapter 3 namely, that an economically correct revaluation of trade flows published in TRs into dollars would require the repricing of all intra-HPE trade at world market prices.

Four different approaches are considered here for estimating the dollar value of intra-CMEA trade (through 1990):

• Revaluing trade flows at hypothetical dollar

prices. Attempts to do this have been made by Marrese and Vanous (1983), Marrese and Wittenberg (1990), and Kenen (1991), for example. The general applicability of their common method—assigning hypothetical dollar prices or values to intra-CMEA trade by commodities or commodity groups—is constrained. There is a scarcity of published commodity data in intra-CMEA trade and, more important, the degree of uncertainty with which hypothetical dollar values can be estimated is high, given varying assumptions about world market prices and dollar-based assessments of the quality and utility of the goods being traded. Due to the complexity and limited commodity coverage of these methods, the results are not shown separately in the Basic Tables.

• Converting TR trade to dollars at the official IBEC TR-dollar exchange rate. This conversion assumes, on average for each country and for each year, that prices in intra-CMEA trade were identical to world market (West-West) prices, from which traders in the CMEA obtained TR values by using the IBEC rate. This approach is simple, and a uniform converter is employed for every country. But price assumptions are unlikely to be accurate. For most years, the IBEC rate overvalues the TR for most manufactured goods and thus understates the resulting dollar values; although the opposite may be true for energy and raw materials.

• Converting each country's TR trade to dollars at its own TR-dollar cross rate. This conversion is more realistic, especially for the exports of countries that have carried out exchange rate reforms. It has two drawbacks, however. For "reforming" countries, the rate is based on the average local-currency cost of earning a dollar and a TR in exports; the coefficient that would link the local-

Table 9.2 Estimated dollar values of Hungary's trade in 1988

	Actual value in TRs	*Estimated value in dollars*	*Dollar value at official TR-dollar exchange rate*	*Dollar value at implicit cross exchange rate*
Hungary's exports to USSR in 1988 (bn)	4.8	4.1	7.6	2.5
Hungary's imports from USSR in 1988 (bn)	4.4	4.9	7.0	2.3
Balance	0.4	-0.8	0.6	0.2

Note: The actual TR value of Hungary's exports to, imports from, and trade balance with the USSR are in column 1. Three alternative estimates of the dollar value of Hungarian-Soviet trade are in columns 2, 3, and 4.
Sources: Columns 1 and 2: Oblath and Tarr, *The Terms-of-Trade Effects from the Elimination of State Trading in Soviet-Hungarian Trade.* World Bank Working Paper No. 690. (May 1991). Table 1, columns 1 and 6; columns 3 and 4: see text.

Table 9.3   Implicit transferable ruble to dollar rates in Hungary and USSR trade (1988)

Commodity	Share in Hungary's TR exports	Share in Hungary's TR imports	Exports	TR-dollar imports
Mining	0.8	34.5	1.11	1.14
Electricity	0.1	8.2	1.11	0.89
Metallurgy	2.8	11.0	0.46	0.50
Machinery	59.5	19.7	1.32	1.09
Chemicals	10.6	16.1	1.27	0.80
Light industry	10.5	7.5	0.95	0.74
Processed food	11.0	1.0	1.06	1.67
Agricultural products	4.2	1.4	1.06	0.55
Building materials	0.4	0.5	1.11	1.17
Other	0.2	0.1	1.11	0.89
Total	100.0	100.0	1.16	1.13
Official TR-dollar				0.63
Hungary's cross rate[a]				1.94[a]

a. Implicit in Hungary's 1988 commercial exchange rates for the dollar (50.41) and the TR (26.00).
Source   Oblath and Tarr, op.cit. Table 1.

currency and TR values in imports may differ because the composition and relative prices of exports and imports are different. More important, the commercial rates introduce a break in data consistency. Older time series were computed using a devisa exchange rate that remained mostly unchanged. These differences in the rates are implicit in the ECE trade series in national currency.

• Converting each country's TR trade to dollars at a uniform composite TR-dollar cross-rate, computed for each year. This method (see chapter 11) takes an unweighted average of cross-rates for CMEA countries immediately after these commercial exchange rates are introduced. A uniform rate is then applied to all countries, following the example of the ECE, which made similar computations for one year. (See *Economic Bulletin for Europe*, November 1990.) The ECE's method, reproduced as time series in the Comparator Tables, uses a single country's cross-rate, rather than making a composite of CMEA country rates, as the authors did. Bilateral TR price levels of the countries are not identical but depend, among other variables, on the commodity composition of bilateral trade; this detracts from the validity of this approach.

Chapter 10. Country Data

Descriptive Notes

The data in the Comparator Tables for seventeen European and non-European HPEs consist of alternative estimates arranged by sources for given indicators, such as GNP per capita. Moreover, the terminology may not correspond precisely to the system of origin but approximates the concept being compared. For example, the term "value added" is not used in MPS, but is used in the Comparator Tables because it approximates the concept (see also box 8.1). The same is true for private consumption in SNA, which is closest to the MPS term "household consumption." The Basic Tables have similar coverage for data series arranged by conceptual or accounting identities, such as Net Material Product by origin and use. They also contain a few alternative estimates, but mostly elaborate data from elsewhere in the Guide.

The majority of indicators are national accounts (production and demand) and international transactions (mainly foreign trade). Only limited time series are shown for debt, balance of payments, and monetary and social indicators, since a wide range of estimates is available from other sources.

These tables, like the Global Tables in Part 2, use documented techniques for gap-filling. Linkage between the tables and the documentation, including footnotes, is explained in Part 4, Technical Notes.

Comparator Tables

The Comparator Tables show alternative estimates available for key economic indicators. How data are derived for each indicator is described in chapter 11. Alternative estimates are an important feature of the statistical landscape for HPEs, since they reflect different approaches used by collectors and producers of data to address statistical problems. They answer two of the most important questions in international comparisons: What does one estimate look like next to another? How do these estimates change relative to one another over time?

Alternative estimates in the Comparator Tables are shown for the following key indicators:

Per capita income is defined loosely to accommodate either GNP or GDP depending on the source's published measure of income. Conversion to U.S. dollars differs among sources: World Bank (Atlas Methodology) and Exchange Rate Conversion (single-year rate) both use exchange rates in their conversion methodology. Other sources include the CIA and LWI estimates and Penn World Tables, which use purchasing power parities.

Gross national product series are provided in current and constant prices to highlight differences in methods of measuring and adjusting for inflation. Substitutions of GDP series are footnoted. World Bank GNP divided by population would not give Atlas GNP per capita owing to different methods of conversion (single year versus three year average).

Conversion factors explain much of the variation among estimates for per capita income. Not all conversion factors are readily published and transparent; thus, selected rates are presented in the Comparator Tables, most of which correspond implicitly to the imputed conversion factor for one of the approaches to estimating per capita income.

Output trends are expressed as indexes rescaled to 1987 from constant price series or volume indexes in their original base years. This presentational rescaling facilitates comparison with World Bank series, which have been partially rebased to the same year; in this process, available components of GDP are presentationally shifted to a 1987 base and then re-added, which alters real growth rates (see SNA accounts (World Bank) in the next chapter for further explanation). But full comparability is impossible at the high level of aggregation available for most alternate sources. Data are shown for three definitions of "overall output" (Gross National Product, Gross Domestic Product, and Net Material Product). A breakdown of trends is also given by sector of origin and expenditure category. Some small differences in trends may result from statistical discrepancies included in one definition and not another. For example, SNA-based measures include discrepancies in services (sector of origin) and private and total consumption (expenditure). For industry and agriculture, a fourth SNA definition of output is shown, Gross Output, which must be reduced by intermediate inputs to reach a value-added measure.

Differences in output trends may reflect methodological and definitional differences in the indexes. These include techniques of accounting for depreciation and nonmaterial services, intermediate consumption, and in some cases, net factor income. Standard sources and methods are cross referenced (in Part 4) for these indicators.

Consumer prices are either national methodology as reported in the IFS or outside estimates reported by the CIA. The two approaches are explained in the Technical Notes. Price index issues are also discussed in the Primer.

Merchandise exports and imports (Total) are published by several sources. The main comparators are from publications of the IMF, UNCTAD, the Arms Control and Disarmament Agency, the Economic Commission for Europe, and the authors' uniform series. Sources and methods for the first four sources and their substitutions are described under International Trade in Sources and Methods.

In the event of gaps in the trade data series, substitutions of data were made using the UN *Monthly Bulletin*, GATT, and CIA or LWI for the first three series shown above. These substitutions were based on comparability of available data for over-

lapping years and countries. All substitutions are signaled by footnotes. The ECE routinely employs trade partner data to fill gaps in its series, but there is no additional gap filling here.

While the authors basically follow the ECE approach to estimating the dollar value of intra-CMEA trade, their estimates differ in the choice of the "uniform" TR-dollar conversion factor adopted. The authors and ECE reconvert nationally reported intra-CMEA trade to TRs. The conversion of the TR data back to dollars employs a "uniform" TR-dollar exchange rate in each case, but the authors chose an average of HPE commercial exchange rates while ECE applies Hungary's TR-dollar rate across all HPEs. This process is detailed in chapter 11. Dollar values of trade outside the CMEA zone can be calculated as the difference between total and intra-CMEA trade for both the ECE and the authors' uniform series.

Basic Tables

The Basic Tables follow the Comparator Tables in this chapter. They provide conceptual and accounting identities for readers to use in exploring the origins of broader aggregates, imputing significance to residual differences among sources, and reaching their own conclusions about appropriate adjustments. Definitions, sources, methods, the choice of indicators, and notes to tables are discussed in the text following the tables. Note that in each set of country pages, the two-page Comparator Tables are shaded to distinguish them from the Basic Tables that follow.

Comparator and Basic Tables

Albania

Comparator tables	1970	1971	1972	1973	1974	1975	1976	1977	1978	1979	1980
PER CAPITA INCOME						*(US dollars)*					
World Bank (Atlas method)	..	..	..	..	..	..	..	..	..	..	..
Single year conversion	..	..	..	..	..	..	..	..	..	..	..
CIA or LWI	..	..	..	..	..	..	..	..	827	..	..
Penn World Tables	..	..	..	..	..	..	..	..	..	..	..
						(thousands)					
POPULATION	2,136	2,188	2,241	2,297	2,349	2,402	2,456	2,508	2,563	2,617	2,671
GROSS NATIONAL PRODUCT, current prices						*(millions of current US dollars)*					
World Bank (Atlas method)	..	..	..	..	..	..	..	..	..	..	..
Single year conversion	..	..	..	..	..	..	..	..	..	..	..
Authors' series	..	..	..	..	..	..	..	..	..	..	..
CIA or LWI	..	..	..	..	..	..	..	..	2,150	..	..
GROSS NATIONAL PRODUCT, constant prices						*(millions of constant 1987 dollars)*					
Single year conversion	..	..	..	..	..	..	..	..	..	..	..
Authors' series, rescaled from 1980 prices	..	..	..	..	..	..	..	..	..	..	..
CIA or LWI, rescaled from 1989 prices	..	..	..	..	..	..	..	..	..	..	..
CONVERSION FACTORS						*(LCUs per US dollar)*					
World Bank (Atlas method)	..	..	..	..	..	..	..	..	..	..	..
Single year convertor	..	..	..	..	..	..	..	..	..	..	..
Authors' series	..	..	..	..	..	..	..	..	..	..	..
Penn World Tables	..	..	..	..	..	..	..	..	..	..	..
OUTPUT TRENDS, OVERALL						*(index, constant prices 1987 = 100)*					
GNP, SNA	..	..	..	..	..	..	..	..	..	..	86.5
NMP, MPS	..	..	..	..	..	..	..	..	..	..	89.1
GNP, "Building block"	..	..	..	..	..	..	..	..	..	..	..
Industry											
Value added, SNA	..	..	..	..	..	..	..	..	..	..	..
Value added, MPS	..	..	..	..	..	..	..	..	..	..	84.4
"Building block"	..	..	..	..	..	..	..	..	..	..	..
Gross output, SNA	..	..	..	..	..	..	..	..	..	..	..
Agriculture											
Value added, SNA	..	..	..	..	..	..	..	..	..	..	..
Value added, MPS	..	..	..	..	..	..	..	..	..	..	89.9
"Building block"	..	..	..	..	..	..	..	..	..	..	..
Gross output, SNA	..	..	..	..	..	..	..	..	..	..	..
Services											
Value added, SNA	..	..	..	..	..	..	..	..	..	..	..
Value added, MPS	..	..	..	..	..	..	..	..	..	..	103.8
"Building block"	..	..	..	..	..	..	..	..	..	..	..
CONSUMPTION											
Total consumption, SNA	..	..	..	..	..	..	..	..	..	..	80.8
Total consumption, MPS	..	..	..	..	..	..	..	..	..	..	82.4
Households, SNA	..	..	..	..	..	..	..	..	..	..	80.4
Households, "building block"	..	..	..	..	..	..	..	..	..	..	..
General government, SNA	..	..	..	..	..	..	..	..	..	..	83.6
General government, "building block"	..	..	..	..	..	..	..	..	..	..	..
INVESTMENT											
Gross fixed investment, SNA	..	..	..	..	..	..	..	..	..	..	84.3
Accumulation, MPS	..	..	..	..	..	..	..	..	..	..	92.4
"Building block"	..	..	..	..	..	..	..	..	..	..	..
CONSUMER PRICES											
National methodology	..	..	..	..	..	..	..	..	..	..	..
Outside estimate	..	..	..	..	..	..	..	..	..	..	..
MERCHANDISE EXPORTS						*(millions of current US dollars)*					
UNCTAD	..	..	..	..	..	175	..	..	..	..	410
IMF: IFS	..	..	..	..	..	..	..	..	..	..	..
ACDA	..	..	..	..	..	..	..	..	151	..	..
ECE	..	..	..	..	..	..	..	..	..	..	..
intra-CMEA	..	..	..	..	..	..	..	..	..	..	..
Authors' uniform TR/$ series	..	..	..	..	..	..	..	..	..	..	..
intra-CMEA	..	..	..	..	..	..	..	..	..	..	..
MERCHANDISE IMPORTS						*(millions of current US dollars)*					
UNCTAD	..	..	..	..	..	..	..	..	..	..	..
IMF: IFS	..	..	..	..	..	..	..	..	..	..	..
ACDA	..	..	..	..	..	..	..	..	173	..	..
ECE	..	..	..	..	..	..	..	..	..	..	..
intra-CMEA	..	..	..	..	..	..	..	..	..	..	..
Authors' uniform series	..	..	..	..	..	..	..	..	..	..	..
intra-CMEA	..	..	..	..	..	..	..	..	..	..	..

Abbreviations in notes column are explained in the General Notes. For sources and methods, see the Technical Notes.

1981	1982	1983	1984	1985	1986	1987	1988	1989	1990	Notes	Comparator tables (continued)
					(US dollars)						**PER CAPITA INCOME**
..	..	..	..	..	..	..	..	..	..	.	World Bank (Atlas method)
..	..	..	..	..	..	..	..	..	..	.	Single year conversion
..	..	..	..	900	933	948	996	1,188	..	A	CIA or LWI
..	..	..	..	..	*(thousands)*	..	..	..	..	.	Penn World Tables
2,725	2,783	2,841	2,901	2,962	3,022	3,083	3,143	3,199	3,255	.	**POPULATION**
				(millions of current US dollars)							**GROSS NATIONAL PRODUCT, current prices**
..	..	..	..	..	..	..	..	..	..	.	World Bank (Atlas method)
..	..	..	..	..	..	..	..	..	..	.	Single year conversion
..	..	..	..	..	..	..	..	..	..	.	Authors' series
..	..	..	..	2,700	2,800	2,940	3,087	3,800	..	.	CIA or LWI
				(millions of constant 1987 dollars)							**GROSS NATIONAL PRODUCT, constant prices**
..	..	..	..	..	..	..	..	..	..	.	Single year conversion
..	..	..	..	..	..	..	..	..	..	.	Authors' series, rescaled from 1980 prices
..	..	..	..	2,975	3,007	3,060	3,111	3,678	..	A	CIA or LWI, rescaled from 1989 prices
				(LCUs per US dollar)							**CONVERSION FACTORS**
..	..	..	..	..	..	..	..	..	..	.	World Bank (Atlas method)
..	..	..	..	..	..	..	..	..	..	.	Single year convertor
..	..	..	..	..	..	..	..	..	..	.	Authors' series
..	..	..	..	..	..	..	..	..	..	.	Penn World Tables
			(index, constant prices 1987 = 100)								**OUTPUT TRENDS, OVERALL**
91.7	94.5	95.3	93.9	95.5	100.8	100.0	98.6	108.2	..	.	GNP, SNA
94.4	96.9	97.5	94.6	96.4	102.3	100.0	99.5	111.1	96.6	.	NMP, MPS
..	..	..	..	..	..	..	..	..	..	.	GNP, "Building block"
											Industry
..	..	..	..	..	..	..	..	..	..	.	Value added, SNA
89.1	94.0	93.9	92.7	92.1	99.7	100.0	100.6	109.2	97.1	.	Value added, MPS
..	..	..	..	..	..	..	..	..	..	.	"Building block"
..	..	..	..	..	..	..	..	..	..	.	Gross output, SNA
											Agriculture
..	..	..	..	..	..	..	..	..	..	.	Value added, SNA
94.3	94.8	102.5	96.7	102.1	104.8	100.0	94.4	108.1	94.3	.	Value added, MPS
..	..	..	..	..	..	..	..	..	..	.	"Building block"
..	..	..	..	..	..	..	..	..	..	.	Gross output, SNA
											Services
..	..	..	..	..	..	..	..	..	..	.	Value added, SNA
113.4	112.4	98.8	96.8	98.6	106.0	100.0	107.0	125.0	100.0	.	Value added, MPS
..	..	..	..	..	..	..	..	..	..	.	"Building block"
											CONSUMPTION
82.4	83.7	88.2	91.4	91.9	96.1	100.0	99.4	104.7	..	.	Total consumption, SNA
84.1	84.9	90.0	92.4	93.0	96.7	100.0	100.7	107.0	108.9	.	Total consumption, MPS
82.5	83.5	88.3	91.2	91.7	95.9	100.0	99.8	105.6	..	.	Households, SNA
..	..	..	..	..	..	..	..	..	..	.	Households, "building block"
82.1	84.9	87.8	92.7	93.6	96.9	100.0	96.7	98.9	..	.	General government, SNA
..	..	..	..	..	..	..	..	..	..	.	General government, "building block"
											INVESTMENT
85.5	94.1	100.0	102.8	90.6	96.4	100.0	96.0	104.8	..	.	Gross fixed investment, SNA
84.4	101.2	103.7	103.4	89.0	95.2	100.0	103.0	114.3	..	.	Accumulation, MPS
..	..	..	..	..	..	..	..	..	..	.	"Building block"
											CONSUMER PRICES
..	..	..	..	..	..	..	..	..	..	.	National methodology
..	..	..	..	..	..	..	..	..	..	.	Outside estimate
				(millions of current US dollars)							**MERCHANDISE EXPORTS**
450	390	340	304	260	405	417	308	..	..	.	UNCTAD
..	..	..	..	..	..	..	..	..	..	.	IMF: IFS
..	..	290	..	345	428	378	..	..	..	.	ACDA
..	..	..	..	..	..	..	..	..	..	.	ECE
..	..	..	..	..	..	..	..	..	..	.	intra-CMEA
..	255	219	193	173	243	194	..	..	..	.	Authors' uniform TR/$ series
..	..	..	..	..	..	..	..	..	..	.	intra-CMEA
				(millions of current US dollars)							**MERCHANDISE IMPORTS**
..	..	..	..	..	..	..	..	..	..	.	UNCTAD
..	..	..	..	..	..	..	..	..	..	.	IMF: IFS
..	137	280	..	335	363	255	..	..	..	.	ACDA
..	..	..	..	..	..	..	..	..	..	.	ECE
..	..	..	..	..	..	..	..	..	..	.	intra-CMEA
..	322	242	227	228	215	228	..	..	..	.	Authors' uniform series
..	..	..	..	..	..	..	..	..	..	.	intra-CMEA

Albania

	1970	1971	1972	1973	1974	1975	1976	1977	1978	1979	1980
SNA ACCOUNTS, current prices					*(millions of current Albanian leks)*						
GNP, at market prices	..	..	..	..	..	..	..	..	..	..	15,571
Net factor income	..	..	..	..	..	..	..	..	..	..	33
GDP at market prices	..	..	..	..	..	..	..	..	..	..	15,538
Net indirect taxes	..	..	..	..	..	..	..	..	..	..	..
GDP at factor cost	..	..	..	..	..	..	..	..	..	..	..
Agriculture	..	..	..	..	..	..	..	..	..	..	..
Industry	..	..	..	..	..	..	..	..	..	..	..
Services, etc.	..	..	..	..	..	..	..	..	..	..	..
Resource balance	..	..	..	..	..	..	..	..	..	..	63
Exports GNFS	..	..	..	..	..	..	..	..	..	..	..
Imports GNFS	..	..	..	..	..	..	..	..	..	..	..
Domestic absorption	..	..	..	..	..	..	..	..	..	..	15,475
Total consumption	..	..	..	..	..	..	..	..	..	..	10,156
Private consumption	..	..	..	..	..	..	..	..	..	..	8,760
General government consumption	..	..	..	..	..	..	..	..	..	..	1,396
Gross domestic investment	..	..	..	..	..	..	..	..	..	..	5,368
Fixed domestic investment	..	..	..	..	..	..	..	..	..	..	5,269
Depreciation	..	..	..	..	..	..	..	..	..	..	..
SNA ACCOUNTS, constant prices					*(millions of constant 1986 Albanian leks)*						
Gross national product (GNP)	..	..	..	..	..	..	..	..	..	..	14,913
GDP at market prices	..	..	..	..	..	..	..	..	..	..	14,881
GDP at factor cost	..	..	..	..	..	..	..	..	..	..	..
Agriculture	..	..	..	..	..	..	..	..	..	..	..
Industry	..	..	..	..	..	..	..	..	..	..	..
Services, etc.	..	..	..	..	..	..	..	..	..	..	..
Resource balance	..	..	..	..	..	..	..	..	..	..	14
Exports GNFS	..	..	..	..	..	..	..	..	..	..	..
Imports GNFS	..	..	..	..	..	..	..	..	..	..	..
Domestic absorption	..	..	..	..	..	..	..	..	..	..	14,867
Total consumption, etc.	..	..	..	..	..	..	..	..	..	..	10,062
Private consumption, etc.	..	..	..	..	..	..	..	..	..	..	8,677
General government consumption	..	..	..	..	..	..	..	..	..	..	1,385
Gross domestic investment	..	..	..	..	..	..	..	..	..	..	4,805
Fixed domestic investment	..	..	..	..	..	..	..	..	..	..	4,712
Depreciation	..	..	..	..	..	..	..	..	..	..	..
MPS ACCOUNTS, current prices					*(millions of current Albanian leks)*						
NMP produced:	6,830	..	..	..	..	..	..	..	..	..	12,862
Agriculture and forestry	2,356	..	..	..	..	..	..	..	..	..	4,319
Industry excluding construction	2,896	..	..	..	..	..	..	..	..	..	5,782
Construction	697	..	..	..	..	..	..	..	..	..	891
Transport and communication	..	..	..	..	..	..	..	..	..	..	372
Trade, etc.	881	..	..	..	..	..	..	..	..	..	..
Other services	..	..	..	..	..	..	..	..	..	..	1,498
Resource balance	..	..	..	..	..	..	..	..	..	..	14
NMP used: domestic market	9,230	..	..	..	..	..	..	..	..	..	12,848
Final consumption, material goods	6,340	..	..	..	..	..	..	..	..	..	9,034
Personal consumption	..	..	..	..	..	..	..	..	..	..	7,721
Collective consumption	..	..	..	..	..	..	..	..	..	..	1,313
Net capital formation	2,890	..	..	..	..	..	..	..	..	..	3,814
Net fixed capital formation	2,120	..	..	..	..	..	..	..	..	..	3,175
Changes in stocks	770	..	..	..	..	..	..	..	..	..	639
Depreciation	..	..	..	..	..	..	..	..	..	..	..
MPS ACCOUNTS, constant prices					*(millions of 1986 Albanian leks)*						
NMP produced:	..	..	..	..	..	..	..	..	..	..	12,199
Agriculture and forestry	..	..	..	..	..	..	..	..	..	..	4,091
Industry and construction	..	..	..	..	..	..	..	..	..	..	6,038
Services	..	..	..	..	..	..	..	..	..	..	2,070
Resource balance	..	..	..	..	..	..	..	..	..	..	15
NMP used: domestic market	..	..	..	..	..	..	..	..	..	..	12,184
Final consumption, material goods	..	..	..	..	..	..	..	..	..	..	8,944
Personal consumption	..	..	..	..	..	..	..	..	..	..	7,631
Collective consumption	..	..	..	..	..	..	..	..	..	..	1,313
Net capital formation	..	..	..	..	..	..	..	..	..	..	3,240
Net fixed capital formation	..	..	..	..	..	..	..	..	..	..	2,972
Depreciation	..	..	..	..	..	..	..	..	..	..	..

Abbreviations in notes column are explained in the General Notes. For sources and methods, see the Technical Notes.

1981	1982	1983	1984	1985	1986	1987	1988	1989	1990	Notes	*Basic tables (continued)*
				(millions of current Albanian leks)							**SNA ACCOUNTS, current prices**
16,164	16,659	16,781	16,538	16,874	17,391	17,256	17,009	18,680	16,219	.	GNP, at market prices
91	115	57	28	11	1	3	1	-1	-15	.	Net factor income
16,073	16,544	16,724	16,510	16,863	17,390	17,253	17,008	18,681	16,234	.	GDP at market prices
..	..	..	..	..	..	..	..	..	..	.	Net indirect taxes
..	..	..	..	..	..	..	..	..	..	.	GDP at factor cost
..	..	..	..	..	..	..	..	..	..	.	Agriculture
..	..	..	..	..	..	..	..	..	..	.	Industry
..	..	..	..	..	..	..	..	..	..	.	Services, etc.
236	-745	-437	-324	-373	-71	-17	-482	-483	-1,316	.	Resource balance
..	..	..	..	..	..	..	..	..	..	.	Exports GNFS
..	..	..	..	..	..	..	..	..	..	.	Imports GNFS
15,837	17,289	17,161	16,834	17,236	17,461	17,270	17,490	19,164	..	.	Domestic absorption
10,354	10,475	10,992	11,393	11,456	11,964	12,455	12.379	13,044	..	.	Total consumption
8,982	9,054	9,524	9,839	9,887	10,351	10,791	10,770	11,398	..	.	Private consumption
1,372	1,421	1,468	1,554	1,569	1,613	1,664	1,609	1,646	..	.	General government consumption
5,645	6,273	6,033	5,247	5,523	5,375	4,903	4,916	5,926	..	.	Gross domestic investment
4,987	5,508	5,923	6,111	5,445	5,385	5,588	5,363	5,854	..	.	Fixed domestic investment
..	..	..	..	..	..	..	..	..	..	.	Depreciation
				(millions of constant 1986 Albanian leks)							**SNA ACCOUNTS, constant prices**
15,826	16,309	16,434	16,201	16,473	17,384	17,249	17,002	18,672	..	.	Gross national product (GNP)
15,736	16,200	16,379	16,174	16,462	17,383	17,246	17,001	18,673	..	f	GDP at market prices
..	..	..	..	..	..	..	..	..	..	.	GDP at factor cost
..	..	..	..	..	..	..	..	..	..	.	Agriculture
..	..	..	..	..	..	..	..	..	..	.	Industry
..	..	..	..	..	..	..	..	..	..	.	Services, etc.
74	-204	-301	-130	-116	51	-105	-287	-289	..	.	Resource balance
..	..	..	..	..	..	..	..	..	..	.	Exports GNFS
..	..	..	..	..	..	..	..	..	..	.	Imports GNFS
15,662	16,404	16,680	16,304	16,578	17,332	17,351	17,288	18,962	..	.	Domestic absorption
10,258	10,415	10,985	11,381	11,444	11,957	12,448	12,372	13,036	..	.	Total consumption, etc.
8,898	9,008	9,530	9,845	9,893	10,351	10,791	10,770	11,398	..	.	Private consumption, etc.
1,360	1,407	1,455	1,536	1,551	1,606	1,657	1,602	1,638	..	.	General government consumption
5,404	5,989	5,695	4,923	5,134	5,375	4,903	4,916	5,926	..	.	Gross domestic investment
4,778	5,261	5,590	5,746	5,060	5,385	5,588	5,363	5,854	..	.	Fixed domestic investment
..	..	..	..	..	..	..	..	..	..	.	Depreciation
				(millions of current Albanian leks)							**MPS ACCOUNTS, current prices**
13,265	13,625	13,696	13,300	13,602	14,013	13,699	13,631	15,223	13,229	.	NMP produced:
4,292	4,314	4,665	4,399	4,703	4,768	4,550	4,296	4,919	4,289	.	Agriculture and forestry
5,704	5,968	5,928	5,848	5,886	6,196	6,276	6,310	6,822	6,087	.	Industry excluding construction
939	1,041	1,070	1,065	979	936	879	891	989	859	.	Construction
375	446	457	461	446	480	479	498	517	449	.	Transport and communication
..	..	..	..	..	..	..	..	..	..	.	Trade, etc.
1,954	1,856	1,577	1,527	1,588	1,633	1,515	1,636	1,976	1,545	f	Other services
74	-204	-301	-130	-116	51	-106	-287	-289	-1,280	f	Resource balance
13,191	13,829	13,997	13,430	13,718	13,962	13,805	13,918	15,512	14,509	.	NMP used: domestic market
9,212	9,262	9,772	10,023	10,095	10,497	10,853	10,928	11,614	11,822	f	Final consumption, material goods
7,863	7,887	8,351	8,563	8,629	9,025	9,335	9,436	10,089	10,291	f	Personal consumption
1,349	1,375	1,422	1,460	1,466	1,472	1,517	1,492	1,525	1,531	.	Collective consumption
3,979	4,567	4,225	3,407	3,623	3,465	2,952	2,990	3,898	2,687	f	Net capital formation
3,173	3,628	3,741	3,754	3,248	3,062	3,218	3,314	3,677	2,616	.	Net fixed capital formation
806	939	484	-347	375	403	-266	-324	221	71	.	Changes in stocks
..	..	..	..	..	..	..	..	..	..	.	Depreciation
				(millions of 1986 Albanian leks)							**MPS ACCOUNTS, constant prices**
12,929	13,281	13,351	12,964	13,200	14,013	13,699	13,631	15,223	13,229	.	NMP produced:
4,292	4,314	4,665	4,399	4,645	4,768	4,550	4,296	4,919	4,289	.	Agriculture and forestry
6,375	6,726	6,716	6,635	6,588	7,132	7,155	7,201	7,811	6,946	.	Industry and construction
2,262	2,241	1,970	1,930	1,967	2,113	1,994	2,134	2,493	1,994	.	Services
75	-204	-300	-130	-116	51	-106	-287	-289	-1,280	f	Resource balance
12,854	13,485	13,651	13,094	13,316	13,962	13,805	13,918	15,512	14,509	.	NMP used: domestic market
9,122	9,210	9,772	10,023	10,095	10,497	10,853	10,928	11,614	11,822	f	Final consumption, material goods
7,773	7,835	8,351	8,563	8,629	9,025	9,335	9,436	10,089	10,291	f	Personal consumption
1,349	1,375	1,422	1,460	1,466	1,472	1,517	1,492	1,525	1,531	.	Collective consumption
3,732	4,275	3,879	3,071	3,221	3,465	2,952	2,990	3,898	2,687	f	Net capital formation
2,716	3,257	3,338	3,328	2,864	3,062	3,218	3,314	3,6/7	..	.	Net fixed capital formation
..	..	..	..	..	..	..	..	..	..	.	Depreciation

Albania

Basic tables (continued)	1970	1971	1972	1973	1974	1975	1976	1977	1978	1979	1980
MPS ACCOUNTS, index					*(index, 1980 = 100)*						
NMP produced:	..	..	..	..	..	..	..	..	..	..	100.0
Agriculture and forestry	..	..	..	..	..	..	..	..	..	..	100.0
Industry excluding construction	..	..	..	..	..	..	..	..	..	..	100.0
Construction	..	..	..	..	..	..	..	..	..	..	100.0
Transport and communication	..	..	..	..	..	..	..	..	..	..	100.0
Trade, etc.	..	..	..	..	..	..	..	..	..	..	..
NMP used: material goods	..	..	..	..	..	..	..	..	..	..	100.0
Final consumption	..	..	..	..	..	..	..	..	..	..	100.0
Net capital formation	..	..	..	..	..	..	..	..	..	..	100.0
EXCHANGE AND CONVERSION RATES					*(LCUs per US dollar: annual average)*						
Single-year converter	..	..	..	..	..	..	..	..	..	..	..
Devisa/official	..	..	..	..	..	..	..	..	..	..	..
Commercial	..	..	..	..	..	3.922	..	..	..	..	3.300
Noncommercial	..	..	..	..	..	..	..	..	..	..	7.000
Informal market	..	..	..	..	..	..	..	..	..	..	..
ICP	..	..	..	..	..	..	..	..	..	..	..
					(ruble per US dollar: annual average)						
Commercial TR/$ cross	..	..	..	..	..	..	..	..	..	..	..
Uniform TR/$ cross	..	..	..	..	..	..	..	..	..	..	..
					(LCUs per ruble: annual average)						
Commercial	..	..	..	..	..	..	..	..	..	..	..
Noncommercial	..	..	..	..	..	..	..	..	..	..	..
Devisa/official	..	..	..	..	..	..	..	..	..	..	..
CONSUMER PRICE INDEXES					*(index)*						
Official, IMF 1985 = 100	..	..	..	..	..	..	..	..	..	..	..
Official, CIA or LWI 1980 = 100	..	..	..	..	..	..	..	..	..	..	..
Alternative, CIA or LWI 1980 = 100	..	..	..	..	..	..	..	..	..	..	..
INTERNATIONAL TRADE (ECE)					*(millions of current Albanian leks)*						
Value of exports, fob	..	..	..	..	..	2,058	..	..	..	..	3,573
to CMEA	..	..	..	..	..	1,147	..	..	..	..	1,825
Value of imports, cif	..	..	..	..	..	3,729	..	..	..	..	3,617
from CMEA	..	..	..	..	..	988	..	..	..	..	1,908
Trade balance	..	..	..	..	..	-1,671	..	..	..	..	-44
CMEA	..	..	..	..	..	159	..	..	..	..	-83
INTERNATIONAL TRADE (Authors')					*(millions of current US dollars)*						
Value of exports, fob	..	..	..	..	..	..	..	..	..	..	..
to developed countries	..	..	..	..	..	..	..	..	..	..	..
to other non-socialist countries	..	..	..	..	..	..	..	..	..	..	..
to socialist countries	..	..	..	..	..	..	..	..	..	..	..
to CMEA	..	..	..	..	..	..	..	..	..	..	..
Value of imports, cif	..	..	..	..	..	..	..	..	..	..	..
from developed countries	..	..	..	..	..	..	..	..	..	..	..
from other non-socialist countries	..	..	..	..	..	..	..	..	..	..	..
from socialist countries	..	..	..	..	..	..	..	..	..	..	..
from CMEA	..	..	..	..	..	..	..	..	..	..	..
Trade balance	..	..	..	..	..	..	..	..	..	..	..
Developed countries	..	..	..	..	..	..	..	..	..	..	..
Other non-socialist countries	..	..	..	..	..	..	..	..	..	..	..
Socialist countries	..	..	..	..	..	..	..	..	..	..	..
CMEA	..	..	..	..	..	..	..	..	..	..	..
PARTNER CONVERTIBLE TRADE (ECE)					*(millions of current US dollars)*						
Exports to non-CMEA (cif)	..	..	..	..	..	..	..	..	..	..	..
Imports from non-CMEA (fob)	..	..	..	..	..	..	..	..	..	..	..
Trade balance	..	..	..	..	..	..	..	..	..	..	..
TRADE PRICE INDEXES (Authors')					*(index, 1980 = 100)*						
Terms of trade	101.8	..	..	..	..	..	..	..	..	..	100.0
Exports	91.7	..	..	..	..	..	..	..	..	..	100.0
Non-socialist countries	..	..	..	..	..	..	..	..	..	..	..
Developed countries	..	..	..	..	..	..	..	..	..	..	..
Other	..	..	..	..	..	..	..	..	..	..	..
Socialist countries	..	..	..	..	..	..	..	..	..	..	..
CMEA	..	..	..	..	..	..	..	..	..	..	..
Imports	90.1	..	..	..	..	..	..	..	..	..	100.0
Non-socialist countries	..	..	..	..	..	..	..	..	..	..	..
Developed countries	..	..	..	..	..	..	..	..	..	..	..
Other	..	..	..	..	..	..	..	..	..	..	..
Socialist countries	..	..	..	..	..	..	..	..	..	..	..
CMEA	..	..	..	..	..	..	..	..	..	..	..

Abbreviations in notes column are explained in the General Notes. For sources and methods, see the Technical Notes.

Albania

1981	1982	1983	1984	1985	1986	1987	1988	1989	1990	Notes	
				(index,1980 = 100)							**MPS ACCOUNTS**, index
106.0	108.9	109.4	106.3	108.2	114.9	112.3	111.7	124.8	108.4	I	NMP produced:
104.9	105.5	114.0	107.5	113.5	116.5	111.2	105.0	120.2	104.8	.	Agriculture and forestry
104.6	109.4	108.7	107.2	107.9	118.6	120.1	120.8	130.6	116.5	.	Industry excluding construction
112.0	124.2	127.6	127.1	116.8	115.0	108.0	109.5	121.5	105.5	.	Construction
98.1	116.7	119.6	120.7	116.7	127.3	127.1	132.1	137.1	119.1	.	Transport and communication
..	..	..	..	..	..	..	..	..	..		Trade, etc.
105.5	110.7	112.0	107.5	109.3	114.6	113.3	114.2	127.3	94.3	I	NMP used: material goods
102.0	103.0	109.3	112.1	112.9	117.4	121.3	122.2	129.9	132.2	.	Final consumption
115.2	131.9	119.7	94.8	99.4	106.9	91.1	92.3	120.3	-10.3	f	Net capital formation
				(LCUs per US dollar: annual average)							**EXCHANGE AND CONVERSION RATES**
..	..	..	..	..	..	..	..	..	..		Single-year converter
..	..	..	..	..	6.660	6.220	5.410	6.480	6.000	.	Devisa/official
3.300	3.300	..	..	..	..	..	..	..	..	f	Commercial
7.000	7.000	..								.	Noncommercial
..	..	..	..	..	..	..	..	..	..	.	Informal market
..	..	..	..	..	..	..	..	..	..	.	ICP
				(ruble per US dollar: annual average)							
..	..	..	..	..	..	..	..	..	..	.	Commercial TR/$ cross
..	..	..	..	..	..	..	..	..	..	.	Uniform TR/$ cross
				(LCUs per ruble: annual average)							
..	..	..	..	..	..	..	..	..	..	.	Commercial
..	..	..	..	..	..	..	..	..	..	.	Noncommercial
..	..	..	..	..	..	..	..	..	..	.	Devisa/official
				(index)							**CONSUMER PRICE INDEXES**
..	..	..	..	..	..	..	..	..	..	.	Official, IMF 1985 = 100
..	..	..	..	..	..	..	..	..	..	.	Official, CIA or LWI 1980 = 100
..	..	..	..	..	..	..	..	..	..	.	Alternative, CIA or LWI 1980 = 100
				(millions of current Albanian leks)							**INTERNATIONAL TRADE** (ECE)
3,513	3,156	2,992	2,800	2,665	2,490	2,490	2,549	3,029	2,289	.	Value of exports, fob
1,686	1,592	1,807	1,652	1,647	1,256	1,260	1,385	1,651	1,059	.	to CMEA
3,391	4,026	3,528	3,257	3,176	2,666	2,650	3,217	3,792	3,797	.	Value of imports, cif
1,507	1,860	1,977	1,782	1,890	1,409	1,400	1,633	1,698	1,556	.	from CMEA
122	-870	-536	-457	-511	-176	-160	-668	-763	-1,508	.	Trade balance
179	-268	-170	-130	-243	-153	-140	-248	-47	-497	.	CMEA
				(millions of current US dollars)							**INTERNATIONAL TRADE** (Authors')
..	255	219	193	173	243	194		..	..	.	Value of exports, fob
..	110	90	95	79	82	74	..	..	..	.	to developed countries
..	..	..	..	..	..	..	..	..	..	.	to other non-socialist countries
..	..	..	..	..	..	..	..	..	..	.	to socialist countries
..	..	..	..	..	..	..	..	..	..	.	to CMEA
..	322	242	227	228	215	228	..	..	..	.	Value of imports, cif
..	152	114	110	101	79	81	..	..	..	.	from developed countries
..	..	..	..	..	..	..	..	..	..	.	from other non-socialist countries
..	..	..	..	..	..	..	..	..	..	.	from socialist countries
..	..	..	..	..	..	..	..	..	..	.	from CMEA
..	-67	-23	-34	-55	28	-34	..	..	..	.	Trade balance
..	-42	-24	-15	-22	3	-7	..	..	..	.	Developed countries
..	..	..	..	..	..	..	..	..	..	.	Other non-socialist countries
..	..	..	..	..	..	..	..	..	..	.	Socialist countries
..	..	..	..	..	..	..	..	..	..	.	CMEA
				(millions of current US dollars)							**PARTNER CONVERTIBLE TRADE** (ECE)
..	..	..	..	..	..	..	..	..	..	.	Exports to non-CMEA (cif)
..	..	..	..	..	..	..	..	..	..	.	Imports from non-CMEA (fob)
..	..	..	..	..	..	..	..	..	..	.	Trade balance
				(index,1980 = 100)							**TRADE PRICE INDEXES** (Authors')
..	..	..	..	179.5	174.3	217.2	227.2	275.4	199.8	f	Terms of trade
..	..	..	..	122.9	103.7	117.4	133.0	176.1	142.2	f	Exports
..	..	..	..	..	..	..	..	..	..	.	Non-socialist countries
..	..	..	..	..	..	..	..	..	..	.·	Developed countries
..	..	..	..	..	..	..	..	..	..	.	Other
..	..	..	..	..	..	..	..	..	..	.	Socialist countries
..	..	..	..	..	..	..	..	..	..	.	CMEA
..	..	..	..	68.5	59.5	54.1	58.6	64.0	71.2	f	Imports
..	..	..	..	..	..	..	..	..	..	.	Non-socialist countries
..	..	..	..	..	..	..	..	..	..	.	Developed countries
..	..	..	..	..	..	..	..	..	..	.	Other
..	..	..	..	..	..	..	..	..	..	.	Socialist countries
..	..	..	..	..	..	..	..	..	..	.	CMEA

Albania

Basic tables (continued)

	1970	1971	1972	1973	1974	1975	1976	1977	1978	1979	1980
TRADE PRICE INDEXES (ECE)						*(index, 1980 = 100)*					
Terms of trade	..	..	..	..	..	..	..	..	..	..	..
Exports	..	..	..	..	..	..	..	..	..	..	..
Imports	..	..	..	..	..	..	..	..	..	..	..
Balance of Payments (ECE)						*(millions of current US dollars)*					
Exports, convertible currency	..	..	..	..	..	..	..	..	..	..	99
Imports, convertible currency	..	..	..	..	..	..	..	..	..	..	105
Trade balance, convertible currency	..	..	..	..	..	..	..	..	..	..	-6
Invisibles, convertible currency	..	..	..	..	..	..	..	..	..	..	-6
Current balance, convertible currency	..	..	..	..	..	..	..	..	..	..	0
External debt, total (World Bank)	..	..	..	..	..	..	..	..	..	..	..
Convertible currency	..	..	..	..	..	..	..	..	..	..	..
CMEA	..	..	..	..	..	..	..	..	..	..	..
External debt service (World Bank)	..	..	..	..	..	..	..	..	..	..	..
Convertible currency	..	..	..	..	..	..	..	..	..	..	..
Total reserves less gold (IMF, IFS)	..	..	..	..	..	..	..	..	..	..	..
Total reserves, including gold at London price	..	..	..	..	..	..	..	..	..	..	..
Total reserves, incl. gold at national valuation	..	..	..	..	..	..	..	..	..	..	..
EMPLOYMENT						*(thousands)*					
Employment, total	..	..	..	..	..	..	..	..	..	..	655
Agriculture	..	..	..	..	..	..	..	..	..	..	137
Industry	..	..	..	..	..	..	..	..	..	..	299
Services	..	..	..	..	..	..	..	..	..	..	219
Labor force, total	901	929	958	986	1,015	1,043	1,077	1,110	1,144	1,177	1,211
Agriculture	596	604	612	620	628	637	645	653	661	669	677
Industry	191	202	213	223	234	245	258	271	285	298	311
Services	114	123	133	142	152	162	174	186	198	210	223
DOMESTIC FINANCE (IMF)						*(millions of current Albanian leks)*					
Money supply, broadly defined	..	..	..	..	..	..	..	..	..	..	2,670
Money, means of payment	..	..	..	..	..	..	..	..	..	..	..
Demand deposits	..	..	..	..	..	..	..	..	..	..	1,967
Currency outside banks	..	..	..	..	..	..	..	..	..	..	..
Quasi-money	..	..	..	..	..	..	..	..	..	..	..
Interest: deposit rate (percent)	..	..	..	..	..	..	..	..	..	..	..
Central government expenditures	..	..	..	..	..	..	..	..	..	..	7,950
Defense	..	..	..	..	..	..	..	..	..	..	..
						(millions of 1989 US dollars)					
Central government exp. (ACDA)	..	..	..	..	..	..	..	..	..	..	..
Military (ACDA)	..	..	..	..	..	..	..	..	..	..	..
LAND AND FORESTS (FAO)											
Pop. density: agr. land (pop. per sq. km)	174	182	191	200	209	222	229	226	230	234	239
Deforestation rate (net)	0	0	0	0	0	-17	0	0	0	0	0
Forest (thousands sq. km)	12	12	12	12	12	10	10	10	10	10	10
SOCIAL INDICATORS											
Population density: total land (pop. per sq. km)	78	80	82	84	86	88	90	92	94	96	98
School enrollment ratio, primary	106	..	..	..	..	..	..	112	110	108	113
secondary	35	..	..	..	..	..	..	53	58	63	67
tertiary	..	..	..	..	..	..	..	..	..	..	5
Energy consumption per capita (kg. of oil eq.)	552	608	711	614	622	666	739	811	881	931	1,055
Daily calorie supply per capita	2,564	2,571	2,558	2,574	2,572	2,544	2,600	2,609	2,702	2,727	2,753
Food production (1979-1981=100)	91	88	84	88	89	86	98	100	97	103	100
Daily protein supply (gm. per capita)	76	76	76	77	78	77	80	80	83	84	85
Population per hospital bed	141	..	..	..	..	..	..	..	..	..	..
per nursing person	..	..	232	..	..	..	..	188	..	..	..
per physician	1,068	..	..	..	..	..	..	950	..	..	..
Female participation in labor force (percent)	34	34	35	35	35	35	35	36	36	36	37
Infant mortality (per 1,000 live births)	66	62	58	56	55	53	52	50	49	48	47
Life expectancy (years)	67	67	68	68	68	69	69	69	69	70	70
Total fertility (births per woman)	5	5	5	5	5	4	4	4	4	4	4
Urban population (percent of total population)	34	34	34	34	34	34	34	34	34	34	34
Population per passenger car	..	..	..	..	..	..	..	..	..	..	..
per telephone	..	..	..	..	..	..	..	..	..	..	..

Abbreviations in notes column are explained in the General Notes. For sources and methods, see the Technical Notes.

1981	1982	1983	1984	1985	1986	1987	1988	1989	1990	Notes	Basic tables (continued)
				(index, 1980 = 100)							**TRADE PRICE INDEXES (ECE)**
..	..	..	..	..	..	..	..	..	..	.	Terms of trade
..	..	..	..	..	..	..	..	..	..	.	Exports
..	..	..	..	..	..	..	..	..	..	.	Imports
				(millions of current US dollars)							**Balance of Payments (ECE)**
151	136	114	108	91	96	100	107	133	123	f	Exports, convertible currency
173	202	157	142	120	96	99	141	219	228	f	Imports, convertible currency
-23	-65	-43	-34	-29	-1	1	-35	-87	-105	f	Trade balance, convertible currency
-10	-11	-4	-3	-1	-1	-7	-11	-21	-15	f	Invisibles, convertible currency
-12	-55	-39	-31	-28	1	8	-24	-66	-91	f	Current balance, convertible currency
..	..	..	..	..	..	..	..	..	..	.	External debt, total (World Bank)
..	..	..	..	..	..	..	..	..	..	.	Convertible currency
..	..	..	..	..	..	..	..	..	..	.	CMEA
..	..	..	..	..	..	..	..	..	..	.	External debt service (World Bank)
..	..	..	..	..	..	..	..	..	..	.	Convertible currency
..	..	..	..	..	..	..	..	..	..	.	Total reserves less gold (IMF, IFS)
..	..	..	..	..	..	..	..	..	..	.	Total reserves, including gold at London price
..	..	..	..	..	..	..	..	..	..	.	Total reserves, incl. gold at national valuation
				(thousands)							**EMPLOYMENT**
..	..	..	..	769	800	830	852	881	908	.	Employment, total
..	..	..	..	168	182	190	197	202	197	.	Agriculture
..	..	..	..	337	350	365	373	387	396	.	Industry
..	..	..	..	264	268	275	282	292	315	.	Services
1,249	1,286	1,323	1,361	1,398	1,437	1,475	1,514	1,552	1,591	.	Labor force, total
..	..	..	..	..	..	..	..	..	..	.	Agriculture
..	..	..	..	..	..	..	..	..	..	.	Industry
..	..	..	..	..	..	..	..	..	..	.	Services
				(millions of current Albanian leks)							**DOMESTIC FINANCE (IMF)**
2,704	2,688	2,980	3,045	3,173	3,403	3,647	3,931	4,514	5,464	.	Money supply, broadly defined
..	..						..			.	Money, means of payment
1,946	1,888	2,069	2,101	2,206	2,368	2,485	2,697	3,273	3,769	.	Demand deposits
..	..	..	..	..	..	..	..	..	..	.	Currency outside banks
..	..	..	..	..	..	..	..	..	..	.	Quasi-money
..	..	..	..	..	..	..	..	..	..	.	Interest: deposit rate (percent)
8,150	8,500	8,750	9,150	9,200	8,870	8,695	..	..	..	.	Central government expenditures
..	..	..	..	..	..	..	..	..	..	.	Defense
				(millions of 1989 US dollars)							
1,570	..	1,520	1,524	1,491	..	1,463	1,434	..	..	.	Central government exp. (ACDA)
180	169	158	168	163	..	162	163	157	..	.	Military (ACDA)
											LAND AND FORESTS (FAO)
244	250	256	261	267	272	278	..	..	..	.	Pop. density: agr. land (pop. per sq. km)
1	1	1	1	0	0	..	..	..	..	.	Deforestation rate (net)
10	10	10	10	10	10	..	..	..	..	.	Forest (thousands sq. km)
											SOCIAL INDICATORS
100	102	104	106	108	110	113	..	..	..	.	Population density: total land (pop. per sq. km)
..	..	..	104	103	101	100	99	99	..	.	School enrollment ratio, primary
..	..	..	65	72	73	76	77	80	..	.	secondary
..	6	7	7	7	7	8	8	..	..	.	tertiary
1,016	1,103	1,124	1,161	1,170	1,179	1,178	..	..	..	.	Energy consumption per capita (kg. of oil eq.)
2,767	2,771	2,770	2,770	2,760	2,749	2,739	2,741	..	..	.	Daily calorie supply per capita
98	100	103	101	98	97	96	96	96	..	.	Food production (1979-1981 = 100)
85	86	87	86	85	83	83	84	..	..	.	Daily protein supply (gm. per capita)
..	..	..	..	..	..	..	..	..	..	.	Population per hospital bed
..	..	..	..	..	..	..	..	..	..	.	per nursing person
..	..	..	..	..	..	..	..	..	..	.	per physician
37	37	37	38	38	38	39	39	39	39	.	Female participation in labor force (percent)
46	45	42	38	35	32	28	27	26	24	.	Infant mortality (per 1,000 live births)
70	70	71	71	71	71	72	72	72	72	.	Life expectancy (years)
4	3	3	3	3	3	3	3	3	3	.	Total fertility (births per woman)
34	34	34	34	34	34	35	35	35	35	.	Urban population (percent of total population)
..	..	..	..	..	..	..	..	..	..	.	Population per passenger car
..	..	..	..	..	..	..	..	..	..	.	per telephone

Bulgaria

Comparator tables	1970	1971	1972	1973	1974	1975	1976	1977	1978	1979	1980
PER CAPITA INCOME						*(US dollars)*					
World Bank (Atlas method)	..	..	..	..	..	..	..	..	..	..	..
Single year conversion	..	..	..	..	..	..	..	..	..	..	2,893
CIA or LWI	1,449	..	..	..	..	2,503	2,731	2,869	3,141	3,546	3,742
Penn World Tables	1,910	2,089	2,271	2,501	2,793	3,302	3,627	3,770	4,138	4,649	4,904
						(thousands)					
POPULATION	8,490	8,536	8,576	8,621	8,679	8,721	8,759	8,804	8,814	8,826	8,862
GROSS NATIONAL PRODUCT, current prices						*(millions of current US dollars)*					
World Bank (Atlas method)	..	..	..	..	..	..	..	..	..	..	
Single year conversion	..	..	..	..	..	..	..	..	..	..	25,639
Authors' series	..	..	..	..	..	..	..	..	..	..	26,000
CIA or LWI	..	..	..	..	..	..	..	..	..	28,870	30,570
GROSS NATIONAL PRODUCT, constant prices						*(millions of constant 1987 dollars)*					
Single year conversion	..	..	..	..	..	..	..	..	..	..	21,251
Authors' series, rescaled from 1980 prices	18,873	..	..	..	..	..	..	..	..	..	35,609
CIA or LWI, rescaled from 1989 prices	34,392	..	..	..	..	43,206	44,502	44,070	45,020	46,749	45,410
CONVERSION FACTORS						*(LCUs per US dollar)*					
World Bank (Atlas method)	..	..	..	..	..	..	..	..	..	..	..
Single year convertor	..	..	..	..	..	..	..	..	1.34	1.30	0.99
Authors' series	..	..	..	..	..	..	..	..	..	..	0.99
Penn World Tables	..	..	..	..	..	..	..	..	..	..	..
OUTPUT TRENDS, OVERALL						*(index, constant prices 1987 = 100)*					
GNP, SNA											76.5
NMP, MPS	38.5	40.8	44.6	47.6	51.4	55.9	59.7	63.5	67.3	71.8	75.6
GNP, "Building block"	70.7	73.1	76.6	79.6	82.0	88.8	91.5	90.6	92.5	96.1	93.3
Industry											
Value added, SNA	..	..	..	..	..	..	..	..	..	..	65.2
Value added, MPS	..	..	36.5	40.0	44.1	47.2	50.3	55.4	60.8	64.2	65.2
"Building block"	57.4	60.9	62.8	66.3	71.4	76.1	78.1	81.3	84.9	87.3	89.3
Gross output, SNA	55.7	..	..	..	..	73.9	..	..	..	..	87.0
Agriculture											
Value added, SNA	..	..	..	..	..	..	..	..	..	..	117.1
Value added, MPS	138.4	135.7	145.3	144.0	134.3	150.9	152.3	131.5	131.5	145.3	116.3
"Building block"	113.5	112.5	120.3	121.6	115.3	128.7	131.4	118.9	120.2	130.7	109.6
Gross output, SNA	88.3	90.1	96.9	94.6	87.0	92.7	100.0	92.8	98.2	105.3	99.1
Services											
Value added, SNA	..	..	..	..	..	..	..	..	..	..	86.4
Value added, MPS	..	..	6.9	10.9	22.9	24.7	32.6	48.3	48.0	50.6	88.6
"Building block"	63.4	66.3	69.3	72.8	76.8	82.4	86.1	86.4	86.4	87.3	89.1
CONSUMPTION											
Total consumption, SNA	..	..	..	..	..	..	..	..	..	..	..
Total consumption, MPS	45.0	48.2	51.3	54.9	58.5	63.0	67.1	69.8	72.0	74.3	77.0
Households, SNA	..	..	..	..	..	..	..	..	..	..	..
Households, "building block"	..	..	..	..	..	79.4	82.4	82.4	83.9	85.5	86.1
General government, SNA	..	..	..	..	..	..	..	..	..	..	70.3
General government, "building block"	..	..	..	..	..	83.1	86.9	87.2	87.9	89.0	92.4
INVESTMENT											
Gross fixed investment, SNA	..	..	..	..	..	..	..	..	..	..	80.7
Accumulation, MPS	..	..	..	..	..	..	..	..	..	..	62.9
"Building block"	..	..	..	..	..	208.3	186.9	178.1	160.4	160.0	135.8
CONSUMER PRICES											
National methodology	..	..	..	..	..	..	..	..	..	..	..
Outside estimate	51.5	53.1	54.8	55.9	58.5	59.8	61.9	65.1	67.2	70.8	83.0
MERCHANDISE EXPORTS						*(millions of current US dollars)*					
UNCTAD	2,004	..	..	..	..	4,691	..	..	..	..	10,372
IMF: IFS	..	..	..	..	..	..	..	..	..	..	10,400
ACDA	..	..	..	..	..	..	..	6,303	7,485	9,013	10,490
ECE	2,004	2,182	2,633	3,318	4,022	5,174	3,764	4,432	5,322	6,218	7,160
intra-CMEA	1,518	1,653	2,057	2,582	2,977	4,098	2,626	3,068	3,648	3,827	4,013
Authors' uniform TR/$ series	1,749	1,797	1,938	2,456	2,913	3,332	4,070	4,896	5,717	6,914	7,979
intra-CMEA	1,275	1,286	1,384	1,742	1,912	2,316	2,923	3,518	4,032	4,502	4,810
MERCHANDISE IMPORTS						*(millions of current US dollars)*					
UNCTAD	1,831	..	..	..	..	5,408	..	..	..	..	9,650
IMF: IFS	..	..	..	..	..	..	..	..	..	..	9,600
ACDA	..	..	..	..	..	..	..	6,344	7,658	8,580	9,776
ECE	1,831	2,120	2,572	3,288	4,520	5,911	4,003	4,464	5,377	5,744	6,321
intra-CMEA	1,337	1,575	2,008	2,549	3,120	4,318	2,652	3,121	3,898	4,040	4,180
Authors' uniform series	1,607	1,755	1,901	2,436	3,365	3,993	4,310	4,931	5,793	6,472	7,170
intra-CMEA	1,122	1,225	1,351	1,720	2,004	2,441	2,952	3,579	4,308	4,753	5,010

Abbreviations in notes column are explained in the General Notes. For sources and methods, see the Technical Notes.

1981	1982	1983	1984	1985	1986	1987	1988	1989	1990	Notes	*Comparator tables (continued)*
				(US dollars)							**PER CAPITA INCOME**
..	3,250	3,230	3,410	3,380	3,230	3,190	2,950	2,740	2,250	.	World Bank (Atlas method)
2,983	2,969	3,028	3,541	3,053	2,700	3,124	2,540	2,385	2,177	.	Single year conversion
4,197	4,597	4,673	4,995	4,990	5,255	5,423	5,562	5,744	5,533	.	CIA or LWI
5,506	6,011	6,150	6,477	6,621						.	Penn World Tables
				(thousands)							
8,878	8,894	8,909	8,925	8,941	8,917	8,894	8,870	8,846	8,823	.	**POPULATION**
			(millions of current US dollars)								**GROSS NATIONAL PRODUCT, current prices**
..	28,940	28,820	30,412	30,181	28,843	28,383	26,192	24,274	19,875	.	World Bank (Atlas method)
26,487	26,405	26,976	31,605	27,294	24,080	27,787	22,532	21,097	19,208	.	Single year conversion
..	..	..	..	..	..	..	23,000	..	..	D	Authors' series
34,420	37,810	38,540	41,270	41,220	43,410	44,870	47,970	49,590	..	.	CIA or LWI
			(millions of constant 1987 dollars)								**GROSS NATIONAL PRODUCT, constant prices**
22,428	22,892	23,884	24,749	25,320	26,339	27,787	28,423	28,102	24,705	.	Single year conversion
..	..	..	..	42,731	..	46,648	49,496	49,496	..	D	Authors' series, rescaled from 1980 prices
46,619	48,131	47,224	48,779	47,310	48,563	48,650	48,348	48,002	44,416	.	CIA or LWI, rescaled from 1989 prices
				(LCUs per US dollar)							**CONVERSION FACTORS**
..	0.99	1.03	1.04	1.08	1.19	1.27	1.44	1.58	2.04	..	World Bank (Atlas method)
1.04	1.09	1.10	1.00	1.19	1.42	1.30	1.67	1.82	2.11	.	Single year convertor
..	..	..	..	..	..	..	1.67	..	..	..	Authors' series
..	..	..	..	..	..	..	..	..	..	.	Penn World Tables
			(index, constant prices 1987 = 100)								**OUTPUT TRENDS, OVERALL**
80.7	82.4	86.0	89.1	91.1	94.8	100.0	102.3	101.1	88.9	.	GNP, SNA
79.4	82.7	85.2	89.0	90.7	95.5	100.0	102.4	102.1	..	f	NMP, MPS
95.8	98.9	97.1	100.3	97.2	99.8	100.0	99.4	98.7	91.3	.	GNP, "Building block"
											Industry
68.7	75.1	80.9	85.8	90.2	94.9	100.0	102.4	108.0	90.4	H	Value added, SNA
68.7	75.1	80.9	85.8	90.2	94.9	100.0	102.4	100.1	..	.	Value added, MPS
91.1	94.1	95.5	97.1	97.0	98.7	100.0	98.7	97.6	84.5	.	"Building block"
..	..	..	..	95.7	96.5	100.0	101.7	100.9	88.7	X	Gross output, SNA
											Agriculture
122.3	129.4	108.3	120.9	96.0	117.1	100.0	98.3	96.4	90.0	H	Value added, SNA
120.9	129.1	108.1	119.8	95.3	116.9	100.0	97.7	95.3	..	.	Value added, MPS
114.4	120.6	106.4	116.1	98.8	104.9	100.0	98.1	96.1	98.2	.	"Building block"
107.2	114.7	100.9	111.3	92.4	107.8	100.0	97.7	102.2	..	f	Gross output, SNA
											Services
90.0	77.8	86.2	79.7	88.8	83.0	100.0	104.9	90.7	89.8	H	Value added, SNA
91.9	80.3	86.2	79.7	88.8	83.0	100.0	104.9	116.0	..	f	Value added, MPS
91.1	92.3	93.5	95.0	96.6	98.2	100.0	101.2	101.8	97.1	.	"Building block"
											CONSUMPTION
..	..	80.1	79.1	86.7	90.6	100.0	96.7	99.0	94.8	.	Total consumption, SNA
81.0	84.1	86.5	90.7	92.3	95.6	100.0	102.2	105.2	..	.	Total consumption, MPS
..	..	80.0	79.3	85.8	88.6	100.0	95.8	97.5	96.6	.	Households, SNA
87.8	91.7	91.7	93.8	95.1	98.6	100.0	99.1	97.1	..	.	Households, "building block"
74.8	79.8	80.5	78.8	89.4	96.1	100.0	99.1	103.1	89.7	.	General government, SNA
94.2	95.0	95.5	96.6	97.6	98.8	100.0	100.7	100.7	..	.	General government, "building block"
											INVESTMENT
82.8	84.3	84.8	84.0	89.0	94.7	100.0	102.2	99.6	73.1	.	Gross fixed investment, SNA
63.5	79.6	73.4	62.6	60.9	56.9	100.0	57.5	51.0	..	.	Accumulation, MPS
154.2	145.6	124.2	135.0	114.6	142.9	100.0	112.7	91.2	..	.	"Building block"
											CONSUMER PRICES
..	..	..	..	..	..	..	..	..	..	.	National methodology
86.3	86.6	90.2	92.3	95.0	96.9	100.0	104.1	112.4	..	.	Outside estimate
			(millions of current US dollars)								**MERCHANDISE EXPORTS**
10,689	11,428	12,130	12,850	13,348	14,192	15,905	17,293	16,216	13,323	.	UNCTAD
10,700	11,400	12,100	12,900	13,300	14,000	15,900	17,300	16,200	..	G	IMF: IFS
10,490	11,500	12,220	12,530	12,780	14,520	16,660	20,350	16,040	..	.	ACDA
7,405	7,512	7,093	7,233	7,390	7,599	7,839	7,554	6,651	5,159	.	ECE
3,991	4,153	4,169	4,015	4,257	5,126	5,009	4,724	4,225	2,841	.	intra-CMEA
8,176	8,679	8,644	8,558	8,741	8,535	9,038	9,029	7,768	5,629	.	Authors' uniform TR/$ series
4,742	5,295	5,697	5,318	5,587	6,045	6,193	6,172	5,322	3,298	.	intra-CMEA
			(millions of current US dollars)								**MERCHANDISE IMPORTS**
10,801	11,527	12,283	12,714	13,656	15,249	16,211	16,706	15,176	12,897	F	UNCTAD
10,800	11,500	12,300	12,700	13,600	15,100	16,200	16,900	15,200	..	G	IMF: IFS
10,610	11,610	12,370	12,350	13,090	15,580	17,060	20,980	14,970	..	.	ACDA
7,174	7,256	6,957	6,831	7,568	8,679	8,220	8,130	7,326	5,484	.	ECE
4,430	4,554	4,400	4,196	4,361	5,115	4,946	4,162	3,467	2,604	.	intra-CMEA
8,024	8,529	8,597	8,217	8,951	9,612	9,408	9,429	8,242	5,911	.	Authors' uniform series
5,263	5,806	6,012	5,558	5,724	6,032	6,114	5,438	4,367	3,022	.	intra-CMEA

Bulgaria

	1970	1971	1972	1973	1974	1975	1976	1977	1978	1979	1980
SNA ACCOUNTS, current prices					*(millions of current Bulgarian leva)*						
GNP, at market prices	..	..	..	..	..	..	..	..	..	..	25,383
Net factor income	..	..	..	..	..	..	..	..	..	..	-408
GDP at market prices	..	..	..	..	..	..	..	..	..	..	25,791
Net indirect taxes	..	..	..	..	..	..	..	..	..	..	339
GDP at factor cost	..	..	..	..	..	..	..	..	..	..	25,452
Agriculture	..	..	..	..	..	..	..	..	..	..	3,719
Industry	..	..	..	..	..	..	..	..	..	..	13,869
Services, etc.	..	..	..	..	..	..	..	..	..	..	8,204
Resource balance	..	..	..	..	..	..	..	..	..	..	1,295
Exports GNFS	..	..	..	..	..	..	..	..	..	..	9,209
Imports GNFS	..	..	..	..	..	..	..	..	..	..	7,915
Domestic absorption	..	..	..	..	..	..	..	..	..	..	24,497
Total consumption	..	..	..	..	..	..	..	..	..	..	15,729
Private consumption	..	..	..	..	..	..	..	..	..	..	11,526
General government consumption	..	..	..	..	..	..	..	..	..	..	4,202
Gross domestic investment	..	..	..	..	..	..	..	..	..	..	8,768
Fixed domestic investment	..	..	..	..	..	..	..	..	..	..	7,289
Depreciation	..	..	..	..	..	..	..	..	..	..	..
SNA ACCOUNTS, constant prices					*(millions of constant 1987 Bulgarian leva)*						
Gross national product (GNP)	..	..	..	..	..	..	..	..	..	..	27,627
GDP at market prices	..	..	..	..	..	..	..	..	..	..	28,118
GDP at factor cost	..	..	..	..	..	..	..	..	..	..	27,748
Agriculture	..	..	..	..	..	..	..	..	..	..	5,046
Industry	..	..	..	..	..	..	..	..	..	..	14,630
Services, etc.	..	..	..	..	..	..	..	..	..	..	8,442
Resource balance	..	..	..	..	..	..	..	..	..	..	..
Exports GNFS	..	..	..	..	..	..	..	..	..	..	..
Imports GNFS	..	..	..	..	..	..	..	..	..	..	..
Domestic absorption	..	..	..	..	..	..	..	..	..	..	..
Total consumption, etc.	..	..	..	..	..	..	..	..	..	..	..
Private consumption, etc.	..	..	..	..	..	..	..	..	..	..	..
General government consumption	..	..	..	..	..	..	..	..	..	..	4,569
Gross domestic investment	..	..	..	..	..	..	..	..	..	..	9,533
Fixed domestic investment	..	..	..	..	..	..	..	..	..	..	7,925
Depreciation	..	..	..	..	..	..	..	..	..	..	..
MPS ACCOUNTS, current prices					*(millions of current Bulgarian leva)*						
NMP produced:	10,527	10,411	11,242	12,148	13,093	14,289	15,145	15,486	16,388	17,666	20,509
Agriculture and forestry	2,310	..	..	..	..	3,063	..	..	..	..	3,384
Industry excluding construction	5,168	..	..	..	..	7,291	..	..	..	..	9,939
Construction	917	..	..	..	..	1,257	..	..	..	..	1,905
Transport and communication	..	..	..	..	..	..	..	..	..	..	..
Trade, etc.	1,040	..	..	..	..	1,120	..	..	..	..	2,821
Other services	1,093	..	..	..	..	1,558	..	..	..	..	2,461
Resource balance	51	-76	-336	-418	-1,039	-1,392	-635	-635	-123	273	-405
NMP used: domestic market	10,476	10,487	11,578	12,566	14,132	15,681	15,780	16,121	16,511	17,393	20,914
Final consumption, material goods	7,416	8,024	8,491	9,085	9,783	10,586	11,263	11,930	12,553	13,701	15,705
Personal consumption	6,655	..	..	..	..	9,075	..	..	..	..	13,717
Collective consumption	762	..	..	..	..	1,512	..	..	..	..	1,988
Net capital formation	3,060	2,463	3,087	3,481	4,349	5,094	4,517	4,191	3,958	3,692	5,209
Net fixed capital formation	1,948	..	..	..	..	2,799	..	..	..	..	3,111
Changes in stocks	..	..	..	..	..	..	..	..	..	..	..
Depreciation	..	..	..	..	..	..	..	..	..	3,095	3,559
MPS ACCOUNTS, constant prices					*(millions of 1982 Bulgarian leva)*						
NMP produced:	10,616	11,241	12,281	13,114	14,155	15,404	16,445	17,485	18,526	19,775	20,816
Agriculture and forestry	..	..	4,901	4,854	4,527	5,087	5,134	4,434	4,434	4,901	3,921
Industry and construction	..	..	7,046	7,729	8,517	9,116	9,727	10,704	11,758	12,413	12,591
Services	..	..	335	531	1,111	1,200	1,584	2,347	2,334	2,461	4,304
Resource balance	-1,789	-1,378	-1,407	-1,857	-2,528	-3,204	-2,163	-2,191	-1,151	-757	-572
NMP used: domestic market	12,405	12,619	13,688	14,972	16,683	18,607	18,607	19,677	19,677	20,532	21,388
Final consumption, material goods	9,381	10,037	10,694	11,444	12,195	13,133	13,977	14,540	15,009	15,478	16,041
Personal consumption	..	..	..	..	..	..	..	..	..	..	13,909
Collective consumption	..	..	..	..	..	..	..	..	..	..	2,132
Net capital formation	2,906	2,557	3,109	3,603	4,475	5,318	4,708	5,144	4,650	4,882	5,347
Net fixed capital formation	..	..	..	..	..	..	..	..	..	..	3,111
Depreciation	..	..	..	..	..	..	..	..	..	..	..

Abbreviations in notes column are explained in the General Notes. For sources and methods, see the Technical Notes.

Basic tables (continued)

	1981	1982	1983	1984	1985	1986	1987	1988	1989	1990	Notes
(millions of current Bulgarian leva)												**SNA ACCOUNTS, current prices**
GNP, at market prices	27,546	28,781	29,674	31,605	32,480	34,194	36,123	37,629	38,397	40,529	.
Net factor income	-272	-232	-141	-66	-116	-230	-408	-717	-1,078	-1,471	.
GDP at market prices	27,818	29,013	29,815	31,671	32,595	34,424	36,531	38,345	39,475	42,000	.
Net indirect taxes	677	-22	31	51	151	585	-1,212	-1,881	-1,217	-1,917	.
GDP at factor cost	27,141	29,035	29,783	31,620	32,445	33,838	37,743	40,226	40,692	43,917	H
Agriculture	4,625	4,984	4,317	5,008	3,869	4,447	4,309	4,394	4,457	7,356	H
Industry	14,448	16,802	17,984	18,988	20,382	22,035	22,454	23,379	23,432	21,688	H
Services, etc.	8,745	7,228	7,514	7,675	8,344	7,942	9,768	10,572	11,586	12,956	H
Resource balance	295	309	57	489	-134	-1,216	-670	-128	-3	-657	.
Exports GNFS	9,823	9,947	11,009	12,075	13,519	13,944	14,892	17,481	17,190	16,751	.
Imports GNFS	9,529	9,637	10,953	11,586	13,653	15,161	15,562	17,609	17,193	17,409	.
Domestic absorption	27,523	28,704	29,758	31,182	32,729	35,640	37,201	38,473	39,478	42,657	.
Total consumption	17,651	18,973	19,951	20,666	22,234	23,290	25,181	25,276	26,374	30,301	.
Private consumption	13,057	13,976	14,945	15,630	16,510	17,048	18,685	18,688	19,305	22,875	.
General government consumption	4,595	4,997	5,006	5,036	5,725	6,242	6,497	6,587	7,069	7,426	.
Gross domestic investment	9,872	9,731	9,807	10,516	10,495	12,350	12,020	13,197	13,104	12,356	.
Fixed domestic investment	7,690	7,973	7,975	8,112	8,613	9,291	9,817	10,260	10,328	9,145	.
Depreciation	..	..	..	..	..	..	..	..	..	..	.
(millions of constant 1987 Bulgarian leva)												**SNA ACCOUNTS, constant prices**
Gross national product (GNP)	29,156	29,760	31,049	32,174	32,917	34,241	36,123	36,949	36,533	32,117	.
GDP at market prices	29,493	30,051	31,242	32,275	33,067	34,464	36,531	37,484	37,274	32,957	.
GDP at factor cost	28,776	30,073	31,210	32,224	32,914	33,879	37,743	39,323	38,427	34,462	H
Agriculture	5,271	5,577	4,666	5,211	4,136	5,048	4,309	4,235	4,153	3,877	H
Industry	15,430	16,872	18,161	19,275	20,257	21,309	22,454	23,000	24,259	20,308	H
Services, etc.	8,791	7,601	8,416	7,790	8,674	8,108	9,768	10,249	8,862	8,773	H
Resource balance	..	..	827	1,658	581	-696	-670	240	-54	-619	.
Exports GNFS	..	..	13,730	16,599	15,935	13,131	14,892	12,909	11,672	9,874	.
Imports GNFS	..	..	12,903	14,940	15,354	13,827	15,562	12,669	11,725	10,493	.
Domestic absorption	..	..	30,415	30,617	32,486	35,160	37,201	37,244	37,328	33,576	.
Total consumption, etc.	..	..	20,175	19,928	21,843	22,802	25,181	24,342	24,917	23,879	.
Private consumption, etc.	..	..	14,947	14,810	16,038	16,556	18,685	17,903	18,222	18,051	.
General government consumption	4,858	5,185	5,228	5,119	5,805	6,246	6,497	6,440	6,695	5,828	.
Gross domestic investment	10,439	10,095	10,240	10,689	10,643	12,358	12,020	12,902	12,411	9,697	.
Fixed domestic investment	8,131	8,272	8,327	8,245	8,734	9,297	9,817	10,030	9,781	7,177	.
Depreciation	..	..	..	..	..	..	..	..	..	..	.
(millions of current Bulgarian leva)												**MPS ACCOUNTS, current prices**
NMP produced:	21,933	22,850	23,479	24,907	25,451	26,851	28,338	29,423	30,840	..	.
Agriculture and forestry	4,186	4,520	3,864	4,512	3,425	3,957	3,712	3,712	3,798	..	.
Industry excluding construction	10,441	12,238	13,265	14,091	15,170	16,677	16,650	17,088	17,625	..	.
Construction	2,063	2,208	2,270	2,367	2,490	2,564	2,675	2,780	2,859	..	.
Transport and communication	..	..	..	..	..	..	..	..	..	..	.
Trade, etc.	2,767	1,384	1,529	1,328	1,801	1,227	2,500	2,471	2,910	..	.
Other services	2,476	2,501	2,550	2,610	2,565	2,426	2,802	3,371	3,648	..	.
Resource balance	-924	-785	-616	-396	-642	-2,088	-778	-979	0	..	.
NMP used: domestic market	22,857	23,634	24,095	25,303	26,093	28,940	29,166	30,402	30,840	..	.
Final consumption, material goods	16,718	17,532	18,299	19,148	20,063	21,351	22,401	23,096	24,809	..	.
Personal consumption	14,575	15,141	15,768	16,484	17,054	18,030	18,823	19,473	21,024	..	.
Collective consumption	2,144	2,392	2,530	2,663	3,008	3,320	3,578	3,623	3,785	..	.
Net capital formation	6,139	6,102	5,796	6,155	6,030	7,589	6,766	7,306	6,031	..	.
Net fixed capital formation	3,143	3,937	3,633	3,096	3,011	2,816	4,946	2,843	2,525	..	.
Changes in stocks	..	..	..	..	..	..	..	..	..	..	.
Depreciation	3,733	3,799	4,011	4,361	4,465	4,761	5,255	5,892	..	..	.
(millions of 1982 Bulgarian leva)												**MPS ACCOUNTS, constant prices**
NMP produced:	21,856	22,770	23,453	24,525	24,973	26,307	27,543	28,194	28,122	..	f
Agriculture and forestry	4,109	4,347	3,637	4,062	3,224	3,935	3,359	3,301	3,142	..	.
Industry and construction	13,280	14,521	15,630	16,589	17,434	18,339	19,324	19,795	19,343	..	.
Services	4,468	3,902	4,186	3,875	4,315	4,033	4,859	5,098	5,638	..	f
Resource balance	-1,165	-678	-287	-450	-292	-1,074	46	-314	0	..	f
NMP used: domestic market	23,022	23,448	23,740	24,975	25,265	27,381	27,497	28,508	28,122	..	f
Final consumption, material goods	16,886	17,517	18,024	18,903	19,242	19,928	20,841	21,296	21,919	..	.
Personal consumption	14,599	15,125	15,505	16,221	16,267	16,692	17,362	17,783	18,288	..	.
Collective consumption	2,286	2,392	2,519	2,681	2,976	3,236	3,479	3,514	3,631	..	.
Net capital formation	6,136	5,931	5,716	6,072	6,022	7,453	6,656	7,212	6,203	..	.
Net fixed capital formation	3,143	3,937	3,633	3,096	3,011	2,816	4,946	2,843	2,525	..	.
Depreciation	..	..	..	..	..	..	..	..	..	..	.

Bulgaria

Basic tables (continued)	1970	1971	1972	1973	1974	1975	1976	1977	1978	1979	1980
MPS ACCOUNTS, index					*(index,1980 = 100)*						
NMP produced:	51.0	54.0	59.0	63.0	68.0	74.0	79.0	84.0	89.0	95.0	100.0
Agriculture and forestry	119.1	116.7	125.0	123.8	115.5	129.8	130.9	113.1	113.1	125.0	100.0
Industry excluding construction	46.7	50.9	54.7	59.8	66.4	71.0	76.6	84.1	93.5	99.1	100.0
Construction	58.5	60.8	63.2	70.2	74.9	80.1	80.7	90.1	93.0	95.9	100.0
Transport and communication	45.3	49.8	54.3	69.7	69.7	76.9	84.2	88.2	93.7	97.7	100.0
Trade, etc.	18.8	20.4	24.2	29.5	33.8	38.6	43.7	51.2	37.7	45.8	100.0
NMP used: material goods	58.0	59.0	64.0	70.0	78.0	87.0	87.0	92.0	92.0	96.0	100.0
Final consumption	58.5	62.6	66.7	71.4	76.0	81.9	87.1	90.6	93.6	96.5	100.0
Net capital formation	54.4	47.8	58.1	67.4	83.7	99.5	88.0	96.2	87.0	91.3	100.0
EXCHANGE AND CONVERSION RATES					*(LCUs per US dollar: annual average)*						
Single-year converter	..	..	..	..	..	..	..	..	1.337	1.297	0.990
Devisa/official	1.170	1.170	1.078	0.988	0.970	0.969	0.966	0.948	0.892	0.865	0.857
Commercial	..	..	..	..	..	1.650	..	..	..	..	0.990
Noncommercial	..	..	..	..	..	1.200	..	..	..	..	1.290
Informal market	3.420	3.080	2.820	2.495	2.483	2.333	2.435	2.581	2.794	2.400	2.357
ICP	..	..	..	..	..	..	..	..	..	..	..
					(ruble per US dollar: annual average)						
Commercial TR/$ cross	..	..	..	..	..	1.660	..	..	..	..	0.990
Uniform TR/$ cross	1.072	1.157	1.232	1.093	1.092	1.167	1.067	1.022	0.973	0.945	0.980
					(LCUs per ruble: annual average)						
Commercial	1.000	..	..	..	..	1.000	..	..	..	..	1.000
Noncommercial	0.780	..	..	..	..	0.880	..	..	..	..	0.880
Devisa/official	1.300	1.300	1.300	1.300	1.300	1.300	1.300	1.300	1.300	1.300	1.300
CONSUMER PRICE INDEXES					*(index)*						
Official, IMF 1985 = 100	..	..	..	..	..	..	..	..	..	..	..
Official, CIA or LWI 1980 = 100	78.7	78.7	78.9	79.0	79.8	80.2	80.5	81.6	83.5	87.0	100.0
Alternative, CIA or LWI 1980 = 100	62.1	64.0	66.0	67.3	70.5	72.0	74.6	78.4	81.0	85.3	100.0
INTERNATIONAL TRADE (ECE)					*(millions of current Bulgarian leva)*						
Value of exports, fob	2,345	2,553	2,837	3,201	3,721	4,541	5,200	6,022	6,650	7,667	8,902
to CMEA	1,776	1,935	2,217	2,476	2,714	3,514	4,054	4,674	5,100	5,531	6,127
Value of imports, cif	2,142	2,480	2,772	3,172	4,196	5,236	5,436	6,062	6,801	7,363	8,283
from CMEA	1,564	1,843	2,164	2,444	2,845	3,703	4,095	4,755	5,449	5,839	6,383
Trade balance	202	73	65	29	-475	-694	-236	-40	-151	303	619
CMEA	212	91	53	31	-131	-189	-41	-81	-349	-309	-255
INTERNATIONAL TRADE (Authors')					*(millions of current US dollars)*						
Value of exports, fob	1,749	1,797	1,938	2,456	2,913	3,332	4,070	4,896	5,717	6,914	7,979
to developed countries	285	301	344	433	448	434	562	608	729	1,277	1,642
to other non-socialist countries	130	147	166	233	473	504	496	662	832	998	1,389
to socialist countries	1,334	1,349	1,428	1,789	1,992	2,394	3,011	3,627	4,156	4,639	4,948
to CMEA	1,275	1,286	1,384	1,742	1,912	2,316	2,923	3,518	4,032	4,502	4,810
Value of imports, cif	1,607	1,755	1,901	2,436	3,365	3,993	4,310	4,931	5,793	6,472	7,170
from developed countries	350	357	385	509	974	1,277	1,038	996	1,146	1,320	1,664
from other non-socialist countries	86	120	135	161	318	222	250	289	267	297	378
from socialist countries	1,171	1,278	1,381	1,766	2,073	2,493	3,022	3,646	4,380	4,855	5,128
from CMEA	1,122	1,225	1,351	1,720	2,004	2,441	2,952	3,579	4,308	4,753	5,010
Trade balance	142	42	37	19	-452	-660	-240	-34	-76	442	809
Developed countries	-65	-56	-41	-76	-526	-843	-475	-388	-417	-43	-22
Other non-socialist countries	44	27	31	72	154	282	246	373	565	701	1,011
Socialist countries	163	71	48	23	-81	-99	-11	-19	-224	-216	-180
CMEA	152	61	33	22	-92	-124	-29	-61	-276	-251	-200
PARTNER CONVERTIBLE TRADE (ECE)					*(millions of current US dollars)*						
Exports to non-CMEA (cif)	247	268	298	387	463	428	522	556	635	973	1,084
Imports from non-CMEA (fob)	349	352	384	537	914	1,154	1,003	943	1,147	1,308	1,710
Trade balance	-102	-84	-86	-150	-451	-726	-481	-387	-512	-335	-626
TRADE PRICE INDEXES (Authors')					*(index,1980 = 100)*						
Terms of trade	125.8	124.2	125.6	125.3	121.1	117.0	114.1	110.5	106.3	103.4	100.0
Exports	64.5	61.3	59.3	68.5	75.0	76.4	82.3	86.6	91.4	97.2	100.0
Non-socialist countries	..	..	..	..	..	..	..	..	..	..	..
Developed countries	..	..	..	..	..	..	..	..	..	..	..
Other	..	..	..	..	..	..	..	..	..	..	..
Socialist countries	..	..	..	..	..	..	..	..	..	..	..
CMEA	71.3	..	63.2	71.3	71.1	78.7	88.4	94.2	99.2	101.2	100.0
Imports	51.2	49.4	47.2	54.7	61.9	65.3	72.1	78.4	85.9	94.0	100.0
Non-socialist countries	..	..	..	..	..	..	..	..	..	..	..
Developed countries	..	..	..	..	..	..	..	..	..	..	..
Other	..	..	..	..	..	..	..	..	..	..	..
Socialist countries	..	..	..	..	..	..	..	..	..	..	..
CMEA	50.8	..	46.0	52.3	53.2	60.0	72.5	80.1	88.4	95.5	100.0

Abbreviations in notes column are explained in the General Notes. For sources and methods, see the Technical Notes.

1981	1982	1983	1984	1985	1986	1987	1988	1989	1990	Notes	Basic tables (continued)
				(index,1980 = 100)							**MPS ACCOUNTS, index**
105.0	109.0	113.0	118.0	120.0	126.0	133.0	136.0	135.0	..	.	NMP produced:
104.0	111.0	93.0	103.0	82.0	100.5	86.0	84.0	82.0	..	.	Agriculture and forestry
106.0	116.0	125.0	133.0	140.0	147.0	156.0	159.0	157.0	..	.	Industry excluding construction
108.0	116.0	119.0	124.0	130.0	133.0	139.0	144.0	145.0	..	.	Construction
110.0	115.0	118.0	123.0	122.0	127.0	133.0	148.0	154.0	..	.	Transport and communication
98.0	68.0	80.0	64.0	83.0	67.0	103.0	102.0	108.0	..	.	Trade, etc.
108.0	110.0	111.0	117.0	119.0	130.0	130.0	135.0	127.0	..	.	NMP used: material goods
105.0	109.0	112.0	118.0	122.0	126.0	132.0	135.0	137.0	..	.	Final consumption
115.0	111.0	107.0	114.0	113.0	140.0	125.0	135.0	99.0	..	.	Net capital formation
				(LCUs per US dollar: annual average)							**EXCHANGE AND CONVERSION RATES**
1.040	1.090	1.100	1.000	1.190	1.420	1.300	1.670	1.820	2.110	.	Single-year converter
0.922	0.951	0.974	1.010	1.030	0.940	0.870	0.830	0.840	..	f	Devisa/official
..	..	..	..	1.190	1.420	1.300	1.670	1.820	..	f	Commercial
..	..	..	..	1.860	1.700	1.280	1.670	1.820	..	f	Noncommercial
2.669	2.989	3.297	3.773	4.756	4.219	4.000	5.419	7.729	..	.	Informal market
..	..	..	..	..	..	..	..	..	..	.	ICP
				(ruble per US dollar: annual average)							
..	..	..	..	1.190	1.350	1.240	1.590	1.730	..	.	Commercial TR/$ cross
1.076	1.105	1.201	1.395	1.433	1.388	1.397	1.484	1.660	1.980	.	Uniform TR/$ cross
				(LCUs per ruble: annual average)							
..	..	..	..	1.000	1.050	1.050	1.050	1.050	..	f	Commercial
..	..	..	..	1.000	1.000	1.000	1.000	1.000	..	.	Noncommercial
1.300	1.300	1.300	1.300	1.300	1.300	1.300	1.300	1.300	..	L	Devisa/official
				(index)							**CONSUMER PRICE INDEXES**
..	..	..	..	..	..	..	..	..	..	.	Official, IMF 1985 = 100
100.5	100.8	102.3	102.9	105.0	109.4	109.4	110.9	119.6	..	f	Official, CIA or LWI 1980 = 100
104.0	104.3	108.6	111.2	114.4	116.8	120.5	125.4	135.4	..	.	Alternative, CIA or LWI 1980 = 100
				(millions of current Bulgarian leva)							**INTERNATIONAL TRADE (ECE)**
9,860	10,880	11,818	12,987	13,739	13,351	13,802	14,417	13,673	10,496	.	Value of exports, fob
6,633	7,607	8,895	9,643	10,408	10,907	11,247	11,907	11,484	8,489	.	to CMEA
9,958	10,976	11,966	12,842	14,067	14,353	14,067	13,928	12,796	10,160	.	Value of imports, cif
7,362	8,341	9,386	10,079	10,663	10,885	11,104	10,491	9,425	7,780	.	from CMEA
-98	-96	-149	145	-327	-1,003	-265	489	877	336	.	Trade balance
-729	-734	-491	-436	-255	23	143	1,416	2,060	709	.	CMEA
				(millions of current US dollars)							**INTERNATIONAL TRADE (Authors')**
8,176	8,679	8,644	8,558	8,741	8,535	9,038	9,029	7,768	5,629	.	Value of exports, fob
1,438	1,300	1,267	1,168	1,133	981	1,074	1,110	1,302	1,140	.	to developed countries
1,869	1,968	1,591	1,984	1,930	1,401	1,690	1,631	1,048	1,095	.	to other non-socialist countries
4,869	5,410	5,786	5,406	5,679	6,153	6,274	6,288	5,418	3,393	.	to socialist countries
4,742	5,295	5,697	5,318	5,587	6,045	6,193	6,172	5,322	3,298	.	to CMEA
8,024	8,529	8,597	8,217	8,951	9,612	9,408	9,429	8,242	5,911	.	Value of imports, cif
2,157	1,920	1,712	1,754	2,076	2,343	2,470	2,580	2,597	1,902	.	from developed countries
499	708	768	808	1,064	1,134	724	1,312	1,199	927	.	from other non-socialist countries
5,368	5,901	6,117	5,654	5,811	6,136	6,214	5,537	4,447	3,081	.	from socialist countries
5,263	5,806	6,012	5,558	5,724	6,032	6,114	5,438	4,367	3,022	.	from CMEA
152	150	47	341	-210	-1,078	-370	-400	-474	-282	.	Trade balance
-718	-619	-445	-586	-943	-1,362	-1,396	-1,470	-1,295	-762	.	Developed countries
1,369	1,260	824	1,175	866	268	966	318	-151	168	.	Other non-socialist countries
-499	-491	-331	-248	-133	17	60	752	971	312	.	Socialist countries
-521	-511	-315	-240	-137	13	79	734	954	275	.	CMEA
				(millions of current US dollars)							**PARTNER CONVERTIBLE TRADE (ECE)**
948	894	783	803	786	808	831	843	920	..	.	Exports to non-CMEA (cif)
1,967	1,641	1,680	1,573	1,984	2,320	2,475	2,495	2,420	..	.	Imports from non-CMEA (fob)
-1,019	-747	-897	-770	-1,198	-1,512	-1,644	-1,652	-1,500	..	.	Trade balance
				(index,1980 = 100)							**TRADE PRICE INDEXES (Authors')**
92.4	85.4	85.0	86.0	83.0	81.4	85.2	87.3	83.8	84.7	.	Terms of trade
94.6	90.2	86.0	81.3	77.4	78.4	81.5	79.6	70.0	66.9	.	Exports
..	..	..	..	..	..	..	..	..	..	.	Non-socialist countries
..	..	..	..	..	..	..	..	..	..	.	Developed countries
..	..	..	..	..	..	..	..	..	..	.	Other
..	..	..	..	..	..	..	..	..	..	.	Socialist countries
93.0	90.1	88.3	80.5	77.6	82.7	83.9	..	..	..	.	CMEA
102.4	105.5	101.1	94.6	93.2	96.4	95.7	91.1	83.5	79.0	.	Imports
..	..	..	..	..	..	..	..	..	..	.	Non-socialist countries
..	..	..	..	..	..	..	..	..	..	.	Developed countries
..	..	..	..	..	..	..	..	..	..	.	Other
..	..	..	..	..	..	..	..	..	..	.	Socialist countries
103.3	112.1	109.8	100.3	100.3	105.3	104.6	..	..	..	.	CMEA

Basic tables (continued)	1970	1971	1972	1973	1974	1975	1976	1977	1978	1979	1980
TRADE PRICE INDEXES (ECE)					*(index, 1980 = 100)*						
Terms of trade	124	131	123	121	119	104	103	101	99	98	100
Exports	62	67	70	78	88	104	73	77	83	92	100
Imports	50	51	57	65	74	101	71	76	84	93	100
Balance of Payments (ECE)					*(millions of current US dollars)*						
Exports, convertible currency	487	489	541	682	917	985	1,054	1,220	1,530	2,362	3,338
Imports, convertible currency	468	524	567	758	1,070	1,757	1,458	1,544	1,472	1,827	2,532
Trade balance, convertible currency	19	-35	-26	-76	-153	-772	-404	-324	58	535	806
Invisibles, convertible currency	-26	-34	1	0	-28	-80	-18	52	18	67	101
Current balance, convertible currency	-7	-69	-25	-76	-181	-852	-422	-272	76	602	907
External debt, total (World Bank)	..	..	..	..	..	..	..	..	..	..	..
Convertible currency	..	..	..	..	..	..	..	..	..	..	..
CMEA	..	..	..	..	..	..	..	..	..	..	..
External debt service (World Bank)	..	..	..	..	..	..	..	..	..	..	..
Convertible currency	..	..	..	..	..	..	..	..	..	..	..
Total reserves less gold (IMF, IFS)	..	..	..	..	..	..	..	..	..	..	..
Total reserves, including gold at London price	..	..	..	..	..	..	..	..	..	..	..
Total reserves, incl. gold at national valuation	..	..	..	..	..	..	..	..	..	..	1,396
EMPLOYMENT					*(thousands)*						
Employment, total	4,151	..	..	..	..	..	..	..	..	..	4,364
Agriculture	1,462	..	..	..	..	..	..	..	..	..	1,039
Industry	1,608	..	..	..	..	..	..	..	..	..	1,892
Services	1,081	..	..	..	..	..	..	..	..	..	1,433
Labor force, total	4,414	4,430	4,447	4,463	4,479	4,496	4,493	4,490	4,487	4,483	4,480
Agriculture	1,535	1,467	1,398	1,329	1,261	1,192	1,116	1,039	963	887	810
Industry	1,667	1,707	1,747	1,786	1,826	1,866	1,899	1,933	1,966	2,000	2,033
Services	1,211	1,257	1,302	1,347	1,393	1,438	1,478	1,518	1,557	1,597	1,637
DOMESTIC FINANCE (IMF)					*(millions of current Bulgarian leva)*						
Money supply, broadly defined	..	..	..	..	..	..	..	..	..	..	..
Money, means of payment	..	..	..	..	..	..	..	..	..	..	..
Demand deposits	..	..	..	..	..	..	..	..	..	..	..
Currency outside banks	..	..	..	..	..	..	..	..	..	..	..
Quasi-money	..	..	..	..	..	..	..	..	..	..	..
Interest: deposit rate (percent)	..	..	..	..	..	..	..	..	..	..	..
Central government expenditures	..	..	..	..	..	9,076	..	..	..	..	12,882
Defense	..	..	..	..	..	..	..	..	..	..	..
					(millions of 1989 US dollars)						
Central government exp. (ACDA)	..	..	..	..	..	..	..	..	..	17,320	16,930
Military (ACDA)	..	..	..	..	..	..	..	..	..	5,739	5,883
LAND AND FORESTS (FAO)											
Pop. density: agr. land (pop. per sq. km)	141	142	142	144	144	146	141	142	142	142	143
Deforestation rate (net)	1	1	1	1	0	0	0	0	0	0	0
Forest (thousands sq. km)	37	37	38	38	38	38	38	38	38	38	38
SOCIAL INDICATORS											
Population density: total land (pop. per sq. km)	77	77	78	78	79	79	79	80	80	80	80
School enrollment ratio, primary	101	..	..	..	..	99	99	99	97	96	98
secondary	79	..	..	..	..	89	90	90	89	87	84
tertiary	..	..	..	..	..	..	..	..	..	..	16
Energy consumption per capita (kg. of oil eq.)	2,657	2,759	2,849	3,025	3,131	3,353	3,424	3,565	3,761	3,956	4,182
Daily calorie supply per capita	3,471	3,553	3,501	3,503	3,479	3,523	3,614	3,512	3,589	3,601	3,608
Food production (1979-1981=100)	88	90	95	93	83	89	96	90	94	101	95
Daily protein supply (gm. per capita)	96	98	99	98	99	102	104	101	104	104	105
Population per hospital bed	129	..	..	..	..	..	..	..	..	..	90
per nursing person	..	..	..	239	..	..	..	..	..	..	..
per physician	537	..	..	..	..	..	..	..	..	..	407
Female participation in labor force (percent)	46	46	46	47	47	47	47	47	47	47	47
Infant mortality (per 1,000 live births)	27	25	26	26	26	23	24	24	22	21	20
Life expectancy (years)	71	71	71	71	71	71	71	71	71	71	71
Total fertility (births per woman)	2	2	2	2	2	2	2	2	2	2	2
Urban population (percent of total population)	52	53	54	55	56	58	58	59	60	61	61
Population per passenger car	..	..	..	..	..	..	..	..	..	..	..
per telephone	..	..	..	..	..	11	..	..	..	..	7

Abbreviations in notes column are explained in the General Notes. For sources and methods, see the Technical Notes.

	1981	1982	1983	1984	1985	1986	1987	1988	1989	1990	Notes
TRADE PRICE INDEXES (ECE) *(index, 1980 = 100)*											
Terms of trade	97	92	88	86	83	79	83	80	..	..	.
Exports	102	97	86	81	80	86	85	79	..	..	.
Imports	105	105	98	94	96	109	103	99	..	..	.
Balance of Payments (ECE) *(millions of current US dollars)*											
Exports, convertible currency	3,360	3,103	2,719	3,299	3,307	2,656	3,277	3,539	3,138	2,488	S
Imports, convertible currency	3,074	2,630	2,653	3,011	3,694	3,488	4,232	4,511	4,337	3,285	S
Trade balance, convertible currency	286	473	66	288	-387	-832	-955	-972	-1,199	-797	.
Invisibles, convertible currency	276	340	226	439	302	117	182	132	-107	-314	.
Current balance, convertible currency	562	813	292	727	-85	-715	-773	-840	-1,306	-1,111	f
External debt, total (World Bank)	..	..	..	..	..	5,244	7,072	9,128	10,213	10,927	.
Convertible currency	..	..	..	..	..	5,244	7,072	9,128	10,213	10,927	.
CMEA	..	..	..	..	..	475	455	670	792	801	.
External debt service (World Bank)	..	..	..	..	..	2,767	2,644	2,582	3,088	1,341	f
Convertible currency	..	..	..	..	..	2,767	2,644	2,582	3,088	1,341	f
Total reserves less gold (IMF, IFS)	..	..	..	..	..	..	..	..	..	..	.
Total reserves, including gold at London price	..	..	..	..	..	..	..	..	..	..	.
Total reserves, incl. gold at national valuation	..	..	..	..	2,136	1,522	1,199	1,801	1,381	..	.
EMPLOYMENT *(thousands)*											
Employment, total	..	..	..	..	4,460	4,473	4,487	4,468	4,327	..	.
Agriculture	..	..	..	..	910	890	859	834	786	..	.
Industry	..	..	..	..	2,037	2,057	2,083	2,069	1,985	..	.
Services	..	..	..	..	1,513	1,526	1,545	1,565	1,557	..	.
Labor force, total	4,481	4,481	4,482	4,483	4,483	4,481	4,480	4,478	4,476	4,475	.
Agriculture	..	..	..	..	..	..	..	..	..	..	.
Industry	..	..	..	..	..	..	..	..	..	..	.
Services	..	..	..	..	..	..	..	..	..	..	.
DOMESTIC FINANCE (IMF) *(millions of current Bulgarian leva)*											
Money supply, broadly defined	..	..	..	..	..	..	..	..	..	..	.
Money, means of payment	..	..	..	..	..	13,213	15,469	17,260	19,855	21,643	.
Demand deposits	..	..	..	..	..	9,835	11,455	12,529	13,886	13,977	.
Currency outside banks	..	..	..	..	..	3,378	4,014	4,731	5,969	7,666	.
Quasi-money	..	..	..	..	..	18,100	18,258	19,811	20,902	27,902	.
Interest: deposit rate (percent)	..	..	..	..	..	2	2	2	2	2	.
Central government expenditures	14,830	15,856	16,008	16,449	18,002	21,143	28,342	28,813	29,521	25,284	.
Defense	..	..	..	..	..	..	1,922	1,934	1,933	..	.
(millions of 1989 US dollars)											
Central government exp. (ACDA)	19,470	20,160	19,470	20,000	20,320	23,850	23,540	19,690	19,800	..	.
Military (ACDA)	5,936	6,507	6,498	6,460	6,612	6,897	6,938	6,109	5,885	..	U
LAND AND FORESTS (FAO)											
Pop. density: agr. land (pop. per sq. km)	144	144	144	145	145	145	144	144	143	..	.
Deforestation rate (net)	0	0	0	0	0	0	0	0	0	..	.
Forest (thousands sq. km)	39	39	39	39	39	39	39	39	39	..	.
SOCIAL INDICATORS											
Population density: total land (pop. per sq. km)	80	81	81	81	81	81	80	80	80	..	.
School enrollment ratio, primary	..	102	102	102	102	104	104	104	97	..	.
secondary	..	82	86	92	102	75	76	75	75	..	.
tertiary	..	15	16	17	19	21	23	25	26	..	.
Energy consumption per capita (kg. of oil eq.)	4,219	4,381	4,447	4,490	4,559	4,681	4,798	4,869	4,801	4,945	.
Daily calorie supply per capita	3,682	3,670	3,639	3,640	3,615	3,654	3,674	3,672	3,707	..	.
Food production (1979-1981=100)	104	111	98	106	87	103	94	95	102	92	.
Daily protein supply (gm. per capita)	107	107	108	108	108	109	110	110	111	..	.
Population per hospital bed	90	..	..	..	..	..	..	..	..	..	.
per nursing person	190	188	..	155	..	..	..	..	..	..	.
per physician	400	385	..	276	..	..	..	..	..	..	.
Female participation in labor force (percent)	46	46	46	46	45	45	45	45	45	45	.
Infant mortality (per 1,000 live births)	20	18	17	16	15	15	15	14	14	13	.
Life expectancy (years)	71	71	72	72	72	72	72	72	72	73	.
Total fertility (births per woman)	2	2	2	2	2	2	2	2	2	2	.
Urban population (percent of total population)	62	63	63	64	65	65	66	66	67	68	.
Population per passenger car	..	..	..	..	9	8	8	8	7	..	.
per telephone	6	5	..	..	..	..	..	..	..	..	.

Comparator tables	1970	1971	1972	1973	1974	1975	1976	1977	1978	1979	1980
PER CAPITA INCOME						*(US dollars)*					
World Bank (Atlas method)	..	..	..	..	..	..	..	..	..	..	..
Single year conversion	..	..	..	..	..	..	..	..	..	..	..
CIA or LWI	..	..	..	..	..	..	..	..	..	..	..
Penn World Tables	..	..	..	..	..	..	..	..	..	..	..
POPULATION	6,938	6,970	7,002	7,034	7,066	*(thousands)* 7,098	6,937	6,780	6,585	6,443	6,400
GROSS NATIONAL PRODUCT, current prices						*(millions of current US dollars)*					
World Bank (Atlas method)	887	861	679	609	566	..	..	..	..	..	..
Single year conversion	718	916	507	702	..	..	..	..	..	..	..
Authors' series	..	..	..	..	..	..	..	..	..	..	..
CIA or LWI	..	..	..	..	..	..	..	..	..	..	..
GROSS NATIONAL PRODUCT, constant prices						*(millions of constant 1987 dollars)*					
Single year conversion	..	..	..	..	..	..	..	..	..	..	..
Authors' series, rescaled from 1980 prices	..	..	..	..	..	..	..	..	..	..	..
CIA or LWI, rescaled from 1989 prices	..	..	..	..	..	..	..	..	..	..	..
CONVERSION FACTORS						*(LCUs per US dollar)*					
World Bank (Atlas method)	..	..	..	..	..	..	..	..	..	..	..
Single year convertor	55.54	75.82	162.25	244.92	..	..	..	..	..	..	..
Authors' series	..	..	..	..	..	..	..	..	..	..	..
Penn World Tables	..	..	..	..	..	..	..	..	..	..	..
OUTPUT TRENDS, OVERALL						*(index, constant prices 1987 = 100)*					
GNP, SNA	..	..	..	..	..	..	..	..	..	..	..
NMP, MPS	..	..	..	..	..	..	..	..	..	..	..
GNP, "Building block"	..	..	..	..	..	..	..	..	..	..	..
Industry											
Value added, SNA	..	..	..	..	..	..	..	..	..	..	..
Value added, MPS	..	..	..	..	..	..	..	..	..	..	..
"Building block"	..	..	..	..	..	..	..	..	..	..	..
Gross output, SNA	..	..	..	..	..	..	..	..	..	..	..
Agriculture											
Value added, SNA	..	..	..	..	..	..	85.1	87.5	75.0	49.4	67.3
Value added, MPS	..	..	..	..	..	..	..	..	..	..	..
"Building block"	..	..	..	..	..	..	..	..	..	..	..
Gross output, SNA	157.5	122.7	99.0	71.3	56.8	79.7	84.5	88.0	75.5	47.5	68.8
Services											
Value added, SNA	..	..	..	..	..	..	..	..	..	..	..
Value added, MPS	..	..	..	..	..	..	..	..	..	..	..
"Building block"	..	..	..	..	..	..	..	..	..	..	..
CONSUMPTION											
Total consumption, SNA	..	..	..	..	..	..	..	..	..	..	..
Total consumption, MPS	..	..	..	..	..	..	..	..	..	..	..
Households, SNA	..	..	..	..	..	..	..	..	..	..	..
Households, "building block"	..	..	..	..	..	..	..	..	..	..	..
General government, SNA	..	..	..	..	..	..	..	..	..	..	..
General government, "building block"	..	..	..	..	..	..	..	..	..	..	..
INVESTMENT											
Gross fixed investment, SNA	..	..	..	..	..	..	..	..	..	..	..
Accumulation, MPS	..	..	..	..	..	..	..	..	..	..	..
"Building block"	..	..	..	..	..	..	..	..	..	..	..
CONSUMER PRICES											
National methodology	..	..	..	..	..	..	..	..	..	..	..
Outside estimate	..	..	..	..	..	..	..	..	..	..	..
MERCHANDISE EXPORTS						*(millions of current US dollars)*					
UNCTAD	..	..	..	..	..	6	..	..	..	..	30
IMF: IFS	39	..	..	..	..	..	..	..	..	..	..
ACDA	..	..	..	..	..	..	..	..	1	..	..
ECE	..	..	..	..	..	..	..	..	..	..	..
intra-CMEA	..	..	..	..	..	..	..	..	..	..	..
Authors' uniform TR/$ series	..	..	..	..	..	6	..	..	..	..	30
intra-CMEA	..	..	..	..	..	..	..	..	..	..	..
MERCHANDISE IMPORTS						*(millions of current US dollars)*					
UNCTAD	52	..	..	..	..	..	..	..	..	..	..
IMF: IFS	54	..	..	..	..	..	..	..	..	..	..
ACDA	..	..	..	..	..	..	..	..	20	..	..
ECE	..	..	..	..	..	..	..	..	..	..	..
intra-CMEA	..	..	..	..	..	..	..	..	..	..	..
Authors' uniform series	..	..	..	..	..	..	..	..	..	..	..
intra-CMEA	..	..	..	..	..	..	..	..	..	..	..

Abbreviations in notes column are explained in the General Notes. For sources and methods, see the Technical Notes.

1981	1982	1983	1984	1985	1986	1987	1988	1989	1990	Notes	*Comparator tables (continued)*
				(US dollars)							**PER CAPITA INCOME**
..	..	..	..	..	..	..	..	..	..	.	World Bank (Atlas method)
..	..	..	..	..	..	..	..	159	156	E	Single year conversion
103	..	..	..	..	..	..	..	..	..	A	CIA or LWI
..	..	..	..	..	..	..	..	..	..	.	Penn World Tables
				(thousands)							**POPULATION**
6,568	6,740	6,917	7,098	7,284	7,472	7,662	7,854	8,048	8,243	.	
			(millions of current US dollars)								**GROSS NATIONAL PRODUCT, current prices**
..	..	..	..	..	..	..	..	..	..	.	World Bank (Atlas method)
..	..	..	..	..	..	..	..	..	..	.	Single year conversion
..	..	..	..	..	..	..	..	1,280	1,288	.	Authors' series
600	..	..	..	..	..	..	..	..	..	.	CIA or LWI
			(millions of constant 1987 dollars)								**GROSS NATIONAL PRODUCT, constant prices**
..	..	..	..	..	..	..	..	..	..	.	Single year conversion
..	..	..	..	..	..	..	..	..	..	.	Authors' series, rescaled from 1980 prices
781	..	..	..	..	..	..	..	..	..	A	CIA or LWI, rescaled from 1989 prices
				(LCUs per US dollar)							**CONVERSION FACTORS**
..	..	..	..	..	..	..	..	..	..	.	World Bank (Atlas method)
..	..	..	..	..	..	..	..	..	..	.	Single year convertor
..	..	..	..	..	..	..	..	..	..	.	Authors' series
..	..	..	..	..	..	..	..	..	..	.	Penn World Tables
			(index, constant prices 1987 = 100)								**OUTPUT TRENDS, OVERALL**
..	..	..	..	..	..	..	..	..	..	.	GNP, SNA
..	..	..	..	..	..	..	..	..	..	.	NMP, MPS
..	..	..	..	..	..	..	..	..	..	.	GNP, "Building block"
											Industry
..	..	..	..	..	..	..	..	..	..	.	Value added, SNA
..	..	..	..	..	..	..	..	..	..	.	Value added, MPS
..	..	..	..	..	..	..	..	..	..	.	"Building block"
..	..	..	..	..	..	..	..	..	..	.	Gross output, SNA
											Agriculture
61.9	69.6	83.3	92.3	100.0	101.2	100.0	105.4	..	..	E	Value added, SNA
..	..	..	..	..	..	..	..	..	..	.	Value added, MPS
..	..	..	..	..	..	..	..	..	..	.	"Building block"
60.8	69.0	84.1	94.5	103.4	103.2	100.0	114.8	110.8	..	f	Gross output, SNA
											Services
..	..	..	..	..	..	..	..	..	..	.	Value added, SNA
..	..	..	..	..	..	..	..	..	..	.	Value added, MPS
..	..	..	..	..	..	..	..	..	..	.	"Building block"
											CONSUMPTION
					..	..	..	..	..	.	Total consumption, SNA
										.	Total consumption, MPS
										.	Households, SNA
										.	Households, "building block"
					..	..	..	..	..	.	General government, SNA
										.	General government, "building block"
											INVESTMENT
					..	..	..	..	..	E	Gross fixed investment, SNA
										.	Accumulation, MPS
										.	"Building block"
											CONSUMER PRICES
..	..	..	..	..	..	..	..	..	..	.	National methodology
..	..	..	..	..	..	..	..	..	..	.	Outside estimate
				(millions of current US dollars)							**MERCHANDISE EXPORTS**
15	16	16	16	16	16	17	17	..	..	.	UNCTAD
..	..	..	..	..	..	..	..	..	..	.	IMF: IFS
..	..	10	..	3	3	..	..	..	..	.	ACDA
..	..	..	..	..	..	..	..	..	..	N	ECE
											intra-CMEA
15	16	16	16	16	16	17	17	..	..	N	Authors' uniform TR/$ series
..	..	..	..	..	..	..	..	..	..	.	intra-CMEA
				(millions of current US dollars)							**MERCHANDISE IMPORTS**
..	..	..	..	..	..	..	..	..	..	M	UNCTAD
..	..	..	..	..	..	..	..	..	..	.	IMF: IFS
..	..	30	..	28	17	..	..	..	..	.	ACDA
..	..	..	..	..	..	..	..	..	..	.	ECE
..	..	..	..	..	..	..	..	..	..	.	intra-CMEA
..	..	..	..	..	..	..	..	..	..	.	Authors' uniform series
..	..	..	..	..	..	..	..	..	..	.	intra-CMEA

Cambodia

Basic tables	1970	1971	1972	1973	1974	1975	1976	1977	1978	1979	1980
SNA ACCOUNTS, current prices	*(billions of current Kampuchean riels)*										
GNP, at market prices	..	..	..	..	..	..	..	..	..	..	..
Net factor income	..	..	..	..	..	..	..	..	..	..	..
GDP at market prices	..	..	..	..	..	..	..	..	..	..	..
Net indirect taxes	..	..	..	..	..	..	..	..	..	..	..
GDP at factor cost	..	..	..	..	..	..	..	..	..	..	..
Agriculture	..	..	..	..	..	..	..	..	..	..	..
Industry	..	..	..	..	..	..	..	..	..	..	..
Services, etc.	..	..	..	..	..	..	..	..	..	..	..
Resource balance	..	..	..	..	..	..	..	..	..	..	..
Exports GNFS	..	..	..	..	..	..	..	..	..	..	..
Imports GNFS	..	..	..	..	..	..	..	..	..	..	..
Domestic absorption	..	..	..	..	..	..	..	..	..	..	..
Total consumption	..	..	..	..	..	..	..	..	..	..	..
Private consumption	..	..	..	..	..	..	..	..	..	..	..
General government consumption	..	..	..	..	..	..	..	..	..	..	..
Gross domestic investment	..	..	..	..	..	..	..	..	..	..	..
Fixed domestic investment	..	..	..	..	..	..	..	..	..	..	..
Depreciation	..	..	..	..	..	..	..	..	..	..	..
SNA ACCOUNTS, constant prices	*(billions of constant 1989 Kampuchean riels)*										
Gross national product (GNP)	..	..	..	..	..	..	..	..	..	..	..
GDP at market prices	..	..	..	..	..	..	..	..	..	..	..
GDP at factor cost	..	..	..	..	..	..	..	..	..	..	..
Agriculture	..	..	..	..	..	..	..	..	..	..	..
Industry	..	..	..	..	..	..	..	..	..	..	..
Services, etc.	..	..	..	..	..	..	..	..	..	..	..
Resource balance	..	..	..	..	..	..	..	..	..	..	..
Exports GNFS	..	..	..	..	..	..	..	..	..	..	..
Imports GNFS	..	..	..	..	..	..	..	..	..	..	..
Domestic absorption	..	..	..	..	..	..	..	..	..	..	..
Total consumption, etc.	..	..	..	..	..	..	..	..	..	..	..
Private consumption, etc.	..	..	..	..	..	..	..	..	..	..	..
General government consumption	..	..	..	..	..	..	..	..	..	..	..
Gross domestic investment	..	..	..	..	..	..	..	..	..	..	..
Fixed domestic investment	..	..	..	..	..	..	..	..	..	..	..
Depreciation	..	..	..	..	..	..	..	..	..	..	..
MPS ACCOUNTS, current prices	*(millions of current Kampuchean riels)*										
NMP produced:											
Agriculture and forestry	..	..	..	..	..	..	..	..	..	..	..
Industry excluding construction	..	..	..	..	..	..	..	..	..	..	..
Construction	..	..	..	..	..	..	..	..	..	..	..
Transport and communication	..	..	..	..	..	..	..	..	..	..	..
Trade, etc.	..	..	..	..	..	..	..	..	..	..	..
Other services	..	..	..	..	..	..	..	..	..	..	..
Resource balance	..	..	..	..	..	..	..	..	..	..	..
NMP used: domestic market	..	..	..	..	..	..	..	..	..	..	..
Final consumption, material goods	..	..	..	..	..	..	..	..	..	..	..
Personal consumption	..	..	..	..	..	..	..	..	..	..	..
Collective consumption	..	..	..	..	..	..	..	..	..	..	..
Net capital formation	..	..	..	..	..	..	..	..	..	..	..
Net fixed capital formation	..	..	..	..	..	..	..	..	..	..	..
Changes in stocks	..	..	..	..	..	..	..	..	..	..	..
Depreciation	..	..	..	..	..	..	..	..	..	..	..
MPS ACCOUNTS, constant prices	*(millions of constant Kampuchean riels)*										
NMP produced:											
Agriculture and forestry	..	..	..	..	..	..	..	..	..	..	..
Industry and construction	..	..	..	..	..	..	..	..	..	..	..
Services	..	..	..	..	..	..	..	..	..	..	..
Resource balance	..	..	..	..	..	..	..	..	..	..	..
NMP used: domestic market	..	..	..	..	..	..	..	..	..	..	..
Final consumption, material goods	..	..	..	..	..	..	..	..	..	..	..
Personal consumption	..	..	..	..	..	..	..	..	..	..	..
Collective consumption	..	..	..	..	..	..	..	..	..	..	..
Net capital formation	..	..	..	..	..	..	..	..	..	..	..
Net fixed capital formation	..	..	..	..	..	..	..	..	..	..	..
Depreciation	..	..	..	..	..	..	..	..	..	..	..

Abbreviations in notes column are explained in the General Notes. For sources and methods, see the Technical Notes.

Cambodia

1981	1982	1983	1984	1985	1986	1987	1988	1989	1990	Notes	Basic tables (continued)
						(billions of current Kampuchean riels)					**SNA ACCOUNTS, current prices**
..	..	..	..	..	..	..	..	248.4	598.8	E	GNP, at market prices
..	..	..	..	..	..	..	..	..	..	.	Net factor income
..	..	..	..	..	..	..	..	248.4	598.8	E	GDP at market prices
..	..	..	..	..	..	..	..	1.4	4.0		Net indirect taxes
..	..	..	..	..	..	98.9	195.6	247.3	594.8	E	GDP at factor cost
..	..	..	..	..	..	42.7	109.5	113.2	291.1	E	Agriculture
..	..	..	..	..	..	20.6	30.1	41.3	73.8	E	Industry
..	..	..	..	..	..	35.6	55.9	92.8	229.8	E	Services, etc.
..	..	..	..	..	..	..	..	..	..	.	Resource balance
..	..	..	..	..	..	..	..	..	..	.	Exports GNFS
..	..	..	..	..	..	..	..	..	..	.	Imports GNFS
..	..	..	..	..	..	..	..	..	..	.	Domestic absorption
..	..	..	..	..	..	..	..	..	..	.	Total consumption
..	..	..	..	..	..	..	..	..	..	.	Private consumption
..	..	..	..	..	..	..	..	..	..	.	General government consumption
..	..	..	..	..	..	..	..	..	..	.	Gross domestic investment
..	..	..	..	..	..	..	..	..	..	.	Fixed domestic investment
..	..	..	..	..	..	..	..	..	..	.	Depreciation
						(billions of constant 1989 Kampuchean riels)					**SNA ACCOUNTS, constant prices**
..	..	..	..	..	..	..	..	..	..	.	Gross national product (GNP)
..	..	..	..	..	..	..	..	..	..	.	GDP at market prices
..	..	..	..	..	..	207.9	241.5	247.3	247.0	E	GDP at factor cost
..	..	..	..	..	..	106.8	106.2	113.2	112.2	E	Agriculture
..	..	..	..	..	..	31.7	40.9	41.3	40.3	E	Industry
..	..	..	..	..	..	69.3	94.4	92.8	94.5	E	Services, etc.
..	..	..	..	..	..	..	..	..	..	.	Resource balance
..	..	..	..	..	..	..	..	..	..	.	Exports GNFS
..	..	..	..	..	..	..	..	..	..	.	Imports GNFS
..	..	..	..	..	..	..	..	..	..	.	Domestic absorption
..	..	..	..	..	..	..	..	..	..	.	Total consumption, etc.
..	..	..	..	..	..	..	..	..	..	.	Private consumption, etc.
..	..	..	..	..	..	..	..	..	..	.	General government consumption
..	..	..	..	..	..	..	..	..	..	.	Gross domestic investment
..	..	..	..	..	..	..	..	..	..	.	Fixed domestic investment
..	..	..	..	..	..	..	..	..	..	.	Depreciation
						(millions of current Kampuchean riels)					**MPS ACCOUNTS, current prices**
..	..	..	..	..	..	..	..	..	..	.	NMP produced:
..	..	..	..	..	..	..	..	..	..	.	Agriculture and forestry
..	..	..	..	..	..	..	..	..	..	.	Industry excluding construction
..	..	..	..	..	..	..	..	..	..	.	Construction
..	..	..	..	..	..	..	..	..	..	.	Transport and communication
..	..	..	..	..	..	..	..	..	..	.	Trade, etc.
..	..	..	..	..	..	..	..	..	..	.	Other services
..	..	..	..	..	..	..	..	..	..	.	Resource balance
..	..	..	..	..	..	..	..	..	..	.	NMP used: domestic market
..	..	..	..	..	..	..	..	..	..	.	Final consumption, material goods
..	..	..	..	..	..	..	..	..	..	.	Personal consumption
..	..	..	..	..	..	..	..	..	..	.	Collective consumption
..	..	..	..	..	..	..	..	..	..	.	Net capital formation
..	..	..	..	..	..	..	..	..	..	.	Net fixed capital formation
..	..	..	..	..	..	..	..	..	..	.	Changes in stocks
..	..	..	..	..	..	..	..	..	..	.	Depreciation
						(millions of constant Kampuchean riels)					**MPS ACCOUNTS, constant prices**
..	..	..	..	..	..	..	..	..	..	.	NMP produced:
..	..	..	..	..	..	..	..	..	..	.	Agriculture and forestry
..	..	..	..	..	..	..	..	..	..	.	Industry and construction
..	..	..	..	..	..	..	..	..	..	.	Services
..	..	..	..	..	..	..	..	..	..	.	Resource balance
..	..	..	..	..	..	..	..	..	..	.	NMP used: domestic market
..	..	..	..	..	..	..	..	..	..	.	Final consumption, material goods
..	..	..	..	..	..	..	..	..	..	.	Personal consumption
..	..	..	..	..	..	..	..	..	..	.	Collective consumption
..	..	..	..	..	..	..	..	..	..	.	Net capital formation
..	..	..	..	..	..	..	..	..	..	.	Net fixed capital formation
..	..	..	..	..	..	..	..	..	..	.	Depreciation

Cambodia

Basic tables (continued)	1970	1971	1972	1973	1974	1975	1976	1977	1978	1979	1980
MPS ACCOUNTS, index					*(index,1980 = 100)*						
NMP produced:	..	..	..	..	..	..	..	..	..	..	..
Agriculture and forestry	..	..	..	..	..	..	..	..	..	..	..
Industry excluding construction	..	..	..	..	..	..	..	..	..	..	..
Construction	..	..	..	..	..	..	..	..	..	..	..
Transport and communication	..	..	..	..	..	..	..	..	..	..	..
Trade, etc.	..	..	..	..	..	..	..	..	..	..	..
NMP used: material goods	..	..	..	..	..	..	..	..	..	..	..
Final consumption	..	..	..	..	..	..	..	..	..	..	..
Net capital formation	..	..	..	..	..	..	..	..	..	..	..
EXCHANGE AND CONVERSION RATES					*(LCUs per US dollar: annual average)*						
Single-year converter	55.540	75.822	162.250	244.917	..	..	..	..	..	..	..
Devisa/official	..	..	..	..	..	..	..	..	..	..	..
Commercial	..	..	..	..	..	..	..	..	..	..	..
Noncommercial	..	..	..	..	..	..	..	..	..	..	..
Informal market	90.070	213.830	202.750	272.750	871.916	5,921.109	2,685.000	..	..	..	..
ICP	..	..	..	..	..	..	..	..	..	..	..
					(ruble per US dollar: annual average)						
Commercial TR/$ cross	..	..	..	..	..	..	..	..	..	..	..
Uniform TR/$ cross	..	..	..	..	..	..	..	..	..	..	..
					(LCUs per ruble: annual average)						
Commercial	..	..	..	..	..	..	..	..	..	..	..
Noncommercial	..	..	..	..	..	..	..	..	..	..	..
Devisa/official	..	..	..	..	..	..	..	..	..	..	..
CONSUMER PRICE INDEXES					*(index)*						
Official, IMF 1985=100	..	..	..	..	..	..	..	..	..	..	..
Official, CIA or LWI 1980=100	..	..	..	..	..	..	..	..	..	..	..
Alternative, CIA or LWI 1980=100	..	..	..	..	..	..	..	..	..	..	..
INTERNATIONAL TRADE (ECE)					*(millions of current Kampuchean riels)*						
Value of exports, fob	..	..	..	..	..	..	..	..	..	..	..
to CMEA	..	..	..	..	..	..	..	..	..	..	..
Value of imports, cif	..	..	..	..	..	..	..	..	..	..	..
from CMEA	..	..	..	..	..	..	..	..	..	..	..
Trade balance	..	..	..	..	..	..	..	..	..	..	..
CMEA	..	..	..	..	..	..	..	..	..	..	..
INTERNATIONAL TRADE (Authors')					*(millions of current US dollars)*						
Value of exports, fob	..	..	..	..	..	6	..	..	..	..	30
to developed countries	..	..	..	..	..	..	..	..	..	..	..
to other non-socialist countries	..	..	..	..	..	..	..	..	..	..	..
to socialist countries	..	..	..	..	..	..	..	..	..	..	..
to CMEA	..	..	..	..	..	..	..	..	..	..	..
Value of imports, cif	..	..	..	..	..	..	..	..	..	..	..
from developed countries	..	..	..	..	..	..	..	..	..	..	..
from other non-socialist countries	..	..	..	..	..	..	..	..	..	..	..
from socialist countries	..	..	..	..	..	..	..	..	..	..	..
from CMEA	..	..	..	..	..	..	..	..	..	..	..
Trade balance	..	..	..	..	..	..	..	..	..	..	..
Developed countries	..	..	..	..	..	..	..	..	..	..	..
Other non-socialist countries	..	..	..	..	..	..	..	..	..	..	..
Socialist countries	..	..	..	..	..	..	..	..	..	..	..
CMEA	..	..	..	..	..	..	..	..	..	..	..
PARTNER CONVERTIBLE TRADE (ECE)					*(millions of current US dollars)*						
Exports to non-CMEA (cif)	..	..	..	..	..	..	..	..	..	..	..
Imports from non-CMEA (fob)	..	..	..	..	..	..	..	..	..	..	..
Trade balance	..	..	..	..	..	..	..	..	..	..	..
TRADE PRICE INDEXES (Authors')					*(index,1980 = 100)*						
Terms of trade	..	..	..	..	..	..	..	..	..	..	..
Exports	..	..	..	..	..	..	..	..	..	..	..
Non-socialist countries	..	..	..	..	..	..	..	..	..	..	..
Developed countries	..	..	..	..	..	..	..	..	..	..	..
Other	..	..	..	..	..	..	..	..	..	..	..
Socialist countries	..	..	..	..	..	..	..	..	..	..	..
CMEA	..	..	..	..	..	..	..	..	..	..	..
Imports	..	..	..	..	..	..	..	..	..	..	..
Non-socialist countries	..	..	..	..	..	..	..	..	..	..	..
Developed countries	..	..	..	..	..	..	..	..	..	..	..
Other	..	..	..	..	..	..	..	..	..	..	..
Socialist countries	..	..	..	..	..	..	..	..	..	..	..
CMEA	..	..	..	..	..	..	..	..	..	..	..

Abbreviations in notes column are explained in the General Notes. For sources and methods, see the Technical Notes.

1981	1982	1983	1984	1985	1986	1987	1988	1989	1990	Notes	Basic tables (continued)
				(index,1980 = 100)							**MPS ACCOUNTS, index**
..	..	..	..	..	..	..	..	..	..	.	NMP produced:
..	..	..	..	..	..	..	..	..	..	.	Agriculture and forestry
..	..	..	..	..	..	..	..	..	..	.	Industry excluding construction
..	..	..	..	..	..	..	..	..	..	.	Construction
..	..	..	..	..	..	..	..	..	..	.	Transport and communication
..	..	..	..	..	..	..	..	..	..	.	Trade, etc.
..	..	..	..	..	..	..	..	..	..	.	NMP used: material goods
..	..	..	..	..	..	..	..	..	..	.	Final consumption
..	..	..	..	..	..	..	..	..	..	.	Net capital formation
				(LCUs per US dollar: annual average)							**EXCHANGE AND CONVERSION RATES**
..	..	..	..	..	..	..	..	194.000	465.000	.	Single-year converter
..	..	..	..	..	..	100.000	142.000	194.000	407.000	.	Devisa/official
..	..	..	..	..	..	..	..	..	..	.	Commercial
..	..	..	..	7.000	30.000	100.000	110.000	159.000	..	.	Noncommercial
15.270	19.060	36.250	..	..	..	..	..	..	..	.	Informal market
..	..	..	..	..	..	..	..	..	..	.	ICP
				(ruble per US dollar: annual average)							
..	..	..	..	..	..	..	..	..	..	.	Commercial TR/$ cross
..	..	..	..	..	..	..	..	..	..	.	Uniform TR/$ cross
				(LCUs per ruble: annual average)							
..	..	..	..	..	..	..	..	..	..	.	Commercial
..	..	..	..	..	..	..	..	..	..	.	Noncommercial
..	..	..	..	..	..	..	..	..	..	.	Devisa/official
				(index)							**CONSUMER PRICE INDEXES**
..	..	..	..	..	..	..	..	..	..	.	Official, IMF 1985 = 100
..	..	..	..	..	..	..	..	..	..	.	Official, CIA or LWI 1980 = 100
..	..	..	..	..	..	..	..	..	..	.	Alternative, CIA or LWI 1980 = 100
				(millions of current Kampuchean riels)							**INTERNATIONAL TRADE (ECE)**
..	..	..	..	..	..	..	..	..	..	.	Value of exports, fob
..	..	..	..	..	..	..	..	..	..	.	to CMEA
..	..	..	..	..	..	..	..	..	..	.	Value of imports, cif
..	..	..	..	..	..	..	..	..	..	.	from CMEA
..	..	..	..	..	..	..	..	..	..	.	Trade balance
..	..	..	..	..	..	..	..	..	..	.	CMEA
				(millions of current US dollars)							**INTERNATIONAL TRADE (Authors')**
15	16	16	16	16	16	17	17	..	..	N	Value of exports, fob
..	..	..	..	..	..	..	..	..	..	.	to developed countries
..	..	..	..	..	..	..	..	..	..	.	to other non-socialist countries
..	..	..	..	..	..	..	..	..	..	.	to socialist countries
..	..	..	..	..	..	..	..	..	..	.	to CMEA
..	..	..	..	..	..	..	..	..	..	.	Value of imports, cif
..	..	..	..	..	..	..	..	..	..	.	from developed countries
..	..	..	..	..	..	..	..	..	..	.	from other non-socialist countries
..	..	..	..	..	..	..	..	..	..	.	from socialist countries
..	..	..	..	..	..	..	..	..	..	.	from CMEA
..	..	..	..	..	..	..	..	..	..	.	Trade balance
..	..	..	..	..	..	..	..	..	..	.	Developed countries
..	..	..	..	..	..	..	..	..	..	.	Other non-socialist countries
..	..	..	..	..	..	..	..	..	..	.	Socialist countries
..	..	..	..	..	..	..	..	..	..	.	CMEA
				(millions of current US dollars)							**PARTNER CONVERTIBLE TRADE (ECE)**
2	3	4	5	6	14	19	8	6	5	f	Exports to non-CMEA (cif)
73	47	51	49	27	12	10	13	29	18	f	Imports from non-CMEA (fob)
-71	-44	-47	-44	-22	2	9	-6	-23	-12	f	Trade balance
				(index,1980 = 100)							**TRADE PRICE INDEXES (Authors')**
..	..	..	..	..	..	..	..	..	..	.	Terms of trade
..	..	..	..	..	..	..	..	..	..	.	Exports
..	..	..	..	..	..	..	..	..	..	.	Non-socialist countries
..	..	..	..	..	..	..	..	..	..	.	Developed countries
..	..	..	..	..	..	..	..	..	..	.	Other
..	..	..	..	..	..	..	..	..	..	.	Socialist countries
..	..	..	..	..	..	..	..	..	..	.	CMEA
..	..	..	..	..	..	..	..	..	..	.	Imports
..	..	..	..	..	..	..	..	..	..	.	Non-socialist countries
..	..	..	..	..	..	..	..	..	..	.	Developed countries
..	..	..	..	..	..	..	..	..	..	.	Other
..	..	..	..	..	..	..	..	..	..	.	Socialist countries
..	..	..	..	..	..	..	..	..	..	.	CMEA

Cambodia

Basic tables (continued)	1970	1971	1972	1973	1974	1975	1976	1977	1978	1979	1980
TRADE PRICE INDEXES (ECE)					*(index, 1980 = 100)*						
Terms of trade	..	..	..	..	..	..	..	..	..	..	..
Exports	..	..	..	..	..	..	..	..	..	..	..
Imports	..	..	..	..	..	..	..	..	..	..	..
Balance of Payments (ECE)					*(millions of current US dollars)*						
Exports, convertible currency	..	..	..	..	..	..	..	..	..	..	..
Imports, convertible currency	..	..	..	..	..	..	..	..	..	..	..
Trade balance, convertible currency	..	..	..	..	..	..	..	..	..	..	..
Invisibles, convertible currency	..	..	..	..	..	..	..	..	..	..	..
Current balance, convertible currency	..	..	..	..	..	..	..	..	..	..	..
External debt, total (World Bank)	..	..	..	..	..	..	..	..	..	..	..
Convertible currency	..	..	..	..	..	..	..	..	..	..	..
CMEA	..	..	..	..	..	..	..	..	..	..	..
External debt service (World Bank)	..	..	..	..	..	..	..	..	..	..	..
Convertible currency	..	..	..	..	..	..	..	..	..	..	..
Total reserves less gold (IMF, IFS)	..	..	..	..	..	..	..	..	..	..	..
Total reserves, including gold at London price	..	..	..	..	..	..	..	..	..	..	..
Total reserves, incl. gold at national valuation	..	..	..	..	..	..	..	..	..	..	..
EMPLOYMENT					*(thousands)*						
Employment, total	..	..	..	..	..	..	..	..	..	..	3,296
Agriculture	..	..	..	..	..	..	..	..	..	..	2,452
Industry	..	..	..	..	..	..	..	..	..	..	..
Services	..	..	..	..	..	..	..	..	..	..	..
Labor force, total	3,069	3,096	3,123	3,150	3,178	3,205	3,224	3,243	3,261	3,280	3,299
Agriculture	2,402	2,411	2,419	2,428	2,436	2,445	2,447	2,448	2,450	2,452	2,454
Industry	129	138	147	156	165	174	184	193	202	211	220
Services	538	547	557	566	576	585	593	601	609	617	625
DOMESTIC FINANCE (IMF)					*(millions of current Kampuchean riels)*						
Money supply, broadly defined	..	..	..	..	..	..	..	..	..	..	..
Money, means of payment	..	..	..	..	..	..	..	..	..	..	..
Demand deposits	..	..	..	..	..	..	..	..	..	..	..
Currency outside banks	..	..	..	..	..	..	..	..	..	..	..
Quasi-money	..	..	..	..	..	..	..	..	..	..	..
Interest: deposit rate (percent)	..	..	..	..	..	..	..	..	..	..	..
Central government expenditures	..	..	..	..	..	..	..	..	..	..	..
Defense	..	..	..	..	..	..	..	..	..	..	..
					(millions of 1989 US dollars)						
Central government exp. (ACDA)	..	..	..	..	..	..	..	..	..	..	..
Military (ACDA)	..	..	..	..	..	..	..	..	..	..	..
LAND AND FORESTS (FAO)											
Pop. density: agr. land (pop. per sq. km)	191	192	193	194	195	196	191	187	182	178	177
Deforestation rate (net)	0	0	0	0	0	0	0	0	0	0	0
Forest (thousands sq. km)	134	134	134	134	134	134	134	134	134	134	134
SOCIAL INDICATORS											
Population density: total land (pop. per sq. km)	39	40	40	40	40	40	39	38	37	37	36
School enrollment ratio, primary	30	..	42	..	..	..	..	..	..	..	..
secondary	8	..	10	..	..	..	..	..	..	..	..
tertiary	..	..	..	..	..	..	..	..	..	..	..
Energy consumption per capita (kg. of oil eq.)	55	57	55	54	54	54	55	56	58	59	61
Daily calorie supply per capita	2,300	2,255	2,218	2,151	1,926	1,671	1,778	1,825	1,789	1,644	1,787
Food production (1979-1981=100)	254	197	153	109	85	124	132	141	124	78	118
Daily protein supply (gm. per capita)	51	52	52	50	46	41	43	44	41	38	41
Population per hospital bed	925	..	..	..	..	..	..	..	..	..	..
per nursing person	..	1,376	..	..	..	..	..	..	..	..	..
per physician	16,248	..	..	..	..	..	..	..	..	..	..
Female participation in labor force (percent)	37	37	37	37	37	38	39	40	41	42	43
Infant mortality (per 1,000 live births)	161	171	181	197	214	230	247	263	242	222	201
Life expectancy (years)	42	41	40	39	37	35	33	31	34	36	39
Total fertility (births per woman)	6	6	6	5	5	5	4	4	4	5	5
Urban population (percent of total population)	12	11	11	11	11	10	10	10	10	10	10
Population per passenger car	268	264	257	387	..	..	..	..	..	..	..
per telephone	..	..	..	..	..	..	..	..	..	..	..

Abbreviations in notes column are explained in the General Notes. For sources and methods, see the Technical Notes.

1981	1982	1983	1984	1985	1986	1987	1988	1989	1990	Notes	*Basic tables (continued)*
				(index, 1980 = 100)							**TRADE PRICE INDEXES (ECE)**
..	..	..	..	..	..	..	..	..	..	.	Terms of trade
..	..	..	..	..	..	..	..	..	..	.	Exports
..	..	..	..	..	..	..	..	..	..	.	Imports
				(millions of current US dollars)							**Balance of Payments (ECE)**
..	..	..	..	..	..	..	..	..	..	.	Exports, convertible currency
..	..	..	..	..	..	..	..	..	..	.	Imports, convertible currency
..	..	..	..	..	..	..	..	..	..	.	Trade balance, convertible currency
..	..	..	..	..	..	..	..	..	..	.	Invisibles, convertible currency
..	..	..	..	..	..	..	..	..	..	.	Current balance, convertible currency
..	390	293	285	318	441	595	717	..	..	O	External debt, total (World Bank)
..	..	..	..	..	..	..	..	..	..	.	Convertible currency
..	128	246	243	269	377	520	649	..	..	.	CMEA
..	3	3	1	14	14	11	13	..	..	Of	External debt service (World Bank)
..	..	..	..	..	..	..	..	..	..	.	Convertible currency
..	..	..	..	..	..	..	..	..	..	.	Total reserves less gold (IMF, IFS)
..	..	..	..	..	..	..	..	..	..	.	Total reserves, including gold at London price
..	..	..	..	..	..	..	..	..	..	.	Total reserves, incl. gold at national valuation
				(thousands)							**EMPLOYMENT**
..	..	..	..	3,606	..	..	..	..	..	.	Employment, total
..	..	..	..	2,607	..	..	..	..	..	.	Agriculture
..	..	..	..	..	..	..	..	..	..	.	Industry
..	..	..	..	..	..	..	..	..	..	.	Services
3,360	3,420	3,481	3,542	3,602	3,633	3,664	3,696	3,727	3,758	.	Labor force, total
..	..	..	..	..	..	..	..	..	..	.	Agriculture
..	..	..	..	..	..	..	..	..	..	.	Industry
..	..	..	..	..	..	..	..	..	..	.	Services
				(millions of current Kampuchean riels)							**DOMESTIC FINANCE (IMF)**
..	..	..	..	..	..	..	..	..	..	.	Money supply, broadly defined
..	..	..	..	..	..	..	..	..	..	.	Money, means of payment
..	..	..	..	..	..	..	..	..	..	.	Demand deposits
..	..	..	..	..	..	..	..	..	..	.	Currency outside banks
..	..	..	..	..	..	..	..	..	..	.	Quasi-money
..	..	..	..	..	..	..	..	..	..	.	Interest: deposit rate (percent)
..	..	..	..	..	..	..	..	..	..	.	Central government expenditures
..	..	..	..	..	..	..	..	..	..	.	Defense
				(millions of 1989 US dollars)							
269	..	..	..	..	..	..	..	..	..	.	Central government exp. (ACDA)
..	..	..	..	..	..	..	..	..	..	.	Military (ACDA)
											LAND AND FORESTS (FAO)
181	186	191	196	200	206	211	..	..	..	.	Pop. density: agr. land (pop. per sq. km)
0	0	0	0	0	0	..	..	..	..	.	Deforestation rate (net)
134	134	134	134	134	134	..	..	..	..	.	Forest (thousands sq. km)
											SOCIAL INDICATORS
37	38	39	40	41	42	43	..	..	..	.	Population density: total land (pop. per sq. km)
..	..	..	..	..	..	..	..	..	..	.	School enrollment ratio, primary
..	..	..	..	..	..	..	..	..	..	.	secondary
..	..	..	..	..	..	..	..	..	..	.	tertiary
60	60	60	59	59	60	59	..	..	..	.	Energy consumption per capita (kg. of oil eq.)
1,769	1,768	1,950	2,106	2,208	2,178	2,152	2,155	..	..	.	Daily calorie supply per capita
103	117	136	149	156	151	143	165	168	162	.	Food production (1979-1981=100)
43	43	46	50	53	52	52	51	..	..	.	Daily protein supply (gm. per capita)
..	..	..	..	..	..	..	..	..	..	.	Population per hospital bed
..	..	..	..	..	..	..	..	..	..	.	per nursing person
..	..	..	..	..	..	..	..	..	..	.	per physician
42	42	41	41	40	39	38	37	36	35	.	Female participation in labor force (percent)
181	160	154	148	142	136	130	126	121	117	.	Infant mortality (per 1,000 live births)
41	43	44	45	46	47	48	49	50	50	.	Life expectancy (years)
5	5	5	5	5	5	5	5	5	5	.	Total fertility (births per woman)
10	11	11	11	11	11	11	11	11	12	.	Urban population (percent of total population)
..	..	..	..	..	..	..	..	..	..	.	Population per passenger car
..	..	..	..	..	..	..	..	..	..	.	per telephone

Comparator tables	1970	1971	1972	1973	1974	1975	1976	1977	1978	1979	1980
PER CAPITA INCOME						*(US dollars)*					
World Bank (Atlas method)	130	130	130	150	160	180	170	190	220	260	300
Single year conversion	114	120	132	152	158	175	160	180	223	265	304
CIA or LWI	..	..	..	..	..	..	..	..	..	165	190
Penn World Tables	340	366	387	433	479	559	551	629	752	866	1,010
						(thousands)					
POPULATION	818,315	841,105	862,030	881,940	900,350	916,395	930,685	943,455	956,165	969,005	981,235
GROSS NATIONAL PRODUCT, current prices						*(millions of current US dollars)*					
World Bank (Atlas method)	103,781	107,639	112,343	130,107	144,865	168,340	159,768	175,121	208,062	248,575	297,645
Single year conversion	93,242	100,529	113,349	134,261	142,582	160,261	148,844	169,423	213,121	257,129	298,398
Authors' series	..	..	..	..	..	..	..	..	..	..	..
CIA or LWI	..	..	..	..	..	..	..	..	..	160,500	186,400
GROSS NATIONAL PRODUCT, constant prices						*(millions of constant 1987 dollars)*					
Single year conversion	90,015	96,837	100,200	108,550	109,697	118,769	112,356	121,185	136,374	146,734	157,884
Authors' series, rescaled from 1980 prices	..	..	..	..	..	..	..	..	..	..	..
CIA or LWI, rescaled from 1989 prices	..	..	..	..	..	..	..	..	..	249,802	265,771
CONVERSION FACTORS						*(LCUs per US dollar)*					
World Bank (Atlas method)	2.21	2.30	2.27	2.05	1.93	1.77	1.81	1.80	1.72	1.61	1.50
Single year convertor	2.46	2.46	2.25	1.99	1.96	1.86	1.94	1.86	1.68	1.55	1.50
Authors' series	..	..	..	..	..	..	..	..	..	..	..
Penn World Tables	0.83	0.80	0.76	0.72	0.65	0.58	0.56	0.53	0.50	0.48	0.45
OUTPUT TRENDS, OVERALL						*(index, constant prices 1987 = 100)*					
GNP, SNA	29.6	31.9	33.0	35.8	36.1	39.1	37.0	39.9	44.9	48.3	52.0
NMP, MPS	29.9	32.0	32.9	35.6	36.0	39.0	38.0	41.0	46.0	46.5	52.4
GNP, "Building block"	..	..	..	..	..	39.4	38.3	41.3	46.4	49.6	52.8
Industry											
Value added, SNA	21.6	24.5	25.8	28.1	28.3	32.3	31.0	35.2	40.9	44.3	49.1
Value added, MPS	21.6	24.4	25.7	27.8	27.8	31.9	31.0	35.1	40.5	43.5	48.9
"Building block"	..	..	..	..	..	..	..	..	..	..	..
Gross output, SNA	18.8	21.4	22.6	24.8	25.0	28.8	29.3	33.7	38.5	41.9	45.7
Agriculture											
Value added, SNA	48.7	49.8	49.1	53.4	55.5	56.7	57.2	56.0	59.0	62.8	61.7
Value added, MPS	51.2	52.0	51.4	56.0	58.3	59.4	58.2	56.8	59.0	62.8	61.6
"Building block"	..	..	..	..	..	..	..	..	..	..	..
Gross output, SNA	..	..	..	..	..	..	..	..	35.4	42.8	48.5
Services											
Value added, SNA	22.5	24.9	27.4	29.4	28.3	31.7	26.1	31.0	36.8	39.4	46.4
Value added, MPS	15.4	17.2	19.9	21.2	18.6	21.2	19.8	28.6	39.3	18.5	45.2
"Building block"	..	..	..	..	..	..	..	..	..	..	..
CONSUMPTION											
Total consumption, SNA	35.6	36.7	38.9	41.5	43.1	45.1	43.4	46.6	51.2	54.7	61.2
Total consumption, MPS	29.5	30.9	32.7	35.1	35.9	37.5	38.7	39.8	42.7	47.4	52.0
Households, SNA	36.8	37.6	40.0	42.9	44.8	46.6	44.8	48.3	52.8	55.5	62.6
Households, "building block"	..	..	..	..	..	..	..	..	..	..	..
General government, SNA	27.7	30.9	31.7	32.8	32.8	35.3	34.5	36.5	41.2	49.8	52.3
General government, "building block"	..	..	..	..	..	..	..	..	..	..	..
INVESTMENT											
Gross fixed investment, SNA	..	..	..	..	..	..	..	..	37.0	37.3	38.3
Accumulation, MPS	..	..	..	..	..	..	..	..	..	..	..
"Building block"	..	..	..	..	..	..	..	..	..	..	..
CONSUMER PRICES											
National methodology	..	..	..	..	..	..	..	..	..	..	..
Outside estimate	..	..	..	..	..	..	..	..	..	..	..
MERCHANDISE EXPORTS						*(millions of current US dollars)*					
UNCTAD	2,307	..	..	..	..	7,689	..	..	..	..	18,270
IMF: IFS	2,307	..	..	..	..	7,689	..	..	..	..	18,099
ACDA	..	..	..	..	..	..	..	..	9,955	13,610	18,100
ECE	..	..	..	..	..	..	..	..	..	..	..
intra-CMEA	..	..	..	..	..	..	..	..	..	..	..
Authors' uniform TR/$ series	2,307	..	..	..	..	7,689	..	..	9,745	13,657	18,132
intra-CMEA	..	..	..	..	..	..	..	..	1,146	1,341	1,380
MERCHANDISE IMPORTS						*(millions of current US dollars)*					
UNCTAD	2,279	..	..	..	..	7,926	..	..	..	..	19,550
IMF: IFS	2,279	..	..	..	..	7,926	..	..	..	..	19,941
ACDA	..	..	..	..	..	..	..	..	10,350	14,490	19,300
ECE	..	..	..	..	..	..	..	..	..	..	..
intra-CMEA	..	..	..	..	..	..	..	..	..	..	..
Authors' uniform series	2,279	..	..	..	..	7,926	..	..	10,915	15,675	19,490
intra-CMEA	..	..	..	..	..	..	..	..	1,086	1,578	1,615

Abbreviations in notes column are explained in the General Notes. For sources and methods, see the Technical Notes.

1981	1982	1983	1984	1985	1986	1987	1988	1989	1990	Notes	Comparator tables (continued)
					(US dollars)						**PER CAPITA INCOME**
320	320	320	330	320	300	300	330	350	370	.	World Bank (Atlas method)
282	272	287	289	278	263	280	341	375	321	.	Single year conversion
215	245	276	322	370	405	454	514	547	..	A	CIA or LWI
1,142	1,273	1,416	1,619	1,883	1,977	2,181	2,472	..	..	.	Penn World Tables
					(thousands)						
993,861	1,008,281	1,023,288	1,036,803	1,051,013	1,066,758	1,083,998	1,101,596	1,118,619	1,133,696	.	**POPULATION**
											GROSS NATIONAL PRODUCT, current prices
319,441	323,939	323,358	338,137	340,944	324,118	328,921	360,804	396,551	415,883	.	World Bank (Atlas method)
279,941	274,399	294,022	300,086	291,742	280,824	303,619	375,717	419,466	363,773	.	Single year conversion
..	..	..	..	..	..	..	..	..	..	.	Authors' series
214,300	247,000	282,200	332,400	386,300	427,700	486,400	559,100	603,500	..	.	CIA or LWI
				(millions of constant 1987 dollars)							**GROSS NATIONAL PRODUCT, constant prices**
164,984	179,342	197,815	226,598	253,748	274,423	303,619	333,376	343,877	359,687	.	Single year conversion
..	..	..	..	..	..	..	..	..	..	.	Authors' series, rescaled from 1980 prices
278,740	301,969	332,069	377,170	425,660	459,341	506,281	563,288	584,096	..	A	CIA or LWI, rescaled from 1989 prices
					(LCUs per US dollar)						**CONVERSION FACTORS**
1.49	1.60	1.80	2.06	2.51	2.99	3.44	3.88	3.98	4.18	.	World Bank (Atlas method)
1.71	1.89	1.98	2.32	2.94	3.45	3.72	3.72	3.76	4.78	.	Single year convertor
..	..	..	..	..	..	..	..	..	..	.	Authors' series
0.42	0.40	0.40	0.42	0.44	0.47	0.49	0.52	..	..	.	Penn World Tables
				(index, constant prices 1987 = 100)							**OUTPUT TRENDS, OVERALL**
54.3	59.1	65.2	74.6	83.6	90.4	100.0	109.8	113.3	118.5	.	GNP, SNA
54.9	59.4	65.4	74.3	84.3	90.7	100.0	111.1	115.0	..	f	NMP, MPS
55.4	60.0	65.9	75.0	84.8	91.4	100.0	111.2	115.6	121.4	.	GNP, "Building block"
											Industry
49.9	52.9	58.1	66.7	79.8	87.5	100.0	120.7	129.9	140.7	H	Value added, SNA
49.8	52.7	58.3	66.8	80.1	88.4	100.0	116.4	121.8	..	.	Value added, MPS
..	..	..	..	..	..	..	..	..	..	.	"Building block"
47.6	51.3	57.0	66.2	79.9	86.9	100.0	117.8	126.2	136.4	X	Gross output, SNA
											Agriculture
66.1	73.8	80.1	90.5	92.0	95.4	100.0	103.2	106.6	114.0	H	Value added, SNA
66.0	73.8	80.1	90.4	92.9	95.7	100.0	102.3	105.5	..	.	Value added, MPS
..	..	..	..	..	..	..	..	..	..	.	"Building block"
55.2	62.6	69.3	81.0	91.6	94.6	100.0	104.2	107.8	115.0	.	Gross output, SNA
											Services
48.8	53.0	59.7	69.0	79.8	88.9	100.0	101.3	98.3	93.8	H	Value added, SNA
51.5	55.1	61.8	69.1	82.3	89.2	100.0	108.0	106.2	..	f	Value added, MPS
..	..	..	..	..	..	..	..	..	..	.	"Building block"
											CONSUMPTION
65.3	68.1	74.7	83.6	88.8	91.5	100.0	110.3	116.9	114.5	.	Total consumption, SNA
56.1	60.3	65.5	74.8	86.5	93.2	100.0	108.2	108.3	..	.	Total consumption, MPS
67.2	69.6	76.4	84.5	90.0	91.6	100.0	111.3	117.7	113.1	.	Households, SNA
..	..	..	..	..	..	..	..	..	..	.	Households, "building block"
53.6	58.8	63.9	78.4	80.7	90.8	100.0	104.3	112.0	123.4	.	General government, SNA
..	..	..	..	..	..	..	..	..	..	.	General government, "building block"
											INVESTMENT
33.6	42.9	49.2	60.3	76.6	87.1	100.0	110.7	93.5	95.8	.	Gross fixed investment, SNA
..	..	..	..	..	..	..	..	..	..	.	Accumulation, MPS
..	..	..	..	..	..	..	..	..	..	.	"Building block"
											CONSUMER PRICES
..	..	..	..	..	..	..	..	..	..	.	National methodology
..	..	..	..	..	..	..	..	..	..	.	Outside estimate
				(millions of current US dollars)							**MERCHANDISE EXPORTS**
22,007	21,913	22,150	24,871	27,343	31,064	39,542	47,650	51,631	52,000	.	UNCTAD
21,465	21,872	22,177	24,831	27,327	31,148	39,542	47,540	51,626	60,921	.	IMF: IFS
21,460	21,870	22,180	24,830	27,330	31,150	39,540	47,540	51,630	..	.	ACDA
..	..	..	..	..	..	..	..	..	..	.	ECE
..	..	..	..	..	..	..	..	..	..	.	intra-CMEA
21,476	21,865	22,096	24,824	27,329	31,367	39,464	47,663	52,914	69,478	W	Authors' uniform TR/$ series
898	919	1,075	1,356	2,147	2,694	2,909	3,233	3,625	2,881	.	intra-CMEA
				(millions of current US dollars)							**MERCHANDISE IMPORTS**
22,014	18,939	21,324	26,183	42,491	43,153	43,393	55,361	58,561	46,400	.	UNCTAD
21,635	18,900	21,336	25,950	42,526	43,172	43,392	55,278	58,282	52,275	.	IMF: IFS
17,940	16,690	21,340	25,950	42,530	43,170	43,390	55,280	58,280	..	.	ACDA
..	..	..	..	..	..	..	..	..	..	.	ECE
..	..	..	..	..	..	..	..	..	..	.	intra-CMEA
21,631	18,920	21,313	25,953	42,480	43,247	43,222	55,352	59,140	58,632	W	Authors' uniform series
1,113	1,418	1,535	1,747	2,591	3,541	3,105	4,194	4,342	3,386	.	intra-CMEA

China

Basic tables	1970	1971	1972	1973	1974	1975	1976	1977	1978	1979	1980
SNA ACCOUNTS, current prices	*(billions of current Chinese yuan)*										
GNP, at market prices	230	248	255	267	280	298	289	315	359	400	447
Net factor income	0	0	0	-9	0	0	0	0	0	1	0
GDP at market prices	230	248	255	276	280	298	289	315	359	398	447
Net indirect taxes	..	..	..	..	..	..	..	..	..	..	..
GDP at factor cost	..	..	..	..	..	..	..	..	..	..	..
Agriculture	78	81	81	89	93	95	96	94	102	126	136
Industry	88	99	104	112	113	128	122	138	160	177	199
Services, etc.	63	67	69	75	74	75	71	83	97	96	112
Resource balance	1	2	3	2	0	1	2	2	-1	-1	0
Exports GNFS	6	8	9	13	15	16	15	15	18	23	30
Imports GNFS	6	5	7	11	16	15	13	14	18	24	30
Domestic absorption	229	245	252	274	280	297	287	313	360	399	447
Total consumption	164	174	183	194	199	207	205	222	240	260	303
Private consumption	146	154	163	173	178	184	183	198	212	227	266
General government consumption	18	20	20	21	21	23	22	24	27	34	37
Gross domestic investment	65	72	69	80	81	90	82	91	120	139	144
Fixed domestic investment	..	..	..	..	..	..	..	..	96	101	107
Depreciation	..	..	..	..	..	..	..	..	..	..	..
SNA ACCOUNTS, constant prices	*(billions of constant 1987 Chinese yuan)*										
Gross national product (GNP)	335	360	373	404	408	442	418	451	508	546	588
GDP at market prices	335	360	373	404	408	442	418	451	508	544	587
GDP at factor cost	..	..	..	..	..	..	..	..	..	..	..
Agriculture	157	160	158	172	179	182	184	180	190	202	199
Industry	99	113	119	129	130	148	142	162	188	204	226
Services, etc.	79	87	96	103	99	111	92	109	129	139	163
Resource balance	1	10	10	7	-2	5	4	0	-15	-20	-21
Exports GNFS	28	34	40	44	42	49	41	40	42	53	66
Imports GNFS	27	24	30	37	44	45	38	40	57	73	86
Domestic absorption	334	351	363	397	410	437	415	451	523	564	608
Total consumption, etc.	245	252	268	286	297	310	298	321	352	376	421
Private consumption, etc.	218	223	237	255	266	277	266	286	313	329	371
General government consumption	26	29	30	31	31	34	33	35	39	47	50
Gross domestic investment	89	99	96	111	113	127	116	130	170	188	187
Fixed domestic investment	..	..	..	..	..	..	..	..	135	136	140
Depreciation	..	..	..	..	..	..	..	..	..	..	..
MPS ACCOUNTS, current prices	*(billions of current Chinese yuan)*										
NMP produced:	193	208	214	232	235	250	243	264	301	335	369
Agriculture and forestry	78	81	81	89	92	95	94	91	99	123	133
Industry excluding construction	79	89	94	102	102	115	111	126	149	163	180
Construction	8	9	9	9	10	11	12	12	13	13	19
Transport and communication	7	8	8	9	9	10	9	11	12	12	13
Trade, etc.	21	21	21	23	23	20	17	24	29	25	25
Other services	..	..	..	..	..	..	..	..	..	..	..
Resource balance	5	7	8	7	6	5	0	7	4	-1	-1
NMP used: domestic market	188	201	205	225	229	245	242	257	298	336	370
Final consumption, material goods	126	132	140	151	155	162	168	174	189	220	253
Personal consumption	115	120	126	136	140	145	150	155	167	191	222
Collective consumption	11	13	14	15	15	17	17	19	22	29	31
Net capital formation	62	68	65	74	74	83	75	83	109	116	117
Net fixed capital formation	42	47	48	50	55	65	62	65	78	84	89
Changes in stocks	20	22	17	24	19	18	13	19	30	32	27
Depreciation	..	..	..	..	..	..	..	..	..	..	..
MPS ACCOUNTS, constant prices	*(billions of 1980 Chinese yuan)*										
NMP produced:	210	225	232	251	254	275	268	288	324	327	369
Agriculture and forestry	110	112	111	121	125	128	125	122	127	135	133
Industry and construction	88	99	105	113	113	130	126	143	165	177	199
Services	13	14	16	18	15	18	16	24	32	15	37
Resource balance	..	..	..	..	..	..	..	..	..	..	..
NMP used: domestic market	..	..	..	..	..	..	..	..	..	..	..
Final consumption, material goods	144	151	159	171	175	182	188	194	208	230	253
Personal consumption	132	137	144	155	158	164	170	174	185	201	222
Collective consumption	12	14	15	16	16	18	19	20	23	30	31
Net capital formation	..	..	..	..	..	..	..	..	..	..	..
Net fixed capital formation	..	..	..	..	..	..	..	..	..	..	..
Depreciation	..	..	..	..	..	..	..	..	..	..	..

Abbreviations in notes column are explained in the General Notes. For sources and methods, see the Technical Notes.

1981	1982	1983	1984	1985	1986	1987	1988	1989	1990	Notes	Basic tables (continued)
				(billions of current Chinese yuan)							**SNA ACCOUNTS, current prices**
477	519	581	696	857	970	1,130	1,398	1,579	1,740	.	GNP, at market prices
0	0	1	2	1	0	-3	-3	-7	-5	.	Net factor income
477	519	580	694	856	970	1,133	1,401	1,586	1,745	f	GDP at market prices
..	..	..	..	..	..	..	..	..	..	.	Net indirect taxes
..	..	..	..	..	..	..	..	..	..	.	GDP at factor cost
155	176	196	229	254	276	322	384	425	480	H	Agriculture
205	216	236	278	345	397	460	579	660	726	H	Industry
117	127	148	187	257	297	351	439	501	539	H	Services, etc.
4	11	7	4	-35	-28	2	-13	-11	62	.	Resource balance
42	47	49	67	89	120	163	193	212	317	.	Exports GNFS
38	37	42	64	124	148	161	206	223	255	.	Imports GNFS
473	508	573	690	891	998	1,131	1,414	1,597	1,684	.	Domestic absorption
334	354	397	466	547	606	688	859	978	1,002	.	Total consumption
295	311	349	405	476	521	593	747	849	859	.	Private consumption
39	43	47	61	72	85	95	112	129	143	.	General government consumption
139	154	176	224	344	392	443	555	619	682	.	Gross domestic investment
96	123	143	183	254	302	364	..	414	445	.	Fixed domestic investment
..	..	..	..	..	..	..	..	..	..	.	Depreciation
				(billions of constant 1987 Chinese yuan)							**SNA ACCOUNTS, constant prices**
614	668	736	843	945	1,021	1,130	1,241	1,280	1,339	.	Gross national product (GNP)
614	667	735	841	944	1,022	1,133	1,243	1,286	1,343	f	GDP at market prices
..	..	..	..	..	..	..	..	..	..	.	GDP at factor cost
213	238	258	291	296	307	322	332	343	367	H	Agriculture
230	243	267	307	367	403	460	555	597	647	H	Industry
172	186	210	242	280	312	351	356	345	329	H	Services, etc.
-13	3	0	-3	-44	-19	2	-13	-28	21	.	Resource balance
81	87	87	101	111	138	163	188	198	217	.	Exports GNFS
93	84	87	105	155	157	161	201	226	196	.	Imports GNFS
627	665	734	844	987	1,041	1,131	1,256	1,313	1,322	.	Domestic absorption
449	469	514	575	611	629	688	759	804	787	.	Total consumption, etc.
399	413	453	501	534	543	593	660	698	670	.	Private consumption, etc.
51	56	61	74	77	86	95	99	106	117	.	General government consumption
177	196	221	269	377	411	443	498	509	534	.	Gross domestic investment
122	156	179	220	279	317	364	403	340	349	.	Fixed domestic investment
..	..	..	..	..	..	..	..	..	..	*	Depreciation
				(billions of current Chinese yuan)							**MPS ACCOUNTS, current prices**
394	426	474	565	702	786	931	1,174	1,313	..	f	NMP produced:
151	172	192	225	249	272	315	382	421	..	.	Agriculture and forestry
184	195	214	252	316	357	426	542	624	..	.	Industry excluding construction
19	21	26	30	41	51	64	78	77	..	.	Construction
13	15	17	21	26	32	38	46	51	..	.	Transport and communication
27	23	25	38	70	73	88	126	139	..	.	Trade, etc.
..	..	..	..	..	..	..	..	..	..	.	Other services
4	-3	-4	-5	-49	-64	-37	-53	-45	..	.	Resource balance
391	429	478	570	751	850	968	1,227	1,358	..	.	NMP used: domestic market
280	305	336	391	488	555	639	804	890	..	.	Final consumption, material goods
247	269	296	340	424	477	550	700	773	..	f	Personal consumption
33	37	40	51	64	78	88	104	117	..	.	Collective consumption
111	124	142	180	263	294	330	423	467	..	.	Net capital formation
78	97	113	145	188	220	272	336	295	..	.	Net fixed capital formation
33	27	30	34	75	75	58	87	172	..	.	Changes in stocks
..	..	..	..	..	..	..	..	..	..	.	Depreciation
				(billions of 1980 Chinese yuan)							**MPS ACCOUNTS, constant prices**
387	418	460	523	593	639	704	782	810	..	f	NMP produced:
142	159	172	195	200	206	215	220	227	..	.	Agriculture and forestry
202	214	237	271	326	359	406	473	495	..	.	Industry and construction
43	46	51	57	68	74	83	89	88	..	f	Services
..	..	..	..	..	..	..	..	..	..	.	Resource balance
..	..	..	..	..	..	..	..	..	..	.	NMP used: domestic market
273	293	319	364	421	454	487	526	527	..	.	Final consumption, material goods
241	257	278	313	359	380	405	439	440	..	f	Personal consumption
32	37	40	51	62	74	82	88	87	..	.	Collective consumption
..	..	..	..	..	..	..	..	..	..	.	Net capital formation
..	..	..	..	..	..	..	..	..	..	.	Net fixed capital formation
..	..	..	..	..	..	..	..	..	..	.	Depreciation

China

	1970	1971	1972	1973	1974	1975	1976	1977	1978	1979	1980
MPS ACCOUNTS, index					*(index, 1980 = 100)*						
NMP produced:	57.1	61.1	62.8	68.0	68.8	74.5	72.5	78.2	87.8	88.7	100.0
Agriculture and forestry	83.0	84.3	83.4	90.9	94.5	96.4	94.5	92.1	95.7	101.8	100.0
Industry excluding construction	42.9	48.6	51.9	56.4	56.1	64.5	62.1	71.3	83.4	90.2	100.0
Construction	55.6	61.8	59.7	60.4	63.9	71.5	75.0	76.4	75.7	77.1	100.0
Transport and communication	58.7	63.5	66.7	70.6	67.5	76.2	73.0	84.1	93.6	96.0	100.0
Trade, etc.	62.5	63.1	65.2	70.4	69.2	69.2	67.4	75.9	93.0	99.4	100.0
NMP used: material goods	..	..	..	..	..	..	..	..	..	..	..
Final consumption	56.7	59.5	62.9	67.5	69.0	72.0	74.3	76.6	82.2	91.1	100.0
Net capital formation	..	..	..	..	..	..	..	..	..	..	..
EXCHANGE AND CONVERSION RATES					*(LCUs per US dollar: annual average)*						
Single-year converter	2.462	2.462	2.245	1.989	1.961	1.860	1.941	1.858	1.684	1.555	1.498
Devisa/official	..	..	..	..	..	..	..	..	..	..	..
Commercial	..	..	..	..	..	..	..	..	..	..	..
Noncommercial	..	..	..	..	..	..	..	..	..	..	..
Informal market	3.380	3.238	2.731	2.122	2.072	2.460	2.377	2.278	2.278	2.359	1.973
ICP	0.826	0.804	0.762	0.722	0.649	0.582	0.563	0.531	0.499	0.477	0.451
					(ruble per US dollar: annual average)						
Commercial TR/$ cross	..	..	..	..	..	..	..	..	..	..	..
Uniform TR/$ cross	..	..	..	..	..	..	..	..	..	..	..
					(LCUs per ruble: annual average)						
Commercial	..	..	..	..	..	..	..	..	..	..	..
Noncommercial	..	..	..	..	..	..	..	..	..	..	..
Devisa/official	..	..	..	..	..	..	..	..	..	..	..
CONSUMER PRICE INDEXES					*(index)*						
Official, IMF 1985 = 100	..	..	..	..	..	71.8	72.1	73.9	74.5	76.0	81.6
Official, CIA or LWI 1980 = 100	..	..	..	..	..	..	..	..	..	..	..
Alternative, CIA or LWI 1980 = 100	..	..	..	..	..	..	..	..	..	..	..
INTERNATIONAL TRADE (ECE)					*(billions of current Chinese yuan)*						
Value of exports, fob	..	..	..	..	..	..	..	..	16	21	27
to CMEA	..	..	..	..	..	..	..	..	2	2	2
Value of imports, cif	..	..	..	..	..	..	..	..	18	24	29
from CMEA	..	..	..	..	..	..	..	..	2	2	2
Trade balance	..	..	..	..	..	..	..	..	-2	-3	-2
CMEA	..	..	..	..	..	..	..	..	0	0	0
INTERNATIONAL TRADE (Authors')					*(millions of current US dollars)*						
Value of exports, fob	2,307	..	..	..	..	7,689	..	..	9,745	13,657	18,132
to developed countries	..	..	..	..	..	..	..	..	3,547	5,639	8,110
to other non-socialist countries	..	..	..	..	..	..	..	..	4,743	6,312	8,221
to socialist countries	..	..	..	..	..	..	..	..	1,455	1,707	1,800
to CMEA	..	..	..	..	..	..	..	..	1,146	1,341	1,380
Value of imports, cif	2,279	..	..	..	..	7,926	..	..	10,915	15,675	19,490
from developed countries	..	..	..	..	..	..	..	..	7,509	11,082	14,356
from other non-socialist countries	..	..	..	..	..	..	..	..	1,995	2,546	3,064
from socialist countries	..	..	..	..	..	..	..	..	1,411	2,047	2,070
from CMEA	..	..	..	..	..	..	..	..	1,086	1,578	1,615
Trade balance	28	..	..	..	..	-237	..	..	-1,170	-2,018	-1,358
Developed countries	..	..	..	..	..	..	..	..	-3,962	-5,443	-6,246
Other non-socialist countries	..	..	..	..	..	..	..	..	2,748	3,765	5,157
Socialist countries	..	..	..	..	..	..	..	..	44	-340	-270
CMEA	..	..	..	..	..	..	..	..	60	-237	-235
PARTNER CONVERTIBLE TRADE (ECE)					*(millions of current US dollars)*						
Exports to non-CMEA (cif)	..	..	..	..	..	..	..	..	..	..	16,926
Imports from non-CMEA (fob)	..	..	..	..	..	..	..	..	..	..	..
Trade balance	..	..	..	..	..	..	..	..	..	..	..
TRADE PRICE INDEXES (Authors')					*(index, 1980 = 100)*						
Terms of trade	79.8	76.9	79.1	77.0	77.0	71.6	77.5	85.1	99.8	99.9	100.0
Exports	29.4	29.8	33.4	47.3	59.9	55.6	60.3	66.6	82.5	92.5	100.0
Non-socialist countries	..	..	..	..	..	..	..	..	..	..	..
Developed countries	..	..	..	..	..	..	..	..	..	..	..
Other	..	..	..	..	..	..	..	..	..	..	..
Socialist countries	..	..	..	..	..	..	..	..	..	..	..
CMEA	..	..	..	..	..	..	..	..	..	..	..
Imports	36.8	38.8	42.2	61.4	77.8	77.6	77.8	78.4	82.6	92.6	100.0
Non-socialist countries	..	..	..	..	..	..	..	..	..	..	..
Developed countries	..	..	..	..	..	..	..	..	..	..	..
Other	..	..	..	..	..	..	..	..	..	..	..
Socialist countries	..	..	..	..	..	..	..	..	..	..	..
CMEA	..	..	..	..	..	..	..	..	..	..	..

Abbreviations in notes column are explained in the General Notes. For sources and methods, see the Technical Notes.

1981	1982	1983	1984	1985	1986	1987	1988	1989	1990	Notes	
				(index,1980 = 100)							**MPS ACCOUNTS, index**
104.9	113.5	124.8	141.8	160.9	173.3	190.9	212.1	219.5	..	f	NMP produced:
107.1	119.7	129.9	146.7	150.6	155.2	162.2	165.9	171.2	..	.	Agriculture and forestry
101.7	107.8	118.4	136.1	162.7	178.4	201.7	236.8	251.0	..	.	Industry excluding construction
101.6	106.5	125.9	139.5	173.0	203.3	230.3	248.6	227.5	..	.	Construction
104.0	116.7	129.4	146.0	175.4	195.2	217.4	242.1	253.9	..	.	Transport and communication
119.0	124.7	140.9	156.7	186.2	199.6	224.3	238.6	226.2	..	.	Trade, etc.
..	..	..	..	..	..	..	..	..			NMP used: material goods
107.9	115.9	125.8	143.8	166.4	179.3	193.7	209.7	209.9	..	.	Final consumption
..	..	..	..	..	..	..	..	..			Net capital formation
				(LCUs per US dollar: annual average)							**EXCHANGE AND CONVERSION RATES**
1.705	1.893	1.976	2.320	2.937	3.453	3.722	3.722	3.764	4.783	.	Single-year converter
											Devisa/official
..	..	..	..	..	..	..	..	..	..	.	Commercial
..	..	..	..	..	..	..	..	..	..	.	Noncommercial
2.038	2.251	2.195	3.048	3.250	3.250					.	Informal market
0.421	0.404	0.400	0.415	0.436	0.467	0.487	0.517			.	ICP
				(ruble per US dollar: annual average)							
..	..	..	..	..	..	..	..		..	.	Commercial TR/$ cross
..	..	..	..	..	..	..	..		..	.	Uniform TR/$ cross
				(LCUs per ruble: annual average)							
..	..	..	..	..	..	..	..	..	..	.	Commercial
..	..	..	..	..	..	..	..	..	..	.	Noncommercial
..	..	..	..	..	..	..	..	..	..	.	Devisa/official
				(index)							**CONSUMER PRICE INDEXES**
83.7	85.4	87.0	89.4	100.0	107.0	116.4	140.5	163.4	..	.	Official, IMF 1985 = 100
..	..	..	..	..	..	..	..	..	..	.	Official, CIA or LWI 1980 = 100
..	..	..	..	..	..	..	..	..	..	.	Alternative, CIA or LWI 1980 = 100
				(billions of current Chinese yuan)							**INTERNATIONAL TRADE (ECE)**
37	41	44	58	80	108	147	177	199	332	W	Value of exports, fob
2	2	2	3	6	9	11	12	14	14	.	to CMEA
37	36	42	60	125	149	161	206	223	280	W	Value of imports, cif
2	3	3	4	8	12	12	16	16	16	.	from CMEA
0	6	2	-3	-45	-41	-14	-29	-23	52	W	Trade balance
0	-1	-1	-1	-1	-3	-1	-4	-3	-2	.	CMEA
				(millions of current US dollars)							**INTERNATIONAL TRADE (Authors')**
21,476	21,865	22,096	24,824	27,329	31,367	39,464	47,663	52,914	69,478	W	Value of exports, fob
9,456	9,397	9,347	10,427	11,430	12,607	14,589	17,470	19,023	26,210	.	to developed countries
10,799	11,253	11,383	12,803	13,496	15,771	21,627	26,540	29,839	39,929	.	to other non-socialist countries
1,221	1,215	1,366	1,594	2,404	2,989	3,248	3,653	4,052	3,343	.	to socialist countries
898	919	1,075	1,356	2,147	2,694	2,909	3,233	3,625	2,881	.	to CMEA
21,631	18,920	21,313	25,953	42,480	43,247	43,222	55,352	59,140	58,632	W	Value of imports, cif
16,105	13,039	14,525	17,967	29,902	28,920	26,499	30,571	31,767	26,007	.	from developed countries
4,088	4,071	4,924	5,910	9,504	10,361	13,173	20,184	22,696	29,008	.	from other non-socialist countries
1,438	1,810	1,864	2,076	3,074	3,966	3,550	4,596	4,677	3,616	.	from socialist countries
1,113	1,418	1,535	1,747	2,591	3,541	3,105	4,194	4,342	3,386	.	from CMEA
-155	2,944	783	-1,129	-15,151	-11,881	-3,758	-7,689	-6,226	10,846	W	Trade balance
-6,649	-3,642	-5,178	-7,540	-18,472	-16,313	-11,910	-13,101	-12,744	202	.	Developed countries
6,712	7,182	6,458	6,892	3,992	5,410	8,454	6,356	7,143	10,921	.	Other non-socialist countries
-217	-596	-497	-481	-671	-977	-302	-943	-625	-273	.	Socialist countries
-215	-499	-460	-391	-445	-847	-195	-961	-717	-505	.	CMEA
				(millions of current US dollars)							**PARTNER CONVERTIBLE TRADE (ECE)**
16,846	14,893	16,708	22,863	35,873	33,330	36,799	48,388	48,889	46,779	W	Exports to non-CMEA (cif)
22,237	21,976	21,785	25,391	28,561	32,502	44,090	56,730	69,610	84,383	W	Imports from non-CMEA (fob)
-5,392	-7,084	-5,077	-2,528	7,312	828	-7,290	-8,342	-20,721	-37,603	W	Trade balance
				(index,1980 = 100)							**TRADE PRICE INDEXES (Authors')**
97.4	95.6	88.3	82.4	76.0	69.9	75.7	75.8	82.1	84.8	K	Terms of trade
99.2	94.6	94.0	93.3	89.4	82.5	87.9	90.0	92.9	99.9	K	Exports
..	..	..	..	..	..	..	..	..	..	.	Non-socialist countries
..	..	..	..	..	..	..	..	..	..	.	Developed countries
..	..	..	..	..	..	..	..	..	..	.	Other
..	..	..	..	..	..	..	..	..	..	.	Socialist countries
..	..	..	..	..	..	..	..	..	..	.	CMEA
101.9	99.0	106.5	113.2	117.6	118.0	116.1	118.7	113.2	117.9	K	Imports
..	..	..	..	..	..	..	..	..	..	.	Non-socialist countries
..	..	..	..	..	..	..	..	..	..	.	Developed countries
..	..	..	..	..	..	..	..	..	..	.	Other
..	..	..	..	..	..	..	..	..	..	.	Socialist countries
..	..	..	..	..	..	..	..	..	..	.	CMEA

China

Basic tables (continued)	1970	1971	1972	1973	1974	1975	1976	1977	1978	1979	1980
TRADE PRICE INDEXES (ECE)					*(index, 1980 = 100)*						
Terms of trade	..	..	..	..	..	..	..	..	..	..	..
Exports	..	..	..	..	..	..	..	..	..	..	..
Imports	..	..	..	..	..	..	..	..	..	..	..
Balance of Payments (ECE)					*(millions of current US dollars)*						
Exports, convertible currency	..	..	..	..	..	..	..	..	..	..	..
Imports, convertible currency	..	..	..	..	..	..	..	..	..	..	..
Trade balance, convertible currency	..	..	..	..	..	..	..	..	..	..	..
Invisibles, convertible currency	..	..	..	..	..	..	..	..	..	..	..
Current balance, convertible currency	..	..	..	..	..	..	..	..	..	..	..
External debt, total (World Bank)	..	..	..	..	..	..	..	..	623	2,183	4,504
Convertible currency	..	..	..	..	..	..	..	..	623	2,183	4,504
CMEA	..	..	..	..	..	..	..	..	..	..	..
External debt service (World Bank)	..	..	..	..	..	..	..	..	..	61	930
Convertible currency	..	..	..	..	..	..	..	..	..	61	930
Total reserves less gold (IMF, IFS)	..	..	..	..	..	..	..	2,345	1,557	2,154	2,545
Total reserves, including gold at London price	..	..	..	..	..	..	..	4,456	4,450	8,708	10,091
Total reserves, incl. gold at national valuation	..	..	..	..	..	..	..	2,889	2,141	2,744	3,116
EMPLOYMENT					*(thousands)*						
Employment, total	..	..	..	..	..	..	..	..	..	..	..
Agriculture	..	..	..	..	..	..	..	..	..	..	..
Industry	..	..	..	..	..	..	..	..	..	..	..
Services	..	..	..	..	..	..	..	..	..	..	..
Labor force, total	428,309	438,999	449,689	460,379	471,069	481,759	494,819	507,879	520,940	534,000	547,060
Agriculture	335,516	341,916	348,316	354,716	361,117	367,517	375,240	382,962	390,685	398,408	406,131
Industry	43,362	46,304	49,245	52,187	55,128	58,070	61,761	65,452	69,144	72,835	76,526
Services	49,431	50,779	52,127	53,475	54,824	56,172	57,818	59,465	61,111	62,757	64,404
DOMESTIC FINANCE (IMF)					*(billions of current Chinese yuan)*						
Money supply, broadly defined	..	..	..	..	..	..	..	86	89	133	167
Money, means of payment	..	..	..	..	..	..	..	58	58	92	115
Demand deposits	..	..	..	..	..	..	..	39	37	65	80
Currency outside banks	..	..	..	..	..	..	..	20	21	27	35
Quasi-money	..	..	..	..	..	..	..	28	31	41	52
Interest: deposit rate (percent)	..	..	..	..	..	..	..	..	..	..	5
Central government expenditures	..	..	..	..	..	..	..	..	..	..	..
Defense	..	..	..	..	..	..	..	..	..	..	..
					(millions of 1989 US dollars)						
Central government exp. (ACDA)	..	..	..	..	..	..	..	..	..	82,090	74,420
Military (ACDA)	..	..	..	..	..	..	..	..	..	26,950	24,120
LAND AND FORESTS (FAO)											
Pop. density: agr. land (pop. per sq. km)	195	200	205	210	214	219	222	225	228	232	234
Deforestation rate (net)	1	1	1	1	1	1	1	1	1	2	2
Forest (thousands sq. km)	1,093	1,100	1,107	1,114	1,121	1,129	1,136	1,143	1,150	1,173	1,196
SOCIAL INDICATORS											
Population density: total land (pop. per sq. km)	88	91	93	95	97	99	100	102	103	104	106
School enrollment ratio, primary	89	..	..	..	..	126	..	106	124	122	112
secondary	24	..	..	..	..	47	..	83	63	56	46
tertiary	..	..	..	..	..	..	..	..	..	..	1
Energy consumption per capita (kg. of oil eq.)	270	298	312	322	324	367	380	416	456	460	456
Daily calorie supply per capita	1,984	2,047	1,994	2,031	2,063	2,074	2,073	2,114	2,212	2,280	2,334
Food production (1979-1981=100)	87	89	87	91	90	91	89	88	94	100	99
Daily protein supply (gm. per capita)	48	50	47	49	49	49	49	50	52	54	55
Population per hospital bed	..	..	..	..	600	600	600	..	..	..	500
per nursing person	..	..	..	..	2,500	2,400	2,300	..	..	..	2,100
per physician	..	..	..	..	1,500	1,400	1,300	..	..	..	1,100
Female participation in labor force (percent)	44	45	45	45	45	45	46	47	48	48	49
Infant mortality (per 1,000 live births)	69	66	61	56	51	46	41	39	38	43	41
Life expectancy (years)	62	63	63	64	64	65	65	66	66	67	67
Total fertility (births per woman)	6	5	5	4	4	3	3	3	3	2	3
Urban population (percent of total population)	18	17	17	17	17	17	17	18	18	19	19
Population per passenger car	..	..	..	12,300	9,971	8,124	6,935	6,328	5,588	4,924	4,126
per telephone	..	..	..	..	..	269	..	..	..	..	225

Abbreviations in notes column are explained in the General Notes. For sources and methods, see the Technical Notes.

122

1981	1982	1983	1984	1985	1986	1987	1988	1989	1990	Notes	*Basic tables (continued)*
				(index,1980 = 100)							**TRADE PRICE INDEXES (ECE)**
..	..	..	..	..	..	..	..	..	..	.	Terms of trade
..	..	..	..	..	..	..	..	..	..	.	Exports
..	..	..	..	..	..	..	..	..	..	.	Imports
				(millions of current US dollars)							**Balance of Payments (ECE)**
..	..	..	..	..	..	..	..	..	..	.	Exports, convertible currency
..	..	..	..	..	..	..	..	..	..	.	Imports, convertible currency
..	..	..	..	..	..	..	..	..	..	.	Trade balance, convertible currency
..	..	..	..	..	..	..	..	..	..	.	Invisibles, convertible currency
..	..	..	..	..	..	..	..	..	..	.	Current balance, convertible currency
5,797	8,358	9,609	12,082	16,722	23,746	35,303	42,406	44,847	52,545	.	External debt, total (World Bank)
5,797	8,358	9,609	12,082	16,722	23,746	35,303	42,406	44,847	52,545	.	Convertible currency
						28	35	30	29	32	.	CMEA
1,744	2,125	2,691	2,285	2,478	2,973	3,812	4,627	5,683	7,006	.	External debt service (World Bank)
1,744	2,125	2,691	2,285	2,478	2,973	3,812	4,627	5,683	7,006	.	Convertible currency
5,058	11,349	14,987	17,366	12,728	11,453	16,305	18,541	17,960	29,586	.	Total reserves less gold (IMF, IFS)
10,106	17,152	19,832	21,281	16,881	16,417	22,453	23,751	23,053	34,476	.	Total reserves, including gold at London price
5,574	11,840	15,451	17,801	13,214	11,994	16,934	19,135	18,547	30,209	.	Total reserves, incl. gold at national valuation
				(thousands)							**EMPLOYMENT**
..	..	..	..	..	..	..	..	..	..	.	Employment, total
..	..	..	..	..	..	..	..	..	..	.	Agriculture
..	..	..	..	..	..	..	..	..	..	.	Industry
..	..	..	..	..	..	..	..	..	..	.	Services
561,229	575,398	589,567	603,737	617,906	630,305	642,704	655,102	667,501	679,900	.	Labor force, total
..	..	..	..	..	..	..	..	..	..	.	Agriculture
..	..	..	..	..	..	..	..	..	..	.	Industry
..	..	..	..	..	..	..	..	..	..	.	Services
				(billions of current Chinese yuan)							**DOMESTIC FINANCE (IMF)**
198	227	271	360	488	635	796	960	1,139	1,468	.	Money supply, broadly defined
135	149	175	245	302	386	457	549	583	701	.	Money, means of payment
95	105	122	166	203	264	312	336	349	437	.	Demand deposits
40	44	53	79	99	122	146	213	234	264	.	Currency outside banks
63	78	96	115	186	249	338	412	556	767	.	Quasi-money
5	6	6	6	7	7	7	9	..	..	.	Interest: deposit rate (percent)
..	..	..	..	..	..	..	..	..	..	.	Central government expenditures
..	..	..	..	..	..	..	..	..	..	.	Defense
				(millions of 1989 US dollars)							
67,210	69,330	76,490	86,740	94,900	113,800	113,100	113,900	117,100	..	.	Central government exp. (ACDA)
23,640	23,780	23,220	22,600	22,600	21,970	22,030	22,720	22,330	..	.	Military (ACDA)
											LAND AND FORESTS (FAO)
237	241	245	249	252	257	261	..	..	..	.	Pop. density: agr. land (pop. per sq. km)
2	-2	-1	-1	-2	0	..	..	..	..	.	Deforestation rate (net)
1,219	1,198	1,185	1,170	1,153	1,150	..	..	..	..	.	Forest (thousands sq. km)
											SOCIAL INDICATORS
107	109	110	112	113	115	117	..	..	..	.	Population density: total land (pop. per sq. km)
..	112	113	118	124	129	132	134	..	..	.	School enrollment ratio, primary
..	36	35	37	39	42	43	44	..	..	.	secondary
..	1	1	1	2	2	2	2	..	..	.	tertiary
445	460	487	521	547	565	570	..	..	..	.	Energy consumption per capita (kg. of oil eq.)
2,367	2,469	2,545	2,612	2,630	2,624	2,654	2,632	..	..	.	Daily calorie supply per capita
101	108	114	121	121	125	128	129	132	139	.	Food production (1979-1981=100)
56	58	60	62	63	63	64	63	..	..	.	Daily protein supply (gm. per capita)
500	500	502	503	505	506	..	..	..	..	.	Population per hospital bed
..	1,800	1,705	1,712	1,617	1,405	..	..	..	..	.	per nursing person
..	1,000	1,003	1,007	1,011	1,012	..	..	..	..	.	per physician
50	50	51	51	52	52	53	53	54	54	.	Female participation in labor force (percent)
41	39	38	36	35	33	32	31	30	29	.	Infant mortality (per 1,000 live births)
67	68	68	69	69	69	70	70	70	70	.	Life expectancy (years)
3	2	2	2	2	3	3	3	3	3	.	Total fertility (births per woman)
19	20	24	32	37	41	47	50	53	56	.	Urban population (percent of total population)
..	..	..	..	4,345	..	..	..	..	..	.	Population per passenger car
211	199	185	166	149	..	..	..	..	..	.	per telephone

Cuba

Comparator tables	1970	1971	1972	1973	1974	1975	1976	1977	1978	1979	1980
PER CAPITA INCOME						*(US dollars)*					
World Bank (Atlas method)	..	..	..	..	..	..	..	..	..	..	
Single year conversion	..	..	..	..	..	..	..	..	..	..	
CIA or LWI	..	..	..	..	..	..	..	1,364	1,545	1,711	1,818
Penn World Tables	..	..	..	..		..	..	..	..	..	..
						(thousands)					
POPULATION	8,551	8,692	8,862	9,036	9,154	9,292	9,423	9,541	9,638	9,720	9,724
GROSS NATIONAL PRODUCT, current prices					*(millions of current US dollars)*						
World Bank (Atlas method)	..	..	..	..	..	..	..	..	..	..	
Single year conversion	..	..	..	..	..	..	..	..	..	..	
Authors' series	..	..	..	..	..	..	..	..	..	..	
CIA or LWI	..	..	..	..	..	..	..	12,960	14,830	16,600	17,630
GROSS NATIONAL PRODUCT, constant prices					*(millions of constant 1987 dollars)*						
Single year conversion	..	..	..	..	..	..	..	..	..	..	
Authors' series, rescaled from 1980 prices	..	..	..	..	..	..	..	..	..	..	
CIA or LWI, rescaled from 1989 prices	..	..	..	..	..	..	..	23,558	25,106	25,832	25,145
CONVERSION FACTORS						*(LCUs per US dollar)*					
World Bank (Atlas method)	..	..	..	..	..	..	..	..	..	..	
Single year convertor	..	..	..	..	..	..	..	..	..	..	
Authors' series	..	..	..	..	..	..	..	..	..	..	
Penn World Tables	..	..	..	..	..	..	..	..	..	..	
OUTPUT TRENDS, OVERALL					*(index, constant prices 1987 = 100)*						
GNP, SNA	..	..	..	..	..	..	..	..	..	..	
NMP, MPS	..	..	..	..	..	62.3	65.4	70.9	75.8	76.3	72.3
GNP, "Building block"	..	..	..	..	..	..	..	..	..	..	
Industry											
Value added, SNA	..	..	..	..	..	..	..	..	..	..	
Value added, MPS	..	..	..	..	..	54.7	57.2	58.7	63.3	61.5	61.4
"Building block"	..	..	..	..	..	..	..	..	..	..	
Gross output, SNA	..	..	..	..	..	..	..	..	..	..	
Agriculture											
Value added, SNA	..	..	..	..	..	..	..	..	..	..	
Value added, MPS	..	..	..	..	..	100.5	103.5	108.4	116.6	114.1	103.4
"Building block"	..	..	..	..	..	..	..	..	..	..	
Gross output, SNA	..	..	..	..	..	..	..	..	..	..	
Services											
Value added, SNA	..	..	..	..	..	..	..	..	..	..	
Value added, MPS	..	..	..	..	..	61.9	65.6	74.7	79.3	82.5	76.2
"Building block"	..	..	..	..	..	..	..	..	..	..	
CONSUMPTION											
Total consumption, SNA	..	..	..	..	..	..	..	..	..	..	
Total consumption, MPS	..	..	..	..	..	66.9	69.8	69.8	73.6	76.6	82.5
Households, SNA	..	..	..	..	..	..	..	..	..	..	
Households, "building block"	..	..	..	..	..	..	..	..	..	..	
General government, SNA	..	..	..	..	..	..	..	..	..	..	
General government, "building block"	..	..	..	..	..	..	..	..	..	..	
INVESTMENT											
Gross fixed investment, SNA	..	..	..	..	..	..	..	..	..	..	
Accumulation, MPS	..	..	..	..	..	71.0	83.1	89.0	75.8	74.3	79.6
"Building block"	..	..	..	..	..	..	..	..	..	..	
CONSUMER PRICES											
National methodology	..	..	..	..	..	..	..	..	..	..	
Outside estimate	..	..	..	..	..	..	..	..	..	..	
MERCHANDISE EXPORTS					*(millions of current US dollars)*						
UNCTAD	1,049	..	..	..	..	3,684	..	..	..	..	5,577
IMF: IFS	..	..	..	..	..	..	..	..	..	..	
ACDA	..	..	..	..	..	..	..	3,669	4,575	4,829	5,593
ECE	..	..	..	..	..	..	..	..	..	..	
intra-CMEA	..	..	..	..	..	..	..	..	..	..	
Authors' uniform TR/$ series	1,049	..	..	..	..	3,684	..	..	..	..	5,577
intra-CMEA	150	..	..	..	..	279	..	..	..	..	569
MERCHANDISE IMPORTS					*(millions of current US dollars)*						
UNCTAD	1,311	..	..	..	..	3,883	..	..	..	..	6,505
IMF: IFS	..	..	..	..	..	..	..	..	..	..	
ACDA	..	..	..	..	..	..	..	4,362	4,751	5,089	6,409
ECE	..	..	..	..	..	..	..	..	..	..	
intra-CMEA	..	..	..	..	..	..	..	..	..	..	
Authors' uniform series	1,311	..	..	..	..	3,883	..	..	..	..	6,505
intra-CMEA	125	..	..	..	..	304	..	..	..	..	826

Abbreviations in notes column are explained in the General Notes. For sources and methods, see the Technical Notes.

1981	1982	1983	1984	1985	1986	1987	1988	1989	1990	Notes	Comparator tables (continued)
				(US dollars)							**PER CAPITA INCOME**
..	..	..	..	..	..	..	..	..	..	.	World Bank (Atlas method)
								..	..	.	Single year conversion
2,149	2,324	2,549	2,699	2,923	3,080	3,272	3,339	3,377	..	A.	CIA or LWI
									..	.	Penn World Tables
				(thousands)							
9,724	9,801	9,897	9,994	10,098	10,199	10,288	10,410	10,522	10,626	.	**POPULATION**
			(millions of current US dollars)								**GROSS NATIONAL PRODUCT, current prices**
..	..	..	..	..	..	..	..	..	..	.	World Bank (Atlas method)
..	..	..	..	..	..	..	..	..	..	.	Single year conversion
..	..	..	..	..	..	..	..	..	..	.	Authors' series
20,840	22,770	25,230	26,990	29,520	31,420	33,700	34,720	35,460	..	.	CIA or LWI
			(millions of constant 1987 dollars)								**GROSS NATIONAL PRODUCT, constant prices**
..	..	..	..	..	..	..	..	..	..	.	Single year conversion
..	..	..	..	..	..	..	..	..	..	.	Authors' series, rescaled from 1980 prices
27,109	27,835	29,694	30,623	32,529	33,749	35,085	34,978	34,320	..	A.	CIA or LWI, rescaled from 1989 prices
				(LCUs per US dollar)							**CONVERSION FACTORS**
..	..	..	..	..	..	..	..	..	..	..	World Bank (Atlas method)
..	..	..	..	..	..	..	..	..	..	..	Single year convertor
..	..	..	..	..	..	..	..	..	..	.	Authors' series
..	..	..	..	..	..	..	..	..	..	.	Penn World Tables
			(index, constant prices 1987 = 100)								**OUTPUT TRENDS, OVERALL**
..	..	..	..	..	..	..	..	..	..	.	GNP, SNA
87.3	91.7	96.7	104.0	108.3	105.8	100.0	102.3	..	..	f	NMP, MPS
..	..	..	..	..	..	..	..	..	..	.	GNP, "Building block"
											Industry
..	..	..	..	..	..	..	..	..	..	.	Value added, SNA
79.1	83.2	90.3	103.9	112.1	106.0	100.0	..	..	..	.	Value added, MPS
..	..	..	..	..	..	..	..	..	..	.	"Building block"
..	..	..	..	..	..	..	..	..	..	.	Gross output, SNA
											Agriculture
..	..	..	..	..	..	..	..	..	..	.	Value added, SNA
122.8	117.2	108.7	111.1	105.6	102.9	100.0	..	..	..	I	Value added, MPS
..	..	..	..	..	..	..	..	..	..	.	"Building block"
..	..	..	..	..	..	..	..	..	..	.	Gross output, SNA
											Services
..	..	..	..	..	..	..	..	..	..	.	Value added, SNA
88.0	94.6	100.3	102.7	105.2	106.2	100.0	..	..	..	.	Value added, MPS
..	..	..	..	..	..	..	..	..	..	.	"Building block"
											CONSUMPTION
..	..	..	..	..	..	..	..	..	..	.	Total consumption, SNA
88.1	90.7	93.1	97.7	100.1	102.5	100.0	101.8	..	..	.	Total consumption, MPS
..	..	..	..	..	..	..	..	..	..	.	Households, SNA
..	..	..	..	..	..	..	..	..	..	.	Households, "building block"
..	..	..	..	..	..	..	..	..	..	.	General government, SNA
..	..	..	..	..	..	..	..	..	..	.	General government, "building block"
											INVESTMENT
..	..	..	..	..	..	..	..	..	..	.	Gross fixed investment, SNA
110.8	89.3	110.6	142.8	152.8	136.6	100.0	106.2	..	..	.	Accumulation, MPS
..	..	..	..	..	..	..	..	..	..	.	"Building block"
											CONSUMER PRICES
..	..	..	..	..	..	..	..	..	..	.	National methodology
..	..	..	..	..	..	..	..	..	..	.	Outside estimate
			(millions of current US dollars)								**MERCHANDISE EXPORTS**
5,406	5,920	6,432	6,213	6,501	6,298	5,401	5,518	6,000	6,200	.	UNCTAD
..	..	..	..	..	..	..	..	..	..	.	IMF: IFS
5,406	5,928	6,416	6,174	6,503	6,438	5,401	5,500	5,392	..	.	ACDA
..	..	..	..	..	..	..	..	..	..	.	ECE
											intra-CMEA
5,406	5,920	6,432	6,213	6,501	6,298	5,401	5,518	6,000	6,200	N	Authors' uniform TR/$ series
..	..	746	826	722	670	820	..	..	..		intra-CMEA
			(millions of current US dollars)								**MERCHANDISE IMPORTS**
6,545	6,637	7,211	8,167	8,749	9,173	7,612	7,579	7,270	7,500	.	UNCTAD
..	..	..	..	..	..	..	..	..	..	.	IMF: IFS
6,546	6,645	7,235	8,213	8,677	9,158	7,612	7,580	8,124	..	.	ACDA
..	..	..	..	..	..	..	..	..	..	.	ECE
											intra-CMEA
6,545	6,637	7,211	8,167	8,749	9,173	7,612	7,579	7,270	7,500	N	Authors' uniform series
..	..	1,120	1,136	1,133	1,120	1,070	..	..	..		intra-CMEA

Cuba

Basic tables	1970	1971	1972	1973	1974	1975	1976	1977	1978	1979	1980
SNA ACCOUNTS, current prices					*(millions of current Cuban pesos)*						
GNP, at market prices	..	..	..	..	..	..	..	..	..	..	..
Net factor income	..	..	..	..	..	..	..	..	..	..	..
GDP at market prices	..	..	..	..	..	..	..	..	..	..	..
Net indirect taxes	..	..	..	..	..	..	..	..	..	..	..
GDP at factor cost	..	..	..	..	..	..	..	..	..	..	..
Agriculture	..	..	..	..	..	..	..	..	..	..	..
Industry	..	..	..	..	..	..	..	..	..	..	..
Services, etc.	..	..	..	..	..	..	..	..	..	..	..
Resource balance	..	..	..	..	..	..	..	..	..	..	..
Exports GNFS	..	..	..	..	..	..	..	..	..	..	..
Imports GNFS	..	..	..	..	..	..	..	..	..	..	..
Domestic absorption	..	..	..	..	..	..	..	..	..	..	..
Total consumption	..	..	..	..	..	..	..	..	..	..	..
Private consumption	..	..	..	..	..	..	..	..	..	..	..
General government consumption	..	..	..	..	..	..	..	..	..	..	..
Gross domestic investment	..	..	..	..	..	..	..	..	..	..	..
Fixed domestic investment	..	..	..	..	..	..	..	..	..	..	..
Depreciation	..	..	..	..	..	..	..	..	..	..	..
SNA ACCOUNTS, constant prices					*(millions of constant 1987 Cuban pesos)*						
Gross national product (GNP)	..	..	..	..	..	..	..	..	..	..	..
GDP at market prices	..	..	..	..	..	..	..	..	..	..	..
GDP at factor cost	..	..	..	..	..	..	..	..	..	..	..
Agriculture	..	..	..	..	..	..	..	..	..	..	..
Industry	..	..	..	..	..	..	..	..	..	..	..
Services, etc.	..	..	..	..	..	..	..	..	..	..	..
Resource balance	..	..	..	..	..	..	..	..	..	..	..
Exports GNFS	..	..	..	..	..	..	..	..	..	..	..
Imports GNFS	..	..	..	..	..	..	..	..	..	..	..
Domestic absorption	..	..	..	..	..	..	..	..	..	..	..
Total consumption, etc.	..	..	..	..	..	..	..	..	..	..	..
Private consumption, etc.	..	..	..	..	..	..	..	..	..	..	..
General government consumption	..	..	..	..	..	..	..	..	..	..	..
Gross domestic investment	..	..	..	..	..	..	..	..	..	..	..
Fixed domestic investment	..	..	..	..	..	..	..	..	..	..	..
Depreciation	..	..	..	..	..	..	..	..	..	..	..
MPS ACCOUNTS, current prices					*(millions of current Cuban pesos)*						
NMP produced:	..	..	..	..	..	8,113	8,355	8,413	9,466	9,621	9,854
Agriculture and forestry	..	..	..	..	..	546	579	600	616	619	617
Industry excluding construction	..	..	..	..	..	3,551	3,763	3,656	3,881	4,105	3,817
Construction	..	..	..	..	..	612	646	717	780	680	785
Transport and communication	..	..	..	..	..	553	580	614	648	704	782
Trade, etc.	..	..	..	..	..	2,851	2,787	2,827	3,542	3,514	3,854
Other services	..	..	..	..	..	..	..	..	..	..	..
Resource balance	..	..	..	..	..	-195	-364	-690	-194	-172	-588
NMP used: domestic market	..	..	..	..	..	8,308	8,719	9,103	9,660	9,793	10,442
Final consumption, material goods	..	..	..	..	..	6,226	6,541	6,773	7,502	7,877	8,336
Personal consumption	..	..	..	..	..	5,408	5,612	5,700	6,104	6,340	6,692
Collective consumption	..	..	..	..	..	818	929	1,073	1,398	1,537	1,644
Net capital formation	..	..	..	..	..	2,082	2,178	2,330	2,158	1,916	2,106
Net fixed capital formation	..	..	..	..	..	1,348	1,600	1,716	1,463	1,432	1,529
Changes in stocks	..	..	..	..	..	734	578	613	695	484	577
Depreciation	..	..	..	..	..	..	..	..	..	..	..
MPS ACCOUNTS, constant prices					*(millions of 1981 Cuban pesos)*						
NMP produced:	..	..	..	..	..	8,204	8,618	9,335	9,986	10,051	9,523
Agriculture and forestry	..	..	..	..	..	1,208	1,244	1,302	1,400	1,370	1,241
Industry and construction	..	..	..	..	..	3,109	3,251	3,338	3,600	3,498	3,495
Services	..	..	..	..	..	3,888	4,123	4,695	4,986	5,183	4,787
Resource balance	..	..	..	..	..	-1,176	-1,153	-588	-165	-160	-1,531
NMP used: domestic market	..	..	..	..	..	9,380	9,771	9,923	10,151	10,211	11,054
Final consumption, material goods	..	..	..	..	..	7,150	7,462	7,458	7,865	8,182	8,817
Personal consumption	..	..	..	..	..	6,297	6,494	6,327	6,410	6,589	7,132
Collective consumption	..	..	..	..	..	853	968	1,131	1,455	1,593	1,685
Net capital formation	..	..	..	..	..	2,230	2,309	2,465	2,286	2,029	2,237
Net fixed capital formation	..	..	..	..	..	1,439	1,686	1,804	1,537	1,507	1,615
Depreciation	..	..	..	..	..	..	..	..	..	..	..

Abbreviations in notes column are explained in the General Notes. For sources and methods, see the Technical Notes.

Cuba

1981	1982	1983	1984	1985	1986	1987	1988	1989	1990	Notes	Basic tables (continued)
				(millions of current Cuban pesos)							**SNA ACCOUNTS, current prices**
..	..	..	..	..	..	..	..	..	..	.	GNP, at market prices
..	..	..	..	..	..	..	..	..	..	.	Net factor income
..	..	..	..	..	..	..	..	..	..	.	GDP at market prices
..	..	..	..	..	..	..	..	..	..	.	Net indirect taxes
..	..	..	..	..	..	..	..	..	..	.	GDP at factor cost
..	..	..	..	..	..	..	..	..	..	.	Agriculture
..	..	..	..	..	..	..	..	..	..	.	Industry
..	..	..	..	..	..	..	..	..	..	.	Services, etc.
..	..	..	..	..	..	..	..	..	..	.	Resource balance
..	..	..	..	..	..	..	..	..	..	.	Exports GNFS
..	..	..	..	..	..	..	..	..	..	.	Imports GNFS
..	..	..	..	..	..	..	..	..	..	.	Domestic absorption
..	..	..	..	..	..	..	..	..	..	.	Total consumption
..	..	..	..	..	..	..	..	..	..	.	Private consumption
..	..	..	..	..	..	..	..	..	..	.	General government consumption
..	..	..	..	..	..	..	..	..	..	.	Gross domestic investment
..	..	..	..	..	..	..	..	..	..	.	Fixed domestic investment
..	..	..	..	..	..	..	..	..	..	.	Depreciation
				(millions of constant 1987 Cuban pesos)							**SNA ACCOUNTS, constant prices**
..	..	..	..	..	..	..	..	..	..	.	Gross national product (GNP)
..	..	..	..	..	..	..	..	..	..	.	GDP at market prices
..	..	..	..	..	..	..	..	..	..	.	GDP at factor cost
..	..	..	..	..	..	..	..	..	..	.	Agriculture
..	..	..	..	..	..	..	..	..	..	.	Industry
..	..	..	..	..	..	..	..	..	..	.	Services, etc.
..	..	..	..	..	..	..	..	..	..	.	Resource balance
..	..	..	..	..	..	..	..	..	..	.	Exports GNFS
..	..	..	..	..	..	..	..	..	..	.	Imports GNFS
..	..	..	..	..	..	..	..	..	..	.	Domestic absorption
..	..	..	..	..	..	..	..	..	..	.	Total consumption, etc.
..	..	..	..	..	..	..	..	..	..	.	Private consumption, etc.
..	..	..	..	..	..	..	..	..	..	.	General government consumption
..	..	..	..	..	..	..	..	..	..	.	Gross domestic investment
..	..	..	..	..	..	..	..	..	..	.	Fixed domestic investment
..	..	..	..	..	..	..	..	..	..	.	Depreciation
				(millions of current Cuban pesos)							**MPS ACCOUNTS, current prices**
11,504	12,176	12,926	13,695	13,952	12,857	12,202	12,654	..	..	f	NMP produced:
1,474	1,397	1,342	1,370	1,362	1,429	1,404	..	..	..	.	Agriculture and forestry
3,568	3,921	4,135	4,734	5,072	4,806	4,499	..	..	..	.	Industry excluding construction
934	942	1,079	1,321	1,313	1,199	1,018	..	..	..	.	Construction
893	909	958	1,051	1,040	986	1,051	..	..	..	.	Transport and communication
4,635	5,008	5,413	5,219	5,166	4,437	4,231	..	..	..	.	Trade, etc.
..	..	..	..	..	..	..	..	..	..	.	Other services
-870	-529	-909	-1,660	-2,175	-2,434	-2,201	-2,272	..	..	.	Resource balance
12,374	12,705	13,835	15,355	16,127	15,291	14,403	14,926	..	..	.	NMP used: domestic market
9,416	10,291	11,040	11,870	12,366	12,809	12,683	12,944	..	..	.	Final consumption, material goods
7,406	8,172	8,667	9,277	9,683	10,047	10,136	10,328	..	..	f	Personal consumption
2,010	2,119	2,373	2,593	2,683	2,762	2,547	2,616	..	..	.	Collective consumption
2,958	2,414	2,795	3,485	3,761	2,482	1,720	1,982	..	..	.	Net capital formation
2,247	1,812	2,243	2,895	3,098	2,729	1,980	2,104	..	..	.	Net fixed capital formation
711	602	553	590	663	-247	-260	-122	..	..	.	Changes in stocks
..	..	..	..	..	..	..	..	..	..	.	Depreciation
				(millions of 1981 Cuban pesos)							**MPS ACCOUNTS, constant prices**
11,504	12,087	12,745	13,696	14,261	13,943	13,174	13,475	..	..	f	NMP produced:
1,474	1,408	1,306	1,335	1,269	1,236	1,201	..	..	..	.	Agriculture and forestry
4,502	4,734	5,138	5,907	6,378	6,029	5,687	..	..	..	.	Industry and construction
5,528	5,945	6,302	6,454	6,614	6,678	6,286	..	..	..	.	Services
-870	13	18	-196	-143	399	649	534	..	..	.	Resource balance
12,374	12,074	12,727	13,892	14,404	13,544	12,525	12,941	..	..	.	NMP used: domestic market
9,416	9,689	9,948	10,437	10,690	10,952	10,684	10,875	..	..	.	Final consumption, material goods
7,406	7,630	7,683	7,961	8,144	8,334	8,280	8,406	..	..	f	Personal consumption
2,010	2,059	2,265	2,476	2,546	2,618	2,404	2,469	..	..	.	Collective consumption
2,958	2,385	2,779	3,455	3,714	2,592	1,841	2,066	..	..	.	Net capital formation
2,247	1,812	2,243	2,895	3,098	2,771	2,028	2,154	..	..	.	Net fixed capital formation
..	..	..	..	..	..	..	..	..	..	.	Depreciation

Basic tables (continued)	1970	1971	1972	1973	1974	1975	1976	1977	1978	1979	1980
MPS ACCOUNTS, index						*(index,1980 = 100)*					
NMP produced:	..	..	..	..	..	86.1	90.5	98.0	104.9	105.5	100.0
Agriculture and forestry	..	..	..	..	..	97.3	100.2	104.9	112.8	110.4	100.0
Industry excluding construction	..	..	..	..	..	..	..	..	..	..	..
Construction	..	..	..	..	..	..	..	..	..	..	..
Transport and communication	..	..	..	..	..	..	..	..	..	..	..
Trade, etc.	..	..	..	..	..	..	..	..	..	..	..
NMP used: material goods	..	..	..	..	..	84.9	88.4	89.8	91.8	92.4	100.0
Final consumption	..	..	..	..	..	81.1	84.6	84.6	89.2	92.8	100.0
Net capital formation	..	..	..	..	..	99.7	103.2	110.2	102.2	90.7	100.0
EXCHANGE AND CONVERSION RATES						*(LCUs per US dollar: annual average)*					
Single-year converter	..	..	..	..	..	..	..	..	..	..	..
Devisa/official	..	..	..	..	..	..	..	..	..	..	..
Commercial	..	..	..	..	..	..	..	..	..	..	..
Noncommercial											
Informal market	6.690	8.910	9.883	9.663	8.993	9.150	9.038	11.041	12.817	14.008	14.879
ICP	..	..	..	..	..	..	..	..	..	..	..
						(ruble per US dollar: annual average)					
Commercial TR/$ cross	..	..	..	..	..	..	..	..	..	..	..
Uniform TR/$ cross	1.072	1.157	1.232	1.093	1.092	1.167	1.067	1.022	0.973	0.945	0.980
						(LCUs per ruble: annual average)					
Commercial	..	..	..	..	..	..	..	..	..	..	..
Noncommercial	..	..	..	..	..	..	..	..	..	..	..
Devisa/official	..	..	..	..	..	..	..	..	..	..	..
CONSUMER PRICE INDEXES						*(index)*					
Official, IMF 1985 = 100	..	..	..	..	..	..	..	..	..	..	..
Official, CIA or LWI 1980 = 100	..	..	..	..	..	..	..	..	..	..	..
Alternative, CIA or LWI 1980 = 100	..	..	..	..	..	..	..	..	..	..	..
INTERNATIONAL TRADE (ECE)						*(millions of current Cuban pesos)*					
Value of exports, fob	..	..	..	..	..	2,953	2,689	2,925	3,440	3,499	3,961
to CMEA	..	..	..	..	..	..	..	..	..	..	..
Value of imports, cif	..	..	..	..	..	3,108	3,181	3,457	3,571	3,686	4,630
from CMEA	..	..	..	..	..	..	..	..	..	..	..
Trade balance	..	..	..	..	..	-155	-492	-532	-132	-187	-669
CMEA	..	..	..	..	..	..	..	..	..	..	..
INTERNATIONAL TRADE (Authors')						*(millions of current US dollars)*					
Value of exports, fob	1,049	..	..	..	..	3,684	..	..	..	..	5,577
to developed countries	272	..	..	..	..	1,171	..	..	..	..	1,671
to other non-socialist countries	..	..	..	..	..	..	..	..	..	..	..
to socialist countries	778	..	..	..	..	2,401	..	..	..	..	3,922
to CMEA	150	..	..	..	..	279	..	..	..	..	569
Value of imports, cif	1,311	..	..	..	..	3,883	..	..	..	..	6,505
from developed countries	406	..	..	..	..	1,832	..	..	..	..	1,426
from other non-socialist countries	..	..	..	..	..	..	..	..	..	..	..
from socialist countries	905	..	..	..	..	1,935	..	..	..	..	4,983
from CMEA	125	..	..	..	..	304	..	..	..	..	826
Trade balance	-262	..	..	..	..	-199	..	..	..	..	-928
Developed countries	-134	..	..	..	..	-661	..	..	..	..	245
Other non-socialist countries	..	..	..	..	..	466	..	..	..	..	..
Socialist countries	-127	..	..	..	..	-25	..	..	..	..	-1,061
CMEA	25	..	..	..	..	..	..	..	..	..	-257
PARTNER CONVERTIBLE TRADE (ECE)						*(millions of current US dollars)*					
Exports to non-CMEA (cif)	..	..	..	..	..	..	..	..	..	..	..
Imports from non-CMEA (fob)	..	..	..	..	..	..	..	..	..	..	..
Trade balance	..	..	..	..	..	..	..	..	..	..	..
TRADE PRICE INDEXES (Authors')						*(index,1980 = 100)*					
Terms of trade	..	..	..	..	..	111.9	106.4	95.3	86.6	87.8	100.0
Exports	..	..	..	..	..	86.6	78.4	74.6	78.0	79.2	100.0
Non-socialist countries	..	..	..	..	..	..	..	..	..	..	..
Developed countries	..	..	..	..	..	..	..	..	..	..	..
Other	..	..	..	..	..	..	..	..	..	..	..
Socialist countries	..	..	..	..	..	..	..	..	..	..	..
CMEA	..	..	..	..	..	..	..	..	..	..	..
Imports	..	..	..	..	..	77.4	73.7	78.3	90.1	90.1	100.0
Non-socialist countries	..	..	..	..	..	..	..	..	..	..	..
Developed countries	..	..	..	..	..	..	..	..	..	..	..
Other	..	..	..	..	..	..	..	..	..	..	..
Socialist countries	..	..	..	..	..	..	..	..	..	..	..
CMEA	..	..	..	..	..	..	..	..	..	..	..

Abbreviations in notes column are explained in the General Notes. For sources and methods, see the Technical Notes.

1981	1982	1983	1984	1985	1986	1987	1988	1989	1990	Notes	Basic tables (continued)
				(index, 1980 = 100)							**MPS ACCOUNTS, index**
120.8	126.9	133.8	143.8	149.8	146.4	138.3	141.5	..	..	I	NMP produced:
118.8	113.4	105.2	107.5	102.2	99.6	96.8	..	..	..	I	Agriculture and forestry
..	..	..	..	..	..	..	..	..	..	.	Industry excluding construction
..	..	..	..	..	..	..	..	..	..	.	Construction
..	..	..	..	..	..	..	..	..	..	.	Transport and communication
..	..	..	..	..	..	..	..	..	..	.	Trade, etc.
111.9	109.2	115.1	125.7	130.3	122.5	113.3	117.1	..	..	I	NMP used: material goods
106.8	109.9	112.8	118.4	121.2	124.2	121.2	123.3	..	..	I	Final consumption
132.2	106.6	124.2	154.4	166.0	115.9	82.3	92.4	..	..	I	Net capital formation
				(LCUs per US dollar: annual average)							**EXCHANGE AND CONVERSION RATES**
..	..	..	..	..	..	..	..	..	..	.	Single-year converter
..	..	..	..	..	..	..	..	..	..	.	Devisa/official
..	..	..	..	..	..	..	..	..	..	.	Commercial
..	..	..	..	..	..	..	..	..	..	.	Noncommercial
19.417	20.916	17.542	..	..	..	..	..	..	..	.	Informal market
..	..	..	..	..	..	..	..	..	..	.	ICP
				(ruble per US dollar: annual average)							
..	..	..	..	..	..	..	..	..	..	.	Commercial TR/$ cross
1.076	1.105	1.201	1.395	1.433	1.388	1.397	1.484	1.660	1.980	.	Uniform TR/$ cross
				(LCUs per ruble: annual average)							
..	..	..	..	..	..	..	..	..	..	.	Commercial
..	..	..	..	..	..	..	..	..	..	.	Noncommercial
..	..	..	..	..	..	..	..	..	..	.	Devisa/official
				(index)							**CONSUMER PRICE INDEXES**
..	..	..	..	..	..	..	..	..	..	.	Official, IMF 1985 = 100
..	..	..	..	..	..	..	..	..	..	.	Official, CIA or LWI 1980 = 100
..	..	..	..	..	..	..	..	..	..	.	Alternative, CIA or LWI 1980 = 100
				(millions of current Cuban pesos)							**INTERNATIONAL TRADE (ECE)**
4,235	4,923	5,549	5,471	5,985	5,330	5,392	5,509	..	..	.	Value of exports, fob
..	..	..	..	..	..	..	..	..	..	.	to CMEA
5,122	5,524	6,206	7,217	8,033	7,584	7,590	7,582	..	..	.	Value of imports, cif
..	..	..	..	..	..	..	..	..	..	.	from CMEA
-887	-601	-657	-1,746	-2,049	-2,254	-2,198	-2,073	..	..	.	Trade balance
..	..	..	..	..	..	..	..	..	..	.	CMEA
				(millions of current US dollars)							**INTERNATIONAL TRADE (Authors')**
5,406	5,920	6,432	6,213	6,501	6,298	5,401	5,518	6,000	6,200	N	Value of exports, fob
..	..	895	644	717	590	..	..	..	..	.	to developed countries
..	..	..	..	..	..	..	..	..	..	.	to other non-socialist countries
..	..	5,521	5,530	5,786	5,700	4,822	..	..	..	.	to socialist countries
..	..	746	826	722	670	820	..	..	..	.	to CMEA
6,545	6,637	7,211	8,167	8,749	9,173	7,612	7,579	7,270	7,500	N	Value of imports, cif
..	..	974	1,307	1,375	1,584	..	..	..	..	.	from developed countries
..	..	..	..	..	..	..	..	..	..	.	from other non-socialist countries
..	..	6,260	6,906	7,302	7,574	6,704	..	..	..	.	from socialist countries
..	..	1,120	1,136	1,133	1,120	1,070	..	..	..	.	from CMEA
-1,139	-717	-779	-1,954	-2,248	-2,875	-2,211	-2,061	-1,270	-1,300	N	Trade balance
..	..	-79	-663	-658	-994	..	..	..	..	.	Developed countries
..	..	..	..	..	..	..	..	..	..	.	Other non-socialist countries
..	..	-739	-1,376	-1,516	-1,874	-1,882	..	..	..	.	Socialist countries
..	..	-374	-310	-411	-450	-250	..	..	..	.	CMEA
				(millions of current US dollars)							**PARTNER CONVERTIBLE TRADE (ECE)**
..	..	1,644	2,217	2,711	2,294	1,489	2,218	2,465	..	W	Exports to non-CMEA (cif)
..	..	1,138	924	932	938	1,012	1,419	1,434	..	W	Imports from non-CMEA (fob)
..	..	506	1,293	1,779	1,356	477	799	1,031	..	W	Trade balance
				(index, 1980 = 100)							**TRADE PRICE INDEXES (Authors')**
82.2	73.3	82.1	70.8	71.0	69.2	74.6	..	..	..	.	Terms of trade
94.3	97.6	113.2	113.8	119.5	114.1	121.7	..	..	..	.	Exports
..	..	..	..	..	..	..	..	..	..	.	Non-socialist countries
..	..	..	..	..	..	..	..	..	..	.	Developed countries
..	..	..	..	..	..	..	..	..	..	.	Other
..	..	..	..	..	..	..	..	..	..	.	Socialist countries
..	..	..	..	..	..	..	..	..	..	.	CMEA
114.8	133.3	137.9	160.7	168.3	164.9	163.1	..	..	..	.	Imports
..	..	..	..	..	..	..	..	..	..	.	Non-socialist countries
..	..	..	..	..	..	..	..	..	..	.	Developed countries
..	..	..	..	..	..	..	..	..	..	.	Other
..	..	..	..	..	..	..	..	..	..	.	Socialist countries
..	..	..	..	..	..	..	..	..	..	.	CMEA

Basic tables (continued)	1970	1971	1972	1973	1974	1975	1976	1977	1978	1979	1980
TRADE PRICE INDEXES (ECE)					*(index, 1980 = 100)*						
Terms of trade	..	..	..	..	..	..	..	..	..	..	..
Exports	..	..	..	..	..	..	..	..	..	..	..
Imports	..	..	..	..	..	..	..	..	..	..	..
Balance of Payments (ECE)					*(millions of current US dollars)*						
Exports, convertible currency	..	..	..	..	..	..	..	..	..	..	..
Imports, convertible currency	..	..	..	..	..	..	..	..	..	..	..
Trade balance, convertible currency	..	..	..	..	..	..	..	..	..	..	..
Invisibles, convertible currency	..	..	..	..	..	..	..	..	..	..	..
Current balance, convertible currency	..	..	..	..	..	..	..	..	..	..	..
External debt, total (World Bank)	..	..	..	..	..	..	..	..	..	..	..
Convertible currency	..	..	..	..	..	..	..	..	..	..	..
CMEA	..	..	..	..	..	..	..	..	..	..	..
External debt service (World Bank)	..	..	..	..	..	..	..	..	..	..	..
Convertible currency	..	..	..	..	..	..	..	..	..	..	..
Total reserves less gold (IMF, IFS)	..	..	..	..	..	..	..	..	..	..	..
Total reserves, including gold at London price	..	..	..	..	..	..	..	..	..	..	..
Total reserves, incl. gold at national valuation	..	..	..	..	..	..	..	..	..	..	..
EMPLOYMENT					*(thousands)*						
Employment, total	..	..	..	..	..	..	..	..	..	..	..
Agriculture	..	..	..	..	..	..	..	..	..	..	..
Industry	..	..	..	..	..	..	..	..	..	..	..
Services	..	..	..	..	..	..	..	..	..	..	..
Labor force, total	2,636	2,718	2,800	2,883	2,965	3,047	3,151	3,255	3,359	3,463	3,567
Agriculture	797	800	804	807	810	813	820	827	834	841	848
Industry	703	731	759	787	815	843	878	913	948	982	1,017
Services	1,136	1,187	1,238	1,288	1,339	1,390	1,452	1,515	1,577	1,639	1,702
DOMESTIC FINANCE (IMF)					*(millions of current Cuban pesos)*						
Money supply, broadly defined	..	..	..	..	..	..	..	..	..	..	..
Money, means of payment	..	..	..	..	..	..	..	..	..	..	..
Demand deposits	..	..	..	..	..	..	..	..	..	..	..
Currency outside banks	..	..	..	..	..	..	..	..	..	..	20
Quasi-money	..	..	..	..	..	..	..	..	..	..	..
Interest: deposit rate (percent)	..	..	..	..	..	..	..	..	..	..	..
Central government expenditures	..	..	..	..	..	..	..	..	..	..	..
Defense	..	..	..	..	..	..	..	..	..	..	..
					(millions of 1989 US dollars)						
Central government exp. (ACDA)	..	..	..	..	..	..	..	..	..	..	..
Military (ACDA)	..	..	..	..	..	..	..	..	1,818	1,865	1,680
LAND AND FORESTS (FAO)											
Pop. density: agr. land (pop. per sq. km)	170	171	159	154	163	162	163	164	167	170	168
Deforestation rate (net)	1	1	1	1	1	1	1	1	1	1	1
Forest (thousands sq. km)	23	23	23	24	24	24	24	24	25	25	25
SOCIAL INDICATORS											
Population density: total land (pop. per sq. km)	77	78	80	82	83	84	85	86	87	88	88
School enrollment ratio, primary	121	..	..	..	..	124	122	119	116	112	108
secondary	22	..	..	..	..	42	48	62	68	71	80
tertiary	..	..	..	..	..	..	..	..	..	..	20
Energy consumption per capita (kg. of oil eq.)	722	748	764	813	826	953	919	988	1,020	1,047	1,033
Daily calorie supply per capita	2,613	2,598	2,622	2,632	2,668	2,598	2,659	2,685	2,759	2,756	2,835
Food production (1979-1981 = 100)	112	90	83	85	87	82	85	91	98	103	94
Daily protein supply (gm. per capita)	70	69	67	69	69	67	68	69	69	70	74
Population per hospital bed	217	..	..	..	..	..	..	..	..	..	..
per nursing person	..	..	..	..	..	..	..	..	..	367	..
per physician	1,222	..	..	..	..	..	..	..	..	..	..
Female participation in labor force (percent)	12	13	14	15	16	16	18	19	20	21	22
Infant mortality (per 1,000 live births)	39	37	28	29	32	25	23	25	22	19	20
Life expectancy (years)	70	71	71	71	72	72	73	73	73	74	74
Total fertility (births per woman)	4	4	4	3	3	3	2	2	2	2	2
Urban population (percent of total population)	60	61	62	63	63	64	65	66	67	67	68
Population per passenger car	119	121	..	129	..	65	..	61	60	64	61
per telephone	..	..	..	..	..	..	..	..	..	..	..

Abbreviations in notes column are explained in the General Notes. For sources and methods, see the Technical Notes.

1981	1982	1983	1984	1985	1986	1987	1988	1989	1990	Notes	
				(index,1980 = 100)							**TRADE PRICE INDEXES (ECE)**
..	..	..	..	..	..	..	..	..	..	.	Terms of trade
..	..	..	..	..	..	..	..	..	..	.	Exports
..	..	..	..	..	..	..	..	..	..	.	Imports
			(millions of current US dollars)								**Balance of Payments (ECE)**
..	..	..	..	..	..	..	..	..	..	.	Exports, convertible currency
..	..	..	..	..	..	..	..	..	..	.	Imports, convertible currency
..	..	..	..	..	..	..	..	..	..	.	Trade balance, convertible currency
..	..	..	..	..	..	..	..	..	..	.	Invisibles, convertible currency
..	..	..	..	..	..	..	..	..	..	.	Current balance, convertible currency
..	5,888	6,689	5,964	7,055	9,509	10,862	11,009	..	..	O	External debt, total (World Bank)
..	..	..	..	..	..	..	..	..	..	.	Convertible currency
..	3,800	4,902	4,285	4,730	6,000	7,000	7,666	..	..	.	CMEA
..	552	568	483	495	602	605	519	..	..	Of	External debt service (World Bank)
..	..	..	..	..	..	..	..	..	..	.	Convertible currency
..	..	..	..	..	..	..	..	..	..	.	Total reserves less gold (IMF, IFS)
..	..	..	..	..	..	..	..	..	..	.	Total reserves, including gold at London price
..	..	..	..	..	..	..	..	..	..	.	Total reserves, incl. gold at national valuation
				(thousands)							**EMPLOYMENT**
..	..	..	..	..	..	..	..	..	..	.	Employment, total
..	..	..	..	..	..	..	..	..	..	.	Agriculture
..	..	..	..	..	..	..	..	..	..	.	Industry
..	..	..	..	..	..	..	..	..	..	.	Services
3,651	3,735	3,819	3,903	3,987	4,082	4,177	4,271	4,366	4,461	.	Labor force, total
..	..	..	..	..	..	..	..	..	..	.	Agriculture
..	..	..	..	..	..	..	..	..	..	.	Industry
..	..	..	..	..	..	..	..	..	..	.	Services
			(millions of current Cuban pesos)								**DOMESTIC FINANCE (IMF)**
..	..	..	..	..	..	..	..	..	..	.	Money supply, broadly defined
..	..	..	..	..	..	..	..	..	..	.	Money, means of payment
..	..	..	..	..	..	..	..	..	..	.	Demand deposits
..	..	..	..	..	..	..	..	..	..	.	Currency outside banks
..	..	..	..	..	..	..	..	..	..	.	Quasi-money
..	..	..	..	..	..	..	..	..	..	.	Interest: deposit rate (percent)
..	..	..	..	..	..	..	..	..	..	.	Central government expenditures
..	..	..	..	..	..	..	..	..	..	.	Defense
				(millions of 1989 US dollars)							
..	..	..	..	..	..	..	..	13,530	..	.	Central government exp. (ACDA)
1,613	1,680	1,788	1,625	1,520	1,450	1,405	1,405	1,377	..	f	Military (ACDA)
											LAND AND FORESTS (FAO)
168	166	167	169	170	167	168	..	..	..	.	Pop. density: agr. land (pop. per sq. km)
4	3	-2	-4	8	0	..	..	..	..	.	Deforestation rate (net)
26	27	26	25	27	27	..	..	..	..	.	Forest (thousands sq. km)
											SOCIAL INDICATORS
88	88	89	90	91	92	93	..	..	..	.	Population density: total land (pop. per sq. km)
..	109	108	106	104	105	104	104	..	..	.	School enrollment ratio, primary
..	80	82	83	85	87	88	91	..	..	.	secondary
..	..	20	20	21	23	23	22	..	..	.	tertiary
1,081	1,136	1,010	1,028	1,052	1,088	1,112	..	..	..	.	Energy consumption per capita (kg. of oil eq.)
2,878	2,980	3,052	3,085	3,088	3,088	3,118	3,103	..	..	.	Daily calorie supply per capita
103	106	103	111	106	107	104	107	108	..	.	Food production (1979-1981=100)
76	76	77	77	79	78	78	77	..	..	.	Daily protein supply (gm. per capita)
..	..	..	..	..	..	..	..	..	..	.	Population per hospital bed
..	..	..	285	..	..	..	..	..	..	.	per nursing person
721	..	..	530	..	..	..	..	..	..	.	per physician
23	23	24	24	25	25	26	26	27	27	.	Female participation in labor force (percent)
19	17	17	15	17	14	13	13	12	12	.	Infant mortality (per 1,000 live births)
74	74	74	75	75	75	75	75	76	76	.	Life expectancy (years)
2	2	2	2	2	2	2	2	2	2	.	Total fertility (births per woman)
69	70	70	71	72	72	73	74	74	75	.	Urban population (percent of total population)
57	54	52	50	49	..	..	..	..	..	.	Population per passenger car
..	..	20	19	19	..	..	..	..	..	.	per telephone

Comparator tables	1970	1971	1972	1973	1974	1975	1976	1977	1978	1979	1980
PER CAPITA INCOME					*(US dollars)*						
World Bank (Atlas method)	..	..	..	..	..	..	..	..	..	..	..
Single year conversion											2,666
CIA or LWI	2,008	..	..	..	..	3,238	3,473	3,844	4,145	4,519	5,041
Penn World Tables	2,809	3,068	3,303	3,606	4,048	4,530	4,821	5,316	5,812	6,352	7,002
						(thousands)					
POPULATION	14,334	14,390	14,465	14,560	14,686	14,802	14,918	15,031	15,138	15,211	15,262
GROSS NATIONAL PRODUCT, current prices					*(millions of current US dollars)*						
World Bank (Atlas method)	..	..	..	..	..	..	..	..	..	..	..
Single year conversion	..	..	..	..	..	..	..	..	..	..	40,687
Authors' series	22,994	..	..	..	..	..	..	..	..	..	41,150
CIA or LWI	..	..	..	..	..	..	..	..	..	63,740	71,160
GROSS NATIONAL PRODUCT, constant prices					*(millions of constant 1987 dollars)*						
Single year conversion	..	..	..	..	..	..	..	..	..	..	46,582
Authors' series, rescaled from 1980 prices	35,506	..	..	..	..	..	..	..	..	..	56,358
CIA or LWI, rescaled from 1989 prices	80,464	..	..	..	..	94,887	96,406	100,770	102,003	102,857	105,704
CONVERSION FACTORS					*(LCUs per US dollar)*						
World Bank (Atlas method)	..	..	..	..	..	..	..	..	..	..	..
Single year convertor	27.00	..	..	..	..	..	..	..	..	..	14.26
Authors' series	16.20	..	..	..	..	..	..	..	..	..	14.26
Penn World Tables	..	..	..	..	..	..	..	..	..	..	..
OUTPUT TRENDS, OVERALL					*(index, constant prices 1987 = 100)*						
GNP, SNA	..	..	..	..	..	..	..	..	..	..	89.8
NMP, MPS	55.5	..	..	..	..	73.4	..	..	..	..	87.5
GNP, "Building block"	69.6	71.9	74.5	77.0	79.7	82.1	83.4	87.2	88.3	89.0	91.5
Industry											
Value added, SNA	..	..	..	..	..	..	..	..	..	..	88.6
Value added, MPS	54.5	..	..	..	..	74.2	..	..	..	..	87.1
"Building block"	66.3	68.6	71.7	74.3	77.1	80.7	83.5	86.5	87.9	89.0	91.7
Gross output, SNA	64.3	..	..	..	..	77.7	..	..	..	..	89.3
Agriculture											
Value added, SNA	..	..	..	..	..	..	..	..	..	..	103.1
Value added, MPS	..	..	..	..	..	..	..	..	..	..	103.1
"Building block"	75.5	78.0	80.4	83.7	85.2	85.2	81.5	91.6	89.0	87.0	91.9
Gross output, SNA	75.5	..	..	..	..	84.5	..	..	..	..	90.9
Services											
Value added, SNA	..	..	..	..	..	..	..	..	..	..	91.3
Value added, MPS	47.8	..	..	..	..	62.6	..	..	..	..	84.3
"Building block"	71.3	73.5	75.6	77.5	80.8	82.6	84.2	86.1	88.4	89.9	91.0
CONSUMPTION											
Total consumption, SNA	..	..	..	..	..	..	..	..	..	..	89.1
Total consumption, MPS	57.8	..	..	..	..	74.9	..	..	..	..	84.7
Households, SNA	..	..	..	..	..	..	..	..	..	..	91.8
Households, "building block"	..	..	..	..	..	84.3	86.1	88.5	91.0	90.8	91.0
General government, SNA	..	..	..	..	..	..	..	..	..	..	83.2
General government, "building block"	..	..	..	..	..	78.2	79.8	82.2	84.3	86.6	88.6
INVESTMENT											
Gross fixed investment, SNA	..	..	..	..	..	..	..	..	..	..	103.9
Accumulation, MPS	73.3	..	..	..	..	122.6	..	..	..	..	126.6
"Building block"	..	..	..	..	..	95.3	100.6	102.0	98.4	95.9	101.6
CONSUMER PRICES											
National methodology	80.5	80.2	79.9	80.2	80.6	81.2	81.8	82.9	84.2	87.5	90.0
Outside estimate	72.1	73.0	75.1	76.6	78.6	80.2	81.5	82.0	83.9	87.2	90.5
MERCHANDISE EXPORTS					*(millions of current US dollars)*						
UNCTAD	3,792	..	..	..	..	8,356	..	..	..	..	12,059
IMF: IFS	..	..	..	..	..	6,154	..	..	..	..	12,063
ACDA	..	..	..	..	..	..	..	10,010	11,670	13,310	15,250
ECE	3,792	4,180	4,916	5,988	7,244	8,704	6,400	7,291	8,545	9,356	10,475
intra-CMEA	2,453	2,690	3,288	3,959	4,553	5,879	3,811	4,266	5,080	5,323	5,559
Authors' uniform TR/$ series	3,363	3,529	3,760	4,613	5,473	5,954	6,860	7,961	9,116	10,363	11,653
intra-CMEA	2,059	2,093	2,212	2,671	2,924	3,323	4,242	4,892	5,614	6,262	6,662
MERCHANDISE IMPORTS					*(millions of current US dollars)*						
UNCTAD	3,695	..	..	..	..	9,077	..	..	..	..	12,161
IMF: IFS	..	..	..	..	..	7,050	..	..	..	..	12,774
ACDA	..	..	..	..	..	..	..	10,880	12,490	14,370	15,520
ECE	3,695	4,010	4,634	6,070	7,721	9,453	7,040	8,067	9,222	10,181	10,619
intra-CMEA	2,357	2,570	3,067	3,897	4,709	6,304	3,899	4,475	5,374	5,704	5,718
Authors' uniform series	3,284	3,391	3,585	4,726	5,899	6,536	7,506	8,759	9,820	11,248	11,827
intra-CMEA	1,979	1,999	2,064	2,629	3,024	3,563	4,340	5,131	5,938	6,711	6,853

Abbreviations in notes column are explained in the General Notes. For sources and methods, see the Technical Notes.

1981	1982	1983	1984	1985	1986	1987	1988	1989	1990	Notes	*Comparator tables (continued)*
				(US dollars)							**PER CAPITA INCOME**
..	2,980	3,000	2,860	2,740	2,790	3,030	3,360	3,460	3,140	.	World Bank (Atlas method)
2,810	2,825	2,802	2,528	2,532	2,974	3,331	3,294	3,223	2,820	.	Single year conversion
5,497	5,942	6,246	6,618	6,845	7,147	7,421	7,815	8,205	8,265	.	CIA or LWI
7,640	8,251	8,713	9,089	9,614		..	..	..	..	.	Penn World Tables
				(thousands)							**POPULATION**
15,314	15,366	15,415	15,459	15,500	15,532	15,565	15,597	15,629	15,662	.	
				(millions of current US dollars)							**GROSS NATIONAL PRODUCT, current prices**
..	45,832	46,176	44,203	42,527	43,323	47,199	52,328	54,036	49,236	.	World Bank (Atlas method)
43,034	43,409	43,187	39,078	39,238	46,187	51,849	51,379	50,379	44,173	.	Single year conversion
..	..	..	..	39,342	..	52,083	51,532	50,279	..	D	Authors' series
77,700	84,230	88,830	94,330	97,790	102,400	106,600	117,100	123,200		.	CIA or LWI
				(millions of constant 1987 dollars)							**GROSS NATIONAL PRODUCT, constant prices**
46,512	47,075	48,356	49,340	50,470	51,460	51,849	53,162	53,921	51,771	.	Single year conversion
..	..	..	..	61,994	..	65,375	66,503	67,630	..	D	Authors' series, rescaled from 1980 prices
105,230	107,223	108,835	111,492	112,251	114,529	115,573	118,040	119,273	115,573	.	CIA or LWI, rescaled from 1989 prices
				(LCUs per US dollar)							**CONVERSION FACTORS**
..	13.00	13.23	14.68	15.85	15.99	15.03	14.10	14.03	16.10	..	World Bank (Atlas method)
13.25	13.73	14.15	16.60	17.18	15.00	13.68	14.36	15.05	17.95	.	Single year convertor
..	..	..	..	17.18	..	13.68	14.36	15.05	..	..	Authors' series
..	..	..	..	..	..	..	..	..	..	.	Penn World Tables
				(index, constant prices 1987 = 100)							**OUTPUT TRENDS, OVERALL**
89.7	90.8	93.3	95.2	97.3	99.2	100.0	102.5	104.0	99.8	.	GNP, SNA
87.4	87.6	89.6	92.7	95.5	98.0	100.0	102.3	103.7	..	.	NMP, MPS
91.0	92.8	94.2	96.5	97.1	99.1	100.0	102.1	103.2	100.0	.	GNP, "Building block"
											Industry
89.9	88.2	89.5	92.3	95.3	97.2	100.0	103.6	104.6	..	H	Value added, SNA
87.3	85.7	87.3	90.2	93.8	96.4	100.0	103.1	..	..		Value added, MPS
93.2	93.5	94.9	95.9	97.3	98.5	100.0	101.3	101.2	96.9	.	"Building block"
..	..	..	..	97.3	99.1	100.0	101.8	102.7	98.2	X	Gross output, SNA
											Agriculture
91.8	100.0	100.2	108.2	101.4	103.4	100.0	100.7	101.7	..	H	Value added, SNA
87.6	97.9	97.9	107.2	100.0	103.1	100.0	99.0	104.1	..		Value added, MPS
83.0	91.2	92.8	100.6	96.8	101.5	100.0	104.6	108.4	104.4	.	"Building block"
..	..	..	..	97.3	100.9	100.0	104.5	109.1	104.5	.	Gross output, SNA
											Services
91.2	94.8	98.8	98.2	100.4	101.8	100.0	101.4	103.2	..	H	Value added, SNA
87.8	90.8	94.6	96.7	99.5	101.6	100.0	100.8	..	..	f	Value added, MPS
91.9	92.6	93.9	95.3	97.1	98.8	100.0	102.1	103.4	102.1	.	"Building block"
											CONSUMPTION
89.9	90.0	94.2	96.0	96.8	98.6	100.0	104.1	106.9	108.4	.	Total consumption, SNA
86.9	85.9	88.3	90.9	93.3	96.5	100.0	104.5	107.2	..	.	Total consumption, MPS
92.7	90.8	93.8	95.2	96.2	97.6	100.0	104.0	106.1	109.8	.	Households, SNA
91.4	92.5	94.0	95.1	97.0	98.5	100.0	102.6	103.9	102.5	.	Households, "building block"
83.4	88.4	95.0	98.0	98.1	100.9	100.0	104.3	108.6	105.0	.	General government, SNA
91.7	92.7	93.7	95.2	97.2	98.9	100.0	102.1	102.8	103.6	.	General government, "building block"
											INVESTMENT
105.4	100.8	95.9	96.9	97.8	102.8	100.0	104.6	111.6	112.0	.	Gross fixed investment, SNA
116.1	107.4	98.0	97.5	100.2	109.5	100.0	105.8	108.4	..	.	Accumulation, MPS
90.7	89.9	87.4	86.7	84.4	97.4	100.0	99.0	112.5	121.3	.	"Building block"
											CONSUMER PRICES
90.8	95.4	96.3	97.2	99.4	99.9	100.0	100.1	101.5	111.7	.	National methodology
92.2	94.0	95.3	96.5	97.9	98.6	100.0	102.4	104.3	114.6	.	Outside estimate
				(millions of current US dollars)							**MERCHANDISE EXPORTS**
11,611	12,061	12,121	11,772	11,900	13,790	15,464	14,880	14,445	12,038	.	UNCTAD
11,611	12,059	12,119	11,775	11,900	13,790	15,469	14,887	14,460	11,840	.	IMF: IFS
15,200	16,180	17,120	28,530	29,370	34,770	36,660	38,450	13,180	..	.	ACDA
10,403	10,338	10,092	10,001	10,552	12,160	12,355	12,381	11,988	10,728	.	ECE
5,691	5,806	5,510	5,469	5,738	6,833	6,869	6,480	5,713	4,066	.	intra-CMEA
11,551	12,054	12,254	11,907	12,592	13,525	14,150	14,577	13,630	11,466	.	Authors' uniform TR/$ series
6,762	7,403	7,529	7,245	7,531	8,058	8,492	8,467	7,196	4,720	.	intra-CMEA
				(millions of current US dollars)							**MERCHANDISE IMPORTS**
11,327	11,689	11,669	11,286	11,570	13,968	15,557	14,579	14,257	13,321	F	UNCTAD
11,894	12,271	12,250	11,852	12,149	14,666	16,340	15,298	14,988	13,712	.	IMF: IFS
14,960	16,000	17,040	27,060	28,200	34,810	37,260	40,160	13,010	..	.	ACDA
10,130	10,015	9,624	9,529	10,216	12,277	12,503	12,180	11,772	11,808	.	ECE
5,726	5,964	5,820	5,871	6,085	7,254	6,497	6,221	5,762	4,602	.	intra-CMEA
11,286	11,775	11,899	11,541	12,348	13,716	14,298	14,288	13,433	12,661	.	Authors' uniform series
6,804	7,604	7,952	7,776	7,986	8,555	8,589	8,129	7,257	5,341	.	intra-CMEA

Czechoslovakia

Basic tables	1970	1971	1972	1973	1974	1975	1976	1977	1978	1979	1980
SNA ACCOUNTS, current prices				*(billions of current Czechoslovakian koruny)*							
GNP, at market prices	..	..	..	..	..	..	..	..	..	..	580
Net factor income	..	..	..	..	..	..	..	..	..	..	-7
GDP at market prices	..	..	..	..	..	..	..	..	..	..	587
Net indirect taxes	..	..	..	..	..	..	..	..	..	..	..
GDP at factor cost	..	..	..	..	..	..	..	..	..	..	..
Agriculture	..	..	..	..	..	..	..	..	..	..	40
Industry	..	..	..	..	..	..	..	..	..	..	350
Services, etc.	..	..	..	..	..	..	..	..	..	..	197
Resource balance	..	..	..	..	..	..	..	..	..	..	0
Exports GNFS	..	..	..	..	..	..	..	..	..	..	199
Imports GNFS	..	..	..	..	..	..	..	..	..	..	198
Domestic absorption	..	..	..	..	..	..	..	..	..	..	587
Total consumption	..	..	..	..	..	..	..	..	..	..	395
Private consumption	..	..	..	..	..	..	..	..	..	..	282
General government consumption	..	..	..	..	..	..	..	..	..	..	114
Gross domestic investment	..	..	..	..	..	..	..	..	..	..	191
Fixed domestic investment	..	..	..	..	..	..	..	..	..	..	155
Depreciation	..	..	..	..	..	..	..	..	..	..	..
SNA ACCOUNTS, constant prices				*(billions of constant 1987 Czechoslovakian koruny)*							
Gross national product (GNP)	..	..	..	..	..	..	..	..	..	..	637
GDP at market prices	..	..	..	..	..	..	..	..	..	..	645
GDP at factor cost	..	..	..	..	..	..	..	..	..	..	..
Agriculture	..	..	..	..	..	..	..	..	..	..	48
Industry	..	..	..	..	..	..	..	..	..	..	363
Services, etc.	..	..	..	..	..	..	..	..	..	..	233
Resource balance	..	..	..	..	..	..	..	..	..	..	-23
Exports GNFS	..	..	..	..	..	..	..	..	..	..	183
Imports GNFS	..	..	..	..	..	..	..	..	..	..	206
Domestic absorption	..	..	..	..	..	..	..	..	..	..	667
Total consumption, etc.	..	..	..	..	..	..	..	..	..	..	439
Private consumption, etc.	..	..	..	..	..	..	..	..	..	..	313
General government consumption	..	..	..	..	..	..	..	..	..	..	126
Gross domestic investment	..	..	..	..	..	..	..	..	..	..	228
Fixed domestic investment	..	..	..	..	..	..	..	..	..	..	192
Depreciation	..	..	..	..	..	..	..	..	..	..	..
MPS ACCOUNTS, current prices				*(billions of current Czechoslovakian koruny)*							
NMP produced:	312	..	..	..	..	408	..	..	..	..	486
Agriculture and forestry	32	..	..	..	..	34	..	..	..	..	35
Industry excluding construction	191	..	..	..	..	264	..	..	..	..	309
Construction	35	..	..	..	..	51	..	..	..	..	51
Transport and communication	..	..	..	..	..	..	..	..	..	..	..
Trade, etc.	29	..	..	..	..	37	..	..	..	..	50
Other services	27	..	..	..	..	23	..	..	..	..	42
Resource balance	12	..	..	..	..	0	..	..	..	..	8
NMP used: domestic market	301	..	..	..	..	408	..	..	..	..	478
Final consumption, material goods	220	..	..	..	..	291	..	..	..	..	354
Personal consumption	168	..	..	..	..	214	..	..	..	..	257
Collective consumption	52	..	..	..	..	78	..	..	..	..	97
Net capital formation	81	..	..	..	..	117	..	..	..	..	124
Net fixed capital formation	50	..	..	..	..	80	..	..	..	..	76
Changes in stocks	31	..	..	..	..	36	..	..	..	..	48
Depreciation	..	..	..	..	..	..	..	..	..	..	..
MPS ACCOUNTS, constant prices				*(billions of 1984 Czechoslovakian koruny)*							
NMP produced:	310	..	..	..	..	410	..	..	..	..	489
Agriculture and forestry	34	..	..	..	..	36	..	..	..	..	37
Industry and construction	218	..	..	..	..	297	..	..	..	..	348
Services	59	..	..	..	..	77	..	..	..	..	104
Resource balance	-29	..	..	..	..	-44	..	..	..	..	-17
NMP used: domestic market	339	..	..	..	..	454	..	..	..	..	506
Final consumption, material goods	262	..	..	..	..	339	..	..	..	..	383
Personal consumption	200	..	..	..	..	253	..	..	..	..	275
Collective consumption	61	..	..	..	..	85	..	..	..	..	108
Net capital formation	77	..	..	..	..	116	..	..	..	..	123
Net fixed capital formation	51	..	..	..	..	85	..	..	..	..	88
Depreciation	..	..	..	..	..	..	..	..	..	..	..

Abbreviations in notes column are explained in the General Notes. For sources and methods, see the Technical Notes.

1981	1982	1983	1984	1985	1986	1987	1988	1989	1990	Notes	Basic tables (continued)
											SNA ACCOUNTS, current prices
570	596	611	649	674	693	709	738	758	793	.	GNP, at market prices
-8	-5	-3	-4	-3	-2	-2	-2	-1	-5	.	Net factor income
578	601	615	653	677	695	711	740	760	798	.	GDP at market prices
..	..	..	..	..	..	..	..	..	..	.	Net indirect taxes
..	..	..	..	..	..	..	..	..	..	.	GDP at factor cost
35	43	46	47	44	47	46	47	60	..	H	Agriculture
332	348	361	375	390	400	410	425	428	..	H	Industry
212	210	208	231	243	248	255	268	272	..	H	Services, etc.
8	12	10	14	20	8	10	22	11	-16	.	Resource balance
180	193	198	228	245	246	251	262	260	265	.	Exports GNFS
172	181	189	214	225	238	241	240	249	281	.	Imports GNFS
571	589	605	639	657	687	701	718	749	814	.	Domestic absorption
403	413	427	449	462	477	493	510	539	574	.	Total consumption
285	292	301	313	324	332	341	354	374	408	.	Private consumption
119	121	126	136	137	145	151	156	164	166	.	General government consumption
167	176	178	189	195	210	208	208	210	240	.	Gross domestic investment
155	162	163	177	181	192	185	197	201	209	.	Fixed domestic investment
..	..	..	..	..	..	..	..	..	..	.	Depreciation
											SNA ACCOUNTS, constant prices
636	644	662	675	690	704	709	727	738	708	.	Gross national product (GNP)
645	650	665	679	693	706	711	729	739	713	.	GDP at market prices
										.	GDP at factor cost
43	46	46	50	47	48	46	47	47	..	H	Agriculture
368	361	367	378	390	398	410	424	428	..	H	Industry
233	242	252	251	256	260	255	259	264	..	H	Services, etc.
-6	3	8	17	23	13	10	16	0	-43	.	Resource balance
187	198	207	230	245	245	251	260	252	246	.	Exports GNFS
193	195	200	214	222	232	241	245	252	289	.	Imports GNFS
651	647	658	662	670	693	701	714	739	756	.	Domestic absorption
443	444	464	473	477	486	493	513	527	534	.	Total consumption, etc.
316	310	320	325	328	333	341	355	362	375	.	Private consumption, etc.
126	134	144	148	149	153	151	158	164	159	.	General government consumption
209	203	193	189	194	207	208	201	212	222	.	Gross domestic investment
194	186	177	179	180	190	185	193	206	207	.	Fixed domestic investment
..	..	..	..	..	..	..	..	..	..	.	Depreciation
											MPS ACCOUNTS, current prices
473	496	508	541	556	570	583	606	618	..	.	NMP produced:
29	37	40	41	37	40	39	39	..	..	.	Agriculture and forestry
285	301	311	318	333	341	349	361	..	..	.	Industry excluding construction
51	52	53	60	61	61	62	65	..	..	.	Construction
..	..	..	..	..	..	..	..	..	..	.	Transport and communication
66	62	59	75	75	76	83	92	..	..	.	Trade, etc.
43	45	45	48	51	52	51	50	..	..	.	Other services
17	22	22	29	29	16	18	27	21	..	f	Resource balance
456	474	486	513	528	555	565	580	596	..	.	NMP used: domestic market
364	378	391	411	426	442	459	480	498	..	.	Final consumption, material goods
263	271	280	287	298	306	315	330	343	..	.	Personal consumption
102	107	112	124	128	136	144	150	155	..	.	Collective consumption
92	97	95	102	102	113	106	100	98	..	.	Net capital formation
85	70	69	84	91	94	76	82	83	..	.	Net fixed capital formation
7	27	26	18	11	19	30	18	15	..	.	Changes in stocks
..	..	..	..	..	..	..	..	..	..	.	Depreciation
											MPS ACCOUNTS, constant prices
489	490	501	519	534	548	559	572	580	..	.	NMP produced:
31	35	35	38	36	37	36	36	..	..	.	Agriculture and forestry
349	343	349	361	376	386	400	412	..	..	.	Industry and construction
108	112	117	119	123	125	123	124	..	..	f	Services
-1	8	16	28	28	17	14	16	5	..	f	Resource balance
490	482	485	491	506	531	546	557	575	..	.	NMP used: domestic market
393	389	399	411	422	437	452	473	485	..	.	Final consumption, material goods
280	274	279	284	289	296	304	319	325	..	.	Personal consumption
113	115	120	127	133	141	148	153	161	..	.	Collective consumption
96	93	86	80	84	94	93	84	90	..	.	Net capital formation
81	75	68	68	70	76	70	74	75	..	.	Net fixed capital formation
..	..	..	..	..	..	..	..	..	..	.	Depreciation

(billions of current Czechoslovakian koruny)

(billions of constant 1987 Czechoslovakian koruny)

(billions of current Czechoslovakian koruny)

(billions of 1984 Czechoslovakian koruny)

Czechoslovakia

Basic tables (continued)	1970	1971	1972	1973	1974	1975	1976	1977	1978	1979	1980
MPS ACCOUNTS, index						*(index, 1980 = 100)*					
NMP produced:	..	..	..	..	..	..	..	..	..	..	100.0
Agriculture and forestry	..	..	..	..	..	..	..	..	..	..	100.0
Industry excluding construction	..	..	..	..	..	..	..	..	..	..	100.0
Construction	..	..	..	..	..	..	..	..	..	..	100.0
Transport and communication	..	..	..	..	..	..	..	..	..	..	100.0
Trade, etc.	..	..	..	..	..	..	..	..	..	..	100.0
NMP used: material goods	..	..	..	..	..	..	..	..	..	..	100.0
Final consumption	..	..	..	..	..	..	..	..	..	..	100.0
Net capital formation	..	..	..	..	..	..	..	..	..	..	100.0
EXCHANGE AND CONVERSION RATES						*(LCUs per US dollar: annual average)*					
Single-year converter	27.000	..	..	..	..	..	..	..	..	..	14.260
Devisa/official	7.200	7.200	6.610	5.860	5.860	5.580	5.770	5.670	5.430	5.320	5.380
Commercial	27.000	27.000	24.790	21.980	21.980	20.980	21.640	15.030	14.390	14.100	14.260
Noncommercial	16.200	16.200	14.870	13.190	10.260	9.770	10.100	9.920	9.500	9.310	9.420
Informal market	42.700	35.050	32.008	25.987	24.563	23.279	25.450	25.554	26.154	25.858	25.688
ICP	..	..	..			..				..	..
						(ruble per US dollar: annual average)					
Commercial TR/$ cross	1.500	1.500	1.377	1.221	1.221	1.166	1.202	1.016	0.972	0.953	0.964
Uniform TR/$ cross	1.072	1.157	1.232	1.093	1.092	1.167	1.067	1.022	0.973	0.945	0.980
						(LCUs per ruble: annual average)					
Commercial	18.000	18.000	18.000	18.000	18.000	18.000	18.000	14.800	14.800	14.800	14.800
Noncommercial	32.810	22.190	22.190	22.190	22.190	22.860	23.000	23.000	19.000	19.000	19.000
Devisa/official	8.000	8.000	8.000	8.000	8.000	8.000	8.000	8.000	8.000	8.000	8.000
CONSUMER PRICE INDEXES						*(index)*					
Official, IMF 1985=100	81.0	80.6	80.4	80.6	81.1	81.6	82.3	83.4	84.7	88.0	90.6
Official, CIA or LWI 1980=100	89.4	89.1	88.8	89.1	89.5	90.0	90.8	92.0	93.5	97.1	100.0
Alternative, CIA or LWI 1980=100	79.7	80.6	82.9	84.6	86.9	88.7	90.1	90.6	92.7	96.4	100.0
INTERNATIONAL TRADE (ECE)						*(billions of current Czechoslovakian koruny)*					
Value of exports, fob	27	30	33	35	41	47	52	58	64	70	80
to CMEA	18	19	22	23	26	31	36	40	44	47	52
Value of imports, cif	27	29	31	36	44	51	56	63	68	76	82
from CMEA	17	19	20	23	26	33	37	42	46	51	54
Trade balance	1	1	2	-1	-3	-4	-4	-5	-5	-6	-1
CMEA	1	1	2	0	-1	-2	-1	-2	-3	-3	-2
INTERNATIONAL TRADE (Authors')						*(millions of current US dollars)*					
Value of exports, fob	3,363	3,529	3,760	4,613	5,473	5,954	6,860	7,961	9,116	10,363	11,653
to developed countries	772	846	963	1,307	1,686	1,658	1,645	1,893	2,117	2,626	3,247
to other non-socialist countries	342	402	421	451	608	720	681	838	987	1,024	1,289
to socialist countries	2,249	2,281	2,377	2,854	3,179	3,575	4,534	5,230	6,012	6,713	7,117
to CMEA	2,059	2,093	2,212	2,671	2,924	3,323	4,242	4,892	5,614	6,262	6,662
Value of imports, cif	3,284	3,391	3,585	4,726	5,899	6,536	7,506	8,759	9,820	11,248	11,827
from developed countries	905	992	1,085	1,541	2,078	2,240	2,418	2,624	2,921	3,430	3,699
from other non-socialist countries	226	230	282	396	550	505	507	730	611	705	830
from socialist countries	2,153	2,168	2,218	2,789	3,271	3,792	4,581	5,405	6,288	7,113	7,298
from CMEA	1,979	1,999	2,064	2,629	3,024	3,563	4,340	5,131	5,938	6,711	6,853
Trade balance	79	138	175	-113	-426	-583	-646	-798	-704	-885	-173
Developed countries	-133	-146	-122	-233	-393	-581	-772	-732	-804	-803	-452
Other non-socialist countries	116	172	138	55	58	215	174	108	376	319	459
Socialist countries	96	112	159	65	-91	-216	-47	-175	-276	-401	-180
CMEA	80	94	149	42	-100	-240	-98	-239	-325	-448	-191
PARTNER CONVERTIBLE TRADE (ECE)						*(millions of current US dollars)*					
Exports to non-CMEA (cif)	808	910	1,025	1,374	1,704	1,826	1,900	2,079	2,391	3,042	3,546
Imports from non-CMEA (fob)	855	1,026	1,119	1,462	1,914	2,101	2,295	2,251	2,565	3,067	3,375
Trade balance	-47	-116	-94	-88	-210	-275	-395	-172	-174	-25	171
TRADE PRICE INDEXES (Authors')						*(index, 1980 = 100)*					
Terms of trade	123.2	..	..	..	..	111.3	109.1	105.5	103.0	100.9	100.0
Exports	54.2	..	..	..	..	68.6	75.4	79.8	85.2	94.0	100.0
Non-socialist countries	35.6	..	..	..	..	67.4	66.6	67.7	73.0	85.0	100.0
Developed countries	..	..	..	..	..	..	..	..	..	..	..
Other	..	..	..	..	..	..	..	..	..	..	..
Socialist countries	63.4	..	..	..	..	69.5	79.9	86.1	91.6	98.8	100.0
CMEA	..	..	..	..	..	..	..	..	..	..	..
Imports	44.0	..	..	..	..	61.7	69.1	75.6	82.8	93.1	100.0
Non-socialist countries	29.7	..	..	..	..	59.8	62.5	68.1	71.5	86.3	100.0
Developed countries	..	..	..	..	..	..	..	..	..	..	..
Other	..	..	..	..	..	..	..	..	..	..	..
Socialist countries	51.5	..	..	..	..	63.0	73.3	80.3	89.1	97.1	100.0
CMEA	..	..	..	..	..	..	..	..	..	..	..

Abbreviations in notes column are explained in the General Notes. For sources and methods, see the Technical Notes.

1981	1982	1983	1984	1985	1986	1987	1988	1989	1990	Notes	Basic tables (continued)
				(index,1980 = 100)							**MPS ACCOUNTS, index**
											NMP produced:
99.9	100.0	102.0	106.0	109.0	111.0	114.0	117.0	117.0	..	.	Agriculture and forestry
85.0	95.0	95.0	104.0	97.0	100.0	97.0	96.0	101.0	..	.	Industry excluding construction
99.7	98.0	99.7	104.0	108.0	111.0	115.0	119.0	124.0	..	.	Construction
102.0	99.1	102.0	98.0	105.0	106.0	109.0	111.0	108.0	..	.	Transport and communication
110.0	107.0	106.0	104.0	98.0	102.0	99.0	105.0	84.0	..	.	Trade, etc.
104.0	109.0	115.0	117.0	122.0	124.0	121.0	123.0	113.0	..	.	
97.0	95.0	96.0	96.0	100.0	104.0	107.0	109.0	113.0	..	.	NMP used: material goods
103.0	101.0	104.0	107.0	110.0	114.0	117.0	123.0	127.0	..	.	Final consumption
78.0	76.0	70.0	65.0	68.0	77.0	76.0	68.0	69.0	..	.	Net capital formation
			(LCUs per US dollar: annual average)								**EXCHANGE AND CONVERSION RATES**
13.250	13.730	14.150	16.600	17.180	15.000	13.680	14.360	15.050	17.950	.	Single-year converter
5.890	6.100	6.290	6.640	6.850	6.000	5.470	5.320	..		f	Devisa/official
13.250	13.730	14.150	16.600	17.180	15.000	13.680	14.360	15.050	..	.	Commercial
10.310	10.680	11.010	11.620	11.990	10.500	9.570	9.310	9.750	..	f	Noncommercial
27.096	28.925	31.154	33.863	41.170	31.718	29.596	34.290	40.854		.	Informal market
..	..									.	ICP
			(ruble per US dollar: annual average)								
1.104	1.144	1.263	1.482	1.534	1.339	1.221	1.381	1.505	..	.	Commercial TR/$ cross
1.076	1.105	1.201	1.395	1.433	1.388	1.397	1.484	1.660	1.980	.	Uniform TR/$ cross
			(LCUs per ruble: annual average)								
12.000	12.000	11.200	11.200	11.200	11.200	11.200	10.400	10.000	..	f	Commercial
19.000	19.000	17.000	17.000	16.000	16.000	16.000	16.000	15.000	..	f	Noncommercial
8.000	8.000	8.000	8.000	8.000	8.000	8.000	8.000		..	.	Devisa/official
				(index)							**CONSUMER PRICE INDEXES**
91.3	95.9	96.9	97.8	100.0	100.5	100.6	100.7	102.1	112.3	.	Official, IMF 1985=100
100.8	105.9	107.0	108.0	109.9	110.4	110.5	110.7	112.2	123.5	.	Official, CIA or LWI 1980=100
101.9	103.9	105.3	106.7	108.2	109.0	110.5	113.1	115.2	126.7	.	Alternative, CIA or LWI 1980=100
		(billions of current Czechoslovakian koruny)									**INTERNATIONAL TRADE (ECE)**
88	95	104	114	197	198	202	214	218	215	.	Value of exports, fob
58	65	72	81	108	112	119	126	120	94	.	to CMEA
86	94	103	114	191	200	204	210	215	238	.	Value of imports, cif
59	67	76	87	114	119	120	121	121	106	.	from CMEA
1	1	1	1	6	-2	-2	4	3	-23	.	Trade balance
0	-2	-4	-6	-7	-7	-1	5	-1	-12	.	CMEA
			(millions of current US dollars)								**INTERNATIONAL TRADE (Authors')**
11,551	12,054	12,254	11,907	12,592	13,525	14,150	14,577	13,630	11,466	.	Value of exports, fob
2,927	2,785	2,712	2,790	2,753	3,182	3,574	4,061	4,502	5,104	.	to developed countries
1,379	1,311	1,480	1,337	1,270	1,365	1,187	1,157	1,159	1,033	.	to other non-socialist countries
7,245	7,958	8,061	7,779	8,570	8,978	9,389	9,358	7,969	5,329	.	to socialist countries
6,762	7,403	7,529	7,245	7,531	8,058	8,492	8,467	7,196	4,720	.	to CMEA
11,286	11,775	11,899	11,541	12,348	13,716	14,298	14,288	13,433	12,661	.	Value of imports, cif
3,248	2,930	2,741	2,593	2,686	3,448	4,098	4,501	4,430	5,675	.	from developed countries
741	681	673	739	704	804	806	806	943	830	.	from other non-socialist countries
7,297	8,164	8,485	8,209	8,957	9,464	9,395	8,981	8,059	6,155	.	from socialist countries
6,804	7,604	7,952	7,776	7,986	8,555	8,589	8,129	7,257	5,341	.	from CMEA
265	279	355	366	244	-192	-149	289	197	-1,195	.	Trade balance
-321	-146	-29	197	66	-266	-524	-440	71	-571	.	Developed countries
639	630	808	599	565	561	381	352	216	203	.	Other non-socialist countries
-53	-205	-424	-429	-387	-486	-6	378	-90	-826	.	Socialist countries
-42	-201	-423	-531	-455	-497	-97	338	-61	-621	.	CMEA
			(millions of current US dollars)								**PARTNER CONVERTIBLE TRADE (ECE)**
3,181	3,107	3,106	3,189	3,036	3,493	3,840	4,056	4,289	..	.	Exports to non-CMEA (cif)
2,851	2,773	2,560	2,424	2,617	3,123	3,699	3,976	3,888	..	.	Imports from non-CMEA (fob)
330	334	546	765	419	370	141	80	401	..	.	Trade balance
				(index,1980 = 100)							**TRADE PRICE INDEXES (Authors')**
95.9	92.6	88.3	90.2	82.2	82.5	86.1	89.5	94.0	97.8	.	Terms of trade
99.1	98.8	94.5	92.5	87.1	92.4	94.7	95.0	91.3	84.4	f	Exports
95.3	90.4	82.8	102.7	76.3	84.9	93.4	101.3	103.0	98.7	.	Non-socialist countries
..	..	..	..	..	..	..	..	..	..	f	Developed countries
..	..	..	..	..	..	..	..	..	..	.	Other
101.3	103.2	100.5	87.1	92.2	96.2	95.3	91.4	82.9	67.9	.	Socialist countries
..	..	..	..	..	..	..	..	..	..	.	CMEA
103.3	106.7	107.0	102.5	106.1	111.9	110.0	106.1	97.1	86.3	f	Imports
97.3	88.9	85.2	84.9	78.0	89.8	97.8	102.6	100.6	96.3	.	Non-socialist countries
..	..	..	..	..	..	..	..	..	..	.	Developed countries
..	..	..	..	..	..	..	..	..	..	.	Other
106.5	114.6	115.7	109.7	116.7	121.9	116.3	108.1	94.7	75.6	.	Socialist countries
..	..	..	..	..	..	..	..	..	..	.	CMEA

Czechoslovakia

Basic tables (continued)	1970	1971	1972	1973	1974	1975	1976	1977	1978	1979	1980
TRADE PRICE INDEXES (ECE)					*(index, 1980 = 100)*						
Terms of trade	117	118	116	115	113	106	103	101	101	100	100
Exports	62	62	68	79	90	105	75	78	88	94	100
Imports	53	53	59	69	80	99	73	78	88	94	100
Balance of Payments (ECE)					*(millions of current US dollars)*						
Exports, convertible currency	836	956	1,185	1,572	2,185	2,149	2,081	2,500	2,909	3,531	4,368
Imports, convertible currency	907	1,023	1,205	1,740	2,358	2,519	2,827	3,086	3,332	4,068	4,380
Trade balance, convertible currency	-71	-68	-19	-168	-174	-371	-746	-586	-423	-537	-12
Invisibles, convertible currency	64	79	130	154	124	113	157	-22	23	4	-264
Current balance, convertible currency	-16	6	104	-22	-61	-281	-612	-635	-434	-570	-316
External debt, total (World Bank)	..	..	..	..	..	..	..	..	..	..	3,988
Convertible currency	..	..	..	..	..	..	..	..	..	..	3,988
CMEA	..	..	..	..	..	..	..	..	..	..	..
External debt service (World Bank)	..	..	..	..	..	..	..	..	..	..	549
Convertible currency	..	..	..	..	..	..	..	..	..	..	549
Total reserves less gold (IMF, IFS)	..	..	..	..	..	..	..	..	..	..	1,839
Total reserves, including gold at London price	69	81	120	207	344	259	249	305	417	946	1,799
Total reserves, incl. gold at national valuation	65	65	65	65	65	80	80	80	80	80	1,920
EMPLOYMENT					*(thousands)*						
Employment, total	6,871	..	..	..	..	7,060	..	..	..	..	7,358
Agriculture	1,178	..	..	..	..	978	..	..	..	..	896
Industry	3,155	..	..	..	..	3,330	..	..	..	..	3,420
Services	2,541	..	..	..	..	1,672	..	..	..	..	3,042
Labor force, total	7,379	7,442	7,506	7,569	7,632	7,695	7,761	7,827	7,893	7,959	8,025
Agriculture	1,247	1,230	1,213	1,196	1,179	1,162	1,143	1,124	1,104	1,085	1,066
Industry	3,573	3,611	3,648	3,685	3,723	3,760	3,800	3,840	3,880	3,921	3,961
Services	2,559	2,602	2,644	2,687	2,730	2,773	2,818	2,863	2,908	2,953	2,999
DOMESTIC FINANCE (IMF)					*(billions of current Czechoslovakian koruny)*						
Money supply, broadly defined	134	..	..	..	..	225	..	..	..	..	312
Money, means of payment	108	..	..	..	..	165	..	..	..	..	207
Demand deposits	90	..	..	..	..	137	..	..	..	..	166
Currency outside banks	18	..	..	..	..	28	..	..	..	..	42
Quasi-money	26	..	..	..	..	61	..	..	..	..	105
Interest: deposit rate (percent)	3	3	3	3	3	3	3	3	3	3	3
Central government expenditures	..	..	..	..	..	0	..	..	..	..	0
Defense	..	..	..	..	..	..	..	..	..	..	..
					(millions of 1989 US dollars)						
Central government exp. (ACDA)	..	..	..	..	..	..	..	..	..	31,430	31,970
Military (ACDA)	..	..	..	..	..	..	..	..	..	7,393	7,734
LAND AND FORESTS (FAO)											
Pop. density: agr. land (pop. per sq. km)	202	203	205	206	209	211	213	216	218	220	223
Deforestation rate (net)	0	0	0	0	0	1	0	0	0	0	1
Forest (thousands sq. km)	45	45	45	45	45	45	45	45	45	45	46
SOCIAL INDICATORS											
Population density: total land (pop. per sq. km)	114	115	115	116	117	118	119	120	121	121	122
School enrollment ratio, primary	98	..	..	..	..	96	97	96	94	92	92
secondary	31	..	..	..	..	35	36	38	40	43	89
tertiary	..	..	..	..	..	..	..	..	..	..	17
Energy consumption per capita (kg. of oil eq.)	3,893	4,084	4,114	4,142	4,207	4,370	4,502	4,622	4,744	4,672	4,770
Daily calorie supply per capita	3,401	3,398	3,400	3,413	3,416	3,418	3,414	3,358	3,422	3,394	3,396
Food production (1979-1981=100)	86	89	91	99	100	96	95	103	106	94	103
Daily protein supply (gm. per capita)	98	99	99	99	100	101	102	101	102	101	102
Population per hospital bed	98	..	..	..	..	..	..	..	..	..	80
per nursing person	..	..	..	167	..	..	..	..	..	..	..
per physician	471	..	..	..	..	..	..	..	..	..	362
Female participation in labor force (percent)	44	44	45	45	46	46	46	47	47	47	47
Infant mortality (per 1,000 live births)	22	22	22	21	21	21	21	20	19	18	18
Life expectancy (years)	70	70	70	70	70	70	70	71	71	71	71
Total fertility (births per woman)	2	2	2	2	3	3	2	2	2	2	2
Urban population (percent of total population)	55	56	58	59	60	61	63	64	65	66	68
Population per passenger car	17	15	13	12	11	10	9	8	8	7	7
per telephone	..	..	..	..	..	6	..	..	..	..	5

Abbreviations in notes column are explained in the General Notes. For sources and methods, see the Technical Notes.

1981	1982	1983	1984	1985	1986	1987	1988	1989	1990	Notes	*Basic tables (continued)*
				(index, 1980 = 100)							**TRADE PRICE INDEXES (ECE)**
98	95	94	93	92	90	91	93	..	..	.	Terms of trade
98	93	86	79	82	93	91	88	..	..	.	Exports
100	99	91	86	89	103	101	94	..	..	.	Imports
				(millions of current US dollars)							**Balance of Payments (ECE)**
4,208	4,069	4,032	4,014	3,852	4,293	4,545	5,014	5,442	5,900	S	Exports, convertible currency
3,866	3,410	3,212	3,114	3,177	4,065	4,666	5,130	5,043	6,100	S	Imports, convertible currency
341	658	820	900	675	228	-122	-117	399	-200	.	Trade balance, convertible currency
-288	-89	68	202	102	222	220	249	-83	-40	.	Invisibles, convertible currency
22	409	854	1,075	740	418	56	90	286	-240	f	Current balance, convertible currency
3,200	2,750	2,276	2,017	4,608	5,568	6,658	7,375	7,917	8,231	.	External debt, total (World Bank)
3,200	2,750	2,276	2,017	4,608	5,568	6,658	7,375	7,917	8,231	.	Convertible currency
..	..	..	..	..	11	9	7	36	44	.	CMEA
553	343	242	206	1,235	1,304	1,438	1,613	1,680	1,545	.	External debt service (World Bank)
553	343	242	206	1,235	1,304	1,438	1,613	1,680	1,545	.	Convertible currency
956	776	803	966	854	1,115	1,382	1,583	2,156	1,102	.	Total reserves less gold (IMF, IFS)
1,248	1,668	1,470	1,205	1,245	1,475	1,772	1,530	1,453	957	.	Total reserves, including gold at London price
1,108	1,046	1,331	1,449	1,324	1,639	1,927	2,113	2,639	1,354	.	Total reserves, incl. gold at national valuation
				(thousands)							**EMPLOYMENT**
7,407	7,435	7,466	7,534	7,606	7,705	7,754	7,804	7,833	..	.	Employment, total
894	883	865	867	865	861	853	839	817	..	.	Agriculture
3,428	3,435	3,454	3,475	3,497	3,558	3,588	3,602	3,615	..	.	Industry
3,085	3,117	3,147	3,192	3,244	3,286	3,313	3,363	3,401	..	.	Services
8,056	8,088	8,119	8,150	8,181	8,222	8,263	8,304	8,345	8,386	.	Labor force, total
..	..	..	..	..	..	..	..	..	..	.	Agriculture
..	..	..	..	..	..	..	..	..	..	.	Industry
..	..	..	..	..	..	..	..	..	..	.	Services
				(billions of current Czechoslovakian koruny)							**DOMESTIC FINANCE (IMF)**
336	363	387	413	431	448	475	529	554	551	.	Money supply, broadly defined
221	237	246	258	260	261	271	310	318	291	.	Money, means of payment
178	191	196	206	206	205	212	247	250	218	.	Demand deposits
43	46	49	52	54	56	59	63	68	74	.	Currency outside banks
115	127	141	156	171	186	204	220	237	260	.	Quasi-money
3	3	3	3	3	3	3	3	3	3	.	Interest: deposit rate (percent)
0	0	0	0	0	0	0	0	447	485	.	Central government expenditures
..	..	..	..	..	..	..	..	35	32	.	Defense
				(millions of 1989 US dollars)							
33,770	32,370	33,450	33,470	34,390	34,520	35,490	38,260	38,540	..	.	Central government exp. (ACDA)
7,858	8,562	8,763	8,835	9,105	9,388	9,508	9,505	8,361	..	U	Military (ACDA)
											LAND AND FORESTS (FAO)
224	225	226	227	228	229	230	231	232	..	.	Pop. density: agr. land (pop. per sq. km)
0	0	0	0	0	0	0	0	0	..	.	Deforestation rate (net)
46	46	46	46	46	46	46	46	46	..	.	Forest (thousands sq. km)
											SOCIAL INDICATORS
122	122	123	123	124	124	124	..	..	..	.	Population density: total land (pop. per sq. km)
91	89	88	99	99	98	96	94	92	..	.	School enrollment ratio, primary
..	..	..	..	84	81	82	85	87	..	.	secondary
..	..	16	16	16	16	16	18	18	..	.	tertiary
4,689	4,630	4,655	4,638	4,724	4,793	4,867	4,864	4,758	5,081	.	Energy consumption per capita (kg. of oil eq.)
3,460	3,529	3,472	3,500	3,476	3,534	3,544	3,660	3,632	..	.	Daily calorie supply per capita
103	108	112	119	115	114	116	119	120	119	.	Food production (1979-1981 = 100)
103	103	103	105	105	105	107	110	109	..	.	Daily protein supply (gm. per capita)
80	..	..	..	..	..	..	..	..	..	.	Population per hospital bed
130	145	..	..	145	..	..	..	..	..	f	per nursing person
350	345	..	..	277	..	..	..	..	..	.	per physician
47	48	48	48	48	48	48	48	48	48	.	Female participation in labor force (percent)
17	16	16	15	14	14	13	13	12	12	.	Infant mortality (per 1,000 live births)
71	71	71	71	71	71	71	71	71	72	.	Life expectancy (years)
2	2	2	2	2	2	2	2	2	2	.	Total fertility (births per woman)
69	70	71	72	73	74	75	76	77	78	.	Urban population (percent of total population)
7	6	6	6	6	6	5	5	5	..	.	Population per passenger car
5	5	..	4	4	4	4	..	..	..	.	per telephone

Comparator tables	1970	1971	1972	1973	1974	1975	1976	1977	1978	1979	1980
PER CAPITA INCOME						*(US dollars)*					
World Bank (Atlas method)	..	..	..	..	..	..	..	..	..	..	..
Single year conversion	2,109	..	..	..	..	..	..	..	..	..	4,421
CIA or LWI	2,016	..	..	..	..	3,413	3,719	4,092	4,468	5,004	5,574
Penn World Tables	2,860	3,103	3,352	3,697	4,245	4,841	5,210	5,724	6,305	7,076	7,891
						(thousands)					
POPULATION	17,068	17,061	17,043	16,980	16,925	16,850	16,786	16,765	16,756	16,745	16,737
GROSS NATIONAL PRODUCT, current prices						*(millions of current US dollars)*					
World Bank (Atlas method)	..	..	..	..	..	..	..	..	..	..	..
Single year conversion	..	..	..	..	..	..	..	..	..	..	..
Authors' series	36,000	..	..	..	..	..	..	..	..	..	74,000
CIA or LWI	..	..	..	..	..	..	..	..	..	80,470	89,570
GROSS NATIONAL PRODUCT, constant prices						*(millions of constant 1987 dollars)*					
Single year conversion	..	..	..	..	..	..	..	..	..	..	..
Authors' series, rescaled from 1980 prices	64,006	..	..	..	..	..	..	..	..	..	101,598
CIA or LWI, rescaled from 1989 prices	96,103	..	..	..	..	104,571	116,143	119,673	121,722	125,138	127,758
CONVERSION FACTORS						*(LCUs per US dollar)*					
World Bank (Atlas method)	..	..	..	..	..	..	..	..	..	..	..
Single year convertor	..	..	..	..	..	..	..	..	..	..	..
Authors' series	4.11	..	..	..	..	..	..	..	..	..	3.31
Penn World Tables	..	..	..	..	..	..	..	..	..	..	..
OUTPUT TRENDS, OVERALL						*(index, constant prices 1987 = 100)*					
GNP, SNA	47.5	..	..	..	..	..	..	..	..	..	75.5
NMP, MPS	46.6	48.7	51.5	54.0	57.4	60.6	62.6	65.8	68.2	71.0	74.1
GNP, "Building block"	..	..	..	..	..	78.6	80.2	82.6	84.0	86.4	88.2
Industry											
Value added, SNA	..	..	..	..	..	..	..	..	..	..	71.8
Value added, MPS	43.2	45.4	47.7	50.5	53.6	56.8	60.1	62.8	65.5	68.2	71.7
"Building block"	..	..	..	..	..	74.9	77.9	79.7	81.9	84.4	86.6
Gross output, SNA	62.4	..	..	..	..	73.5	..	..	..	..	85.5
Agriculture											
Value added, SNA	..	..	..	..	..	..	..	..	..	..	84.3
Value added, MPS	75.7	71.9	79.5	80.3	85.5	83.3	74.2	83.3	80.3	84.0	84.0
"Building block"	..	..	..	..	..	81.1	74.4	81.5	79.8	84.1	84.7
Gross output, SNA	73.1	..	..	..	..	87.0	..	..	..	..	92.6
Services											
Value added, SNA	..	..	..	..	..	..	..	..	..	..	80.6
Value added, MPS	41.1	47.2	48.8	51.7	55.2	61.6	66.9	68.3	72.8	75.2	78.9
"Building block"	..	..	..	..	..	82.8	85.7	87.0	88.6	90.2	92.0
CONSUMPTION											
Total consumption, SNA	..	..	..	..	..	..	..	..	..	..	81.9
Total consumption, MPS	52.5	54.9	58.2	61.5	65.6	68.0	71.3	74.6	77.0	79.5	82.0
Households, SNA	..	..	..	..	..	..	..	..	..	..	80.4
Households, "building block"	..	..	..	..	..	82.1	84.9	85.8	87.6	89.3	90.7
General government, SNA	..	..	..	..	..	..	..	..	..	..	89.7
General government, "building block"	..	..	..	..	..	80.7	84.0	85.6	87.1	88.8	90.0
INVESTMENT											
Gross fixed investment, SNA	..	..	..	..	..	..	..	..	..	..	90.1
Accumulation, MPS	78.9	76.8	78.9	87.4	91.6	90.5	98.9	104.2	98.9	93.7	105.3
"Building block"	..	..	..	..	..	128.5	133.4	141.9	134.7	133.4	140.6
CONSUMER PRICES											
National methodology	..	..	..	..	..	..	..	..	..	..	..
Outside estimate	79.8	80.9	81.2	79.2	81.5	81.7	82.4	84.8	85.5	87.3	89.7
MERCHANDISE EXPORTS						*(millions of current US dollars)*					
UNCTAD	4,581	..	..	..	..	10,088	..	..	..	..	17,312
IMF: IFS	..	..	..	..	..	..	..	..	..	..	17,300
ACDA	..	..	..	..	..	..	..	12,780	14,960	16,610	18,860
ECE	4,581	5,076	6,186	7,581	9,127	11,050	8,347	8,757	10,237	11,416	12,523
intra-CMEA	3,144	3,518	4,445	5,323	6,031	7,899	4,818	5,401	6,529	7,109	6,884
Authors' uniform TR/$ series	4,038	4,236	4,659	5,771	6,849	7,423	8,922	9,596	10,957	12,727	13,961
intra-CMEA	2,640	2,736	2,991	3,591	3,873	4,465	5,363	6,194	7,215	8,363	8,250
MERCHANDISE IMPORTS						*(millions of current US dollars)*					
UNCTAD	4,847	..	..	..	..	11,290	..	..	..	..	19,082
IMF: IFS	..	..	..	..	..	..	..	..	..	..	19,100
ACDA	..	..	..	..	..	..	..	15,050	16,450	18,380	20,790
ECE	4,847	4,981	5,906	7,909	10,014	12,271	10,078	10,758	11,450	12,773	14,247
intra-CMEA	3,203	3,244	3,760	4,930	5,904	8,106	5,038	5,979	6,745	6,689	6,852
Authors' uniform series	4,307	4,221	4,622	6,245	7,804	8,576	10,673	11,676	12,192	14,010	15,699
intra-CMEA	2,689	2,523	2,530	3,327	3,792	4,581	5,608	6,857	7,454	7,870	8,212

Abbreviations in notes column are explained in the General Notes. For sources and methods, see the Technical Notes.

1981	1982	1983	1984	1985	1986	1987	1988	1989	1990	Notes	Comparator tables (continued)
				(US dollars)							**PER CAPITA INCOME**
											World Bank (Atlas method)
..	..	..	..	..	..	..	6,900	..	..	DE	Single year conversion
6,235	6,628	7,015	7,496	7,972	8,306	8,703	9,078	9,718	..		CIA or LWI
8,816	9,345	9,946	10,463	11,310						.	Penn World Tables
				(thousands)							
16,736	16,697	16,699	16,671	16,644	16,624	16,641	16,666	16,630	15,229	.	**POPULATION**
			(millions of current US dollars)								**GROSS NATIONAL PRODUCT, current prices**
..	..	..	..	..	..	..	..	..	..		World Bank (Atlas method)
..	..	..	..	..	..	..	..	..	..	.	Single year conversion
..	..	..	..	..	..	..	115,000	..	..	D	Authors' series
100,300	106,300	112,600	120,000	127,400	132,600	139,100	151,300	159,400		.	CIA or LWI
			(millions of constant 1987 dollars)								**GROSS NATIONAL PRODUCT, constant prices**
..	..	..	..	..	..	..	..	..	..		Single year conversion
..	..	..	..	124,965	..	134,109	139,189	142,237	..	D	Authors' series, rescaled from 1980 prices
130,376	129,921	132,426	136,184	140,397	142,446	144,837	146,431	148,140	..	.	CIA or LWI, rescaled from 1989 prices
				(LCUs per US dollar)							**CONVERSION FACTORS**
..	..	..	..	..	..	..	..	..	..		World Bank (Atlas method)
..	..	..	..	..	..	..	..	..	..		Single year convertor
..	..	..	..	..	..	..	3.01	..	..		Authors' series
..	..	..	..	..	..	..	..	..	..	.	Penn World Tables
			(index, constant prices 1987 = 100)								**OUTPUT TRENDS, OVERALL**
78.6	80.8	84.5	88.7	93.1	96.8	100.0	103.1	105.5	..	DEf	GNP, SNA
77.7	79.7	83.4	88.0	92.6	96.6	100.0	102.8	104.5		.	NMP, MPS
90.0	89.7	91.4	94.0	96.9	98.3	100.0	101.1	102.3	..	.	GNP, "Building block"
											Industry
75.7	78.3	82.5	86.9	91.8	96.5	100.0	103.9	106.5	..	H	Value added, SNA
75.6	78.0	82.2	86.8	91.7	96.4	100.0	103.8				Value added, MPS
88.7	88.9	90.2	92.7	95.9	98.0	100.0	102.4	103.9	..	.	"Building block"
..	..	..	..	95.7	98.3	100.0	102.6	104.3	..	X	Gross output, SNA
											Agriculture
86.8	85.4	89.5	97.7	101.3	100.4	100.0	94.0	96.7	..	H	Value added, SNA
86.3	84.8	88.6	96.9	101.4	100.7	100.0	92.4	95.0			Value added, MPS
87.0	86.1	89.9	97.3	101.5	100.3	100.0	93.6	94.3	..	.	"Building block"
..	..	..	..	100.9	100.9	100.0	98.1	98.1			Gross output, SNA
											Services
82.2	85.0	87.3	89.6	93.2	96.2	100.0	104.4	106.4	..	H	Value added, SNA
81.6	84.8	85.3	87.2	90.7	94.7	100.0	106.1		..		Value added, MPS
93.1	92.2	93.7	94.5	96.4	98.0	100.0	102.1	102.9	..	.	"Building block"
											CONSUMPTION
83.4	84.7	85.6	88.7	92.6	96.2	100.0	103.5	106.2	..	.	Total consumption, SNA
83.6	85.2	85.2	88.5	92.6	95.9	100.0	104.1	106.6	..	.	Total consumption, MPS
82.6	84.0	84.7	88.3	92.2	96.3	100.0	103.7	106.7	..	.	Households, SNA
91.6	91.1	93.0	94.1	96.1	97.9	100.0	102.6	104.0	..	.	Households, "building block"
88.0	88.6	90.5	90.7	94.4	95.3	100.0	102.8	103.1	..	.	General government, SNA
91.8	93.9	95.8	97.2	98.3	99.0	100.0	101.0	102.0	..	.	General government, "building block"
											INVESTMENT
92.1	88.3	87.7	83.6	87.4	92.5	100.0	106.0	106.6	..	.	Gross fixed investment, SNA
102.1	84.2	84.2	86.3	91.6	94.7	100.0	110.5	107.4	..	Y	Accumulation, MPS
132.5	107.8	92.5	91.4	92.7	97.0	100.0	97.6	99.1	..	.	"Building block"
											CONSUMER PRICES
..	..	..	..	..	..	..	..	..	..	.	National methodology
91.1	93.1	92.2	95.1	96.7	99.3	100.0	100.7	102.7	..	.	Outside estimate
			(millions of current US dollars)								**MERCHANDISE EXPORTS**
19,858	21,743	23,793	24,836	18,210	16,351	16,396	16,619	17,334	11,842		UNCTAD
19,900	21,800	23,800	24,800	24,900	25,100	27,300	..	..	..	G	IMF: IFS
19,650	22,200	24,290	24,550	23,890	27,830	30,740	32,000				ACDA
14,027	15,173	15,592	15,521	17,636	16,856	16,474	15,812	16,004	16,542	.	ECE
6,990	6,963	6,790	6,545	6,910	7,695	7,500	6,743	6,243	6,041	.	intra-CMEA
15,404	17,179	18,174	17,729	19,928	18,327	18,362	18,028	17,740	17,558	f	Authors' uniform TR/$ series
8,305	8,878	9,278	8,670	9,068	9,075	9,272	8,810	7,863	7,012	.	intra-CMEA
			(millions of current US dollars)								**MERCHANDISE IMPORTS**
20,181	20,196	21,524	22,940	15,760	16,128	16,710	17,408	17,778	10,876	F	UNCTAD
20,200	20,200	21,500	23,000	23,100	24,900	26,900	..	..	..	G	IMF: IFS
19,970	20,620	21,970	21,930	22,150	27,500	30,990	30,800				ACDA
14,181	13,644	13,831	14,110	15,163	16,674	16,788	16,617	16,516	19,659	.	ECE
7,146	6,952	6,306	6,155	7,201	8,277	7,455	6,510	5,845	4,102	.	intra-CMEA
15,597	15,645	16,254	16,203	17,548	18,264	18,682	18,788	18,163	20,372	f	Authors' uniform series
8,491	8,864	8,617	8,152	9,450	9,761	9,216	8,506	7,363	4,762	.	intra-CMEA

German Democratic Republic

Basic tables	1970	1971	1972	1973	1974	1975	1976	1977	1978	1979	1980
SNA ACCOUNTS, current prices	*(billions of current German Democratic Republic marks)*										
GNP, at market prices	..	..	..	..	..	..	..	..	..	..	..
Net factor income	..	..	..	..	..	..	..	..	..	..	..
GDP at market prices	148	..	..	..	..	..	..	..	..	..	245
Net indirect taxes	..	..	..	..	..	..	..	..	..	..	..
GDP at factor cost	..	..	..	..	..	..	..	..	..	..	..
Agriculture	..	..	..	..	..	..	..	..	..	..	19
Industry	..	..	..	..	..	..	..	..	..	..	160
Services, etc.	..	..	..	..	..	..	..	..	..	..	66
Resource balance	..	..	..	..	..	..	..	..	..	..	2
Exports GNFS	..	..	..	..	..	..	..	..	..	..	..
Imports GNFS	..	..	..	..	..	..	..	..	..	..	..
Domestic absorption	..	..	..	..	..	..	..	..	..	..	243
Total consumption	..	..	..	..	..	..	..	..	..	..	178
Private consumption	..	..	..	..	..	..	..	..	..	..	150
General government consumption	..	..	..	..	..	..	..	..	..	..	28
Gross domestic investment	..	..	..	..	..	..	..	..	..	..	65
Fixed domestic investment	..	..	..	..	..	..	..	..	..	..	58
Depreciation	..	..	..	..	..	..	..	..	..	..	..
SNA ACCOUNTS, constant prices	*(billions of constant 1987 German Democratic Republic marks)*										
Gross national product (GNP)	..	..	..	..	..	..	..	..	..	..	..
GDP at market prices	..	..	..	..	..	..	..	..	..	..	250
GDP at factor cost	..	..	..	..	..	..	..	..	..	..	..
Agriculture	..	..	..	..	..	..	..	..	..	..	29
Industry	..	..	..	..	..	..	..	..	..	..	148
Services, etc.	..	..	..	..	..	..	..	..	..	..	75
Resource balance	..	..	..	..	..	..	..	..	..	..	-29
Exports GNFS	..	..	..	..	..	..	..	..	..	..	..
Imports GNFS	..	..	..	..	..	..	..	..	..	..	..
Domestic absorption	..	..	..	..	..	..	..	..	..	..	279
Total consumption, etc.	..	..	..	..	..	..	..	..	..	..	196
Private consumption, etc.	..	..	..	..	..	..	..	..	..	..	161
General government consumption	..	..	..	..	..	..	..	..	..	..	35
Gross domestic investment	..	..	..	..	..	..	..	..	..	..	83
Fixed domestic investment	..	..	..	..	..	..	..	..	..	..	75
Depreciation	..	..	..	..	..	..	..	..	..	..	..
MPS ACCOUNTS, current prices	*(billions of current German Democratic Republic marks)*										
NMP produced:											
Agriculture and forestry	..	..	..	..	..	..	..	..	..	..	..
Industry excluding construction	..	..	..	..	..	..	..	..	..	..	..
Construction	..	..	..	..	..	..	..	..	..	..	..
Transport and communication	..	..	..	..	..	..	..	..	..	..	..
Trade, etc.	..	..	..	..	..	..	..	..	..	..	..
Other services	..	..	..	..	..	..	..	..	..	..	..
Resource balance	..	..	..	..	..	..	..	..	..	..	..
NMP used: domestic market	..	..	..	..	..	..	..	..	..	..	..
Final consumption, material goods	..	..	..	..	..	..	..	..	..	..	..
Personal consumption	..	..	..	..	..	..	..	..	..	..	..
Collective consumption	..	..	..	..	..	..	..	..	..	..	..
Net capital formation	..	..	..	..	..	..	..	..	..	..	..
Net fixed capital formation	..	..	..	..	..	..	..	..	..	..	..
Changes in stocks	..	..	..	..	..	..	..	..	..	..	..
Depreciation	..	..	..	..	..	..	..	..	..	..	..
MPS ACCOUNTS, constant prices	*(billions of 1985 German Democratic Republic marks)*										
NMP produced:	122	127	135	141	150	158	164	172	178	186	194
Agriculture and forestry	23	22	24	24	26	25	22	25	24	25	25
Industry and construction	84	88	92	98	104	110	116	122	127	132	139
Services	15	18	18	19	21	23	25	26	27	28	30
Resource balance	..	..	..	..	..	..	..	..	..	..	..
NMP used: domestic market	..	..	..	..	..	..	..	..	..	..	..
Final consumption, material goods	..	..	..	..	..	..	..	..	..	..	..
Personal consumption	..	..	..	..	..	..	..	..	..	..	..
Collective consumption	..	..	..	..	..	..	..	..	..	..	..
Net capital formation	..	..	..	..	..	..	..	..	..	..	..
Net fixed capital formation	..	..	..	..	..	..	..	..	..	..	..
Depreciation	..	..	..	..	..	..	..	..	..	..	..

Abbreviations in notes column are explained in the General Notes. For sources and methods, see the Technical Notes.

1981	1982	1983	1984	1985	1986	1987	1988	1989	1990	Notes	Basic tables (continued)
				(billions of current German Democratic Republic marks)							**SNA ACCOUNTS, current prices**
..	..	..	..	..	..	..	..	..	..	.	GNP, at market prices
..	..	..	..	..	..	..	..	..	..	.	Net factor income
253	264	277	293	312	322	333	346	353	..	.	GDP at market prices
..	..	..	..	..	..	..	..	..	..	.	Net indirect taxes
..	..	..	..	..	..	..	..	..	..	.	GDP at factor cost
20	19	21	32	33	34	34	33	34	..	H	Agriculture
166	173	181	177	192	200	207	216	219	..	H	Industry
67	72	74	84	87	88	92	98	101	..	H	Services, etc.
2	14	18	17	16	9	5	-4	-4	..	.	Resource balance
..	..	..	..	..	..	..	..	..	..	.	Exports GNFS
..	..	..	..	..	..	..	..	..	..	.	Imports GNFS
252	250	258	277	296	313	328	350	357	..	.	Domestic absorption
184	189	193	207	219	229	239	249	257	..	.	Total consumption
155	160	162	174	184	192	200	207	214	..	.	Private consumption
29	29	31	32	35	36	40	41	43	..	.	General government consumption
68	60	65	69	76	83	88	101	100	..	.	Gross domestic investment
62	59	63	61	68	75	83	93	92	..	.	Fixed domestic investment
..	..	..	..	..	..	..	..	..	..	.	Depreciation
			(billions of constant 1987 German Democratic Republic marks)								**SNA ACCOUNTS, constant prices**
..	..	..	..	..	..	..	..	..	..	.	Gross national product (GNP)
261	269	281	295	310	322	333	343	351	..	.	GDP at market prices
..	..	..	..	..	..	..	..	..	..	.	GDP at factor cost
29	29	30	33	34	34	34	32	33	..	H	Agriculture
156	162	170	179	190	199	207	215	220	..	H	Industry
76	79	81	83	86	89	92	97	98	..	H	Services, etc.
-21	-8	2	7	8	8	6	0	1	..	.	Resource balance
..	..	..	..	..	..	..	..	..	..	.	Exports GNFS
..	..	..	..	..	..	..	..	..	..	.	Imports GNFS
282	277	280	289	302	314	327	343	350	..	.	Domestic absorption
200	203	205	212	222	230	239	248	254	..	.	Total consumption, etc.
165	168	169	176	184	193	200	207	213	..	.	Private consumption, etc.
35	35	36	36	37	38	40	41	41	..	.	General government consumption
83	74	75	76	81	84	88	95	96	..	.	Gross domestic investment
77	73	73	69	73	77	83	88	89	..	.	Fixed domestic investment
..	..	..	..	..	..	..	..	..	..	.	Depreciation
			(billions of current German Democratic Republic marks)								**MPS ACCOUNTS, current prices**
..	..	..	..	..	..	..	..	..	..	.	NMP produced:
..	..	..	..	..	..	..	..	..	..	.	Agriculture and forestry
..	..	..	..	..	..	..	..	..	..	.	Industry excluding construction
..	..	..	..	..	..	..	..	..	..	.	Construction
..	..	..	..	..	..	..	..	..	..	.	Transport and communication
..	..	..	..	..	..	..	..	..	..	.	Trade, etc.
..	..	..	..	..	..	..	..	..	..	.	Other services
..	..	..	..	..	..	..	..	..	..	.	Resource balance
..	..	..	..	..	..	..	..	..	..	.	NMP used: domestic market
..	..	..	..	..	..	..	..	..	..	.	Final consumption, material goods
..	..	..	..	..	..	..	..	..	..	.	Personal consumption
..	..	..	..	..	..	..	..	..	..	.	Collective consumption
..	..	..	..	..	..	..	..	..	..	.	Net capital formation
..	..	..	..	..	..	..	..	..	..	.	Net fixed capital formation
..	..	..	..	..	..	..	..	..	..	.	Changes in stocks
..	..	..	..	..	..	..	..	..	..	.	Depreciation
			(billions of 1985 German Democratic Republic marks)								**MPS ACCOUNTS, constant prices**
203	208	218	230	242	252	261	268	273	..	.	NMP produced:
26	25	27	29	30	30	30	27	..	..	.	Agriculture and forestry
147	151	159	168	178	187	194	201	..	..	.	Industry and construction
31	32	32	33	34	36	38	40	..	..	.	Services
..	..	..	..	..	..	..	..	..	..	.	Resource balance
..	..	..	..	..	..	..	..	..	..	.	NMP used: domestic market
..	..	..	..	..	..	..	..	..	..	.	Final consumption, material goods
..	..	..	..	..	..	..	..	..	..	.	Personal consumption
..	..	..	..	..	..	..	..	..	..	.	Collective consumption
..	..	..	..	..	..	..	..	..	..	.	Net capital formation
..	..	..	..	..	..	..	..	..	..	.	Net fixed capital formation
..	..	..	..	..	..	..	..	..	..	.	Depreciation

Basic tables (continued)	1970	1971	1972	1973	1974	1975	1976	1977	1978	1979	1980
MPS ACCOUNTS, index						*(index, 1980 = 100)*					
NMP produced:	62.8	65.7	69.5	72.9	77.5	81.7	84.5	88.8	92.0	95.8	100.0
Agriculture and forestry	90.1	85.6	94.6	95.5	101.8	99.1	88.3	99.1	95.5	100.0	100.0
Industry excluding construction	59.2	62.1	65.7	69.2	74.0	78.1	82.8	86.4	90.5	94.7	100.0
Construction	69.4	72.9	75.7	78.5	82.6	87.5	91.7	95.8	97.9	97.2	100.0
Transport and communication	67.6	72.3	73.6	77.0	81.1	87.2	91.2	93.9	98.0	99.3	100.0
Trade, etc.	63.7	67.5	72.0	75.8	81.5	84.1	86.6	91.1	94.9	96.8	100.0
NMP used: material goods	66.0	68.0	72.0	77.0	81.0	83.0	89.0	93.0	94.0	95.0	100.0
Final consumption	64.0	67.0	71.0	75.0	80.0	83.0	87.0	91.0	94.0	97.0	100.0
Net capital formation	75.0	73.0	75.0	83.0	87.0	86.0	94.0	99.0	94.0	89.0	100.0
EXCHANGE AND CONVERSION RATES					*(LCUs per US dollar: annual average)*						
Single-year converter	..	..	..	..	..	..	..	..	..	..	..
Devisa/official	4.200	4.200	3.870	3.480	3.480	3.480	3.480	3.480	3.480	3.480	3.300
Commercial	..	..	..	..	..	..	..	..	..	..	..
Noncommercial	3.660	3.491	3.189	2.673	2.588	2.460	2.518	2.322	2.009	1.833	1.818
Informal market	13.280	13.170	12.833	9.767	9.692	8.840	9.583	9.571	8.688	8.300	9.060
ICP	..	..	..	..	..	..	..	..	..	..	..
					(ruble per US dollar: annual average)						
Commercial TR/$ cross	..	..	..	..	..	..	..	..	..	..	..
Uniform TR/$ cross	1.072	1.157	1.232	1.093	1.092	1.167	1.067	1.022	0.973	0.945	0.980
					(LCUs per ruble: annual average)						
Commercial	..	..	..	..	..	..	..	..	..	..	..
Noncommercial	..	..	..	..	..	..	..	..	..	..	..
Devisa/official	4.667	4.667	4.667	4.667	4.667	4.667	4.667	4.667	4.667	4.667	4.667
CONSUMER PRICE INDEXES						*(index)*					
Official, IMF 1985 = 100	..	..	..	..	..	..	..	..	..	..	..
Official, CIA or LWI 1980 = 100	100.6	101.0	100.5	99.9	99.5	99.5	99.5	99.4	99.3	99.6	100.0
Alternative, CIA or LWI 1980 = 100	89.0	90.2	90.5	88.3	90.8	91.1	91.8	94.6	95.3	97.3	100.0
INTERNATIONAL TRADE (ECE)				*(billions of current German Democratic Republic marks)*							
Value of exports, fob	19	21	24	26	30	35	40	42	46	52	57
to CMEA	13	15	17	18	20	24	27	30	33	37	38
Value of imports, cif	20	21	23	27	34	39	46	50	51	56	63
from CMEA	14	14	15	17	19	25	28	33	34	35	38
Trade balance	-1	0	1	-1	-3	-4	-6	-8	-5	-4	-6
CMEA	0	1	3	1	0	-1	-1	-3	-1	2	0
INTERNATIONAL TRADE (Authors')					*(millions of current US dollars)*						
Value of exports, fob	4,038	4,236	4,659	5,771	6,849	7,423	8,922	9,596	10,957	12,727	13,961
to developed countries	1,003	1,070	1,296	1,726	2,393	2,263	2,764	2,472	2,615	3,136	4,172
to other non-socialist countries	192	223	224	288	368	444	500	571	768	853	1,105
to socialist countries	2,843	2,943	3,139	3,757	4,088	4,716	5,658	6,552	7,574	8,737	8,684
to CMEA	2,640	2,736	2,991	3,591	3,873	4,465	5,363	6,194	7,215	8,363	8,250
Value of imports, cif	4,307	4,221	4,622	6,245	7,804	8,576	10,673	11,676	12,192	14,010	15,699
from developed countries	1,296	1,374	1,818	2,557	3,294	3,281	4,192	3,780	3,708	4,991	5,816
from other non-socialist countries	189	186	162	234	542	491	626	723	677	776	1,117
from socialist countries	2,822	2,661	2,642	3,453	3,967	4,803	5,854	7,173	7,807	8,243	8,766
from CMEA	2,689	2,523	2,530	3,327	3,792	4,581	5,608	6,857	7,454	7,870	8,212
Trade balance	-270	15	37	-474	-955	-1,153	-1,750	-2,080	-1,235	-1,283	-1,738
Developed countries	-293	-304	-522	-831	-901	-1,018	-1,428	-1,309	-1,093	-1,855	-1,644
Other non-socialist countries	3	37	62	53	-175	-48	-126	-151	91	78	-11
Socialist countries	20	282	497	303	121	-88	-196	-620	-232	494	-82
CMEA	-49	213	461	265	82	-117	-245	-663	-238	493	38
PARTNER CONVERTIBLE TRADE (ECE)					*(millions of current US dollars)*						
Exports to non-CMEA (cif)	988	1,142	1,312	1,749	2,302	2,534	2,753	3,046	3,509	4,351	5,383
Imports from non-CMEA (fob)	1,144	1,275	1,626	1,955	2,541	2,910	3,181	3,282	4,004	5,225	5,719
Trade balance	-156	-133	-314	-206	-239	-376	-428	-236	-495	-874	-336
TRADE PRICE INDEXES (Authors')						*(index, 1980 = 100)*					
Terms of trade	119.1	118.1	114.3	110.3	105.2	101.7	102.7	101.1	102.4	100.8	100.0
Exports	59.6	56.8	56.0	64.7	71.0	71.9	81.4	83.9	88.9	94.5	100.0
Non-socialist countries	..	..	..	..	..	..	..	..	..	..	..
Developed countries	47.1	..	..	..	..	75.9	..	..	..	..	100.0
Other	45.5	..	..	..	..	88.1	..	..	..	..	100.0
Socialist countries	..	..	..	..	..	..	..	..	..	..	..
CMEA	..	..	..	..	..	..	..	..	..	..	100.0
Imports	..	..	..	..	..	..	..	..	..	..	100.0
Non-socialist countries	..	..	..	..	..	..	..	..	..	..	..
Developed countries	..	..	..	..	..	..	..	..	..	..	100.0
Other	..	..	..	..	..	..	..	..	..	..	100.0
Socialist countries	..	..	..	..	..	..	..	..	..	..	..
CMEA	..	..	..	..	..	..	..	..	..	..	100.0

Abbreviations in notes column are explained in the General Notes. For sources and methods, see the Technical Notes.

1981	1982	1983	1984	1985	1986	1987	1988	1989	1990	Notes	Basic tables (continued)
				(index, 1980 = 100)							**MPS ACCOUNTS, index**
104.8	107.5	112.5	118.7	124.9	130.0	135.0	138.0	141.0	..	.	NMP produced:
102.7	100.9	105.4	115.3	120.7	119.8	119.0	110.0	113.0	..	.	Agriculture and forestry
105.3	109.5	115.4	121.3	128.4	135.0	140.0	145.0	148.0	..	.	Industry excluding construction
104.9	104.9	110.4	117.4	125.0	133.0	138.0	144.0	144.0	..	.	Construction
104.1	106.1	110.8	115.5	117.6	120.3	122.3	124.0	126.0	..	.	Transport and communication
103.8	104.5	107.0	110.8	114.6	119.1	124.0	130.0	133.0	..	.	Trade, etc.
101.0	97.0	98.0	101.0	106.0	110.0	115.0	121.0	123.0	..	.	NMP used: material goods
102.0	104.0	104.0	108.0	113.0	117.0	122.0	127.0	130.0	..	.	Final consumption
97.0	80.0	80.0	82.0	87.0	90.0	95.0	105.0	102.0	..	.	Net capital formation
				(LCUs per US dollar: annual average)							**EXCHANGE AND CONVERSION RATES**
..	..	..	..	..	..	..	..	..	..	.	Single-year converter
3.320	3.460	3.540	3.640	3.700	3.300	3.010	2.945	..	..	.	Devisa/official
..	..	..	..	8.140	8.140	8.140	8.140	8.140	8.140	f	Commercial
2.260	2.427	2.553	2.846	2.944	2.172	1.797	1.756	1.880	..	.	Noncommercial
9.788	10.867	12.050	13.826	16.837	16.950	15.000	18.394	19.667	..	.	Informal market
..	..	..	..	..	..	..	..	..	..	.	ICP
				(ruble per US dollar: annual average)							
..	..	..	..	1.740	1.740	1.740	1.740	1.740	..	f	Commercial TR/$ cross
1.076	1.105	1.201	1.395	1.433	1.388	1.397	1.484	1.660	1.980	.	Uniform TR/$ cross
				(LCUs per ruble: annual average)							
..	..	..	..	..	..	..	..	..	..	.	Commercial
..	..	..	..	..	..	..	..	..	..	.	Noncommercial
4.667	4.667	4.667	4.667	4.667	4.667	4.667	4.667	4.667	..	.	Devisa/official
				(index)							**CONSUMER PRICE INDEXES**
..	..	..	..	..	..	..	..	..	..	.	Official, IMF 1985 = 100
100.2	100.2	100.2	100.2	100.1	100.1	100.1	100.1	102.1	..	.	Official, CIA or LWI 1980 = 100
101.6	103.8	102.8	106.0	107.8	110.7	111.5	112.3	114.5	..	.	Alternative, CIA or LWI 1980 = 100
				(billions of current German Democratic Republic marks)							**INTERNATIONAL TRADE (ECE)**
66	75	84	90	148	133	134	135	141	151	f	Value of exports, fob
42	46	52	56	61	59	61	61	61	65	.	to CMEA
67	70	76	84	128	131	136	142	145	172	f	Value of imports, cif
43	46	48	53	63	63	60	59	57	44	.	from CMEA
-1	5	8	7	20	2	-3	-6	-4	-21	f	Trade balance
-1	0	4	3	-3	-4	0	2	4	21	.	CMEA
				(millions of current US dollars)							**INTERNATIONAL TRADE (Authors')**
15,404	17,179	18,174	17,729	19,928	18,327	18,362	18,028	17,740	17,558	f	Value of exports, fob
5,446	6,296	7,102	7,461	8,764	7,323	7,246	7,678	8,407	9,361	.	to developed countries
1,268	1,578	1,441	1,255	1,534	1,326	1,239	907	905	860	.	to other non-socialist countries
8,690	9,305	9,631	9,012	9,630	9,678	9,876	9,443	8,428	7,337	.	to socialist countries
8,305	8,878	9,278	8,670	9,068	9,075	9,272	8,810	7,863	7,012	.	to CMEA
15,597	15,645	16,254	16,203	17,548	18,264	18,682	18,788	18,163	20,372	f	Value of imports, cif
5,952	5,509	6,219	6,651	6,308	6,738	7,914	8,843	9,439	14,570	.	from developed countries
702	858	1,000	1,009	1,219	1,064	858	694	731	651	.	from other non-socialist countries
8,943	9,279	9,035	8,543	10,020	10,462	9,910	9,251	7,994	5,151	.	from socialist countries
8,491	8,864	8,617	8,152	9,450	9,761	9,216	8,506	7,363	4,762	.	from CMEA
-194	1,534	1,921	1,526	2,380	63	-320	-760	-423	-2,814	f	Trade balance
-507	788	884	810	2,456	585	-667	-1,165	-1,032	-5,209	.	Developed countries
566	721	441	246	315	262	381	213	175	209	.	Other non-socialist countries
-253	26	596	469	-391	-785	-34	192	434	2,186	.	Socialist countries
-186	14	661	518	-382	-686	56	304	501	2,251	.	CMEA
				(millions of current US dollars)							**PARTNER CONVERTIBLE TRADE (ECE)**
5,182	5,399	5,390	5,299	5,166	5,368	6,512	6,861	3,038	..	.	Exports to non-CMEA (cif)
5,273	4,692	5,041	4,422	4,496	5,686	7,003	7,270	3,598	..	.	Imports from non-CMEA (fob)
-91	707	349	877	670	-318	-491	-409	-560	..	.	Trade balance
				(index, 1980 = 100)							**TRADE PRICE INDEXES (Authors')**
99.4	97.6	95.1	95.3	100.6	95.7	102.3	104.8	108.8	81.6	.	Terms of trade
100.5	105.5	99.6	95.0	104.3	100.4	100.7	99.1	97.1	96.1	.	Exports
..	..	..	..	..	..	..	..	..	..	.	Non-socialist countries
..	..	..	..	123.7	107.8	107.9	111.5	119.7	..	.	Developed countries
..	..	..	..	151.7	147.4	149.5	161.9	172.8	..	.	Other
..	..	..	..	..	..	..	..	..	..	.	Socialist countries
..	..	..	..	88.4	92.4	92.2	86.7	77.6	..	.	CMEA
101.1	108.1	104.8	99.7	103.7	104.9	98.4	94.5	89.2	117.7	.	Imports
..	..	..	..	..	..	..	..	..	..	.	Non-socialist countries
..	..	..	..	92.6	88.2	86.2	89.1	91.7	..	.	Developed countries
..	..	..	..	93.9	114.4	94.2	86.9	83.0	..	.	Other
..	..	..	..	..	..	..	..	..	..	.	Socialist countries
..	..	..	..	116.1	121.2	116.2	105.1	90.6	..	.	CMEA

German Democratic Republic

	1970	1971	1972	1973	1974	1975	1976	1977	1978	1979	1980
TRADE PRICE INDEXES (ECE)					*(index, 1980 = 100)*						
Terms of trade	125	125	125	120	117	109	104	104	104	100	100
Exports	62	63	69	80	91	105	76	78	88	92	100
Imports	50	51	56	67	78	97	72	75	85	93	100
Balance of Payments (ECE)					*(millions of current US dollars)*						
Exports, convertible currency	1,281	1,417	1,643	2,152	2,952	2,941	3,515	3,366	3,708	4,328	5,679
Imports, convertible currency	1,535	1,631	2,081	2,894	3,986	3,986	5,059	4,779	4,679	6,097	7,382
Trade balance, convertible currency	-254	-214	-438	-742	-1,034	-1,045	-1,544	-1,413	-971	-1,769	-1,703
Invisibles, convertible currency	179	245	245	274	148	234	292	280	288	452	83
Current balance, convertible currency	-75	31	-193	-468	-886	-811	-1,252	-1,133	-683	-1,317	-1,620
External debt, total (World Bank)	..	..	..	..	..	..	..	..	..	..	..
Convertible currency	..	..	..	..	..	..	..	..	..	..	..
CMEA	..	..	..	..	..	..	..	..	..	..	..
External debt service (World Bank)	..	..	..	..	..	..	..	..	..	..	..
Convertible currency	..	..	..	..	..	..	..	..	..	..	..
Total reserves less gold (IMF, IFS)	..	..	..	..	..	..	..	..	..	..	..
Total reserves, including gold at London price	..	..	..	..	..	..	..	..	..	..	..
Total reserves, incl. gold at national valuation	..	..	..	..	..	..	..	..	..	..	..
EMPLOYMENT					*(thousands)*						
Employment, total	8,167	..	..	..	..	..	..	..	..	..	..
Agriculture	1,060	..	..	..	..	..	..	..	..	..	..
Industry	4,052	..	..	..	..	..	..	..	..	..	..
Services	3,056	..	..	..	..	..	..	..	..	..	..
Labor force, total	8,553	8,588	8,622	8,656	8,691	8,725	8,804	8,882	8,960	9,038	9,117
Agriculture	1,075	1,062	1,049	1,036	1,023	1,011	1,002	993	984	975	966
Industry	4,295	4,311	4,327	4,343	4,359	4,375	4,413	4,450	4,488	4,525	4,562
Services	3,183	3,215	3,246	3,277	3,308	3,339	3,389	3,439	3,489	3,538	3,588
DOMESTIC FINANCE (IMF)				*(billions of current German Democratic Republic marks)*							
Money supply, broadly defined	..	..	..	..	..	..	..	..	..	..	..
Money, means of payment	..	..	..	..	..	..	..	..	..	..	..
Demand deposits	..	..	..	..	..	..	..	..	..	..	..
Currency outside banks	..	..	..	..	..	..	..	..	..	..	..
Quasi-money	..	..	..	..	..	..	..	..	..	..	..
Interest: deposit rate (percent)	..	..	..	..	..	..	..	..	..	..	..
Central government expenditures	..	..	..	..	..	..	..	..	..	..	..
Defense	..	..	..	..	..	..	..	..	..	..	..
					(millions of 1989 US dollars)						
Central government exp. (ACDA)	..	..	..	..	..	..	..	..	..	60,480	63,470
Military (ACDA)	..	..	..	..	..	..	..	..	..	10,190	10,370
LAND AND FORESTS (FAO)											
Pop. density: agr. land (pop. per sq. km)	272	271	271	270	269	268	267	267	267	267	267
Deforestation rate (net)	0	0	0	0	0	0	0	0	0	0	0
Forest (thousands sq. km)	30	30	30	30	30	30	30	30	30	30	30
SOCIAL INDICATORS											
Population density: total land (pop. per sq. km)	161	161	161	160	159	159	158	158	158	158	158
School enrollment ratio, primary	93	..	..	..	..	94	94	93	97	97	108
secondary	92	..	..	..	..	89	92	93	89	88	80
tertiary	..	..	..	..	..	..	..	..	..	..	30
Energy consumption per capita (kg. of oil eq.)	4,216	4,304	4,330	4,453	4,546	4,607	4,789	4,929	5,059	5,210	5,386
Daily calorie supply per capita	3,344	3,343	3,369	3,353	3,387	3,440	3,520	3,497	3,560	3,628	3,640
Food production (1979-1981=100)	79	76	84	86	96	90	85	92	96	100	99
Daily protein supply (gm. per capita)	93	94	94	96	96	99	101	100	103	104	105
Population per hospital bed	90	..	..	..	..	..	..	..	..	..	..
per nursing person	..	..	..	..	..	..	..	..	..	..	..
per physician	626	..	..	..	..	..	..	..	..	..	494
Female participation in labor force (percent)	43	43	44	44	44	45	45	46	46	47	47
Infant mortality (per 1,000 live births)	19	18	18	16	16	16	14	13	13	13	12
Life expectancy (years)	70	70	70	71	71	71	71	71	71	71	72
Total fertility (births per woman)	2	2	2	2	2	2	2	2	2	2	2
Urban population (percent of total population)	74	74	74	75	75	75	75	76	76	76	76
Population per passenger car	15	14	12	11	10	9	8	8	7	7	6
per telephone	..	..	..	..	..	7	..	..	..	..	5

Abbreviations in notes column are explained in the General Notes. For sources and methods, see the Technical Notes.

1981	1982	1983	1984	1985	1986	1987	1988	1989	1990	Notes	Basic tables (continued)
				(index, 1980 = 100)							**TRADE PRICE INDEXES (ECE)**
102	101	98	96	103	93	89	90	..	..	.	Terms of trade
103	101	94	88	98	95	93	91	..	..	.	Exports
101	100	95	91	96	101	104	100	..	..	.	Imports
				(millions of current US dollars)							**Balance of Payments (ECE)**
7,125	8,277	8,952	9,096	10,622	8,979	8,771	8,857	9,580	..	.	Exports, convertible currency
7,103	6,817	7,694	8,116	7,888	8,170	9,139	9,913	10,511	..	.	Imports, convertible currency
22	1,460	1,258	980	2,734	809	-368	-1,056	-931	..	.	Trade balance, convertible currency
-406	-326	-77	-41	46	339	581	461	181	..	.	Invisibles, convertible currency
-384	1,134	1,181	939	2,780	1,148	213	-595	-750	..	f	Current balance, convertible currency
..	..	..	..	..	..	..	..	..	..	.	External debt, total (World Bank)
..	..	..	..	..	..	..	..	..	..	.	Convertible currency
..	..	..	..	..	..	..	..	..	..	.	CMEA
..	..	..	..	..	..	..	..	..	..	.	External debt service (World Bank)
..	..	..	..	..	..	..	..	..	..	.	Convertible currency
..	..	..	..	..	..	..	..	..	..	.	Total reserves less gold (IMF, IFS)
..	..	..	..	..	..	..	..	..	..	.	Total reserves, including gold at London price
..	..	..	..	..	..	..	..	..	..	.	Total reserves, incl. gold at national valuation
				(thousands)							**EMPLOYMENT**
..	..	..	..	..	..	..	8,952	..	..	.	Employment, total
..	..	..	..	..	..	..	947	..	..	.	Agriculture
..	..	..	..	..	..	..	4,441	..	..	.	Industry
..	..	..	..	..	..	..	3,564	..	..	.	Services
9,197	9,277	9,357	9,438	9,518	9,548	9,579	9,609	9,639	9,670	.	Labor force, total
..	..	..	..	..	..	..	..	..	..	.	Agriculture
..	..	..	..	..	..	..	..	..	..	.	Industry
..	..	..	..	..	..	..	..	..	..	.	Services
				(billions of current German Democratic Republic marks)							**DOMESTIC FINANCE (IMF)**
..	..	..	..	..	..	..	..	..	..	.	Money supply, broadly defined
..	..	..	..	..	..	..	..	..	..	.	Money, means of payment
..	..	..	..	..	..	..	..	..	..	.	Demand deposits
..	..	..	..	..	..	..	..	..	..	.	Currency outside banks
..	..	..	..	..	..	..	..	..	..	.	Quasi-money
..	..	..	..	..	..	..	..	..	..	.	Interest: deposit rate (percent)
..	..	..	..	..	..	..	..	..	..	.	Central government expenditures
..	..	..	..	..	..	..	..	..	..	.	Defense
				(millions of 1989 US dollars)							
65,790	70,210	73,680	76,870	83,270	83,270	86,660	91,540	93,780	..	.	Central government exp. (ACDA)
10,660	11,500	11,770	12,050	12,310	12,650	13,030	13,290	13,970	..	U	Military (ACDA)
											LAND AND FORESTS (FAO)
267	267	267	267	267	268	269	..	..	..	.	Pop. density: agr. land (pop. per sq. km)
0	0	0	0	0	0	..	..	..	..	.	Deforestation rate (net)
30	30	30	30	30	30	..	..	..	..	.	Forest (thousands sq. km)
											SOCIAL INDICATORS
158	158	158	157	157	158	158	..	..	..	.	Population density: total land (pop. per sq. km)
..	93	97	99	102	105	106	105	..	..	.	School enrollment ratio, primary
..	82	80	79	78	78	77	78	..	..	.	secondary
..	..	31	30	31	31	32	33	..	..	.	tertiary
5,440	5,436	5,468	5,627	5,784	5,826	6,031	..	..	..	.	Energy consumption per capita (kg. of oil eq.)
3,651	3,729	3,752	3,802	3,828	3,821	3,855	3,890	..	..	.	Daily calorie supply per capita
102	95	96	107	116	116	118	112	113	..	.	Food production (1979-1981=100)
106	108	109	112	112	112	114	115	..	..	.	Daily protein supply (gm. per capita)
..	..	..	..	..	..	..	..	..	..	.	Population per hospital bed
..	..	..	..	143	..	..	..	..	..	.	per nursing person
490	472	..	..	439	..	..	..	..	..	.	per physician
48	48	49	49	49	50	50	50	50	50	.	Female participation in labor force (percent)
12	12	11	10	10	9	9	8	8	8	.	Infant mortality (per 1,000 live births)
72	72	72	73	73	73	73	73	74	74	.	Life expectancy (years)
2	2	2	2	2	2	2	2	2	2	.	Total fertility (births per woman)
76	76	76	77	77	77	77	77	77	77	.	Urban population (percent of total population)
6	6	6	5	5	..	..	..	..	..	.	Population per passenger car
5	5	5	5	4	..	..	..	..	..	.	per telephone

Hungary

Comparator tables	1970	1971	1972	1973	1974	1975	1976	1977	1978	1979	1980
PER CAPITA INCOME						*(US dollars)*					
World Bank (Atlas method)	..	..	..	..	..	..	..	1,320	1,500	1,680	1,930
Single year conversion	..	..	..	..	..	1,026	1,191	1,320	1,531	1,757	2,033
CIA or LWI	1,554	..	..	..	..	2,534	2,690	3,035	3,324	3,617	3,980
Penn World Tables	1,180	1,358	1,448	1,600	1,897	2,220	2,452	2,811	3,294	3,586	4,038
POPULATION						*(thousands)*					
	10,337	10,365	10,394	10,436	10,471	10,532	10,589	10,637	10,673	10,698	10,710
GROSS NATIONAL PRODUCT, current prices						*(millions of current US dollars)*					
World Bank (Atlas method)	..	..	..	..	..	..	..	13,989	16,028	18,013	20,634
Single year conversion	..	..	..	..	..	10,807	12,613	14,036	16,345	18,797	21,774
Authors' series	5,543	..	..	..	..	..	..	..	..	..	22,232
CIA or LWI	..	..	..	..	..	..	..	..	..	35,700	39,310
GROSS NATIONAL PRODUCT, constant prices						*(millions of constant 1987 dollars)*					
Single year conversion	..	..	..	16,737	17,690	18,783	19,595	20,865	21,774	22,025	22,083
Authors' series, rescaled from 1980 prices	19,183	..	..	..	..	..	..	..	..	..	30,449
CIA or LWI, rescaled from 1989 prices	44,909	..	..	..	..	52,834	52,992	56,320	57,694	57,800	58,381
CONVERSION FACTORS						*(LCUs per US dollar)*					
World Bank (Atlas method)	..	..	..	..	..	..	..	41.10	38.66	37.13	34.33
Single year convertor	60.00	59.82	55.26	48.97	46.75	43.97	41.58	40.96	37.91	35.58	32.53
Authors' series	60.00	..	..	..	..	..	..	..	..	..	32.43
Penn World Tables	27.25	25.63	25.98	25.69	22.60	20.65	20.37	19.47	17.91	17.79	16.67
OUTPUT TRENDS, OVERALL						*(index, constant prices 1987 = 100)*					
GNP, SNA	..	..	..	66.7	70.5	74.9	78.1	83.2	86.8	87.8	88.0
NMP, MPS	57.4	60.8	64.6	69.1	73.2	77.7	80.0	85.7	89.1	90.1	89.3
GNP, "Building block"	71.6	74.8	76.4	80.4	82.5	84.2	84.5	89.8	92.0	92.2	93.1
Industry											
Value added, SNA	50.7	54.2	57.7	62.2	67.4	72.2	76.4	81.2	85.7	90.1	88.6
Value added, MPS	50.9	54.2	57.6	62.5	67.8	72.9	76.8	82.7	87.2	92.4	88.9
"Building block"	75.5	77.2	78.1	81.3	83.7	86.3	88.6	92.4	95.8	96.2	94.6
Gross output, SNA	71.8	..	..	..	..	81.8	..	..	..	..	90.9
Agriculture											
Value added, SNA	63.7	67.8	69.6	73.3	75.4	77.1	74.1	83.2	83.9	82.8	85.9
Value added, MPS	86.7	91.9	93.6	97.1	97.1	97.1	90.2	100.6	97.1	91.9	97.1
"Building block"	72.9	80.3	82.0	88.6	87.8	87.9	82.3	93.2	92.3	89.7	95.2
Gross output, SNA	71.7	..	..	..	..	87.7	..	..	..	..	94.3
Services											
Value added, SNA	52.4	55.5	59.9	64.7	67.8	72.7	75.9	80.0	84.4	83.8	84.2
Value added, MPS	52.3	55.0	59.1	63.3	67.7	73.3	80.5	83.4	87.6	87.7	86.1
"Building block"	66.9	69.0	71.2	74.5	78.0	79.9	81.5	85.0	87.8	89.4	90.3
CONSUMPTION											
Total consumption, SNA	62.4	66.1	68.4	72.0	80.1	79.4	81.3	82.1	84.9	86.7	87.3
Total consumption, MPS	60.8	64.1	66.0	68.5	73.2	76.6	78.2	82.1	85.6	88.5	88.7
Households, SNA	61.8	65.4	68.1	72.0	81.3	80.0	81.8	82.6	85.6	87.0	87.7
Households, "building block"	..	..	..	..	..	84.1	84.9	88.3	90.9	92.2	93.4
General government, SNA	65.8	70.1	70.5	71.8	73.0	75.6	78.4	79.0	80.7	84.7	84.8
General government, "building block"	..	..	..	..	..	73.2	75.9	77.5	79.3	81.6	83.2
INVESTMENT											
Gross fixed investment, SNA	55.6	66.9	66.3	68.5	76.9	86.9	86.9	98.9	103.9	104.7	99.0
Accumulation, MPS	112.2	114.0	124.1	131.2	123.8	173.0	151.0	149.3	164.2	170.6	158.8
"Building block"	..	..	..	..	..	126.4	120.9	129.6	146.7	123.3	120.5
CONSUMER PRICES											
National methodology	..	..	42.6	44.0	44.8	46.5	49.0	50.9	53.3	58.0	63.4
Outside estimate	36.8	38.7	40.2	42.1	43.3	45.0	48.0	49.8	51.8	56.8	61.3
MERCHANDISE EXPORTS						*(millions of current US dollars)*					
UNCTAD	2,317	..	..	..	..	6,091	..	..	..	..	8,677
IMF: IFS	1,726	..	..	..	..	4,519	..	..	..	..	8,671
ACDA	..	..	..	..	..	..	..	7,959	8,814	11,120	11,640
ECE	2,317	2,500	3,291	4,370	5,130	6,063	4,927	5,816	6,351	7,930	8,609
intra-CMEA	1,444	1,625	2,165	2,823	3,375	4,155	2,785	3,289	3,489	4,217	4,431
Authors' uniform TR/$ series	2,068	2,113	2,539	3,400	3,898	4,159	5,265	6,346	6,757	8,737	9,551
intra-CMEA	1,212	1,264	1,457	1,905	2,167	2,349	3,100	3,772	3,856	4,962	5,310
MERCHANDISE IMPORTS						*(millions of current US dollars)*					
UNCTAD	2,506	..	..	..	..	7,176	..	..	..	..	9,235
IMF: IFS	1,877	..	..	..	..	5,400	..	..	..	..	9,245
ACDA	..	..	..	..	..	..	..	8,558	10,580	11,920	12,610
ECE	2,505	2,990	3,153	3,877	5,576	7,152	5,534	6,516	7,940	8,683	9,188
intra-CMEA	1,565	1,892	1,989	2,355	3,133	4,539	2,853	3,263	3,891	4,389	4,350
Authors' uniform series	2,241	2,547	2,474	3,082	4,436	5,110	5,872	7,020	8,371	9,502	10,110
intra-CMEA	1,314	1,472	1,338	1,589	2,012	2,565	3,176	3,741	4,300	5,164	5,213

Abbreviations in notes column are explained in the General Notes. For sources and methods, see the Technical Notes.

1981	1982	1983	1984	1985	1986	1987	1988	1989	1990	Notes	Comparator tables (continued)
				(US dollars)							**PER CAPITA INCOME**
2,150	2,220	2,120	2,030	1,930	2,010	2,250	2,480	2,620	2,780	.	World Bank (Atlas method)
2,044	2,057	1,891	1,828	1,854	2,140	2,362	2,615	2,638	2,980	.	Single year conversion
4,394	4,846	4,989	5,322	5,355	5,622	5,949	6,315	6,483	6,371	.	CIA or LWI
4,526	4,835	4,885	5,037	5,170	5,417	5,795	5,924	..	..	.	Penn World Tables
				(thousands)							**POPULATION**
10,713	10,711	10,700	10,679	10,657	10,640	10,621	10,596	10,576	10,554	.	
				(millions of current US dollars)							**GROSS NATIONAL PRODUCT, current prices**
23,018	23,738	22,634	21,687	20,580	21,388	23,914	26,249	27,685	29,319	.	World Bank (Atlas method)
21,901	22,033	20,232	19,518	19,757	22,766	25,084	27,711	27,903	31,451	.	Single year conversion
..	..	..	..	20,624	..	26,110	27,959	28,883	..	D	Authors' series
43,430	47,870	49,210	52,360	52,580	55,130	57,850	63,340	64,740	..	.	CIA or LWI
				(millions of constant 1987 dollars)							**GROSS NATIONAL PRODUCT, constant prices**
22,503	22,653	23,095	23,592	23,563	23,947	25,084	24,994	24,762	23,882	.	Single year conversion
..	..	..	..	33,189	..	35,000	35,016	35,016	..	D	Authors' series, rescaled from 1980 prices
58,804	60,917	60,283	61,868	60,336	61,657	62,714	63,823	62,661	58,962	.	CIA or LWI, rescaled from 1989 prices
				(LCUs per US dollar)							**CONVERSION FACTORS**
32.65	34.00	38.14	43.24	48.11	48.78	49.27	53.22	59.53	67.80	..	World Bank (Atlas method)
34.31	36.63	42.67	48.04	50.12	45.83	46.97	50.41	59.07	63.21	.	Single year convertor
				50.12	..	46.97	50.41	59.07	..	..	Authors' series
16.09	16.37	17.15	18.19	18.76	18.89	19.93	22.46	..	..	.	Penn World Tables
				(index, constant prices 1987 = 100)							**OUTPUT TRENDS, OVERALL**
89.7	90.3	92.1	94.1	93.9	95.5	100.0	99.6	98.7	95.2	.	GNP, SNA
91.6	94.0	94.3	96.6	95.2	96.1	100.0	99.5	98.4	..	f	NMP, MPS
93.8	97.1	96.1	98.7	96.2	98.3	100.0	101.8	99.9	94.0	.	GNP, "Building block"
											Industry
94.8	95.9	97.8	99.1	96.6	96.2	100.0	92.5	91.2	83.2	Hf	Value added, SNA
92.8	97.1	100.0	100.3	97.6	96.8	100.0	..	..	..	.	Value added, MPS
95.1	95.9	96.4	98.2	96.3	98.3	100.0	98.3	95.8	88.3	.	"Building block"
..	..	..	..	97.3	99.1	100.0	99.1	96.4	88.2	X	Gross output, SNA
											Agriculture
89.4	99.2	99.2	103.9	99.6	103.1	100.0	107.9	107.9	98.9	Hf	Value added, SNA
97.1	105.8	102.9	108.7	101.0	104.9	100.0	108.7	..	..	.	Value added, MPS
94.6	106.8	100.5	107.0	97.9	100.3	100.0	107.6	106.3	98.8	.	"Building block"
..	..	..	..	96.2	100.0	100.0	108.5	105.7	99.1	.	Gross output, SNA
											Services
84.9	84.2	84.0	86.7	90.3	92.6	100.0	103.1	104.5	106.2	Hf	Value added, SNA
90.2	90.6	89.7	92.0	92.0	94.3	100.0	..	..	..	.	Value added, MPS
91.9	92.8	93.3	94.3	95.1	97.2	100.0	102.0	100.6	97.2	.	"Building block"
											CONSUMPTION
91.3	91.6	91.2	92.6	94.9	96.2	100.0	97.2	97.9	94.8	.	Total consumption, SNA
91.3	92.6	93.1	93.9	95.1	97.0	100.0	96.5	..	..	.	Total consumption, MPS
91.7	91.9	91.4	92.9	94.8	95.7	100.0	95.9	97.6	93.3	.	Households, SNA
95.3	95.7	95.0	95.3	96.0	97.1	100.0	97.2	97.3	93.4	.	Households, "building block"
88.3	89.8	90.0	91.1	95.1	99.7	100.0	105.8	99.7	104.4	.	General government, SNA
84.3	85.1	87.0	88.4	90.3	96.3	100.0	105.5	109.5	113.5	.	General government, "building block"
											INVESTMENT
94.9	93.4	90.4	87.1	84.5	90.5	100.0	91.6	95.8	87.9	.	Gross fixed investment, SNA
134.3	113.1	130.4	118.5	74.6	123.7	100.0	76.9	..	..	.	Accumulation, MPS
114.2	115.3	104.6	104.3	95.7	104.2	100.0	103.5	94.3	78.8	.	"Building block"
											CONSUMER PRICES
66.3	70.9	75.5	82.0	87.8	92.4	100.0	116.3	136.0	174.4	.	National methodology
64.6	69.1	74.8	81.4	87.6	92.2	100.0	111.8	131.7	169.4	.	Outside estimate
				(millions of current US dollars)							**MERCHANDISE EXPORTS**
8,712	8,767	8,696	8,563	8,542	9,183	9,577	9,999	9,673	9,550	.	UNCTAD
8,707	8,773	8,702	8,563	8,538	9,165	9,556	9,949	10,067	9,599	.	IMF: IFS
11,830	12,420	13,200	13,280	13,440	16,180	18,050	19,050	20,210	..	.	ACDA
8,725	8,858	8,768	8,617	8,472	9,171	9,583	9,999	9,672	9,550	.	ECE
4,745	4,726	4,412	4,274	4,545	5,018	4,885	4,548	4,045	3,049	.	intra-CMEA
9,680	10,249	10,513	10,123	10,023	10,159	10,826	11,549	10,861	10,129	.	Authors' uniform TR/$ series
5,638	6,025	6,028	5,661	5,965	5,918	6,039	5,942	5,095	3,540	.	intra-CMEA
				(millions of current US dollars)							**MERCHANDISE IMPORTS**
9,128	8,814	8,503	8,091	8,228	9,613	9,858	9,372	8,863	8,621	.	UNCTAD
9,139	8,819	8,509	8,091	8,224	9,599	9,841	9,345	8,709	8,669	.	IMF: IFS
12,590	12,870	13,370	12,940	12,930	16,470	17,360	18,290	18,630	..	.	ACDA
9,159	8,867	8,554	8,128	8,183	9,593	9,859	9,372	8,863	8,621	.	ECE
4,392	4,417	4,152	3,948	4,088	4,902	4,714	4,147	3,512	2,930	.	intra-CMEA
10,047	10,166	10,202	9,530	9,574	10,552	11,076	10,781	9,883	9,133	.	Authors' uniform series
5,218	5,631	5,673	5,229	5,365	5,781	5,828	5,419	4,423	3,401	.	intra-CMEA

Basic tables	1970	1971	1972	1973	1974	1975	1976	1977	1978	1979	1980
SNA ACCOUNTS, current prices					*(billions of current Hungarian forint)*						
GNP, at market prices	..	..	..	..	..	475	524	575	620	669	708
Net factor income	..	..	..	..	..	-8	-5	-7	-10	-14	-13
GDP at market prices	333	361	391	429	449	483	529	582	630	682	721
Net indirect taxes	..	..	..	..	..	..	..	..	..	..	..
GDP at factor cost	..	..	..	..	..	..	..	..	..	..	..
Agriculture	61	69	71	82	85	86	95	105	108	109	124
Industry	151	164	179	201	225	248	259	286	309	332	297
Services, etc.	122	128	142	146	139	149	175	191	213	241	301
Resource balance	-8	-23	5	20	-20	-36	-21	-26	-58	-22	-16
Exports GNFS	100	108	133	164	187	200	205	241	244	283	282
Imports GNFS	108	131	129	144	207	236	227	267	302	306	297
Domestic absorption	340	383	386	409	469	519	550	608	687	705	737
Total consumption	229	247	262	282	308	336	361	392	428	473	515
Private consumption	194	210	224	242	261	286	307	334	362	401	441
General government consumption	34	38	39	41	47	50	53	58	66	71	74
Gross domestic investment	112	136	124	127	161	182	190	217	260	232	221
Fixed domestic investment	100	113	117	123	139	161	168	198	214	221	208
Depreciation	..	..	..	..	..	..	..	..	..	..	..
SNA ACCOUNTS, constant prices					*(billions of constant 1987 Hungarian forint)*						
Gross national product (GNP)	..	..	..	786	831	882	920	980	1,023	1,035	1,037
GDP at market prices	655	697	742	798	844	898	930	994	1,041	1,057	1,057
GDP at factor cost	..	..	..	..	..	..	..	..	..	..	..
Agriculture	121	128	132	139	143	146	140	157	159	157	163
Industry	251	268	285	308	334	357	378	402	424	446	438
Services, etc.	284	301	325	351	368	395	412	434	458	455	457
Resource balance	-90	-133	-84	-61	-112	-120	-112	-83	-134	-76	-69
Exports GNFS	139	150	185	217	225	235	254	294	299	339	341
Imports GNFS	229	282	269	278	337	355	366	377	434	415	410
Domestic absorption	746	830	826	859	956	1,018	1,042	1,077	1,175	1,133	1,127
Total consumption, etc.	565	598	619	652	725	718	736	743	769	784	790
Private consumption, etc.	481	509	530	561	633	623	637	643	667	678	683
General government consumption	83	89	89	91	92	96	99	100	102	107	107
Gross domestic investment	181	232	207	207	231	300	306	334	406	348	337
Fixed domestic investment	169	203	201	208	234	264	264	300	315	318	301
Depreciation	..	..	..	..	..	..	..	..	..	..	..
MPS ACCOUNTS, current prices					*(billions of current Hungarian forint)*						
NMP produced:	276	297	322	355	369	394	433	477	515	556	583
Agriculture and forestry	49	57	57	67	67	66	70	76	75	73	85
Industry excluding construction	113	121	133	152	172	190	197	214	228	248	212
Construction	31	35	38	41	46	48	52	61	68	71	60
Transport and communication	21	22	23	26	28	30	35	38	41	42	45
Trade, etc.	36	40	45	48	57	60	61	69	75	78	69
Other services	..	..	..	..	..	..	..	..	..	..	..
Resource balance	-8	-23	5	20	-20	-36	-21	-26	-58	-22	-16
NMP used: domestic market	283	319	317	335	389	430	454	503	572	579	599
Final consumption, material goods	208	224	236	254	278	303	326	355	389	430	470
Personal consumption	180	193	205	222	241	262	283	308	333	370	407
Collective consumption	28	30	31	32	37	40	44	48	56	60	63
Net capital formation	75	96	81	81	110	127	128	148	184	149	129
Net fixed capital formation	55	57	65	72	70	101	93	98	112	120	110
Changes in stocks	20	39	16	9	40	26	35	50	71	29	19
Depreciation	..	..	..	..	..	..	..	..	..	..	..
MPS ACCOUNTS, constant prices					*billions of 1981 Hungarian forint)*						
NMP produced:	385	407	433	463	490	521	536	574	597	604	598
Agriculture and forestry	80	85	87	90	90	90	83	93	90	86	91
Industry and construction	157	167	177	193	209	225	237	255	269	285	274
Services	73	77	82	88	94	102	112	116	122	122	120
Resource balance	-50	-76	-33	-12	-44	-49	-40	-36	-70	-24	-19
NMP used: domestic market	434	483	465	474	535	569	576	610	666	628	617
Final consumption, material goods	340	359	370	383	410	429	438	460	479	495	496
Personal consumption	301	316	327	340	360	378	384	403	418	428	429
Collective consumption	40	43	43	44	49	51	54	57	62	67	67
Net capital formation	93	128	94	88	128	136	138	151	187	133	121
Net fixed capital formation	75	76	83	87	82	115	100	99	109	113	106
Depreciation	..	..	..	..	..	..	..	..	..	..	..

Abbreviations in notes column are explained in the General Notes. For sources and methods, see the Technical Notes.

1981	1982	1983	1984	1985	1986	1987	1988	1989	1990	Notes	Basic tables (continued)
(billions of current Hungarian forint)											**SNA ACCOUNTS, current prices**
752	807	863	938	990	1,043	1,178	1,397	1,648	1,988	.	GNP, at market prices
-28	-41	-33	-41	-44	-45	-48	-55	-82	-93	.	Net factor income
780	848	896	978	1,034	1,089	1,226	1,452	1,730	2,081	.	GDP at market prices
..	..	..	..	..	..	..	..	..	..	.	Net indirect taxes
											GDP at factor cost
..	..	..	..	..	..	..	..	..	..		
137	149	153	166	167	183	189	210	236	259	Hf	Agriculture
324	350	369	401	426	440	495	527	630	658	Hf	Industry
319	349	374	412	441	466	543	715	865	1,165	Hf	Services, etc.
-8	7	17	31	21	-15	-6	39	57	80	.	Resource balance
308	322	361	402	436	432	464	530	621	685	.	Exports GNFS
316	315	344	371	415	447	470	492	564	605	.	Imports GNFS
788	841	879	948	1,012	1,104	1,232	1,414	1,673	2,001	.	Domestic absorption
557	599	642	696	754	812	905	1,055	1,228	1,522	.	Total consumption
478	515	551	601	649	696	779	887	1,050	1,300	.	Private consumption
79	84	91	95	105	116	126	169	178	222	.	General government consumption
231	242	237	252	258	293	328	358	445	479	.	Gross domestic investment
207	214	220	225	232	261	304	296	348	370	.	Fixed domestic investment
..	..	..	..	..	..	..	..	..	..	.	Depreciation
(billions of constant 1987 Hungarian forint)											**SNA ACCOUNTS, constant prices**
1,057	1,064	1,085	1,108	1,107	1,125	1,178	1,174	1,163	1,122	.	Gross national product (GNP)
1,098	1,119	1,127	1,157	1,156	1,174	1,226	1,221	1,222	1,175	.	GDP at market prices
										.	GDP at factor cost
..	..	..	..	..	..	..	..	..	..		
169	188	188	197	189	195	189	204	204	187	Hf	Agriculture
469	475	484	490	478	476	495	457	451	412	Hf	Industry
461	457	456	470	490	502	543	559	567	576	Hf	Services, etc.
-57	-28	-5	19	8	-14	-6	24	21	33	.	Resource balance
360	373	400	429	452	442	464	496	502	500	.	Exports GNFS
417	402	405	410	444	457	470	472	481	468	.	Imports GNFS
1,155	1,147	1,132	1,138	1,148	1,188	1,232	1,197	1,201	1,143	.	Domestic absorption
826	829	825	838	858	871	905	880	886	858	.	Total consumption, etc.
714	716	711	723	738	745	779	746	760	726	.	Private consumption, etc.
112	113	114	115	120	126	126	134	126	132	.	General government consumption
329	318	308	300	290	317	328	317	315	285	.	Gross domestic investment
288	284	274	264	257	275	304	278	291	267	.	Fixed domestic investment
..	..	..	..	..	..	..	..	..	..	.	Depreciation
(billions of current Hungarian forint)											**MPS ACCOUNTS, current prices**
635	696	738	804	842	881	1,000	1,152	1,414	..	f	NMP produced:
94	97	98	106	100	111	113	127	..	..	.	Agriculture and forestry
237	260	277	302	330	336	402	405	..	..	.	Industry excluding construction
63	71	78	85	86	94	105	106	..	..	.	Construction
51	57	58	59	61	68	75	80	..	..	.	Transport and communication
73	76	81	93	101	114	115	158	..	..	.	Trade, etc.
..	..	..	..	..	..	..	..	..	..	.	Other services
-8	7	17	31	21	-15	-6	38	..	..	.	Resource balance
643	690	721	773	821	897	1,006	1,114	..	..	.	NMP used: domestic market
508	549	587	631	677	726	807	887	..	..	.	Final consumption, material goods
439	475	508	549	586	627	700	771	..	..	.	Personal consumption
69	74	79	82	91	99	107	131	..	..	.	Collective consumption
135	141	134	142	144	171	199	227	..	..	.	Net capital formation
101	96	121	123	105	154	199	186	..	..	.	Net fixed capital formation
34	45	14	19	39	17	-1	41	..	..	.	Changes in stocks
..	..	..	..	..	..	..	..	..	..	.	Depreciation
billions of 1981 Hungarian forint)											**MPS ACCOUNTS, constant prices**
613	630	631	647	638	643	670	666	659	..	f	NMP produced:
90	99	96	101	94	98	93	..	..	..	.	Agriculture and forestry
286	299	308	309	301	298	308	..	..	..	.	Industry and construction
126	126	125	128	128	131	139	..	..	..	.	Services
-8	15	33	53	47	30	38	56	..	..	.	Resource balance
622	615	598	594	590	614	632	611	..	..	.	NMP used: domestic market
511	518	521	526	532	543	560	540	..	..	.	Final consumption, material goods
442	448	450	454	458	467	483	461	..	..	.	Personal consumption
69	70	71	71	75	77	77	79	..	..	.	Collective consumption
111	97	77	69	58	71	73	71	..	..	.	Net capital formation
89	75	87	79	50	82	66	51	..	..	.	Net fixed capital formation
..	..	..	..	..	..	..	..	..	..	.	Depreciation

Basic tables (continued)	1970	1971	1972	1973	1974	1975	1976	1977	1978	1979	1980
MPS ACCOUNTS, index					*(index, 1980 = 100)*						
NMP produced:	64.0	68.0	72.0	77.0	82.0	87.0	90.0	96.0	100.0	101.0	100.0
Agriculture and forestry	89.3	94.6	96.4	100.0	100.0	100.0	92.9	103.6	100.0	94.6	100.0
Industry excluding construction	56.8	60.2	64.8	71.0	77.3	82.4	86.9	93.2	97.7	104.0	100.0
Construction	59.5	64.3	65.5	68.5	73.8	81.5	85.1	92.9	99.4	103.6	100.0
Transport and communication	68.5	71.2	75.3	80.1	83.6	89.7	89.7	95.2	98.6	101.4	100.0
Trade, etc.	62.9	66.7	72.3	78.0	84.9	92.5	96.9	98.1	104.4	103.1	100.0
NMP used: material goods	70.0	78.0	75.0	77.0	86.0	92.0	93.0	99.0	108.0	102.0	100.0
Final consumption	68.5	71.9	74.7	77.4	82.2	86.3	88.4	92.5	96.6	100.0	100.0
Net capital formation	78.7	102.4	80.3	77.2	103.9	115.7	114.2	124.4	155.1	110.2	100.0
EXCHANGE AND CONVERSION RATES					*(LCUs per US dollar: annual average)*						
Single-year converter	60.000	59.822	55.260	48.966	46.752	43.971	41.575	40.961	37.911	35.578	32.532
Devisa/official	11.740	11.740	10.812	9.620	9.148	8.604	..	..	..	..	..
Commercial	60.000	59.822	55.260	48.966	48.752	43.971	41.575	40.961	37.911	35.578	32.532
Noncommercial	30.000	29.911	27.630	24.483	23.376	20.666	20.788	20.480	18.956	20.013	22.139
Informal market	49.530	42.620	42.288	35.850	33.213	31.896	36.517	36.729	33.633	32.720	31.075
ICP	27.252	25.634	25.978	25.693	22.605	20.649	20.368	19.469	17.913	17.789	16.669
					(ruble per US dollar: annual average)						
Commercial TR/$ cross	1.500	1.496	1.382	1.224	1.219	1.099	1.188	1.170	1.140	1.112	1.171
Uniform TR/$ cross	1.072	1.157	1.232	1.093	1.092	1.167	1.067	1.022	0.973	0.945	0.980
					(LCUs per ruble: annual average)						
Commercial	40.000	40.000	40.000	40.000	40.000	40.000	35.000	35.000	33.250	32.000	27.790
Noncommercial	..	..	..	..	..	..	..	..	..	..	..
Devisa/official	13.044	13.044	13.044	13.044	13.044	13.044	..	..	..	..	..
CONSUMER PRICE INDEXES					*(index)*						
Official, IMF 1985=100	..	..	48.5	50.2	51.1	53.0	55.8	58.0	60.7	66.1	72.3
Official, CIA or LWI 1980=100	64.4	65.6	67.5	69.8	71.0	73.7	77.4	80.4	84.2	91.6	100.0
Alternative, CIA or LWI 1980=100	60.0	63.1	65.5	68.7	70.6	73.4	78.2	81.2	84.4	92.6	100.0
INTERNATIONAL TRADE (ECE)					*(billions of current Hungarian forint)*						
Value of exports, fob	27	29	36	42	47	52	205	239	241	282	281
to CMEA	17	19	23	27	31	36	116	135	132	150	145
Value of imports, cif	29	35	34	37	51	62	230	267	301	309	300
from CMEA	18	22	22	23	29	39	119	134	148	156	142
Trade balance	-2	-6	2	5	-4	-9	-25	-29	-60	-27	-19
CMEA	-1	-3	2	5	2	-3	-3	1	-15	-6	3
INTERNATIONAL TRADE (Authors')					*(millions of current US dollars)*						
Value of exports, fob	2,068	2,113	2,539	3,400	3,898	4,159	5,265	6,346	6,757	8,737	9,551
to developed countries	616	606	816	1,171	1,345	1,301	1,522	1,693	1,892	2,561	2,926
to other non-socialist countries	150	150	178	218	343	384	423	517	589	799	939
to socialist countries	1,302	1,357	1,546	2,011	2,211	2,475	3,320	4,136	4,276	5,377	5,686
to CMEA	1,212	1,264	1,457	1,905	2,167	2,349	3,100	3,772	3,856	4,962	5,310
Value of imports, cif	2,241	2,547	2,474	3,082	4,436	5,110	5,872	7,020	8,371	9,502	10,110
from developed countries	661	820	883	1,168	1,939	1,942	2,009	2,413	3,108	3,306	3,632
from other non-socialist countries	195	175	195	265	452	512	541	670	725	736	906
from socialist countries	1,385	1,552	1,396	1,649	2,046	2,655	3,322	3,937	4,539	5,460	5,572
from CMEA	1,314	1,472	1,338	1,589	2,012	2,565	3,176	3,741	4,300	5,164	5,213
Trade balance	-173	-434	65	318	-538	-950	-607	-675	-1,614	-765	-560
Developed countries	-45	-214	-67	3	-593	-642	-487	-720	-1,216	-745	-707
Other non-socialist countries	-45	-24	-18	-47	-109	-129	-118	-153	-135	63	33
Socialist countries	-83	-195	150	362	165	-180	-2	199	-263	-83	114
CMEA	-101	-208	119	315	155	-217	-76	30	-444	-203	98
PARTNER CONVERTIBLE TRADE (ECE)					*(millions of current US dollars)*						
Exports to non-CMEA (cif)	541	604	813	1,119	1,376	1,287	1,484	1,792	2,069	2,635	2,920
Imports from non-CMEA (fob)	671	800	884	1,164	1,879	1,913	1,904	2,406	3,105	3,134	3,468
Trade balance	-130	-196	-71	-45	-503	-626	-420	-614	-1,036	-499	-548
TRADE PRICE INDEXES (Authors')					*(index, 1980 = 100)*						
Terms of trade	..	..	..	..	..	..	..	..	..	..	100.0
Exports	..	..	..	..	..	..	..	..	..	..	100.0
Non-socialist countries	..	..	..	..	..	..	..	..	..	..	100.0
Developed countries	..	..	..	..	..	..	..	..	..	..	100.0
Other	..	..	..	..	..	..	..	..	..	..	100.0
Socialist countries	..	..	..	..	..	..	..	..	..	..	100.0
CMEA	..	..	..	..	..	..	..	..	..	..	100.0
Imports	..	..	..	..	..	..	..	..	..	..	100.0
Non-socialist countries	..	..	..	..	..	..	..	..	..	..	100.0
Developed countries	..	..	..	..	..	..	..	..	..	..	100.0
Other	..	..	..	..	..	..	..	..	..	..	100.0
Socialist countries	..	..	..	..	..	..	..	..	..	..	100.0
CMEA	..	..	..	..	..	..	..	..	..	..	100.0

Abbreviations in notes column are explained in the General Notes. For sources and methods, see the Technical Notes.

1981	1982	1983	1984	1985	1986	1987	1988	1989	1990	Notes	Basic tables (continued)
				(index, 1980 = 100)							**MPS ACCOUNTS, index**
103.0	105.0	106.0	108.0	107.0	108.0	112.0	111.0	110.0	..	.	NMP produced:
100.0	109.0	106.0	112.0	104.0	108.0	103.0	112.0	..	..	.	Agriculture and forestry
105.0	111.0	115.0	117.0	115.0	114.0	118.0	114.0		..	.	Industry excluding construction
103.0	105.0	105.0	99.0	90.0	91.0	93.0	80.0	..	..	.	Construction
105.0	106.0	105.0	108.0	104.0	108.0	113.0	113.0	..	..	.	Transport and communication
105.0	106.0	101.0	103.0	103.0	104.0	111.0	96.0	..	..	.	Trade, etc.
101.0	99.0	97.0	96.0	96.0	99.0	102.0	97.0	97.0	..	.	NMP used: material goods
103.0	104.0	105.0	106.0	107.0	109.0	113.0	109.0	109.0	..	.	Final consumption
91.0	80.0	64.0	57.0	48.0	59.0	60.0	48.0	47.0	..	.	Net capital formation
				(LCUs per US dollar: annual average)							**EXCHANGE AND CONVERSION RATES**
34.314	36.631	42.671	48.042	50.119	45.832	46.971	50.413	59.066	63.206	.	Single-year converter
..	..	..	..	..	..	..	..	..		.	Devisa/official
34.314	36.631	42.671	48.042	50.119	45.832	46.971	50.413	59.066	..	.	Commercial
34.314	36.631	42.671	48.042	50.119	45.832	46.971	50.413	59.066	..	.	Noncommercial
36.250	42.150	51.260	56.827	84.010	70.850	68.510	72.271	92.048	..	.	Informal market
16.086	16.370	17.150	18.189	18.760	18.892	19.925	22.464	..	..	.	ICP
				(ruble per US dollar: annual average)							
1.279	1.409	1.641	1.848	1.881	1.637	1.727	1.939	2.091	..	.	Commercial TR/$ cross
1.076	1.105	1.201	1.395	1.433	1.388	1.397	1.484	1.660	1.980	.	Uniform TR/$ cross
				(LCUs per ruble: annual average)							
26.840	26.000	26.000	26.000	26.650	28.000	27.200	26.000	28.250	..	.	Commercial
..	..	..	..	..	..	..	..	..	..	.	Noncommercial
..	..	..	..	..	..	..	..	..	..	.	Devisa/official
				(index)							**CONSUMER PRICE INDEXES**
75.5	80.8	86.0	93.5	100.0	105.3	113.9	132.5	155.0	198.7	.	Official, IMF 1985=100
104.6	111.8	119.9	129.9	139.0	146.3	158.9	183.6	214.8	278.8	.	Official, CIA or LWI 1980=100
105.3	112.7	122.0	132.7	142.8	150.2	163.0	182.3	214.6	276.1	.	Alternative, CIA or LWI 1980=100
				(billions of current Hungarian forint)							**INTERNATIONAL TRADE (ECE)**
299	325	374	414	425	420	450	504	571	604	f	Value of exports, fob
163	173	188	205	228	230	229	229	239	193	.	to CMEA
314	325	365	391	410	440	463	473	524	545	f	Value of imports, cif
151	162	177	190	205	225	221	209	207	185	.	from CMEA
-15	0	9	23	15	-19	-13	32	48	59	f	Trade balance
12	11	11	16	23	5	8	20	32	8	.	CMEA
				(millions of current US dollars)							**INTERNATIONAL TRADE (Authors')**
9,680	10,249	10,513	10,123	10,023	10,159	10,826	11,549	10,861	10,129	.	Value of exports, fob
2,593	2,630	2,860	2,946	2,558	2,865	3,438	3,951	4,171	5,032	.	to developed countries
1,059	1,171	1,144	1,029	948	793	887	991	924	922	.	to other non-socialist countries
6,028	6,448	6,509	6,148	6,517	6,501	6,502	6,607	5,766	4,174	.	to socialist countries
5,638	6,025	6,028	5,661	5,965	5,918	6,039	5,942	5,095	3,540	.	to CMEA
10,047	10,166	10,202	9,530	9,574	10,552	11,076	10,781	9,883	9,133	.	Value of imports, cif
3,660	3,210	2,935	2,826	3,141	3,611	4,041	4,057	4,370	4,536	.	from developed countries
783	934	1,120	986	589	635	671	721	562	905	.	from other non-socialist countries
5,604	6,023	6,146	5,718	5,844	6,306	6,364	6,002	4,951	3,691	.	from socialist countries
5,218	5,631	5,673	5,229	5,365	5,781	5,828	5,419	4,423	3,401	.	from CMEA
-367	83	312	593	449	-393	-249	768	977	996	.	Trade balance
-1,066	-580	-75	120	-583	-746	-603	-106	-199	495	.	Developed countries
276	237	24	43	360	157	215	270	361	17	.	Other non-socialist countries
424	425	362	430	673	196	138	605	815	483	.	Socialist countries
420	394	355	432	600	136	210	523	672	139	.	CMEA
				(millions of current US dollars)							**PARTNER CONVERTIBLE TRADE (ECE)**
2,626	2,429	2,507	2,720	2,770	3,130	3,796	4,209	4,701	..	.	Exports to non-CMEA (cif)
3,461	3,139	2,856	2,784	3,079	3,711	4,111	4,153	4,943	..	.	Imports from non-CMEA (fob)
-835	-710	-349	-64	-309	-581	-315	56	-242	..	.	Trade balance
				(index, 1980 = 100)							**TRADE PRICE INDEXES (Authors')**
98.8	96.1	93.6	91.5	90.3	86.9	88.4	91.2	93.2	..	.	Terms of trade
98.3	97.3	92.0	83.5	82.4	85.0	87.6	89.8	85.2	..	.	Exports
95.2	89.2	81.3	77.7	76.3	82.1	88.9	95.5	91.8	..	.	Non-socialist countries
96.3	90.5	81.8	77.9	76.8	83.1	89.7	94.9	91.9	..	.	Developed countries
92.6	86.2	80.1	77.2	74.9	78.7	86.0	98.1	91.4	..	.	Other
100.2	102.2	98.6	87.2	85.7	86.7	86.6	85.4	79.4	..	.	Socialist countries
99.5	101.8	98.0	86.3	84.7	85.7	86.1	84.0	77.4	..	.	CMEA
99.5	101.3	98.3	91.2	91.3	97.8	99.1	98.4	91.4	..	.	Imports
95.0	87.5	80.7	78.1	78.0	90.4	97.8	104.0	99.8	..	.	Non-socialist countries
95.9	90.5	84.8	80.9	80.0	91.5	100.0	106.3	103.0	..	.	Developed countries
90.4	77.2	69.9	69.8	67.3	84.1	84.8	91.0	74.9	..	.	Other
103.2	110.9	109.9	100.0	99.8	102.8	100.0	94.0	83.1	..	.	Socialist countries
103.4	111.6	110.9	100.8	100.7	103.9	100.8	93.2	81.8	..	.	CMEA

Basic tables (continued)	1970	1971	1972	1973	1974	1975	1976	1977	1978	1979	1980
TRADE PRICE INDEXES (ECE)					*(index, 1980 = 100)*						
Terms of trade	125	125	124	124	115	108	106	101	100	103	100
Exports	61	62	68	80	90	104	75	78	84	96	100
Imports	49	50	55	65	78	96	71	77	84	93	100
Balance of Payments (ECE)					*(millions of current US dollars)*						
Exports, convertible currency	609	611	877	1,463	2,066	2,209	2,344	2,661	3,178	4,063	4,863
Imports, convertible currency	686	829	936	1,354	2,492	2,500	2,519	3,020	3,959	4,230	4,587
Trade balance, convertible currency	-77	-218	-59	109	-426	-291	-175	-359	-781	-167	276
Invisibles, convertible currency	-47	-36	-32	-90	-115	-240	-190	-396	-461	-657	-647
Current balance, convertible currency	-124	-254	-91	19	-541	-531	-365	-755	-1,242	-824	-371
External debt, total (World Bank)	..	..	..	0	0	0	2	45	8,248	8,861	9,757
Convertible currency	..	..	..	0	0	0	2	45	8,248	8,861	9,757
CMEA	..	..	..	..	..	..	..	..	..	70	70
External debt service (World Bank)	..	..	..	..	..	..	..	0	330	526	1,922
Convertible currency	..	..	..	..	..	..	..	0	330	526	1,922
Total reserves less gold (IMF, IFS)	..	..	..	..	..	..	..	..	..	..	..
Total reserves, including gold at London price	..	..	..	..	..	..	..	..	..	..	..
Total reserves, incl. gold at national valuation	..	61	71	77	56	67	66	70	249	402	468
EMPLOYMENT					*(thousands)*						
Employment, total	4,980	..	..	..	..	..	..	..	..	..	..
Agriculture	1,313	..	..	..	..	..	..	..	..	..	..
Industry	2,151	..	..	..	..	..	..	..	..	..	..
Services	1,516	..	..	..	..	..	..	..	..	..	..
Labor force, total	5,495	5,485	5,475	5,465	5,455	5,445	5,400	5,355	5,310	5,265	5,219
Agriculture	1,379	1,339	1,299	1,259	1,219	1,179	1,133	1,087	1,041	995	950
Industry	2,464	2,453	2,441	2,430	2,419	2,408	2,381	2,355	2,328	2,302	2,276
Services	1,652	1,694	1,735	1,776	1,817	1,858	1,885	1,913	1,940	1,967	1,994
DOMESTIC FINANCE (IMF)					*(billions of current Hungarian forint)*						
Money supply, broadly defined	..	..	..	..	..	..	..	..	..	..	..
Money, means of payment	..	..	..	..	..	..	..	..	..	..	..
Demand deposits	..	..	..	..	..	..	..	..	..	..	..
Currency outside banks	..	..	..	..	..	..	..	..	..	..	..
Quasi-money	..	..	..	..	..	..	..	..	..	..	..
Interest: deposit rate (percent)	3	3	3	3	3	3	3	3	3	3	3
Central government expenditures	..	..	..	..	..	..	..	..	..	..	..
Defense	..	..	..	..	..	..	..	..	..	..	..
					(millions of 1989 US dollars)						
Central government exp. (ACDA)	..	..	..	..	..	..	..	..	..	29,070	27,630
Military (ACDA)	..	..	..	..	..	..	..	..	..	4,017	4,173
LAND AND FORESTS (FAO)											
Pop. density: agr. land (pop. per sq. km)	150	151	152	153	154	156	157	158	159	161	162
Deforestation rate (net)	1	1	0	1	3	1	1	1	1	1	1
Forest (thousands sq. km)	15	15	15	15	15	15	16	16	16	16	16
SOCIAL INDICATORS											
Population density: total land (pop. per sq. km)	112	112	113	113	113	114	115	115	116	116	116
School enrollment ratio, primary	97	..	..	..	..	99	99	98	97	96	96
secondary	63	..	..	..	..	63	..	..	..	70	69
tertiary											13
Energy consumption per capita (kg. of oil eq.)	2,053	2,118	2,129	2,259	2,312	2,391	2,554	2,657	2,796	2,763	2,767
Daily calorie supply per capita	3,341	3,340	3,355	3,370	3,401	3,468	3,388	3,457	3,477	3,449	3,507
Food production (1979-1981=100)	71	80	85	90	91	93	89	96	98	95	104
Daily protein supply (gm. per capita)	95	95	96	96	97	100	100	99	100	99	99
Population per hospital bed	123	..	..	..	..	..	..	..	..	..	110
per nursing person	..	..	..	214	..	..	..	..	..	..	..
per physician	507	..	..	..	..	..	..	..	..	..	400
Female participation in labor force (percent)	41	41	42	42	42	42	42	42	42	42	42
Infant mortality (per 1,000 live births)	36	35	33	34	34	33	30	26	24	24	23
Life expectancy (years)	70	70	70	70	70	70	70	70	70	70	70
Total fertility (births per woman)	2	2	2	2	2	2	2	2	2	2	2
Urban population (percent of total population)	46	46	47	48	49	50	50	51	52	53	54
Population per passenger car	43	35	31	26	21	18	16	15	13	12	11
per telephone	..	..	..	..	..	10	..	..	..	..	9

Abbreviations in notes column are explained in the General Notes. For sources and methods, see the Technical Notes.

				(index, 1980 = 100)							**TRADE PRICE INDEXES (ECE)**
97	97	96	94	91	88	90	93	..	..	.	Terms of trade
98	95	87	80	77	86	87	85	..	..	.	Exports
101	98	91	86	85	98	97	92	..	..	.	Imports
				(millions of current US dollars)							**Balance of Payments (ECE)**
4,879	4,831	4,832	4,916	4,188	4,186	5,050	5,505	6,446	6,349	f	Exports, convertible currency
4,432	4,163	4,059	4,025	4,060	4,668	5,014	5,016	5,910	5,998	f	Imports, convertible currency
447	668	772	891	127	-482	36	489	537	348	f	Trade balance, convertible currency
-1,176	-967	-702	-825	-974	-1,013	-913	-1,297	-1,974	-221	.	Invisibles, convertible currency
-729	-299	70	66	-847	-1,495	-877	-808	-1,437	127	f	Current balance, convertible currency
9,781	10,216	10,745	10,983	13,955	16,907	19,584	19,602	20,390	21,316	.	External debt, total (World Bank)
9,781	10,216	10,745	10,983	13,955	16,907	19,584	19,602	20,390	21,316	.	Convertible currency
71	64	57	47	40	33	31	30	31	26	.	CMEA
2,362	2,432	2,351	2,705	3,689	4,182	3,746	3,512	3,569	4,283	f	External debt service (World Bank)
2,362	2,432	2,351	2,705	3,689	4,182	3,746	3,512	3,569	4,283	.	Convertible currency
..	..	1,231	1,560	2,153	2,302	1,634	1,467	1,246	1,070	.	Total reserves less gold (IMF, IFS)
..	..	1,816	2,196	2,914	3,219	2,429	2,121	1,846	1,186	.	Total reserves, including gold at London price
381	146	1,577	2,026	2,793	3,053	2,159	1,977	1,725	1,167	.	Total reserves, incl. gold at national valuation
				(thousands)							**EMPLOYMENT**
..	..	..	..	..	..	..	4,845	..	..	.	Employment, total
..	..	..	..	..	..	..	991	..	..	.	Agriculture
..	..	..	..	..	..	..	1,843	..	..	.	Industry
..	..	..	..	..	..	..	2,011	..	..	.	Services
5,219	5,218	5,217	5,216	5,215	5,227	5,239	5,252	5,264	5,276	.	Labor force, total
..	..	..	..	..	..	..	..	..	..	.	Agriculture
..	..	..	..	..	..	..	..	..	..	.	Industry
..	..	..	..	..	..	..	..	..	..	.	Services
				(billions of current Hungarian forint)							**DOMESTIC FINANCE (IMF)**
..	..	..	..	..	554	595	..	..	..	.	Money supply, broadly defined
..	188	192	201	240	266	307	302	355	449	.	Money, means of payment
..	103	97	95	123	136	153	138	174	239	.	Demand deposits
..	85	95	105	117	131	154	164	181	210	.	Currency outside banks
..	230	235	248	259	276	288	311	351	464	.	Quasi-money
3	5	5	5	5	4	4	9	14	23	.	Interest: deposit rate (percent)
438	454	492	520	550	637	700	792	958	1,089	.	Central government expenditures
19	20	22	23	38	26	28	38	35	39	.	Defense
				(millions of 1989 US dollars)							
30,010	29,020	30,300	29,680	28,060	27,490	26,780	27,320	20,260	..	.	Central government exp. (ACDA)
4,129	4,407	4,412	4,326	4,305	4,345	4,361	4,576	4,064	..	U	Military (ACDA)
											LAND AND FORESTS (FAO)
162	163	163	163	163	163	163	..	..	..	.	Pop. density: agr. land (pop. per sq. km)
1	0	0	0	1	1	..	..	..	..	.	Deforestation rate (net)
16	16	16	16	17	17	..	..	..	..	.	Forest (thousands sq. km)
											SOCIAL INDICATORS
116	116	116	116	115	115	115	..	..	..	.	Population density: total land (pop. per sq. km)
..	99	99	99	98	98	97	96	..	..	.	School enrollment ratio, primary
..	73	73	73	72	70	70	71	..	..	.	secondary
..	14	15	15	16	15	15	15	..	..	.	tertiary
2,796	2,861	2,840	2,887	3,038	3,056	3,062	..	..	..	.	Energy consumption per capita (kg. of oil eq.)
3,478	3,551	3,544	3,514	3,558	3,578	3,727	3,601	..	..	.	Daily calorie supply per capita
101	113	106	113	109	110	110	117	116	106	.	Food production (1979-1981=100)
100	102	102	101	102	103	104	102	..	..	.	Daily protein supply (gm. per capita)
109	..	..	..	..	..	..	..	..	..	.	Population per hospital bed
157	..	..	..	174	..	..	..	..	..	.	per nursing person
391	381	..	..	307	..	..	..	..	..	.	per physician
42	42	42	42	42	42	42	43	43	43	.	Female participation in labor force (percent)
21	20	19	20	20	19	17	17	16	16	.	Infant mortality (per 1,000 live births)
70	70	70	70	70	70	70	70	71	71	.	Life expectancy (years)
2	2	2	2	2	2	2	2	2	2	.	Total fertility (births per woman)
54	55	56	57	58	58	59	60	61	61	.	Urban population (percent of total population)
10	9	9	8	7	..	..	..	..	..	.	Population per passenger car
8	8	8	7	7	..	..	..	..	..	.	per telephone

Comparator tables	1970	1971	1972	1973	1974	1975	1976	1977	1978	1979	1980
PER CAPITA INCOME					*(US dollars)*						
World Bank (Atlas method)	..	..	..	..	..	..	..	..	..	..	..
Single year conversion	272	272	299	396	449	568	572	616	757	848	739
CIA or LWI	..	..	..	..	..	..	..	..	..	1,181	1,217
Penn World Tables	..	..	..	..	..	..	..	..	..	..	..
POPULATION					*(thousands)*						
	14,619	15,030	15,430	15,819	16,196	16,562	16,917	17,263	17,600	17,931	18,260
GROSS NATIONAL PRODUCT, current prices					*(millions of current US dollars)*						
World Bank (Atlas method)	..	..	..	..	..	..	..	..	..	..	..
Single year conversion	..	..	..	..	..	..	..	..	..	..	..
Authors' series	3,980	4,090	4,620	6,270	7,270	9,400	9,680	10,640	13,320	15,200	13,500
CIA or LWI									20,200	20,900	21,900
GROSS NATIONAL PRODUCT, constant prices					*(millions of constant 1987 dollars)*						
Single year conversion	..	..	..	..	..	..	..	..	..	..	..
Authors' series, rescaled from 1980 prices	..	..	..	..	..	..	..	..	..	..	..
CIA or LWI, rescaled from 1989 prices	..	..	..	..	..	..	..	..	34,193	32,520	31,232
CONVERSION FACTORS					*(LCUs per US dollar)*						
World Bank (Atlas method)	..	..	..	..	..	..	..	..	..	..	..
Single year convertor	..	..	..	..	..	..	..	..	..	..	..
Authors' series	2.57	2.57	2.57	2.37	2.37	2.04	2.15	2.15	1.86	1.79	1.70
Penn World Tables	..	..	..	..	..	..	..	..	..	..	..
OUTPUT TRENDS, OVERALL					*(index, constant prices 1987 = 100)*						
GNP, SNA	..	..	..	..	..	..	..	..	..	..	..
NMP, MPS	..	..	..	..	..	..	..	..	..	..	..
GNP, "Building block"	..	..	..	..	..	..	..	..	..	..	..
Industry											
Value added, SNA	..	..	..	..	..	..	..	..	..	..	..
Value added, MPS	..	..	..	..	..	..	..	..	..	..	..
"Building block"	..	..	..	..	..	..	..	..	..	..	..
Gross output, SNA	..	..	..	..	..	..	..	..	..	..	..
Agriculture											
Value added, SNA	..	..	..	..	..	..	..	..	..	..	..
Value added, MPS	..	..	..	..	..	..	..	..	..	..	..
"Building block"	..	..	..	..	..	..	..	..	..	..	..
Gross output, SNA	44.3	47.9	51.3	52.4	56.3	60.4	65.2	69.6	72.1	74.3	76.4
Services											
Value added, SNA	..	..	..	..	..	..	..	..	..	..	..
Value added, MPS	..	..	..	..	..	..	..	..	..	..	..
"Building block"	..	..	..	..	..	..	..	..	..	..	..
CONSUMPTION											
Total consumption, SNA	..	..	..	..	..	..	..	..	..	..	..
Total consumption, MPS	..	..	..	..	..	..	..	..	..	..	..
Households, SNA	..	..	..	..	..	..	..	..	..	..	..
Households, "building block"	..	..	..	..	..	..	..	..	..	..	..
General government, SNA	..	..	..	..	..	..	..	..	..	..	..
General government, "building block"	..	..	..	..	..	..	..	..	..	..	..
INVESTMENT											
Gross fixed investment, SNA	..	..	..	..	..	..	..	..	..	..	..
Accumulation, MPS	..	..	..	..	..	..	..	..	..	..	..
"Building block"	..	..	..	..	..	..	..	..	..	..	..
CONSUMER PRICES											
National methodology	..	..	..	..	..	..	..	..	..	..	..
Outside estimate	..	..	..	..	..	..	..	..	..	..	..
MERCHANDISE EXPORTS					*(millions of current US dollars)*						
UNCTAD	..	..	..	..	502	..	..	..	..	..	1,135
IMF: IFS	..	..	..	..	..	..	..	..	..	..	..
ACDA	..	..	..	..	..	..	..	..	967	1,320	..
ECE	..	..	..	..	..	..	..	..	..	..	..
intra-CMEA	..	..	..	..	..	..	..	..	..	..	..
Authors' uniform TR/$ series	..	..	..	..	..	..	..	..	..	..	..
intra-CMEA	..	..	..	..	..	..	..	..	..	..	..
MERCHANDISE IMPORTS					*(millions of current US dollars)*						
UNCTAD	..	..	..	..	..	..	..	..	..	..	..
IMF: IFS	..	..	..	..	..	..	..	..	..	..	..
ACDA	..	..	..	..	..	..	..	..	902	1,300	..
ECE	..	..	..	..	..	..	..	..	..	..	..
intra-CMEA	..	..	..	..	..	..	..	..	..	..	..
Authors' uniform series	..	..	..	..	..	..	..	..	..	..	..
intra-CMEA	..	..	..	..	..	..	..	..	..	..	..

Abbreviations in notes column are explained in the General Notes. For sources and methods, see the Technical Notes.

1981	1982	1983	1984	1985	1986	1987	1988	1989	1990	Notes	Comparator tables (continued)
				(US dollars)							**PER CAPITA INCOME**
..	..	..	..	..	..	..	..	..	..	.	World Bank (Atlas method)
730	719	752	752	..	..	..	..	..	..	E	Single year conversion
1,240	1,263	1,291	1,311	1,342	1,367	1,389	1,418	1,429	..	A	CIA or LWI
..	..	..	..	..	*(thousands)*	..	..	..	..	.	Penn World Tables
18,586	18,911	19,236	19,561	19,888	20,217	20,550	20,887	21,229	21,576	.	**POPULATION**
				(millions of current US dollars)							**GROSS NATIONAL PRODUCT, current prices**
..	..	..	..	..	..	..	..	..	..	.	World Bank (Atlas method)
..	..	..	..	..	..	..	..	..	..	.	Single year conversion
13,560	13,600	14,470	14,700	..	..	..	..	..	..	f	Authors' series
22,700	23,500	24,400	25,300	26,300	27,200	28,200	29,200	30,000	..	.	CIA or LWI
				(millions of constant 1987 dollars)							**GROSS NATIONAL PRODUCT, constant prices**
..	..	..	..	..	..	..	..	..	..	.	Single year conversion
..	..	..	..	..	..	..	..	..	..	.	Authors' series, rescaled from 1980 prices
29,529	28,726	28,716	28,706	28,977	29,210	29,355	29,423	29,035	..	A	CIA or LWI, rescaled from 1989 prices
				(LCUs per US dollar)							**CONVERSION FACTORS**
..	..	..	..	..	..	..	..	..	..	.	World Bank (Atlas method)
..	..	..	..	..	..	..	..	..	..	.	Single year convertor
1.77	2.12	2.18	2.21	..	..	..	..	..	..	.	Authors' series
..	..	..	..	..	..	..	..	..	..	.	Penn World Tables
				(index, constant prices 1987 = 100)							**OUTPUT TRENDS, OVERALL**
..	..	..	..	..	..	..	..	..	..	.	GNP, SNA
..	..	..	..	..	..	..	..	..	..	.	NMP, MPS
..	..	..	..	..	..	..	..	..	..	.	GNP, "Building block"
											Industry
..	..	..	..	..	..	..	..	..	..	.	Value added, SNA
..	..	..	..	..	..	..	..	..	..	.	Value added, MPS
..	..	..	..	..	..	..	..	..	..	.	"Building block"
..	..	..	..	..	..	..	..	..	..	.	Gross output, SNA
											Agriculture
..	..	..	..	..	..	..	..	..	..	.	Value added, SNA
..	..	..	..	..	..	..	..	..	..	.	Value added, MPS
..	..	..	..	..	..	..	..	..	..	.	"Building block"
78.7	80.7	84.8	88.8	93.3	96.8	100.0	102.5	104.4	..	f	Gross output, SNA
											Services
..	..	..	..	..	..	..	..	..	..	.	Value added, SNA
..	..	..	..	..	..	..	..	..	..	.	Value added, MPS
..	..	..	..	..	..	..	..	..	..	.	"Building block"
											CONSUMPTION
..	..	..	..	..	..	..	..	..	..	.	Total consumption, SNA
..	..	..	..	..	..	..	..	..	..	.	Total consumption, MPS
..	..	..	..	..	..	..	..	..	..	.	Households, SNA
..	..	..	..	..	..	..	..	..	..	.	Households, "building block"
..	..	..	..	..	..	..	..	..	..	.	General government, SNA
..	..	..	..	..	..	..	..	..	..	.	General government, "building block"
											INVESTMENT
..	..	..	..	..	..	..	..	..	..	.	Gross fixed investment, SNA
..	..	..	..	..	..	..	..	..	..	E	Accumulation, MPS
..	..	..	..	..	..	..	..	..	..	A	"Building block"
											CONSUMER PRICES
..	..	..	..	..	..	..	..	..	..	.	National methodology
..	..	..	..	..	..	..	..	..	..	.	Outside estimate
				(millions of current US dollars)							**MERCHANDISE EXPORTS**
935	868	1,150	1,309	1,335	1,410	1,551	1,865	..	..	.	UNCTAD
											IMF: IFS
1,410	1,700	1,400	1,600	1,380	1,700	..	2,400	..	..	.	ACDA
..	..	..	..	..	..	..	..	..	..	.	ECE
											intra-CMEA
1,410	1,700	1,400	1,600	1,380	1,700	..	2,400	..	..	A	Authors' uniform TR/$ series
..	..	..	..	..	..	..	..	..	..	.	intra-CMEA
				(millions of current US dollars)							**MERCHANDISE IMPORTS**
..	..	..	..	..	..	..	..	..	..	.	UNCTAD
											IMF: IFS
1,645	1,600	1,500	1,360	1,720	2,000	..	3,100	..	..	.	ACDA
..	..	..	..	..	..	..	..	..	..	.	ECE
											intra-CMEA
1,645	1,600	1,500	1,360	1,720	2,000	..	3,100	..	..	A	Authors' uniform series
..	..	..	..	..	..	..	..	..	..	.	intra-CMEA

Korea, Democratic People's Republic

	1970	1971	1972	1973	1974	1975	1976	1977	1978	1979	1980
SNA ACCOUNTS, current prices	*(millions of current Korean Dem Peoples Rep. won)*										
GNP, at market prices	..	..	..	..	..	..	..	..	..	..	..
Net factor income	..	..	..	..	..	..	..	..	..	..	..
GDP at market prices	..	..	..	..	..	..	..	..	..	..	..
Net indirect taxes	..	..	..	..	..	..	..	..	..	..	..
GDP at factor cost	..	..	..	..	..	..	..	..	..	..	..
Agriculture	..	..	..	..	..	..	..	..	..	..	..
Industry	..	..	..	..	..	..	..	..	..	..	..
Services, etc.	..	..	..	..	..	..	..	..	..	..	..
Resource balance	..	..	..	..	..	..	..	..	..	..	..
Exports GNFS	..	..	..	..	..	..	..	..	..	..	..
Imports GNFS	..	..	..	..	..	..	..	..	..	..	..
Domestic absorption	..	..	..	..	..	..	..	..	..	..	..
Total consumption	..	..	..	..	..	..	..	..	..	..	..
Private consumption	..	..	..	..	..	..	..	..	..	..	..
General government consumption	..	..	..	..	..	..	..	..	..	..	..
Gross domestic investment	..	..	..	..	..	..	..	..	..	..	..
Fixed domestic investment	..	..	..	..	..	..	..	..	..	..	..
Depreciation	..	..	..	..	..	..	..	..	..	..	..
SNA ACCOUNTS, constant prices	*(millions of constant 1987 Korean Dem Peoples Rep. won)*										
Gross national product (GNP)	..	..	..	..	..	..	..	..	..	..	..
GDP at market prices	..	..	.	..	..	..	..	..	..	..	..
GDP at factor cost	..	..	..	..	..	..	..	..	..	..	..
Agriculture	..	..	..	..	..	..	..	..	..	..	..
Industry	..	..	..	..	..	..	..	..	..	..	..
Services, etc.	..	..	..	..	..	..	..	..	..	..	..
Resource balance	..	..	..	..	..	..	..	..	..	..	..
Exports GNFS	..	..	..	..	..	..	..	..	..	..	..
Imports GNFS	..	..	..	..	..	..	..	..	..	..	..
Domestic absorption	..	..	..	..	..	..	..	..	..	..	..
Total consumption, etc.	..	..	..	..	..	..	..	..	..	..	..
Private consumption, etc.	..	..	..	..	..	..	..	..	..	..	..
General government consumption	..	..	..	..	..	..	..	..	..	..	..
Gross domestic investment	..	..	..	..	..	..	..	..	..	..	..
Fixed domestic investment	..	..	..	..	..	..	..	..	..	..	..
Depreciation	..	..	..	..	..	..	..	..	..	..	..
MPS ACCOUNTS, current prices	*(millions of current Korean Dem Peoples Rep. won)*										
NMP produced:											
Agriculture and forestry	..	..	..	..	..	..	..	..	..	..	..
Industry excluding construction	..	..	..	..	..	..	..	..	..	..	..
Construction	..	..	..	..	..	..	..	..	..	..	..
Transport and communication	..	..	..	..	..	..	..	..	..	..	..
Trade, etc.	..	..	..	..	..	..	..	..	..	..	..
Other services	..	..	..	..	..	..	..	..	..	..	..
Resource balance	..	..	..	..	..	..	..	..	..	..	..
NMP used: domestic market	..	..	..	..	..	..	..	..	..	..	..
Final consumption, material goods	..	..	..	..	..	..	..	..	..	..	..
Personal consumption	..	..	..	..	..	..	..	..	..	..	..
Collective consumption	..	..	..	..	..	..	..	..	..	..	..
Net capital formation	..	..	..	..	..	..	..	..	..	..	..
Net fixed capital formation	..	..	..	..	..	..	..	..	..	..	..
Changes in stocks	..	..	..	..	..	..	..	..	..	..	..
Depreciation	..	..	..	..	..	..	..	..	..	..	..
MPS ACCOUNTS, constant prices	*(millions of constant Korean Dem Peoples Rep. won)*										
NMP produced:											
Agriculture and forestry	..	..	..	..	..	..	..	..	..	..	..
Industry and construction	..	..	..	..	..	..	..	..	..	..	..
Services	..	..	..	..	..	..	..	..	..	..	..
Resource balance	..	..	..	..	..	..	..	..	..	..	..
NMP used: domestic market	..	..	..	..	..	..	..	..	..	..	..
Final consumption, material goods	..	..	..	..	..	..	..	..	..	..	..
Personal consumption	..	..	..	..	..	..	..	..	..	..	..
Collective consumption	..	..	..	..	..	..	..	..	..	..	..
Net capital formation	..	..	..	..	..	..	..	..	..	..	..
Net fixed capital formation	..	..	..	..	..	..	..	..	..	..	..
Depreciation	..	..	..	..	..	..	..	..	..	..	..

Abbreviations in notes column are explained in the General Notes. For sources and methods, see the Technical Notes.

1981	1982	1983	1984	1985	1986	1987	1988	1989	1990	Notes	*Basic tables (continued)*

(millions of current Korean Dem Peoples Rep. won) — **SNA ACCOUNTS, current prices**

1981	1982	1983	1984	1985	1986	1987	1988	1989	1990	Notes	
..	..	..	..	..	..	..	..	..	..	.	GNP, at market prices
..	..	..	..	..	..	..	..	..	..	.	Net factor income
..	..	..	..	..	..	..	..	..	..	.	GDP at market prices
..	..	..	..	..	..	..	..	..	..	.	Net indirect taxes
..	..	..	..	..	..	..	..	..	..	.	GDP at factor cost
..	..	..	..	..	..	..	..	..	..	.	Agriculture
..	..	..	..	..	..	..	..	..	..	.	Industry
..	..	..	..	..	..	..	..	..	..	.	Services, etc.
..	..	..	..	..	..	..	..	..	..	.	Resource balance
..	..	..	..	..	..	..	..	..	..	.	Exports GNFS
..	..	..	..	..	..	..	..	..	..	.	Imports GNFS
..	..	..	..	..	..	..	..	..	..	.	Domestic absorption
..	..	..	..	..	..	..	..	..	..	.	Total consumption
..	..	..	..	..	..	..	..	..	..	.	Private consumption
..	..	..	..	..	..	..	..	..	..	.	General government consumption
..	..	..	..	..	..	..	..	..	..	.	Gross domestic investment
..	..	..	..	..	..	..	..	..	..	.	Fixed domestic investment
..	..	..	..	..	..	..	..	..	..	.	Depreciation

(millions of constant 1987 Korean Dem Peoples Rep. won) — **SNA ACCOUNTS, constant prices**

1981	1982	1983	1984	1985	1986	1987	1988	1989	1990	Notes	
..	..	..	..	..	..	..	..	..	..	.	Gross national product (GNP)
..	..	..	..	..	..	..	..	..	..	.	GDP at market prices
..	..	..	..	..	..	..	..	..	..	.	GDP at factor cost
..	..	..	..	..	..	..	..	..	..	.	Agriculture
..	..	..	..	..	..	..	..	..	..	.	Industry
..	..	..	..	..	..	..	..	..	..	.	Services, etc.
..	..	..	..	..	..	..	..	..	..	.	Resource balance
..	..	..	..	..	..	..	..	..	..	.	Exports GNFS
..	..	..	..	..	..	..	..	..	..	.	Imports GNFS
..	..	..	..	..	..	..	..	..	..	.	Domestic absorption
..	..	..	..	..	..	..	..	..	..	.	Total consumption, etc.
..	..	..	..	..	..	..	..	..	..	.	Private consumption, etc.
..	..	..	..	..	..	..	..	..	..	.	General government consumption
..	..	..	..	..	..	..	..	..	..	.	Gross domestic investment
..	..	..	..	..	..	..	..	..	..	.	Fixed domestic investment
..	..	..	..	..	..	..	..	..	..	.	Depreciation

(millions of current Korean Dem Peoples Rep. won) — **MPS ACCOUNTS, current prices**

1981	1982	1983	1984	1985	1986	1987	1988	1989	1990	Notes	
..	..	..	..	..	..	..	..	..	..	.	NMP produced:
..	..	..	..	..	..	..	..	..	..	.	Agriculture and forestry
..	..	..	..	..	..	..	..	..	..	.	Industry excluding construction
..	..	..	..	..	..	..	..	..	..	.	Construction
..	..	..	..	..	..	..	..	..	..	.	Transport and communication
..	..	..	..	..	..	..	..	..	..	.	Trade, etc.
..	..	..	..	..	..	..	..	..	..	.	Other services
..	..	..	..	..	..	..	..	..	..	.	Resource balance
..	..	..	..	..	..	..	..	..	..	.	NMP used: domestic market
..	..	..	..	..	..	..	..	..	..	.	Final consumption, material goods
..	..	..	..	..	..	..	..	..	..	.	Personal consumption
..	..	..	..	..	..	..	..	..	..	.	Collective consumption
..	..	..	..	..	..	..	..	..	..	.	Net capital formation
..	..	..	..	..	..	..	..	..	..	.	Net fixed capital formation
..	..	..	..	..	..	..	..	..	..	.	Changes in stocks
..	..	..	..	..	..	..	..	..	..	.	Depreciation

(millions of constant Korean Dem Peoples Rep. won) — **MPS ACCOUNTS, constant prices**

1981	1982	1983	1984	1985	1986	1987	1988	1989	1990	Notes	
..	..	..	..	..	..	..	..	..	..	.	NMP produced:
..	..	..	..	..	..	..	..	..	..	.	Agriculture and forestry
..	..	..	..	..	..	..	..	..	..	.	Industry and construction
..	..	..	..	..	..	..	..	..	..	.	Services
..	..	..	..	..	..	..	..	..	..	.	Resource balance
..	..	..	..	..	..	..	..	..	..	.	NMP used: domestic market
..	..	..	..	..	..	..	..	..	..	.	Final consumption, material goods
..	..	..	..	..	..	..	..	..	..	.	Personal consumption
..	..	..	..	..	..	..	..	..	..	.	Collective consumption
..	..	..	..	..	..	..	..	..	..	.	Net capital formation
..	..	..	..	..	..	..	..	..	..	.	Net fixed capital formation
..	..	..	..	..	..	..	..	..	..	.	Depreciation

Basic tables *(continued)*	1970	1971	1972	1973	1974	1975	1976	1977	1978	1979	1980
MPS ACCOUNTS, index					*(index,1980 = 100)*						
NMP produced:	..	..	..	..	..	..	..	..	..	..	..
Agriculture and forestry	..	..	..	..	..	..	..	..	..	..	..
Industry excluding construction	..	..	..	..	..	..	..	..	..	..	..
Construction	..	..	..	..	..	..	..	..	..	..	..
Transport and communication	..	..	..	..	..	..	..	..	..	..	..
Trade, etc.	..	..	..	..	..	..	..	..	..	..	..
NMP used: material goods	..	..	..	..	..	..	..	..	..	..	..
Final consumption	..	..	..	..	..	..	..	..	..	..	..
Net capital formation	..	..	..	..	..	..	..	..	..	..	..
EXCHANGE AND CONVERSION RATES					*(LCUs per US dollar: annual average)*						
Single-year converter	..	..	..	..	..	..	..	..	..	..	..
Devisa/official	..	..	..	..	..	..	..	..	..	..	..
Commercial	2.570	2.570	2.570	2.370	2.370	2.050	2.150	2.150	1.860	1.790	1.700
Noncommercial	..	..	..	..	..	..	..	..	..	..	..
Informal market	..	..	..	..	..	..	..	..	..	..	..
ICP	..	..	..	..	..	..	..	..	..	..	..
					(ruble per US dollar: annual average)						
Commercial TR/$ cross	..	..	..	..	..	..	..	..	..	..	..
Uniform TR/$ cross	..	..	..	..	..	..	..	..	..	..	..
					(LCUs per ruble: annual average)						
Commercial	..	..	..	..	..	..	..	..	..	..	..
Noncommercial	..	..	..	..	..	..	..	..	..	..	..
Devisa/official	..	..	..	..	..	..	..	..	..	..	..
CONSUMER PRICE INDEXES					*(index)*						
Official, IMF 1985=100	..	..	..	..	..	..	..	..	..	..	..
Official, CIA or LWI 1980=100	..	..	..	..	..	..	..	..	..	..	..
Alternative, CIA or LWI 1980=100	..	..	..	..	..	..	..	..	..	..	..
INTERNATIONAL TRADE (ECE)					*(millions of current Korean Dem Peoples Rep. won)*						
Value of exports, fob	..	..	..	..	..	..	..	..	..	..	..
to CMEA	..	..	..	..	..	..	..	..	..	..	..
Value of imports, cif	..	..	..	..	..	..	..	..	..	..	..
from CMEA	..	..	..	..	..	..	..	..	..	..	..
Trade balance	..	..	..	..	..	..	..	..	..	..	..
CMEA	..	..	..	..	..	..	..	..	..	..	..
INTERNATIONAL TRADE (Authors')					*(millions of current US dollars)*						
Value of exports, fob	..	..	..	..	..	..	..	..	..	..	..
to developed countries	..	..	..	..	..	..	..	..	..	..	..
to other non-socialist countries	..	..	..	..	..	..	..	..	..	..	..
to socialist countries	..	..	..	..	..	..	..	..	..	..	..
to CMEA	..	..	..	..	..	..	..	..	..	..	..
Value of imports, cif	..	..	..	..	..	..	..	..	..	..	..
from developed countries	..	..	..	..	..	..	..	..	..	..	..
from other non-socialist countries	..	..	..	..	..	..	..	..	..	..	..
from socialist countries	..	..	..	..	..	..	..	..	..	..	..
from CMEA	..	..	..	..	..	..	..	..	..	..	..
Trade balance	..	..	..	..	..	..	..	..	..	..	..
Developed countries	..	..	..	..	..	..	..	..	..	..	..
Other non-socialist countries	..	..	..	..	..	..	..	..	..	..	..
Socialist countries	..	..	..	..	..	..	..	..	..	..	..
CMEA	..	..	..	..	..	..	..	..	..	..	..
PARTNER CONVERTIBLE TRADE (ECE)					*(millions of current US dollars)*						
Exports to non-CMEA (cif)	..	..	..	..	..	..	..	..	..	..	..
Imports from non-CMEA (fob)	..	..	..	..	..	..	..	..	..	..	..
Trade balance	..	..	..	..	..	..	..	..	..	..	..
TRADE PRICE INDEXES (Authors')					*(index,1980 = 100)*						
Terms of trade	..	..	..	..	..	..	..	..	..	..	..
Exports	..	..	..	..	..	..	..	..	..	..	..
Non-socialist countries	..	..	..	..	..	..	..	..	..	..	..
Developed countries	..	..	..	..	..	..	..	..	..	..	..
Other	..	..	..	..	..	..	..	..	..	..	..
Socialist countries	..	..	..	..	..	..	..	..	..	..	..
CMEA	..	..	..	..	..	..	..	..	..	..	..
Imports	..	..	..	..	..	..	..	..	..	..	..
Non-socialist countries	..	..	..	..	..	..	..	..	..	..	..
Developed countries	..	..	..	..	..	..	..	..	..	..	..
Other	..	..	..	..	..	..	..	..	..	..	..
Socialist countries	..	..	..	..	..	..	..	..	..	..	..
CMEA	..	..	..	..	..	..	..	..	..	..	..

Abbreviations in notes column are explained in the General Notes. For sources and methods, see the Technical Notes.

1981	1982	1983	1984	1985	1986	1987	1988	1989	1990	Notes	*Basic tables (continued)*
				(index, 1980 = 100)							**MPS ACCOUNTS, index**
..	..	..	..	..	..	..	..	..	..	.	NMP produced:
..	..	..	..	..	..	..	..	..	..	.	Agriculture and forestry
..	..	..	..	..	..	..	..	..	..	.	Industry excluding construction
..	..	..	..	..	..	..	..	..	..	.	Construction
..	..	..	..	..	..	..	..	..	..	.	Transport and communication
..	..	..	..	..	..	..	..	..	..	.	Trade, etc.
..	..	..	..	..	..	..	..	..	..	.	NMP used: material goods
..	..	..	..	..	..	..	..	..	..	.	Final consumption
..	..	..	..	..	..	..	..	..	..	.	Net capital formation
				(LCUs per US dollar: annual average)							**EXCHANGE AND CONVERSION RATES**
..	..	..	..	..	..	..	..	..	..	.	Single-year converter
..	..	..	1.070	0.940	0.940	0.940	0.940	0.940	..	.	Devisa/official
1.770	2.120	2.180	2.210						..	.	Commercial
..	..	..	..	..	..	..	..	..	..	.	Noncommercial
..	..	..	..	..	..	..	..	..	..	.	Informal market
..	..	..	..	..	..	..	..	..	..	.	ICP
				(ruble per US dollar: annual average)							
..	..	..	..	..	..	..	..	..	..	.	Commercial TR/$ cross
..	..	..	..	..	..	..	..	..	..	.	Uniform TR/$ cross
				(LCUs per ruble: annual average)							
..	..	..	..	..	..	..	..	..	..	.	Commercial
..	..	..	..	..	..	..	..	..	..	.	Noncommercial
..	..	..	..	..	..	..	..	..	..	.	Devisa/official
				(index)							**CONSUMER PRICE INDEXES**
..	..	..	..	..	..	..	..	..	..	.	Official, IMF 1985 = 100
..	..	..	..	..	..	..	..	..	..	.	Official, CIA or LWI 1980 = 100
..	..	..	..	..	..	..	..	..	..	.	Alternative, CIA or LWI 1980 = 100
				(millions of current Korean Dem Peoples Rep. won)							**INTERNATIONAL TRADE (ECE)**
..	..	..	..	..	..	..	..	..	..	.	Value of exports, fob
..	..	..	..	..	..	..	..	..	..	.	to CMEA
..	..	..	..	..	..	..	..	..	..	.	Value of imports, cif
..	..	..	..	..	..	..	..	..	..	.	from CMEA
..	..	..	..	..	..	..	..	..	..	.	Trade balance
..	..	..	..	..	..	..	..	..	..	.	CMEA
				(millions of current US dollars)							**INTERNATIONAL TRADE (Authors')**
1,410	1,700	1,400	1,600	1,380	1,700	..	2,400	..	..	A	Value of exports, fob
..	..	..	..	..	..	..	..	..	..	.	to developed countries
..	..	..	..	..	..	..	..	..	..	.	to other non-socialist countries
..	..	..	..	..	..	..	..	..	..	.	to socialist countries
..	..	..	..	..	..	..	..	..	..	.	to CMEA
1,645	1,600	1,500	1,360	1,720	2,000	..	3,100	..	..	A	Value of imports, cif
..	..	..	..	..	..	..	..	..	..	.	from developed countries
..	..	..	..	..	..	..	..	..	..	.	from other non-socialist countries
..	..	..	..	..	..	..	..	..	..	.	from socialist countries
..	..	..	..	..	..	..	..	..	..	.	from CMEA
-235	100	-100	240	-340	-300	..	-700	..	..	A	Trade balance
..	..	..	..	..	..	..	..	..	..	.	Developed countries
..	..	..	..	..	..	..	..	..	..	.	Other non-socialist countries
..	..	..	..	..	..	..	..	..	..	.	Socialist countries
..	..	..	..	..	..	..	..	..	..	.	CMEA
				(millions of current US dollars)							**PARTNER CONVERTIBLE TRADE (ECE)**
..	..	..	..	..	..	..	..	..	..	.	Exports to non-CMEA (cif)
..	..	..	..	..	..	..	..	..	..	.	Imports from non-CMEA (fob)
..	..	..	..	..	..	..	..	..	..	.	Trade balance
				(index, 1980 = 100)							**TRADE PRICE INDEXES (Authors')**
..	..	..	..	..	..	..	..	..	..	.	Terms of trade
..	..	..	..	..	..	..	..	..	..	.	Exports
..	..	..	..	..	..	..	..	..	..	.	Non-socialist countries
..	..	..	..	..	..	..	..	..	..	.	Developed countries
..	..	..	..	..	..	..	..	..	..	.	Other
..	..	..	..	..	..	..	..	..	..	.	Socialist countries
..	..	..	..	..	..	..	..	..	..	.	CMEA
..	..	..	..	..	..	..	..	..	..	.	Imports
..	..	..	..	..	..	..	..	..	..	.	Non-socialist countries
..	..	..	..	..	..	..	..	..	..	.	Developed countries
..	..	..	..	..	..	..	..	..	..	.	Other
..	..	..	..	..	..	..	..	..	..	.	Socialist countries
..	..	..	..	..	..	..	..	..	..	.	CMEA

Basic tables (continued)	1970	1971	1972	1973	1974	1975	1976	1977	1978	1979	1980
TRADE PRICE INDEXES (ECE)					*(index, 1980 = 100)*						
Terms of trade	..	..	..	..	..	..	..	..	..	..	..
Exports	..	..	..	..	..	..	..	..	..	..	..
Imports	..	..	..	..	..	..	..	..	..	..	..
Balance of Payments (ECE)					*(millions of current US dollars)*						
Exports, convertible currency	..	..	..	..	..	..	..	..	..	..	..
Imports, convertible currency	..	..	..	..	..	..	..	..	..	..	..
Trade balance, convertible currency	..	..	..	..	..	..	..	..	..	..	..
Invisibles, convertible currency	..	..	..	..	..	..	..	..	..	..	..
Current balance, convertible currency	..	..	..	..	..	..	..	..	..	..	..
External debt, total (World Bank)	..	..	..	..	..	..	..	..	..	..	..
Convertible currency	..	..	..	..	..	..	..	..	..	..	..
CMEA	..	..	..	..	..	..	..	..	..	..	..
External debt service (World Bank)	..	..	..	..	..	..	..	..	..	..	..
Convertible currency	..	..	..	..	..	..	..	..	..	..	..
Total reserves less gold (IMF, IFS)	..	..	..	..	..	..	..	..	..	..	..
Total reserves, including gold at London price	..	..	..	..	..	..	..	..	..	..	..
Total reserves, incl. gold at national valuation	..	..	..	..	..	..	..	..	..	..	..
EMPLOYMENT					*(thousands)*						
Employment, total	..	..	..	..	..	..	..	..	..	..	..
Agriculture	..	..	..	..	..	..	..	..	..	..	..
Industry	..	..	..	..	..	..	..	..	..	..	..
Services	..	..	..	..	..	..	..	..	..	..	..
Labor force, total	5,908	6,088	6,269	6,450	6,631	6,812	7,017	7,222	7,428	7,633	7,838
Agriculture	3,118	3,146	3,173	3,200	3,227	3,254	3,274	3,295	3,315	3,335	3,355
Industry	1,516	1,594	1,673	1,751	1,829	1,907	2,000	2,094	2,187	2,280	2,373
Services	1,273	1,348	1,424	1,499	1,575	1,650	1,742	1,834	1,926	2,018	2,110
DOMESTIC FINANCE (IMF)				*(millions of current Korean Dem Peoples Rep. won)*							
Money supply, broadly defined	..	..	..	..	..	..	..	..	..	..	..
Money, means of payment	..	..	..	..	..	..	..	..	..	..	..
Demand deposits	..	..	..	..	..	..	..	..	..	..	..
Currency outside banks	..	..	..	..	..	..	..	..	..	..	..
Quasi-money	..	..	..	..	..	..	..	..	..	..	..
Interest: deposit rate (percent)	..	..	..	..	..	..	..	..	..	..	..
Central government expenditures	..	..	..	..	..	..	..	..	..	..	..
Defense	..	..	..	..	..	..	..	..	..	..	..
					(millions of 1989 US dollars)						
Central government exp. (ACDA)	..	..	..	..	..	..	..	..	..	..	..
Military (ACDA)	..	..	..	..	..	..	..	..	7,066	6,720	6,454
LAND AND FORESTS (FAO)											
Pop. density: agr. land (pop. per sq. km)	713	716	735	736	753	753	762	764	775	786	797
Deforestation rate (net)	0	0	0	0	0	0	0	0	0	0	0
Forest (thousands sq. km)	90	90	90	90	90	90	90	90	90	90	90
SOCIAL INDICATORS											
Population density: total land (pop. per sq. km)	121	125	128	131	135	138	141	143	146	149	152
School enrollment ratio, primary	..	..	..	..	..	..	116	..	..	..	..
secondary	..	..	..	..	..	..	..	..	..	..	..
tertiary	..	..	..	..	..	..	..	..	..	..	..
Energy consumption per capita (kg. of oil eq.)	1,550	2,118	1,748	1,841	1,891	1,973	1,969	1,984	2,044	2,034	2,102
Daily calorie supply per capita	2,462	2,533	2,482	2,633	2,659	2,727	2,815	2,820	2,935	2,982	3,022
Food production (1979-1981 = 100)	75	79	83	82	87	90	95	99	100	100	100
Daily protein supply (gm. per capita)	73	74	74	79	79	80	81	79	81	82	83
Population per hospital bed	..	..	..	..	..	..	..	..	..	..	..
per nursing person	..	..	..	..	..	..	..	..	..	..	..
per physician	..	..	..	..	..	..	..	..	..	..	..
Female participation in labor force (percent)	38	38	38	38	38	39	39	39	39	39	39
Infant mortality (per 1,000 live births)	51	49	47	45	42	40	37	35	34	33	32
Life expectancy (years)	60	61	62	62	63	64	65	66	66	66	67
Total fertility (births per woman)	6	6	5	5	5	4	4	3	3	3	3
Urban population (percent of total population)	53	54	55	55	56	57	57	57	57	57	57
Population per passenger car	..	..	..	..	..	..	..	..	..	..	..
per telephone	..	..	..	..	..	..	..	..	..	..	..

Abbreviations in notes column are explained in the General Notes. For sources and methods, see the Technical Notes.

Korea, Democratic People's Republic

1981	1982	1983	1984	1985	1986	1987	1988	1989	1990	Notes	
				(index, 1980 = 100)							**TRADE PRICE INDEXES (ECE)**
..	..	..	..	..	..	..	..	..	..	.	Terms of trade
..	..	..	..	..	..	..	..	..	..	.	Exports
..	..	..	..	..	..	..	..	..	..	.	Imports
				(millions of current US dollars)							**Balance of Payments (ECE)**
..	..	..	1,100	1,100	1,300	1,500	2,000	..	..	.	Exports, convertible currency
..	..	..	1,100	1,500	1,800	3,000	3,200	..	..	.	Imports, convertible currency
..	..	..	0	-400	-500	-1,500	-1,200	..	..	.	Trade balance, convertible currency
..	..	..	..	..	..	..	..	..	..	.	Invisibles, convertible currency
..	..	..	..	..	..	..	..	..	..	.	Current balance, convertible currency
..	1,108	895	865	1,171	1,520	1,356	1,208	..	..	O	External debt, total (World Bank)
											Convertible currency
..	160	145	168	121	100	120	141	..	..	.	CMEA
..	122	122	71	98	75	118	102	..	..	Of	External debt service (World Bank)
..	..	..	..	..	..	..	..	..	..	.	Convertible currency
..	..	..	..	..	..	..	..	..	..	.	Total reserves less gold (IMF, IFS)
..	..	..	..	..	..	..	..	..	..	.	Total reserves, including gold at London price
..	..	..	..	..	..	..	..	..	..	.	Total reserves, incl. gold at national valuation
				(thousands)							**EMPLOYMENT**
..	..	..	..	..	..	..	..	..	..	.	Employment, total
..	..	..	..	..	..	..	..	..	..	.	Agriculture
..	..	..	..	..	..	..	..	..	..	.	Industry
..	..	..	..	..	..	..	..	..	..	.	Services
8,087	8,336	8,586	8,835	9,084	9,361	9,638	9,915	10,193	10,470	.	Labor force, total
..	..	..	..	..	..	..	..	..	..	.	Agriculture
..	..	..	..	..	..	..	..	..	..	.	Industry
..	..	..	..	..	..	..	..	..	..	.	Services
			(millions of current Korean Dem Peoples Rep. won)								**DOMESTIC FINANCE (IMF)**
..	..	..	..	..	..	..	..	..	..	.	Money supply, broadly defined
..	..	..	..	..	..	..	..	..	..	.	Money, means of payment
..	..	..	..	..	..	..	..	..	..	.	Demand deposits
..	..	..	..	..	..	..	..	..	..	.	Currency outside banks
..	..	..	..	..	..	..	..	..	..	.	Quasi-money
..	..	..	..	..	..	..	..	..	..	.	Interest: deposit rate (percent)
..	..	..	..	..	..	..	..	..	..	.	Central government expenditures
..	..	..	..	..	..	..	..	..	..	.	Defense
				(millions of 1989 US dollars)							
..	..	..	..	..	..	..	..	..	..	.	Central government exp. (ACDA)
6,103	5,936	5,934	5,932	5,988	6,037	6,066	6,079	6,000	..	.	Military (ACDA)
											LAND AND FORESTS (FAO)
806	815	822	828	825	828	842	..	..	..	.	Pop. density: agr. land (pop. per sq. km)
0	0	0	0	0	0	..	..	..	..	.	Deforestation rate (net)
90	90	90	90	90	90	..	..	..	..	.	Forest (thousands sq. km)
											SOCIAL INDICATORS
154	157	160	163	165	168	171	..	..	..	.	Population density: total land (pop. per sq. km)
..	..	..	..	..	..	100	..	..	..	.	School enrollment ratio, primary
..	..	..	..	..	..	..	..	..	..	.	secondary
..	..	..	..	..	..	..	..	..	..	.	tertiary
2,064	2,078	2,166	2,144	2,180	2,173	2,165	..	..	..	.	Energy consumption per capita (kg. of oil eq.)
3,033	3,045	3,084	3,071	3,061	3,128	3,195	3,193	..	..	.	Daily calorie supply per capita
100	100	102	105	107	108	109	109	108	..	.	Food production (1979-1981=100)
83	83	84	85	86	88	90	90	..	..	.	Daily protein supply (gm. per capita)
..	..	..	..	..	..	..	..	..	..	.	Population per hospital bed
..	..	..	..	..	..	..	..	..	..	.	per nursing person
..	419									.	per physician
40	40	40	40	41	41	41	41	41	42	.	Female participation in labor force (percent)
31	30	30	29	29	28	28	27	27	26	.	Infant mortality (per 1,000 live births)
67	68	68	68	69	69	69	70	70	71	.	Life expectancy (years)
3	3	3	3	3	3	3	2	2	2	.	Total fertility (births per woman)
57	58	58	58	59	59	59	59	60	60	.	Urban population (percent of total population)
..	..	..	..	..	..	..	..	..	..	.	Population per passenger car
..	..	..	..	..	..	..	..	..	..	.	per telephone

Lao PDR

Comparator tables	1970	1971	1972	1973	1974	1975	1976	1977	1978	1979	1980
PER CAPITA INCOME					*(US dollars)*						
World Bank (Atlas method)	..	..	..	..	..	..	..	..	..	..	..
Single year conversion	..	..	..	..	..	..	..	..	..	..	..
CIA or LWI	..	..	..	..	..	..	..	..	..	..	..
Penn World Tables	..	..	..	..	..	..	..	..	..	..	..
POPULATION					*(thousands)*						
	2,713	2,777	2,844	2,912	2,973	3,024	3,066	3,097	3,126	3,159	3,205
GROSS NATIONAL PRODUCT, current prices					*(millions of current US dollars)*						
World Bank (Atlas method)	..	..	..	..	..	..	..	..	..	..	..
Single year conversion	..	..	..	..	..	..	..	..	..	..	..
Authors' series	..	..	..	..	..	..	..	..	..	..	..
CIA or LWI	..	..	..	..	..	..	..	..	..	..	..
GROSS NATIONAL PRODUCT, constant prices					*(millions of constant 1987 dollars)*						
Single year conversion	..	..	..	..	..	..	..	..	..	..	..
Authors' series, rescaled from 1980 prices	..	..	..	..	..	..	..	..	..	..	..
CIA or LWI, rescaled from 1989 prices	..	..	..	..	..	..	..	..	..	..	..
CONVERSION FACTORS					*(LCUs per US dollar)*						
World Bank (Atlas method)	..	..	..	..	..	..	..	..	..	..	..
Single year convertor	0.12	0.12	0.25	0.30	0.30	0.36	1.63	2.52	4.20	5.71	10.22
Authors' series	..	..	..	..	..	..	..	..	..	..	..
Penn World Tables	..	..	..	..	..	..	..	..	..	..	..
OUTPUT TRENDS, OVERALL					*(index, constant prices 1987 = 100)*						
GNP, SNA	..	..	..	..	..	..	..	..	..	..	..
NMP, MPS											69.3
GNP, "Building block"	..	..	..	..	..	..	..	..	..	..	..
Industry											
Value added, SNA	..	..	..	..	..	..	..	..	..	..	..
Value added, MPS											46.2
"Building block"	..	..	..	..	..	..	..	..	..	..	..
Gross output, SNA	..	..	..	..	..	..	..	..	..	..	..
Agriculture											
Value added, SNA	..	..	..	..	..	..	..	..	..	..	..
Value added, MPS											73.6
"Building block"	..	..	..	..	..	..	..	..	..	..	..
Gross output, SNA	..	..	..	..	..	..	..	..	..	..	..
Services											
Value added, SNA	..	..	..	..	..	..	..	..	..	..	..
Value added, MPS											70.0
"Building block"	..	..	..	..	..	..	..	..	..	..	..
CONSUMPTION											
Total consumption, SNA	..	..	..	..	..	..	..	..	..	..	..
Total consumption, MPS	..	..	..	..	..	..	..	..	..	..	..
Households, SNA	..	..	..	..	..	..	..	..	..	..	..
Households, "building block"	..	..	..	..	..	..	..	..	..	..	..
General government, SNA	..	..	..	..	..	..	..	..	..	..	..
General government, "building block"	..	..	..	..	..	..	..	..	..	..	..
INVESTMENT											
Gross fixed investment, SNA	..	..	..	..	..	..	..	..	..	..	..
Accumulation, MPS	..	..	..	..	..	..	..	..	..	..	..
"Building block"	..	..	..	..	..	..	..	..	..	..	..
CONSUMER PRICES											
National methodology	..	..	..	..	..	..	..	..	..	..	..
Outside estimate	..	..	..	..	..	..	..	..	..	..	..
MERCHANDISE EXPORTS					*(millions of current US dollars)*						
UNCTAD	7	..	..	..	..	11	..	..	..	..	31
IMF: IFS	7	..	..	..	..	12	..	..	..	..	5
ACDA	..	..	..	..	..	..	..	4	3	5	5
ECE	..	..	..	..	..	..	..	..	..	..	..
intra-CMEA	..	..	..	..	..	..	..	..	..	..	..
Authors' uniform TR/$ series	7	..	..	..	..	11	..	..	..	..	31
intra-CMEA	..	..	..	..	..	..	..	..	..	..	..
MERCHANDISE IMPORTS					*(millions of current US dollars)*						
UNCTAD	114	..	..	..	..	43	..	..	..	..	131
IMF: IFS	114	..	..	..	..	45	..	..	..	..	29
ACDA	..	..	..	..	..	..	..	14	16	20	29
ECE	..	..	..	..	..	..	..	..	..	..	..
intra-CMEA	..	..	..	..	..	..	..	..	..	..	..
Authors' uniform series	114	..	..	..	..	43	..	..	..	..	131
intra-CMEA	..	..	..	..	..	..	..	..	..	..	..

Abbreviations in notes column are explained in the General Notes. For sources and methods, see the Technical Notes.

1981	1982	1983	1984	1985	1986	1987	1988	1989	1990	Notes	Comparator tables (continued)
					(US dollars)						**PER CAPITA INCOME**
..	..	..			590	440	260	220	200	.	World Bank (Atlas method)
..	..	..	529	694	504	298	160	190	206	.	Single year conversion
..	135	..	150	..	..	..	..	..	..	A	CIA or LWI
..	..	..	..	..	..	..	..	..	..	.	Penn World Tables
					(thousands)						
3,261	3,328	3,406	3,495	3,594	3,701	3,813	3,931	4,055	4,186	.	**POPULATION**
				(millions of current US dollars)							**GROSS NATIONAL PRODUCT, current prices**
..	..	..	..	..	2,182	1,695	1,007	888	848	.	World Bank (Atlas method)
..	..	..	1,848	2,494	1,864	1,137	628	771	863	.	Single year conversion
..	..	..	..	..	..	..	..	..	..	.	Authors' series
..	460	..	525	..	..	..	..	..	..	.	CIA or LWI
				(millions of constant 1987 dollars)							**GROSS NATIONAL PRODUCT, constant prices**
..	..	..	1,042	1,096	1,148	1,137	1,113	1,265	1,349	.	Single year conversion
..	..	..	..	..	..	..	..	..	..	.	Authors' series, rescaled from 1980 prices
..	562	..	595	..	..	..	..	..	..	A	CIA or LWI, rescaled from 1989 prices
					(LCUs per US dollar)						**CONVERSION FACTORS**
..	..	..	..	..	81.15	117.47	244.66	506.16	721.05	..	World Bank (Atlas method)
20.00	35.00	35.00	35.00	45.00	95.00	175.12	392.01	583.02	708.57	.	Single year convertor
..	..	..	..	..	..	..	..	..	..	..	Authors' series
..	..	..	..	..	..	..	..	..	..	..	Penn World Tables
				(index, constant prices 1987 = 100)							**OUTPUT TRENDS, OVERALL**
..	..	..	91.7	96.4	101.0	100.0	97.9	111.2	118.6	.	GNP, SNA
73.6	75.0	78.6	84.2	92.0	98.8	100.0	..	..	..	.	NMP, MPS
..	..	..	..	..	..	..	..	..	..	.	GNP, "Building block"
											Industry
											Value added, SNA
48.7	57.3	63.5	69.2	86.3	94.3	100.0	..	..	..	.	Value added, MPS
..	..	..	..	..	..	..	..	..	..	.	"Building block"
..	..	..	..	..	..	..	..	..	..	.	Gross output, SNA
											Agriculture
											Value added, SNA
78.7	78.4	80.8	86.7	93.3	100.2	100.0	..	..	..	I	Value added, MPS
..	..	..	..	..	..	..	..	..	..	.	"Building block"
..	..	..	..	..	..	..	..	..	..	.	Gross output, SNA
											Services
											Value added, SNA
72.0	75.9	83.0	86.9	91.0	95.7	100.0	..	..	..	.	Value added, MPS
..	..	..	..	..	..	..	..	..	..	.	"Building block"
											CONSUMPTION
..	..	..	89.2	96.7	100.4	100.0	99.9	113.6	120.3	.	Total consumption, SNA
..	..	..	..	..	..	..	..	..	..	.	Total consumption, MPS
..	..	..	87.8	94.4	99.5	100.0	99.9	115.8	123.9	.	Households, SNA
..	..	..	..	..	..	..	..	..	..	.	Households, "building block"
..	..	..	103.0	119.2	109.5	100.0	100.0	91.2	84.5	.	General government, SNA
..	..	..	..	..	..	..	..	..	..	.	General government, "building block"
											INVESTMENT
..	..	..	110.3	104.1	104.0	100.0	85.9	92.9	97.8	.	Gross fixed investment, SNA
..	..	..	..	..	..	..	..	..	..	.	Accumulation, MPS
..	..	..	..	..	..	..	..	..	..	A	"Building block"
											CONSUMER PRICES
..	..	..	..	..	..	..	..	..	..	.	National methodology
..	..	..	..	..	..	..	..	..	..	.	Outside estimate
				(millions of current US dollars)							**MERCHANDISE EXPORTS**
33	40	26	12	54	60	62	81	80	80	.	UNCTAD
2	..	..	5	5	5	..	..	..	..	.	IMF: IFS
2	..	..	36	..	56	49	..	58	..	.	ACDA
24	40	41	44	50	33	64	63	57	72	f	ECE
..	..	..	..	..	..	..	..	..	..	.	intra-CMEA
33	40	26	12	54	60	62	81	80	80	N	Authors' uniform TR/$ series
..	..	..	..	..	..	..	..	..	..	.	intra-CMEA
				(millions of current US dollars)							**MERCHANDISE IMPORTS**
125	130	92	48	131	131	146	162	150	155	.	UNCTAD
21	..	..	29	29	29	..	..	..	..	.	IMF: IFS
21	..	..	98	..	205	219	..	219	..	.	ACDA
110	132	150	162	192	186	216	186	219	256	f	ECE
..	..	..	..	..	..	..	..	..	..	.	intra-CMEA
125	130	92	48	131	131	146	162	150	155	N	Authors' uniform series
..	..	..	..	..	..	..	..	..	..	.	intra-CMEA

Lao PDR

Basic tables	1970	1971	1972	1973	1974	1975	1976	1977	1978	1979	1980
SNA ACCOUNTS, current prices					*(millions of current Lao kip)*						
GNP, at market prices	..	..	..	..	..	..	..	..	..	..	..
Net factor income	..	..	..	..	..	..	..	..	..	..	..
GDP at market prices	..	..	..	..	..	..	..	..	..	..	..
Net indirect taxes	..	..	..	..	..	..	..	..	..	..	..
GDP at factor cost	..	..	..	..	..	..	..	..	..	..	..
Agriculture	..	..	..	..	..	..	..	..	..	..	..
Industry	..	..	..	..	..	..	..	..	..	..	..
Services, etc.	..	..	..	..	..	..	..	..	..	..	..
Resource balance	..	..	..	..	..	..	..	..	..	..	..
Exports GNFS	..	..	..	..	..	..	..	..	..	..	..
Imports GNFS	..	..	..	..	..	..	..	..	..	..	..
Domestic absorption	..	..	..	..	..	..	..	..	..	..	..
Total consumption	..	..	..	..	..	..	..	..	..	..	..
Private consumption	..	..	..	..	..	..	..	..	..	..	..
General government consumption	..	..	..	..	..	..	..	..	..	..	..
Gross domestic investment	..	..	..	..	..	..	..	..	..	..	..
Fixed domestic investment	..	..	..	..	..	..	..	..	..	..	..
Depreciation	..	..	..	..	..	..	..	..	..	..	..
SNA ACCOUNTS, constant prices					*(millions of constant 1987 Lao kip)*						
Gross national product (GNP)	..	..	..	..	..	..	..	..	..	..	..
GDP at market prices	..	..	..	..	..	..	..	..	..	..	..
GDP at factor cost	..	..	..	..	..	..	..	..	..	..	..
Agriculture	..	..	..	..	..	..	..	..	..	..	..
Industry	..	..	..	..	..	..	..	..	..	..	..
Services, etc.	..	..	..	..	..	..	..	..	..	..	..
Resource balance	..	..	..	..	..	..	..	..	..	..	..
Exports GNFS	..	..	..	..	..	..	..	..	..	..	..
Imports GNFS	..	..	..	..	..	..	..	..	..	..	..
Domestic absorption	..	..	..	..	..	..	..	..	..	..	..
Total consumption, etc.	..	..	..	..	..	..	..	..	..	..	..
Private consumption, etc.	..	..	..	..	..	..	..	..	..	..	..
General government consumption	..	..	..	..	..	..	..	..	..	..	..
Gross domestic investment	..	..	..	..	..	..	..	..	..	..	..
Fixed domestic investment	..	..	..	..	..	..	..	..	..	..	..
Depreciation	..	..	..	..	..	..	..	..	..	..	..
MPS ACCOUNTS, current prices					*(millions of current Lao kip)*						
NMP produced:	..	..	..	..	..	..	..	..	..	..	..
Agriculture and forestry	..	..	..	..	..	..	..	..	..	..	..
Industry excluding construction	..	..	..	..	..	..	..	..	..	..	..
Construction	..	..	..	..	..	..	..	..	..	..	..
Transport and communication	..	..	..	..	..	..	..	..	..	..	..
Trade, etc.	..	..	..	..	..	..	..	..	..	..	..
Other services	..	..	..	..	..	..	..	..	..	..	..
Resource balance	..	..	..	..	..	..	..	..	..	..	..
NMP used: domestic market	..	..	..	..	..	..	..	..	..	..	..
Final consumption, material goods	..	..	..	..	..	..	..	..	..	..	..
Personal consumption	..	..	..	..	..	..	..	..	..	..	..
Collective consumption	..	..	..	..	..	..	..	..	..	..	..
Net capital formation	..	..	..	..	..	..	..	..	..	..	..
Net fixed capital formation	..	..	..	..	..	..	..	..	..	..	..
Changes in stocks	..	..	..	..	..	..	..	..	..	..	..
Depreciation	..	..	..	..	..	..	..	..	..	..	..
MPS ACCOUNTS, constant prices					*(millions of 1986 Lao kip)*						
NMP produced:	..	..	..	..	..	..	..	..	..	..	37,493
Agriculture and forestry	..	..	..	..	..	..	..	..	..	..	29,430
Industry and construction	..	..	..	..	..	..	..	..	..	..	3,600
Services	..	..	..	..	..	..	..	..	..	..	4,463
Resource balance	..	..	..	..	..	..	..	..	..	..	..
NMP used: domestic market	..	..	..	..	..	..	..	..	..	..	..
Final consumption, material goods	..	..	..	..	..	..	..	..	..	..	..
Personal consumption	..	..	..	..	..	..	..	..	..	..	..
Collective consumption	..	..	..	..	..	..	..	..	..	..	..
Net capital formation	..	..	..	..	..	..	..	..	..	..	..
Net fixed capital formation	..	..	..	..	..	..	..	..	..	..	..
Depreciation	..	..	..	..	..	..	..	..	..	..	..

Abbreviations in notes column are explained in the General Notes. For sources and methods, see the Technical Notes.

1981	1982	1983	1984	1985	1986	1987	1988	1989	1990	Notes	Basic tables (continued)
											(millions of current Lao kip) **SNA ACCOUNTS, current prices**
..	..	..	64,668	112,223	177,104	199,161	246,288	449,602	611,217	.	GNP, at market prices
..	..	..	-112	-105	-285	-95	-855	-1,200	-1,632	.	Net factor income
..	..	..	64,780	112,328	177,389	199,256	247,143	450,802	612,848	.	GDP at market prices
..	..	..	..	..	..	..	..	..	..	.	Net indirect taxes
..	..	..	..	..	..	..	..	..	..	.	GDP at factor cost
..	..	..	..	..	..	..	..	..	..	.	Agriculture
..	..	..	..	..	..	..	٠٠	..	..	.	Industry
..	..	..	..	..	..	..	..	..	..	.	Services, etc.
..	..	..	-2,193	-6,064	-6,893	-15,046	-33,128	-59,493	-85,130	.	Resource balance
..	..	..	1,745	4,319	6,098	11,606	25,676	44,352	61,541	.	Exports GNFS
..	..	..	3,938	10,383	12,991	26,652	58,804	103,845	146,671	.	Imports GNFS
..	..	..	66,973	118,392	184,282	214,302	280,271	510,295	697,978	.	Domestic absorption
..	..	..	63,114	110,868	172,570	194,797	248,435	455,823	622,406	.	Total consumption
..	..	..	58,600	100,039	156,909	176,916	214,092	402,962	545,855	.	Private consumption
..	..	..	4,514	10,829	15,661	17,881	34,343	52,861	76,551	.	General government consumption
..	..	..	3,859	7,524	11,712	19,505	31,836	54,472	75,572	.	Gross domestic investment
..	..	..	3,856	7,514	11,712	19,505	31,836	54,472	75,572	.	Fixed domestic investment
..	..	..	..	..	..	..	..	..	..	.	Depreciation
											(millions of constant 1987 Lao kip) **SNA ACCOUNTS, constant prices**
..	..	..	182,536	191,917	201,084	199,161	194,950	221,467	236,178	.	Gross national product (GNP)
..	..	..	182,859	192,103	201,417	199,256	195,597	222,031	236,769	.	GDP at market prices
..	..	..	..	..	..	..	..	..	..	.	GDP at factor cost
..	..	..	..	..	..	..	..	..	..	.	Agriculture
..	..	..	..	..	..	..	..	..	..	.	Industry
..	..	..	..	..	..	..	..	..	..	.	Services, etc.
..	..	..	-12,403	-16,600	-14,454	-15,046	-15,804	-17,342	-16,683	.	Resource balance
..	..	..	8,824	11,492	11,648	11,606	11,689	13,772	16,071	.	Exports GNFS
..	..	..	21,227	28,092	26,102	26,652	27,493	31,113	32,753	.	Imports GNFS
..	..	..	195,262	208,704	215,871	214,302	211,400	239,373	253,452	.	Domestic absorption
..	..	..	173,749	188,406	195,588	194,797	194,646	221,251	234,369	.	Total consumption, etc.
..	..	..	155,337	167,097	176,003	176,916	176,772	204,949	219,253	.	Private consumption, etc.
..	..	..	18,412	21,309	19,584	17,881	17,875	16,302	15,116	.	General government consumption
..	..	..	21,513	20,297	20,283	19,505	16,754	18,122	19,083	.	Gross domestic investment
..	..	..	21,513	20,297	20,283	19,505	16,754	18,122	19,083	.	Fixed domestic investment
..	..	..	..	..	..	..	..	..	..	.	Depreciation
											(millions of current Lao kip) **MPS ACCOUNTS, current prices**
											NMP produced:
..	..	..	..	..	..	..	..	..	..	.	Agriculture and forestry
..	..	..	..	..	..	..	..	..	..	.	Industry excluding construction
..	..	..	..	..	..	..	..	..	..	.	Construction
..	..	..	..	..	..	..	..	..	..	.	Transport and communication
..	..	..	..	..	..	..	..	..	..	.	Trade, etc.
..	..	..	..	..	..	..	..	..	..	.	Other services
..	..	..	..	..	..	..	..	..	..	.	Resource balance
..	..	..	..	..	..	..	..	..	..	.	NMP used: domestic market
..	..	..	..	..	..	..	..	..	..	.	Final consumption, material goods
..	..	..	..	..	..	..	..	..	..	.	Personal consumption
..	..	..	..	..	..	..	..	..	..	.	Collective consumption
..	..	..	..	..	..	..	..	..	..	.	Net capital formation
..	..	..	..	..	..	..	..	..	..	.	Net fixed capital formation
..	..	..	..	..	..	..	..	..	..	.	Changes in stocks
..	..	..	..	..	..	..	..	..	..	.	Depreciation
											(millions of 1986 Lao kip) **MPS ACCOUNTS, constant prices**
											NMP produced:
39,838	40,629	42,531	45,579	49,825	53,479	54,139	..	..	..	.	Agriculture and forestry
31,442	31,324	32,292	34,638	37,292	40,026	39,965	..	..	..	.	Agriculture and forestry
3,800	4,463	4,947	5,398	6,730	7,348	7,795	..	..	..	.	Industry and construction
4,596	4,842	5,292	5,543	5,803	6,105	6,379	..	..	..	.	Services
..	..	..	..	..	..	..	..	..	..	.	Resource balance
..	..	..	..	..	..	..	..	..	..	.	NMP used: domestic market
..	..	..	..	..	..	..	..	..	..	.	Final consumption, material goods
..	..	..	..	..	..	..	..	..	..	.	Personal consumption
..	..	..	..	..	..	..	..	..	..	.	Collective consumption
..	..	..	..	..	..	..	..	..	..	.	Net capital formation
..	..	..	..	..	..	..	..	..	..	.	Net fixed capital formation
..	..	..	..	..	..	..	..	..	..	.	Depreciation

Basic tables (continued)	1970	1971	1972	1973	1974	1975	1976	1977	1978	1979	1980
MPS ACCOUNTS, index					*(index, 1980 = 100)*						
NMP produced:	..	..	..	..	..	..	..	..	..	..	100.0
Agriculture and forestry	..	..	..	..	..	..	..	..	..	..	100.0
Industry excluding construction	..	..	..	..	..	..	..	..	..	..	..
Construction	..	..	..	..	..	..	..	..	..	..	..
Transport and communication	..	..	..	..	..	..	..	..	..	..	..
Trade, etc.	..	..	..	..	..	..	..	..	..	..	..
NMP used: material goods	..	..	..	..	..	..	..	..	..	..	..
Final consumption	..	..	..	..	..	..	..	..	..	..	..
Net capital formation	..	..	..	..	..	..	..	..	..	..	..
EXCHANGE AND CONVERSION RATES					*(LCUs per US dollar: annual average)*						
Single-year converter	0.120	0.120	0.248	0.300	0.300	0.360	1.626	2.520	4.199	5.714	10.218
Devisa/official	..	..	..	..	..	..	..	2.000	4.000	10.000	10.000
Commercial	..	..	..	..	..	0.350	1.190	1.190	3.000	4.000	10.000
Noncommercial	..	..	..	..	..	..	..	..	..	..	..
Informal market	0.292	0.303	0.393	0.465	0.478	1.266	8.250	16.600	22.580	19.375	17.938
ICP	..	..	..							..	..
					(ruble per US dollar: annual average)						
Commercial TR/$ cross	..	..	..	..	..	..	..	..	..	..	..
Uniform TR/$ cross	..	..	..	..	..	..	..	..	..	..	..
					(LCUs per ruble: annual average)						
Commercial	..	..	..	..	..	..	..	..	..	..	..
Noncommercial	..	..	..	..	..	..	..	..	..	..	..
Devisa/official	..	..	..	..	..	..	..	..	..	..	..
CONSUMER PRICE INDEXES					*(index)*						
Official, IMF 1985 = 100	..	..	..	..	..	..	..	..	..	..	..
Official, CIA or LWI 1980 = 100	..	..	..	..	..	..	..	..	..	..	..
Alternative, CIA or LWI 1980 = 100	..	..	..	..	..	..	..	..	..	..	..
INTERNATIONAL TRADE (ECE)					*(millions of current Lao kip)*						
Value of exports, fob	..	..	..	..	..	..	..	..	..	..	..
to CMEA	..	..	..	..	..	..	..	..	..	..	..
Value of imports, cif	..	..	..	..	..	..	..	..	..	..	..
from CMEA	..	..	..	..	..	..	..	..	..	..	..
Trade balance	..	..	..	..	..	..	..	..	..	..	..
CMEA	..	..	..	..	..	..	..	..	..	..	..
INTERNATIONAL TRADE (Authors')					*(millions of current US dollars)*						
Value of exports, fob	7	..	..	..	..	11	..	..	..	..	31
to developed countries	..	..	..	..	..	..	..	..	..	..	..
to other non-socialist countries	..	..	..	..	..	..	..	..	..	..	..
to socialist countries	..	..	..	..	..	..	..	..	..	..	..
to CMEA	..	..	..	..	..	..	..	..	..	..	..
Value of imports, cif	114	..	..	..	..	43	..	..	..	..	131
from developed countries	..	..	..	..	..	..	..	..	..	..	..
from other non-socialist countries	..	..	..	..	..	..	..	..	..	..	..
from socialist countries	..	..	..	..	..	..	..	..	..	..	..
from CMEA	..	..	..	..	..	..	..	..	..	..	..
Trade balance	-107	..	..	..	..	-32	..	..	..	..	-100
Developed countries	..	..	..	..	..	..	..	..	..	..	..
Other non-socialist countries	..	..	..	..	..	..	..	..	..	..	..
Socialist countries	..	..	..	..	..	..	..	..	..	..	..
CMEA	..	..	..	..	..	..	..	..	..	..	..
PARTNER CONVERTIBLE TRADE (ECE)					*(millions of current US dollars)*						
Exports to non-CMEA (cif)	..	..	..	..	..	..	..	..	..	..	..
Imports from non-CMEA (fob)	..	..	..	..	..	..	..	..	..	..	..
Trade balance	..	..	..	..	..	..	..	..	..	..	..
TRADE PRICE INDEXES (Authors')					*(index, 1980 = 100)*						
Terms of trade	..	..	..	..	..	..	..	..	..	..	..
Exports	..	..	..	..	..	..	..	..	..	..	..
Non-socialist countries	..	..	..	..	..	..	..	..	..	..	..
Developed countries	..	..	..	..	..	..	..	..	..	..	..
Other	..	..	..	..	..	..	..	..	..	..	..
Socialist countries	..	..	..	..	..	..	..	..	..	..	..
CMEA	..	..	..	..	..	..	..	..	..	..	..
Imports	..	..	..	..	..	..	..	..	..	..	..
Non-socialist countries	..	..	..	..	..	..	..	..	..	..	..
Developed countries	..	..	..	..	..	..	..	..	..	..	..
Other	..	..	..	..	..	..	..	..	..	..	..
Socialist countries	..	..	..	..	..	..	..	..	..	..	..
CMEA	..	..	..	..	..	..	..	..	..	..	..

Abbreviations in notes column are explained in the General Notes. For sources and methods, see the Technical Notes.

Lao PDR

1981	1982	1983	1984	1985	1986	1987	1988	1989	1990	Notes	Basic tables (continued)
				(index, 1980 = 100)							**MPS ACCOUNTS, index**
106.3	108.4	113.4	121.6	132.9	142.6	144.4	..	..	..	I	NMP produced:
106.8	106.4	109.7	117.7	126.7	136.0	135.8	..	..	..	I	Agriculture and forestry
..	..	..	..	..	..	..	..	..	..	.	Industry excluding construction
..	..	..	..	..	..	..	..	..	..	.	Construction
..	..	..	..	..	..	..	..	..	..	.	Transport and communication
..	..	..	..	..	..	..	..	..	..	.	Trade, etc.
..	..	..	..	..	..	..	..	..	..	.	NMP used: material goods
..	..	..	..	..	..	..	..	..	..	.	Final consumption
..	..	..	..	..	..	..	..	..	..	.	Net capital formation
				(LCUs per US dollar: annual average)							**EXCHANGE AND CONVERSION RATES**
20.000	35.000	35.000	35.000	45.000	95.000	175.117	392.012	583.015	708.570	.	Single-year converter
10.000	10.000	10.000	10.000	10.000	10.000	10.000	..	..	..	.	Devisa/official
20.000	35.000	35.000	35.000	95.000	95.000	350.000	450.000	689.000	..	.	Commercial
..	..	..	..	..	..	..	..	..	..	.	Noncommercial
33.917	51.063	113.166	..	..	..	..	..	..	..	.	Informal market
..	..	..	..	..	..	..	..	..	..	.	ICP
				(ruble per US dollar: annual average)							
..	..	..	..	..	..	..	..	..	..	.	Commercial TR/$ cross
..	..	..	..	..	..	..	..	..	..	.	Uniform TR/$ cross
				(LCUs per ruble: annual average)							
..	..	..	..	..	..	..	..	..	..	.	Commercial
..	..	..	..	..	..	..	..	..	..	.	Noncommercial
..	..	..	..	..	..	..	..	..	..	.	Devisa/official
				(index)							**CONSUMER PRICE INDEXES**
..	..	..	..	..	..	..	..	..	..	.	Official, IMF 1985 = 100
..	..	..	..	..	..	..	..	..	..	.	Official, CIA or LWI 1980 = 100
..	..	..	..	..	..	..	..	..	..	.	Alternative, CIA or LWI 1980 = 100
				(millions of current Lao kip)							**INTERNATIONAL TRADE (ECE)**
..	..	..	..	..	..	..	..	..	..	.	Value of exports, fob
..	..	..	..	..	..	..	..	..	..	.	to CMEA
..	..	..	..	..	..	..	..	..	..	.	Value of imports, cif
..	..	..	..	..	..	..	..	..	..	.	from CMEA
..	..	..	..	..	..	..	..	..	..	.	Trade balance
..	..	..	..	..	..	..	..	..	..	.	CMEA
				(millions of current US dollars)							**INTERNATIONAL TRADE (Authors')**
33	40	26	12	54	60	62	81	80	80	N	Value of exports, fob
..	..	..	..	..	..	..	..	..	..	.	to developed countries
..	..	..	..	..	..	..	..	..	..	.	to other non-socialist countries
..	..	..	..	..	..	..	..	..	..	.	to socialist countries
..	..	..	..	..	..	..	..	..	..	.	to CMEA
125	130	92	48	131	131	146	162	150	155	N	Value of imports, cif
..	..	..	..	..	..	..	..	..	..	.	from developed countries
..	..	..	..	..	..	..	..	..	..	.	from other non-socialist countries
..	..	..	..	..	..	..	..	..	..	.	from socialist countries
..	..	..	..	..	..	..	..	..	..	.	from CMEA
-92	-90	-66	-36	-77	-71	-84	-81	-70	-75	N	Trade balance
..	..	..	..	..	..	..	..	..	..	.	Developed countries
..	..	..	..	..	..	..	..	..	..	.	Other non-socialist countries
..	..	..	..	..	..	..	..	..	..	.	Socialist countries
..	..	..	..	..	..	..	..	..	..	.	CMEA
				(millions of current US dollars)							**PARTNER CONVERTIBLE TRADE (ECE)**
..	..	24	11	16	13	64	96	98	..	W	Exports to non-CMEA (cif)
..	..	80	36	51	56	83	111	122	..	W	Imports from non-CMEA (fob)
..	..	-56	-25	-35	-43	-18	-15	-24	..	W	Trade balance
				(index, 1980 = 100)							**TRADE PRICE INDEXES (Authors')**
..	..	..	..	..	..	..	..	..	..	.	Terms of trade
..	..	..	..	..	..	..	..	..	..	.	Exports
..	..	..	..	..	..	..	..	..	..	.	Non-socialist countries
..	..	..	..	..	..	..	..	..	..	.	Developed countries
..	..	..	..	..	..	..	..	..	..	.	Other
..	..	..	..	..	..	..	..	..	..	.	Socialist countries
..	..	..	..	..	..	..	..	..	..	.	CMEA
..	..	..	..	..	..	..	..	..	..	.	Imports
..	..	..	..	..	..	..	..	..	..	.	Non-socialist countries
..	..	..	..	..	..	..	..	..	..	.	Developed countries
..	..	..	..	..	..	..	..	..	..	.	Other
..	..	..	..	..	..	..	..	..	..	.	Socialist countries
..	..	..	..	..	..	..	..	..	..	.	CMEA

Lao PDR

Basic tables (continued)	1970	1971	1972	1973	1974	1975	1976	1977	1978	1979	1980
TRADE PRICE INDEXES (ECE)					*(index, 1980 = 100)*						
Terms of trade	..	..	..	..	..	..	..	..	..	..	..
Exports	..	..	..	..	..	..	..	..	..	..	..
Imports	..	..	..	..	..	..	..	..	..	..	..
Balance of Payments (ECE)					*(millions of current US dollars)*						
Exports, convertible currency	..	..	..	..	..	..	..	..	..	..	28
Imports, convertible currency	..	..	..	..	..	..	..	..	..	..	92
Trade balance, convertible currency	..	..	..	..	..	..	..	..	..	..	-64
Invisibles, convertible currency	..	..	..	..	..	..	..	..	..	..	-2
Current balance, convertible currency	..	..	..	..	..	..	..	..	..	..	-66
External debt, total (World Bank)	8	16	19	33	41	64	115	163	225	255	293
Convertible currency	8	16	19	33	41	44	55	72	104	104	112
CMEA	..	..	..	..	..	20	60	91	121	151	181
External debt service (World Bank)	2	2	3	5	6	6	6	7	10	13	2
Convertible currency	2	2	3	5	6	6	6	7	10	13	2
Total reserves less gold (IMF, IFS)	6	8	7	11	15	..	..	..	..	..	13
Total reserves, including gold at London price	6	8	7	11	15	..	..	..	..	..	13
Total reserves, incl. gold at national valuation	..	..	..	..	..	..	..	..	..	..	..
EMPLOYMENT					*(thousands)*						
Employment, total	..	..	..	..	..	..	..	..	..	..	..
Agriculture	..	..	..	..	..	..	..	..	..	..	..
Industry	..	..	..	..	..	..	..	..	..	..	..
Services	..	..	..	..	..	..	..	..	..	..	..
Labor force, total	1,610	1,640	1,670	1,700	1,730	1,760	1,776	1,792	1,808	1,823	1,839
Agriculture	1,270	1,289	1,307	1,325	1,343	1,361	1,368	1,374	1,380	1,386	1,393
Industry	84	89	94	98	103	108	113	117	121	126	130
Services	256	263	270	277	284	291	296	301	306	311	316
DOMESTIC FINANCE (IMF)					*(millions of current Lao kip)*						
Money supply, broadly defined	..	..	..	..	..	..	..	..	..	..	..
Money, means of payment	..	..	..	..	..	..	..	..	..	..	..
Demand deposits	..	..	..	..	..	..	..	..	..	..	..
Currency outside banks	..	..	..	..	..	..	..	..	..	..	..
Quasi-money	..	..	..	..	..	..	..	..	..	..	..
Interest: deposit rate (percent)	..	..	..	..	..	..	..	..	..	7	7
Central government expenditures	..	..	..	..	..	22	54	490	573	636	1,777
Defense	..	..	..	..	..	..	..	..	..	..	..
					(millions of 1989 US dollars)						
Central government exp. (ACDA)	..	..	..	..	..	..	..	..	..	277	..
Military (ACDA)	..	..	..	..	..	..	..	..	..	80	..
LAND AND FORESTS (FAO)											
Pop. density: agr. land (pop. per sq. km)	165	169	173	177	180	184	186	187	188	190	191
Deforestation rate (net)	-1	-1	-1	-1	-1	-1	-1	-1	-1	-1	-1
Forest (thousands sq. km)	147	146	145	144	143	142	141	140	139	138	137
SOCIAL INDICATORS											
Population density: total land (pop. per sq. km)	12	12	12	13	13	13	13	13	14	14	14
School enrollment ratio, primary	53	..	..	..	..	58	92	92	96	96	116
secondary	3	..	..	..	..	7	11	14	16	17	21
tertiary											1
Energy consumption per capita (kg. of oil eq.)	73	55	63	66	42	44	44	47	47	46	33
Daily calorie supply per capita	2,256	2,226	2,203	2,169	2,125	2,047	1,951	1,980	2,168	2,310	2,412
Food production (1979-1981=100)	89	83	81	82	81	78	66	71	76	89	102
Daily protein supply (gm. per capita)	61	60	59	58	56	54	51	52	58	62	65
Population per hospital bed	1,078	..	..	..	..	..	..	..	..	..	..
per nursing person	..	..	..	1,386	..	..	2,983	..	2,267	..	..
per physician	15,156	..	..	..	..	..	19,654	..	..	..	..
Female participation in labor force (percent)	50	50	49	49	48	48	48	47	47	47	47
Infant mortality (per 1,000 live births)	146	145	145	143	141	139	137	135	132	130	127
Life expectancy (years)	40	40	40	41	42	42	43	44	44	45	45
Total fertility (births per woman)	6	6	6	6	6	7	7	7	7	7	7
Urban population (percent of total population)	10	10	10	11	11	11	12	12	13	13	13
Population per passenger car	247	230	222	214	211	..	..	..	..	..	..
per telephone	..	..	..	..	..	..	..	..	..	..	..

Abbreviations in notes column are explained in the General Notes. For sources and methods, see the Technical Notes.

1981	1982	1983	1984	1985	1986	1987	1988	1989	1990	Notes	Basic tables (continued)
				(index, 1980 = 100)							**TRADE PRICE INDEXES (ECE)**
..	..	..	..	..	..	..	..	..	..	.	Terms of trade
..	..	..	..	..	..	..	..	..	..	.	Exports
..	..	..	..	..	..	..	..	..	..	.	Imports
				(millions of current US dollars)							**Balance of Payments (ECE)**
23	40	41	44	54	53	49	52	..	..	.	Exports, convertible currency
110	132	150	162	193	206	219	240		..	.	Imports, convertible currency
-86	-92	-109	-118	-140	-153	-170	-187	..	..	.	Trade balance, convertible currency
17	24	13	35	46	45	47	51	..	..	.	Invisibles, convertible currency
-69	-68	-96	-83	-94	-107	-123	-137	..	..	.	Current balance, convertible currency
321	355	391	434	476	597	726	824	947	1,060	.	External debt, total (World Bank)
110	112	113	115	135	165	190	193	252	334	.	Convertible currency
212	243	278	319	342	432	536	631	695	726	.	CMEA
2	4	3	6	9	10	13	13	13	11	f	External debt service (World Bank)
2	2	3	4	5	9	11	12	12	10	.	Convertible currency
13	8	19	11	25	32	21	16	16	61	.	Total reserves less gold (IMF, IFS)
13	8	19	11	25	32	21	16	16	61	.	Total reserves, including gold at London price
..	..	..	11	26	33	21	17	17	62	.	Total reserves, incl. gold at national valuation
				(thousands)							**EMPLOYMENT**
..	..	..	..	..	..	..	..	..	..	.	Employment, total
..	..	..	..	..	..	..	..	..	..	.	Agriculture
..	..	..	..	..	..	..	..	..	..	.	Industry
..	..	..	..	..	..	..	..	..	..	.	Services
1,874	1,909	1,944	1,979	2,014	2,059	2,104	2,149	2,194	2,239	.	Labor force, total
..	..	..	..	..	..	..	..	..	..	.	Agriculture
..	..	..	..	..	..	..	..	..	..	.	Industry
..	..	..	..	..	..	..	..	..	..	.	Services
				(millions of current Lao kip)							**DOMESTIC FINANCE (IMF)**
..	..	..	..	2,280	3,876	15,842	21,715	41,114	..	.	Money supply, broadly defined
785	1,205	1,668	1,655	2,226	3,881	6,904	12,102	25,127	..	.	Money, means of payment
616	969	1,348	1,205	1,591	2,834	4,797	8,616	8,285	..	.	Demand deposits
169	236	320	450	635	1,047	2,107	3,486	16,842	..	.	Currency outside banks
..	..	..	..	54	95	8,954	10,119	15,987	..	.	Quasi-money
7	7	7	7	10	10	10	14	..	..	.	Interest: deposit rate (percent)
1,956	5,475	6,696	8,385	20,806	27,615	28,675	79,350	123,021	..	.	Central government expenditures
..	..	..	..	..	..	..	..	..	..	.	Defense
				(millions of 1989 US dollars)							
..	..	..	302	..	..	..	302	..	..	.	Central government exp. (ACDA)
..	..	..	64	63	..	..	..	..	..	.	Military (ACDA)
											LAND AND FORESTS (FAO)
194	197	202	207	211	218	224	..	..	..	.	Pop. density: agr. land (pop. per sq. km)
-1	-1	-1	-1	-1	-1	..	..	..	..	.	Deforestation rate (net)
136	135	134	133	132	131	..	..	..	..	.	Forest (thousands sq. km)
											SOCIAL INDICATORS
14	14	15	15	16	16	17	..	..	..	.	Population density: total land (pop. per sq. km)
..	109	108	107	111	..	110	..	..	..	.	School enrollment ratio, primary
..	22	23	23	23	..	27	..	..	..	.	secondary
1	1	2	2	2	2	..	..	..	..	.	tertiary
44	47	44	37	40	37	37	..	..	..	.	Energy consumption per capita (kg. of oil eq.)
2,486	2,489	2,532	2,577	2,608	2,590	2,616	2,637	..	..	.	Daily calorie supply per capita
109	106	107	118	122	123	112	102	118	123	.	Food production (1979-1981 = 100)
66	67	68	69	70	70	71	71	..	..	.	Daily protein supply (gm. per capita)
..	..	..	..	..	..	..	..	..	..	.	Population per hospital bed
..	..	..	..	532	..	..	..	..	..	.	per nursing person
..	..	..	..	1,362	..	..	..	..	..	.	per physician
46	46	45	45	45	44	44	44	43	43	.	Female participation in labor force (percent)
125	122	120	117	115	112	110	108	105	103	.	Infant mortality (per 1,000 live births)
46	46	47	47	48	48	49	49	49	50	.	Life expectancy (years)
7	7	7	7	7	7	7	7	7	7	.	Total fertility (births per woman)
14	14	15	15	16	16	17	18	18	19	.	Urban population (percent of total population)
..	..	..	..	..	..	..	..	..	..	.	Population per passenger car
..	..	..	426	..	..	..	..	..	..	.	per telephone

Comparator tables	1970	1971	1972	1973	1974	1975	1976	1977	1978	1979	1980
PER CAPITA INCOME					*(US dollars)*						
Authors' series	..	..	..	..	..	..	..	..	..	..	..
Single year conversion	..	..	..	..	..	..	..	..	..	..	1,431
CIA or LWI	..	..	..	..	..	..	..	..	..	..	..
Penn World Tables	..	..	..	..	..	..	..	..	..	..	..
POPULATION					*(thousands)*						
	1,256	1,287	1,317	1,346	1,378	1,412	1,449	1,488	1,530	1,573	1,619
GROSS NATIONAL PRODUCT, current prices					*(millions of current US dollars)*						
World Bank (Atlas method)	..	..	..	..	..	..	..	..	..	..	..
Single year conversion	..	..	..	..	..	..	..	..	..	..	2,318
Authors' series	..	..	..	..	..	..	..	..	..	..	..
CIA or LWI	..	..	..	..	..	..	..	..	..	..	..
GROSS NATIONAL PRODUCT, constant prices					*(millions of constant 1987 dollars)*						
Single year conversion	..	..	..	..	..	..	..	..	..	..	2,135
Authors' series, rescaled from 1980 prices	..	..	..	..	..	..	..	..	..	..	..
CIA or LWI, rescaled from 1989 prices	..	..	..	..	..	..	..	..	..	..	..
CONVERSION FACTORS					*(LCUs per US dollar)*						
World Bank (Atlas method)	..	..	..	..	..	..	..	..	..	..	..
Single year convertor	4.00	..	..	..	..	3.19	..	..	..	..	2.90
Authors' series	..	..	..	..	..	..	..	..	..	..	..
Penn World Tables	..	..	..	..	..	..	..	..	..	..	..
OUTPUT TRENDS, OVERALL					*(index, constant prices 1987 = 100)*						
GNP, SNA	..	..	..	..	..	..	..	..	..	..	..
NMP, MPS	..	..	..	..	..	..	..	..	..	..	66.8
GNP, "Building block"	..	..	..	..	..	..	..	..	..	..	..
Industry											
Value added, SNA	..	..	..	..	..	..	..	..	..	..	..
Value added, MPS	..	..	..	..	..	..	..	..	..	..	63.6
"Building block"	..	..	..	..	..	..	..	..	..	..	..
Gross output, SNA	..	..	..	..	..	..	..	..	..	..	..
Agriculture											
Value added, SNA	..	..	..	..	..	..	..	..	..	..	..
Value added, MPS	..	..	..	..	..	..	..	..	..	..	75.2
"Building block"	..	..	..	..	..	..	..	..	..	..	..
Gross output, SNA	..	..	..	..	..	..	..	..	..	..	..
Services											
Value added, SNA	..	..	..	..	..	..	..	..	..	..	..
Value added, MPS	..	..	..	..	..	..	..	..	..	..	66.2
"Building block"	..	..	..	..	..	..	..	..	..	..	..
CONSUMPTION											
Total consumption, SNA	..	..	..	..	..	..	..	..	..	..	..
Total consumption, MPS	..	..	..	..	..	..	..	..	..	..	66.7
Households, SNA	..	..	..	..	..	..	..	..	..	..	..
Households, "building block"	..	..	..	..	..	..	..	..	..	..	..
General government, SNA	..	..	..	..	..	..	..	..	..	..	..
General government, "building block"	..	..	..	..	..	..	..	..	..	..	..
INVESTMENT											
Gross fixed investment, SNA	..	..	..	..	..	..	..	..	..	..	..
Accumulation, MPS	..	..	..	..	..	..	..	..	..	..	72.5
"Building block"	..	..	..	..	..	..	..	..	..	..	..
CONSUMER PRICES											
National methodology	..	..	..	..	..	..	..	..	..	..	..
Outside estimate	..	..	..	..	..	..	..	..	..	..	..
MERCHANDISE EXPORTS					*(millions of current US dollars)*						
UNCTAD	..	..	..	..	..	213	..	..	..	..	403
IMF: IFS	..	..	..	..	..	..	..	..	..	..	..
ACDA	..	..	..	..	..	..	..	..	..	..	..
ECE	..	..	..	..	..	..	..	..	..	..	..
intra-CMEA	..	..	..	..	..	..	..	..	..	..	..
Authors' uniform TR/$ series	..	..	..	..	..	..	..	..	..	..	413
intra-CMEA	..	..	..	..	..	..	..	..	..	..	..
MERCHANDISE IMPORTS					*(millions of current US dollars)*						
UNCTAD	121	..	..	..	..	266	..	..	..	..	566
IMF: IFS	..	..	..	..	..	..	..	..	..	..	..
ACDA	..	..	..	..	..	..	..	..	..	..	..
ECE	..	..	..	..	..	..	..	..	..	..	..
intra-CMEA	..	..	..	..	..	..	..	..	..	..	..
Authors' uniform series	..	..	..	..	..	..	..	..	..	..	562
intra-CMEA	..	..	..	..	..	..	..	..	..	..	..

Abbreviations in notes column are explained in the General Notes. For sources and methods, see the Technical Notes.

1981	1982	1983	1984	1985	1986	1987	1988	1989	1990	Notes	*Comparator tables (continued)*
				(US dollars)							**PER CAPITA INCOME**
..	1,610	1,580	1,550	1,500	1,540	1,620	1,750	1,820	..	.	Authors' series
1,395	1,474	1,502	1,398	1,355	1,535	1,712	1,764	1,719	..	.	Single year conversion
..	..	..	..	..	..	..	..	..	..	.	CIA or LWI
..	..	..	..	..	..	..	..	..	..	.	Penn World Tables
				(thousands)							**POPULATION**
1,666	1,714	1,762	1,810	1,856	1,907	1,960	2,014	2,070	2,124	.	
			(millions of current US dollars)								**GROSS NATIONAL PRODUCT, current prices**
..	..	..	..	..	..	..	..	..	..	.	World Bank (Atlas method)
2,324	2,526	2,646	2,530	2,514	2,927	3,356	3,552	3,558	..	.	Single year conversion
	2,760	2,778	2,810	2,785	2,930	3,169	3,531	3,775	..	.	Authors' series
..	..	..	..	..	..	..	..	..	..	.	CIA or LWI
			(millions of constant 1987 dollars)								**GROSS NATIONAL PRODUCT, constant prices**
2,319	2,500	2,644	2,799	2,958	3,217	3,356	3,518	3,661	..	.	Single year conversion
..	..	..	..	..	..	..	..	..	..	.	Authors' series, rescaled from 1980 prices
..	..	..	..	..	..	..	..	..	..	.	CIA or LWI, rescaled from 1989 prices
			(LCUs per US dollar)								**CONVERSION FACTORS**
..	..	..	..	..	..	..	..	..	..	.	World Bank (Atlas method)
3.19	3.24	3.30	3.54	3.71	3.18	2.89	2.89	3.00	..	f	Single year convertor
..	..	..	..	..	..	..	..	..	..	.	Authors' series
..	..	..	..	..	..	..	..	..	..	.	Penn World Tables
			(index, constant prices 1987 = 100)								**OUTPUT TRENDS, OVERALL**
..	..	..	..	..	..	..	..	..	..	.	GNP, SNA
72.5	78.6	83.3	87.0	91.7	96.8	100.0	104.2	114.4	..	.	NMP, MPS
..	..	..	..	..	..	..	..	..	..	.	GNP, "Building block"
											Industry
..	..	..	..	..	..	..	..	..	..	.	Value added, SNA
68.2	74.4	80.9	87.4	91.9	95.1	100.0	105.1	116.7	..	.	Value added, MPS
..	..	..	..	..	..	..	..	..	..	.	"Building block"
..	..	..	..	..	..	..	..	..	..	.	Gross output, SNA
											Agriculture
..	..	..	..	..	..	..	..	..	..	.	Value added, SNA
88.7	100.8	100.8	92.5	100.8	106.8	100.0	102.3	116.5	..	.	Value added, MPS
..	..	..	..	..	..	..	..	..	..	.	"Building block"
..	..	..	..	..	..	..	..	..	..	.	Gross output, SNA
											Services
..	..	..	..	..	..	..	..	..	..	.	Value added, SNA
71.6	75.1	80.0	84.1	87.1	93.8	100.0	104.2	111.0	..	.	Value added, MPS
..	..	..	..	..	..	..	..	..	..	.	"Building block"
											CONSUMPTION
..	..	..	..	..	82.1	100.0	108.9	115.2	124.4	.	Total consumption, SNA
72.7	77.3	81.3	85.3	89.3	97.3	100.0	104.7	108.7	..	V	Total consumption, MPS
..	..	..	..	..	76.5	100.0	111.0	119.7	131.4	.	Households, SNA
..	..	..	..	..	..	..	..	..	..	.	Households, "building block"
..	..	..	..	..	95.3	100.0	103.8	104.5	107.5	.	General government, SNA
..	..	..	..	..	..	..	..	..	..	.	General government, "building block"
											INVESTMENT
..	..	..	..	..	129.7	100.0	94.7	78.8	60.5	YE	Gross fixed investment, SNA
100.7	100.7	107.2	100.0	114.5	113.8	100.0	94.2	99.3	..	YV	Accumulation, MPS
..	..	..	..	..	..	..	..	..	..	.	"Building block"
											CONSUMER PRICES
..	..	..	..	..	..	..	..	..	..	.	National methodology
..	..	..	..	..	..	..	..	..	..	.	Outside estimate
			(millions of current US dollars)								**MERCHANDISE EXPORTS**
455	422	580	595	607	710	780	820	..	..	.	UNCTAD
..	..	..	..	..	..	..	..	..	..	.	IMF: IFS
..	..	..	..	388	..	..	..	..	..	.	ACDA
..	..	..	..	..	..	..	..	..	..	.	ECE
..	..	..	..	..	..	..	..	..	..	.	intra-CMEA
437	516	550	569	553	670	739	761	716	..	f	Authors' uniform TR/$ series
..	..	..	..	..	..	..	..	..	..	.	intra-CMEA
			(millions of current US dollars)								**MERCHANDISE IMPORTS**
655	..	..	..	..	..	..	..	..	..	M	UNCTAD
..	..	..	..	..	..	..	..	..	..	.	IMF: IFS
..	..	..	..	1,000	..	..	..	..	..	.	ACDA
..	..	..	..	..	..	..	..	..	..	.	ECE
..	..	..	..	..	..	..	..	..	..	.	intra-CMEA
656	726	837	820	878	1,066	1,137	1,146	956	..	f	Authors' uniform series
..	..	..	..	..	..	..	..	..	..	.	intra-CMEA

Mongolia

Basic tables	1970	1971	1972	1973	1974	1975	1976	1977	1978	1979	1980
SNA ACCOUNTS, current prices			*(millions of current Mongolian tughriks)*								
GNP, at market prices	..	..	..	..	..	..	..	..	..	..	5,718
Net factor income											-1,037
GDP at market prices	..	..	..	..	..	..	..	..	..	..	6,755
Net indirect taxes											..
GDP at factor cost	..	..	..	..	..	..	..	..	..	..	..
Agriculture	..	..	..	..	..	..	..	..	..	..	..
Industry	..	..	..	..	..	..	..	..	..	..	..
Services, etc.	..	..	..	..	..	..	..	..	..	..	..
Resource balance	..	..	..	..	..	..	..	..	..	..	-1,324
Exports GNFS											1,285
Imports GNFS											2,609
Domestic absorption	..	..	..	..	..	..	..	..	..	..	8,079
Total consumption											4,956
Private consumption	..	..	..	..	..	..	..	..	..	..	..
General government consumption	..	..	..	..	..	..	..	..	..	..	..
Gross domestic investment	..	..	..	..	..	..	..	..	..	..	3,123
Fixed domestic investment											3,104
Depreciation	..	..	..	..	..	..	..	..	..	..	..
SNA ACCOUNTS, constant prices			*(millions of constant 1987 Mongolian tughriks)*								
Gross national product (GNP)	..	..	..	..	..	..	..	..	..	..	..
GDP at market prices	..	..	..	..	..	..	..	..	..	..	6,235
GDP at factor cost											
Agriculture	..	..	..	..	..	..	..	..	..	..	..
Industry	..	..	..	..	..	..	..	..	..	..	..
Services, etc.	..	..	..	..	..	..	..	..	..	..	..
Resource balance	..	..	..	..	..	..	..	..	..	..	-2,518
Exports GNFS	..	..	..	..	..	..	..	..	..	..	1,786
Imports GNFS	..	..	..	..	..	..	..	..	..	..	4,304
Domestic absorption	..	..	..	..	..	..	..	..	..	..	8,753
Total consumption, etc.	..	..	..	..	..	..	..	..	..	..	..
Private consumption, etc.	..	..	..	..	..	..	..	..	..	..	..
General government consumption	..	..	..	..	..	..	..	..	..	..	..
Gross domestic investment	..	..	..	..	..	..	..	..	..	..	..
Fixed domestic investment	..	..	..	..	..	..	..	..	..	..	..
Depreciation	..	..	..	..	..	..	..	..	..	..	..
MPS ACCOUNTS, current prices			*(millions of current Mongolian tughriks)*								
NMP produced:	..	..	..	..	..	..	..	..	..	..	5,577
Agriculture and forestry	..	..	..	..	..	..	..	..	..	..	838
Industry excluding construction	..	..	..	..	..	..	..	..	..	..	1,635
Construction	..	..	..	..	..	..	..	..	..	..	342
Transport and communication	..	..	..	..	..	..	..	..	..	..	624
Trade, etc.	..	..	..	..	..	..	..	..	..	..	2,025
Other services	..	..	..	..	..	..	..	..	..	..	113
Resource balance	..	..	..	..	..	..	..	..	..	..	-1,830
NMP used: domestic market	..	..	..	..	..	..	..	..	..	..	7,407
Final consumption, material goods	..	..	..	..	..	..	..	..	..	..	4,629
Personal consumption	..	..	..	..	..	..	..	..	..	..	3,501
Collective consumption	..	..	..	..	..	..	..	..	..	..	1,129
Net capital formation	..	..	..	..	..	..	..	..	..	..	2,778
Net fixed capital formation	..	..	..	..	..	..	..	..	..	..	2,883
Changes in stocks	..	..	..	..	..	..	..	..	..	..	-105
Depreciation	..	..	..	..	..	..	..	..	..	..	..
MPS ACCOUNTS, constant prices			*(millions of 1986 Mongolian tughriks)*								
NMP produced:	..	..	..	..	..	..	..	..	..	..	5,006
Agriculture and forestry	..	..	..	..	..	..	..	..	..	..	1,071
Industry and construction	..	..	..	..	..	..	..	..	..	..	1,917
Services	..	..	..	..	..	..	..	..	..	..	2,018
Resource balance	..	..	..	..	..	..	..	..	..	..	..
NMP used: domestic market	..	..	..	..	..	..	..	..	..	..	..
Final consumption, material goods	..	..	..	..	..	..	..	..	..	..	..
Personal consumption	..	..	..	..	..	..	..	..	..	..	..
Collective consumption	..	..	..	..	..	..	..	..	..	..	..
Net capital formation	..	..	..	..	..	..	..	..	..	..	..
Net fixed capital formation	..	..	..	..	..	..	..	..	..	..	..
Depreciation	..	..	..	..	..	..	..	..	..	..	..

Abbreviations in notes column are explained in the General Notes. For sources and methods, see the Technical Notes.

1981	1982	1983	1984	1985	1986	1987	1988	1989	1990	Notes	Basic tables (continued)
				(millions of current Mongolian tughriks)							**SNA ACCOUNTS, current prices**
6,352	7,106	7,631	7,827	8,155	8,052	8,351	9,013	9,545	9,295	.	GNP, at market prices
-1,074	-1,099	-1,132	-1,168	-1,217	-1,258	-1,359	-1,288	-1,186	-1,219	.	Net factor income
7,426	8,205	8,762	8,996	9,372	9,310	9,710	10,301	10,731	10,514	.	GDP at market prices
..	..	..	2,142	2,172	1,679	1,664	1,630	1,763	1,518	.	Net indirect taxes
..	..	..	6,854	7,200	7,361	8,045	8,671	8,968	8,997	.	GDP at factor cost
..	..	..	1,362	1,354	1,664	1,569	1,683	1,832	1,820	.	Agriculture
..	..	..	2,578	2,767	2,975	3,246	3,483	3,681	3,550	.	Industry
..	..	..	2,915	3,079	2,993	3,231	3,505	3,456	3,627	.	Services, etc.
-2,540	-2,676	-2,619	-2,481	-2,851	-3,367	-2,829	-2,886	-3,551	-2,819	.	Resource balance
1,520	1,840	2,023	2,300	2,369	2,624	2,618	2,669	2,497	2,410	.	Exports GNFS
4,059	4,516	4,642	4,781	5,219	5,990	5,447	5,555	6,048	5,230	.	Imports GNFS
9,965	10,881	11,381	11,477	12,222	12,677	12,539	13,187	14,282	13,333	.	Domestic absorption
5,360	5,688	6,883	6,915	6,749	6,493	8,102	8,852	9,341	10,191	.	Total consumption
..	..	..	5,046	4,788	4,221	5,718	6,378	6,849	7,629	.	Private consumption
..	..	..	1,869	1,961	2,273	2,384	2,475	2,492	2,562	.	General government consumption
4,606	5,193	4,499	4,562	5,474	6,184	4,437	4,335	4,941	3,142	.	Gross domestic investment
4,289	4,646	3,924	4,282	4,634	4,763	4,552	4,538	4,807	3,380	.	Fixed domestic investment
..	..	..	..	..	..	..	..	..	..	.	Depreciation
				(millions of constant 1987 Mongolian tughriks)							**SNA ACCOUNTS, constant prices**
..	..	..	..	..	..	..	..	..	9,295	.	Gross national product (GNP)
6,757	7,324	7,741	8,199	8,581	9,291	9,710	10,206	10,632	10,599	.	GDP at market prices
..	..	..	..	..	..	..	..	..	..	.	GDP at factor cost
..	..	..	..	..	..	..	..	..	..	.	Agriculture
..	..	..	..	..	..	..	..	..	..	.	Industry
..	..	..	..	..	..	..	..	..	..	.	Services, etc.
-3,202	-2,875	-3,279	-2,832	-3,474	-3,113	-2,829	-2,819	-2,198	-2,160	.	Resource balance
1,956	2,146	2,443	2,535	2,439	2,711	2,618	2,572	2,423	2,186	.	Exports GNFS
5,158	5,020	5,722	5,368	5,913	5,824	5,447	5,391	4,621	4,346	.	Imports GNFS
9,958	10,199	11,020	11,032	12,055	12,404	12,539	13,024	12,830	12,759	.	Domestic absorption
..	..	..	6,650	6,879	6,648	8,102	8,823	9,335	10,077	.	Total consumption, etc.
..	..	..	4,894	4,926	4,376	5,718	6,348	6,843	7,514	.	Private consumption, etc.
..	..	..	1,756	1,953	2,273	2,384	2,475	2,492	2,562	.	General government consumption
..	..	..	4,319	5,193	5,755	4,437	4,202	3,495	2,683	.	Gross domestic investment
..	..	..	..	..	..	..	..	..	..	.	Fixed domestic investment
..	..	..	..	..	..	..	..	..	..	.	Depreciation
				(millions of current Mongolian tughriks)							**MPS ACCOUNTS, current prices**
6,151	6,826	7,325	7,378	7,637	7,248	7,479	7,890	8,646	8,320	f	NMP produced:
1,008	1,220	1,320	1,250	1,238	1,521	1,406	1,510	1,723	1,687	.	Agriculture and forestry
1,807	2,111	2,358	2,384	2,493	2,443	2,520	2,639	2,920	2,915	.	Industry excluding construction
342	346	353	368	382	423	504	563	617	454	.	Construction
669	718	767	813	880	845	861	906	904	841	.	Transport and communication
2,211	2,308	2,400	2,436	2,516	1,865	2,036	2,130	2,327	2,281	f	Trade, etc.
114	124	127	127	127	151	153	142	155	141	.	Other services
-2,648	-2,318	-2,304	-2,351	-2,890	-3,570	-2,957	-2,838	-2,591	..	.	Resource balance
8,798	9,144	9,630	9,729	10,526	10,817	10,436	10,728	11,237	..	.	NMP used: domestic market
5,036	5,302	5,611	5,895	6,169	6,547	6,841	7,215	7,523	..	.	Final consumption, material goods
3,647	3,856	4,068	4,263	4,430	4,619	4,844	5,067	5,348	..	.	Personal consumption
1,389	1,446	1,543	1,632	1,740	1,929	1,997	2,148	2,175	..	.	Collective consumption
3,763	3,841	4,018	3,834	4,357	4,270	3,595	3,513	3,714	..	.	Net capital formation
2,358	2,643	2,544	4,299	4,759	2,506	3,213	2,825	3,196	..	.	Net fixed capital formation
1,404	1,199	1,474	-464	-402	1,764	381	688	519	..	.	Changes in stocks
..	..	..	..	..	..	..	..	..	..	.	Depreciation
				(millions of 1986 Mongolian tughriks)							**MPS ACCOUNTS, constant prices**
5,427	5,886	6,242	6,516	6,866	7,248	7,489	7,802	8,565	..	.	NMP produced:
1,186	1,353	1,365	1,314	1,437	1,521	1,424	1,457	1,659	..	.	Agriculture and forestry
2,057	2,244	2,438	2,635	2,772	2,866	3,015	3,168	3,520	..	.	Industry and construction
2,185	2,289	2,439	2,566	2,657	2,861	3,050	3,178	3,386	..	.	Services
..	..	..	..	..	..	..	..	..	..	.	Resource balance
..	..	..	..	..	..	..	..	..	..	.	NMP used: domestic market
..	..	..	..	..	..	..	..	..	..	.	Final consumption, material goods
..	..	..	..	..	..	..	..	..	..	.	Personal consumption
..	..	..	..	..	..	..	..	..	..	.	Collective consumption
..	..	..	..	..	..	..	..	..	..	.	Net capital formation
..	..	..	..	..	..	..	..	..	..	.	Net fixed capital formation
..	..	..	..	..	..	..	..	..	..	.	Depreciation

Basic tables (continued)	1970	1971	1972	1973	1974	1975	1976	1977	1978	1979	1980
MPS ACCOUNTS, index						*(index,1980 = 100)*					
NMP produced:	..	..	..	..	..	..	..	..	..	..	100.0
Agriculture and forestry	..	..	..	..	..	..	..	..	..	..	100.0
Industry excluding construction	..	..	..	..	..	..	..	..	..	..	100.0
Construction	..	..	..	..	..	..	..	..	..	..	100.0
Transport and communication	..	..	..	..	..	..	..	..	..	..	100.0
Trade, etc.	..	..	..	..	..	..	..	..	..	..	100.0
NMP used: material goods	..	..	..	..	..	..	..	..	..	..	100.0
Final consumption	..	..	..	..	..	..	..	..	..	..	100.0
Net capital formation	..	..	..	..	..	..	..	..	..	..	100.0
EXCHANGE AND CONVERSION RATES						*(LCUs per US dollar: annual average)*					
Single-year converter	4.000	..	..	..	..	3.190	..	..	..	..	2.900
Devisa/official	..	..	..	..	..	..	..	..	..	..	
Commercial	4.000	..	..	..	..	3.190	..	..	..	..	2.900
Noncommercial	..	..	..	..	..	..	..	..	..	..	..
Informal market	..	..	..	..	..	..	..	..	..	..	
ICP	..	..	..	..	..	..	..	..	..	..	
						(ruble per US dollar: annual average)					
Commercial TR/$ cross	..	..	..	..	..	0.719	..	..	..	..	0.653
Uniform TR/$ cross	1.072	1.157	1.232	1.093	1.092	1.167	1.067	1.022	0.973	0.945	0.980
						(LCUs per ruble: annual average)					
Commercial	4.440	..	..	..	..	4.440	..	..	..	..	4.440
Noncommercial	9.610	..	..	..	..	9.610	..	..	..	..	7.110
Devisa/official	..	..	..	..	..	..	..	..	..	..	
CONSUMER PRICE INDEXES						*(index)*					
Official, IMF 1985 = 100	..	..	..	..	..	..	..	..	97.0	..	97.1
Official, CIA or LWI 1980 = 100	..	..	..	..	..	..	..	..	..	..	
Alternative, CIA or LWI 1980 = 100	..	..	..	..	..	..	..	..	..	..	
INTERNATIONAL TRADE (ECE)						*(millions of current Mongolian tughriks)*					
Value of exports, fob	..	..	..	..	..	..	..	..	..	..	1,198
to CMEA	..	..	..	..	..	..	..	..	..	..	
Value of imports, cif	..	..	..	..	..	..	..	..	..	..	1,630
from CMEA	..	..	..	..	..	..	..	..	..	..	
Trade balance	..	..	..	..	..	..	..	..	..	..	-431
CMEA	..	..	..	..	..	..	..	..	..	..	
INTERNATIONAL TRADE (Authors')						*(millions of current US dollars)*					
Value of exports, fob	..	..	..	..	..	..	..	..	..	..	413
to developed countries	..	..	..	..	..	..	..	..	..	..	
to other non-socialist countries	..	..	..	..	..	..	..	..	..	..	
to socialist countries	..	..	..	..	..	..	..	..	..	..	
to CMEA	..	..	..	..	..	..	..	..	..	..	..
Value of imports, cif	..	..	..	..	..	..	..	..	..	..	562
from developed countries	..	..	..	..	..	..	..	..	..	..	
from other non-socialist countries	..	..	..	..	..	..	..	..	..	..	
from socialist countries	..	..	..	..	..	..	..	..	..	..	
from CMEA	..	..	..	..	..	..	..	..	..	..	
Trade balance	..	..	..	..	..	..	..	..	..	..	-149
Developed countries	..	..	..	..	..	..	..	..	..	..	
Other non-socialist countries	..	..	..	..	..	..	..	..	..	..	
Socialist countries	..	..	..	..	..	..	..	..	..	..	
CMEA	..	..	..	..	..	..	..	..	..	..	
PARTNER CONVERTIBLE TRADE (ECE)						*(millions of current US dollars)*					
Exports to non-CMEA (cif)	..	..	..	..	..	..	..	..	..	..	..
Imports from non-CMEA (fob)	..	..	..	..	..	..	..	..	..	..	..
Trade balance	..	..	..	..	..	..	..	..	..	..	..
TRADE PRICE INDEXES (Authors')						*(index,1980 = 100)*					
Terms of trade	..	..	..	..	..	..	..	..	..	..	
Exports	..	..	..	..	..	..	..	..	..	..	
Non-socialist countries	..	..	..	..	..	..	..	..	..	..	
Developed countries	..	..	..	..	..	..	..	..	..	..	
Other	..	..	..	..	..	..	..	..	..	..	
Socialist countries	..	..	..	..	..	..	..	..	..	..	
CMEA	..	..	..	..	..	..	..	..	..	..	
Imports	..	..	..	..	..	..	..	..	..	..	
Non-socialist countries	..	..	..	..	..	..	..	..	..	..	
Developed countries	..	..	..	..	..	..	..	..	..	..	
Other	..	..	..	..	..	..	..	..	..	..	
Socialist countries	..	..	..	..	..	..	..	..	..	..	
CMEA	..	..	..	..	..	..	..	..	..	..	

Abbreviations in notes column are explained in the General Notes. For sources and methods, see the Technical Notes.

1981	1982	1983	1984	1985	1986	1987	1988	1989	1990	Notes	Basic tables (continued)
				(index, 1980 = 100)							**MPS ACCOUNTS, index**
108.0	118.0	125.0	130.0	137.0	145.0	150.0	156.0	171.0	..	V	NMP produced:
118.0	134.0	134.0	123.0	134.0	142.0	133.0	136.0	155.0	..	.	Agriculture and forestry
109.0	121.0	132.0	144.0	152.0	155.0	159.0	162.0	184.0	..	.	Industry excluding construction
100.0	101.0	103.0	107.0	112.0	124.0	147.0	180.0	180.0	..	.	Construction
107.0	115.0	123.0	130.0	141.0	159.0	162.0	170.0	170.0	..	.	Transport and communication
107.0	112.0	117.0	122.0	125.0	132.0	144.0	156.0	171.0	..	.	Trade, etc.
120.0	125.0	131.0	132.0	143.0	150.0	146.0	147.0	153.0	..	V	NMP used: material goods
109.0	116.0	122.0	128.0	134.0	146.0	150.0	157.0	163.0	..	V	Final consumption
139.0	139.0	148.0	138.0	158.0	157.0	138.0	130.0	137.0	..	V	Net capital formation
				(LCUs per US dollar: annual average)							**EXCHANGE AND CONVERSION RATES**
3.190	3.240	3.300	3.540	3.710	3.180	2.890	2.890	3.000	..	f	Single-year converter
..	..	..	..	..	..	..	..	..	..	.	Devisa/official
3.190	3.240	3.300	3.540	3.710	3.180	2.890	2.890	3.000	5.630	f	Commercial
..	..	..	..	..	..	..	20.000	20.000	..	f	Noncommercial
..	..	..	..	..	..	..	..	..	..	.	Informal market
..	..	..	..	..	..	..	..	..	..	.	ICP
				(ruble per US dollar: annual average)							
0.719	0.730	0.743	0.797	0.836	0.716	0.651	0.651	0.676	..	f	Commercial TR/$ cross
1.076	1.105	1.201	1.395	1.433	1.388	1.397	1.484	1.660	1.980	.	Uniform TR/$ cross
				(LCUs per ruble: annual average)							
4.440	4.440	4.440	4.440	4.440	4.440	4.440	4.440	4.440	..	f	Commercial
7.110	7.110	7.110	7.110	7.110	6.690	6.690	6.690	6.690	..	f	Noncommercial
..	..	..	..	..	..	..	..	..	..	.	Devisa/official
				(index)							**CONSUMER PRICE INDEXES**
97.0	99.4	99.4	99.4	100.0	99.0	99.0	99.0	99.0	..	.	Official, IMF 1985 = 100
..	..	..	..	..	..	..	..	..	..	.	Official, CIA or LWI 1980 = 100
..	..	..	..	..	..	..	..	..	..	.	Alternative, CIA or LWI 1980 = 100
				(millions of current Mongolian tughriks)							**INTERNATIONAL TRADE (ECE)**
1,394	1,671	1,814	2,015	2,050	2,130	2,136	2,199	2,148	..	f	Value of exports, fob
..	..	..	..	..	..	..	..	..	..	.	to CMEA
2,094	2,353	2,761	2,901	3,259	3,390	3,286	3,313	2,868	..	f	Value of imports, cif
..	..	..	..	..	..	..	..	..	..	.	from CMEA
-699	-682	-947	-886	-1,209	-1,260	-1,150	-1,114	-720	..	f	Trade balance
..	..	..	..	..	..	..	..	..	..	.	CMEA
				(millions of current US dollars)							**INTERNATIONAL TRADE (Authors')**
437	516	550	569	553	670	739	761	716	..	f	Value of exports, fob
..	..	..	..	..	..	..	..	..	..	.	to developed countries
..	..	..	..	..	..	..	..	..	..	.	to other non-socialist countries
..	..	..	..	..	..	..	..	..	..	.	to socialist countries
..	..	..	..	..	..	..	..	..	..	.	to CMEA
656	726	837	820	878	1,066	1,137	1,146	956	..	f	Value of imports, cif
..	..	..	..	..	..	..	..	..	..	.	from developed countries
..	..	..	..	..	..	..	..	..	..	.	from other non-socialist countries
..	..	..	..	..	..	..	..	..	..	.	from socialist countries
..	..	..	..	..	..	..	..	..	..	.	from CMEA
-219	-210	-287	-250	-326	-396	-398	-385	-240	..	f	Trade balance
..	..	..	..	..	..	..	..	..	..	.	Developed countries
..	..	..	..	..	..	..	..	..	..	.	Other non-socialist countries
..	..	..	..	..	..	..	..	..	..	.	Socialist countries
..	..	..	..	..	..	..	..	..	..	.	CMEA
				(millions of current US dollars)							**PARTNER CONVERTIBLE TRADE (ECE)**
..	..	..	..	..	..	..	..	..	..	.	Exports to non-CMEA (cif)
..	..	..	..	..	..	..	..	..	..	.	Imports from non-CMEA (fob)
..	..	..	..	..	..	..	..	..	..	.	Trade balance
				(index, 1980 = 100)							**TRADE PRICE INDEXES (Authors')**
..	..	..	..	..	..	..	..	..	..	.	Terms of trade
..	..	..	..	..	..	..	..	..	..	.	Exports
..	..	..	..	..	..	..	..	..	..	.	Non-socialist countries
..	..	..	..	..	..	..	..	..	..	.	Developed countries
..	..	..	..	..	..	..	..	..	..	.	Other
..	..	..	..	..	..	..	..	..	..	.	Socialist countries
..	..	..	..	..	..	..	..	..	..	.	CMEA
..	..	..	..	..	..	..	..	..	..	.	Imports
..	..	..	..	..	..	..	..	..	..	.	Non-socialist countries
..	..	..	..	..	..	..	..	..	..	.	Developed countries
..	..	..	..	..	..	..	..	..	..	.	Other
..	..	..	..	..	..	..	..	..	..	.	Socialist countries
..	..	..	..	..	..	..	..	..	..	.	CMEA

Mongolia

Basic tables (continued)	1970	1971	1972	1973	1974	1975	1976	1977	1978	1979	1980
TRADE PRICE INDEXES (ECE)					*(index, 1980 = 100)*						
Terms of trade	..	..	..	..	..	..	..	..	..	..	..
Exports	..	..	..	..	..	..	..	..	..	..	..
Imports	..	..	..	..	..	..	..	..	..	..	..
Balance of Payments (ECE)					*(millions of current US dollars)*						
Exports, convertible currency	..	..	..	..	..	2	..	..	..	..	7
Imports, convertible currency	..	..	..	..	..	4	..	..	..	..	9
Trade balance, convertible currency	..	..	..	..	..	-2	..	..	..	..	-2
Invisibles, convertible currency	..	..	..	..	..	1	..	..	..	..	2
Current balance, convertible currency	..	..	..	..	..	-1	..	..	..	..	0
External debt, total (World Bank)	..	..	..	..	..	..	..	..	..	..	973
Convertible currency	..	..	..	..	..	..	..	..	..	..	..
CMEA	..	..	..	..	..	..	..	..	..	..	973
External debt service (World Bank)	..	..	..	..	..	..	..	..	..	..	10
Convertible currency	..	..	..	..	..	..	..	..	..	..	..
Total reserves less gold (IMF, IFS)	..	..	..	..	..	..	..	..	..	..	9
Total reserves, including gold at London price	..	..	..	..	..	..	..	..	..	..	..
Total reserves, incl. gold at national valuation	..	..	..	..	..	..	..	..	..	..	23
EMPLOYMENT					*(thousands)*						
Employment, total	..	..	..	..	..	..	..	..	..	..	511
Agriculture	..	..	..	..	..	..	..	..	..	..	203
Industry	..	..	..	..	..	..	..	..	..	..	112
Services	..	..	..	..	..	..	..	..	..	..	196
Labor force, total	582	599	616	634	651	668	689	710	731	751	772
Agriculture	279	281	284	287	290	293	296	299	302	305	308
Industry	122	126	129	133	137	140	145	149	153	158	162
Services	181	192	203	213	224	235	248	262	275	289	303
DOMESTIC FINANCE (IMF)					*(millions of current Mongolian tughriks)*						
Money supply, broadly defined	..	..	..	..	..	..	..	..	..	..	..
Money, means of payment											
Demand deposits	..	..	..	..	..	..	..	..	..	..	..
Currency outside banks	..	..	..	..	..	..	..	..	..	..	..
Quasi-money	..	..	..	..	..	..	..	..	..	..	..
Interest: deposit rate (percent)	..	..	..	..	..	..	..	..	..	..	..
Central government expenditures	..	..	..	..	..	..	..	..	..	..	..
Defense	..	..	..	..	..	..	..	..	..	..	..
					(millions of 1989 US dollars)						
Central government exp. (ACDA)	..	..	..	..	..	..	..	..	..	..	..
Military (ACDA)	..	..	..	..	..	..	..	..	..	257	296
LAND AND FORESTS (FAO)											
Pop. density: agr. land (pop. per sq. km)	1	1	1	1	1	1	1	1	1	1	1
Deforestation rate (net)	0	0	0	0	2	0	0	0	0	0	0
Forest (thousands sq. km)	150	150	150	150	152	152	152	152	152	152	152
SOCIAL INDICATORS											
Population density: total land (pop. per sq. km)	1	1	1	1	1	1	1	1	1	1	1
School enrollment ratio, primary	113	..	..	..	..	108	..	106	104	104	106
secondary	87	..	..	..	..	81	..	86	87	88	88
tertiary	..	..	..	..	..	..	..	..	..	..	..
Energy consumption per capita (kg. of oil eq.)	613	635	663	685	717	754	793	878	1,008	1,087	1,168
Daily calorie supply per capita	2,288	2,355	2,400	2,373	2,365	2,397	2,409	2,410	2,472	2,464	2,436
Food production (1979-1981=100)	111	107	107	110	111	123	111	100	109	105	98
Daily protein supply (gm. per capita)	87	86	89	86	88	90	89	90	92	88	86
Population per hospital bed	105	..	..	..	..	..	..	..	..	..	87
per nursing person	..	..	..	248	..	..	..	..	..	..	..
per physician	578	..	..	..	..	..	..	..	..	..	..
Female participation in labor force (percent)	42	42	42	42	42	42	42	42	42	42	42
Infant mortality (per 1,000 live births)	102	100	98	96	94	92	90	88	86	84	82
Life expectancy (years)	53	53	54	54	55	55	56	56	57	57	58
Total fertility (births per woman)	6	6	6	6	6	6	6	6	5	5	5
Urban population (percent of total population)	45	46	47	47	48	49	49	50	50	51	51
Population per passenger car	..	..	..	..	..	..	..	..	..	..	..
per telephone	..	..	..	..	..	..	..	..	..	..	..

Abbreviations in notes column are explained in the General Notes. For sources and methods, see the Technical Notes.

178

1981	1982	1983	1984	1985	1986	1987	1988	1989	1990	Notes	*Basic tables (continued)*
				(index, 1980 = 100)							**TRADE PRICE INDEXES (ECE)**
..	..	..	..	..	..	..	..	..	..	.	Terms of trade
..	..	..	..	..	..	..	..	..	..	.	Exports
..	..	..	..	..	..	..	..	..	..	.	Imports
				(millions of current US dollars)							**Balance of Payments (ECE)**
6	9	5	20	23	18	32	34	52	..	.	Exports, convertible currency
10	10	13	8	9	18	17	22	34	..	.	Imports, convertible currency
-4	..	-8	12	14	0	14	13	18	..	.	Trade balance, convertible currency
4	4	3	2	3	7	8	7	13	..	.	Invisibles, convertible currency
0	3	-4	14	17	7	23	20	31	..	.	Current balance, convertible currency
1,233	1,652	2,007	2,343	2,800	4,070	4,125	4,596	5,187	..	f	External debt, total (World Bank)
..	..	..	..	..	..	..	..	..	..	f	Convertible currency
1,233	1,652	2,007	2,343	2,779	4,044	4,103	4,576	5,169	..	f	CMEA
11	16	21	25	30	7	10	18	26	..	f	External debt service (World Bank)
..	..	..	..	..	..	..	..	..	..	.	Convertible currency
9	11	7	22	52	74	148	145	121	..	f	Total reserves less gold (IMF, IFS)
..	..	..	..	..	..	..	..	..	..	.	Total reserves, including gold at London price
22	24	19	33	69	92	168	164	140	..	f	Total reserves, incl. gold at national valuation
				(thousands)							**EMPLOYMENT**
518	532	543	550	562	581	598	616	633	..	.	Employment, total
195	196	196	190	187	186	185	184	186	..	.	Agriculture
117	124	129	134	139	145	153	158	161	..	.	Industry
206	212	218	227	236	250	261	274	286	..	.	Services
797	821	845	869	894	921	948	975	1,002	1,029	.	Labor force, total
..	..	..	..	..	..	..	..	..	..	.	Agriculture
..	..	..	..	..	..	..	..	..	..	.	Industry
..	..	..	..	..	..	..	..	..	..	.	Services
				(millions of current Mongolian tughriks)							**DOMESTIC FINANCE (IMF)**
..	..	..	..	..	..	..	..	..	..	.	Money supply, broadly defined
..	..	..	..	..	..	..	..	..	..	.	Money, means of payment
..	..	..	..	..	..	..	..	..	..	.	Demand deposits
..	..	..	..	..	..	..	..	..	..	.	Currency outside banks
..	..	..	..	..	..	..	..	..	..	.	Quasi-money
..	..	..	..	..	..	..	..	..	..	.	Interest: deposit rate (percent)
..	..	..	..	..	..	..	..	..	..	.	Central government expenditures
..	..	..	..	..	..	..	..	..	..	.	Defense
				(millions of 1989 US dollars)							
..	..	..	..	..	..	..	..	..	..	.	Central government exp. (ACDA)
266	250	244	229	219	276	295	293	259	..	.	Military (ACDA)
											LAND AND FORESTS (FAO)
1	1	1	2	2	2	2	..	..	..	.	Pop. density: agr. land (pop. per sq. km)
0	0	0	0	0	0	..	..	..	..	.	Deforestation rate (net)
152	152	152	152	152	152	..	..	..	..	.	Forest (thousands sq. km)
											SOCIAL INDICATORS
1	1	1	1	1	1	1	..	..	..	.	Population density: total land (pop. per sq. km)
106	107	106	105	..	102	..	..	..	..	.	School enrollment ratio, primary
88	87	87	88	..	92	..	..	..	..	.	secondary
..	..	..	..	..	22	..	..	..	..	.	tertiary
1,134	1,259	1,244	1,251	1,211	1,179	1,181	..	..	..	.	Energy consumption per capita (kg. of oil eq.)
2,461	2,445	2,451	2,443	2,446	2,486	2,499	2,458	..	..	.	Daily calorie supply per capita
97	99	101	95	95	99	92	91	90	..	.	Food production (1979-1981=100)
86	84	84	84	83	85	84	83	..	..	.	Daily protein supply (gm. per capita)
88	..	..	..	..	..	..	..	..	..	.	Population per hospital bed
206	212	..	..	..	..	..	..	..	..	.	per nursing person
99	102	..	..	..	..	..	..	..	..	.	per physician
42	43	43	43	43	43	43	43	43	43	.	Female participation in labor force (percent)
80	78	76	74	72	70	68	66	64	62	.	Infant mortality (per 1,000 live births)
58	59	59	60	60	61	61	62	62	63	.	Life expectancy (years)
5	5	5	5	5	5	5	5	5	5	.	Total fertility (births per woman)
51	52	52	52	52	52	52	52	52	52	.	Urban population (percent of total population)
..	..	..	..	..	..	..	..	..	..	.	Population per passenger car
..	..	..	..	..	..	..	..	..	..	f	per telephone

Comparator tables	1970	1971	1972	1973	1974	1975	1976	1977	1978	1979	1980
PER CAPITA INCOME						*(US dollars)*					
World Bank (Atlas method)	380	390	390	430	560	630	700	780	740	560	650
Single year conversion	370	376	379	456	622	623	695	795	738	555	698
CIA or LWI	..	..	..	..	..	..	..	..	..	279	308
Penn World Tables	1,135	1,192	1,176	1,424	1,685	1,663	1,841	2,147	1,895	1,290	1,969
POPULATION						*(thousands)*					
	2,053	2,121	2,192	2,265	2,337	2,408	2,478	2,546	2,615	2,689	2,771
GROSS NATIONAL PRODUCT, current prices						*(millions of current US dollars)*					
World Bank (Atlas method)	773	819	852	965	1,303	1,525	1,726	1,980	1,947	1,518	1,788
Single year conversion	760	796	831	1,033	1,453	1,500	1,722	2,025	1,929	1,491	1,935
Authors' series	..	..	..	..	..	..	..	..	..	..	..
CIA or LWI	..	..	..	..	..	..	..	..	..	752	862
GROSS NATIONAL PRODUCT, constant prices						*(millions of constant 1987 dollars)*					
Single year conversion	3,219	3,316	3,367	3,521	4,096	4,161	4,338	4,707	4,273	3,084	3,240
Authors' series, rescaled from 1980 prices	..	..	..	..	..	..	..	..	..	..	..
CIA or LWI, rescaled from 1989 prices	..	..	..	..	..	..	..	..	..	1,169	1,228
CONVERSION FACTORS						*(LCUs per US dollar)*					
World Bank (Atlas method)	0.01	0.01	0.01	0.01	0.01	0.01	0.01	0.01	0.01	0.01	0.01
Single year convertor	0.01	0.01	0.01	0.01	0.01	0.01	0.01	0.01	0.01	0.01	0.01
Authors' series	..	..	..	..	..	..	..	..	..	..	..
Penn World Tables	0.00	0.00	0.00	0.00	0.00	0.00	0.00	0.00	0.00	0.00	0.00
OUTPUT TRENDS, OVERALL						*(index, constant prices 1987 = 100)*					
GNP, SNA	101.1	104.2	105.8	110.6	128.7	130.7	136.3	147.9	134.2	96.9	101.8
NMP, MPS	..	..	..	..	..	..	..	..	..	..	..
GNP, "Building block"	..	..	..	..	..	..	..	..	..	..	..
Industry											
Value added, SNA	86.4	89.3	94.3	98.5	116.4	115.5	121.5	138.3	122.8	81.1	95.0
Value added, MPS	..	..	..	..	..	..	..	..	..	..	..
"Building block"	..	..	..	..	..	..	..	..	..	..	..
Gross output, SNA	..	..	..	..	..	..	..	..	..	..	..
Agriculture											
Value added, SNA	105.7	109.8	109.7	119.6	131.8	134.1	136.4	144.1	154.1	130.4	105.6
Value added, MPS	..	..	..	..	..	..	..	..	..	..	..
"Building block"	..	..	..	..	..	..	..	..	..	..	..
Gross output, SNA	..	..	..	..	..	..	..	..	..	..	..
Services											
Value added, SNA	96.9	99.7	101.5	107.4	123.7	122.4	130.6	141.8	120.0	82.3	99.8
Value added, MPS	..	..	..	..	..	..	..	..	..	..	..
"Building block"	..	..	..	..	..	..	..	..	..	..	..
CONSUMPTION											
Total consumption, SNA	91.0	93.4	94.7	97.9	110.8	114.5	120.2	128.9	124.0	92.9	103.9
Total consumption, MPS	..	..	..	..	..	..	..	..	..	..	..
Households, SNA	141.8	145.6	146.8	152.7	173.1	177.2	185.4	198.8	187.4	134.5	145.9
Households, "building block"	..	..	..	..	..	..	..	..	..	..	..
General government, SNA	13.9	14.2	15.7	14.5	16.2	19.2	21.3	23.0	27.8	29.8	40.1
General government, "building block"	..	..	..	..	..	..	..	..	..	..	..
INVESTMENT											
Gross fixed investment, SNA	74.0	76.4	70.4	93.8	117.4	110.6	115.9	153.7	85.2	29.9	75.4
Accumulation, MPS	..	..	..	..	..	..	..	..	..	..	..
"Building block"	..	..	..	..	..	..	..	..	..	..	..
CONSUMER PRICES											
National methodology	..	..	..	..	..	..	..	..	..	..	..
Outside estimate	..	..	..	..	..	..	..	..	..	..	..
MERCHANDISE EXPORTS						*(millions of current US dollars)*					
UNCTAD	179	..	..	..	..	375	..	..	..	..	450
IMF: IFS	179	..	..	..	..	375	..	..	..	..	451
ACDA	..	..	..	..	..	..	..	637	646	567	451
ECE	..	..	..	..	..	..	..	..	..	..	..
intra-CMEA	..	..	..	..	..	..	..	..	..	..	..
Authors' uniform TR/$ series	179	..	..	..	..	375	..	..	..	..	451
intra-CMEA	..	..	..	..	..	..	..	..	..	..	..
MERCHANDISE IMPORTS						*(millions of current US dollars)*					
UNCTAD	198	..	..	..	..	517	..	..	..	..	887
IMF: IFS	199	..	..	..	..	517	..	..	..	..	887
ACDA	..	..	..	..	..	..	..	762	596	360	887
ECE	..	..	..	..	..	..	..	..	..	..	..
intra-CMEA	..	..	..	..	..	..	..	..	..	..	..
Authors' uniform series	199	210	218	327	562	517	532	762	596	360	887
intra-CMEA	..	..	..	..	..	..	..	..	..	..	..

Abbreviations in notes column are explained in the General Notes. For sources and methods, see the Technical Notes.

1981	1982	1983	1984	1985	1986	1987	1988	1989	1990	Notes	Comparator tables (continued)
				(US dollars)							**PER CAPITA INCOME**
760	800	810	790	760	760	810	..	..	..	.	World Bank (Atlas method)
802	769	770	865	798	731	910	..	..	..	.	Single year conversion
347	353	386	367	338	304	348	313	307	..	A	CIA or LWI
1,968	1,900	1,945	1,947	1,890	1,888	..	..	..	..	.	Penn World Tables
				(thousands)							
2,860	2,956	3,058	3,164	3,272	3,383	3,497	3,614	3,732	3,853	.	**POPULATION**
			(millions of current US dollars)								**GROSS NATIONAL PRODUCT, current prices**
2,174	2,351	2,486	2,487	2,495	2,585	2,815	..	..	..	.	World Bank (Atlas method)
2,295	2,272	2,356	2,737	2,611	2,473	3,183	..	..	..	.	Single year conversion
..	..	..	..	..	..	..	..	..	..	.	Authors' series
1,006	1,059	1,159	1,136	1,114	1,032	1,182	1,094	1,106	..	.	CIA or LWI
			(millions of constant 1987 dollars)								**GROSS NATIONAL PRODUCT, constant prices**
3,450	3,407	3,584	3,399	3,209	3,140	3,183	2,401	2,436	..	.	Single year conversion
..	..	..	..	..	..	..	..	..	..	.	Authors' series, rescaled from 1980 prices
1,309	1,294	1,365	1,288	1,227	1,108	1,231	1,102	1,070	..	A	CIA or LWI, rescaled from 1989 prices
			(LCUs per US dollar)								**CONVERSION FACTORS**
0.01	0.01	0.01	0.02	0.04	0.15	0.89	..	..	..	.	World Bank (Atlas method)
0.01	0.01	0.01	0.02	0.04	0.16	0.79	..	..	..	.	Single year convertor
										.	Authors' series
0.00	0.01	0.01	0.01	0.02	0.07	..	..	..	..	.	Penn World Tables
			(index, constant prices 1987 = 100)								**OUTPUT TRENDS, OVERALL**
108.4	107.0	112.6	106.8	100.8	98.6	100.0	75.4	76.5	..	.	GNP, SNA
..	..	..	..	..	..	..	..	..	..	.	NMP, MPS
..	..	..	..	..	..	..	..	..	..	.	GNP, "Building block"
											Industry
97.7	94.8	100.3	101.2	98.3	101.7	100.0	69.2	63.1	60.5	Hf	Value added, SNA
..	..	..	..	..	..	..	..	..	..	.	Value added, MPS
..	..	..	..	..	..	..	..	..	..	.	"Building block"
..	..	..	..	..	..	..	..	..	..	.	Gross output, SNA
											Agriculture
115.6	118.9	125.7	119.0	113.3	103.3	100.0	89.8	92.0	93.8	Hf	Value added, SNA
..	..	..	..	..	..	..	..	..	..	.	Value added, MPS
..	..	..	..	..	..	..	..	..	..	.	"Building block"
..	..	..	..	..	..	..	..	..	..	.	Gross output, SNA
											Services
103.7	101.3	104.6	103.4	98.8	98.8	100.0	97.5	91.1	92.3	Hf	Value added, SNA
..	..	..	..	..	..	..	..	..	..	.	Value added, MPS
..	..	..	..	..	..	..	..	..	..	.	"Building block"
											CONSUMPTION
98.7	97.6	102.7	104.6	101.7	99.9	100.0	92.5	90.8	93.5	.	Total consumption, SNA
..	..	..	..	..	..	..	..	..	..	.	Total consumption, MPS
133.8	126.8	122.3	117.1	108.4	103.1	100.0	113.2	120.3	123.7	.	Households, SNA
..	..	..	..	..	..	..	..	..	..	.	Households, "building block"
45.5	53.2	73.0	85.6	91.6	95.2	100.0	61.1	46.0	47.6	.	General government, SNA
..	..	..	..	..	..	..	..	..	..	.	General government, "building block"
											INVESTMENT
120.7	97.4	102.0	104.3	105.4	99.0	100.0	88.0	75.9	63.8	.	Gross fixed investment, SNA
..	..	..	..	..	..	..	..	..	..	.	Accumulation, MPS
..	..	..	..	..	..	..	..	..	..	.	"Building block"
											CONSUMER PRICES
..	..	..	..	..	..	..	..	..	..	.	National methodology
..	..	..	..	..	..	..	..	..	..	.	Outside estimate
			(millions of current US dollars)								**MERCHANDISE EXPORTS**
500	406	429	385	302	247	300	236	250	280	.	UNCTAD
508	406	429	386	301	247	300	236	..	..	.	IMF: IFS
508	406	429	386	302	247	300	236	250	..	.	ACDA
..	..	..	..	..	..	..	..	..	..	.	ECE
											intra-CMEA
528	406	429	386	302	247	300	236	..	..	f	Authors' uniform TR/$ series
..	..	..	..	..	..	..	..	..	..	.	intra-CMEA
			(millions of current US dollars)								**MERCHANDISE IMPORTS**
999	776	807	826	964	857	923	900	1,000	1,050	.	UNCTAD
999	776	826	848	964	857	923	..	..	..	.	IMF: IFS
999	776	826	848	964	857	923	800	550	..	.	ACDA
..	..	..	..	..	..	..	..	..	..	.	ECE
											intra-CMEA
999	776	807	826	964	857	923	900	1,000	1,050	f	Authors' uniform series
..	..	..	..	..	..	..	..	..	..	.	intra-CMEA

Nicaragua

Basic tables	1970	1971	1972	1973	1974	1975	1976	1977	1978	1979	1980
SNA ACCOUNTS, current prices					*(millions of current Nicaraguan New cordobas)*						
GNP, at market prices	5	6	6	7	10	11	12	14	14	14	19
Net factor income	0	0	0	0	-1	0	-1	-1	-1	-1	-1
GDP at market prices	6	6	6	8	11	11	13	15	14	15	21
Net indirect taxes	0	1	1	1	1	1	1	2	1	1	1
GDP at factor cost	5	5	6	7	10	10	11	13	13	13	19
Agriculture	1	1	2	2	3	3	3	4	4	4	5
Industry	1	2	2	2	3	3	4	4	4	4	7
Services, etc.	3	3	3	4	5	5	6	7	6	6	9
Resource balance	0	0	0	-1	-1	-1	0	-1	1	2	-4
Exports GNFS	2	2	2	2	3	3	4	5	5	6	5
Imports GNFS	2	2	2	3	5	4	4	6	5	4	9
Domestic absorption	6	6	6	8	12	12	12	16	14	13	25
Total consumption	5	5	5	7	9	10	10	12	12	13	21
Private consumption	4	4	4	6	8	9	9	10	10	11	17
General government consumption	1	1	1	1	1	1	1	1	2	3	4
Gross domestic investment	1	1	1	2	3	2	2	4	2	-1	4
Fixed domestic investment	1	1	1	2	3	3	3	4	2	1	3
Depreciation	..	..	..	..	..	..	..	..	..	..	..
SNA ACCOUNTS, constant prices					*(millions of constant 1987 Nicaraguan New cordobas)*						
Gross national product (GNP)	2,532	2,608	2,648	2,770	3,221	3,273	3,412	3,702	3,360	2,425	2,548
GDP at market prices	2,615	2,701	2,756	2,936	3,352	3,347	3,509	3,818	3,517	2,586	2,705
GDP at factor cost	2,416	2,479	2,526	2,654	3,031	3,044	3,198	3,447	3,202	2,355	2,538
Agriculture	823	854	854	931	1,026	1,044	1,062	1,121	1,199	1,015	822
Industry	538	557	588	614	726	720	757	862	765	506	592
Services, etc.	1,254	1,290	1,314	1,391	1,601	1,584	1,690	1,835	1,553	1,065	1,292
Resource balance	189	208	339	220	158	320	340	198	372	543	-27
Exports GNFS	448	464	609	602	612	657	683	664	724	828	492
Imports GNFS	259	257	270	382	454	337	343	466	352	286	519
Domestic absorption	2,426	2,493	2,417	2,715	3,195	3,027	3,169	3,620	3,145	2,043	2,732
Total consumption, etc.	2,114	2,171	2,201	2,274	2,574	2,660	2,793	2,996	2,881	2,159	2,413
Private consumption, etc.	1,986	2,040	2,057	2,140	2,425	2,483	2,596	2,784	2,624	1,884	2,043
General government consumption	128	131	145	134	149	177	197	212	257	275	370
Gross domestic investment	312	323	216	442	621	368	376	624	264	-116	319
Fixed domestic investment	263	272	250	333	417	393	412	546	303	106	268
Depreciation	..	..	..	..	..	..	..	..	..	..	..
MPS ACCOUNTS, current prices					*(millions of current Nicaraguan New cordobas)*						
NMP produced:	..	..	..	..	..	..	..	..	..	..	..
Agriculture and forestry	..	..	..	..	..	..	..	..	..	..	..
Industry excluding construction	..	..	..	..	..	..	..	..	..	..	..
Construction	..	..	..	..	..	..	..	..	..	..	..
Transport and communication	..	..	..	..	..	..	..	..	..	..	..
Trade, etc.	..	..	..	..	..	..	..	..	..	..	..
Other services	..	..	..	..	..	..	..	..	..	..	..
Resource balance	..	..	..	..	..	..	..	..	..	..	..
NMP used: domestic market	..	..	..	..	..	..	..	..	..	..	..
Final consumption, material goods	..	..	..	..	..	..	..	..	..	..	..
Personal consumption	..	..	..	..	..	..	..	..	..	..	..
Collective consumption	..	..	..	..	..	..	..	..	..	..	..
Net capital formation	..	..	..	..	..	..	..	..	..	..	..
Net fixed capital formation	..	..	..	..	..	..	..	..	..	..	..
Changes in stocks	..	..	..	..	..	..	..	..	..	..	..
Depreciation	..	..	..	..	..	..	..	..	..	..	..
MPS ACCOUNTS, constant prices					*(millions of 1981 Nicaraguan New cordobas)*						
NMP produced:	..	..	..	..	..	..	..	..	..	..	..
Agriculture and forestry	..	..	..	..	..	..	..	..	..	..	..
Industry and construction	..	..	..	..	..	..	..	..	..	..	..
Services	..	..	..	..	..	..	..	..	..	..	..
Resource balance	..	..	..	..	..	..	..	..	..	..	..
NMP used: domestic market	..	..	..	..	..	..	..	..	..	..	..
Final consumption, material goods	..	..	..	..	..	..	..	..	..	..	..
Personal consumption	..	..	..	..	..	..	..	..	..	..	..
Collective consumption	..	..	..	..	..	..	..	..	..	..	..
Net capital formation	..	..	..	..	..	..	..	..	..	..	..
Net fixed capital formation	..	..	..	..	..	..	..	..	..	..	..
Depreciation	..	..	..	..	..	..	..	..	..	..	..

Abbreviations in notes column are explained in the General Notes. For sources and methods, see the Technical Notes.

Nicaragua

				(millions of current Nicaraguan New cordobas)							**SNA ACCOUNTS, current prices**
23	27	31	41	105	393	2,504	..	..	..	.	GNP, at market prices
-1	-2	-2	-4	-11	-43	-192	..	..	..	.	Net factor income
25	28	33	45	115	436	2,696	312,000	15,167,039	1,151,686,000	.	GDP at market prices
3	5	7	11	25	89	504	..	..	..	.	Net indirect taxes
21	24	26	34	91	346	2,192	..	..	..	Hf	GDP at factor cost
5	6	8	11	27	91	778	88,853	4,476,000	348,342,000	Hf	Agriculture
8	9	10	14	40	146	623	66,843	3,030,000	229,873,000	Hf	Industry
12	13	15	20	48	199	1,294	156,304	7,661,040	573,471,000	Hf	Services, etc.
-5	-3	-4	-6	-8	-35	-54	-134,000	-5,018,000	-261,297,000	.	Resource balance
6	5	6	7	17	56	317	59,000	5,038,000	267,333,000	.	Exports GNFS
10	7	10	13	25	91	371	193,000	10,056,000	528,630,000	.	Imports GNFS
29	31	36	51	124	471	2,750	446,000	20,185,038	1,412,983,000	.	Domestic absorption
24	26	29	41	97	397	2,324	365,000	16,180,039	1,178,975,000	.	Total consumption
18	19	19	25	56	243	1,401	262,000	12,086,040	840,833,000	.	Private consumption
5	7	10	16	41	154	923	103,000	4,094,000	338,142,000	.	General government consumption
6	5	7	10	27	74	426	81,000	4,005,000	234,008,000	.	Gross domestic investment
5	5	6	9	24	60	355	85,000	4,195,000	235,202,000	.	Fixed domestic investment
..	..	..	..	..	..	..	..	..	..	.	Depreciation
				(millions of constant 1987 Nicaraguan New cordobas)							**SNA ACCOUNTS, constant prices**
2,714	2,679	2,819	2,673	2,524	2,469	2,504	1,889	1,916	..	.	Gross national product (GNP)
2,850	2,827	2,957	2,896	2,773	2,717	2,696	2,393	2,288	2,302	.	GDP at market prices
2,467	2,391	2,375	2,220	2,180	2,160	2,192	..	..	..	Hf	GDP at factor cost
900	925	979	926	882	804	778	699	716	730	Hf	Agriculture
609	591	625	631	612	634	623	431	393	377	Hf	Industry
1,342	1,311	1,354	1,339	1,279	1,279	1,294	1,262	1,179	1,195	Hf	Services, etc.
69	158	134	25	-29	-38	-54	-58	-80	-102	.	Resource balance
565	520	557	441	389	321	317	306	352	399	.	Exports GNFS
496	362	423	416	419	358	371	364	432	501	.	Imports GNFS
2,781	2,669	2,823	2,871	2,802	2,755	2,750	2,451	2,368	2,404	.	Domestic absorption
2,294	2,267	2,387	2,430	2,364	2,322	2,324	2,150	2,109	2,172	.	Total consumption, etc.
1,874	1,776	1,713	1,641	1,519	1,443	1,401	1,586	1,685	1,732	.	Private consumption, etc.
420	491	673	790	845	879	923	564	424	439	.	General government consumption
487	402	437	441	438	433	426	301	259	233	.	Gross domestic investment
429	346	363	371	375	352	355	313	270	227	.	Fixed domestic investment
..	..	..	..	..	..	..	..	..	..	.	Depreciation
				(millions of current Nicaraguan New cordobas)							**MPS ACCOUNTS, current prices**
											NMP produced:
..	..	..	..	..	..	..	..	..	..	.	Agriculture and forestry
..	..	..	..	..	..	..	..	..	..	.	Industry excluding construction
..	..	..	..	..	..	..	..	..	..	.	Construction
..	..	..	..	..	..	..	..	..	..	.	Transport and communication
..	..	..	..	..	..	..	..	..	..	.	Trade, etc.
..	..	..	..	..	..	..	..	..	..	.	Other services
..	..	..	..	..	..	..	..	..	..	.	Resource balance
..	..	..	..	..	..	..	..	..	..	.	NMP used: domestic market
..	..	..	..	..	..	..	..	..	..	.	Final consumption, material goods
..	..	..	..	..	..	..	..	..	..	.	Personal consumption
..	..	..	..	..	..	..	..	..	..	.	Collective consumption
..	..	..	..	..	..	..	..	..	..	.	Net capital formation
..	..	..	..	..	..	..	..	..	..	.	Net fixed capital formation
..	..	..	..	..	..	..	..	..	..	.	Changes in stocks
..	..	..	..	..	..	..	..	..	..	.	Depreciation
				(millions of 1981 Nicaraguan New cordobas)							**MPS ACCOUNTS, constant prices**
											NMP produced:
..	..	..	..	..	..	..	..	..	..	.	Agriculture and forestry
..	..	..	..	..	..	..	..	..	..	.	Industry and construction
..	..	..	..	..	..	..	..	..	..	.	Services
..	..	..	..	..	..	..	..	..	..	.	Resource balance
..	..	..	..	..	..	..	..	..	..	.	NMP used: domestic market
..	..	..	..	..	..	..	..	..	..	.	Final consumption, material goods
..	..	..	..	..	..	..	..	..	..	.	Personal consumption
..	..	..	..	..	..	..	..	..	..	.	Collective consumption
..	..	..	..	..	..	..	..	..	..	.	Net capital formation
..	..	..	..	..	..	..	..	..	..	.	Net fixed capital formation
..	..	..	..	..	..	..	..	..	..	.	Depreciation

Basic tables (continued)	1970	1971	1972	1973	1974	1975	1976	1977	1978	1979	1980
MPS ACCOUNTS, index				*(index, 1980 = 100)*							
NMP produced:	..	..	..	..	..	..	..	..	..	..	..
Agriculture and forestry	..	..	..	..	..	..	..	..	..	..	..
Industry excluding construction	..	..	..	..	..	..	..	..	..	..	..
Construction	..	..	..	..	..	..	..	..	..	..	..
Transport and communication	..	..	..	..	..	..	..	..	..	..	..
Trade, etc.	..	..	..	..	..	..	..	..	..	..	..
NMP used: material goods	..	..	..	..	..	..	..	..	..	..	..
Final consumption	..	..	..	..	..	..	..	..	..	..	..
Net capital formation	..	..	..	..	..	..	..	..	..	..	..
EXCHANGE AND CONVERSION RATES				*(LCUs per US dollar: annual average)*							
Single-year converter	0.007	0.007	0.007	0.007	0.007	0.007	0.007	0.007	0.007	0.009	0.010
Devisa/official	..	..	..	..	..	..	..	..	..	..	..
Commercial	..	..	..	..	..	..	..	..	..	..	..
Noncommercial	..	..	..	..	..	..	..	..	..	..	..
Informal market	0.008	0.008	0.008	0.008	0.008	0.003	0.008	0.008	0.009	0.018	0.017
ICP	0.002	0.002	0.002	0.002	0.003	0.003	0.003	0.003	0.003	0.004	0.004
				(ruble per US dollar: annual average)							
Commercial TR/$ cross	..	..	..	..	..	..	..	..	..	..	..
Uniform TR/$ cross	..	..	..	..	..	..	..	..	..	..	..
				(LCUs per ruble: annual average)							
Commercial	..	..	..	..	..	..	..	..	..	..	..
Noncommercial	..	..	..	..	..	..	..	..	..	..	..
Devisa/official	..	..	..	..	..	..	..	..	..	..	..
CONSUMER PRICE INDEXES				*(index)*							
Official, IMF 1985 = 100	..	..	3.1	3.9	4.4	4.8	4.9	5.4	5.7	8.4	11.4
Official, CIA or LWI 1980 = 100	..	..	..	..	..	..	..	..	..	..	..
Alternative, CIA or LWI 1980 = 100	..	..	..	..	..	..	..	..	..	..	..
INTERNATIONAL TRADE (ECE)				*(millions of current Nicaraguan New cordobas)*							
Value of exports, fob	..	..	..	..	..	..	..	..	..	..	..
to CMEA	..	..	..	..	..	..	..	..	..	..	..
Value of imports, cif	..	..	..	..	..	..	..	..	..	..	..
from CMEA	..	..	..	..	..	..	..	..	..	..	..
Trade balance	..	..	..	..	..	..	..	..	..	..	..
CMEA	..	..	..	..	..	..	..	..	..	..	..
INTERNATIONAL TRADE (Authors')				*(millions of current US dollars)*							
Value of exports, fob	179	187	249	278	381	375	542	637	646	567	451
to developed countries	..	..	..	..	..	..	..	..	..	..	..
to other non-socialist countries	..	..	..	..	..	..	..	..	..	..	..
to socialist countries	..	..	..	..	..	..	..	..	..	..	..
to CMEA	..	..	..	..	..	..	..	..	..	..	..
Value of imports, cif	199	210	218	327	562	517	532	762	596	360	887
from developed countries	..	..	..	..	..	..	..	..	..	..	..
from other non-socialist countries	..	..	..	..	..	..	..	..	..	..	..
from socialist countries	..	..	..	..	..	..	..	..	..	..	..
from CMEA	..	..	..	..	..	..	..	..	..	..	..
Trade balance	-20	-23	31	-49	-181	-142	10	-125	50	207	-436
Developed countries	..	..	..	..	..	..	..	..	..	..	..
Other non-socialist countries	..	..	..	..	..	..	..	..	..	..	..
Socialist countries	..	..	..	..	..	..	..	..	..	..	..
CMEA	..	..	..	..	..	..	..	..	..	..	..
PARTNER CONVERTIBLE TRADE (ECE)				*(millions of current US dollars)*							
Exports to non-CMEA (cif)	..	..	..	..	..	..	..	..	..	..	..
Imports from non-CMEA (fob)	..	..	..	..	..	..	..	..	..	..	..
Trade balance	..	..	..	..	..	..	..	..	..	..	..
TRADE PRICE INDEXES (Authors')				*(index, 1980 = 100)*							
Terms of trade	128.6	121.5	119.8	136.7	115.6	94.4	126.3	132.9	109.6	106.4	100.0
Exports	33.3	33.5	36.6	51.8	59.9	53.4	72.5	83.0	77.9	92.2	100.0
Non-socialist countries	..	..	..	..	..	..	..	..	..	..	..
Developed countries	..	..	..	..	..	..	..	..	..	..	..
Other	..	..	..	..	..	..	..	..	..	..	..
Socialist countries	..	..	..	..	..	..	..	..	..	..	..
CMEA	..	..	..	..	..	..	..	..	..	..	..
Imports	25.9	27.6	30.5	37.9	51.8	56.6	57.4	62.4	71.1	86.7	100.0
Non-socialist countries	..	..	..	..	..	..	..	..	..	..	..
Developed countries	..	..	..	..	..	..	..	..	..	..	..
Other	..	..	..	..	..	..	..	..	..	..	..
Socialist countries	..	..	..	..	..	..	..	..	..	..	..
CMEA	..	..	..	..	..	..	..	..	..	..	..

Abbreviations in notes column are explained in the General Notes. For sources and methods, see the Technical Notes.

1981	1982	1983	1984	1985	1986	1987	1988	1989	1990	Notes	Basic tables (continued)
				(index,1980 = 100)							**MPS ACCOUNTS, index**
..	..	..	..	..	..	..	..	..	..	.	NMP produced:
..	..	..	..	..	..	..	..	..	..	.	Agriculture and forestry
..	..	..	..	..	..	..	..	..	..	.	Industry excluding construction
..	..	..	..	..	..	..	..	..	..	.	Construction
..	..	..	..	..	..	..	..	..	..	.	Transport and communication
..	..	..	..	..	..	..	..	..	..	.	Trade, etc.
..	..	..	..	..	..	..	..	..	..	.	NMP used: material goods
..	..	..	..	..	..	..	..	..	..	.	Final consumption
..	..	..	..	..	..	..	..	..	..	.	Net capital formation
				(LCUs per US dollar: annual average)							**EXCHANGE AND CONVERSION RATES**
0.010	0.012	0.013	0.015	0.040	0.159	0.787	..	..	..	.	Single-year converter
..	..	..	..	..	..	..	..	..	..	.	Devisa/official
..	..	..	..	..	..	..	..	..	..	.	Commercial
..	..	..	..	..	..	..	..	..	..	.	Noncommercial
0.026	0.036	0.081	0.104	0.603	1.235	1.965	2.190	..	..	.	Informal market
0.004	0.005	0.006	0.007	0.019	0.068	..	..	..	..	.	ICP
				(ruble per US dollar: annual average)							
..	..	..	..	..	..	..	..	..	..	.	Commercial TR/$ cross
..	..	..	..	..	..	..	..	..	..	.	Uniform TR/$ cross
				(LCUs per ruble: annual average)							
..	..	..	..	..	..	..	..	..	..	.	Commercial
..	..	..	..	..	..	..	..	..	..	.	Noncommercial
..	..	..	..	..	..	..	..	..	..	.	Devisa/official
				(index)							**CONSUMER PRICE INDEXES**
14.1	17.6	23.1	31.3	100.0	781.4	7,907.4	814,860.0	..	..	.	Official, IMF 1985=100
..	..	..	..	..	..	..	..	..	..	.	Official, CIA or LWI 1980=100
..	..	..	..	..	..	..	..	..	..	.	Alternative, CIA or LWI 1980=100
				(millions of current Nicaraguan New cordobas)							**INTERNATIONAL TRADE (ECE)**
..	..	..	..	..	..	..	..	..	..	.	Value of exports, fob
..	..	..	..	..	..	..	..	..	..	.	to CMEA
..	..	..	..	..	..	..	..	..	..	.	Value of imports, cif
..	..	..	..	..	..	..	..	..	..	.	from CMEA
..	..	..	..	..	..	..	..	..	..	.	Trade balance
..	..	..	..	..	..	..	..	..	..	.	CMEA
				(millions of current US dollars)							**INTERNATIONAL TRADE (Authors')**
528	406	429	386	302	247	300	236	250	280	f	Value of exports, fob
..	..	..	..	..	..	..	..	..	..	.	to developed countries
..	..	..	..	..	..	..	..	..	..	.	to other non-socialist countries
..	..	..	..	..	..	..	..	..	..	.	to socialist countries
..	..	..	..	..	..	..	..	..	..	.	to CMEA
999	776	807	826	964	857	923	900	1,000	1,050	f	Value of imports, cif
..	..	..	..	..	..	..	..	..	..	.	from developed countries
..	..	..	..	..	..	..	..	..	..	.	from other non-socialist countries
..	..	..	..	..	..	..	..	..	..	.	from socialist countries
..	..	..	..	..	..	..	..	..	..	.	from CMEA
-471	-370	-378	-440	-662	-610	-623	-664	-750	-770	f	Trade balance
..	..	..	..	..	..	..	..	..	..	.	Developed countries
..	..	..	..	..	..	..	..	..	..	.	Other non-socialist countries
..	..	..	..	..	..	..	..	..	..	.	Socialist countries
..	..	..	..	..	..	..	..	..	..	.	CMEA
				(millions of current US dollars)							**PARTNER CONVERTIBLE TRADE (ECE)**
..	..	671	590	477	392	416	466	435	..	Wf	Exports to non-CMEA (cif)
..	..	464	462	309	305	240	299	297	..	Wf	Imports from non-CMEA (fob)
..	..	207	128	168	87	176	167	138	..	Wf	Trade balance
				(index,1980 = 100)							**TRADE PRICE INDEXES (Authors')**
86.5	87.6	91.6	92.3	86.8	94.8	77.8	79.4	..	..	K	Terms of trade
88.4	86.2	87.8	85.8	78.9	89.1	80.3	87.2	..	..	K	Exports
..	..	..	..	..	..	..	..	..	..	.	Non-socialist countries
..	..	..	..	..	..	..	..	..	..	.	Developed countries
..	..	..	..	..	..	..	..	..	..	.	Other
..	..	..	..	..	..	..	..	..	..	.	Socialist countries
..	..	..	..	..	..	..	..	..	..	.	CMEA
102.3	98.5	95.9	93.0	90.9	94.0	103.2	109.8	..	..	K	Imports
..	..	..	..	..	..	..	..	..	..	.	Non-socialist countries
..	..	..	..	..	..	..	..	..	..	.	Developed countries
..	..	..	..	..	..	..	..	..	..	.	Other
..	..	..	..	..	..	..	..	..	..	.	Socialist countries
..	..	..	..	..	..	..	..	..	..	.	CMEA

Basic tables (continued)	1970	1971	1972	1973	1974	1975	1976	1977	1978	1979	1980
TRADE PRICE INDEXES (ECE)					*(index, 1980 = 100)*						
Terms of trade	..	..	..	..	..	..	..	..	..	..	..
Exports	..	..	..	..	..	..	..	..	..	..	..
Imports	..	..	..	..	..	..	..	..	..	..	..
Balance of Payments (ECE)					*(millions of current US dollars)*						
Exports, convertible currency	213	220	286	316	437	447	616	719	720	672	495
Imports, convertible currency	229	238	256	390	647	588	592	841	665	511	906
Trade balance, convertible currency	-15	-18	30	-75	-210	-142	23	-122	55	162	-411
Invisibles, convertible currency	..	..	..	..	..	..	..	..	..	..	..
Current balance, convertible currency	-40	-45	22	-66	-257	-185	-39	-182	-25	180	-411
External debt, total (World Bank)	155	191	234	339	465	611	673	1,276	1,429	1,487	2,170
Convertible currency	155	191	234	339	465	611	673	1,276	1,429	1,487	2,170
CMEA	..	..	..	..	..	..	..	..	..	..	5
External debt service (World Bank)	36	31	38	78	56	64	84	107	107	56	115
Convertible currency	36	31	38	78	56	64	84	107	107	56	115
Total reserves less gold (IMF, IFS)	49	58	80	116	104	122	146	148	51	147	65
Total reserves, including gold at London price	49	59	81	118	108	124	148	153	57	156	75
Total reserves, incl. gold at national valuation	49	59	80	117	105	122	147	149	52	147	65
EMPLOYMENT					*(thousands)*						
Employment, total	..	..	..	..	..	..	..	..	..	..	..
Agriculture	..	..	..	..	..	..	..	..	..	..	..
Industry	..	..	..	..	..	..	..	..	..	..	..
Services	..	..	..	..	..	..	..	..	..	..	..
Labor force, total	619	640	660	681	702	722	743	763	784	805	825
Agriculture	319	326	333	340	347	354	360	366	372	378	384
Industry	96	99	103	106	109	113	116	120	123	127	130
Services	204	214	225	235	245	255	266	277	288	299	311
DOMESTIC FINANCE (IMF)					*(millions of current Nicaraguan New cordobas)*						
Money supply, broadly defined	1	1	1	2	2	2	3	3	3	3	6
Money, means of payment	1	1	1	1	1	1	2	2	2	3	4
Demand deposits	0	0	0	1	1	1	1	1	1	1	2
Currency outside banks	0	0	0	0	1	0	1	1	1	2	2
Quasi-money	0	0	1	1	1	1	1	1	1	1	2
Interest: deposit rate (percent)	..	..	..	..	..	..	..	..	..	8	8
Central government expenditures	1	1	1	1	2	2	2	3	3	3	6
Defense	0	0	0	0	0	0	0	0	1	0	1
					(millions of 1989 US dollars)						
Central government exp. (ACDA)	..	..	..	..	..	..	..	..	..	270	416
Military (ACDA)	..	..	..	..	..	..	..	..	..	39	78
LAND AND FORESTS (FAO)											
Pop. density: agr. land (pop. per sq. km)	37	38	39	40	40	41	42	43	44	44	45
Deforestation rate (net)	-2	-2	-2	-2	-2	-2	-2	-2	-2	-3	-2
Forest (thousands sq. km)	56	55	54	53	52	51	49	48	47	46	45
SOCIAL INDICATORS											
Population density: total land (pop. per sq. km	17	18	19	19	20	20	21	21	22	23	23
School enrollment ratio, primary	80	..	..	..	..	82	88	87	84	90	99
secondary	18	..	..	..	..	24	28	30	28	30	43
tertiary	..	..	..	..	..	..	..	..	..	..	14
Energy consumption per capita (kg. of oil eq.)	254	249	284	301	306	293	325	369	339	240	273
Daily calorie supply per capita	2,430	2,413	2,351	2,419	2,340	2,374	2,413	2,432	2,380	2,326	2,312
Food production (1979-1981=100)	112	111	110	106	105	115	119	120	126	133	87
Daily protein supply (gm. per capita)	74	72	69	70	67	69	69	69	68	65	60
Population per hospital bed	424	..	..	..	..	400	..	..	..	..	..
per nursing person	..	..	..	..	..	..	..	..	..	..	591
per physician	2,136	..	..	..	..	2,098	..	..	..	..	2,283
Female participation in labor force (percent)	12	12	12	12	12	12	12	13	13	13	13
Infant mortality (per 1,000 live births)	106	103	100	99	97	96	94	93	90	86	83
Life expectancy (years)	54	54	55	55	55	56	56	56	57	58	58
Total fertility (births per woman)	7	7	7	7	7	7	6	6	6	6	6
Urban population (percent of total population	47	48	48	49	50	50	51	52	52	53	53
Population per passenger car	60	66	..	71	74	66	69	59	64	..	73
per telephone	..	..	..	..	..	67	..	..	..	..	..

Abbreviations in notes column are explained in the General Notes. For sources and methods, see the Technical Notes.

Nicaragua

1981	1982	1983	1984	1985	1986	1987	1988	1989	1990	Notes	
				(index, 1980 = 100)							**TRADE PRICE INDEXES (ECE)**
..	..	..	..	..	..	..	..	..	..	.	Terms of trade
..	..	..	..	..	..	..	..	..	..	.	Exports
..	..	..	..	..	..	..	..	..	..	.	Imports
				(millions of current US dollars)							**Balance of Payments (ECE)**
553	447	498	461	344	287	325	273	340	375	f	Exports, convertible currency
1,031	826	870	884	924	836	895	856	666	719	f	Imports, convertible currency
-478	-379	-372	-424	-579	-549	-570	-583	-325	-345	f	Trade balance, convertible currency
..	..	..	..	..	..	..	..	..	..	f	Invisibles, convertible currency
-592	-514	-507	-597	-726	-688	-688	-715	-326	-369	f	Current balance, convertible currency
2,439	2,913	4,058	4,751	5,736	6,730	7,864	8,587	9,568	10,497	.	External debt, total (World Bank)
2,439	2,913	4,058	4,751	5,736	6,730	7,864	8,587	9,568	10,497	.	Convertible currency
31	112	222	399	1,014	1,675	2,061	2,413	2,954	3,360	.	CMEA
223	201	107	86	64	40	40	26	14	16	f	External debt service (World Bank)
223	201	107	86	64	40	40	26	14	16	.	Convertible currency
111	171	175	..	..	..	..	..	..	..	.	Total reserves less gold (IMF, IFS)
119	179	221	..	..	..	..	..	..	..	.	Total reserves, including gold at London price
112	172	180	..	..	..	..	..	..	..	.	Total reserves, incl. gold at national valuation
				(thousands)							**EMPLOYMENT**
..	..	..	..	..	..	..	..	..	..	.	Employment, total
..	..	..	..	..	..	..	..	..	..	.	Agriculture
..	..	..	..	..	..	..	..	..	..	.	Industry
..	..	..	..	..	..	..	..	..	..	.	Services
859	892	926	960	993	1,035	1,078	1,120	1,162	1,204	.	Labor force, total
..	..	..	..	..	..	..	..	..	..	.	Agriculture
..	..	..	..	..	..	..	..	..	..	.	Industry
..	..	..	..	..	..	..	..	..	..	.	Services
			(millions of current Nicaraguan New cordobas)								**DOMESTIC FINANCE (IMF)**
8	10	17	31	74	..	..	..	..	..	.	Money supply, broadly defined
5	7	11	21	55	193	1,422	..	..	..	.	Money, means of payment
3	4	6	10	26	94	692	..	..	..	.	Demand deposits
2	3	5	11	29	99	730	..	..	..	.	Currency outside banks
3	3	6	10	20	57	200	..	..	..	.	Quasi-money
9	..	..	..	..	..	..	..	..	..	.	Interest: deposit rate (percent)
10	14	22	29	69	228	..	155,126	4,869,000	402,335,000	.	Central government expenditures
..	..	..	..	..	..	..	..	..	..	.	Defense
				(millions of 1989 US dollars)							
564	704	1,010	934	834	664	..	594	254	..	.	Central government exp. (ACDA)
100	151	159	195	218	..	..	..	..	..	.	Military (ACDA)
											LAND AND FORESTS (FAO)
46	47	48	50	51	52	54	..	..	..	.	Pop. density: agr. land (pop. per sq. km)
-3	-3	-3	-3	-3	-3	..	..	..	..	.	Deforestation rate (net)
44	43	42	40	39	38	..	..	..	..	.	Forest (thousands sq. km)
											SOCIAL INDICATORS
24	25	26	27	28	29	29	..	..	..	.	Population density: total land (pop. per sq. km)
..	100	103	99	101	98	99	..	..	..	.	School enrollment ratio, primary
..	39	44	43	39	42	43	..	..	..	.	secondary
..	..	13	11	10	9	8	..	..	..	.	tertiary
278	257	265	244	267	260	256	..	..	..	.	Energy consumption per capita (kg. of oil eq.)
2,307	2,315	2,356	2,378	2,367	2,381	2,378	2,361	..	..	.	Daily calorie supply per capita
80	81	79	76	68	61	58	54	60	60	.	Food production (1979-1981=100)
59	58	59	59	58	59	58	57	..	..	.	Daily protein supply (gm. per capita)
..	..	..	..	400	..	..	..	..	..	.	Population per hospital bed
590	..	..	535	..	..	..	..	..	..	.	per nursing person
2,229	..	..	1,500	..	..	..	..	..	..	.	per physician
13	13	14	14	14	15	15	15	15	16	.	Female participation in labor force (percent)
79	76	73	70	68	65	62	60	57	55	.	Infant mortality (per 1,000 live births)
59	60	61	61	62	63	63	64	64	65	.	Life expectancy (years)
6	6	6	6	6	6	6	5	5	5	.	Total fertility (births per woman)
54	55	55	56	57	57	58	59	59	60	.	Urban population (percent of total population)
..	..	..	..	84	..	..	..	..	..	.	Population per passenger car
..	..	61	..	..	..	..	..	..	..	.	per telephone

Poland

Comparator tables	1970	1971	1972	1973	1974	1975	1976	1977	1978	1979	1980
PER CAPITA INCOME						*(US dollars)*					
World Bank (Atlas method)	..	..	..	..	..	..	..	..	..	..	..
Single year conversion	..	..	..	..	..	..	..	..	..	..	1,530
CIA or LWI	1,245	..	..	..	..	2,303	2,487	2,676	2,948	3,128	3,294
Penn World Tables	..	..	..	..	..	..	..	..	..	..	3,403
						(thousands)					
POPULATION	32,526	32,805	33,068	33,363	33,691	34,022	34,362	34,698	35,010	35,225	35,578
GROSS NATIONAL PRODUCT, current prices						*(millions of current US dollars)*					
World Bank (Atlas method)	..	..	..	..	..	..	..	..	..	..	..
Single year conversion	..	..	..	..	..	..	..	..	..	..	54,432
Authors' series	16,000	..	..	..	..	..	..	..	..	..	52,000
CIA or LWI	..	..	..	..	..	..	..	..	..	101,700	108,100
GROSS NATIONAL PRODUCT, constant prices						*(millions of constant 1987 dollars)*					
Single year conversion	..	..	..	..	..	..	..	..	..	..	57,520
Authors' series, rescaled from 1980 prices	42,474	..	..	..	..	..	..	..	..	..	..
CIA or LWI, rescaled from 1989 prices	113,232	..	..	..	..	155,113	158,991	161,938	167,832	164,730	160,541
CONVERSION FACTORS						*(LCUs per US dollar)*					
World Bank (Atlas method)	..	..	..	..	..	..	..	..	..	..	..
Single year convertor	..	..	..	..	..	..	..	..	..	..	44.22
Authors' series	60.25	..	..	..	..	..	..	..	..	..	48.29
Penn World Tables	..	..	..	..	..	..	..	..	..	..	20.74
OUTPUT TRENDS, OVERALL						*(index, constant prices 1987 = 100)*					
GNP, SNA											94.3
NMP, MPS	57.5	62.3	69.1	76.0	84.7	91.5	98.4	103.2	106.1	103.2	97.4
GNP, "Building block"	67.3	72.1	77.3	83.0	87.9	92.1	94.4	96.1	99.6	97.8	95.3
Industry											
Value added, SNA	..	..	..	..	..	..	..	..	..	..	..
Value added, MPS	57.4	62.3	70.2	79.2	88.7	97.8	106.0	111.8	114.0	110.4	100.6
"Building block"	68.5	73.3	79.9	88.6	97.0	106.4	108.9	110.4	112.3	110.1	107.5
Gross output, SNA	71.3	..	..	..	..	103.2	..	..	..	..	106.4
Agriculture											
Value added, SNA	..	..	..	..	..	..	..	..	..	..	..
Value added, MPS	95.3	104.9	109.6	113.5	109.6	100.1	102.0	103.0	109.6	103.9	87.7
"Building block"	78.2	84.5	89.4	93.4	92.8	86.6	88.0	88.5	95.9	90.2	82.1
Gross output, SNA	82.6	..	..	..	..	86.8	..	..	..	..	82.6
Services											
Value added, SNA	..	..	..	..	..	..	..	..	..	..	..
Value added, MPS	36.0	38.3	43.6	46.8	61.0	71.6	78.1	82.9	85.4	85.8	95.8
"Building block"	58.8	62.6	66.8	70.7	75.8	81.6	84.3	87.2	89.6	90.7	92.0
CONSUMPTION											
Total consumption, SNA	..	..	..	..	..	..	..	..	..	..	92.4
Total consumption, MPS	50.4	54.6	59.4	63.3	68.0	75.7	83.3	89.1	91.4	94.1	97.9
Households, SNA	..	..	..	..	..	..	..	..	..	..	93.4
Households, "building block"	..	..	..	..	..	85.6	90.5	93.9	94.1	95.2	96.1
General government, SNA	..	..	..	..	..	..	..	..	..	..	86.0
General government, "building block"	..	..	..	..	..	75.6	77.2	78.5	79.7	81.5	82.6
INVESTMENT											
Gross fixed investment, SNA	..	..	..	..	..	..	..	..	..	..	104.8
Accumulation, MPS	..	..	..	..	..	..	..	..	..	..	..
"Building block"	..	..	..	..	..	140.1	138.1	130.3	135.3	121.7	110.6
CONSUMER PRICES											
National methodology	11.0	11.1	11.1	11.4	12.2	12.4	13.0	13.6	14.7	15.8	17.3
Outside estimate	8.6	8.8	9.1	9.7	10.5	11.1	12.0	13.0	14.2	15.5	17.4
MERCHANDISE EXPORTS						*(millions of current US dollars)*					
UNCTAD	3,548	..	..	..	..	10,282	..	..	..	..	16,997
IMF: IFS	3,548	..	..	..	..	10,289	..	..	..	..	14,191
ACDA	..	..	..	..	..	..	..	14,530	14,490	16,860	17,540
ECE	3,550	3,875	4,927	6,453	8,628	11,113	8,586	9,597	11,077	12,532	13,072
intra-CMEA	2,149	2,302	2,986	3,792	4,701	6,642	3,953	4,487	5,426	5,882	5,302
Authors' uniform TR/$ series	3,186	3,332	3,903	5,165	6,859	8,074	9,055	10,289	11,678	13,625	14,177
intra-CMEA	1,804	1,791	2,009	2,559	3,019	3,754	4,400	5,146	5,996	6,920	6,354
MERCHANDISE IMPORTS						*(millions of current US dollars)*					
UNCTAD	3,608	..	..	..	..	12,536	..	..	..	..	19,089
IMF: IFS	..	..	..	..	..	11,155	..	..	..	..	16,690
ACDA	..	..	..	..	..	..	..	14,770	16,490	18,160	19,700
ECE	3,610	4,040	5,329	7,868	10,797	13,313	11,468	11,878	12,978	13,996	14,706
intra-CMEA	2,374	2,596	3,103	3,940	4,727	6,234	3,923	4,646	5,533	5,690	5,957
Authors' uniform series	3,213	3,435	4,262	6,528	9,020	10,480	11,931	12,589	13,585	15,050	15,939
intra-CMEA	1,993	2,019	2,087	2,659	3,035	3,524	4,367	5,327	6,114	6,695	7,139

Abbreviations in notes column are explained in the General Notes. For sources and methods, see the Technical Notes.

Poland

1981	1982	1983	1984	1985	1986	1987	1988	1989	1990	Notes	Comparator tables (continued)
				(US dollars)							**PER CAPITA INCOME**
..	1,520	1,790	2,070	2,080	2,030	1,870	1,850	1,890	1,690	.	World Bank (Atlas method)
1,409	1,721	1,992	1,980	1,839	1,905	1,623	1,744	2,080	1,578	.	Single year conversion
3,389	3,542	3,824	4,076	4,208	4,424	4,473	4,698	4,791	4,531	.	CIA or LWI
3,214	3,161	3,343	3,549	3,817	4,026	4,189	..	..	..	.	Penn World Tables
				(thousands)							
35,902	36,227	36,571	36,914	37,203	37,396	37,591	37,786	37,983	38,180	.	**POPULATION**
				(millions of current US dollars)							**GROSS NATIONAL PRODUCT, current prices**
..	55,246	65,417	76,264	77,559	75,973	70,127	70,059	71,665	64,480	.	World Bank (Atlas method)
50,588	62,351	72,837	73,091	68,429	71,234	61,001	65,891	79,018	60,234	.	Single year conversion
..	..	..	..	70,987	..	63,905	69,000	51,361	..	D	Authors' series
112,300	118,300	129,000	138,700	144,400	152,800	155,400	170,900	174,700		.	CIA or LWI
				(millions of constant 1987 dollars)							**GROSS NATIONAL PRODUCT, constant prices**
50,616	48,242	51,357	54,490	57,503	59,924	61,001	63,560	63,548	55,548	.	Single year conversion
..	..	..	..	70,791	..	75,746	78,577	77,870	..	D	Authors' series, rescaled from 1980 prices
152,010	150,614	158,060	163,954	165,660	170,935	168,453	172,176	169,073	154,182	.	CIA or LWI, rescaled from 1989 prices
				(LCUs per US dollar)							**CONVERSION FACTORS**
..	95.73	101.93	108.53	129.82	164.35	230.59	404.93	1,586.83	8,874.40	..	World Bank (Atlas method)
51.15	84.82	91.55	113.24	147.14	175.29	265.08	430.55	1,439.18	9,500.00	.	Single year convertor
..	..	..	..	147.14	..	265.08	429.41	1,439.20	..	..	Authors' series
23.86	48.43	56.63	65.46	73.56	85.91	107.57	..	..	..	.	Penn World Tables
				(index, constant prices 1987 = 100)							**OUTPUT TRENDS, OVERALL**
83.0	79.1	84.2	89.3	94.3	98.2	100.0	104.2	104.2	91.1	.	GNP, SNA
85.7	80.8	85.7	90.6	93.5	98.1	100.0	104.9	104.6	..	f	NMP, MPS
90.2	89.4	93.8	97.3	98.3	101.5	100.0	102.2	100.4	91.5	.	GNP, "Building block"
											Industry
..	..	..	91.7	93.2	97.1	100.0	104.8	..	..	H	Value added, SNA
83.3	79.6	83.9	89.1	92.9	97.0	100.0	105.1	102.9	..	.	Value added, MPS
93.4	89.7	95.4	98.5	99.4	100.8	100.0	101.2	96.1	78.7	.	"Building block"
..	..	..	..	101.1	102.1	100.0	102.1	96.8	77.7	X	Gross output, SNA
											Agriculture
..	..	..	95.3	101.3	106.6	100.0	101.6	..	..	H	Value added, SNA
88.6	93.0	98.2	103.5	103.5	109.6	100.0	101.8	103.5	..	.	Value added, MPS
85.7	89.8	94.2	98.8	99.0	106.9	100.0	103.2	104.1	102.4	.	"Building block"
..	..	..	..	..	107.4	100.0	104.1	105.0	103.3	.	Gross output, SNA
											Services
..	..	..	84.0	92.7	96.2	100.0	103.7	..	..	H	Value added, SNA
90.7	77.5	83.7	87.4	89.9	94.7	100.0	106.4	110.5	..	f	Value added, MPS
90.2	88.8	92.0	95.2	96.9	98.6	100.0	102.6	102.1	96.9	.	"Building block"
											CONSUMPTION
88.2	79.1	82.8	86.4	93.2	97.3	100.0	102.0	100.6	85.8	.	Total consumption, SNA
91.7	81.5	86.9	90.6	92.7	97.2	100.0	102.9	101.2	..	f	Total consumption, MPS
89.1	78.4	82.2	85.4	92.4	97.0	100.0	102.3	102.7	85.7	.	Households, SNA
92.8	87.2	92.0	94.5	96.2	99.2	100.0	102.6	103.5	96.2	.	Households, "building block"
82.1	84.1	86.7	93.3	98.9	99.0	100.0	100.2	86.1	86.2	.	General government, SNA
85.3	87.4	90.5	94.4	98.2	98.5	100.0	100.6	100.5	100.3	.	General government, "building block"
											INVESTMENT
84.8	73.2	79.6	87.4	91.9	96.1	100.0	105.5	103.8	92.8	.	Gross fixed investment, SNA
..	..	..	..	89.9	95.2	100.0	109.3	101.2	..	.	Accumulation, MPS
102.4	98.7	102.2	106.3	105.7	109.4	100.0	101.3	93.3	79.7	.	"Building block"
											CONSUMER PRICES
20.9	42.0	51.3	59.0	67.9	79.9	100.0	160.2	562.5	3857.5	.	National methodology
22.2	40.6	49.2	56.9	65.5	77.9	100.0	163.2	581.6	3576.5	.	Outside estimate
				(millions of current US dollars)							**MERCHANDISE EXPORTS**
13,182	11,172	11,572	11,750	11,488	12,074	12,205	13,834	12,914	14,311	.	UNCTAD
10,675	11,213	11,572	11,750	11,489	12,074	12,205	13,960	13,466	13,500	.	IMF: IFS
13,640	15,260	16,430	17,270	17,710	23,360	24,690	30,750	28,480	..	.	ACDA
10,084	10,526	10,441	10,897	11,100	13,130	14,094	14,875	15,831	18,100	.	ECE
4,436	4,962	4,874	4,965	5,255	6,539	6,727	6,546	6,733	7,074	.	intra-CMEA
10,953	11,988	12,347	12,645	12,947	14,486	15,939	17,147	17,854	19,377	.	Authors' uniform TR/$ series
5,271	6,326	6,660	6,576	6,897	7,712	8,317	8,553	8,481	8,212	.	intra-CMEA
				(millions of current US dollars)							**MERCHANDISE IMPORTS**
15,224	10,244	10,590	10,638	10,791	11,070	10,595	12,239	11,343	9,542	F	UNCTAD
12,792	10,648	10,927	10,985	11,855	11,535	11,215	12,712	10,659	8,229	.	IMF: IFS
15,980	14,610	15,750	16,540	17,420	22,310	22,840	26,610	24,380	..	.	ACDA
11,392	9,502	9,377	9,722	10,430	12,315	12,686	13,056	12,058	12,356	.	ECE
5,714	5,350	5,190	5,322	5,571	6,787	6,575	5,714	4,785	5,370	.	intra-CMEA
12,512	11,080	11,419	11,597	12,358	13,735	14,485	15,073	13,580	13,337	.	Authors' uniform series
6,789	6,822	7,092	7,050	7,311	8,004	8,128	7,466	6,026	6,233	.	intra-CMEA

Poland

Basic tables	1970	1971	1972	1973	1974	1975	1976	1977	1978	1979	1980
SNA ACCOUNTS, current prices					*(billions of current Polish zlotys)*						
GNP, at market prices	..	..	..	..	..	..	..	..	..	..	2,407
Net factor income	..	..	..	..	..	..	..	..	..	..	-104
GDP at market prices	..	..	..	..	..	..	..	..	..	..	2,511
Net indirect taxes	..	..	..	..	..	..	..	..	..	..	..
GDP at factor cost	..	..	..	..	..	..	..	..	..	..	..
Agriculture	..	..	..	..	..	..	..	..	..	..	..
Industry	..	..	..	..	..	..	..	..	..	..	..
Services, etc.	..	..	..	..	..	..	..	..	..	..	..
Resource balance	..	..	..	..	..	..	..	..	..	..	-74
Exports GNFS	..	..	..	..	..	..	..	..	..	..	707
Imports GNFS	..	..	..	..	..	..	..	..	..	..	780
Domestic absorption	..	..	..	..	..	..	..	..	..	..	2,585
Total consumption	..	..	..	..	..	..	..	..	..	..	1,923
Private consumption	..	..	..	..	..	..	..	..	..	..	1,692
General government consumption	..	..	..	..	..	..	..	..	..	..	231
Gross domestic investment	..	..	..	..	..	..	..	..	..	..	662
Fixed domestic investment	..	..	..	..	..	..	..	..	..	..	621
Depreciation	..	..	..	..	..	..	..	..	..	..	..
SNA ACCOUNTS, constant prices					*(billions of constant 1987 Polish zlotys)*						
Gross national product (GNP)	..	..	..	..	..	..	..	..	..	..	15,248
GDP at market prices	..	..	..	..	..	..	..	..	..	..	15,839
GDP at factor cost	..	..	..	..	..	..	..	..	..	..	..
Agriculture	..	..	..	..	..	..	..	..	..	..	..
Industry	..	..	..	..	..	..	..	..	..	..	..
Services, etc.	..	..	..	..	..	..	..	..	..	..	..
Resource balance	..	..	..	..	..	..	..	..	..	..	-275
Exports GNFS	..	..	..	..	..	..	..	..	..	..	3,114
Imports GNFS	..	..	..	..	..	..	..	..	..	..	3,389
Domestic absorption	..	..	..	..	..	..	..	..	..	..	16,114
Total consumption, etc.	..	..	..	..	..	..	..	..	..	..	10,766
Private consumption, etc.	..	..	..	..	..	..	..	..	..	..	9,462
General government consumption	..	..	..	..	..	..	..	..	..	..	1,305
Gross domestic investment	..	..	..	..	..	..	..	..	..	..	5,348
Fixed domestic investment	..	..	..	..	..	..	..	..	..	..	4,003
Depreciation	..	..	..	..	..	..	..	..	..	..	..
MPS ACCOUNTS, current prices					*(billions of current Polish zlotys)*						
NMP produced:	767	875	973	1,089	1,237	1,388	1,639	1,786	1,957	1,991	1,992
Agriculture and forestry	136	169	191	208	214	215	265	290	323	323	315
Industry excluding construction	400	424	460	530	668	785	808	890	971	1,000	1,039
Construction	83	106	129	151	160	171	227	229	264	244	202
Transport and communication	51	57	64	75	79	92	124	128	131	135	143
Trade, etc.	92	121	131	123	101	93	202	230	247	257	254
Other services	9	9	10	12	14	22	26	29	33	40	39
Resource balance	11	9	0	-32	-58	-66	-64	-55	-40	-40	-61
NMP used: domestic market	736	847	957	1,121	1,308	1,468	1,711	1,841	1,985	2,019	2,053
Final consumption, material goods	553	600	656	734	840	955	1,103	1,242	1,356	1,489	1,664
Personal consumption	470	509	554	620	706	808	928	1,044	1,135	1,250	1,409
Collective consumption	83	92	102	113	134	147	175	198	221	239	255
Net capital formation	262	360	418	542	671	691	836	755	789	617	388
Net fixed capital formation	133	176	224	286	337	391	456	482	507	444	348
Changes in stocks	129	184	193	255	334	299	380	273	282	173	41
Depreciation	..	..	..	..	..	..	..	..	..	..	..
MPS ACCOUNTS, constant prices					*(billions of 1984 Polish zlotys)*						
NMP produced:	4,320	4,686	5,199	5,712	6,371	6,883	7,396	7,762	7,982	7,762	7,323
Agriculture and forestry	1,019	1,121	1,172	1,213	1,172	1,070	1,091	1,101	1,172	1,111	938
Industry and construction	2,636	2,859	3,222	3,635	4,071	4,490	4,863	5,130	5,232	5,065	4,616
Services	665	707	805	864	1,128	1,323	1,442	1,531	1,577	1,586	1,769
Resource balance	-18	-101	-187	-422	-511	-672	-683	-466	-322	-167	-158
NMP used: domestic market	4,339	4,787	5,386	6,134	6,882	7,555	8,079	8,228	8,303	7,929	7,480
Final consumption, material goods	3,032	3,285	3,570	3,808	4,086	4,550	5,008	5,354	5,494	5,656	5,886
Personal consumption	..	..	..	..	..	..	..	..	..	..	..
Collective consumption	..	..	..	..	..	..	..	..	..	..	..
Net capital formation	1,307	1,503	1,816	2,326	2,796	3,005	3,071	2,875	2,809	2,273	1,594
Net fixed capital formation	..	..	..	..	..	..	..	..	..	..	..
Depreciation	..	..	..	..	..	..	..	..	..	..	..

Abbreviations in notes column are explained in the General Notes. For sources and methods, see the Technical Notes.

1981	1982	1983	1984	1985	1986	1987	1988	1989	1990	Notes	*Basic tables (continued)*
				(billions of current Polish zlotys)							**SNA ACCOUNTS, current prices**
2,588	5,289	6,668	8,277	10,069	12,486	16,170	28,369	113,721	572,222	.	GNP, at market prices
-165	-258	-256	-299	-376	-467	-770	-1,260	-4,598	-31,882	.	Net factor income
2,753	5,546	6,924	8,576	10,445	12,953	16,940	29,629	118,319	604,104	.	GDP at market prices
..	..	..	..	..	..	..	..	..	..	.	Net indirect taxes
											GDP at factor cost
..	..	..	1,236	1,519	1,797	2,050	3,892	14,435	83,366	H	Agriculture
..	..	..	4,510	5,328	6,632	8,838	15,530	48,511	218,201	H	Industry
..	..	..	2,830	3,598	4,524	6,052	10,207	55,373	302,537	H	Services, etc.
-58	116	122	169	139	184	407	811	4,963	49,507	.	Resource balance
638	1,078	1,192	1,516	1,901	2,358	3,625	6,745	22,570	156,211	.	Exports GNFS
697	962	1,070	1,346	1,761	2,174	3,218	5,934	17,608	106,704	.	Imports GNFS
2,811	5,430	6,802	8,407	10,305	12,769	16,533	28,818	113,356	554,597	.	Domestic absorption
2,303	3,880	5,068	6,150	7,417	9,029	11,649	19,161	67,824	370,219	.	Total consumption
2,042	3,425	4,458	5,348	6,456	7,851	10,133	16,732	60,756	325,174	.	Private consumption
260	455	610	801	962	1,178	1,516	2,429	7,067	45,045	.	General government consumption
508	1,551	1,734	2,257	2,888	3,740	4,884	9,657	45,533	184,378	.	Gross domestic investment
514	1,117	1,395	1,781	2,211	2,836	3,821	6,663	19,351	115,732	.	Fixed domestic investment
..	..	..	..	..	..	..	..	..	..	.	Depreciation
				(billions of constant 1987 Polish zlotys)							**SNA ACCOUNTS, constant prices**
13,417	12,788	13,614	14,444	15,243	15,885	16,170	16,849	16,846	14,725	.	Gross national product (GNP)
14,259	13,580	14,335	15,144	15,921	16,591	16,940	17,624	17,675	15,563	.	GDP at market prices
											GDP at factor cost
..	..	..	1,954	2,077	2,185	2,050	2,083	..	..	H	Agriculture
..	..	..	8,107	8,237	8,584	8,838	9,266	..	..	H	Industry
..	..	..	5,084	5,607	5,822	6,052	6,275	..	..	H	Services, etc.
-174	349	459	575	394	376	407	458	386	1,378	.	Resource balance
2,547	2,705	2,953	3,303	3,313	3,453	3,625	3,966	4,071	4,685	.	Exports GNFS
2,721	2,356	2,494	2,729	2,920	3,076	3,218	3,508	3,684	3,307	.	Imports GNFS
14,433	13,232	13,876	14,570	15,527	16,214	16,533	17,166	17,289	14,185	.	Domestic absorption
10,275	9,216	9,643	10,069	10,858	11,335	11,649	11,888	11,715	9,993	.	Total consumption, etc.
9,030	7,941	8,328	8,654	9,358	9,834	10,133	10,369	10,410	8,686	.	Private consumption, etc.
1,245	1,276	1,315	1,414	1,500	1,501	1,516	1,519	1,305	1,307	.	General government consumption
4,158	4,015	4,233	4,501	4,669	4,879	4,884	5,278	5,574	4,192	.	Gross domestic investment
3,240	2,797	3,043	3,341	3,513	3,671	3,821	4,031	3,967	3,547	.	Fixed domestic investment
..	..	..	..	..	..	..	..	..	..	.	Depreciation
				(billions of current Polish zlotys)							**MPS ACCOUNTS, current prices**
2,160	4,753	5,924	7,182	8,658	10,697	14,013	24,995	104,952	..	f	NMP produced:
638	925	1,089	1,256	1,399	1,650	1,849	3,543	15,089	..	.	Agriculture and forestry
910	2,388	2,968	3,562	4,117	5,061	6,804	12,031	52,672	..	.	Industry excluding construction
158	510	644	833	1,064	1,379	1,801	3,207	10,055	..	.	Construction
141	207	318	420	563	667	851	1,462	5,184	..	.	Transport and communication
270	656	802	982	1,344	1,708	2,385	4,111	19,502	..	.	Trade, etc.
43	68	103	128	171	232	323	641	2,450	..	.	Other services
-57	65	94	90	157	28	383	627	4,503	..	.	Resource balance
2,217	4,688	5,831	7,092	8,501	10,579	13,631	24,368	100,450	..	.	NMP used: domestic market
1,998	3,455	4,438	5,341	6,290	7,725	9,956	16,588	57,573	..	.	Final consumption, material goods
1,721	2,929	3,750	4,456	5,206	6,403	8,255	13,822	50,071	..	.	Personal consumption
276	526	688	885	1,084	1,321	1,701	2,766	7,502	..	.	Collective consumption
220	1,233	1,393	1,751	2,211	2,855	3,675	7,780	42,877	..	.	Net capital formation
225	800	1,054	1,275	1,534	1,950	2,612	4,785	16,695	..	.	Net fixed capital formation
-6	433	339	476	678	905	1,063	2,994	26,182	..	.	Changes in stocks
..	..	..	..	..	..	..	..	..	..	.	Depreciation
				(billions of 1984 Polish zlotys)							**MPS ACCOUNTS, constant prices**
6,444	6,078	6,444	6,810	7,030	7,376	7,520	7,885	7,869	..	f	NMP produced:
947	994	1,050	1,107	1,107	1,176	1,084	1,098	1,107	..	f	Agriculture and forestry
3,822	3,653	3,848	4,089	4,263	4,452	4,589	4,822	4,720	..	.	Industry and construction
1,675	1,431	1,546	1,615	1,660	1,748	1,847	1,965	2,042	..	f	Services
-214	94	86	153	148	153	164	181	161	..	.	Resource balance
6,657	5,984	6,358	6,657	6,882	7,223	7,356	7,704	7,708	..	.	NMP used: domestic market
5,510	4,900	5,226	5,446	5,575	5,845	6,011	6,187	6,084	..	f	Final consumption, material goods
..	..	..	..	4,624	4,855	5,000	5,164	5,206	..	.	Personal consumption
..	..	..	..	951	990	1,011	1,024	878	..	.	Collective consumption
1,148	1,084	1,132	1,212	1,307	1,378	1,345	1,517	1,624	..	.	Net capital formation
..	..	..	..	838	888	933	1,019	944	..	.	Net fixed capital formation
..	..	..	..	..	..	..	..	..	..	.	Depreciation

Poland

Basic tables (continued)	1970	1971	1972	1973	1974	1975	1976	1977	1978	1979	1980
MPS ACCOUNTS, index					*(index, 1980 = 100)*						
NMP produced:	59.0	64.0	71.0	78.0	87.0	94.0	101.0	106.0	109.0	106.0	100.0
Agriculture and forestry	108.7	119.6	125.0	129.3	125.0	114.1	116.3	117.4	125.0	118.5	100.0
Industry excluding construction	52.9	57.7	63.5	70.9	79.4	88.4	96.3	103.7	106.3	104.8	100.0
Construction	71.9	77.0	92.1	106.5	119.4	128.8	137.4	137.4	138.1	127.3	100.0
Transport and communication	45.2	50.7	57.0	62.0	71.9	81.9	87.8	91.4	96.8	93.2	100.0
Trade, etc.	50.5	55.1	60.1	67.7	76.8	85.9	92.4	97.0	97.5	100.0	100.0
NMP used: material goods	58.0	64.0	72.0	82.0	92.0	101.0	108.0	110.0	111.0	106.0	100.0
Final consumption	53.2	57.4	62.2	67.6	72.3	80.9	87.8	93.6	95.2	98.4	100.0
Net capital formation	82.0	94.3	113.9	145.9	175.4	188.5	192.6	180.3	176.2	142.6	100.0
EXCHANGE AND CONVERSION RATES					*(LCUs per US dollar: annual average)*						
Single-year converter	..	..	..	..	..	..	..	..	..	..	44.217
Devisa/official	4.000	4.000	3.680	3.365	3.320	3.320	3.320	3.320	3.240	3.095	3.049
Commercial	..	60.000	55.200	50.480	49.800	49.800	43.160	43.160	42.170	40.160	44.220
Noncommercial	40.000	40.000	36.800	33.650	33.200	33.200	33.200	33.200	32.440	30.950	30.490
Informal market	132.540	107.630	84.750	77.250	85.440	101.625	121.125	126.729	118.229	105.188	119.833
ICP	..	..	..	..	..	..	..	..	..	..	20.741
					(ruble per US dollar: annual average)						
Commercial TR/$ cross	..	1.500	1.380	1.262	1.245	1.245	1.079	1.079	1.054	1.004	1.106
Uniform TR/$ cross	1.072	1.157	1.232	1.093	1.092	1.167	1.067	1.022	0.973	0.945	0.980
					(LCUs per ruble: annual average)						
Commercial	40.000	40.000	40.000	40.000	40.000	40.000	40.000	40.000	40.000	40.000	40.000
Noncommercial	..	..	..	..	..	..	..	..	..	..	..
Devisa/official	4.440	4.440	4.440	4.440	4.440	4.440	4.440	4.440	4.440	4.440	4.440
CONSUMER PRICE INDEXES					*(index)*						
Official, IMF 1985 = 100	16.2	16.4	16.3	16.7	17.9	18.3	19.1	20.1	21.7	23.2	25.4
Official, CIA or LWI 1980 = 100	63.2	63.1	63.1	64.9	69.5	71.6	74.7	78.4	86.2	92.2	100.0
Alternative, CIA or LWI 1980 = 100	49.4	50.9	52.6	55.6	60.5	64.1	69.2	75.0	81.8	89.2	100.0
INTERNATIONAL TRADE (ECE)					*(billions of current Polish zlotys)*						
Value of exports, fob	14	16	18	21	28	34	37	41	45	50	52
to CMEA	9	9	11	12	15	20	21	23	26	29	28
Value of imports, cif	14	16	20	26	35	42	46	49	51	54	58
from CMEA	10	10	11	13	15	18	21	24	26	28	31
Trade balance	0	-1	-2	-5	-7	-8	-10	-8	-6	-4	-6
CMEA	-1	-1	0	-1	0	1	0	-1	-1	1	-3
INTERNATIONAL TRADE (Authors')					*(millions of current US dollars)*						
Value of exports, fob	3,186	3,332	3,903	5,165	6,859	8,074	9,055	10,289	11,678	13,625	14,177
to developed countries	1,007	1,156	1,499	2,170	3,016	3,243	3,527	3,837	4,311	5,047	5,859
to other non-socialist countries	275	274	297	325	667	880	915	1,042	1,045	1,291	1,649
to socialist countries	1,904	1,902	2,107	2,670	3,176	3,951	4,613	5,411	6,321	7,287	6,669
to CMEA	1,804	1,791	2,009	2,559	3,019	3,754	4,400	5,146	5,996	6,920	6,354
Value of imports, cif	3,213	3,435	4,262	6,528	9,020	10,480	11,931	12,589	13,585	15,050	15,939
from developed countries	930	1,102	1,815	3,446	5,326	6,186	6,786	6,334	6,362	6,652	6,701
from other non-socialist countries	204	215	253	303	504	610	589	699	839	1,370	1,790
from socialist countries	2,078	2,118	2,194	2,779	3,190	3,684	4,557	5,555	6,384	7,028	7,448
from CMEA	1,993	2,019	2,087	2,659	3,035	3,524	4,367	5,327	6,114	6,695	7,139
Trade balance	-27	-104	-359	-1,363	-2,161	-2,406	-2,877	-2,300	-1,907	-1,425	-1,763
Developed countries	77	54	-316	-1,276	-2,310	-2,943	-3,258	-2,498	-2,051	-1,605	-843
Other non-socialist countries	71	59	45	21	163	270	326	342	207	-79	-141
Socialist countries	-174	-217	-88	-108	-15	267	56	-144	-62	259	-780
CMEA	-189	-228	-78	-78	-100	-16	231	33	-182	-118	225	-784
PARTNER CONVERTIBLE TRADE (ECE)					*(millions of current US dollars)*						
Exports to non-CMEA (cif)	1,032	1,197	1,490	2,117	2,820	3,182	3,611	3,852	4,330	5,036	5,471
Imports from non-CMEA (fob)	922	1,114	1,746	3,233	4,669	5,593	5,633	5,145	5,725	6,210	6,670
Trade balance	110	83	-256	-1,116	-1,849	-2,411	-2,022	-1,293	-1,395	-1,174	-1,199
TRADE PRICE INDEXES (Authors')					*(index, 1980 = 100)*						
Terms of trade	..	..	..	..	..	..	..	..	..	..	100.0
Exports	..	..	..	..	..	..	..	..	..	..	100.0
Non-socialist countries	..	..	..	..	..	..	..	..	..	..	100.0
Developed countries	..	..	..	..	..	..	..	..	..	..	..
Other	..	..	..	..	..	..	..	..	..	..	..
Socialist countries	..	..	..	..	..	..	..	..	..	..	100.0
CMEA	..	..	..	..	..	..	..	..	..	..	..
Imports	..	..	..	..	..	..	..	..	..	..	100.0
Non-socialist countries	..	..	..	..	..	..	..	..	..	..	100.0
Developed countries	..	..	..	..	..	..	..	..	..	..	..
Other	..	..	..	..	..	..	..	..	..	..	..
Socialist countries	..	..	..	..	..	..	..	..	..	..	100.0
CMEA	..	..	..	..	..	..	..	..	..	..	..

Abbreviations in notes column are explained in the General Notes. For sources and methods, see the Technical Notes.

1981	1982	1983	1984	1985	1986	1987	1988	1989	1990	Notes	Basic tables (continued)
				(index, 1980 = 100)							**MPS ACCOUNTS, index**
88.0	83.0	88.0	93.0	96.0	101.0	103.0	108.0	108.0	..	V	NMP produced:
101.0	106.0	112.0	118.0	118.0	125.0	114.0	116.0	118.0	..	.	Agriculture and forestry
85.0	82.0	86.0	91.0	95.0	99.0	102.0	107.0	105.0	..	.	Industry excluding construction
75.0	69.0	74.0	80.0	83.0	87.0	89.0	94.0	94.0	..	.	Construction
91.0	79.0	87.0	95.0	99.0	104.0	110.0	115.0	..	..	.	Transport and communication
93.0	81.0	84.0	87.0	91.0	96.0	101.0	108.0	..	..	.	Trade, etc.
89.0	80.0	85.0	89.0	92.0	97.0	99.0	103.0	104.0	..	.	NMP used: material goods
95.0	84.0	89.0	93.0	96.0	101.0	103.0	107.0	106.0	..	.	Final consumption
72.0	68.0	71.0	76.0	82.0	86.0	84.0	95.0	99.5		.	Net capital formation
				(LCUs per US dollar: annual average)							**EXCHANGE AND CONVERSION RATES**
51.152	84.824	91.550	113.240	147.142	175.287	265.082	430.546	1,439.180	9,500.000	.	Single-year converter
3.350	..	..	..	..	..	..	..	..	..	Lf	Devisa/official
51.150	84.820	91.550	113.240	147.140	175.290	265.080	430.550	1,439.200	..	f	Commercial
33.500	84.820	91.550	113.240	147.140	175.290	265.080	430.550	1,439.180	..	f	Noncommercial
272.417	479.167	587.917	507.333	707.354	745.548	900.895	1,763.958	5,196.457	..	.	Informal market
23.857	48.432	56.633	65.464	73.555	85.910	107.570	..	..	..	.	ICP
				(ruble per US dollar: annual average)							
1.279	1.247	1.346	1.588	1.764	1.904	2.277	2.212	2.964	..	.	Commercial TR/$ cross
1.076	1.105	1.201	1.395	1.433	1.388	1.397	1.484	1.660	1.980	.	Uniform TR/$ cross
				(LCUs per ruble: annual average)							
40.000	68.000	68.000	71.330	83.420	92.080	116.420	194.670	485.640	..	f	Commercial
..	..	..	..	..	..	..	..	..	..	.	Noncommercial
4.440	..	..	..	..	..	..	..	..	..	Lf	Devisa/official
				(index)							**CONSUMER PRICE INDEXES**
30.8	61.9	75.5	86.9	100.0	117.7	147.4	236.1	828.9	5,684.3	.	Official, IMF 1985 = 100
121.2	247.9	300.9	345.5	397.3	466.8	585.0	943.5	3,243.9	22,211.1	.	Official, CIA or LWI 1980 = 100
127.5	233.4	282.8	327.4	376.7	448.3	575.3	938.7	3,346.4	20,576.9	.	Alternative, CIA or LWI 1980 = 100
				(billions of current Polish zlotys)							**INTERNATIONAL TRADE (ECE)**
45	951	1,060	1,336	1,691	2,116	3,237	6,012	19,476	134,847	f	Value of exports, fob
25	475	544	654	825	986	1,353	2,471	6,837	34,146	.	to CMEA
52	869	970	1,210	1,595	1,964	2,876	5,272	14,864	88,865	f	Value of imports, cif
32	513	579	702	874	1,023	1,322	2,157	4,858	25,919	.	from CMEA
-8	82	90	126	96	152	361	739	4,612	45,982	f	Trade balance
-7	-37	-35	-47	-50	-37	31	314	1,979	8,227	.	CMEA
				(millions of current US dollars)							**INTERNATIONAL TRADE (Authors')**
10,953	11,988	12,347	12,645	12,947	14,486	15,939	17,147	17,854	19,377	.	Value of exports, fob
3,921	3,662	3,753	4,062	3,983	4,092	5,082	6,077	6,646	8,803	.	to developed countries
1,543	1,545	1,486	1,449	1,207	1,473	1,206	1,388	1,390	1,357	.	to other non-socialist countries
5,490	6,781	7,107	7,134	7,756	8,921	9,651	9,682	9,817	9,217	.	to socialist countries
5,271	6,326	6,660	6,576	6,897	7,712	8,317	8,553	8,481	8,212	.	to CMEA
12,512	11,080	11,419	11,597	12,358	13,735	14,485	15,073	13,580	13,337	.	Value of imports, cif
4,489	3,168	3,049	3,139	3,495	3,702	4,315	5,618	5,480	5,619	.	from developed countries
949	596	755	805	762	692	759	857	712	635	.	from other non-socialist countries
7,074	7,316	7,615	7,653	8,102	9,341	9,411	8,598	7,388	7,083	.	from socialist countries
6,789	6,822	7,092	7,050	7,311	8,004	8,128	7,466	6,026	6,233	.	from CMEA
-1,559	909	928	1,048	588	751	1,455	2,074	4,274	6,040	.	Trade balance
-568	494	704	923	488	391	767	459	1,166	3,184	.	Developed countries
593	949	732	643	445	781	447	531	678	722	.	Other non-socialist countries
-1,584	-535	-508	-519	-345	-420	241	1,084	2,430	2,134	.	Socialist countries
-1,518	-496	-432	-474	-414	-293	189	1,087	2,455	1,979	.	CMEA
				(millions of current US dollars)							**PARTNER CONVERTIBLE TRADE (ECE)**
3,624	3,392	3,400	4,032	4,073	4,350	5,062	5,805	6,297	..	.	Exports to non-CMEA (cif)
4,469	3,385	3,115	3,227	3,455	3,678	4,252	5,139	6,605	..	.	Imports from non-CMEA (fob)
-845	7	285	805	618	672	810	666	-308	..	.	Trade balance
				(index, 1980 = 100)							**TRADE PRICE INDEXES (Authors')**
98.3	95.6	91.4	91.2	93.0	93.6	97.9	102.3	120.1	..	.	Terms of trade
96.3	97.8	92.1	85.6	86.7	92.6	97.4	95.2	98.8	..	.	Exports
93.4	88.3	79.0	76.2	76.8	81.2	85.6	89.4	94.5	..	.	Non-socialist countries
..	..	..	..	..	..	..	..	..	..	.	Developed countries
..	..	..	..	..	..	..	..	..	..	.	Other
99.2	105.1	101.7	92.8	93.3	99.8	105.0	99.7	102.3	..	.	Socialist countries
..	..	..	..	..	..	..	..	..	..	.	CMEA
97.9	102.3	100.8	93.8	93.2	99.0	99.5	93.1	82.3	..	.	Imports
93.5	85.4	80.9	78.1	74.4	78.3	81.7	84.9	76.3	..	.	Non-socialist countries
..	..	..	..	..	..	..	..	..	..	.	Developed countries
..	..	..	..	..	..	..	..	..	..	.	Other
101.4	111.1	110.7	101.9	103.2	108.7	109.1	99.2	87.3	..	.	Socialist countries
..	..	..	..	..	..	..	..	..	..	.	CMEA

Poland

Basic tables (continued)	1970	1971	1972	1973	1974	1975	1976	1977	1978	1979	1980
TRADE PRICE INDEXES (ECE)					*(index, 1980 = 100)*						
Terms of trade	107	109	110	110	103	108	100	100	101	100	100
Exports	52	53	60	70	81	98	74	77	85	93	100
Imports	49	49	54	63	79	91	74	77	85	92	100
Balance of Payments (ECE)					*(millions of current US dollars)*						
Exports, convertible currency	1,064	1,262	1,633	2,278	3,477	4,109	4,310	4,746	5,280	5,940	7,174
Imports, convertible currency	991	1,108	1,798	3,595	5,559	6,949	6,968	6,608	7,371	8,009	8,108
Trade balance, convertible currency	73	154	-165	-1,317	-2,082	-2,840	-2,658	-1,862	-2,091	-2,069	-934
Invisibles, convertible currency	71	121	205	229	11	-173	-124	-250	-353	-1,050	-1,720
Current balance, convertible currency	144	275	40	-1,088	-2,071	-3,013	-2,782	-2,112	-2,444	-3,119	-2,654
External debt, total (World Bank)	24	41	77	207	401	698	1,487	1,839	2,770	3,872	8,894
Convertible currency	24	41	77	207	401	698	1,487	1,839	2,770	3,872	8,678
CMEA	..	..	..	..	..	..	..	..	..	..	224
External debt service (World Bank)	6	6	8	40	85	190	305	430	522	761	2,899
Convertible currency	6	6	8	40	85	190	305	430	522	761	2,844
Total reserves less gold (IMF, IFS)	..	..	..	..	..	..	..	..	..	565	128
Total reserves, including gold at London price	..	..	..	..	..	..	..	..	..	658	447
Total reserves, incl. gold at national valuation	..	..	..	..	..	..	..	..	..	832	431
EMPLOYMENT					*(thousands)*						
Employment, total	..	..	..	..	..	..	..	..	..	..	..
Agriculture	..	..	..	..	..	..	..	..	..	..	..
Industry	..	..	..	..	..	..	..	..	..	..	..
Services	..	..	..	..	..	..	..	..	..	..	..
Labor force, total	17,336	17,493	17,650	17,806	17,963	18,120	18,200	18,280	18,360	18,440	18,520
Agriculture	6,748	6,621	6,493	6,366	6,238	6,111	5,945	5,779	5,614	5,448	5,282
Industry	5,936	6,073	6,211	6,349	6,487	6,625	6,740	6,856	6,971	7,086	7,201
Services	4,652	4,799	4,945	5,091	5,238	5,384	5,514	5,645	5,775	5,906	6,036
DOMESTIC FINANCE (IMF)					*(billions of current Polish zlotys)*						
Money supply, broadly defined	..	..	..	..	..	..	..	..	..	1,386	1,546
Money, means of payment	..	..	..	..	..	..	..	..	..	826	910
Demand deposits	..	..	..	..	..	..	..	..	..	591	618
Currency outside banks	..	..	..	..	..	..	..	..	..	235	293
Quasi-money	..	..	..	..	..	..	..	..	..	561	636
Interest: deposit rate (percent)	..	..	..	..	..	..	..	..	..	..	3
Central government expenditures	..	..	..	..	..	..	..	..	..	..	..
Defense	..	..	..	..	..	..	..	..	..	..	..
					(millions of 1989 US dollars)						
Central government exp. (ACDA)	..	..	..	..	..	..	..	..	56,640	57,440	61,180
Military (ACDA)	..	..	..	..	..	..	..	..	..	13,730	14,210
LAND AND FORESTS (FAO)											
Pop. density: agr. land (pop. per sq. km)	166	168	171	173	175	177	179	181	183	185	187
Deforestation rate (net)	0	0	0	0	0	0	0	0	0	0	0
Forest (thousands sq. km)	86	86	86	86	86	86	86	86	87	87	87
SOCIAL INDICATORS											
Population density: total land (pop. per sq. km)	107	108	109	110	111	112	113	114	115	116	117
School enrollment ratio, primary	101	..	..	..	..	100	100	100	100	99	100
secondary	62	..	..	69	..	73	..	74	75	76	77
tertiary	..	..	..	..	..	..	..	..	..	..	18
Energy consumption per capita (kg. of oil eq.)	2,512	2,561	2,675	2,694	2,751	2,971	3,133	3,260	3,351	3,432	3,456
Daily calorie supply per capita	3,402	3,406	3,440	3,477	3,485	3,518	3,585	3,573	3,565	3,579	3,583
Food production (1979-1981=100)	100	96	101	106	108	108	111	103	111	111	95
Daily protein supply (gm. per capita)	101	102	104	106	106	110	110	109	110	110	111
Population per hospital bed	131	..	..	..	..	..	..	..	..	..	..
per nursing person	..	..	..	255	..	..	..	..	..	214	..
per physician	700	..	..	..	..	..	..	..	..	..	..
Female participation in labor force (percent)	47	47	47	47	47	47	47	47	46	46	46
Infant mortality (per 1,000 live births)	33	30	28	26	24	25	24	25	22	21	21
Life expectancy (years)	70	70	71	71	71	71	71	71	71	71	71
Total fertility (births per woman)	2	2	2	2	2	2	2	2	2	2	2
Urban population (percent of total population)	52	53	54	54	55	55	56	57	57	58	58
Population per passenger car	68	59	50	43	37	32	27	22	19	17	15
per telephone	..	..	..	..	..	13	..	..	..	..	11

Abbreviations in notes column are explained in the General Notes. For sources and methods, see the Technical Notes.

1981	1982	1983	1984	1985	1986	1987	1988	1989	1990	Notes	*Basic tables (continued)*
				(index, 1980 = 100)							**TRADE PRICE INDEXES (ECE)**
100	97	95	95	93	92	93	92	..	..	.	Terms of trade
96	89	82	76	75	84	83	80	..	..	.	Exports
96	92	86	81	81	90	89	88	..	..	.	Imports
				(millions of current US dollars)							**Balance of Payments (ECE)**
5,482	4,974	5,402	5,828	5,768	6,226	6,920	7,911	8,113	10,863	.	Exports, convertible currency
6,233	4,616	4,317	4,372	4,594	5,108	5,878	6,991	7,987	8,649	.	Imports, convertible currency
-751	358	1,085	1,456	1,174	1,118	1,042	920	126	2,214	.	Trade balance, convertible currency
-2,390	-2,575	-2,271	-2,153	-1,697	-1,692	-1,434	-1,483	-2,048	-1,546	.	Invisibles, convertible currency
-3,141	-2,217	-1,186	-697	-523	-574	-392	-563	-1,922	668	f	Current balance, convertible currency
13,065	18,767	20,177	21,161	33,336	36,670	42,620	42,146	43,029	49,386	.	External debt, total (World Bank)
12,525	17,583	18,642	19,479	31,389	34,104	40,070	39,491	41,668	48,155	.	Convertible currency
577	1,333	1,713	1,879	2,153	2,781	2,772	2,868	1,539	1,516	.	CMEA
1,296	755	981	1,186	2,045	1,816	2,060	1,763	1,542	953	f	External debt service (World Bank)
1,293	706	912	1,083	1,929	1,731	1,832	1,522	1,415	754	.	Convertible currency
278	647	765	1,106	870	698	1,495	2,055	2,314	4,492	.	Total reserves less gold (IMF, IFS)
187	215	180	146	154	185	228	194	189	182	.	Total reserves, including gold at London price
466	835	954	1,295	1,059	887	1,684	2,244	2,503	4,681	.	Total reserves, incl. gold at national valuation
				(thousands)							**EMPLOYMENT**
..	..	..	..	..	..	..	..	..	..	.	Employment, total
..	..	..	..	..	..	..	..	..	..	.	Agriculture
..	..	..	..	..	..	..	..	..	..	.	Industry
..	..	..	..	..	..	..	..	..	..	.	Services
18,660	18,800	18,940	19,080	19,221	19,317	19,414	19,510	19,607	19,704	.	Labor force, total
..	..	..	..	..	..	..	..	..	..	.	Agriculture
..	..	..	..	..	..	..	..	..	..	.	Industry
..	..	..	..	..	..	..	..	..	..	.	Services
				(billions of current Polish zlotys)							**DOMESTIC FINANCE (IMF)**
1,907	2,643	3,039	3,576	4,366	5,532	7,416	12,110	74,433	198,004	.	Money supply, broadly defined
1,105	1,573	1,747	2,001	2,449	2,998	3,786	5,748	19,975	101,670	.	Money, means of payment
703	968	1,029	1,177	1,435	1,832	2,474	3,225	10,095	62,334	.	Demand deposits
402	605	718	824	1,014	1,166	1,312	2,523	9,880	39,336	.	Currency outside banks
802	1,070	1,292	1,575	1,917	2,534	3,631	6,362	54,458	96,334	.	Quasi-money
4	6	6	6	6	6	6	21	21	28	.	Interest: deposit rate (percent)
..	..	..	3,795	4,719	5,417	6,751	11,458	..	..	.	Central government expenditures
..	..	..					..	..	..	.	Defense
				(millions of 1989 US dollars)							
62,200	42,060	36,680	40,610	41,050	40,240	35,690	35,160	66,160	..	.	Central government exp. (ACDA)
14,100	15,710	15,480	16,030	16,700	16,900	16,620	15,980	15,480	..	U	Military (ACDA)
											LAND AND FORESTS (FAO)
190	192	194	195	197	198	199	201	202	..	.	Pop. density: agr. land (pop. per sq. km)
0	0	0	0	0	0	0	0	0	..	.	Deforestation rate (net)
87	87	87	87	87	87	87	87	88	..	.	Forest (thousands sq. km)
											SOCIAL INDICATORS
118	119	120	121	122	123	124	..	..	..	.	Population density: total land (pop. per sq. km)
..	100	101	101	101	101	101	100	99	..	.	School enrollment ratio, primary
..	75	75	78	78	80	80	81	81	..	.	secondary
..	..	..	16	17	17	18	20	20	..	.	tertiary
3,152	3,217	3,198	3,166	3,231	3,325	3,426	3,425	3,326	3,417	.	Energy consumption per capita (kg. of oil eq.)
3,367	3,284	3,364	3,353	3,353	3,403	3,401	3,479	3,505	..	.	Daily calorie supply per capita
94	97	101	104	106	111	104	106	110	111	.	Food production (1979-1981 = 100)
106	97	98	97	99	102	99	103	103	..	.	Daily protein supply (gm. per capita)
..	..	..	..	187	..	..	..	..	..	.	Population per hospital bed
..	..	..	..								per nursing person
550	541	..	..	487							per physician
46	46	46	46	46	46	46	46	46	46	.	Female participation in labor force (percent)
21	20	19	19	18	18	18	17	17	16	.	Infant mortality (per 1,000 live births)
71	71	71	71	71	71	71	71	71	71	.	Life expectancy (years)
2	2	2	2	2	2	2	2	2	2	.	Total fertility (births per woman)
59	59	59	60	60	60	61	61	61	62	.	Urban population (percent of total population)
14	13	12	11	10	9	9	8	8	..	.	Population per passenger car
10	9	..	9	9	9	8	..	..	..	.	per telephone

Romania

Comparator tables	1970	1971	1972	1973	1974	1975	1976	1977	1978	1979	1980
PER CAPITA INCOME						*(US dollars)*					
World Bank (Atlas method)	..	..	..	..	..	..	..	..	..	..	..
Single year conversion	..	..	..	..	..	..	..	..	..	..	..
CIA or LWI	1,155	..	..	..	..	2,150	2,382	2,573	2,825	3,136	3,406
Penn World Tables	1,256	1,514	1,665	1,818	2,073	2,349	2,723	2,953	3,307	3,713	3,946
						(thousands)					
POPULATION	20,253	20,470	20,663	20,828	21,029	21,245	21,446	21,658	21,855	22,048	22,201
GROSS NATIONAL PRODUCT, current prices						*(millions of current US dollars)*					
World Bank (Atlas method)	..	..	..	..	..	..	..	..	..	..	..
Single year conversion	..	..	..	..	..	..	..	..	..	..	..
Authors' series	10,000	..	..	..	..	..	..	..	..	..	34,000
CIA or LWI	..	..	..	..	..	..	..	..	..	68,590	74,990
GROSS NATIONAL PRODUCT, constant prices						*(millions of constant 1987 dollars)*					
Single year conversion	..	..	..	..	..	22,306	24,727	26,575	28,689	30,527	31,065
Authors' series, rescaled from 1980 prices	21,194	..	..	..	..	..	..	..	..	..	47,098
CIA or LWI, rescaled from 1989 prices	65,386	..	..	..	..	90,437	95,049	97,220	100,385	103,279	103,550
CONVERSION FACTORS						*(LCUs per US dollar)*					
World Bank (Atlas method)	..	..	..	..	..	..	..	..	..	..	..
Single year convertor	..	..	..	..	..	..	..	..	..	..	..
Authors' series	24.89	..	..	..	..	..	..	..	..	..	18.21
Penn World Tables	..	..	..	..	..	..	..	..	..	..	..
OUTPUT TRENDS, OVERALL						*(index, constant prices 1987 = 100)*					
GNP, SNA	..	..	..	..	..	59.0	65.4	70.3	75.9	80.7	82.2
NMP, MPS	30.1	34.6	38.2	41.9	47.8	52.2	57.4	62.5	67.7	71.3	73.5
GNP, "Building block"	62.0	70.8	75.3	77.7	82.1	85.8	90.1	92.2	95.2	97.9	98.2
Industry											
Value added, SNA	..	..	..	..	..	..	..	61.8	67.1	69.3	80.3
Value added, MPS	25.6	28.5	31.9	36.8	41.3	45.8	51.0	57.4	62.4	66.5	69.9
"Building block"	55.4	61.4	65.8	71.2	78.8	82.2	87.4	91.3	94.9	97.8	99.2
Gross output, SNA	52.4	..	..	..	..	..	..	..	..	..	97.1
Agriculture											
Value added, SNA	..	..	..	..	..	..	..	137.8	144.2	131.4	106.1
Value added, MPS	64.0	80.6	88.9	83.8	81.9	81.9	100.4	96.6	100.4	102.4	89.6
"Building block"	75.6	97.1	104.6	100.8	98.5	99.4	102.5	100.5	100.7	101.7	98.6
Gross output, SNA	53.7	64.0	71.5	68.6	70.5	71.8	88.0	86.9	87.7	92.3	89.1
Services											
Value added, SNA	..	..	..	..	..	..	..	63.5	69.5	87.3	81.1
Value added, MPS	22.7	23.6	24.9	30.5	47.7	54.8	49.9	56.7	63.7	66.8	75.7
"Building block"	62.8	66.5	69.1	71.3	75.6	81.5	85.5	87.7	91.8	95.5	96.3
CONSUMPTION											
Total consumption, SNA	..	..	..	..	..	..	..	..	..	..	122.3
Total consumption, MPS	..	..	..	..	..	..	..	..	..	..	77.8
Households, SNA	..	..	..	..	..	..	..	..	..	..	..
Households, "building block"	..	..	..	..	..	87.6	86.7	90.1	92.1	94.7	97.5
General government, SNA	..	..	..	..	..	..	..	..	..	..	..
General government, "building block"	..	..	..	..	..	102.8	106.3	105.3	104.8	108.2	109.2
INVESTMENT											
Gross fixed investment, SNA	..	..	..	..	..	..	..	..	..	..	101.6
Accumulation, MPS	..	..	..	..	..	..	..	..	..	..	109.9
"Building block"	..	..	..	..	..	144.3	154.1	153.5	156.4	161.9	154.4
CONSUMER PRICES											
National methodology	..	..	..	..	..	..	..	..	..	..	..
Outside estimate	44.2	..	..	..	..	51.1	56.9	57.4	62.0	66.1	69.4
MERCHANDISE EXPORTS						*(millions of current US dollars)*					
UNCTAD	1,851	..	..	..	..	5,341	..	..	..	..	11,209
IMF: IFS	1,851	..	..	..	..	5,341	..	..	..	..	11,209
ACDA	..	..	..	..	..	..	..	7,064	8,093	9,949	11,210
ECE	1,852	2,102	2,604	3,728	5,010	5,664	5,091	5,792	6,616	8,008	9,217
intra-CMEA	931	1,009	1,246	1,722	1,895	2,342	1,485	1,870	2,153	2,144	2,509
Authors' uniform TR/$ series	1,679	1,837	2,128	3,091	4,205	4,455	5,291	6,108	6,883	8,469	9,795
intra-CMEA	782	785	838	1,162	1,217	1,324	1,653	2,144	2,379	2,522	3,007
MERCHANDISE IMPORTS						*(millions of current US dollars)*					
UNCTAD	1,960	..	..	..	..	5,342	..	..	..	..	12,818
IMF: IFS	2,117	..	..	..	..	5,769	..	..	..	..	13,843
ACDA	..	..	..	..	..	..	..	7,060	8,926	11,170	12,810
ECE	1,961	2,104	2,620	3,491	5,272	5,647	5,066	5,807	7,480	9,154	11,061
intra-CMEA	948	975	1,189	1,442	1,799	2,246	1,537	1,877	2,106	2,265	2,358
Authors' uniform series	1,791	1,852	2,178	2,945	4,506	4,503	5,263	6,119	7,740	9,628	11,627
intra-CMEA	796	758	800	973	1,155	1,269	1,711	2,152	2,328	2,665	2,826

Abbreviations in notes column are explained in the General Notes. For sources and methods, see the Technical Notes.

1981	1982	1983	1984	1985	1986	1987	1988	1989	1990	Notes	*Comparator tables (continued)*
				(US dollars)							**PER CAPITA INCOME**
..	..	..	..	..	..	..	..	1,720	1,620	.	World Bank (Atlas method)
..	..	..	..	..	..	1,650	1,751	1,792	1,516	.	Single year conversion
3,685	3,903	4,005	4,306	4,408	4,575	4,597	4,718	4,740	4,151	.	CIA or LWI
4,306	4,641	4,834	5,217	5,529						.	Penn World Tables
				(thousands)							**POPULATION**
22,353	22,478	22,553	22,625	22,725	22,819	22,914	23,009	23,104	23,200	.	
				(millions of current US dollars)							**GROSS NATIONAL PRODUCT, current prices**
..	..	..	..	..	..	..	..	39,839	37,573	.	World Bank (Atlas method)
..	..	..	..	..	..	37,811	40,292	41,409	35,168	.	Single year conversion
..	..	..	..	..	..	..	74,000	..	..	D	Authors' series
81,750	87,040	89,640	96,620	99,330	103,600	104,600	112,300	113,400	..	.	CIA or LWI
				(millions of constant 1987 dollars)							**GROSS NATIONAL PRODUCT, constant prices**
31,037	32,478	34,487	36,534	36,673	37,495	37,811	37,833	35,800	32,999	.	Single year conversion
..	..	..	..	58,402	..	64,995	66,879	0	..	D	Authors' series, rescaled from 1980 prices
102,917	103,007	102,103	106,173	105,992	107,711	105,449	105,269	102,012	85,915	.	CIA or LWI, rescaled from 1989 prices
				(LCUs per US dollar)							**CONVERSION FACTORS**
..	..	..	..	..	..	..	..	20.06	21.00	..	World Bank (Atlas method)
..	..	..	..	..	..	22.20	21.20	19.30	22.43	.	Single year convertor
..	..	..	..	..	..	..	14.19	..	..	.	Authors' series
..	..	..	..	..	..	..	..	..	..	.	Penn World Tables
				(index, constant prices 1987 = 100)							**OUTPUT TRENDS, OVERALL**
82.1	85.9	91.2	96.6	97.0	99.2	100.0	100.1	94.7	87.3	.	GNP, SNA
73.2	76.3	80.8	97.5	96.7	99.0	100.0	97.7	91.8	81.4	f	NMP, MPS
97.6	97.7	96.8	100.7	100.5	102.2	100.0	99.7	96.7	81.5	.	GNP, "Building block"
											Industry
78.8	82.9	91.0	95.7	94.2	99.3	100.0	97.1	90.7	73.3	H	Value added, SNA
68.9	72.2	78.3	95.2	94.8	98.2	100.0	94.7	88.3	70.7	.	Value added, MPS
97.0	95.8	95.9	100.3	98.8	101.7	100.0	98.2	95.8	68.3	.	"Building block"
..	..	..	..	98.1	101.0	100.0	97.1	94.2	76.7	X	Gross output, SNA
											Agriculture
105.4	109.1	108.0	117.6	119.0	110.7	100.0	109.1	102.6	115.4	H	Value added, SNA
89.7	92.7	90.7	119.2	110.7	108.0	100.0	108.3	101.4	115.6	I	Value added, MPS
97.8	102.2	100.4	106.5	108.8	107.4	100.0	99.8	88.9	82.3	.	"Building block"
88.8	95.4	92.7	104.1	96.8	108.6	100.0	104.8	101.4	..	f	Gross output, SNA
											Services
85.0	86.1	87.1	92.9	95.3	94.8	100.0	101.5	97.4	103.7	H	Value added, SNA
77.9	79.6	83.1	90.1	93.5	95.4	100.0	101.3	98.3	97.4	.	Value added, MPS
98.3	97.3	95.7	97.2	97.3	99.1	100.0	102.1	103.9	101.2	.	"Building block"
											CONSUMPTION
118.1	106.8	97.1	110.5	99.2	96.9	100.0	117.3	126.0	134.6	.	Total consumption, SNA
79.3	78.0	77.5	98.7	94.6	96.1	100.0	103.1	104.7	117.8	.	Total consumption, MPS
..	..	..	..	..	..	..	..	..	..	.	Households, SNA
96.2	96.3	91.5	91.2	96.0	97.5	100.0	100.2	96.3	..	.	Households, "building table"
..	..	..	..	..	..	..	..	..	..	.	General government, SNA
109.7	110.5	106.9	106.1	106.5	105.8	100.0	100.6	100.6	..	.	General government, "building block"
											INVESTMENT
94.4	90.8	93.0	98.6	100.3	101.4	100.0	97.9	96.3	59.4	.	Gross fixed investment, SNA
94.7	86.3	86.3	107.7	106.9	108.6	100.0	91.4	86.2	29.4	.	Accumulation, MPS
147.3	145.3	154.1	141.6	120.9	131.7	100.0	74.2	74.5	..	.	"Building block"
											CONSUMER PRICES
..	..	..	..	..	..	..	..	..	..	.	National methodology
75.8	87.9	92.4	96.2	98.1	100.0	100.0	100.3	108.3	..	.	Outside estimate
				(millions of current US dollars)							**MERCHANDISE EXPORTS**
12,610	11,559	11,512	12,646	12,167	12,543	12,948	11,391	10,486	5,982	.	UNCTAD
12,610	11,559	11,512	12,646	12,167	12,543	..	..	..	..	.	IMF: IFS
12,610	11,560	11,510	12,650	12,170	12,540	13,180				.	ACDA
10,294	8,972	8,601	9,466	8,376	8,159	8,580	8,971	8,076	4,570	.	ECE
2,755	2,429	2,191	2,178	2,342	2,754	2,552	2,406	2,083	1,136	.	intra-CMEA
10,893	9,746	9,501	10,296	9,219	8,722	9,251	9,816	8,686	4,776	.	Authors' uniform TR/$ series
3,274	3,097	2,994	2,885	3,073	3,248	3,155	3,143	2,623	1,318	.	intra-CMEA
				(millions of current US dollars)							**MERCHANDISE IMPORTS**
12,457	9,745	9,643	10,334	10,432	10,590	10,820	7,641	8,436	9,207	F	UNCTAD
13,454	10,525	10,414	11,161	11,267	11,437	..	..	..	..	.	IMF: IFS
12,460	9,745	9,643	10,330	10,430	10,600	11,480				.	ACDA
10,090	7,270	6,156	6,430	6,700	6,411	6,355	5,361	5,834	6,889	.	ECE
2,765	2,234	2,069	2,021	2,275	2,982	2,625	2,307	2,296	1,971	.	intra-CMEA
10,690	7,979	7,014	7,176	7,498	6,998	7,042	6,157	6,493	7,242	.	Authors' uniform series
3,285	2,848	2,827	2,678	2,986	3,516	3,245	3,015	2,893	2,287	.	intra-CMEA

Romania

	1970	1971	1972	1973	1974	1975	1976	1977	1978	1979	1980
SNA ACCOUNTS, current prices					*(billions of current Romanian lei)*						
GNP, at market prices	..	..	..	..	..	437	489	510	549	594	603
Net factor income	..	..	..	..	..	0	-2	-3	-3	-5	-14
GDP at market prices	..	..	..	..	..	437	491	513	552	599	617
Net indirect taxes	..	..	..	..	..	..	..	..	..	..	..
GDP at factor cost	..	..	..	..	..		..	..		..	..
Agriculture	..	..	..	..	..	64	80	75	76	81	78
Industry	..	..	..	..	..	266	293	314	340	365	373
Services, etc.	..	..	..	..	..	107	118	124	136	153	166
Resource balance	..	..	..	..	..	..	..	..	..	..	-30
Exports GNFS	..	..	..	..	..	..	..	..	..	..	218
Imports GNFS	..	..	..	..	..	..	..	..	..	..	247
Domestic absorption	..	..	..	..	..	441	490	508	561	607	647
Total consumption	..	..	..	..	..	264	287	304	336	370	401
Private consumption	..	..	..	..	..	..	..	..	..	..	370
General government consumption	..	..	..	..	..	..	..	..	..	..	31
Gross domestic investment	..	..	..	..	..	177	203	204	225	237	246
Fixed domestic investment	..	..	..	..	..	146	154	171	199	207	213
Depreciation	..	..	..	..	..	..	..	..	..	..	..
SNA ACCOUNTS, constant prices					*(billions of constant 1987 Romanian lei)*						
Gross national product (GNP)	..	..	..	..	..	495	549	590	637	678	690
GDP at market prices	..	..	..	..	..	495	552	593	640	683	706
GDP at factor cost	..	..	..	..	..	..	..	..	..	..	..
Agriculture	..	..	..	..	..	..	..	143	149	136	110
Industry	..	..	..	..	..	..	..	323	351	362	420
Services, etc.	..	..	..	..	..	..	..	139	152	191	178
Resource balance	..	..	..	..	..	..	..	..	..	..	-245
Exports GNFS	..	..	..	..	..	..	..	..	..	..	209
Imports GNFS	..	..	..	..	..	..	..	..	..	..	454
Domestic absorption	..	..	..	..	..	..	..	..	..	..	950
Total consumption, etc.	..	..	..	..	..	..	..	..	..	..	661
Private consumption, etc.	..	..	..	..	..	..	..	..	..	..	..
General government consumption	..	..	..	..	..	..	..	..	..	..	..
Gross domestic investment	..	..	..	..	..	210	254	258	299	294	289
Fixed domestic investment	..	..	..	..	..	..	..	..	..	..	249
Depreciation	..	..	..	..	..	..	..	..	..	..	..
MPS ACCOUNTS, current prices					*(billions of current Romanian lei)*						
NMP produced:	212	238	261	289	325	362	400	432	464	499	514
Agriculture and forestry	39	53	55	53	52	59	74	69	71	74	71
Industry excluding construction	123	133	148	168	184	216	235	246	269	292	306
Construction	22	23	25	26	27	28	28	46	47	48	44
Transport and communication	13	13	14	16	18	21	21	25	27	29	31
Trade, etc.	15	16	19	25	45	38	42	46	50	56	62
Other services	..	..	..	..	..	..	..	..	..	..	..
Resource balance	..	..	..	..	..	..	..	..	..	..	-17
NMP used: domestic market	..	..	..	..	..	..	..	..	..	..	530
Final consumption, material goods	..	..	..	..	..	..	..	..	..	..	341
Personal consumption	..	..	..	..	..	..	..	..	..	..	327
Collective consumption	..	..	..	..	..	..	..	..	..	..	13
Net capital formation	..	..	..	..	..	..	..	..	..	..	190
Net fixed capital formation	..	..	..	..	..	..	..	..	..	..	157
Changes in stocks	..	..	..	..	..	..	..	..	..	..	33
Depreciation	..	..	..	..	..	..	..	..	..	..	..
MPS ACCOUNTS, constant prices					*(billions of 1981 Romanian lei)*						
NMP produced:	211	242	267	293	334	365	401	437	473	499	514
Agriculture and forestry	59	75	83	78	76	76	93	90	93	95	83
Industry and construction	123	137	154	177	199	221	246	277	300	321	337
Services	28	29	31	38	60	68	62	71	80	83	95
Resource balance	..	..	..	..	..	..	..	..	..	..	-46
NMP used: domestic market	..	..	..	..	..	..	..	..	..	..	560
Final consumption, material goods	..	..	..	..	..	..	..	..	..	..	354
Personal consumption	..	..	..	..	..	..	..	..	..	..	341
Collective consumption	..	..	..	..	..	..	..	..	..	..	13
Net capital formation	..	..	..	..	..	..	..	..	..	..	207
Net fixed capital formation	..	..	..	..	..	..	..	..	..	..	169
Depreciation	..	..	..	..	..	..	..	..	..	..	..

Abbreviations in notes column are explained in the General Notes. For sources and methods, see the Technical Notes.

Romania

			(billions of current Romanian lei)								**SNA ACCOUNTS, current prices**
608	715	757	802	807	830	839	854	799	789	.	GNP, at market prices
-15	-13	-12	-14	-10	-9	-6	-3	1	-55	.	Net factor income
624	727	769	816	817	839	845	857	798	844	.	GDP at market prices
..	..	..	..	..	..	..	..	..	..		Net indirect taxes
..	..	..	..	..	..	..	..	..	..	.	GDP at factor cost
92	126	108	111	114	107	103	116	111	152	H	Agriculture
356	413	464	499	491	520	520	523	473	455	H	Industry
176	189	197	207	212	212	219	221	215	237	H	Services, etc.
3	28	32	51	35	32	36	59	37	-77	.	Resource balance
202	186	210	287	188	169	164	175	169	146	.	Exports GNFS
199	157	178	236	153	137	129	116	133	223	.	Imports GNFS
621	699	737	766	783	807	809	798	762	921	.	Domestic absorption
395	454	475	487	513	519	541	555	548	631	.	Total consumption
363	424	444	456	481	488	513	524	515	592	.	Private consumption
32	30	31	31	32	30	28	31	33	40	.	General government consumption
226	245	262	279	270	288	269	243	213	289	.	Gross domestic investment
209	216	231	245	246	249	246	240	236	168	.	Fixed domestic investment
..	..	..	..	..	..	..	..	..	..		Depreciation
			(billions of constant 1987 Romanian lei)								**SNA ACCOUNTS, constant prices**
689	721	766	811	814	832	839	840	795	733	.	Gross national product (GNP)
706	734	778	825	824	841	845	843	794	730	.	GDP at market prices
..	..	..	..	..	..	..	..	..	..		GDP at factor cost
109	113	112	122	123	115	103	113	106	119	H	Agriculture
412	433	475	500	492	519	523	507	474	383	H	Industry
186	189	191	204	209	208	219	222	213	227	H	Services, etc.
-182	-98	-9	-46	19	31	36	-36	-125	-230	.	Resource balance
194	160	149	218	166	154	164	199	189	103	.	Exports GNFS
376	257	158	264	147	123	129	235	314	332	.	Imports GNFS
889	831	787	871	805	811	809	879	918	959	.	Domestic absorption
638	577	525	597	536	524	541	634	681	727	.	Total consumption, etc.
..	..	..	..	..	..	..	..	..	..		Private consumption, etc.
..	..	..	..	..	..	..	..	..	..		General government consumption
250	254	262	274	269	287	269	245	238	232	.	Gross domestic investment
232	223	228	242	246	249	246	240	237	146	.	Fixed domestic investment
..	..	..	..	..	..	..	..	..	..		Depreciation
			(billions of current Romanian lei)								**MPS ACCOUNTS, current prices**
512	610	640	684	672	694	697	697	633	672	f	NMP produced:
83	117	98	104	104	100	96	103	96	139	.	Agriculture and forestry
290	341	385	416	396	417	417	411	368	359	.	Industry excluding construction
418	45	50	53	55	57	58	57	45	46	.	Construction
31	32	32	33	33	35	35	36	36	32	.	Transport and communication
66	75	76	79	83	85	91	90	88	96	f	Trade, etc.
..	..	..	..	..	..	..	..	..	..	.	Other services
-12	16	37	43	54	48	62	81	45	-99	f	Resource balance
524	594	603	641	618	647	635	616	588	770	f	NMP used: domestic market
361	417	415	441	432	440	458	472	478	581	.	Final consumption, material goods
349	406	402	427	419	427	446	460	466	565	.	Personal consumption
12	11	13	14	13	13	12	12	12	16	.	Collective consumption
163	177	188	200	186	207	178	144	110	189	.	Net capital formation
146	148	158	166	162	167	154	141	133	70	.	Net fixed capital formation
17	29	31	34	24	39	23	3	-23	121	.	Changes in stocks
63	68	73	79	84	82	91	99	104	101	.	Depreciation
			(billions of 1981 Romanian lei)								**MPS ACCOUNTS, constant prices**
512	533	565	682	676	692	699	683	642	570	f	NMP produced:
83	86	84	111	103	100	93	101	94	107	.	Agriculture and forestry
332	348	377	459	457	473	482	456	425	341	.	Industry and construction
97	99	104	112	117	119	125	126	123	122	.	Services
-12	16	48	38	58	48	67	70	56	-84	.	Resource balance
524	517	517	644	619	644	633	613	586	653	.	NMP used: domestic market
361	355	352	449	430	437	455	469	476	536	.	Final consumption, material goods
349	344	340	436	417	424	443	457	464	520	.	Personal consumption
12	10	12	13	13	13	12	12	12	16	.	Collective consumption
163	162	165	195	189	207	178	144	110	118	.	Net capital formation
146	133	133	166	165	167	154	141	133	45	.	Net fixed capital formation
..	..	..	..	..	..	..	..	..	..	.	Depreciation

Romania

Basic tables (continued)	1970	1971	1972	1973	1974	1975	1976	1977	1978	1979	1980
MPS ACCOUNTS, index					*(index, 1980 = 100)*						
NMP produced:	41.0	47.0	52.0	57.0	65.0	71.0	78.0	85.0	92.0	97.0	100.0
Agriculture and forestry	71.4	90.0	99.3	93.6	91.4	91.4	112.1	107.9	112.1	114.3	100.0
Industry excluding construction	34.0	38.1	43.2	50.7	57.5	63.9	71.4	79.6	87.4	94.2	100.0
Construction	53.2	58.5	61.7	65.4	69.1	76.1	83.0	98.9	101.1	101.6	100.0
Transport and communication	43.1	47.4	52.2	57.8	62.9	74.1	77.6	81.9	85.8	92.7	100.0
Trade, etc.	44.2	49.6	54.4	57.1	61.5	67.7	77.4	81.4	88.9	91.6	100.0
NMP used: material goods	..	..	..	..	..	..	..	..	..	..	100.0
Final consumption	..	..	..	..	..	..	..	..	..	..	100.0
Net capital formation	..	..	..	..	..	..	..	..	..	..	100.0
EXCHANGE AND CONVERSION RATES					*(LCUs per US dollar: annual average)*						
Single-year converter	..	..	..	..	..	..	..	..	..	..	..
Devisa/official	6.000	6.000	5.520	5.062	4.970	4.970	4.970	4.970	4.574	4.470	4.470
Commercial	24.000	24.000	24.000	20.253	20.000	20.000	20.000	20.000	18.355	18.000	18.000
Noncommercial	18.000	18.000	16.000	14.578	13.791	12.000	12.000	12.000	12.000	12.000	12.000
Informal market	39.025	39.745	38.817	30.192	28.692	29.713	36.138	34.575	31.954	29.479	29.429
ICP	..	..	..	..	..	..	..	..	..	..	..
					(ruble per US dollar: annual average)						
Commercial TR/$ cross	1.200	1.200	1.200	1.013	1.017	1.111	1.111	1.111	1.020	1.000	1.000
Uniform TR/$ cross	1.072	1.157	1.232	1.093	1.092	1.167	1.067	1.022	0.973	0.945	0.980
					(LCUs per ruble: annual average)						
Commercial	20.000	20.000	20.000	20.000	19.670	18.000	18.000	18.000	18.000	18.000	18.000
Noncommercial	..	..	..	..	..	..	..	..	..	..	..
Devisa/official	6.660	6.660	6.660	6.660	6.660	6.660	6.660	6.660	6.660	6.660	6.660
CONSUMER PRICE INDEXES					*(index)*						
Official, IMF 1985 = 100	..	..	..	..	..	..	..	..	..	..	..
Official, CIA or LWI 1980 = 100	91.0	91.6	91.6	92.1	93.2	93.4	93.9	94.4	96.0	97.9	100.0
Alternative, CIA or LWI 1980 = 100	63.6	..	..	..	..	73.6	82.0	82.6	89.4	95.2	100.0
INTERNATIONAL TRADE (ECE)					*(billions of current Romanian lei)*						
Value of exports, fob	11	13	14	19	24	27	31	35	37	44	51
to CMEA	6	6	7	9	9	10	12	15	15	16	20
Value of imports, cif	12	13	15	17	26	27	30	35	41	49	59
from CMEA	6	6	7	7	8	10	12	15	15	17	18
Trade balance	-1	0	0	1	-1	0	0	0	-4	-5	-8
CMEA	0	0	0	1	0	0	0	0	0	-1	1
INTERNATIONAL TRADE (Authors')					*(millions of current US dollars)*						
Value of exports, fob	1,679	1,837	2,128	3,091	4,205	4,455	5,291	6,108	6,883	8,469	9,795
to developed countries	610	728	904	1,337	2,069	1,855	2,129	2,112	2,638	3,527	3,968
to other non-socialist countries	166	180	247	434	692	1,029	1,193	1,526	1,443	1,866	2,337
to socialist countries	904	929	978	1,320	1,444	1,571	1,969	2,470	2,802	3,076	3,490
to CMEA	782	785	838	1,162	1,217	1,324	1,653	2,144	2,379	2,522	3,007
Value of imports, cif	1,791	1,852	2,178	2,945	4,506	4,503	5,263	6,119	7,740	9,628	11,627
from developed countries	783	841	1,078	1,487	2,525	2,279	2,208	2,588	3,414	3,914	4,114
from other non-socialist countries	120	130	190	325	606	737	1,118	1,098	1,589	2,558	4,094
from socialist countries	888	881	910	1,132	1,375	1,487	1,937	2,433	2,736	3,156	3,419
from CMEA	796	758	800	973	1,155	1,269	1,711	2,152	2,328	2,665	2,826
Trade balance	-112	-15	-49	147	-301	-48	29	-11	-857	-1,159	-1,832
Developed countries	-173	-113	-174	-150	-456	-424	-79	-476	-776	-387	-146
Other non-socialist countries	46	50	57	109	86	292	76	429	-146	-692	-1,757
Socialist countries	15	48	67	188	68	84	32	37	65	-80	71
CMEA	-14	27	38	189	62	55	-59	-8	51	-142	180
PARTNER CONVERTIBLE TRADE (ECE)					*(millions of current US dollars)*						
Exports to non-CMEA (cif)	543	624	796	1,137	1,620	1,677	2,060	1,979	2,401	3,259	3,466
Imports from non-CMEA (fob)	728	787	1,038	1,432	2,157	2,091	2,104	2,395	3,082	3,881	4,016
Trade balance	-185	-163	-242	-295	-537	-414	-44	-416	-681	-622	-550
TRADE PRICE INDEXES (Authors')					*(index, 1980 = 100)*						
Terms of trade	..	..	..	..	..	..	..	..	..	..	100.0
Exports	..	..	..	..	..	..	..	..	..	..	100.0
Non-socialist countries	..	..	..	..	..	..	..	..	..	..	100.0
Developed countries	..	..	..	..	..	..	..	..	..	..	..
Other	..	..	..	..	..	..	..	..	..	..	..
Socialist countries	..	..	..	..	..	..	..	..	..	..	100.0
CMEA	..	..	..	..	..	..	..	..	..	..	..
Imports	..	..	..	..	..	..	..	..	..	..	100.0
Non-socialist countries	..	..	..	..	..	..	..	..	..	..	100.0
Developed countries	..	..	..	..	..	..	..	..	..	..	..
Other	..	..	..	..	..	..	..	..	..	..	..
Socialist countries	..	..	..	..	..	..	..	..	..	..	100.0
CMEA	..	..	..	..	..	..	..	..	..	..	..

Abbreviations in notes column are explained in the General Notes. For sources and methods, see the Technical Notes.

Romania

	1981	1982	1983	1984	1985	1986	1987	1988	1989	1990	Notes	
					(index, 1980 = 100)							**MPS ACCOUNTS, index**
	99.6	103.7	109.9	132.6	131.5	134.6	136.0	132.8	124.8	110.8	I	NMP produced:
	100.1	103.5	101.3	133.1	123.6	120.6	111.7	120.9	113.2	129.1	I	Agriculture and forestry
	99.5	104.2	112.7	139.1	137.7	142.4	145.3	136.9	130.3	102.1	I	Industry excluding construction
	92.9	98.0	107.8	117.8	122.7	128.2	128.9	126.7	100.2	95.8	I	Construction
	104.0	105.0	105.3	108.3	108.3	113.3	116.7	123.3	116.7	92.7	I	Transport and communication
	102.3	105.3	111.8	123.9	130.5	131.9	139.2	138.6	136.0	145.3	I	Trade, etc.
	93.5	92.3	92.3	115.0	110.4	114.9	112.9	109.4	104.6	116.6	I	NMP used: material goods
	102.0	100.3	99.6	127.0	121.6	123.6	128.6	132.5	134.6	151.5	I	Final consumption
	78.9	78.6	79.8	94.4	91.2	100.1	86.1	69.9	53.1	56.9	I	Net capital formation
					(LCUs per US dollar: annual average)							**EXCHANGE AND CONVERSION RATES**
	..	..	..	..	..	..	22.200	21.200	19.300	22.432	.	Single-year converter
	..	..	..	..	..	..	..	..	..	..	Lf	Devisa/official
	15.000	15.000	17.179	21.280	17.141	16.153	14.557	14.277	14.922	22.083	f	Commercial
	11.125	11.012	13.120	14.013	12.241	11.337	9.759	8.747	8.992	..	f	Noncommercial
	39.838	48.104	58.246	64.840	74.390	81.176	82.914	91.708	131.125	..	.	Informal market
	..	..	..	..	..	..	..	..	..	..	.	ICP
					(ruble per US dollar: annual average)							
	1.000	1.000	1.011	1.239	1.106	1.042	0.939	0.921	0.963	..	.	Commercial TR/$ cross
	1.076	1.105	1.201	1.395	1.433	1.388	1.397	1.484	1.660	1.980	.	Uniform TR/$ cross
					(LCUs per ruble: annual average)							
	15.000	15.000	17.000	17.170	15.500	15.500	15.500	15.500	15.500	17.000	.	Commercial
	..	..	..	..	..	..	..	..	..	..	.	Noncommercial
	..	..	..	..	..	..	..	..	..	..	Lf	Devisa/official
					(index)							**CONSUMER PRICE INDEXES**
	..	..	..	..	..	..	..	..	..	..	.	Official, IMF 1985 = 100
	102.1	119.5	125.6	127.1	126.5	126.5	126.5	126.5	127.9	..	.	Official, CIA or LWI 1980 = 100
	109.3	126.7	133.1	138.7	141.3	144.1	144.1	144.5	156.1	..	.	Alternative, CIA or LWI 1980 = 100
					(billions of current Romanian lei)							**INTERNATIONAL TRADE (ECE)**
	168	152	173	228	178	164	168	182	168	135	f	Value of exports, fob
	53	51	61	69	68	70	68	72	68	53	.	to CMEA
	165	125	130	161	147	136	133	122	135	210	f	Value of imports, cif
	53	47	58	64	66	76	70	69	74	92	.	from CMEA
	3	27	43	67	31	28	35	60	33	-75	f	Trade balance
	0	4	3	5	2	-6	-2	3	-7	-39	.	CMEA
					(millions of current US dollars)							**INTERNATIONAL TRADE (Authors')**
	10,893	9,746	9,501	10,296	9,219	8,722	9,251	9,816	8,686	4,776	.	Value of exports, fob
	3,753	3,259	3,514	3,988	3,637	3,190	3,833	4,009	3,855	2,373	.	to developed countries
	3,358	2,900	2,630	2,924	2,038	1,828	1,910	2,206	1,870	917	.	to other non-socialist countries
	3,781	3,586	3,357	3,384	3,544	3,704	3,508	3,600	2,961	1,486	.	to socialist countries
	3,274	3,097	2,994	2,885	3,073	3,248	3,155	3,143	2,623	1,318	.	to CMEA
	10,690	7,979	7,014	7,176	7,498	6,998	7,042	6,157	6,493	7,242	.	Value of imports, cif
	3,509	1,890	1,317	1,502	1,467	1,454	1,128	986	1,003	2,174	.	from developed countries
	3,392	2,805	2,499	2,630	2,677	1,680	2,320	1,778	2,293	2,526	.	from other non-socialist countries
	3,789	3,284	3,198	3,044	3,354	3,864	3,593	3,393	3,196	2,543	.	from socialist countries
	3,285	2,848	2,827	2,678	2,986	3,516	3,245	3,015	2,893	2,287	.	from CMEA
	203	1,767	2,487	3,120	1,721	1,724	2,209	3,659	2,193	-2,466	.	Trade balance
	245	1,369	2,196	2,486	2,170	1,736	2,705	3,023	2,852	199	.	Developed countries
	-34	96	132	294	-639	148	-411	428	-423	-1,609	.	Other non-socialist countries
	-8	303	159	340	189	-160	-85	207	-236	-1,057	.	Socialist countries
	-11	249	168	207	87	-269	-90	129	-269	-969	.	CMEA
					(millions of current US dollars)							**PARTNER CONVERTIBLE TRADE (ECE)**
	3,517	2,576	2,750	3,686	3,453	3,639	4,067	4,095	3,920	..	.	Exports to non-CMEA (cif)
	3,108	1,771	1,366	1,453	1,512	1,763	1,338	1,248	1,157	..	.	Imports from non-CMEA (fob)
	409	805	1,384	2,233	1,941	1,876	2,729	2,847	2,763	..	.	Trade balance
					(index, 1980 = 100)							**TRADE PRICE INDEXES (Authors')**
	97.8	97.3	98.2	98.7	92.8	109.5	110.8	..	..	..	.	Terms of trade
	99.5	97.2	91.1	84.6	77.0	74.0	80.6	..	..	..	.	Exports
	99.6	93.8	86.7	83.0	72.5	64.9	77.7	..	..	..	f	Non-socialist countries
	..	..	..	..	..	..	..	..	..	..	.	Developed countries
	..	..	..	..	..	..	..	..	..	..	.	Other
	99.4	103.0	99.1	87.9	84.1	86.2	85.3	..	..	..	.	Socialist countries
	..	..	..	..	..	..	..	..	..	..	.	CMEA
	101.7	99.9	92.7	85.7	82.9	67.5	72.7	..	..	..	.	Imports
	101.8	98.4	89.8	87.3	83.0	59.0	75.4	..	..	..	.	Non-socialist countries
	..	..	..	..	..	..	..	..	..	..	.	Developed countries
	..	..	..	..	..	..	..	..	..	..	.	Other
	101.6	102.0	96.2	83.5	82.8	74.5	70.1	..	..	..	.	Socialist countries
	..	..	..	..	..	..	..	..	..	..	Lf	CMEA

Romania

Basic tables (continued)	1970	1971	1972	1973	1974	1975	1976	1977	1978	1979	1980
TRADE PRICE INDEXES (ECE)					*(index, 1980 = 100)*						
Terms of trade	103	103	108	108	107	105	105	106	104	104	100
Exports	39	40	48	57	75	82	67	71	77	88	100
Imports	38	39	44	53	71	79	63	67	74	84	100
Balance of Payments (ECE)					*(millions of current US dollars)*						
Exports, convertible currency	708	830	1,076	1,666	2,619	2,839	3,403	3,700	4,040	5,363	6,503
Imports, convertible currency	819	881	1,148	1,734	2,945	2,950	3,327	3,783	4,632	6,518	8,037
Trade balance, convertible currency	-111	-51	-72	-68	-326	-111	76	-83	-592	-1,155	-1,534
Invisibles, convertible currency	-110	-90	-105	-112	-190	-149	-137	-190	-187	-513	-865
Current balance, convertible currency	-221	-141	-177	-180	-516	-260	-61	-273	-779	-1,668	-2,399
External debt, total (World Bank)	..	..	..	57	58	122	419	616	787	3,583	9,762
Convertible currency	..	..	..	57	58	122	419	616	787	3,583	9,762
CMEA	..	..	..	..	..	..	..	..	..	..	..
External debt service (World Bank)	..	..	..	..	1	1	8	76	114	142	1,529
Convertible currency	..	..	..	..	1	1	8	76	114	142	1,529
Total reserves less gold (IMF, IFS)	..	..	..	215	241	539	562	256	376	525	323
Total reserves, including gold at London price	..	..	..	255	456	364	370	504	756	1,810	2,188
Total reserves, incl. gold at national valuation	..	..	..	311	346	645	674	386	529	566	366
EMPLOYMENT					*(thousands)*						
Employment, total	..	..	..	..	..	..	..	..	..	..	..
Agriculture	..	..	..	..	..	..	..	..	..	..	..
Industry	..	..	..	..	..	..	..	..	..	..	..
Services	..	..	..	..	..	..	..	..	..	..	..
Labor force, total	11,037	11,051	11,065	11,079	11,093	11,107	11,093	11,079	11,066	11,052	11,039
Agriculture	5,375	5,180	4,985	4,790	4,595	4,400	4,194	3,988	3,783	3,577	3,371
Industry	3,434	3,577	3,719	3,861	4,003	4,146	4,277	4,408	4,539	4,670	4,801
Services	2,227	2,294	2,361	2,428	2,494	2,561	2,622	2,683	2,744	2,806	2,867
DOMESTIC FINANCE (IMF)					*(billions of current Romanian lei)*						
Money supply, broadly defined	..	..	..	80	102	113	132	150	176	194	218
Money, means of payment	..	..	..	45	61	66	76	84	95	102	115
Demand deposits	..	..	..	27	42	45	52	57	66	68	75
Currency outside banks	..	..	..	18	18	21	24	27	28	34	39
Quasi-money	..	..	..	36	41	48	56	66	81	92	104
Interest: deposit rate (percent)	..	..	..	..	..	..	..	..	..	..	..
Central government expenditures	115	116	124	145	185	216	228	259	277	316	276
Defense	7	7	8	8	9	10	11	11	12	12	10
					(millions of 1989 US dollars)						
Central government exp. (ACDA)	..	..	..	..	..	..	..	..	46,620	51,370	43,840
Military (ACDA)	..	..	..	..	..	..	..	..	..	6,835	6,759
LAND AND FORESTS (FAO)											
Pop. density: agr. land (pop. per sq. km)	136	137	138	140	141	142	143	145	146	147	148
Deforestation rate (net)	0	0	0	0	0	0	0	0	0	0	0
Forest (thousands sq. km)	63	63	63	63	63	63	63	63	63	63	63
SOCIAL INDICATORS											
Population density: total land (pop. per sq. km)	88	89	90	90	91	92	93	94	95	96	96
School enrollment ratio, primary	112	..	..	..	..	107	103	99	97	98	102
secondary	44	..	..	..	..	65	74	84	87	83	71
tertiary	..	..	..	..	..	..	..	..	..	..	11
Energy consumption per capita (kg. of oil eq.)	2,136	2,258	2,358	2,546	2,564	2,726	2,914	3,079	3,281	3,263	3,367
Daily calorie supply per capita	3,027	3,094	3,159	3,225	3,217	3,275	3,445	3,427	3,407	3,410	3,418
Food production (1979-1981=100)	67	78	87	83	84	84	100	99	97	105	99
Daily protein supply (gm. per capita)	90	92	94	96	97	98	101	102	101	104	105
Population per hospital bed	121	..	..	..	..	..	..	..	..	..	107
per nursing person	..	..	..	430	..	..	..	..	..	..	..
per physician	844	..	..	..	..	..	..	..	..	..	678
Female participation in labor force (percent)	47	46	46	46	46	46	46	46	46	45	45
Infant mortality (per 1,000 live births)	49	42	40	38	35	35	31	31	30	32	29
Life expectancy (years)	69	69	69	69	69	70	70	70	70	70	70
Total fertility (births per woman)	3	3	3	2	3	3	3	3	3	3	2
Urban population (percent of total population)	42	43	44	44	45	46	47	47	48	48	49
Population per passenger car	..	..	..	..	..	..	..	..	..	..	..
per telephone	..	..	..	..	..	..	..	..	..	..	..

Abbreviations in notes column are explained in the General Notes. For sources and methods, see the Technical Notes.

1981	1982	1983	1984	1985	1986	1987	1988	1989	1990	Notes	*Basic tables (continued)*
					(index, 1980 = 100)						**TRADE PRICE INDEXES (ECE)**
102	104	110	111	102	122	122	130	..	..	.	Terms of trade
100	95	89	84	74	72	79	80	..	..	.	Exports
98	91	80	76	73	59	65	61	..	..	.	Imports
				(millions of current US dollars)							**Balance of Payments (ECE)**
7,216	6,235	6,246	6,892	6,280	5,127	5,864	6,511	5,990	3,467	.	Exports, convertible currency
7,012	4,710	4,558	4,706	4,835	3,238	3,428	2,903	3,471	5,100	.	Imports, convertible currency
204	1,525	1,688	2,186	1,445	1,889	2,436	3,608	2,600	-1,600	.	Trade balance, convertible currency
-1,022	-870	-766	-650	-530	-391	-200	..	338	100	.	Invisibles, convertible currency
-818	655	922	1,536	915	1,498	2,236	3,608	2,938	-1,500	f	Current balance, convertible currency
10,447	10,003	9,128	7,758	7,008	6,983	6,580	2,524	500	369	.	External debt, total (World Bank)
10,447	10,003	9,128	7,758	7,008	6,983	6,580	2,524	500	369	.	Convertible currency
..	..	..	..	..	..	..	..	..	..	.	CMEA
2,057	2,910	1,874	2,116	2,064	1,981	2,493	4,274	1,946	30	.	External debt service (World Bank)
2,057	2,910	1,874	2,116	2,064	1,981	2,493	4,274	1,946	30	.	Convertible currency
404	450	525	709	199	582	1,402	780	1,859	524	.	Total reserves less gold (IMF, IFS)
1,427	1,623	1,381	1,150	1,248	1,269	660	594	872	850	.	Total reserves, including gold at London price
453	499	566	753	249	626	1,423	2,016	3,704	1,304	.	Total reserves, incl. gold at national valuation
				(thousands)							**EMPLOYMENT**
..	..	..	..	..	..	..	..	..	..	.	Employment, total
..	..	..	..	..	..	..	..	..	..	.	Agriculture
..	..	..	..	..	..	..	..	..	..	.	Industry
..	..	..	..	..	..	..	..	..	..	.	Services
11,115	11,190	11,266	11,342	11,418	11,499	11,581	11,662	11,744	11,825	.	Labor force, total
..	..	..	..	..	..	..	..	..	..	.	Agriculture
..	..	..	..	..	..	..	..	..	..	.	Industry
..	..	..	..	..	..	..	..	..	..	.	Services
				(billions of current Romanian lei)							**DOMESTIC FINANCE (IMF)**
253	289	287	305	323	342	353	389	411	505	.	Money supply, broadly defined
136	167	156	162	166	170	171	199	205	233	.	Money, means of payment
94	122	111	113	111	110	111	134	130	141	.	Demand deposits
41	45	45	49	55	60	61	65	75	92	.	Currency outside banks
118	122	131	143	157	172	182	190	206	280	.	Quasi-money
..	..	..	..	..	..	..	..	..	..	.	Interest: deposit rate (percent)
250	234	212	236	340	356	344	314	321	290	.	Central government expenditures
11	11	12	12	27	29	25	28	29	30	.	Defense
				(millions of 1989 US dollars)							
38,490	29,970	25,720	27,530	39,010	41,510	37,470	39,120	40,970	..	.	Central government exp. (ACDA)
6,704	7,178	7,628	7,637	7,787	7,833	8,050	7,291	6,916	..	U	Military (ACDA)
											LAND AND FORESTS (FAO)
150	150	151	151	151	152	152	152	157	..	.	Pop. density: agr. land (pop. per sq. km)
0	0	0	0	0	0	0	0	0	..	.	Deforestation rate (net)
63	63	63	63	63	63	63	64	64	..	.	Forest (thousands sq. km)
											SOCIAL INDICATORS
97	98	98	98	99	99	100	..	..	..	.	Population density: total land (pop. per sq. km)
..	..	99	98	98	97	97	96	95	..	.	School enrollment ratio, primary
..	..	72	73	75	74	79	85	88	..	.	secondary
..	..	12	12	11	11	10	9	9	..	.	tertiary
3,343	3,309	3,285	3,326	3,411	3,418	3,519	3,566	3,526	3,623	.	Energy consumption per capita (kg. of oil eq.)
3,301	3,341	3,364	3,442	3,391	3,398	3,341	3,255	3,155	..	.	Daily calorie supply per capita
96	104	104	115	106	105	91	94	93	89	.	Food production (1979-1981=100)
103	102	104	106	103	103	101	98	96	..	.	Daily protein supply (gm. per capita)
114	..	..	..	..	..	..	..	..	..	.	Population per hospital bed
280	277	..	..	..	..	..	..	..	..	.	per nursing person
700	612	..	..	567	..	..	..	..	..	.	per physician
45	45	45	45	45	45	45	46	46	46	.	Female participation in labor force (percent)
29	28	24	23	26	26	25	25	24	23	.	Infant mortality (per 1,000 live births)
70	70	70	70	69	69	69	69	70	70	.	Life expectancy (years)
2	2	2	2	2	2	2	2	2	2	.	Total fertility (births per woman)
49	49	50	50	51	51	51	52	52	53	.	Urban population (percent of total population)
..	..	..	..	24	23	22	21	19	..	.	Population per passenger car
..	..	..	..			..				.	per telephone

Comparator tables	1970	1971	1972	1973	1974	1975	1976	1977	1978	1979	1980
PER CAPITA INCOME						(US dollars)					
Authors' series	..	..	..	..	..	..	..	..	..	..	2,776
Single year conversion	1,302	..	..	..	..	..	..	..	..	..	
CIA or LWI	2,461	2,652	2,778	3,192	3,562	3,905	4,277	4,628	5,064	5,481	5,985
Penn World Tables	2,191	2,394	2,517	2,865	3,219	3,576	3,885	4,252	4,631	5,090	5,626
						(thousands)					
POPULATION	242,757	245,083	247,459	249,747	252,131	254,469	256,760	259,029	261,253	263,425	265,542
GROSS NATIONAL PRODUCT, current prices						(millions of current US dollars)					
World Bank (Atlas method)	..	..	..	..	..	..	..	..	..	..	..
Single year conversion	..	..	..	..	..	..	..	..	..	..	..
Authors' series	316,000	..	..	..	..	..	..	..	..	..	737,000
CIA or LWI	..	..	..	..	..	..	..	..	1,274,000	1,390,000	1,532,000
GROSS NATIONAL PRODUCT, constant prices						(millions of constant 1987 dollars)					
Single year conversion	..	..	..	..	..	..	..	..	..	..	..
Authors' series, rescaled from 1980 prices	595,532	..	..	..	..	..	..	..	..	..	1,009,377
CIA or LWI, rescaled from 1989 prices	1,670,371	1,719,635	1,736,367	1,891,599	1,953,878	1,969,680	2,045,902	2,094,237	2,155,587	2,162,092	2,183,473
CONVERSION FACTORS						(LCUs per US dollar)					
World Bank (Atlas method)	..	..	..	..	..	..	..	..	..	..	..
Single year convertor	..	..	..	..	..	..	..	..	..	..	..
Authors' series	1.19	..	..	..	..	..	..	..	..	..	0.84
Penn World Tables	..	..	..	..	..	..	..	..	..	..	..
OUTPUT TRENDS, OVERALL						(index, constant prices 1987 = 100)					
GNP, SNA	46.3	..	..	..	..	..	..	..	..	..	78.6
NMP, MPS	50.0	53.3	54.9	59.8	63.1	66.4	70.5	73.8	77.0	78.7	82.0
GNP, "Building block"	67.2	69.1	69.8	76.1	78.6	79.2	82.3	84.2	86.7	86.9	87.8
Industry											
Value added, SNA	44.2	..	..	..	..	..	..	..	..	..	81.9
Value added, MPS	45.3	48.6	51.9	55.7	60.4	65.1	68.9	72.4	76.0	78.6	81.3
"Building block"	60.6	64.1	66.4	70.5	74.7	79.2	80.2	84.2	82.4	84.8	87.8
Gross output, SNA	58.6	61.2	63.8	68.1	72.4	76.7	79.3	81.9	83.6	85.3	86.2
Agriculture											
Value added, SNA	76.1	..	..	..	..	..	..	..	..	..	83.6
Value added, MPS	72.0	75.1	66.8	79.2	75.5	70.8	78.4	80.2	82.3	79.9	85.8
"Building block"	94.0	93.3	83.8	102.7	98.2	87.1	94.6	96.8	99.7	95.6	87.8
Gross output, SNA	83.9	83.1	78.0	90.7	89.0	81.4	88.1	91.5	94.1	89.0	84.7
Services											
Value added, SNA	35.8	..	..	..	..	..	..	..	..	..	72.4
Value added, MPS	52.1	55.7	59.0	62.7	66.6	71.2	74.3	78.0	81.2	82.9	86.3
"Building block"	60.3	62.0	66.2	68.3	72.5	75.1	78.0	77.7	84.4	84.7	87.8
CONSUMPTION											
Total consumption, SNA	48.4	..	..	..	..	..	..	..	..	..	83.3
Total consumption, MPS	51.6	54.6	57.7	60.8	64.4	68.1	71.1	74.2	77.3	80.4	84.0
Households, SNA	..	..	..	..	..	..	..	..	..	..	..
Households, "building block"	..	..	..	..	..	..	..	..	..	..	..
General government, SNA	..	..	..	..	..	..	..	..	..	..	..
General government, "building block"	..	..	..	..	..	..	..	..	..	..	..
INVESTMENT											
Gross fixed investment, SNA	45.6	..	..	..	..	..	..	..	..	..	74.7
Accumulation, MPS	65.5	68.7	68.1	76.6	78.6	77.9	83.8	85.1	89.7	87.1	87.7
"Building block"	58.8	62.7	63.3	68.9	73.6	74.2	77.1	78.9	81.2	81.5	82.3
CONSUMER PRICES											
National methodology	..	..	..	..	..	..	..	..	..	..	..
Outside estimate	70.6	71.4	73.9	74.8	74.8	75.6	76.5	77.3	80.7	81.5	84.0
MERCHANDISE EXPORTS						(millions of current US dollars)					
UNCTAD	12,800	..	..	..	..	33,316	..	..	..	..	76,449
IMF: IFS	..	..	..	..	..	..	..	..	..	..	76,600
ACDA	..	..	..	..	..	..	..	45,230	52,430	64,910	76,440
ECE	12,800	13,806	15,402	21,359	28,541	35,198	29,200	35,529	40,936	49,907	57,932
intra-CMEA	6,956	7,423	9,112	10,348	14,140	20,259	12,573	14,890	18,409	19,520	20,723
Authors' uniform TR/$ series	11,458	11,803	12,131	17,339	22,883	25,585	30,767	37,921	43,013	53,659	62,477
intra-CMEA	5,840	5,775	6,131	6,982	9,081	11,451	13,995	17,076	20,343	22,966	24,836
MERCHANDISE IMPORTS						(millions of current US dollars)					
UNCTAD	11,732	..	..	..	..	36,971	..	..	..	..	68,522
IMF: IFS	..	..	..	..	..	..	..	..	..	..	68,600
ACDA	..	..	..	..	..	..	..	40,930	50,800	57,970	68,470
ECE	11,731	12,480	16,091	21,009	25,946	38,770	30,792	32,208	39,572	44,350	52,208
intra-CMEA	6,692	7,338	9,367	11,093	13,454	19,534	11,692	13,477	17,947	17,939	18,253
Authors' uniform series	10,506	10,663	12,728	16,944	20,690	29,563	32,231	34,358	41,599	47,754	56,205
intra-CMEA	5,618	5,708	6,302	7,485	8,641	11,041	13,015	15,455	19,833	21,106	21,875

Abbreviations in notes column are explained in the General Notes. For sources and methods, see the Technical Notes.

Former USSR

1981	1982	1983	1984	1985	1986	1987	1988	1989	1990	Notes	
				(US dollars)							**PER CAPITA INCOME**
..	..	..	..	2,522	3,064	3,511	3,783	..	..	f	Authors' series
										.	Single year conversion
6,581	7,103	7,475	7,770	8,004	8,413	8,758	9,166	9,558	9,521	.	CIA or LWI
6,197	6,731	7,180	7,550	8,108						.	Penn World Tables
				(thousands)							
267,722	270,042	272,540	275,066	277,537	280,236	283,100	285,463	287,845	288,734	.	**POPULATION**
				(millions of current US dollars)							**GROSS NATIONAL PRODUCT, current prices**
..	..	..	..	..	..	..	..	..	..	.	World Bank (Atlas method)
										.	Single year conversion
				700,000	858,602	993,976	1,080,000	..	..	f	Authors' series
1,699,000	1,849,999	1,965,000	2,063,000	2,145,000	2,275,000	2,393,000	2,526,000	2,664,000	..	.	CIA or LWI
				(millions of constant 1987 dollars)							**GROSS NATIONAL PRODUCT, constant prices**
..	..	..	..	..	..	..	..	..	..	.	Single year conversion
				1,211,252	1,250,618	1,285,946	1,357,612	1,397,987	..		Authors' series, rescaled from 1980 prices
2,209,500	2,260,624	2,311,748	2,339,634	2,361,943	2,443,184	2,487,244	2,540,785	2,565,045	2,472,558		CIA or LWI, rescaled from 1989 prices
				(LCUs per US dollar)							**CONVERSION FACTORS**
..	..	..	..	..	..	..	..	..	..	..	World Bank (Atlas method)
..	..	..	..	..	..	..	..	..	..	.	Single year convertor
..	..	..	..	1.11	0.93	0.83	0.81	..	..	..	Authors' series
..	..	..	..	..	..	..	..	..	..	.	Penn World Tables
				(index, constant prices 1987 = 100)							**OUTPUT TRENDS, OVERALL**
81.5	84.7	88.5	92.1	94.2	97.3	100.0	105.7	108.8	..	Ef	GNP, SNA
84.4	87.7	91.0	94.3	95.8	98.4	100.0	103.9	106.6	..	.	NMP, MPS
88.8	90.9	92.9	94.1	95.0	98.2	100.0	102.2	103.1	99.4	f	GNP, "Building block"
											Industry
84.9	87.2	90.7	93.9	93.7	96.3	100.0	106.9	109.4	..	Ef	Value added, SNA
84.4	86.7	90.1	93.3	93.8	..	100.0	106.9	109.4	..	.	Value added, MPS
88.8	88.7	90.7	94.1	95.0	95.8	100.0	102.2	100.6	97.0	f	"Building block"
87.1	87.9	90.5	93.1	94.8	97.4	100.0	102.6	101.7	99.1	X	Gross output, SNA
											Agriculture
84.1	90.2	95.6	95.6	93.4	101.0	100.0	104.4	105.0	..	Ef	Value added, SNA
84.1	96.0	99.5	104.5	90.0	97.0	100.0	97.8	102.6	..	I	Value added, MPS
84.4	95.4	97.6	94.1	90.2	103.1	100.0	97.0	103.1	99.4	f	"Building block"
83.9	89.8	95.8	94.9	94.1	101.7	100.0	100.0	103.4	100.0	.	Gross output, SNA
											Services
76.4	79.3	82.8	88.4	95.0	97.0	100.0	104.7	109.8	..	Ef	Value added, SNA
89.7	90.4	93.4	96.2	98.2	..	100.0	104.7	111.3	..	.	Value added, MPS
91.1	90.9	92.9	94.1	97.4	98.2	100.0	104.8	105.8	102.0	f	"Building block"
											CONSUMPTION
87.0	87.8	90.8	94.7	96.0	98.1	100.0	104.8	107.0	..	Ef	Total consumption, SNA
87.4	88.2	90.8	95.0	96.6	98.3	100.0	104.2	110.1	..	.	Total consumption, MPS
..	..	..	..	..	..	..	..	..	..	.	Households, SNA
..	..	..	..	..	..	..	..	..	..	.	Households, "building block"
..	..	..	..	..	..	..	..	..	..	.	General government, SNA
..	..	..	..	..	..	..	..	..	..	.	General government, "building block"
											INVESTMENT
76.4	84.6	90.3	89.8	93.6	97.4	100.0	107.9	115.0	..	YEK	Gross fixed investment, SNA
88.6	98.2	102.6	100.0	101.8	104.4	100.0	105.3	102.6	..	Y	Accumulation, MPS
86.1	85.2	90.0	91.1	92.0	98.2	100.0	105.3	103.1	96.3	f	"Building block"
											CONSUMER PRICES
..	..	..	..	..	..	..	..	..	..	.	National methodology
87.4	89.9	91.6	91.6	94.1	98.3	100.0	103.4	110.1	125.2	.	Outside estimate
				(millions of current US dollars)							**MERCHANDISE EXPORTS**
79,003	86,912	91,343	91,652	87,281	97,247	107,874	110,507	109,121	103,834	.	UNCTAD
79,100	87,000	91,600	91,300	87,300	97,300	107,700	110,500	109,400	..	G	IMF: IFS
79,380	87,170	91,650	91,490	87,200	97,050	107,700	110,700	109,300	..	.	ACDA
60,442	64,214	63,596	62,344	57,332	60,060	63,415	62,038	62,283	59,066	.	ECE
22,343	22,110	20,992	20,656	21,388	25,755	23,563	20,138	18,154	13,488	.	intra-CMEA
65,033	70,877	72,017	69,740	64,718	65,058	69,463	68,819	67,525	61,525	.	Authors' uniform TR/$ series
26,549	28,190	28,684	27,360	28,070	30,373	29,131	26,312	22,866	15,657	.	intra-CMEA
				(millions of current US dollars)							**MERCHANDISE IMPORTS**
72,960	77,752	80,412	80,680	83,140	88,871	96,061	107,090	114,512	120,874	F	UNCTAD
72,900	77,700	80,400	80,500	83,000	88,900	95,900	107,400	114,800	..	G	IMF: IFS
73,190	77,850	80,440	80,410	83,310	88,870	95,970	107,300	114,700	..	.	ACDA
56,924	57,128	55,383	53,932	54,778	55,031	53,802	58,064	64,981	64,974	.	ECE
18,474	19,556	18,775	18,737	20,144	23,091	22,498	20,542	19,412	17,142	.	intra-CMEA
60,860	63,143	62,906	60,653	61,836	59,614	59,565	64,922	70,524	68,045	.	Authors' uniform series
21,951	24,934	25,655	24,818	26,437	27,231	27,814	26,840	24,451	19,899	.	intra-CMEA

Basic tables	1970	1971	1972	1973	1974	1975	1976	1977	1978	1979	1980
SNA ACCOUNTS, current prices	*(billions of current USSR rubles)*										
GNP, at market prices	376	..	..	..	..	..	..	..	..	..	619
Net factor income	..	..	..	..	..	..	..	..	..	..	..
GDP at market prices	376	..	..	..	..	..	..	..	..	..	619
Net indirect taxes	..	..	..	..	..	..	..	..	..	..	..
GDP at factor cost	..	..	..	..	..	..	..	..	..	..	..
Agriculture	..	..	..	..	..	..	..	..	..	..	81
Industry	..	..	..	..	..	..	..	..	..	..	310
Services, etc.	..	..	..	..	..	..	..	..	..	..	229
Resource balance	..	..	..	..	..	..	..	..	..	..	8
Exports GNFS	..	..	..	..	..	..	..	..	..	..	..
Imports GNFS	..	..	..	..	..	..	..	..	..	..	..
Domestic absorption	..	..	..	..	..	..	..	..	..	..	611
Total consumption	..	..	..	..	..	..	..	..	..	..	421
Private consumption	..	..	..	..	..	..	..	..	..	..	351
General government consumption	..	..	..	..	..	..	..	..	..	..	70
Gross domestic investment	..	..	..	..	..	..	..	..	..	..	190
Fixed domestic investment	..	..	..	..	..	..	..	..	..	..	151
Depreciation	..	..	..	..	..	..	..	..	..	..	73
SNA ACCOUNTS, constant prices	*(billions of constant 1987 USSR rubles)*										
Gross national product (GNP)	382	..	..	..	..	..	..	..	..	..	648
GDP at market prices	382	..	..	..	..	..	..	..	..	..	648
GDP at factor cost	..	..	..	..	..	..	..	..	..	..	..
Agriculture	105	..	..	..	..	..	..	..	..	..	115
Industry	165	..	..	..	..	..	..	..	..	..	307
Services, etc.	112	..	..	..	..	..	..	..	..	..	227
Resource balance	-3	..	..	..	..	..	..	..	..	..	..
Exports GNFS	..	..	..	..	..	..	..	..	..	..	..
Imports GNFS	..	..	..	..	..	..	..	..	..	..	..
Domestic absorption	385	..	..	..	..	..	..	..	..	..	653
Total consumption, etc.	265	..	..	..	..	..	..	..	..	..	455
Private consumption, etc.	..	..	..	..	..	..	..	..	..	..	..
General government consumption	..	..	..	..	..	..	..	..	..	..	..
Gross domestic investment	121	..	..	..	..	..	..	..	..	..	198
Fixed domestic investment	..	..	..	..	..	..	..	..	..	..	..
Depreciation	..	..	..	..	..	..	..	..	..	..	..
MPS ACCOUNTS, current prices	*(billions of current USSR rubles)*										
NMP produced:	289	305	314	338	354	363	386	406	427	441	462
Agriculture and forestry	63	63	60	69	66	62	66	72	74	73	69
Industry excluding construction	148	157	164	173	186	191	200	207	220	227	238
Construction	30	33	35	36	39	41	43	45	46	47	48
Transport and communication	16	18	19	20	22	24	24	25	25	26	27
Trade, etc.	32	35	37	39	41	46	53	57	61	69	81
Other services	..	..	..	..	..	..	..	..	..	..	..
Resource balance	4	5	3	3	6	0	3	6	6	8	8
NMP used: domestic market	286	300	311	335	348	363	383	399	421	433	454
Final consumption, material goods	201	213	225	237	250	266	280	293	308	324	346
Personal consumption	195	206	217	228	240	256	269	281	295	311	331
Collective consumption	7	7	8	9	10	11	11	12	13	13	14
Net capital formation	84	87	85	98	98	97	103	107	113	109	109
Net fixed capital formation	51	54	55	60	63	63	60	60	66	62	69
Changes in stocks	33	33	30	37	36	34	44	47	47	47	39
Depreciation	..	..	..	..	..	..	..	..	..	..	..
MPS ACCOUNTS, constant prices	*(billions of 1980 USSR rubles)*										
NMP produced:	282	300	310	337	356	374	398	416	435	444	462
Agriculture and forestry	58	60	54	64	61	57	63	64	66	64	69
Industry and construction	159	171	183	196	212	229	242	254	267	276	286
Services	65	70	74	78	83	89	93	97	101	103	108
Resource balance	-13	-8	-13	-8	-7	-3	2	7	8	8	8
NMP used: domestic market	295	309	322	345	363	377	395	409	427	436	454
Final consumption, material goods	..	..	..	..	..	..	..	..	..	..	..
Personal consumption	..	..	..	..	..	..	..	..	..	..	..
Collective consumption	..	..	..	..	..	..	..	..	..	..	..
Net capital formation	..	..	..	..	..	..	..	..	..	..	..
Net fixed capital formation	..	..	..	..	..	..	..	..	..	..	..
Depreciation	..	..	..	..	..	..	..	..	..	..	..

Abbreviations in notes column are explained in the General Notes. For sources and methods, see the Technical Notes.

1981	1982	1983	1984	1985	1986	1987	1988	1989	1990	Notes	Basic tables (continued)
				(billions of current USSR rubles)							**SNA ACCOUNTS, current prices**
650	693	725	760	777	799	825	875	924	..	Ef	GNP, at market prices
..	..	..	..	..	..	..	..	..	..	.	Net factor income
650	693	725	760	777	799	825	875	924	..	Ef	GDP at market prices
..	..	..	..	..	..	..	..	..	..	.	Net indirect taxes
..	..	..	..	..	..	..	..	..	..	.	GDP at factor cost
85	93	127	132	129	137	137	161	170	..	Ef	Agriculture
323	347	335	350	353	358	374	382	392	..	Ef	Industry
243	253	263	277	295	303	313	333	362	..	Ef	Services, etc.
9	11	12	12	10	11	14	12	5	..	.	Resource balance
..	..	..	..	..	..	..	..	..	..	.	Exports GNFS
..	..	..	..	..	..	..	..	..	..	.	Imports GNFS
641	682	713	749	767	787	811	864	919	..	E	Domestic absorption
445	464	483	503	519	532	546	588	632	..	E	Total consumption
				422	432	445	473	509	..	.	Private consumption
				97	100	102	115	123	..	.	General government consumption
196	218	230	246	248	256	265	276	288	..	E	Gross domestic investment
				178	194	215	212	217	..	E	Fixed domestic investment
..	..	..	..	103	..	..	..	..	..	E	Depreciation
				(billions of constant 1987 USSR rubles)							**SNA ACCOUNTS, constant prices**
673	699	730	760	777	803	825	872	898	..	Ef	Gross national product (GNP)
673	699	730	760	777	803	825	872	898	..	Ef	GDP at market prices
..	..	..	..	..	..	..	..	..	..	.	GDP at factor cost
116	124	131	131	128	139	137	143	144	..	Ef	Agriculture
318	327	340	351	351	360	374	400	410	..	Ef	Industry
239	249	260	277	298	304	313	328	344	..	Ef	Services, etc.
-5	-5	-5	4	4	9	14	14	9	..	.	Resource balance
..	..	..	..	..	..	..	..	..	..	.	Exports GNFS
..	..	..	..	..	..	..	..	..	..	.	Imports GNFS
678	704	735	755	772	794	811	858	889	..	Ef	Domestic absorption
476	480	496	517	524	536	546	573	584	..	Ef	Total consumption, etc.
..	..	..	..	..	..	..	..	..	..	.	Private consumption, etc.
..	..	..	..	..	..	..	..	..	..	.	General government consumption
202	224	239	238	248	258	265	286	304	..	Ef	Gross domestic investment
..	..	..	..	..	..	..	..	..	..	.	Fixed domestic investment
..	..	..	..	..	..	..	..	..	..	.	Depreciation
				(billions of current USSR rubles)							**MPS ACCOUNTS, current prices**
487	524	548	571	579	587	600	631	657	..	f	NMP produced:
73	81	111	116	113	122	123	143	150	..	.	Agriculture and forestry
248	267	254	262	263	258	269	270	277	..	.	Industry excluding construction
49	52	53	59	62	71	75	81	83	..	.	Construction
28	32	33	34	35	36	37	39	40	..	.	Transport and communication
89	93	97	100	105	101	97	99	107	..	.	Trade, etc.
..	..	..	..	..	..	..	..	..	..	.	Other services
9	11	12	12	10	11	14	12	5	..	.	Resource balance
478	513	536	559	569	576	586	619	652	..	.	NMP used: domestic market
365	379	393	407	418	428	442	466	502	..	.	Final consumption, material goods
350	363	376	389	399	407	419	441	475	..	.	Personal consumption
15	16	17	18	20	21	23	25	27	..	.	Collective consumption
113	134	143	152	150	148	144	153	150	..	.	Net capital formation
66	70	74	81	80	87	94	90	80	..	.	Net fixed capital formation
47	65	70	71	70	61	50	64	70	..	.	Changes in stocks
..	..	..	..	..	..	..	..	..	..	.	Depreciation
				(billions of 1980 USSR rubles)							**MPS ACCOUNTS, constant prices**
476	495	513	532	540	555	564	586	601	..	.	NMP produced:
68	77	80	84	72	78	80	79	82	..	.	Agriculture and forestry
297	305	317	328	330	..	351	376	384	..	.	Industry and construction
112	113	117	120	122	..	125	131	139	..	.	Services
8	9	9	18	18	23	28	28	24	..	.	Resource balance
468	486	504	513	522	531	536	559	577	..	.	NMP used: domestic market
..	..	..	..	..	..	..	..	..	..	.	Final consumption, material goods
..	..	..	..	..	..	..	..	..	..	.	Personal consumption
..	..	..	..	..	..	..	..	..	..	.	Collective consumption
..	..	..	..	..	..	..	..	..	..	.	Net capital formation
..	..	..	..	..	..	..	..	..	..	.	Net fixed capital formation
..	..	..	..	..	..	..	..	..	..	.	Depreciation

Basic tables (continued)	1970	1971	1972	1973	1974	1975	1976	1977	1978	1979	1980
MPS ACCOUNTS, index						*(index, 1980 = 100)*					
NMP produced:	61.0	65.0	67.0	73.0	77.0	81.0	86.0	90.0	94.0	96.0	100.0
Agriculture and forestry	83.9	87.5	77.9	92.3	88.0	82.5	91.3	93.4	95.9	93.1	100.0
Industry excluding construction	54.1	57.8	62.2	67.0	73.0	78.9	83.8	88.6	93.0	96.8	100.0
Construction	64.1	69.2	72.4	75.6	80.8	85.9	89.1	91.0	96.2	96.2	100.0
Transport and communication	58.5	62.6	66.7	71.3	76.6	83.0	86.5	90.6	94.7	95.3	100.0
Trade, etc.	61.0	65.2	68.9	73.2	77.4	82.3	86.0	90.2	93.9	96.3	100.0
NMP used: material goods	65.0	68.0	71.0	76.0	80.0	83.0	87.0	90.0	94.0	96.0	100.0
Final consumption	61.3	65.0	68.7	72.4	76.7	81.0	84.7	88.3	92.0	95.7	100.0
Net capital formation	74.6	78.4	77.6	87.3	89.6	88.8	95.5	97.0	102.2	99.3	100.0
EXCHANGE AND CONVERSION RATES						*(LCUs per US dollar: annual average)*					
Single-year converter	..	..	..	..	..	..	..	..	..	..	..
Devisa/official	0.900	0.900	0.823	0.743	0.758	0.722	0.754	0.736	0.681	0.656	0.649
Commercial	..	..	..	..	..	..	..	..	..	..	..
Noncommercial	0.900	0.900	0.823	0.743	0.758	0.722	0.754	0.736	0.681	0.656	0.649
Informal market	5.886	5.400	4.158	3.957	3.049	3.175	3.722	3.867	4.049	4.051	3.978
ICP	..	..	..	..	..	..	..	..	..	..	..
						(ruble per US dollar: annual average)					
Commercial TR/$ cross	..	..	..	..	..	..	..	..	..	..	..
Uniform TR/$ cross	1.072	1.157	1.232	1.093	1.092	1.167	1.067	1.022	0.973	0.945	0.980
						(LCUs per ruble: annual average)					
Commercial	..	..	..	..	..	..	..	..	..	..	..
Noncommercial	..	..	..	..	..	..	..	..	..	..	..
Devisa/official	1.000	1.000	1.000	1.000	1.000	1.000	1.000	1.000	1.000	1.000	1.000
CONSUMER PRICE INDEXES						*(index)*					
Official, IMF 1985 = 100	..	..	..	..	..	..	..	..	..	..	..
Official, CIA or LWI 1980 = 100	..	..	..	..	..	..	..	..	..	..	..
Alternative, CIA or LWI 1980 = 100	84.0	85.0	88.0	89.0	89.0	90.0	91.0	92.0	96.0	97.0	100.0
INTERNATIONAL TRADE (ECE)						*(billions of current USSR rubles)*					
Value of exports, fob	12	12	13	16	21	24	28	33	36	42	50
to CMEA	6	7	8	8	10	13	15	18	20	22	24
Value of imports, cif	11	11	13	16	19	27	29	30	35	38	45
from CMEA	6	7	8	8	9	13	14	16	19	20	21
Trade balance	1	1	-1	0	2	-3	-1	3	1	5	5
CMEA	0	0	0	-1	1	1	1	2	1	2	3
INTERNATIONAL TRADE (Authors')						*(millions of current US dollars)*					
Value of exports, fob	11,458	11,803	12,131	17,339	22,883	25,585	30,767	37,921	43,013	53,659	62,477
to developed countries	2,393	2,758	2,966	5,047	8,255	8,504	10,390	11,980	12,777	19,064	24,440
to other non-socialist countries	2,040	2,030	2,440	3,952	4,471	4,584	4,961	7,251	8,392	9,590	10,585
to socialist countries	7,025	7,015	6,725	8,340	10,157	12,497	15,415	18,690	21,844	25,004	27,452
to CMEA	5,840	5,775	6,131	6,982	9,081	11,451	13,995	17,076	20,343	22,966	24,836
Value of imports, cif	10,506	10,663	12,728	16,944	20,690	29,563	32,231	34,358	41,599	47,754	56,205
from developed countries	2,822	2,890	4,181	6,176	8,109	13,440	14,355	13,484	16,122	20,206	24,224
from other non-socialist countries	1,273	1,412	1,633	2,336	3,145	4,153	3,720	4,072	4,157	4,862	7,846
from socialist countries	6,411	6,362	6,914	8,432	9,436	11,969	14,156	16,802	21,320	22,686	24,135
from CMEA	5,618	5,708	6,302	7,485	8,641	11,041	13,015	15,455	19,833	21,106	21,875
Trade balance	951	1,140	-597	395	2,193	-3,978	-1,464	3,563	1,414	5,905	6,273
Developed countries	-429	-132	-1,215	-1,129	146	-4,936	-3,965	-1,504	-3,345	-1,141	216
Other non-socialist countries	767	618	807	1,617	1,325	431	1,241	3,179	4,235	4,729	2,739
Socialist countries	613	653	-189	-92	722	528	1,259	1,889	524	2,318	3,317
CMEA	222	66	-171	-503	441	410	980	1,621	510	1,860	2,961
PARTNER CONVERTIBLE TRADE (ECE)						*(millions of current US dollars)*					
Exports to non-CMEA (cif)	2,501	2,860	3,163	4,904	8,078	9,000	11,041	12,554	13,949	19,846	25,958
Imports from non-CMEA (fob)	2,813	2,847	4,133	5,954	7,946	13,173	14,422	14,334	16,642	20,040	22,949
Trade balance	-312	13	-970	-1,050	132	-4,173	-3,381	-1,780	-2,693	-194	3,009
TRADE PRICE INDEXES (Authors')						*(index, 1980 = 100)*					
Terms of trade	78.8	..	..	..	..	76.2	82.6	86.0	88.5	94.6	100.0
Exports	34.8	..	..	..	..	52.8	58.5	65.6	73.0	87.4	100.0
Non-socialist countries	23.2	..	..	..	..	47.9	48.8	54.8	60.2	81.1	100.0
Developed countries	14.2	..	..	..	..	39.9	41.3	45.5	49.4	76.4	100.0
Other	33.7	..	..	..	..	62.8	64.6	70.2	76.7	90.2	100.0
Socialist countries	42.2	40.4	38.9	44.6	..	58.0	68.1	76.7	85.4	94.7	100.0
CMEA	38.5	36.4	38.9	40.9	..	58.2	68.0	76.7	87.2	95.8	100.0
Imports	44.2	..	..	..	..	69.3	70.8	76.2	82.5	92.5	100.0
Non-socialist countries	32.8	..	..	..	..	71.2	66.9	70.4	74.4	88.2	100.0
Developed countries	34.7	..	..	..	..	75.1	69.6	71.9	75.6	89.5	100.0
Other	28.6	..	..	..	..	58.5	56.5	65.3	69.6	82.7	100.0
Socialist countries	51.4	48.7	46.4	53.1	..	66.6	75.7	82.4	90.2	97.2	100.0
CMEA	47.7	46.3	44.8	49.9	..	66.8	75.5	81.6	90.3	97.2	100.0

Abbreviations in notes column are explained in the General Notes. For sources and methods, see the Technical Notes.

1981	1982	1983	1984	1985	1986	1987	1988	1989	1990	Notes	Basic tables (continued)
				(index, 1980 = 100)							**MPS ACCOUNTS, index**
103.0	107.0	111.0	115.0	117.0	120.0	122.0	127.0	130.0	..	V	NMP produced:
98.0	111.9	116.0	121.8	104.9	113.1	116.5	113.9	119.6	..	I	Agriculture and forestry
104.0	107.0	111.0	115.0	115.0	116.0	120.0	128.0	131.0	..	.	Industry excluding construction
103.0	105.0	110.0	113.0	117.0	131.0	138.0	149.0	152.0	..	.	Construction
104.0	107.0	112.0	113.0	116.0	120.0	121.0	128.0	128.0	..	.	Transport and communication
104.0	104.0	107.0	111.0	113.0	114.0	113.0	119.0	128.0	..	.	Trade, etc.
103.0	107.0	111.0	113.0	115.0	117.0	118.0	123.0	127.0	..	.	NMP used: material goods
104.0	105.0	108.0	113.0	115.0	117.0	119.0	124.0	131.0	..	.	Final consumption
101.0	112.0	117.0	114.0	116.0	119.0	114.0	120.0	117.0	..	.	Net capital formation
				(LCUs per US dollar: annual average)							**EXCHANGE AND CONVERSION RATES**
..	..	..	..	..	..	..	..	..	..	.	Single-year converter
0.719	0.726	0.743	0.816	0.836	0.704	0.633	0.607	0.630	..	L	Devisa/official
..	..	..	..	..	..	..	..	..	..	f	Commercial
0.719	0.726	0.743	0.816	0.836	0.704	0.633	0.607	0.630	..	.	Noncommercial
3.747	3.880	4.078	4.639	5.313	5.238	5.438	5.845	12.373	..	.	Informal market
..	..	..	..	..	..	..	..	..	..	.	ICP
				(ruble per US dollar: annual average)							
..	..	..	..	..	..	..	..	..	..	.	Commercial TR/$ cross
1.076	1.105	1.201	1.395	1.433	1.388	1.397	1.484	1.660	1.980	.	Uniform TR/$ cross
				(LCUs per ruble: annual average)							
..	..	..	..	..	..	..	..	..	..	.	Commercial
..	..	..	..	..	..	..	..	..	..	.	Noncommercial
1.000	1.000	0.980	1.040	1.030	1.000	0.980	0.960	0.960	..	L	Devisa/official
				(index)							**CONSUMER PRICE INDEXES**
..	..	..	..	..	..	..	..	..	..	.	Official, IMF 1985 = 100
..	..	..	..	..	..	..	..	..	..	.	Official, CIA or LWI 1980 = 100
104.0	107.0	109.0	109.0	112.0	117.0	119.0	123.0	131.0	149.0	.	Alternative, CIA or LWI 1980 = 100
				(billions of current USSR rubles)							**INTERNATIONAL TRADE (ECE)**
57	63	68	74	73	68	68	67	69	61	.	Value of exports, fob
29	31	34	38	40	42	41	39	38	31	.	to CMEA
53	56	60	65	69	63	61	65	72	71	.	Value of imports, cif
24	28	31	35	38	38	39	40	41	39	.	from CMEA
5	7	8	9	3	6	7	2	-3	-10	.	Trade balance
5	4	4	4	2	4	2	-1	-3	-8	.	CMEA
				(millions of current US dollars)							**INTERNATIONAL TRADE (Authors')**
65,033	70,877	72,017	69,740	64,718	65,058	69,463	68,819	67,525	61,525	.	Value of exports, fob
23,987	25,963	26,451	26,163	22,200	18,621	22,410	24,161	26,020	29,227	.	to developed countries
12,057	14,022	14,164	13,391	11,487	13,565	15,414	15,761	16,067	14,546	.	to other non-socialist countries
28,988	30,892	31,402	30,186	31,031	32,871	31,639	28,897	25,438	17,753	.	to socialist countries
26,549	28,190	28,684	27,360	28,070	30,373	29,131	26,312	22,866	15,657	.	to CMEA
60,860	63,143	62,906	60,653	61,836	59,614	59,565	64,922	70,524	68,045	.	Value of imports, cif
25,190	26,023	25,194	23,994	23,052	22,519	21,916	26,887	32,535	34,360	.	from developed countries
10,817	9,233	9,656	9,232	9,131	6,952	7,498	8,808	11,088	11,519	.	from other non-socialist countries
24,854	27,888	28,056	27,427	29,652	30,143	30,151	29,227	26,900	22,166	.	from socialist countries
21,951	24,934	25,655	24,818	26,437	27,231	27,814	26,840	24,451	19,899	.	from CMEA
4,173	7,735	9,110	9,087	2,883	5,444	9,898	3,896	-2,999	-6,519	.	Trade balance
-1,203	-60	1,257	2,169	-852	-3,898	494	-2,727	-6,515	-5,133	.	Developed countries
1,241	4,789	4,507	4,159	2,356	6,613	7,916	6,954	4,979	3,027	.	Other non-socialist countries
4,135	3,005	3,346	2,759	1,379	2,728	1,488	-331	-1,462	-4,413	.	Socialist countries
4,598	3,256	3,029	2,542	1,633	3,142	1,317	-528	-1,585	-4,242	.	CMEA
				(millions of current US dollars)							**PARTNER CONVERTIBLE TRADE (ECE)**
25,364	26,444	25,845	26,621	23,567	21,103	23,189	23,754	25,718	..	.	Exports to non-CMEA (cif)
24,943	25,690	24,650	24,086	23,730	22,952	22,299	26,221	28,726	..	.	Imports from non-CMEA (fob)
421	754	1,195	2,535	-163	-1,849	890	-2,467	-3,008	..	.	Trade balance
				(index, 1980 = 100)							**TRADE PRICE INDEXES (Authors')**
103.7	..	..	..	114.8	..	..	94.7	91.6	94.0	.	Terms of trade
103.4	..	..	..	96.7	..	..	88.6	85.2	91.9	f	Exports
100.8	..	..	..	83.9	..	..	83.4	87.1	102.4	f	Non-socialist countries
101.5	..	..	..	79.1	..	..	61.4	68.2	86.2	.	Developed countries
99.3	..	..	..	93.3	..	..	117.2	117.7	134.7	.	Other
106.7	116.5	117.5	108.5	110.5	110.7	105.6	95.6	82.0	66.2	.	Socialist countries
107.2	118.5	120.6	111.3	112.0	116.6	110.8	100.1	85.4	67.6	.	CMEA
99.7	..	..	..	84.2	..	..	93.5	93.0	97.8	f	Imports
100.4	..	..	..	81.6	..	..	100.3	103.4	112.2	f	Non-socialist countries
9.2	..	..	..	80.2	..	..	107.8	112.9	115.4	.	Developed countries
103.0	..	..	..	85.2	..	..	77.4	75.6	102.7	.	Other
98.7	98.2	95.7	86.7	87.1	88.5	88.5	85.2	76.3	67.9	.	Socialist countries
98.4	98.0	95.9	87.3	89.6	91.6	92.3	89.0	79.4	69.8	.	CMEA

Basic tables (continued)	1970	1971	1972	1973	1974	1975	1976	1977	1978	1979	1980
TRADE PRICE INDEXES (ECE)					*(index, 1980 = 100)*						
Terms of trade	78	79	79	88	85	86	82	91	92	98	100
Exports	41	41	46	60	69	80	61	69	77	90	100
Imports	52	52	58	69	81	93	74	76	83	91	100
Balance of Payments (ECE)					*(millions of current US dollars)*						
Exports, convertible currency	4,759	5,114	5,745	9,451	13,623	14,172	16,573	20,715	22,796	30,946	38,226
Imports, convertible currency	4,347	4,585	6,160	8,960	11,992	18,669	19,269	18,850	21,850	26,728	34,824
Trade balance, convertible currency	412	529	-415	491	1,631	-4,497	-2,696	1,865	946	4,218	3,402
Invisibles, convertible currency	467	303	255	636	730	326	111	14	26	52	-425
Current balance, convertible currency	879	832	-161	1,127	2,361	-4,171	-2,585	1,879	972	4,270	2,977
External debt, total (World Bank)	..	..	..	..	..	..	..	..	..	..	..
Convertible currency	..	..	..	..	..	..	..	..	..	..	..
CMEA	..	..	..	..	..	..	..	..	..	..	..
External debt service (World Bank)	..	..	..	..	..	..	..	..	..	..	..
Convertible currency	..	..	..	..	..	..	..	..	..	..	..
Total reserves less gold (IMF, IFS)	..	..	..	..	..	..	..	..	..	..	..
Total reserves, including gold at London price	..	..	..	..	..	..	..	..	..	..	..
Total reserves, incl. gold at national valuation	..	..	..	..	..	..	..	..	..	..	..
EMPLOYMENT					*(thousands)*						
Employment, total	..	..	..	..	..	..	..	..	..	..	..
Agriculture	..	..	..	..	..	..	..	..	..	..	..
Industry	..	..	..	..	..	..	..	..	..	..	..
Services	..	..	..	..	..	..	..	..	..	..	..
Labor force, total	117,276	119,136	120,996	122,857	124,717	126,577	128,648	130,719	132,791	134,862	136,933
Agriculture	30,091	29,852	29,612	29,373	29,134	28,895	28,590	28,285	27,980	27,676	27,371
Industry	44,156	45,024	45,893	46,762	47,630	48,499	49,486	50,473	51,461	52,448	53,435
Services	43,030	44,260	45,491	46,722	47,952	49,183	50,572	51,961	53,350	54,739	56,128
DOMESTIC FINANCE (IMF)					*(billions of current USSR rubles)*						
Money supply, broadly defined	..	..	..	..	..	..	..	..	..	..	..
Money, means of payment	..	..	..	..	..	..	..	..	..	..	..
Demand deposits	..	..	..	..	..	..	..	..	..	..	..
Currency outside banks	..	..	..	..	..	..	..	..	..	..	..
Quasi-money	..	..	..	..	..	..	..	..	..	..	..
Interest: deposit rate (percent)	..	..	..	..	..	..	..	..	..	..	..
Central government expenditures	..	..	..	..	..	..	..	..	..	..	..
Defense	..	..	..	..	..	..	..	..	..	..	..
					(millions of 1989 US dollars)						
Central government exp. (ACDA)	..	..	..	..	..	..	..	..	..	509,600	546,600
Military (ACDA)	..	..	..	..	..	..	..	..	279,089	284,400	292,000
LAND AND FORESTS (FAO)											
Pop. density: agr. land (pop. per sq. km)	40	40	41	41	42	42	42	43	43	44	44
Deforestation rate (net)	1	1	1	1	0	0	0	0	0	0	0
Forest (thousands sq. km)	8,770	8,810	8,850	8,890	8,930	8,970	9,010	9,050	9,090	9,120	9,160
SOCIAL INDICATORS											
Population density: total land (pop. per sq. km)	11	11	11	11	11	11	12	12	12	12	12
School enrollment ratio, primary	104	..	..	..	..	97	97	98	104	106	104
secondary	85	..	..	..	..	92	93	92	91	92	93
tertiary	..	..	..	..	..	..	..	..	..	..	21
Energy consumption per capita (kg. of oil eq.)	3,109	3,262	3,405	3,524	3,646	3,801	3,948	4,082	4,202	4,275	4,358
Daily calorie supply per capita	3,343	3,331	3,288	3,314	3,354	3,344	3,393	3,372	3,377	3,372	3,384
Food production (1979-1981=100)	102	103	96	112	106	102	108	104	113	104	100
Daily protein supply (gm. per capita)	102	102	102	102	105	106	106	104	105	104	103
Population per hospital bed	91	..	..	..	..	..	..	..	..	..	..
per nursing person	..	..	..	169	..	..	..	..	..	..	..
per physician	421	..	..	..	..	..	..	..	..	..	..
Female participation in labor force (percent)	46	46	46	46	47	47	47	47	47	48	48
Infant mortality (per 1,000 live births)	24	23	25	26	28	28	27	27	27	27	26
Life expectancy (years)	69	69	69	69	68	68	68	68	68	68	68
Total fertility (births per woman)	2	2	2	2	2	2	2	2	2	2	2
Urban population (percent of total population)	57	57	58	59	59	60	61	61	62	62	63
Population per passenger car	..	..	..	..	..	..	..	..	35	32	29
per telephone	..	..	..	..	..	15	..	..	..	..	11

Abbreviations in notes column are explained in the General Notes. For sources and methods, see the Technical Notes.

210

1981	1982	1983	1984	1985	1986	1987	1988	1989	1990	Notes	Basic tables (continued)
				(index, 1980 = 100)							**TRADE PRICE INDEXES (ECE)**
103	117	123	121	109	100	104	100	..	..	.	Terms of trade
104	114	110	102	89	91	94	89	..	..	.	Exports
101	97	90	84	82	91	90	89	..	..	.	Imports
				(millions of current US dollars)							**Balance of Payments (ECE)**
39,123	43,390	44,214	43,326	36,924	34,638	40,817	42,688	45,148	48,759	S	Exports, convertible currency
39,851	39,092	37,982	36,625	36,189	33,254	32,683	39,211	47,445	50,196	.	Imports, convertible currency
-728	4,298	6,232	6,701	735	1,384	8,134	3,477	-2,297	-1,437	.	Trade balance, convertible currency
-915	-717	-391	-20	-656	-940	-1,030	-1,213	-1,680	-3,100	.	Invisibles, convertible currency
-1,643	3,581	5,841	6,681	79	444	7,104	2,265	-3,977	-4,537	.	Current balance, convertible currency
..	..	..	..		..		..	..	..	.	External debt, total (World Bank)
..	..	..	..	28,900	31,400	39,200	43,000	54,000	..	f	Convertible currency
..	..	..	..	..	..	..	..	..	..		CMEA
..	..	..	..		..		..	..	..	.	External debt service (World Bank)
..	..	..	..	..	7,800	8,800	8,200	9,400	..	f	Convertible currency
..	..	..	..	12,900	14,700	14,100	15,300	14,700	..	f	Total reserves less gold (IMF, IFS)
..	..	..	..	..	..	..	..	..	..	.	Total reserves, including gold at London price
..	..	..	..	..	..	..	..	..	..	.	Total reserves, incl. gold at national valuation
				(thousands)							**EMPLOYMENT**
..	..	..	..	..	..	..	..	..	..	.	Employment, total
..	..	..	..	..	..	..	..	..	..	.	Agriculture
..	..	..	..	..	..	..	..	..	..	.	Industry
..	..	..	..	..	..	..	..	..	..	.	Services
138,204	139,475	140,747	142,018	143,289	143,958	144,627	145,296	145,965	146,634	.	Labor force, total
..	..	..	..	..	..	..	..	..	..	.	Agriculture
..	..	..	..	..	..	..	..	..	..	.	Industry
..	..	..	..	..	..	..	..	..	..	.	Services
				(billions of current USSR rubles)							**DOMESTIC FINANCE (IMF)**
..	..	..	..	..	..	..	..	..	..	.	Money supply, broadly defined
..	..	..	..	..	..	..	..	..	..	.	Money, means of payment
..	..	..	..	..	..	..	..	..	..	.	Demand deposits
..	..	..	..	..	..	..	..	..	..	.	Currency outside banks
..	..	..	..	..	..	..	..	..	..	.	Quasi-money
..	..	..	..	..	..	..	..	..	..	.	Interest: deposit rate (percent)
..	..	..	..	..	..	..	..	..	..	.	Central government expenditures
..	..	..	..	..	..	..	..	..	..	.	Defense
				(millions of 1989 US dollars)							
571,300	616,400	606,800	615,500	630,700	680,300	709,900	712,500	680,000	..	f	Central government exp. (ACDA)
295,200	300,500	304,900	309,200	315,600	319,200	325,900	330,900	311,000	..	U	Military (ACDA)
											LAND AND FORESTS (FAO)
44	45	45	45	46	46	47	..	..	..	.	Pop. density: agr. land (pop. per sq. km)
0	0	0	0	0	0	..	..	..	..	.	Deforestation rate (net)
9,200	9,240	9,280	9,320	9,350	9,380	..	..	..	..	.	Forest (thousands sq. km)
											SOCIAL INDICATORS
12	12	12	12	13	13	13	..	..	..	.	Population density: total land (pop. per sq. km)
..	107	106	105	105	105	106	105	..	..	.	School enrollment ratio, primary
..	97	99	98	98	99	98	98	..	..	.	secondary
..	..	..	22	22	22	23	24	..	..	.	tertiary
4,412	4,510	4,584	4,725	4,843	4,935	5,006	..	..	..	.	Energy consumption per capita (kg. of oil eq.)
3,353	3,377	3,380	3,387	3,365	3,375	3,386	3,386	..	..	.	Daily calorie supply per capita
97	103	107	107	106	112	112	110	113	..	.	Food production (1979-1981=100)
102	103	103	104	105	106	106	106	..	..	.	Daily protein supply (gm. per capita)
..	..	..	..	..	..	..	..	..	..	.	Population per hospital bed
..	..	..	..	..	..	..	..	..	..	.	per nursing person
270										.	per physician
48	48	47	47	47	47	47	47	46	46	.	Female participation in labor force (percent)
26	26	26	26	26	25	25	25	24	24	.	Infant mortality (per 1,000 live births)
68	68	68	69	69	69	70	70	70	71	.	Life expectancy (years)
2	2	2	2	2	3	3	2	2	2	.	Total fertility (births per woman)
63	64	64	65	65	65	65	66	66	66	.	Urban population (percent of total population)
28	..	..	..	..	..	..	..	..	..	.	Population per passenger car
10	..	9	9	..	..	..	..	..	..	.	per telephone

Viet Nam

Comparator tables	1970	1971	1972	1973	1974	1975	1976	1977	1978	1979	1980
PER CAPITA INCOME						*(US dollars)*					
World Bank (Atlas method)	..	..	..	..	..	..	..	..	..	..	..
Single year conversion	..	..	..	..	..	..	..	..	..	..	..
CIA or LWI	..	..	..	..	..	..	..	..	..	..	157
Penn World Tables	..	..	..	..	..	..	..	..	..	..	..
						(thousands)					
POPULATION	42,729	43,725	44,758	45,825	46,918	48,030	49,158	50,295	51,436	52,574	53,700
GROSS NATIONAL PRODUCT, current prices						*(millions of current US dollars)*					
World Bank (Atlas method)	..	..	..	..	..	..	..	..	..	..	..
Single year conversion	..	..	..	..	..	..	..	..	..	..	..
Authors' series	..	..	..	..	..	..	..	..	..	..	..
CIA or LWI	..	..	..	..	..	..	..	..	..	..	8,400
GROSS NATIONAL PRODUCT, constant prices						*(millions of constant 1987 dollars)*					
Single year conversion	..	..	..	..	..	..	..	..	..	..	..
Authors' series, rescaled from 1980 prices	..	..	..	..	..	..	..	..	..	..	..
CIA or LWI, rescaled from 1989 prices	..	..	..	..	..	..	..	..	..	..	11,982
CONVERSION FACTORS						*(LCUs per US dollar)*					
World Bank (Atlas method)											
Single year convertor	0.02	0.02	0.33	0.10	0.13	0.16	0.18	0.18	0.20	0.21	0.21
Authors' series	..	..	..	..	..	..	..	..	..	..	..
Penn World Tables	..	..	..	..	..	..	..	..	..	..	..
OUTPUT TRENDS, OVERALL						*(index, constant prices 1987 = 100)*					
GNP, SNA	..	..	..	..	..	..	..	..	..	..	..
NMP, MPS	..	..	..	..	..	..	..	..	..	..	69.1
GNP, "Building block"	..	..	..	..	..	..	..	..	..	..	..
Industry											
Value added, SNA	..	..	..	..	..	..	..	..	..	..	..
Value added, MPS	..	..	..	..	..	..	..	..	..	..	60.3
"Building block"	..	..	..	..	..	..	..	..	..	..	..
Gross output, SNA	..	..	..	..	..	..	..	..	..	..	..
Agriculture											
Value added, SNA	..	..	..	..	..	..	..	..	..	..	..
Value added, MPS	..	..	..	..	..	..	..	..	..	..	74.0
"Building block"	..	..	..	..	..	..	..	..	..	..	..
Gross output, SNA	..	..	..	..	..	..	..	..	..	..	..
Services											
Value added, SNA	..	..	..	..	..	..	..	..	..	..	..
Value added, MPS	..	..	..	..	..	..	..	..	..	..	72.8
"Building block"	..	..	..	..	..	..	..	..	..	..	..
CONSUMPTION											
Total consumption, SNA	..	..	..	..	..	..	..	..	..	..	..
Total consumption, MPS	..	..	..	..	..	..	..	..	..	..	75.7
Households, SNA	..	..	..	..	..	..	..	..	..	..	..
Households, "building block"	..	..	..	..	..	..	..	..	..	..	..
General government, SNA	..	..	..	..	..	..	..	..	..	..	..
General government, "building block"	..	..	..	..	..	..	..	..	..	..	..
INVESTMENT											
Gross fixed investment, SNA	..	..	..	..	..	..	80.0	99.8	109.1	106.4	99.6
Accumulation, MPS	..	..	..	..	..	..	..	..	..	..	46.0
"Building block"	..	..	..	..	..	..	..	..	..	..	..
CONSUMER PRICES											
National methodology	..	..	..	..	..	..	..	..	..	..	..
Outside estimate	..	..	..	..	..	..	..	..	..	..	..
MERCHANDISE EXPORTS						*(millions of current US dollars)*					
UNCTAD	..	..	..	..	..	..	..	..	..	..	570
IMF: IFS	8	..	..	..	..	229	..	..	..	..	537
ACDA	..	..	..	..	..	..	..	594	648	587	537
ECE	..	..	..	..	..	..	..	..	..	..	..
intra-CMEA	..	..	..	..	..	..	..	..	..	..	..
Authors' uniform TR/S series	8	..	..	..	..	229	..	..	..	..	537
intra-CMEA	..	..	..	..	..	..	..	..	..	..	..
MERCHANDISE IMPORTS						*(millions of current US dollars)*					
UNCTAD	..	..	..	..	..	..	..	..	..	..	..
IMF: IFS	373	..	..	..	..	1,102	..	..	..	..	1,296
ACDA	..	..	..	..	..	..	..	1,372	1,485	1,599	1,296
ECE	..	..	..	..	..	..	..	..	..	..	..
intra-CMEA	..	..	..	..	..	..	..	..	..	..	..
Authors' uniform series	373	..	..	..	..	1,102	..	..	..	..	1,296
intra-CMEA	..	..	..	..	..	..	..	..	..	..	..

Abbreviations in notes column are explained in the General Notes. For sources and methods, see the Technical Notes.

Viet Nam

1981	1982	1983	1984	1985	1986	1987	1988	1989	1990	Notes	Comparator tables (continued)
					(US dollars)						**PER CAPITA INCOME**
..	..	..	..	..					.		World Bank (Atlas method)
..	..	..	..	..	587	811	513	143	137		Single year conversion
..	..	..	..	..	204	203	208	219	..	A	CIA or LWI
..	..	..	..	..	..	..	..	..	.		Penn World Tables
					(thousands)						**POPULATION**
54,722	55,687	56,655	57,692	58,868	60,249	61,750	63,263	64,800	66,473	.	
					(millions of current US dollars)						**GROSS NATIONAL PRODUCT, current prices**
..	..	..	..	..					.		World Bank (Atlas method)
..	..	..	..	..	35,333	50,097	32,458	9,243	9,072	.	Single year conversion
..	..	..	..	..	..	..	..	..	.		Authors' series
..	..	..	..	..	12,400	12,600	13,200	14,200	..		CIA or LWI
					(millions of constant 1987 dollars)						**GROSS NATIONAL PRODUCT, constant prices**
..	..	..	..	..	48,114	50,097	53,019	56,776	59,490	.	Single year conversion
..	..	..	..	..	..	..	..	..	.		Authors' series, rescaled from 1980 prices
..	..	..	..	..	13,318	13,114	13,298	13,743	..	A	CIA or LWI, rescaled from 1989 prices
					(LCUs per US dollar)						**CONVERSION FACTORS**
..	..	..	..	..	..	..	..	..	..		World Bank (Atlas method)
0.58	0.94	1.00	1.03	6.70	18.00	61.96	480.00	3,532.78	5,130.50		Single year convertor
..	..	..	..	..	..	..	..	..	..		Authors' series
..	..	..	..	..	..	..	..	..	..		Penn World Tables
					(index, constant prices 1987 = 100)						**OUTPUT TRENDS, OVERALL**
..	..	..	..	..	96.0	100.0	105.8	113.3	118.8	.	GNP, SNA
..	77.0	82.5	89.3	94.4	97.5	100.0	105.8	108.3	..	.	NMP, MPS
..	..	..	..	..	..	..	..	..	.		GNP, "Building block"
											Industry
..	..	..	..	..	..	..	..	..	..		Value added, SNA
..	64.3	69.0	77.3	86.6	90.2	100.0	103.2	99.5	..		Value added, MPS
..	..	..	..	..	..	..	..	..	.		"Building block"
..	..	..	..	85.7	90.9	100.0	114.3	110.6	115.6	.	Gross output, SNA
											Agriculture
..	..	..	..	..	..	..	..	..	..		Value added, SNA
..	85.4	92.3	96.0	100.3	103.4	100.0	105.3	113.6	..	I	Value added, MPS
..	..	..	..	..	..	..	..	..	.		"Building block"
..	99.6	102.9	104.9	102.1	104.4	100.0	103.9	105.4	..	f	Gross output, SNA
											Services
..	..	..	..	..	..	..	..	..	..		Value added, SNA
..	78.4	81.9	94.3	93.3	95.7	100.0	105.4	110.6	..	.	Value added, MPS
..	..	..	..	..	..	..	..	..	.		"Building block"
											CONSUMPTION
..	..	..	..	..	..	..	..	..	..		Total consumption, SNA
..	..	..	..	..	97.3	100.0	105.9	108.9	..	.	Total consumption, MPS
..	..	..	..	..	..	..	..	..	..		Households, SNA
..	..	..	..	..	..	..	..	..	.		Households, "building block"
..	..	..	..	..	..	..	..	..	..		General government, SNA
..	..	..	..	..	..	..	..	..	.		General government, "building block"
											INVESTMENT
89.6	89.9	115.7	145.0	155.0	128.3	100.0	84.5	72.7	..	YK	Gross fixed investment, SNA
..	..	..	..	..	97.3	100.0	110.1	67.8	..	YI	Accumulation, MPS
..	..	..	..	..	..	..	..	..	..		"Building block"
											CONSUMER PRICES
..	..	..	..	..	..	..	..	..	..		National methodology
..	..	..	..	..	..	..	..	..	.		Outside estimate
					(millions of current US dollars)						**MERCHANDISE EXPORTS**
560	520	636	675	776	896	983	1,182	..	..	.	UNCTAD
467	595	..	269	332	324	..	..	..	..	.	IMF: IFS
467	595	652	763	..	785	880	1,100	..	..	.	ACDA
..	..	..	..	..	..	..	..	..	..		ECE
..	..	..	..	..	..	..	..	..	..		intra-CMEA
467	595	..	269	332	324	..	..	..	..	f	Authors' uniform TR/$ series
..	..	..	..	..	..	..	..	..	..		intra-CMEA
					(millions of current US dollars)						**MERCHANDISE IMPORTS**
..	..	..	..	..	..	..	..	..	..	.	UNCTAD
1,398	1,438	..	1,300	1,300	1,300	..	..	..	..	.	IMF: IFS
1,398	1,438	1,550	1,823	..	1,590	2,190	2,500	..	..	.	ACDA
..	..	..	..	..	..	..	..	..	..		ECE
..	..	..	..	..	..	..	..	..	..		intra-CMEA
1,398	1,438	..	1,300	1,300	1,300	..	..	..	..	f	Authors' uniform series
..	..	..	..	..	..	..	..	..	..		intra-CMEA

Viet Nam

Basic tables	1970	1971	1972	1973	1974	1975	1976	1977	1978	1979	1980
SNA ACCOUNTS, current prices				*(millions of current Vietnamese dong)*							
GNP, at market prices	..	..	..	..	..	..	..	..	..	..	..
Net factor income	..	..	..	..	..	..	..	..	..	..	..
GDP at market prices	..	..	..	..	..	..	..	..	..	..	..
Net indirect taxes	..	..	..	..	..	..	..	..	..	..	..
GDP at factor cost	..	..	..	..	..	..	..	..	..	..	..
Agriculture	..	..	..	..	..	..	..	..	..	..	..
Industry	..	..	..	..	..	..	..	..	..	..	..
Services, etc.	..	..	..	..	..	..	..	..	..	..	..
Resource balance	..	..	..	..	..	..	..	..	..	..	..
Exports GNFS	..	..	..	..	..	..	..	..	..	..	..
Imports GNFS	..	..	..	..	..	..	..	..	..	..	..
Domestic absorption	..	..	..	..	..	..	..	..	..	..	..
Total consumption	..	..	..	..	..	..	..	..	..	..	..
Private consumption	..	..	..	..	..	..	..	..	..	..	..
General government consumption	..	..	..	..	..	..	..	..	..	..	..
Gross domestic investment	..	..	..	..	..	..	..	..	..	..	..
Fixed domestic investment	..	..	..	..	..	..	..	..	..	..	..
Depreciation	..	..	..	..	..	..	..	..	..	..	..
SNA ACCOUNTS, constant prices				*(millions of constant 1987 Vietnamese dong)*							
Gross national product (GNP)	..	..	..	..	..	..	..	..	..	..	..
GDP at market prices	..	..	..	..	..	..	..	..	..	..	..
GDP at factor cost	..	..	..	..	..	..	..	..	..	..	..
Agriculture	..	..	..	..	..	..	..	..	..	..	..
Industry	..	..	..	..	..	..	..	..	..	..	..
Services, etc.	..	..	..	..	..	..	..	..	..	..	..
Resource balance	..	..	..	..	..	..	..	..	..	..	..
Exports GNFS	..	..	..	..	..	..	..	..	..	..	..
Imports GNFS	..	..	..	..	..	..	..	..	..	..	..
Domestic absorption	..	..	..	..	..	..	..	..	..	..	..
Total consumption, etc.	..	..	..	..	..	..	..	..	..	..	..
Private consumption, etc.	..	..	..	..	..	..	..	..	..	..	..
General government consumption	..	..	..	..	..	..	..	..	..	..	..
Gross domestic investment	..	..	..	..	..	..	..	..	..	..	..
Fixed domestic investment	..	..	..	..	..	..	..	..	..	..	..
Depreciation	..	..	..	..	..	..	..	..	..	..	..
MPS ACCOUNTS, current prices				*(millions of current Vietnamese dong)*							
NMP produced:	..	..	..	..	..	..	..	..	..	..	2,577
Agriculture and forestry	..	..	..	..	..	..	..	..	..	..	1,336
Industry excluding construction	..	..	..	..	..	..	..	..	..	..	520
Construction	..	..	..	..	..	..	..	..	..	..	87
Transport and communication	..	..	..	..	..	..	..	..	..	..	60
Trade, etc.	..	..	..	..	..	..	..	..	..	..	457
Other services	..	..	..	..	..	..	..	..	..	..	117
Resource balance	..	..	..	..	..	..	..	..	..	..	..
NMP used: domestic market	..	..	..	..	..	..	..	..	..	..	2,985
Final consumption, material goods	..	..	..	..	..	..	..	..	..	..	2,678
Personal consumption	..	..	..	..	..	..	..	..	..	..	2,418
Collective consumption	..	..	..	..	..	..	..	..	..	..	260
Net capital formation	..	..	..	..	..	..	..	..	..	..	307
Net fixed capital formation	..	..	..	..	..	..	..	..	..	..	..
Changes in stocks	..	..	..	..	..	..	..	..	..	..	..
Depreciation	..	..	..	..	..	..	..	..	..	..	..
MPS ACCOUNTS, constant prices				*(millions of 1982 Vietnamese dong)*							
NMP produced:	..	..	..	..	..	..	..	..	..	..	120,130
Agriculture and forestry	..	..	..	..	..	..	..	..	..	..	61,530
Industry and construction	..	..	..	..	..	..	..	..	..	..	35,700
Services	..	..	..	..	..	..	..	..	..	..	22,930
Resource balance	..	..	..	..	..	..	..	..	..	..	..
NMP used: domestic market	..	..	..	..	..	..	..	..	..	..	146,400
Final consumption, material goods	..	..	..	..	..	..	..	..	..	..	132,230
Personal consumption	..	..	..	..	..	..	..	..	..	..	124,620
Collective consumption	..	..	..	..	..	..	..	..	..	..	7,610
Net capital formation	..	..	..	..	..	..	..	..	..	..	14,170
Net fixed capital formation	..	..	..	..	..	..	..	..	..	..	..
Depreciation	..	..	..	..	..	..	..	..	..	..	..

Abbreviations in notes column are explained in the General Notes. For sources and methods, see the Technical Notes.

1981	1982	1983	1984	1985	1986	1987	1988	1989	1990	Notes	
				(millions of current Vietnamese dong)							**SNA ACCOUNTS, current prices**
..	..	..	..	..	636,000	3,104,000	15,580,000	32,653,999	46,544,007	.	GNP, at market prices
					0	0	0	0	0	.	Net factor income
..	..	..	64,800	131,100	636,000	3,104,000	15,580,000	32,653,999	46,544,007	.	GDP at market prices
			..	..	0	0	0	0	0	.	Net indirect taxes
..	..	..	64,800	131,100	636,000	3,104,000	15,580,000	32,653,999	46,544,007	.	GDP at factor cost
..	..	..	..	..	..	..	..	..	..	.	Agriculture
..	..	..	..	..	..	..	..	..	..	.	Industry
..	..	..	..	..	..	..	..	..	..	.	Services, etc.
..	..	..	..	..	..	..	..	..	..	.	Resource balance
..	..	..	..	..	..	..	..	..	..	.	Exports GNFS
..	..	..	..	..	..	..	..	..	..	.	Imports GNFS
..	..	..	..	..	..	..	..	..	..	.	Domestic absorption
..	..	..	..	..	..	..	..	..	..	.	Total consumption
..	..	..	..	..	..	..	..	..	..	.	Private consumption
..	..	..	..	..	..	..	..	..	..	.	General government consumption
..	..	..	..	..	..	..	..	4,572,000	..	.	Gross domestic investment
..	..	..	..	..	..	..	..	..	..	.	Fixed domestic investment
..	..	..	..	..	..	..	..	..	..	.	Depreciation
				(millions of constant 1987 Vietnamese dong)							**SNA ACCOUNTS, constant prices**
..	..	..	..	..	2,981,134	3,104,000	3,285,067	3,517,868	3,686,000	.	Gross national product (GNP)
..	..	..	2,731,520	2,886,720	2,981,134	3,104,000	3,285,067	3,517,868	3,686,000	.	GDP at market prices
..	..	..	2,731,520	2,886,720	2,981,134	3,104,000	3,285,067	3,517,868	3,686,000	.	GDP at factor cost
..	..	..	..	..	..	..	..	..	..	.	Agriculture
..	..	..	..	..	..	..	..	..	..	.	Industry
..	..	..	..	..	..	..	..	..	..	.	Services, etc.
..	..	..	..	..	..	..	..	..	..	.	Resource balance
..	..	..	..	..	..	..	..	..	..	.	Exports GNFS
..	..	..	..	..	..	..	..	..	..	.	Imports GNFS
..	..	..	..	..	..	..	..	..	..	.	Domestic absorption
..	..	..	..	..	..	..	..	..	..	.	Total consumption, etc.
..	..	..	..	..	..	..	..	..	..	.	Private consumption, etc.
..	..	..	..	..	..	..	..	..	..	.	General government consumption
..	..	..	..	..	..	..	..	..	..	.	Gross domestic investment
..	..	..	..	..	..	..	..	..	..	.	Fixed domestic investment
..	..	..	..	..	..	..	..	..	..	.	Depreciation
				(millions of current Vietnamese dong)							**MPS ACCOUNTS, current prices**
..	133,800	..	..	..	378,237	1,807,334	9,400,000	15,995,360		f	NMP produced:
..	71,000	..	..	..	163,937	853,359	5,269,139	8,269,698		.	Agriculture and forestry
..	..	..	..	..	110,953	525,318	2,012,055	3,842,380		.	Industry excluding construction
..	..	..	..	..	13,315	58,198	343,827	729,000		.	Construction
..	..	..	..	..	3,814	17,316	138,328	267,466		.	Transport and communication
..	..	..	..	..	75,766	317,004	1,421,719	2,536,911		.	Trade, etc.
..	..	..	..	..	10,452	36,139	214,896	349,404		.	Other services
..	..	..	..	..	-39,249	-185,444	-1,450,000	7,939,782	..	f	Resource balance
..	..	..	..	..	417,486	1,992,778	10,850,000	8,055,578	..	.	NMP used: domestic market
..	..	..	..	..	382,605	1,833,638	9,732,000	6,420,578	..	.	Final consumption, material goods
..	..	..	..	..	371,457	1,750,425	9,412,000	5,892,578	..	.	Personal consumption
..	..	..	..	..	11,146	83,213	320,000	528,000	..	.	Collective consumption
..	..	..	..	..	34,881	159,140	1,118,000	1,635,001	..	.	Net capital formation
..	..	..	..	..	..	..	..	..	..	.	Net fixed capital formation
..	..	..	..	..	..	..	..	..	..	.	Changes in stocks
..	..	..	..	..	..	..	..	..	..	.	Depreciation
				(millions of 1982 Vietnamese dong)							**MPS ACCOUNTS, constant prices**
..	133,800	143,400	155,300	164,100	169,560	173,879	183,878	188,273	..	.	NMP produced:
..	71,000	76,700	79,800	83,400	85,980	83,143	87,553	94,481	..	.	Agriculture and forestry
..	38,100	40,900	45,800	51,300	53,430	59,236	61,137	58,962	..	.	Industry and construction
..	24,700	25,800	29,700	29,400	30,150	31,500	33,188	34,830	..	.	Services
..	..	..	..	..	-30,252	-31,563	-34,936	-22,736	..	.	Resource balance
..	..	..	..	..	199,812	205,442	218,814	211,009	..	.	NMP used: domestic market
..	..	..	..	..	169,850	174,652	184,928	190,118	..	.	Final consumption, material goods
..	..	..	..	..	162,060	165,529	176,407	181,575	..	.	Personal consumption
..	..	..	..	..	7,790	9,123	821	8,543	..	.	Collective consumption
..	..	..	..	..	29,962	30,790	33,886	20,891	..	.	Net capital formation
..	..	..	..	..	..	..	..	..	..	.	Net fixed capital formation
..	..	..	..	..	..	..	..	..	..	.	Depreciation

Basic tables (continued)	1970	1971	1972	1973	1974	1975	1976	1977	1978	1979	1980
MPS ACCOUNTS, index					*(index, 1980 = 100)*						
NMP produced:	..	..	..	..	..	..	..	..	..	..	100.0
Agriculture and forestry	..	..	..	..	..	..	..	..	..	..	100.0
Industry excluding construction	..	..	..	..	..	..	..	..	..	..	100.0
Construction	..	..	..	..	..	..	..	..	..	..	100.0
Transport and communication	..	..	..	..	..	..	..	..	..	..	..
Trade, etc.	..	..	..	..	..	..	..	..	..	..	..
NMP used: material goods	..	..	..	..	..	..	..	..	..	..	100.0
Final consumption	..	..	..	..	..	..	..	..	..	..	100.0
Net capital formation	..	..	..	..	..	..	..	..	..	..	100.0
EXCHANGE AND CONVERSION RATES					*(LCUs per US dollar: annual average)*						
Single-year converter	0.024	0.024	0.327	0.100	0.127	0.164	0.185	0.182	0.197	0.206	0.205
Devisa/official	..	..	..	..	..	0.164	..	..	..	..	0.205
Commercial	..	..	..	..	..	..	..	..	..	..	..
Noncommercial	..	..	..	..	..	..	..	..	..	..	..
Informal market	..	..	..	..	..	..	..	..	..	..	..
ICP	..	..	..	..	..	..	..	..	..	..	..
					(ruble per US dollar: annual average)						
Commercial TR/$ cross	..	..	..	..	..	..	..	..	..	..	..
Uniform TR/$ cross	1.072	1.157	1.232	1.093	1.092	1.167	1.067	1.022	0.973	0.945	0.980
					(LCUs per ruble: annual average)						
Commercial	..	..	..	..	..	..	..	..	..	..	..
Noncommercial	..	..	..	..	..	..	..	..	..	..	..
Devisa/official	..	..	..	..	..	..	..	..	..	..	..
CONSUMER PRICE INDEXES					*(index)*						
Official, IMF 1985 = 100	..	..	..	..	..	..	..	..	..	..	..
Official, CIA or LWI 1980 = 100	..	..	..	..	..	..	..	..	..	..	..
Alternative, CIA or LWI 1980 = 100	..	..	..	..	..	..	..	..	..	..	..
INTERNATIONAL TRADE (ECE)					*(millions of current Vietnamese dong)*						
Value of exports, fob	..	..	..	..	..	..	..	..	..	..	..
to CMEA	..	..	..	..	..	..	..	..	..	..	..
Value of imports, cif	..	..	..	..	..	..	..	..	..	..	..
from CMEA	..	..	..	..	..	..	..	..	..	..	..
Trade balance	..	..	..	..	..	..	..	..	..	..	..
CMEA	..	..	..	..	..	..	..	..	..	..	..
INTERNATIONAL TRADE (Authors')					*(millions of current US dollars)*						
Value of exports, fob	8	..	..	..	..	229	..	..	..	..	537
to developed countries	..	..	..	..	..	..	..	..	..	..	..
to other non-socialist countries	..	..	..	..	..	..	..	..	..	..	..
to socialist countries	..	..	..	..	..	..	..	..	..	..	..
to CMEA	..	..	..	..	..	..	..	..	..	..	..
Value of imports, cif	373	..	..	..	..	1,102	..	..	..	..	1,296
from developed countries	..	..	..	..	..	..	..	..	..	..	..
from other non-socialist countries	..	..	..	..	..	..	..	..	..	..	..
from socialist countries	..	..	..	..	..	..	..	..	..	..	..
from CMEA	..	..	..	..	..	..	..	..	..	..	..
Trade balance	-365	..	..	..	..	-873	..	..	..	..	-759
Developed countries	..	..	..	..	..	..	..	..	..	..	..
Other non-socialist countries	..	..	..	..	..	..	..	..	..	..	..
Socialist countries	..	..	..	..	..	..	..	..	..	..	..
CMEA	..	..	..	..	..	..	..	..	..	..	..
PARTNER CONVERTIBLE TRADE (ECE)					*(millions of current US dollars)*						
Exports to non-CMEA (cif)	..	..	..	..	..	..	..	..	..	..	..
Imports from non-CMEA (fob)	..	..	..	..	..	..	..	..	..	..	..
Trade balance	..	..	..	..	..	..	..	..	..	..	..
TRADE PRICE INDEXES (Authors')					*(index, 1980 = 100)*						
Terms of trade	..	..	..	..	..	..	..	..	..	..	..
Exports	..	..	..	..	..	..	..	..	..	..	..
Non-socialist countries	..	..	..	..	..	..	..	..	..	..	..
Developed countries	..	..	..	..	..	..	..	..	..	..	..
Other	..	..	..	..	..	..	..	..	..	..	..
Socialist countries	..	..	..	..	..	..	..	..	..	..	..
CMEA	..	..	..	..	..	..	..	..	..	..	..
Imports	..	..	..	..	..	..	..	..	..	..	..
Non-socialist countries	..	..	..	..	..	..	..	..	..	..	..
Developed countries	..	..	..	..	..	..	..	..	..	..	..
Other	..	..	..	..	..	..	..	..	..	..	..
Socialist countries	..	..	..	..	..	..	..	..	..	..	..
CMEA	..	..	..	..	..	..	..	..	..	..	..

Abbreviations in notes column are explained in the General Notes. For sources and methods, see the Technical Notes.

1981	1982	1983	1984	1985	1986	1987	1988	1989	1990	Notes	**Basic tables (continued)**
				(index, 1980 = 100)							**MPS ACCOUNTS, index**
..	111.4	119.4	129.3	136.6	141.1	144.7	153.1	156.7	..	I	NMP produced:
..	115.4	124.7	129.7	135.5	139.7	135.1	142.3	153.6	..	.	Agriculture and forestry
..	110.3	117.7	131.8	148.1	154.8	172.5	179.2	172.8	..	.	Industry excluding construction
..	81.3	92.6	103.8	112.9	113.1	119.4	115.2	111.4	..	.	Construction
..	..	..	..	..	..	120.0	122.0	124.0	126.0	..	.	Transport and communication
..	..	..	..	120.0	127.2	132.2	140.2	147.9	..	.	Trade, etc.
..	..	..	..	..	136.5	140.3	149.5	144.1	..	I	NMP used: material goods
..	..	..	..	..	128.5	132.1	139.9	143.8	..	.	Final consumption
..	..	..	..	..	211.4	217.3	239.1	147.4	..	.	Net capital formation
				(LCUs per US dollar: annual average)							**EXCHANGE AND CONVERSION RATES**
0.578	0.943	1.002	1.030	6.698	18.000	61.960	480.000	3,532.780	5,130.500	.	Single-year converter
0.578	0.943	1.002	1.030	6.698	18.000	61.960	480.000	3,532.780		.	Devisa/official
..	..	..	..	..	..	..	..	..	..	.	Commercial
..	..	..	..	..	..	..	..	..	..	.	Noncommercial
..	..	..	..	..	..	..	..	..	..	.	Informal market
..	..	..	..	..	..	..	..	..	..	.	ICP
				(ruble per US dollar: annual average)							
..	..	..	..	..	..	..	..	..	..	.	Commercial TR/$ cross
1.076	1.105	1.201	1.395	1.433	1.388	1.397	1.484	1.660	1.980	.	Uniform TR/$ cross
				(LCUs per ruble: annual average)							
..	..	..	..	..	..	..	..	..	..	.	Commercial
..	..	..	..	..	..	..	..	..	..	.	Noncommercial
..	..	..	..	..	..	..	..	..	..	.	Devisa/official
				(index)							**CONSUMER PRICE INDEXES**
..	..	..	..	..	..	..	..	..	..	.	Official, IMF 1985 = 100
..	..	..	..	..	..	..	..	..	..	.	Official, CIA or LWI 1980 = 100
..	..	..	..	..	..	..	..	..	..	.	Alternative, CIA or LWI 1980 = 100
				(millions of current Vietnamese dong)							**INTERNATIONAL TRADE (ECE)**
..	..	..	..	..	..	..	..	..	..	.	Value of exports, fob
..	..	..	..	..	..	..	..	..	..	.	to CMEA
..	..	..	..	..	..	..	..	..	..	.	Value of imports, cif
..	..	..	..	..	..	..	..	..	..	.	from CMEA
..	..	..	..	..	..	..	..	..	..	.	Trade balance
..	..	..	..	..	..	..	..	..	..	.	CMEA
				(millions of current US dollars)							**INTERNATIONAL TRADE (Authors')**
467	595	..	269	332	324	..	..	..	..	f	Value of exports, fob
..	..	..	..	..	..	..	..	..	..	.	to developed countries
..	..	..	..	..	..	..	..	..	..	.	to other non-socialist countries
..	..	..	..	..	..	..	..	..	..	.	to socialist countries
..	..	..	..	..	..	..	..	..	..	.	to CMEA
1,398	1,438	..	1,300	1,300	1,300	..	..	..	..	f	Value of imports, cif
..	..	..	..	..	..	..	..	..	..	.	from developed countries
..	..	..	..	..	..	..	..	..	..	.	from other non-socialist countries
..	..	..	..	..	..	..	..	..	..	.	from socialist countries
..	..	..	..	..	..	..	..	..	..	.	from CMEA
-931	-843	..	-1,031	-968	-976	..	..	..	..	f	Trade balance
..	..	..	..	..	..	..	..	..	..	.	Developed countries
..	..	..	..	..	..	..	..	..	..	.	Other non-socialist countries
..	..	..	..	..	..	..	..	..	..	.	Socialist countries
..	..	..	..	..	..	..	..	..	..	.	CMEA
				(millions of current US dollars)							**PARTNER CONVERTIBLE TRADE (ECE)**
..	..	206	238	296	291	366	458	740	..	W	Exports to non-CMEA (cif)
..	..	413	509	554	533	541	462	741	..	W	Imports from non-CMEA (fob)
..	..	-207	-271	-258	-243	-175	-4	-1	..	W	Trade balance
				(index, 1980 = 100)							**TRADE PRICE INDEXES (Authors')**
..	..	..	..	100.0	100.2	97.9	95.6	91.9	..	f	Terms of trade
..	..	..	..	100.0	100.6	100.4	99.4	98.0	..	f	Exports
..	..	..	..	..	..	..	..	..	..	.	Non-socialist countries
..	..	..	..	..	..	..	..	..	..	.	Developed countries
..	..	..	..	..	..	..	..	..	..	.	Other
..	..	..	..	..	..	..	..	..	..	.	Socialist countries
..	..	..	..	..	..	..	..	..	..	.	CMEA
..	..	..	..	100.0	100.4	102.6	104.0	106.6	..	.	Imports
..	..	..	..	..	..	..	..	..	..	.	Non-socialist countries
..	..	..	..	..	..	..	..	..	..	.	Developed countries
..	..	..	..	..	..	..	..	..	..	.	Other
..	..	..	..	..	..	..	..	..	..	.	Socialist countries
..	..	..	..	..	..	..	..	..	..	.	CMEA

Basic tables (continued)	1970	1971	1972	1973	1974	1975	1976	1977	1978	1979	1980
TRADE PRICE INDEXES (ECE)					*(index, 1980 = 100)*						
Terms of trade	..	..	..	..	..	..	..	..	..	..	..
Exports	..	..	..	..	..	..	..	..	..	..	..
Imports	..	..	..	..	..	..	..	..	..	..	..
Balance of Payments (ECE)					*(millions of current US dollars)*						
Exports, convertible currency	..	..	..	..	..	..	..	..	..	..	..
Imports, convertible currency	..	..	..	..	..	..	..	..	..	..	..
Trade balance, convertible currency	..	..	..	..	..	..	..	..	..	..	..
Invisibles, convertible currency	..	..	..	..	..	..	..	..	..	..	..
Current balance, convertible currency	..	..	..	..	..	..	..	..	..	..	..
External debt, total (World Bank)	..	..	..	..	..	..	..	..	..	..	..
Convertible currency	..	..	..	..	..	..	..	..	..	..	..
CMEA	..	..	..	..	..	..	..	..	..	..	..
External debt service (World Bank)	..	..	..	..	..	..	..	..	..	..	..
Convertible currency	..	..	..	..	..	..	..	..	..	..	..
Total reserves less gold (IMF, IFS)	217	243	245	165	210	..	..	..	..	..	..
Total reserves, including gold at London price	243	273	290	242	339	..	..	..	..	..	..
Total reserves, incl. gold at national valuation	..	..	..	..	..	..	..	..	..	..	..
EMPLOYMENT					*(thousands)*						
Employment, total	..	..	..	..	..	..	..	..	..	..	..
Agriculture	..	..	..	..	..	..	..	..	..	..	..
Industry	..	..	..	..	..	..	..	..	..	..	..
Services	..	..	..	..	..	..	..	..	..	..	..
Labor force, total	20,272	20,681	21,090	21,499	21,907	22,316	22,839	23,362	23,884	24,407	24,930
Agriculture	15,529	15,639	15,748	15,858	15,967	16,077	16,226	16,375	16,524	16,673	16,822
Industry	1,316	1,461	1,607	1,753	1,898	2,044	2,225	2,406	2,588	2,769	2,950
Services	3,427	3,581	3,734	3,888	4,042	4,195	4,388	4,580	4,773	4,966	5,158
DOMESTIC FINANCE (IMF)					*(millions of current Vietnamese dong)*						
Money supply, broadly defined	400	557	736	866	1,206	..	..	..	..	..	..
Money, means of payment	328	421	460	526	668	..	..	..	..	..	..
Demand deposits	76	97	93	126	177	..	..	..	..	..	..
Currency outside banks	252	324	367	400	491	..	..	..	..	..	..
Quasi-money	72	135	276	340	538	..	..	..	..	..	..
Interest: deposit rate (percent)	..	..	..	..	..	..	..	..	..	..	..
Central government expenditures	..	..	..	..	..	..	..	..	..	..	..
Defense	..	..	..	..	..	..	..	..	..	..	..
					(millions of 1989 US dollars)						
Central government exp. (ACDA)	..	..	..	..	..	..	..	..	..	..	..
Military (ACDA)	..	..	..	..	..	..	..	..	..	..	..
LAND AND FORESTS (FAO)											
Pop. density: agr. land (pop. per sq. km)	674	690	704	716	731	739	732	739	753	824	786
Deforestation rate (net)	0	0	0	0	0	0	0	0	0	0	0
Forest (thousands sq. km)	138	138	137	137	136	136	135	135	134	134	133
SOCIAL INDICATORS											
Population density: total land (pop. per sq. km)	131	134	138	141	144	148	151	155	158	162	165
School enrollment ratio, primary	..	..	..	..	..	119	123	120	110	116	109
secondary	..	..	..	..	..	46	49	50	44	48	42
tertiary	..	..	..	..	..	..	..	..	..	..	2
Energy consumption per capita (kg. of oil eq.)	215	181	166	172	122	133	78	83	83	87	91
Daily calorie supply per capita	2,164	2,157	2,106	2,109	2,068	1,981	1,987	2,041	2,003	2,042	2,067
Food production (1979-1981=100)	97	96	96	96	94	88	96	91	90	97	100
Daily protein supply (gm. per capita)	50	50	50	50	48	46	46	47	46	47	47
Population per hospital bed	..	..	..	..	..	..	..	..	..	..	286
per nursing person	..	..	4,305	..	..	..	..	..	..	..	
per physician	..	..	..	..	..	..	..	..	..	..	4,151
Female participation in labor force (percent)	44	44	44	44	43	43	43	43	43	43	43
Infant mortality (per 1,000 live births)	104	97	90	84	79	73	68	62	60	58	57
Life expectancy (years)	55	57	58	59	60	60	61	62	62	63	63
Total fertility (births per woman)	6	6	6	6	6	6	6	6	5	5	5
Urban population (percent of total population)	18	18	19	19	19	19	19	19	19	19	19
Population per passenger car	..	..	..	..	..	..	..	..	..	..	..
per telephone	..	..	..	..	..	..	..	..	..	..	..

Abbreviations in notes column are explained in the General Notes. For sources and methods, see the Technical Notes.

218

1981	1982	1983	1984	1985	1986	1987	1988	1989	1990	Notes	Basic tables (continued)
				(index, 1980 = 100)							**TRADE PRICE INDEXES (ECE)**
..	..	..	..	..	..	..	..	..	..		Terms of trade
..	..	..	..	..	..	..	..	..	..		Exports
..	..	..	..	..	..	..	..	..	..		Imports
				(millions of current US dollars)							**Balance of Payments (ECE)**
149	210	224	276	336	307	430	465	977	..	.	Exports, convertible currency
310	335	330	468	459	453	465	603	985	..	.	Imports, convertible currency
-161	-125	-106	-192	-123	-146	-35	-138	-8	..	.	Trade balance, convertible currency
-54	56	-8	-31	-47	-28	-50	-70	-210	..	.	Invisibles, convertible currency
-215	-69	-114	-223	-170	-174	-85	-208	-218	..	.	Current balance, convertible currency
..	3,572	4,776	4,899	5,428	7,894	10,076	11,597		..	O	External debt, total (World Bank)
..	..	..	..	..	..	..	..	..	..		Convertible currency
..	2,500	3,870	4,000	4,300	6,500	8,500	9,997	..	..	.	CMEA
..	295	66	47	169	262	371	236	..	..	Of	External debt service (World Bank)
..	..	..	..	..	..	..	..	..	..		Convertible currency
17	16	12	12	12	12	..	..	..	..		Total reserves less gold (IMF, IFS)
291	331	275	225	238	282	..	..	..	..		Total reserves, including gold at London price
..	..	..	..	..	..	..	..	..	..		Total reserves, incl. gold at national valuation
				(thousands)							**EMPLOYMENT**
..	..	24,400	25,100	26,025	27,399	27,968	28,922	28,745	..		Employment, total
..	..	..	..	18,979	19,974	20,419	21,102	20,471	..		Agriculture
..	..	..	..	3,632	3,799	3,872	4,005	3,948	..		Industry
..	..	..	..	3,414	3,626	3,677	2,815	4,326	..		Services
25,695	26,460	27,225	27,990	28,755	29,587	30,420	31,252	32,084	32,916	.	Labor force, total
..	..	..	..	..	..	..	..	..	..		Agriculture
..	..	..	..	..	..	..	..	..	..		Industry
..	..	..	..	..	..	..	..	..	..		Services
				(millions of current Vietnamese dong)							**DOMESTIC FINANCE (IMF)**
..	..	..	..	..	..	..	..	..	..		Money supply, broadly defined
..	..	..	..	..	..	..	..	..	..		Money, means of payment
..	..	..	..	..	..	..	..	..	..		Demand deposits
..	..	..	..	..	..	..	..	..	..		Currency outside banks
..	..	..	..	..	..	..	..	..	..		Quasi-money
..	..	..	..	..	..	..	..	..	..		Interest: deposit rate (percent)
..	..	..	..	..	..	..	..	..	..		Central government expenditures
..	..	..	..	..	..	..	..	..	..		Defense
				(millions of 1989 US dollars)							
..	..	..	..	..	6,547	4,507	..	..	..	.	Central government exp. (ACDA)
..	..	..	..	..	2,670		..	..	..		Military (ACDA)
											LAND AND FORESTS (FAO)
801	816	830	845	862	886	910	..	..	..		Pop. density: agr. land (pop. per sq. km)
0	0	0	0	0	..	..	..	..	..		Deforestation rate (net)
133	132	132	131	131	..	..	..	..	..		Forest (thousands sq. km)
											SOCIAL INDICATORS
168	171	174	177	181	185	190	..	..	..	.	Population density: total land (pop. per sq. km)
..	..	..	104	102	..	..	..	..	..	.	School enrollment ratio, primary
..	..	..	40	42	..	..	..	..	..	.	secondary
..	..	..	..	..	..	..	..	..	..	.	tertiary
94	93	94	82	86	87	88	..	..	..	.	Energy consumption per capita (kg. of oil eq.)
2,133	2,186	2,164	2,214	2,212	2,215	2,204	2,233	..	..		Daily calorie supply per capita
103	112	113	117	117	118	116	122	129	131	.	Food production (1979-1981=100)
48	49	49	50	50	50	50	51	..	..		Daily protein supply (gm. per capita)
271	..	..	..	..	..	..	..	..	..		Population per hospital bed
1,241	..	..	..	..	594	..	..	..	..		per nursing person
4,048	..	..	..	..	947	..	..	..	..		per physician
43	43	44	44	44	45	45	45	45	46	.	Female participation in labor force (percent)
55	53	51	50	49	47	46	44	43	42	.	Infant mortality (per 1,000 live births)
64	64	64	65	65	65	66	66	66	67	.	Life expectancy (years)
5	5	5	5	5	4	4	4	4	4	.	Total fertility (births per woman)
20	20	20	20	20	21	21	21	22	22	.	Urban population (percent of total population)
..	..	..	..	..	..	..	..	..	..		Population per passenger car
..	541	535	529	512	..	..	..	..	..		per telephone

Yugoslavia

Comparator tables	1970	1971	1972	1973	1974	1975	1976	1977	1978	1979	1980
PER CAPITA INCOME						*(US dollars)*					
World Bank (Atlas method)	660	740	780	870	1,150	1,380	1,620	1,970	2,400	2,880	3,250
Single year conversion	672	719	758	969	1,266	1,449	1,728	2,098	2,491	3,080	3,241
CIA or LWI	1,236	..	..	..	..	2,080	2,259	2,560	2,873	3,313	3,763
Penn World Tables	1,143	1,317	1,374	1,475	1,859	2,063	2,226	2,552	2,977	3,357	3,743
POPULATION						*(thousands)*					
	20,371	20,572	20,772	20,956	21,164	21,365	21,573	21,775	21,968	22,166	22,304
GROSS NATIONAL PRODUCT, current prices						*(millions of current US dollars)*					
World Bank (Atlas method)	13,347	15,167	16,280	18,281	24,410	29,462	34,912	42,853	52,818	63,758	72,482
Single year conversion	13,688	14,787	15,745	20,308	26,792	30,949	37,270	45,681	54,724	68,265	72,282
Authors' series	..	..	..	..	..	..	..	..	..	..	..
CIA or LWI	..	..	..	..	..	..	..	..	..	35,100	38,960
GROSS NATIONAL PRODUCT, constant prices						*(millions of constant 1987 dollars)*					
Single year conversion	36,022	39,242	40,665	41,847	48,062	48,243	50,766	55,090	60,079	62,987	64,262
Authors' series, rescaled from 1980 prices	..	..	..	..	..	..	..	..	..	..	..
CIA or LWI, rescaled from 1989 prices	70,369	..	..	..	..	87,962	90,688	97,286	102,651	109,688	114,966
CONVERSION FACTORS						*(LCUs per US dollar)*					
World Bank (Atlas method)	0.00	0.00	0.00	0.00	0.00	0.00	0.00	0.00	0.00	0.00	0.00
Single year convertor	0.00	0.00	0.00	0.00	0.00	0.00	0.00	0.00	0.00	0.00	0.00
Authors' series	..	..	..	..	..	..	..	..	..	..	..
Penn World Tables	0.01	0.01	0.01	0.01	0.01	0.01	0.01	0.02	0.02	0.02	0.02
OUTPUT TRENDS, OVERALL						*(index, constant prices 1987 = 100)*					
GNP, SNA	55.4	60.4	62.6	64.4	73.9	74.2	78.1	84.7	92.4	96.9	98.9
NMP, MPS	54.1	58.4	60.9	63.9	69.4	71.9	74.7	80.7	86.3	92.4	94.5
GNP, "Building block"	55.7	59.3	60.4	63.4	67.9	69.6	71.8	77.0	81.3	86.8	91.0
Industry											
Value added, SNA	41.6	44.6	54.0	55.9	61.4	65.9	68.5	75.0	81.9	87.5	90.3
Value added, MPS	47.6	51.2	54.5	56.6	62.1	66.6	69.3	75.6	82.4	89.2	92.2
"Building block"	49.8	53.8	56.2	58.0	63.4	65.9	66.5	73.7	81.3	88.9	95.4
Gross output, SNA	55.0	..	..	..	..	69.4	..	..	..	..	90.1
Agriculture											
Value added, SNA	64.3	68.5	71.2	77.5	81.7	79.6	84.7	89.6	84.8	87.9	87.9
Value added, MPS	68.7	73.3	72.0	78.3	82.7	80.5	85.7	90.7	86.0	90.6	90.6
"Building block"	69.0	73.5	71.0	77.1	81.4	79.3	84.8	89.5	84.7	89.2	89.2
Gross output, SNA	68.8	..	..	..	..	79.8	..	..	..	..	91.7
Services											
Value added, SNA	56.6	62.8	56.4	57.5	63.5	63.9	67.5	72.1	82.5	85.0	90.5
Value added, MPS	58.3	63.9	66.9	69.9	75.8	77.1	79.1	84.8	93.3	98.8	100.5
"Building block"	56.6	59.5	60.7	63.6	67.4	69.7	72.2	75.7	80.0	84.0	87.4
CONSUMPTION											
Total consumption, SNA	63.0	69.6	68.9	71.0	87.2	85.1	83.1	94.2	104.4	109.6	107.4
Total consumption, MPS	61.0	65.3	68.4	70.3	75.5	78.6	82.7	88.6	94.7	99.8	100.2
Households, SNA	61.7	72.5	68.0	70.5	95.3	89.8	82.8	99.0	114.3	120.1	115.3
Households, "building block"	..	..	..	..	..	77.5	80.9	83.0	86.8	90.2	93.0
General government, SNA	64.6	65.9	70.0	71.6	76.7	79.1	83.5	87.9	91.6	95.9	97.0
General government, "building block"	..	..	..	..	..	66.6	73.8	77.5	80.4	82.7	84.7
INVESTMENT											
Gross fixed investment, SNA	86.7	90.6	93.4	96.1	104.8	115.0	124.3	136.1	150.4	160.1	150.6
Accumulation, MPS	87.5	91.5	94.4	97.1	105.9	116.1	125.6	137.4	151.9	161.6	152.1
"Building block"	..	..	..	..	..	77.5	71.6	89.5	94.0	113.3	116.6
CONSUMER PRICES											
National methodology	0.6	0.7	0.8	1.0	1.2	1.5	1.7	1.9	2.2	2.7	3.5
Outside estimate	0.5	0.7	0.8	0.9	1.2	1.4	1.6	1.9	2.2	2.7	3.5
MERCHANDISE EXPORTS						*(millions of current US dollars)*					
UNCTAD	1,679	..	..	..	..	4,072	..	..	..	..	10,770
IMF: IFS	1,679	..	..	..	..	4,072	..	..	..	..	8,977
ACDA	..	..	..	..	..	..	..	5,354	5,671	6,491	8,978
ECE	..	..	..	..	..	..	..	..	..	..	..
intra-CMEA											
Authors' uniform TR/$ series	1,650	1,781	2,186	2,789	3,769	4,031	4,780	5,151	5,518	6,334	8,811
intra-CMEA	541	663	786	917	1,457	1,879	2,039	2,089	2,388	2,670	3,987
MERCHANDISE IMPORTS						*(millions of current US dollars)*					
UNCTAD	2,874	..	..	..	..	7,697	..	..	..	..	18,279
IMF: IFS	2,874	..	..	..	..	7,697	..	..	..	..	15,076
ACDA	..	..	..	..	..	..	..	9,634	9,988	12,860	15,080
ECE	..	..	..	..	..	..	..	..	..	..	..
intra-CMEA											
Authors' uniform series	2,822	3,205	3,183	4,463	7,468	7,619	7,315	9,550	9,930	12,763	15,010
intra-CMEA	589	778	797	1,095	1,715	1,859	2,212	2,734	2,896	3,462	4,421

Abbreviations in notes column are explained in the General Notes. For sources and methods, see the Technical Notes.

1981	1982	1983	1984	1985	1986	1987	1988	1989	1990	Notes	Comparator tables (continued)
				(US dollars)							**PER CAPITA INCOME**
3,450	3,230	2,640	2,270	2,040	2,290	2,510	2,710	2,940	3,060	.	World Bank (Atlas method)
3,135	2,787	2,051	1,928	1,998	2,778	2,776	2,545	3,243	3,670	.	Single year conversion
4,160	4,434	4,613	4,861	5,012	5,316	5,390	5,453	5,596	5,438	.	CIA or LWI
4,061	4,302	4,306	4,392	4,485	4,790	4,857	..	..	..	.	Penn World Tables
				(thousands)							
22,471	22,642	22,805	22,966	23,124	23,274	23,417	23,566	23,690	23,800	.	**POPULATION**
				(millions of current US dollars)							**GROSS NATIONAL PRODUCT, current prices**
77,539	73,187	60,149	52,090	47,188	53,188	58,813	63,964	69,581	72,860	.	World Bank (Atlas method)
70,454	63,108	46,775	44,274	46,197	64,664	65,003	59,968	76,825	87,356	.	Single year conversion
..	..	..	..	..	..	..	..	..	..	.	Authors' series
43,050	45,710	46,890	49,440	51,150	54,740	55,610	55,890	58,640	..	.	CIA or LWI
				(millions of constant 1987 dollars)							**GROSS NATIONAL PRODUCT, constant prices**
64,618	64,579	63,691	64,634	64,207	66,857	65,003	64,111	64,996	60,508	.	Single year conversion
..	..	..	..	..	..	..	..	..	..	.	Authors' series, rescaled from 1980 prices
116,813	117,868	118,924	121,651	122,618	127,632	126,225	124,378	123,234	115,582	.	CIA or LWI, rescaled from 1989 prices
				(LCUs per US dollar)							**CONVERSION FACTORS**
0.00	0.00	0.01	0.01	0.03	0.05	0.08	0.24	3.18	13.57	..	World Bank (Atlas method)
0.00	0.01	0.01	0.02	0.03	0.04	0.07	0.25	2.88	11.32	.	Single year convertor
..	..	..	..	..	..	..	..	..	..	..	Authors' series
0.03	0.03	0.05	0.07	0.12	0.23	0.43	..	..	..	.	Penn World Tables
				(index, constant prices 1987 = 100)							**OUTPUT TRENDS, OVERALL**
99.4	99.3	98.0	99.4	98.8	102.9	100.0	98.6	100.0	93.1	.	GNP, SNA
95.8	96.3	95.3	97.2	97.7	101.1	100.0	98.3	..	..	f	NMP, MPS
92.5	93.3	94.1	96.3	97.1	101.2	100.0	98.6	97.6	91.5	.	GNP, "Building block"
											Industry
92.2	90.7	89.3	92.3	94.1	97.8	100.0	99.3	100.2	89.9	.	Value added, SNA
94.3	93.1	92.1	95.3	97.3	99.7	100.0	98.7	..	..	.	Value added, MPS
96.0	94.1	94.6	96.8	98.8	101.2	100.0	99.6	99.2	87.1	.	"Building block"
..	..	..	..	97.3	99.1	100.0	100.9	100.0	..	X	Gross output, SNA
											Agriculture
90.4	97.0	96.3	98.4	91.8	98.2	100.0	96.4	100.7	93.1	.	Value added, SNA
93.1	99.9	99.1	101.2	94.5	104.2	100.0	96.7	..	..	I	Value added, MPS
91.7	98.4	97.6	99.9	93.1	104.2	100.0	93.2	95.5	92.8	.	"Building block"
..	..	..	..	94.5	102.8	100.0	99.1	99.1	..	.	Gross output, SNA
											Services
89.8	92.4	89.5	90.4	96.8	98.5	100.0	97.9	96.7	93.0	.	Value added, SNA
99.9	100.1	99.3	98.6	99.9	102.1	100.0	98.4	..	..	.	Value added, MPS
89.3	90.7	92.4	94.5	97.0	100.0	100.0	99.5	96.9	95.4	.	"Building block"
											CONSUMPTION
104.5	102.9	100.9	99.9	97.8	105.7	100.0	96.8	95.8	106.7	.	Total consumption, SNA
98.7	98.5	96.3	95.5	95.7	100.0	100.0	98.9	..	..	.	Total consumption, MPS
113.7	110.7	108.7	106.4	101.4	112.3	100.0	95.5	93.5	118.7	.	Households, SNA
93.3	93.6	93.6	92.9	92.5	99.1	100.0	97.5	98.8	..	.	Households, "building block"
92.5	92.7	90.7	91.6	93.0	97.1	100.0	98.5	98.7	91.2	.	General government, SNA
87.2	89.2	90.9	92.8	95.1	97.5	100.0	101.4	101.2	..	.	General government, "building block"
											INVESTMENT
135.8	128.3	115.9	104.7	100.6	96.4	100.0	95.3	92.3	92.8	.	Gross fixed investment, SNA
137.2	129.6	117.0	105.8	101.9	105.4	100.0	94.2	..	..	YI	Accumulation, MPS
113.4	109.2	105.1	103.0	105.0	108.4	100.0	99.6	101.3	..	.	"Building block"
											CONSUMER PRICES
4.9	6.4	9.0	13.9	23.9	45.3	100.0	294.1	3940.5	26915.6	.	National methodology
4.9	6.5	9.0	14.0	24.9	45.5	100.0	311.2	4201.6	..	.	Outside estimate
				(millions of current US dollars)							**MERCHANDISE EXPORTS**
10,929	10,241	9,913	10,254	10,642	10,298	11,425	12,597	13,363	14,300	.	UNCTAD
10,940	10,284	9,913	10,254	10,700	10,353	11,443	12,663	13,460	14,669	.	IMF: IFS
10,940	10,250	9,914	10,250	10,700	10,350	11,440	12,660	13,460	..	.	ACDA
..	..	..	..	..	..	..	..	..	..	.	ECE
											intra-CMEA
10,866	10,246	9,913	10,249	10,642	10,311	11,433	12,601	13,599	14,356	W	Authors' uniform TR/$ series
5,358	5,115	4,551	4,673	5,283	4,915	3,908	4,079	4,446	4,034	.	intra-CMEA
				(millions of current US dollars)							**MERCHANDISE IMPORTS**
15,817	13,334	12,154	11,956	12,164	11,750	12,603	13,154	14,802	17,300	.	UNCTAD
15,727	13,453	12,154	11,996	12,207	11,750	12,632	13,171	14,829	19,191	.	IMF: IFS
15,730	13,450	12,150	12,000	12,210	11,750	12,630	13,170	14,830	..	.	ACDA
..	..	..	..	..	..	..	..	..	..	.	ECE
											intra-CMEA
15,661	13,150	12,154	11,995	12,163	11,762	12,603	13,155	14,832	19,226	W	Authors' uniform series
4,845	4,528	4,414	3,859	3,861	3,754	3,702	3,589	4,215	4,315	.	intra-CMEA

Yugoslavia

Basic tables	1970	1971	1972	1973	1974	1975	1976	1977	1978	1979	1980
SNA ACCOUNTS, current prices					*(millions of current Yugoslav new dinars)*						
GNP, at market prices	17	22	27	33	43	54	68	84	102	130	178
Net factor income	0	0	0	0	0	0	0	0	0	-1	-2
GDP at market prices	17	22	27	33	43	54	68	84	102	130	180
Net indirect taxes	2	2	2	2	5	5	6	8	10	13	15
GDP at factor cost	16	20	25	31	38	49	62	76	93	117	165
Agriculture	3	3	4	6	6	8	9	11	11	14	20
Industry	6	8	12	13	16	22	26	32	39	51	72
Services, etc.	7	9	9	13	16	19	27	33	43	53	73
Resource balance	-1	-1	-1	-1	-4	-4	-2	-5	-5	-9	-8
Exports GNFS	3	4	6	7	9	11	13	15	17	20	34
Imports GNFS	4	6	7	8	13	15	15	20	22	29	41
Domestic absorption	18	23	28	34	47	58	70	89	107	139	188
Total consumption	13	16	20	25	34	40	48	59	72	89	116
Private consumption	10	13	15	20	26	30	36	44	54	67	88
General government consumption	3	4	5	5	7	10	12	15	18	22	28
Gross domestic investment	6	7	8	9	13	18	22	30	35	50	72
Fixed domestic investment	5	7	8	9	12	16	21	27	36	45	55
Depreciation	..	..	..	..	..	..	..	..	..	..	..
SNA ACCOUNTS, constant prices					*(millions of constant 1987 Yugoslav new dinars)*						
Gross national product (GNP)	2,655	2,892	2,997	3,084	3,542	3,556	3,741	4,060	4,428	4,642	4,736
GDP at market prices	2,645	2,878	2,980	3,058	3,511	3,534	3,722	4,032	4,403	4,635	4,755
GDP at factor cost	2,280	2,476	2,595	2,697	2,951	3,037	3,190	3,438	3,756	3,935	4,102
Agriculture	404	430	447	486	513	500	532	562	532	552	552
Industry	936	1,003	1,213	1,257	1,381	1,482	1,541	1,687	1,842	1,967	2,030
Services, etc.	947	1,050	942	961	1,061	1,068	1,129	1,205	1,378	1,421	1,513
Resource balance	-264	-333	-155	-221	-427	-396	-159	-397	-380	-540	-293
Exports GNFS	847	917	1,034	1,120	1,059	1,070	1,182	1,158	1,214	1,246	1,336
Imports GNFS	1,111	1,250	1,189	1,341	1,486	1,466	1,340	1,556	1,594	1,785	1,629
Domestic absorption	2,908	3,211	3,135	3,279	3,938	3,929	3,881	4,429	4,783	5,175	5,047
Total consumption, etc.	2,356	2,606	2,577	2,657	3,263	3,186	3,110	3,525	3,907	4,100	4,018
Private consumption, etc.	1,304	1,532	1,435	1,490	2,013	1,897	1,749	2,092	2,413	2,537	2,436
General government consumption	1,052	1,075	1,141	1,167	1,250	1,289	1,361	1,433	1,494	1,563	1,582
Gross domestic investment	553	605	559	622	675	743	770	904	876	1,075	1,030
Fixed domestic investment	859	899	926	953	1,040	1,140	1,233	1,349	1,491	1,587	1,493
Depreciation	..	..	..	..	..	..	..	..	..	..	..
MPS ACCOUNTS, current prices					*(millions of current Yugoslav new dinars)*						
NMP produced:	16	20	25	31	41	50	59	73	90	117	155
Agriculture and forestry	3	4	4	6	7	8	10	12	12	16	21
Industry excluding construction	6	8	9	12	17	20	24	30	37	46	64
Construction	2	2	3	3	4	5	6	8	10	13	17
Transport and communication	1	2	2	3	3	4	5	6	8	10	13
Trade, etc.	4	5	5	7	8	10	12	15	20	27	34
Other services	0	1	1	1	1	3	2	3	4	6	7
Resource balance	1	1	2	2	2	2	3	1	3	1	1
NMP used: domestic market	15	20	22	28	39	48	56	73	87	115	154
Final consumption, material goods	10	13	16	20	26	33	39	47	57	73	96
Personal consumption	9	11	14	17	22	28	33	40	49	62	82
Collective consumption	2	2	2	3	4	5	6	7	9	11	14
Net capital formation	5	7	6	9	13	16	17	26	30	42	58
Net fixed capital formation	4	5	5	6	7	12	14	20	27	34	39
Changes in stocks	1	2	2	3	6	5	3	6	3	8	19
Depreciation	..	..	..	..	..	..	..	..	..	..	..
MPS ACCOUNTS, constant prices					*(millions of 1972 Yugoslav new dinars)*						
NMP produced:	22	24	25	26	28	29	30	33	35	37	38
Agriculture and forestry	4	5	4	5	5	5	5	6	5	6	6
Industry and construction	11	11	12	12	14	15	15	17	18	20	20
Services	7	8	8	9	9	9	10	10	11	12	12
Resource balance	1	1	1	2	2	2	1	1	1	1	3
NMP used: domestic market	21	22	23	24	26	27	29	31	34	36	35
Final consumption, material goods	14	15	16	16	18	18	19	21	22	23	23
Personal consumption	12	13	14	14	15	16	16	18	19	20	20
Collective consumption	2	2	2	2	2	3	3	3	3	3	3
Net capital formation	7	7	8	8	8	9	10	11	12	13	12
Net fixed capital formation	..	..	..	..	..	..	..	..	..	..	..
Depreciation	..	..	..	..	..	..	..	..	..	..	..

Abbreviations in notes column are explained in the General Notes. For sources and methods, see the Technical Notes.

Yugoslavia

1981	1982	1983	1984	1985	1986	1987	1988	1989	1990	Notes	
											(millions of current Yugoslav new dinars) — **SNA ACCOUNTS, current prices**
246	317	434	677	1,248	2,452	4,791	15,128	220,978	988,692	.	GNP, at market prices
-4	-8	-12	-21	-38	-56	-124	-453	-4,226	-9,937	.	Net factor income
251	325	446	697	1,286	2,508	4,915	15,581	225,204	998,629	.	GDP at market prices
22	26	40	60	88	171	366	1,040	15,154	67,072	.	Net indirect taxes
229	299	406	638	1,199	2,337	4,548	14,541	210,050	931,557	.	GDP at factor cost
30	41	60	87	139	273	628	1,556	24,576	109,117	.	Agriculture
104	130	173	279	553	984	2,249	6,465	103,975	447,675	.	Industry
95	128	173	272	507	1,081	1,672	6,520	81,499	374,765	.	Services, etc.
-6	0	1	6	23	44	142	955	6,829	-8,093	.	Resource balance
50	71	122	207	384	598	1,207	5,616	55,877	240,337	.	Exports GNFS
56	71	121	202	361	554	1,065	4,662	49,048	248,430	.	Imports GNFS
257	325	445	692	1,264	2,464	4,772	14,626	218,375	1,006,830	.	Domestic absorption
159	210	286	432	765	1,501	3,742	8,753	119,177	792,153	.	Total consumption
122	161	222	337	593	1,162	2,112	7,456	103,709	723,564	.	Private consumption
38	49	64	95	171	340	1,630	1,297	15,468	68,589	.	General government consumption
98	116	159	260	499	963	1,030	5,873	99,199	214,681	.	Gross domestic investment
69	86	103	146	261	505	992	2,719	34,152	164,749	.	Fixed domestic investment
..	..	..	..	..	..	..	..	..	..	.	Depreciation
											(millions of constant 1987 Yugoslav new dinars) — **SNA ACCOUNTS, constant prices**
4,762	4,760	4,694	4,764	4,732	4,927	4,791	4,725	4,790	4,459	.	Gross national product (GNP)
4,813	4,843	4,788	4,871	4,840	5,013	4,915	4,837	4,865	4,496	.	GDP at market prices
4,140	4,199	4,108	4,205	4,309	4,463	4,548	4,476	4,501	4,160	.	GDP at factor cost
567	609	605	618	576	617	628	606	632	585	.	Agriculture
2,075	2,039	2,007	2,075	2,116	2,200	2,249	2,233	2,253	2,021	.	Industry
1,501	1,545	1,496	1,512	1,617	1,646	1,672	1,637	1,616	1,554	.	Services, etc.
-139	-18	10	102	168	63	142	230	198	14	.	Resource balance
1,273	1,200	1,127	1,208	1,268	1,230	1,207	1,198	1,242	1,277	.	Exports GNFS
1,412	1,218	1,117	1,106	1,100	1,167	1,065	968	1,044	1,263	.	Imports GNFS
4,952	4,861	4,778	4,769	4,672	4,950	4,772	4,607	4,666	4,482	.	Domestic absorption
3,910	3,851	3,775	3,739	3,659	3,954	3,742	3,622	3,584	3,994	.	Total consumption, etc.
2,401	2,339	2,296	2,246	2,143	2,372	2,112	2,017	1,976	2,508	.	Private consumption, etc.
1,508	1,512	1,478	1,492	1,516	1,583	1,630	1,605	1,608	1,486	.	General government consumption
1,042	1,010	1,004	1,031	1,013	996	1,030	986	1,082	488	.	Gross domestic investment
1,347	1,273	1,149	1,039	997	956	992	945	916	920	.	Fixed domestic investment
..	..	..	..	..	..	..	..	..	..	.	Depreciation
											(millions of current Yugoslav new dinars) — **MPS ACCOUNTS, current prices**
221	293	406	633	1,129	2,204	4,921	14,832	..	..	f	NMP produced:
31	45	64	93	141	298	582	1,680	..	..	.	Agriculture and forestry
93	123	173	285	546	1,022	2,427	7,664	..	..	.	Industry excluding construction
22	27	31	44	78	152	330	867	..	..	.	Construction
17	22	29	45	83	162	350	1,045	..	..	.	Transport and communication
48	64	92	141	233	475	1,000	2,956	..	..	.	Trade, etc.
9	12	16	26	47	96	233	621	..	..	.	Other services
9	26	44	59	112	207	636	1,797	..	..	.	Resource balance
212	267	363	573	1,017	1,997	4,286	13,035	..	..	.	NMP used: domestic market
134	177	243	373	663	1,312	2,895	8,753	..	..	.	Final consumption, material goods
114	151	209	321	566	1,121	2,480	7,456	..	..	.	Personal consumption
20	26	35	52	97	191	415	1,297	..	..	.	Collective consumption
78	90	120	200	354	685	1,391	4,282	..	..	.	Net capital formation
48	53	56	77	145	290	427	1,128	..	..	.	Net fixed capital formation
30	37	63	123	209	395	964	3,154	..	..	.	Changes in stocks
..	..	..	..	..	..	..	..	..	..	.	Depreciation
											(millions of 1972 Yugoslav new dinars) — **MPS ACCOUNTS, constant prices**
39	39	38	39	39	41	40	40	..	..	f	NMP produced:
6	6	6	6	6	6	6	6	..	..	.	Agriculture and forestry
21	21	20	21	21	22	22	22	..	..	.	Industry and construction
12	12	12	12	12	13	12	12	..	..	.	Services
5	6	7	9	9	9	9	9	..	..	.	Resource balance
34	33	32	31	30	32	31	30	..	..	.	NMP used: domestic market
23	23	22	22	22	23	23	23	..	..	.	Final consumption, material goods
20	20	19	19	19	20	20	20	..	..	.	Personal consumption
3	3	3	3	3	3	3	3	..	..	.	Collective consumption
11	10	9	8	8	8	8	8	..	..	.	Net capital formation
..	..	..	..	..	..	..	..	..	..	.	Net fixed capital formation
..	..	..	..	..	..	..	..	..	..	.	Depreciation

Basic tables (continued)	1970	1971	1972	1973	1974	1975	1976	1977	1978	1979	1980
MPS ACCOUNTS, index					*(index, 1980 = 100)*						
NMP produced:	57.2	61.8	64.5	67.7	73.4	76.1	79.1	85.4	91.3	97.8	100.0
Agriculture and forestry	75.9	80.9	79.5	86.4	91.2	88.8	94.6	100.1	94.9	100.0	100.0
Industry excluding construction	49.8	54.5	58.4	61.6	68.2	72.5	75.2	82.1	89.0	96.0	100.0
Construction	58.8	59.7	61.9	60.7	64.5	71.4	74.9	81.8	91.1	99.8	100.0
Transport and communication	..	..	..	..	..	..	..	..	..	..	..
Trade, etc.	..	..	..	..	..	..	..	..	..	..	..
NMP used: material goods	59.7	63.4	66.1	68.0	73.4	77.7	82.5	89.1	96.3	101.9	100.0
Final consumption	60.8	65.1	68.2	70.2	75.3	78.5	82.5	88.4	94.5	99.6	100.0
Net capital formation	57.6	60.2	62.1	63.8	69.6	76.4	82.6	90.4	99.9	106.3	100.0
EXCHANGE AND CONVERSION RATES					*(LCUs per US dollar: annual average)*						
Single-year converter	0.001	0.002	0.002	0.002	0.002	0.002	0.002	0.002	0.002	0.002	0.003
Devisa/official	..	..	..	..	..	..	..	..	..	..	..
Commercial	0.001	0.002	0.002	0.002	0.002	0.002	0.002	0.002	0.002	0.002	0.003
Noncommercial	0.001	0.002	0.002	0.002	0.002	0.002	0.002	0.002	0.002	0.002	0.003
Informal market	0.001	0.002	0.002	0.002	0.002	0.002	0.002	0.002	0.002	0.002	0.003
ICP	0.007	0.008	0.009	0.011	0.011	0.011	0.012	0.014	0.015	0.016	0.018	0.022
					(ruble per US dollar: annual average)						
Commercial TR/$ cross	..	..	..	..	..	..	..	..	..	..	..
Uniform TR/$ cross	1.450	1.386	1.418	1.837	2.859	2.460	2.491	2.659	2.523	2.906	3.498
					(LCUs per ruble: annual average)						
Commercial	..	..	..	..	..	..	..	..	..	..	..
Noncommercial	..	..	..	..	..	..	..	..	..	..	..
Devisa/official	..	..	..	..	..	..	..	..	..	..	..
CONSUMER PRICE INDEXES					*(index)*						
Official, IMF 1985 = 100	2.6	3.0	3.5	4.2	5.1	6.3	7.0	8.1	9.2	11.1	14.6
Official, CIA or LWI 1980 = 100	17.6	20.6	23.5	27.9	35.3	44.6	49.0	55.4	62.7	76.5	100.0
Alternative, CIA or LWI 1980 = 100	15.5	18.7	22.3	26.8	33.2	40.3	45.7	54.4	63.7	78.3	100.0
INTERNATIONAL TRADE (ECE)					*(millions of current Yugoslav new dinars)*						
Value of exports, fob	2	3	4	5	6	7	9	9	10	12	22
to CMEA	1	1	1	2	2	3	4	4	4	5	10
Value of imports, cif	4	5	5	7	12	13	13	18	19	24	37
from CMEA	1	1	1	2	3	3	4	5	5	7	11
Trade balance	-2	-2	-2	-3	-6	-6	-5	-8	-8	-12	-15
CMEA	0	0	0	0	0	0	0	-1	-1	-2	-1
INTERNATIONAL TRADE (Authors')					*(millions of current US dollars)*						
Value of exports, fob	1,650	1,781	2,186	2,789	3,769	4,031	4,780	5,151	5,518	6,334	8,811
to developed countries	902	910	1,215	1,509	1,705	1,390	1,925	1,970	1,987	2,472	3,101
to other non-socialist countries	199	200	164	306	472	715	783	1,026	1,088	1,118	1,555
to socialist countries	549	671	807	974	1,592	1,926	2,072	2,154	2,443	2,744	4,155
to CMEA	541	663	786	917	1,457	1,879	2,039	2,089	2,388	2,670	3,987
Value of imports, cif	2,822	3,205	3,183	4,463	7,468	7,619	7,315	9,550	9,930	12,763	15,010
from developed countries	1,932	2,092	2,063	2,760	4,463	4,589	3,977	5,387	5,553	7,255	7,835
from other non-socialist countries	296	327	314	583	1,226	1,121	1,084	1,359	1,372	1,952	2,632
from socialist countries	595	786	806	1,120	1,780	1,910	2,254	2,804	3,005	3,556	4,542
from CMEA	589	778	797	1,095	1,715	1,859	2,212	2,734	2,896	3,462	4,421
Trade balance	-1,172	-1,423	-997	-1,674	-3,699	-3,588	-2,535	-4,400	-4,412	-6,429	-6,198
Developed countries	-1,030	-1,182	-848	-1,251	-2,758	-3,199	-2,052	-3,417	-3,566	-4,783	-4,734
Other non-socialist countries	-97	-127	-150	-277	-754	-406	-301	-333	-284	-834	-1,077
Socialist countries	-46	-115	1	-146	-188	16	-182	-650	-562	-812	-387
CMEA	-48	-115	-11	-178	-258	20	-173	-645	-508	-792	-434
PARTNER CONVERTIBLE TRADE (ECE)					*(millions of current US dollars)*						
Exports to non-CMEA (cif)	..	..	..	..	..	..	..	..	..	..	..
Imports from non-CMEA (fob)	..	..	..	..	..	..	..	..	..	..	..
Trade balance	..	..	..	..	..	..	..	..	..	..	..
TRADE PRICE INDEXES (Authors')					*(index, 1980 = 100)*						
Terms of trade	106.0	106.8	107.1	106.5	95.6	99.3	100.7	99.6	103.6	101.0	100.0
Exports	29.8	31.2	33.0	39.5	52.1	56.9	59.1	66.8	72.4	84.0	100.0
Non-socialist countries	..	..	..	..	..	..	..	..	..	..	..
Developed countries	..	..	..	..	..	..	..	..	..	..	..
Other	..	..	..	..	..	..	..	..	..	..	..
Socialist countries	..	..	..	..	..	..	..	..	..	..	..
CMEA	..	..	..	..	..	..	..	..	..	..	..
Imports	28.1	29.2	30.8	37.1	54.5	57.3	58.7	67.1	69.9	83.2	100.0
Non-socialist countries	..	..	..	..	..	..	..	..	..	..	..
Developed countries	..	..	..	..	..	..	..	..	..	..	..
Other	..	..	..	..	..	..	..	..	..	..	..
Socialist countries	..	..	..	..	..	..	..	..	..	..	..
CMEA	..	..	..	..	..	..	..	..	..	..	..

Abbreviations in notes column are explained in the General Notes. For sources and methods, see the Technical Notes.

1981	1982	1983	1984	1985	1986	1987	1988	1989	1990	Notes	Basic tables (continued)
				(index,1980 = 100)							**MPS ACCOUNTS, index**
101.4	101.9	100.9	102.9	103.4	107.1	105.8	104.0	..	..	I	NMP produced:
102.8	110.3	109.4	111.8	104.3	115.0	110.4	106.7	..	..	.	Agriculture and forestry
104.2	104.4	106.0	111.2	114.3	117.9	118.4	117.8	..	..	.	Industry excluding construction
95.3	88.1	76.6	73.5	72.2	71.2	70.6	66.0	..	..	.	Construction
..	..	..	..	..	..	..	..	..	..	.	Transport and communication
											Trade, etc.
95.6	93.8	89.6	86.5	85.7	89.3	88.1	86.1	..	..	I	NMP used: material goods
98.4	98.3	96.1	95.2	95.5	99.7	99.8	98.7	..	..	.	Final consumption
90.2	85.2	77.0	69.6	67.0	69.3	65.8	61.9	..	..	.	Net capital formation
				(LCUs per US dollar: annual average)							**EXCHANGE AND CONVERSION RATES**
0.004	0.005	0.009	0.015	0.027	0.038	0.074	0.252	2.876	11.318	.	Single-year converter
..	..	..	..	..	..	..	..	..	..	.	Devisa/official
0.004	0.005	0.009	0.015	0.027	0.038	0.074	0.252	2.876		f	Commercial
0.004	0.005	0.009	0.015	0.027	0.038	0.074	0.252	2.876	..	.	Noncommercial
0.004	0.006	0.011	0.014	0.029	0.035	0.037	0.287	2.809	..	.	Informal market
0.028	0.033	0.045	0.069	0.124	0.225	0.432	..	..	..	.	ICP
				(ruble per US dollar: annual average)							
..	..	..	..	..	..	..	..	..	..	.	Commercial TR/$ cross
3.265	2.816	2.598	2.478	2.298	1.769	1.925	1.876	1.900	..	.	Uniform TR/$ cross
				(LCUs per ruble: annual average)							
..	..	..	..	..	..	..	..	..	..	.	Commercial
..	..	..	..	..	..	..	..	..	..	.	Noncommercial
..	..	..	..	..	..	..	..	..	..	.	Devisa/official
				(index)							**CONSUMER PRICE INDEXES**
20.3	26.8	37.5	58.0	100.0	189.8	419.0	1,232.3	16,511.2	112,780.0	.	Official, IMF 1985=100
146.0	189.1	263.6	411.7	725.3	1,364.3	2,965.9	8,722.6	117,873.6	..	.	Official, CIA or LWI 1980=100
139.8	185.0	257.0	400.1	712.3	1,303.9	2,863.7	8,912.6	120,322.2	..	.	Alternative, CIA or LWI 1980=100
				(millions of current Yugoslav new dinars)							**INTERNATIONAL TRADE (ECE)**
38	52	92	157	288	391	843	3,179	39,116	162,471	W	Value of exports, fob
19	26	42	71	143	186	288	1,029	12,789	45,656	.	to CMEA
55	66	113	183	329	446	929	3,319	42,665	217,598	W	Value of imports, cif
17	23	41	59	104	142	273	905	12,124	48,840	.	from CMEA
-17	-15	-21	-27	-41	-55	-83	-140	-3,549	-55,127	W	Trade balance
2	3	1	12	38	44	15	124	666	-3,184	.	CMEA
				(millions of current US dollars)							**INTERNATIONAL TRADE (Authors')**
10,866	10,246	9,913	10,249	10,642	10,311	11,433	12,601	13,599	14,356	W	Value of exports, fob
3,371	2,839	3,248	3,663	3,631	3,656	5,545	6,492	7,124	8,368	.	to developed countries
2,061	2,164	2,040	1,767	1,550	1,597	1,822	1,915	1,933	1,890	.	to other non-socialist countries
5,433	5,243	4,625	4,819	5,461	5,057	4,065	4,194	4,542	4,098	.	to socialist countries
5,358	5,115	4,551	4,673	5,283	4,915	3,908	4,079	4,446	4,034	.	to CMEA
15,661	13,150	12,154	11,995	12,163	11,762	12,603	13,155	14,832	19,226	W	Value of imports, cif
8,236	6,573	5,547	5,290	5,563	5,633	7,095	7,275	8,285	12,007	.	from developed countries
2,459	1,946	2,122	2,782	2,670	2,290	1,703	2,206	2,248	2,696	.	from other non-socialist countries
4,966	4,631	4,485	3,922	3,930	3,840	3,806	3,674	4,299	4,523	.	from socialist countries
4,845	4,528	4,414	3,859	3,861	3,754	3,702	3,589	4,215	4,315	.	from CMEA
-4,895	-2,904	-2,241	-1,746	-1,522	-1,452	-1,171	-554	-1,234	-487	W	Trade balance
-4,865	-3,734	-2,299	-1,627	-1,932	-1,977	-1,550	-783	-1,161	-3,639	.	Developed countries
-398	218	-82	-1,015	-1,120	-693	119	-291	-315	-806	.	Other non-socialist countries
467	612	140	897	1,531	1,217	259	520	243	-425	.	Socialist countries
513	587	137	814	1,422	1,161	206	490	231	-281	.	CMEA
				(millions of current US dollars)							**PARTNER CONVERTIBLE TRADE (ECE)**
5,115	5,693	6,064	6,167	6,446	7,730	9,494	11,138	11,699	14,047	W	Exports to non-CMEA (cif)
8,860	7,211	7,255	7,535	8,195	9,391	9,195	10,633	11,376	15,966	W	Imports from non-CMEA (fob)
-3,745	-1,518	-1,191	-1,368	-1,749	-1,661	299	505	323	-1,920	W	Trade balance
				(index,1980 = 100)							**TRADE PRICE INDEXES (Authors')**
98.5	102.8	100.8	..	..	..	..	..	..	..	f	Terms of trade
108.1	115.8	113.5	..	..	..	..	..	..	..	f	Exports
..	..	..	..	..	..	..	..	..	..	.	Non-socialist countries
..	..	..	..	..	..	..	..	..	..	.	Developed countries
..	..	..	..	..	..	..	..	..	..	.	Other
..	..	..	..	..	..	..	..	..	..	.	Socialist countries
..	..	..	..	..	..	..	..	..	..	.	CMEA
109.8	112.6	112.6	..	..	..	..	..	..	..	f	Imports
..	..	..	..	..	..	..	..	..	..	.	Non-socialist countries
..	..	..	..	..	..	..	..	..	..	.	Developed countries
..	..	..	..	..	..	..	..	..	..	.	Other
..	..	..	..	..	..	..	..	..	..	.	Socialist countries
..	..	..	..	..	..	..	..	..	..	.	CMEA

Basic tables (continued)	1970	1971	1972	1973	1974	1975	1976	1977	1978	1979	1980
TRADE PRICE INDEXES (ECE)					*(index, 1980 = 100)*						
Terms of trade	..	..	..	..	..	..	..	..	..	..	..
Exports	..	..	..	..	..	..	..	..	..	..	..
Imports	..	..	..	..	..	..	..	..	..	..	..
Balance of Payments (ECE)					*(millions of current US dollars)*						
Exports, convertible currency	..	..	..	..	..	..	..	..	..	..	5,656
Imports, convertible currency	..	..	..	..	..	..	..	..	..	..	11,321
Trade balance, convertible currency	..	..	..	..	..	..	..	..	..	..	-5,665
Invisibles, convertible currency	..	..	..	..	..	..	..	..	..	..	1,934
Current balance, convertible currency	..	..	..	..	..	..	..	..	..	..	-2,204
External debt, total (World Bank)	2,053	2,777	3,529	4,308	5,094	5,999	7,542	10,119	12,528	15,970	18,486
Convertible currency	1,993	2,701	3,417	4,215	5,010	5,921	7,468	10,064	12,482	15,934	18,459
CMEA	201	230	254	239	253	299	355	410	496	589	615
External debt service (World Bank)	524	671	898	1,128	1,280	1,454	1,486	1,800	2,096	3,313	3,735
Convertible currency	523	670	897	1,105	1,269	1,448	1,479	1,781	2,086	3,300	3,724
Total reserves less gold (IMF, IFS)	89	157	675	1,276	1,085	811	1,990	2,044	2,388	1,257	1,384
Total reserves, including gold at London price	143	221	772	1,439	1,359	1,017	2,187	2,294	2,757	2,138	2,478
Total reserves, incl. gold at national valuation	140	213	732	1,337	1,147	873	2,052	2,108	2,457	1,329	1,462
EMPLOYMENT					*(thousands)*						
Employment, total	..	..	..	..	..	..	..	..	..	..	..
Agriculture	..	..	..	..	..	..	..	..	..	..	..
Industry	..	..	..	..	..	..	..	..	..	..	..
Services	..	..	..	..	..	..	..	..	..	..	..
Labor force, total	9,177	9,267	9,357	9,448	9,538	9,629	9,694	9,760	9,826	9,892	9,958
Agriculture	4,571	4,447	4,323	4,200	4,076	3,952	3,804	3,656	3,508	3,360	3,212
Industry	2,677	2,743	2,810	2,876	2,942	3,009	3,070	3,132	3,194	3,256	3,318
Services	1,929	2,077	2,224	2,372	2,520	2,668	2,820	2,972	3,124	3,276	3,428
DOMESTIC FINANCE (IMF)					*(millions of current Yugoslav new dinars)*						
Money supply, broadly defined	10	13	16	21	26	34	47	57	73	90	123
Money, means of payment	4	4	6	8	10	14	22	25	29	34	45
Demand deposits	2	2	4	5	7	9	17	19	22	25	34
Currency outside banks	2	2	2	3	4	4	5	6	8	9	12
Quasi-money	7	9	10	13	15	20	25	32	44	55	78
Interest: deposit rate (percent)	..	..	..	..	..	..	..	3	5	5	6
Central government expenditures	3	4	6	7	10	12	16	9	10	12	16
Defense	1	1	1	1	2	3	3	4	4	6	8
					(millions of 1989 US dollars)						
Central government exp. (ACDA)	..	..	..	..	..	..	..	..	..	5,299	5,064
Military (ACDA)	..	..	..	..	..	..	..	..	..	2,400	2,459
LAND AND FORESTS (FAO)											
Pop. density: agr. land (pop. per sq. km)	139	142	143	145	147	149	151	153	154	156	156
Deforestation rate (net)	1	0	1	0	1	1	0	1	1	0	0
Forest (thousands sq. km)	89	89	90	89	90	90	91	92	92	93	93
SOCIAL INDICATORS											
Population density: total land (pop. per sq. km)	80	81	81	82	83	84	85	85	86	87	87
School enrollment ratio, primary	106	..	..	..	..	103	101	99	99	99	100
secondary	63	..	..	..	..	76	78	79	82	82	83
tertiary	..	..	..	..	..	..	..	..	..	..	22
Energy consumption per capita (kg. of oil eq.)	1,140	1,224	1,209	1,392	1,418	1,430	1,480	1,524	1,605	1,713	1,784
Daily calorie supply per capita	3,316	3,345	3,305	3,328	3,475	3,478	3,522	3,525	3,487	3,488	3,612
Food production (1979-1981=100)	82	89	85	89	96	96	99	102	95	99	100
Daily protein supply (gm. per capita)	93	94	93	94	98	99	101	102	102	102	103
Population per hospital bed	177	..	..	..	..	200	..	..	..	..	167
per nursing person	..	..	..	423	..	..	..	..	..	..	..
per physician	1,000	..	..	..	..	1,000	..	..	..	..	679
Female participation in labor force (percent)	32	32	33	33	33	33	33	33	33	33	33
Infant mortality (per 1,000 live births)	56	50	44	40	41	40	37	36	34	33	31
Life expectancy (years)	68	68	68	69	69	69	69	69	69	69	69
Total fertility (births per woman)	2	2	2	2	2	2	2	2	2	2	2
Urban population (percent of total population)	35	36	37	38	39	40	41	42	43	44	45
Population per passenger car	28	24	21	18	16	14	13	11	10	10	9
per telephone	..	..	..	..	..	16	..	..	..	..	10

Abbreviations in notes column are explained in the General Notes. For sources and methods, see the Technical Notes.

226

Yugoslavia

1981	1982	1983	1984	1985	1986	1987	1988	1989	1990	Notes	
				(index, 1980 = 100)							**TRADE PRICE INDEXES (ECE)**
..	..	..	..	..	..	..	..	..	..	.	Terms of trade
..	..	..	..	..	..	..	..	..	..	.	Exports
..	..	..	..	..	..	..	..	..	..	.	Imports
				(millions of current US dollars)							**Balance of Payments (ECE)**
6,441	5,854	6,271	6,588	6,496	7,249	8,572	9,624	10,519	..	.	Exports, convertible currency
11,746	9,635	8,069	7,759	8,267	9,739	9,610	10,212	11,971	..	.	Imports, convertible currency
-5,305	-3,781	-1,798	-1,171	-1,771	-2,490	-1,038	-588	-1,452	..	.	Trade balance, convertible currency
923	1,110	426	241	480	1,115	127	1,310	1,965	..	.	Invisibles, convertible currency
-1,430	-1,420	299	682	344	245	1,067	2,210	2,010	..	.	Current balance, convertible currency
20,646	19,900	20,477	19,644	22,278	21,507	22,476	20,987	19,998	20,690	.	External debt, total (World Bank)
20,628	19,891	20,477	19,644	22,278	21,507	22,476	20,987	19,998	20,690	.	Convertible currency
643	600	545	474	478	652	570	508	495	486	.	CMEA
3,726	4,077	3,648	4,491	3,336	4,014	3,875	3,741	3,807	4,219	f	External debt service (World Bank)
3,717	4,066	3,638	4,491	3,336	4,014	3,875	3,741	3,807	4,219	.	Convertible currency
1,597	775	976	1,158	1,095	1,460	698	2,298	4,136	5,474	.	Total reserves less gold (IMF, IFS)
2,335	1,624	1,687	1,732	1,704	2,189	1,601	3,074	4,899	6,208	.	Total reserves, including gold at London price
1,676	854	1,055	1,237	1,173	1,538	777	2,378	4,216	5,554	.	Total reserves, incl. gold at national valuation
				(thousands)							**EMPLOYMENT**
..	..	..	..	..	..	..	..	..	..	.	Employment, total
..	..	..	..	..	..	..	..	..	..	.	Agriculture
..	..	..	..	..	..	..	..	..	..	.	Industry
..	..	..	..	..	..	..	..	..	..	.	Services
10,063	10,168	10,274	10,379	10,484	10,559	10,633	10,708	10,783	10,858	.	Labor force, total
..	..	..	..	..	..	..	..	..	..	.	Agriculture
..	..	..	..	..	..	..	..	..	..	.	Industry
..	..	..	..	..	..	..	..	..	..	.	Services
				(millions of current Yugoslav new dinars)							**DOMESTIC FINANCE (IMF)**
162	215	299	436	702	1,279	2,960	10,122	247,683	344,968	.	Money supply, broadly defined
57	73	87	125	182	383	764	2,407	51,030	126,283	.	Money, means of payment
42	53	63	93	127	267	549	1,822	38,655	73,766	.	Demand deposits
15	20	25	33	55	116	215	585	12,375	52,517	.	Currency outside banks
105	142	211	311	520	896	2,196	7,715	196,653	218,685	.	Quasi-money
7	12	12	31	61	56	79	279	5,645	..	.	Interest: deposit rate (percent)
20	24	33	49	84	161	357	1,167	11,448	..	f	Central government expenditures
10	12	16	24	46	97	197	568	6,113	..	.	Defense
				(millions of 1989 US dollars)							
4,703	4,289	4,366	4,244	3,910	4,000	4,465	5,406	3,981	..	.	Central government exp. (ACDA)
2,372	2,152	2,030	2,112	2,144	2,398	2,460	2,631	2,126	..	.	Military (ACDA)
											LAND AND FORESTS (FAO)
157	159	161	162	164	165	166	..	..	..	.	Pop. density: agr. land (pop. per sq. km)
0	0	0	1	0	0	..	..	..	..	.	Deforestation rate (net)
92	92	93	93	94	93	..	..	..	..	.	Forest (thousands sq. km)
											SOCIAL INDICATORS
88	89	89	90	91	91	92	..	..	..	.	Population density: total land (pop. per sq. km)
..	101	100	98	97	96	95	94	..	..	.	School enrollment ratio, primary
..	83	82	81	80	80	80	80	..	..	.	secondary
..	21	20	2	19	19	19	18	..	..	.	tertiary
1,818	1,726	1,806	1,936	1,941	2,038	2,115	..	..	..	.	Energy consumption per capita (kg. of oil eq.)
3,624	3,559	3,609	3,524	3,500	3,671	3,533	3,505	..	..	.	Daily calorie supply per capita
101	109	104	106	97	107	101	96	98	90	.	Food production (1979-1981=100)
103	101	103	101	100	102	100	100	..	..	.	Daily protein supply (gm. per capita)
..	..	..	..	..	..	..	..	..	..	.	Population per hospital bed
300	301	..	..	..	255	..	..	..	..	.	per nursing person
700	644	..	..	..	549	..	..	..	..	.	per physician
34	34	34	34	34	35	35	35	35	35	.	Female participation in labor force (percent)
31	30	32	29	29	27	25	25	24	23	.	Infant mortality (per 1,000 live births)
69	69	69	70	70	71	71	72	72	72	.	Life expectancy (years)
2	2	2	2	2	2	2	2	2	2	.	Total fertility (births per woman)
46	48	49	50	51	52	53	54	55	56	.	Urban population (percent of total population)
9	8	8	8	8	..	..	..	..	..	.	Population per passenger car
9	8	8	..	6	..	..	..	..	..	.	per telephone

Part 4. Technical Notes

Chapter 11. Sources and Methods

The sources and methods pertaining to data in the Guide are explained in this chapter. Descriptions are of general practices—how the data are derived and compiled. The next chapter, *General Notes*, explains deviations from general practices.

In principal, the Comparator and Basic Tables use the same underlying data and methods as the Global Tables. For an explanation of the format, scope, indicators, and country groupings in the Global Tables, see chapters 5.

The text tables in chapters 8 and 9 also share the same database and sources and methods as the other tables, but have not been linked for this version of the Guide to the notation system described below, for practical reasons. If future editions of the Guide prove necessary, a fully integrated notation system is envisaged.

Throughout the Guide, readers are advised to consult chapter 11 in using the data. As with other data publications, care must be taken in identifying the definitions and descriptions of concepts used. In the Guide, technical documentation is especially important owing to the basic incomparability of certain data series, despite their superficial appearance of measuring the same economic or social phenomena (e.g., per capita income). Similarly, variations in national statistical practices also reduce the comparability of data. Data in the Guide should be interpreted only as indicating trends and characterizing major differences among economies, rather than as precise quantitative indications of such differences.

The indicators below are grouped by broad economic category (SNA Accounts, MPS Accounts, Exchange and Conversion Rates, etc.) and are presented in the order of their appearance in the Basic Tables. Selected indicators may be discussed that are not shown in the Basic Tables to allow for a logical flow between related indicators: GNP in dollars (Comparator Tables), for example, is explained below under SNA accounts. In general, indicators shown in the Basic Tables are presented first.

Broad classifications from the Basic Tables include: SNA Accounts (World Bank, and other series), MPS Accounts, Exchange and Conversion Rates, Consumer Prices, International Trade, Partner Convertible Trade, Trade Price Indexes, Balance of Payments and External Debt, Domestic Finance, Land and Forest, and Social Indicators.

SNA accounts (World Bank)

The World Bank is the primary source for SNA-based series on the origin and use of resources in the Basic Tables, and for most data series shown in the Global Tables. World Bank series are an alternative presented for most indicators in the Comparator Tables as well. Since the World Bank is more a user than compiler of national accounts, its series are themselves drawn from various published sources and information provided directly by national authorities. For more detailed information on World Bank series, readers are encouraged to consult appropriate World Bank publications, notably the footnotes to *World Tables*.

National accounts data are based mainly on national sources as collected by World Bank regional country economists. They generally accord with the System of National Accounts. Most definitions of indicators given below are those in UN SNA, series F, no. 2, revision 3. (See table 7.1 for SNA concepts, coverage, and measurement.)

SNA data are expressed in national currency units and shown both in current prices and in "chain-linked" 1987 constant prices. Growth rates and output trends are based on constant price series. Chain-linking describes a process that facilitates intertemporal comparisons: constant price data are computed with weights relevant to distinct time periods and then spliced, so that trends in each time segment are determined by the relative importance of components during that time span. The World Bank applies a uniform chain-linking that begins by partially rebasing each country's national accounts to three base years (1987, 1980, and 1970). The base year 1970 determines trends for 1960–75, 1980 base year applies to 1976–82, and the 1987 base year applies for 1983 and beyond. Linking these three constant price time series is thought to provide the most meaningful basis for long-term trend analysis.

The first step, for each of the three sub-periods, is rescaling to move the year in which current and constant price versions of the same time series have the same value without altering the trend of either, for the most detailed level of data available. Components of GDP are individually rescaled and summed to provide GDP and its subaggregates. To the extent that the sum based on new weights changes GDP, a rescaling deviation arises between constant price GDP by industrial origin and constant price GDP by expenditure. In World Bank Series, these rescaling deviations are absorbed in "private consumption, etc." on the assumption that GDP by industrial origin is a more reliable estimate than GDP by expenditure (with private consumption often a residual in the original national accounts).

The Bank's approach to partial rebasing takes into account the effects of changes in intersectoral relative prices between the original and new base periods (original base periods are noted at the end of chapter 12). Because private consumption is calculated as a residual, the national accounting identities are maintained. This method of accounting does, however, involve "burying" in private consumption whatever statistical discrepancies arise on the expenditures side in the rebasing and chain-linking process.

The Bank's partial rebasing begins with constant price estimates by industrial origin at a rather aggregated level, although usually more disaggregated than is shown in these tables. If sufficient data are not available for partial rebasing to 1987, then 1980 is used; the original base year is used if 1980 data are not available. If only GDP or GNP is available, the original constant price estimates of GDP are directly rescaled to 1987 prices.

The GNP per capita figures in U.S. dollars are calculated according to the World Bank Atlas method of converting GNP data in national currency to U.S. dollars. In this method (discussed in more detail in the *Atlas*), the conversion factor for any year is the average exchange rate for that year and the two preceding years, adjusted for differences in rates of inflation between the country and the United States. This averaging smooths fluctuations in prices and exchange rates. The resulting estimate of GNP in U.S. dollars is divided by the midyear population to obtain the per capita GNP in current U.S. dollars.

The following formulas describe the procedures for computing the conversion factor for year t:

$$(e^*_{t-2,t} = \frac{1}{3}\left[e_{t-2}\left(\frac{P_t}{P_{t-2}}\bigg/\frac{P^\$_t}{P^\$_{t-2}}\right) + e_{t-1}\left(\frac{P_t}{P_{t-1}}\bigg/\frac{P^\$_t}{P^\$_{t-1}}\right) + e_t\right]$$

and for calculating GNP per capita in U.S. dollars for year t:

$$(\gamma^\$_t) = (\gamma_t \mid N_t / e^*_{t-2,t})$$

where

γ_t	=	current GNP (local currency) for year t
P_t	=	GNP deflator for year t
e_t	=	annual average exchange rate (local currency/U.S. dollar) for year t
N_t	=	midyear population for year t
$P^\$_t$	=	U.S. GNP deflator for year t.

Gross National Income (GNY) per capita in the Global Tables is an adjusted measure of GNP that takes into account changes in the terms of trade. The terms of trade are calculated as the difference between exports expressed as a capacity to import (i.e., export of goods and non-factor services deflated by the import price index) and exports at constant prices (deflated by the export prices index). It should be noted that the terms of trade adjustment used here is based on implicit trade deflators from national accounts, where available; from foreign trade data otherwise. The two tend to differ, often significantly, for reasons that are poorly documented even for market economies.

The Comparator Tables present dollar GNP at current prices using both the Atlas method and single-year conversion factors. For further explanation of World Bank exchange rates, see *Exchange rates and conversion factors* on page 235.

SNA accounts (authors' series)

The authors' series, used mainly for gap-filling, was the backbone of the database until early 1991, when massive amounts of new information became available for many HPEs. They continue to be used where new national sources have not become available or have not yet been evaluated by the World Bank, or to show somewhat different interpretations of these sources. The authors' series remain useful in any event, for historical perspective, since recently released official reports rarely extend to earlier periods. They appear mainly in the text and Comparator Tables.

The authors relied on data from several published sources, especially the annual statistical yearbooks from central statistical offices. In all cases where the official national statistical authorities published data on GDP or reported such data directly to the World Bank, they were adapted without any changes or adjustments.

GDP at current prices was estimated by the authors for five European countries for 1970 (see Country Notes). This was done by scaling up NMP by an adjusted ratio between GDP/NMP, obtained for the same countries in the 1980s. It was assumed that in 1970 the GDP/NMP ratio was 3–4 percentage points lower than in 1980, because depreciation in this period increased more rapidly than net value added; and employment in the nonmaterial sectors increased faster than in the material sectors. Country exceptions to these assumptions are footnoted in the tables.

For countries where a breakdown of GDP by sector of origin at current prices was unavailable during the 1980s, gaps were filled by comparing shares of GDP with shares of NMP, and extrapolating on the basis of these ratios. In countries where a breakdown of depreciation by sector was available for 1970 and 1980, the change in their shares was taken into account in estimating for other countries the gross value added by sector for 1970. For countries where depreciation data were not available by sector of origin, NMP to GDP adjustments were made on the basis of the 1980s ratios.

A breakdown of GDP by end-use categories at current prices was available for all or several years in the 1980s for most HPEs in Europe; the difference between GDP produced and domestically absorbed, i.e., the resource balance, was taken to be the same as the difference in NMP produced and used. This is recognized as a weak assumption, given the vagaries of how international transactions are valued in MPS accounts, but there was little choice. To calculate ratios between GDP and NMP end-use categories, the GDP components were derived from officially published NMP aggregates by upscaling or as a residual. In the latter cases, gross investment was first defined by adding the value of depreciation to net accumulation as defined in MPS, and then consumption was obtained as a residual.

Estimates of GDP at constant prices (shown in the text tables as volume indexes) for selected countries were derived from GDP current price series in a selected base year (1980) by using the officially published volume indexes of GDP for the whole period 1970–89. The volume indexes of NMP were used in the same way for Czechoslovakia and Bulgaria with minor adjustments (see Country Foot-

notes for these countries).

A breakdown of GDP by sector of origin at constant prices was estimated for the USSR, Czechoslovakia, and Bulgaria for all years (1970–89), and for the German Democratic Republic and Poland for 1970. The starting point for the estimation was the magnitude and growth of NMP components at constant prices, which were adjusted by the published or estimated increases of depreciation in the different sectors.

A breakdown of GDP by end-use aggregates at constant prices was derived from the current values of a selected year by extrapolating these values with volume indexes published for material consumption. In the case of gross investment, data for gross fixed capital formation were used, and the original volume of stockbuilding added. In most cases, mainly for 1970, gross capital formation was accepted as a more realistic estimate, and final consumption was derived as a residual.

GDP in dollars as calculated by the authors is described under conversion factors (authors' series) later in this chapter.

SNA accounts (CIA or LWI, ACDA)

The terms CIA or LWI, and the "building block approach" as used in the tables, denote series taken directly or derived from data published by the CIA or LWI, which follow a similar methodology but are not always identical. In the Comparator Tables, these are featured. In the Global Tables, the series are shown where other series are unavailable.

The main features of this methodology, adjusted factor costs, and the "building block" method of calculating growth, are described in detail in chapter 8 (see *Alternative computations*).

LWI's *Research Project On National Income* in East and Central Europe is the primary source of data in this section for Bulgaria, Czechoslovakia, the German Democratic Republic, Hungary, Poland, Romania, and Yugoslavia. The LWI project does not cover the USSR. Gross output data and other selected data for the USSR are from the CIA *Handbook of Economic Statistics*. Analytically similar data are available from the CIA for Eastern European countries other than the USSR, for GNP, GNP per capita in 1989 U.S. dollars, and alternative consumer price indexes. For these overlapping indicators, LWI data in most cases supercede CIA data, as the data from the two sources agree, with the exception of Romania in recent years. CIA and LWI data also differ in the alternative price indexes for Poland and Yugoslavia for some years.

Methodologies for specific indicators are described below.

- *GNP volume index.* Indexes shown in the Comparator Tables are from data in domestic currencies at factor cost. They are derived by aggregating the sectoral volume indexes according to their share in GNP by origin of production. The original indexes in 1975 prices were rebased in the Guide to 1980.

- *Agriculture: value added in GNP.* Derived by the authors by combining agriculture and forestry indexes from LWI.

- *Industry: value added in GNP.* Derived by combining industry and construction indexes from LWI.

- *Services: value added in GNP.* Derived by combining transportation, communications, trade, finance, government, and other sectors of origin of production from LWI. Also see notes to GNP at market prices.

- *Consumption in GNP.* Derived by combining personal consumption and government consumption from LWI, based on shares in domestic absorption.

- *Personal (household) consumption.* Refers to gross national product distributed for personal consumption in domestic final use (shown in the Country Tables as household consumption). Also see notes on domestic absorption.

- *Government consumption.* Refers to the government consumption component in GNP distributed for domestic final use. Includes administration, justice, internal security, education, culture, health, and social welfare components. Also see notes on domestic absorption and investment.

- *Investment in GNP.* Derived as the residual of domestic absorption and consumption. Consequently, it includes the statistical discrepancy normally included under consumption. May include defense expenditures.

- *Gross industrial output.* Official data are adjusted by the CIA to conform to industrial production indexes used by the Federal Reserve Board to measure the U.S. industrial output. Construction is excluded. Indexes are very close to LWI indexes for industry.

- *Gross agricultural output.* Adjusted output. See note on gross industrial output. Excludes forestry. Intermediate costs of seeds, feed, and waste are excluded. Data differ from LWI indexes for agriculture.

- *GNP per capita in constant 1989 U.S. dollars.* Data for USSR are from CIA, remaining data are from LWI.

- *Overall GNP in constant 1989 U.S. dollars.* Data for USSR are from the CIA, remaining data are from LWI. Total GNP is derived from per capita estimates by multiplying the per capita numbers by mid-year population. See also notes to GNP volume indexes.

The GNP and per capita income sections of the Comparator Tables for the USSR refer to U.S. dollar series, constructed using a bilateral comparison method for valuing output; that is, in essence, an estimation of purchasing power parity. For more details on this method, see chapter 9. For other countries of Eastern Europe, see Alton in the Bibliography.

ACDA (U.S. Arms Control and Disarmament Agency) data has been used in the comparator pages in cases where CIA and LWI series are unavailable. For HPEs outside Europe, data are ACDA estimates. For China, ACDA GNP data uses World Bank series in LCUs, converted to dollars at a benchmark PPP rate, which is based on traded goods only.

MPS accounts

The Guide presents information on the Material Product System (MPS) somewhat differently from the sources and methods provided above for the SNA. Here, sources of data and the recommendations of MPS are presented first. Country practices are detailed in, *General Notes.*

The main channels of publication for national accounts data are basically the same in countries using SNA and MPS. All countries now publish their national accounts data in statistical yearbooks, and more detailed information is sometimes provided in specialized national accounts publications. A second channel of publication is dissemination by international agencies. The United Nations Statistical Office (UNSO) is the official authority among international agencies in this area and publishes a Yearbook of National Accounts Statistics that covers most countries. It uses separate sets of questionnaires to collect information from the countries using SNA and MPS, respectively. In addition to the UN, the World Bank, the IMF, the OECD, and EUROSTAT (until 1991) also collect and publish national accounts data for a number of HPEs.

There are great differences in the amount, completeness, and timeliness of data published about HPEs in the various publications. This is the case for market economies as well, except for OECD member countries and a few other high-income economies. In general, HPEs publish a more limited set of national accounts data than do the market economies. The publication of long time-series value estimates at constant prices is especially restricted. The UNSO national accounts questionnaire sent to countries using MPS requests much more detail than the CMEA questionnaire. The replies to the CMEA questionnaire were, as a result, generally more complete than the UNSO questionnaire.

The standard concepts and methods of macroeconomic aggregates described below are generally followed by all European HPEs. However, there are also some important deviations from these rules that are discussed in the *General Notes*.

The Material Product System (MPS) was adopted by the CMEA Standing Commission for Statistical Cooperation in 1969 and revised in 1989. All forms of economic activities are classified according to the nature and results of the application of labor. The CMEA Standing Commission for Statistical Cooperation adopted a Standard Classification of Branches of the National Economy (CBNE) which is used in various statistical areas and serves also as an important guide in the construction of MPS. This was adopted by the UN as a parallel standard to SNA. The CBNE clearly distinguishes between "productive" and "non-productive" activities, with productive activity as the fundamental basis for defining output and consumption. In MPS only those activities that produce material goods or bring them from the producer to the consumer, or extend their service life, are considered productive and included in creation of national income. Other activities are considered "nonmaterial" services that do not create national income (NMP), and are more akin to transfers.

The two main spheres of activities are further detailed by branches, sub-branches, and groups of activities that are roughly similar to the ISIC categories used in SNA. Industrial activity is separated from agricultural, transportation, and trade activities. Within industrial activity, mining is distinguished from manufacturing, etc. The large activity categories basically cover the same branches in MPS and SNA. Note the following specific features of the CBNE:

- Mining and quarrying; manufacturing; and electricity, gas, and water are shown as one category under "Industry". Construction is a separate division of branches, although some of the series in the Basic Tables include it in "Industry" to facilitate comparisons between MPS and SNA series.

- Hunting and collection of forestry products are treated as a part of forestry and logging. Timber extraction is included in industry, while forestry covers plantation and maintenance of forests only.

- The distribution of gas, electricity, and water to households is treated as a nonmaterial service that is included in housing. This activity is therefore not reflected in NMP.

- Cleaning, dyeing, and repair services are included with industrial activity (manufacturing).

- Other branches of material activities include news gathering and editorial agencies, industrial services other than architectural design services, printing and publishing services, the production of motion pictures, phonograph records and prerecorded tapes, data processing and tabulating services, waterway-maintenance services and the operation of flood-control systems, and services related to the conservation of natural resources and the protection of the environment.

- Restaurants and cafes are included in trade as contributors to NMP.

The unit of classification is not the organizational unit, or enterprise, but a smaller unit that performs one type of activity (i.e., establishment). If an enterprise or institution or other organizational unit carries on more than one type of economic activity, it is considered to consist of two or more establishments that perform different activities.

NMP produced is equal to global product (i.e., gross output) of goods and material services less intermediate material consumption, including consumption of fixed assets (depreciation). At the enterprise or sector level the net value added is called the "net production" of the given producing unit. The term "net value added" is also used, although this risks confusion with the similar SNA terms, which differs mainly by including nonmaterial services (in both gross output and deductions of intermediate inputs) and by not deducting depreciation as an intermediate input.

In more detail, Global Social Product is used for indicating the total production of all material branches; included are only goods and material services sold or provided free to employees. The production of a given enterprise or branch is called "Gross output" of the given producing unit or sector. Gross output of material goods and services is valued at both producers' and purchasers' values. The difference between the two sets of values gives the distributive trade margins and the transportation margins. The gross output of the distributive-trade units is equal to the value of their gross margins on internal and external trade. Internal trade also includes restaurants, cafes and other catering, net of food and drinks purchased by these units. Gross margins on external trade are equivalent to the sum in domestic currency of (a) the value of imports of goods and material services in the domestic market less the actual value at which these imports are purchased from abroad and (b) the actual value at which exports of goods and material services are sold to abroad less the value of these exports, in the domestic market.

NMP can also be defined as the sum of goods and material services used for final purposes; this is termed "NMP used." In this "expenditure" approach net material product is the sum of the final uses of goods and material services, that is, personal consumption, and material consumption of units in the nonmaterial sphere serving individuals, and that of similar units serving the community as a whole (government and nonprofit organizations), net capital formation (i.e., net of depreciation), replacement for losses, and the balance between exports and imports of goods and material services.

The accounting identity for amounts produced and used or purchased holds true in both MPS and SNA. However, MPS accounts are traditionally reported with NMP produced differing from NMP used by the value of the resource balance, with considerable scope for national differences in the valuation of this resource balance.

Resource balance, or net exports of goods and material services, are defined to include:

* Outward-bound goods that cross the border of the country, including re-exports, or imported goods exported without being processed
* Goods purchased outside the country by a foreign trade organization of the country in question and shipped directly to a third country
* Outward-bound monetary and non-monetary gold and other precious metals
* Unilateral transfers of goods by the government and public organizations, balanced by unrequited transfers, often called foreign aid

* Material services, such as transport; forwarding and communications services; rental, including rental payments for time-charters of ships and other transport equipment; and export contract services rendered to other countries

Imports cover the same categories of goods and material services when they are inward bound. Exports are valued free-on-board (f.o.b.); imports include cost, insurance, and freight (c.i.f.). This is broadly in line with reports from market economies, although the values may be those reported by FTOs or domestic enterprises rather than the customs service, depending on national methodology.

Personal consumption consists of all consumer goods, irrespective of durability, and material services (repair, transport, communication, and similar services) purchased by households, received in kind as payment for work in state and collective enterprises and in private plots, or produced on own account on personal plots. Household purchases of dwellings are regarded as capital formation, as in SNA, but since rent is rarely based on market prices, the housing component of personal consumption is generally approximated by including the maintenance and depreciation of dwellings, implying a significant undervaluation of housing. Also included are reimbursable expenditures for material goods and services purchased during business trips. In MPS as in SNA, the domestic concept of consumption is used, so that direct purchases by foreign tourists, diplomatic personnel, and other non-residents in the domestic market are included, while similar purchases abroad by residents are excluded.

Material consumption in the nonmaterial sphere serving individuals (not shown in tables) covers expenditures on non-durable goods and material services by these units, reduced by the increases in their stocks of goods. This includes the materials used in health, education, social, welfare and personal services serving individuals, and consumption of fixed assets used by these units (depreciation).

Consumption of the population (not shown) is the sum of personal consumption and material consumption in the units of the nonmaterial sphere serving individuals. Material consumption of the nonmaterial sphere serving the community as a whole consists of non-durable goods and material services purchased during a period of account by units, reduced by the increases in their stocks of goods during the period of account. It includes consumption of fixed assets by these units. This item shows the material inputs of general administration, defense (to the extent it is reported to statistical offices), financial services, research institutions, and the like.

Final consumption is the sum of personal consumption and material consumption in the units of the nonmaterial sphere serving individuals and of those serving the community as a whole (shown in the tables as collective consumption).

Net fixed capital formation consists of the value of new fixed assets purchased or built and completed capital repairs to these assets, less the consumption of fixed assets for renewal of assets and capital repairs, capital losses due to fire, floods, and other calamities, and the remaining value of scrapped fixed assets. Thus, it measures the net increase in the value of fixed assets during a period of account. Fixed assets include

- Completed dwellings, buildings, and other structures
- Machinery, equipment, and other durable goods acquired by units of the material and nonmaterial sphere
- Cattle, excluding young cattle and cattle raised for meat
- Perennial plants
- Expenditures to improve land, forests and other natural resources.

New fixed assets put into use are generally valued inclusive of acquisition and installation cost. Capital repairs cover outlays on repairs, which make up at least in part for the physical depreciation of fixed assets and/or significantly raise the capacity and productivity of fixed assets. As mentioned above, capital repair was included in fixed capital formation in the USSR only; in other HPEs these outlays were treated as current inputs, i.e., intermediate consumption.

Gross fixed capital formation is equal to net fixed capital formation plus depreciation.

An increase in material circulating assets and stocks consists of increases during the period of account in the stocks of enterprises. Also covered (at least in principle) are increases in government stockpiles, including stocks of defense items and state reserves of precious metals and precious stones. The stocks in the material sphere consist of raw materials, fuels, supplies, and other non-durable goods; young cattle and cattle raised for meat; work in progress; including uncompleted construction projects, and finished goods not yet sold.

Depreciation, or consumption of fixed assets, includes an allowance for normal wear and tear and foreseen obsolescence of fixed assets based on standard ranges of depreciation and the difference between the book and scrap values of scrapped fixed assets. Allowances for depreciation are often based on the original cost of the assets, which may be periodically adjusted to replacement cost.

Exchange rates and conversion factors

The presentation below distinguishes between exchange rates and conversion factors. Exchange rates are shown in the Basic Tables, conversion factors are shown in the Comparator Tables, with two exceptions described below.

Some HPEs have, or have had, several types of exchange rates or "coefficients" that have certain similarities with exchange rates. Since the early 1960s, most HPEs have introduced reforms that changed the prevailing "accounting" exchange rate, establishing one or more new kinds of exchange rates or coefficients, or assigned new roles to them in the economy. In most cases, coefficients take into account the impact of price equalization funds, foreign trade differentials, etc. Hence, they embody elements of fiscal and monetary policy instruments as distinguished in market economies. In recent years, some countries have unified their exchange rates, for example, Poland in 1990.

Exchange rates and exchange rate type coefficients can be grouped into the "commercial rate", the "devisa or official rate", the "informal rate", and the "transferable ruble/$ cross rate." GNP conversion factors shown in the Comparator Tables, directly or implicitly weight each of these four rates in the overall conversion factor.

Exchange rates

The Atlas annual rate in the Basic Tables is conceptually the same as the single year converter in the Comparator Tables. The difference is the World Bank's use of this rate as an annual exchange rate that is generally appropriate for converting trade flows for the specified period, but not as a conversion factor for GNP per capita, where the Atlas Methodology is used.

Dollar exchange rates

The *Atlas annual rate*, as a rule, is the official exchange rate reported in the IMF's *International Financial Statistics*, line rf. Exceptions arise where IFS-style measures are recast to report on a fiscal year basis or to average multiple exchange rates. Where multiple exchange rate practices are officially maintained and the spread between the rates is analytically significant, a transactions-weighted average is given, if possible. However, no account of unofficial parallel market rates is taken in the calculations. When the official exchange rate, including any multiple rates, is judged to overvalue the domestic currency by an exceptionally large margin from the rate effectively applied to international transactions, a substitute conversion factor is used by the World Bank (essentially using a simplified PPP). There are a few such cases in any given year and none in the case of HPEs (largely because the relationship among domestic prices, the price of foreign currency, and wages is still too imperfectly understood).

DEVISA AND OFFICIAL RATES ARE CONCEPTUALLY SIMILAR. The "devisa" prefix, used mainly in HPEs in Europe, indicates that the currency is an official but artificial unit of account. Transactions in a foreign currency (or unit of account) are converted at the "devisa" rate into what appears to be the local currency, but is not the same because domestic prices are set and maintained independently of export and import prices. Various kinds of exchange rates are designated as "official" in HPE publications. In some cases, the "devisa" (or "official") prefix is implied for local currency series but is not explicitly stated. Conversion of these series to other currencies requires verification of the original conversion rate.

COMMERCIAL EXCHANGE RATES vis-à-vis the dollar link foreign and domestic prices for some or all convertible-currency transactions. In the tabulation that follows, commercial rates are defined as coefficients that link foreign and domestic prices in the enterprise sector.

Exchange rate labeling in the official publications of some HPEs can be misleading. In some cases a country publishes a "commercial" exchange rate that may be a commercial rate only in a pro

forma sense; that is, it functions in the economy like the so-called devisa or official rate, described above. Such conversion factors are reported here as devisa or official rates rather than commercial rates.

Conversely, countries in some cases have introduced de facto commercial exchange rates retroactively. The commercial rate may be shown simply as an "adjustment coefficient" applied to the devisa or official rate, in which case it can be readily computed. In such cases, an alternative commercial rate was derived by the authors to convert GNP to dollars, as documented below.

NONCOMMERCIAL (TOURIST) EXCHANGE RATES. These rates were established by each country either as explicit rates for tourists or as premia or discounts from the official rates. In some cases the buying and selling rates differed by very large margins. The basis for establishing the tourist exchange rates was the purchasing powers of a tourist basket, from which deviations in either direction reflected such factors as the desire of the authorities to encourage or discourage the inflow/outflow of tourists to/from the country.

INFORMAL RATES (BLACK OR GRAY MARKET RATES) emerged as the official tourist exchange rates became out of line with the supply and demand for foreign currencies for tourists. In some cases, these rates deviated from the official rates by several hundred percent. For example, as the black market rate of the zloty against the dollar depreciated sharply in Poland, before the introduction of a convertible zloty in 1990, the demand increased, say, for Hungarian forints by residents of Poland who could obtain dollars cheaper via the Hungarian currency than directly in Poland. For this reason, during 1988-89, Hungary experienced a huge inflow of "tourists" from Poland who were selling goods for forints, in order to take back dollars to Poland, eventually prompting restrictions by the authorities in both countries.

ICP RATES, strictly speaking, is neither an exchange rate nor a conversion factor. Rather, it is the explicit rate at which income in national currency is expressed in equivalent purchasing power. ICP rates are available for benchmark years only and the rate shown in the Basic Tables are from Penn World Tables (see below).

TRANSFERABLE RUBLE/$ CROSS-RATES are useful for reconverting HPE merchandise trade and balance of payments data from national currency into dollars or other *convertible currencies*. Official sources generally used the devisa (or official) rate or the commercial rate. However, the dollar value of international transactions denominated in *transferable rubles* cannot be established with any degree of confidence (see chapter 3).

For the Guide, a composite or *uniform* TR/$ rate was derived as the simple average of the CMEA TR/$ cross rates for 1970–90, as shown in table 11.1. This approach does not address the many conceptual issues in estimating such a rate, but provides plausible results, especially for the 1980s, when countries trading with the West adjusted their exchange rates to reflect changing terms of trade.

For the USSR, the rate introduced in November 1990 is used because it corresponds most closely with the cross rates of the other countries. Since each country's structure of trade influences its rate, in addition to its policy on exchange rates, it can be argued that a simple average is better than a weighted one, which would tilt too much in favor of countries with larger volumes of trade. Moreover, this approach would give greater weights to countries trading most with the West. The simple average discounts the trade weight of the USSR.

Ruble exchange rates

The various types of **Ruble exchange rates** report local currency units vis-à-vis the transferable ruble or the Soviet domestic ruble, more or less paralleling those listed against the dollar. However, some important differences should be noted.

The devisa rates, the commercial rates, and the auction rates are against the TR; the noncommercial rates and the parallel market rates are vis-à-vis the domestic ruble of the USSR. In 1990, some countries also introduced commercial rates vis-à-vis the *domestic* currencies of some of the CMEA countries.

OFFICIAL DEVISA RATES VIS-À-VIS THE TR were established during the traditional phase of the CMEA. These rates had only bookkeeping significance since foreign and domestic prices were completely isolated; the instrument of separation was the system of automatic "price equalization", discussed in the Primer.

THE COMMERCIAL RATE per ruble was initially calculated the same way and was intended to play the same role as the dollar commercial exchange rate. But it was soon realized that the structure of world market prices differed so substantially from the structure of intra-CMEA prices, especially after the 1973 oil price shock, that it was not possible to link domestic prices to prices on both markets simultaneously. Therefore, a decision had to be made as to which set of prices should be relevant for domestic price formation. In countries where a linkage was made, Western world market prices were selected. This meant that the introduction of a commercial exchange rate vis-à-vis the TR did not change the situation much, compared with the period when only a devisa rate existed, so that a comprehensive system of automatic price equalization had to be maintained in ruble trade.

NONCOMMERCIAL (TOURIST) EXCHANGE RATES. These rates were established among CMEA countries in February 8, 1963, and updated in July 28, 1971. They were determined on the basis of the hypothetical annual consumption of a four-member diplomatic family. In 1974 another basket, for short-term tourists, was added (comprised of forty-five food, twenty-five industrial consumer, and twenty-one service items). The exchange rate became an average of the PPPs of the two baskets.

Table 11.1 Uniform TR/$ rates[a]

	1980	1985	1986	1987	1988	1989	1990
Bulgaria	0.990	1.190	1.350	1.240	1.590	1.730	2.300
Czechoslovakia	0.960	1.530	1.340	1.220	1.380	1.510	1.840
German Dem. Rep.	1.740	1.740	1.740	1.740	1.740	..	..
Hungary	1.170	1.880	1.640	1.730	1.940	2.090	..
Poland	1.110	1.760	1.900	2.280	2.210	2.960	..
Romania	1.000	1.110	1.040	0.940	0.920	0.960	..
USSR	0.650	0.820	0.700	0.630	0.610	0.630	1.800
Average	0.980	1.433	1.388	1.397	1.484	1.660	1.980

a. Average of national commercial TR/$ cross rates (unweighted). Calculated by the authors.

In the HPEs, tourist transactions were planned as part of intergovernmental trade agreements, and the authorities provided each other domestic currencies for sale in their own countries to departing tourists. A country that agreed to be a net exporter of tourist services provided its partner a net supply of its currency, with an understanding about the kinds of goods that the deficit country would agree to ship as payment for importing tourist services. In addition to tourist transactions, the noncommercial rate was used to settle royalties, costs incurred in connection with fairs and exhibits in other CMEA countries, the media, and cross-country telecommunications.

The deposits/credits to banking accounts arising from tourist transactions were converted into TRs on the basis of agreed coefficients (e.g., the number of Bulgarian leva per TR) and cleared through the IBEC.

Although it remained in effect until 1990, the system described in the preceding three paragraphs began to break down several years earlier as the number of tourists increased greatly and member countries pursued increasingly divergent economic and tourist policies.

Conversion factors

Conversion factors are either implicit or explicit: the main ones examined here are World Bank Atlas, single year conversion; authors' series; and Penn World Tables.

The World Bank Atlas method. This was described earlier in this chapter under SNA Accounts (World Bank).

The single year conversion factor. This is also described above under Atlas annual rate.

Table 11.2 Proxy commercial exchange rates

Country	1970	1980	1988
Bulgaria (leva/$)	..	0.99	1.67
Czechoslovakia (koruna/$)	16.20	14.26	4.36
German Dem. Rep. (mark/$)	4.20	3.30	3.01
Hungary (forint/$)	60.00	32.43	50.41
Poland (zloty/$)	60.00	48.58	430.55
Romania (leu/$)	24.00	18.00	14.28
Yugoslavia (dinar/$)	12.50	24.64	2,523.00
USSR (ruble/$)	1.19	0.84	0.81

The authors' series. This was calculated for the eight Central and East European countries (benchmarks shown below in table 11.2), estimated as commercial exchange rates. These estimates were based on the coefficient: *local currency cost of exports at producer prices*/export revenues ($). The results were reasonably consistent with the Atlas' annual rate for any single year.

These conversion rates were used for current value GDP figures in national currency units and then divided by the population to arrive at authors' series GNP in U.S. dollars.

Penn World Tables. PPPs are an implicit series calculated from ICP benchmark series moved by national volume indexes (with some adjustment) and an inferred set of price indexes (excluding exchange rates) from UN cost of living adjustment data, and other price data commercially available. The series was derived as the price level times the exchange rate reported by Summers and Heston in the *Quarterly Journal of Economics*, May 1991.

Consumer price indexes

The consumer price index (CPI) based on IFS data (line 64) reflects prices of goods and services used for private consumption of households. The GDP deflator in the Global Tables is an implicit deflator, derived as the ratio of current and constant price GDP series.

Consumer price indexes reported by the CIA are indicated as such in the Basic Tables, and as "outside estimates" in the Comparator Tables. The CIA and LWI also report "Official price indexes" in 1970 prices, rebased in the Guide to 1980; these may appear in "official" lines, with their source clearly indicated.

The alternative consumer price index is derived by dividing an index of official personal consumption in current prices by an index of independently calculated, personal consumption in 1976 constant prices. Original data in 1970 prices are rescaled in the Guide to 1980.

International trade

The Guide's primary source for international trade data is IFS, which provides a consistent series for worldwide comparisons, and the Economic Commision for Europe's DMAP database, which is electronically accessible to the World Bank, but conceptually the same as reported in ECE publications (see bibliography).

ECE data for CMEA countries are similar to UN global sources described below except that ECE makes a special effort to fill gaps for the European HPEs from mirror (partner trade) statistics and from other sources, and it reports the original data sources for the comparative presentation of these countries' international trade data.

The ECE trade data in national currency include, by country, series in local currencies for total exports and imports as well as their composition by developed, developing, and socialist (mainly CMEA) groups of countries. These trade flows are from national statistical sources, expressed in national currencies, converted by national authorities from convertible currency (dollar) and ruble values

For ECE trade data in dollars, shown in the Comparator Tables, a separate total is shown for trade with CMEA countries. Separate series on intra-CMEA trade facilitate comparison across sources. As discussed above, the ECE's dollar values of ruble-denominated intra-CMEA trade are obtained by converting from national currency to rubles at the national rate, and to dollars at the Hungary's ruble/dollar cross rate. The authors provide an alternative dollar estimate of intra-CMEA trade, using a similar approach as ECE's, except for the choice of a different uniform ruble/dollar cross-rate series.

The alternative estimates of dollar trade shown in the Comparator Tables vary widely, due to differing methodologies. The decision to use a uniform ruble/dollar cross-rate converter sets ECE and the authors apart from other sources, including national statistical offices. This decision reflects an attempt to deal with broken ruble/dollar cross rates used in the region (see the Primer), which result in asymmetric measures of intra-CMEA trade in other published series. Although a uniform ruble/dollar converter may be inappropriate for converting ruble trade to dollars for a given country, it is considered by ECE and the authors as a workable solution because it standardizes the dollar values of transactions in the ruble zone, and in both cases converts these to dollars at the more realistic commercial rather than official rates.

Authors series trade data in dollars, like ECE trade data in dollars, is first converted from national currency to dollars and rubles, respectively, at national rates. Next, the authors' intra-CMEA trade is converted to dollars at a uniform (composite) TR/$ cross rate, calculated as an average of CMEA countries' own commercial ruble/dollar cross rates, as describe

previously under *Conversion factors*. A composite cross rate is chosen by the authors in preference to a single country's cross rate on the logic that the trend will be smoother, and corresponds to ruble-dollar movements as perceived by all the CMEA countries as they began to trade increasingly with the non-socialist world.

Other UN sources of trade data in dollars. In addition to the ECE, there are several other UN publications. In general, they all take the same approach or rely on a common source, although there are relatively minor country- or year-specific differences among them, depending on their vintage and whether and how gaps are filled. A basic source for these series is UNCTAD's *Handbook of International Trade and Development Statistics*, which reports export and import dollar totals for the HPEs; attempts to fill gaps in the data obtained from original publications; and presents data, whenever possible, in an analytical way, through the use of rank orderings, growth rates, shares, and so on, to facilitate their interpretation.

In these other publications, intra-CMEA trade is converted from local currencies to dollars at the prevailing commercial *or* devisa exchange rates, as believed to be appropriate, unless otherwise noted in the documentation by country. This causes fundamental problems of comparability owing to broken cross rates, as discussed above. Their East-West trade data basically originates from national sources, as compiled by the ECE for the European HPEs, with a number of series for the other countries representing UNCTAD secretariat estimates and judgments of the best source of data for a particular country. Detailed methods and sources for gap-filling are not published. Regional totals for some countries have been adjusted where necessary to approximate imports c.i.f. and exports f.o.b. The Eastern European countries covered are Albania, Bulgaria, Czechoslovakia, the German Democratic Republic, Hungary, Poland, Romania and the USSR. Asian socialist countries covered are China, Korea People's Democratic Republic, Mongolia, and Viet Nam.

To fill gaps in the UN series, the Guide uses data found in various issues of the UN *Monthly Bulletin of Statistics*. Its definitions are broadly the same as those of the Guide except it includes trade between the Federal Republic of Germany and German Democratic Republic before unification. In all other respects, both publications try to adhere to the international statistical terms and definitions in current use, as found in UN *International Trade Statistics*.

UNCTAD

UNCTAD's export data consist of the following outward moving goods: (a) national goods, i.e., those wholly or partly produced in the country; (b) foreign goods, neither transformed nor declared for domestic consumption in the country, and (c) nationalized goods, i.e., foreign goods declared from domestic consumption that move outward without having been transformed. These general exports comprise all three categories; in the general trade system, the sum of (b) and (c) may be tabulated as re-exports. Special exports comprise categories (a) and (c). Direct transit trade, consisting of goods entering or leaving for transport purposes only, is excluded from both import and export statistics.

UNCTAD's import data accord with the general trade system and cover both goods entering directly for domestic consumption and goods recorded into customs storage, at the time of their first arrival, as imports. Under the special trade system, goods are recorded as imports when declared for domestic consumption whether at time of entry or on withdrawal from customs storage. For more complete information on these definitions, see *International Trade Statistics: Concepts and Definitions* (UNCTAD Statistical Papers, Series M, No. 52). The UN *Monthly Bulletin of Statistics* is used as an alternative source.

IMF international financial statistics

Merchandise exports f.o.b. and imports c.i.f. are, in general, customs statistics reported under the general trade system, according to the recommendations of *UN International Trade Statistics: Concepts and Definitions*, 1982. For some countries data relate to the special trade system. The difference between general and special trade lies mainly in the treatment of recording the movement of goods through customs-bonded storage areas, such as warehouses. Where customs data are used as the primary source, the data should be the same as merchandise trade shown in the balance of payments, allowing for differences of classification in respect of international shipment services, timing adjustments for change of ownership, and some coverage adjustments. However, in practice, many of the adjustments to the balance of payments data for merchandise trade are carried out on an annual basis and cannot be applied regularly to monthly or quarterly data. For this reason, the data shown may differ from those reported in the balance of payments. The data for merchandise imports f.o.b. are derived by applying c.i.f. over f.o.b. factors that are principally taken from balance of payments statistics.

U.S. Arms Control and Disarmament Agency data

Although the publication of the Arms Control and Disarmament Agency (ACDA) itself does not elaborate on the details of how dollar export and import totals are obtained for the HPEs, the series are practically identical to those in the CIA's *Handbook of Economic Statistics*, which does document its methodology. Intra-HPE trade is derived by converting local currency volumes to TR and then to dollars at the prevailing TR/official exchange rate. This overstates substantially the dollar value of such trade and, therefore total trade.

CIA Handbook of Economic Statistics

The handbook relies upon official Soviet statistics, using U.S. dollar exchange rates for the Soviet foreign exchange ruble as announced by the State Bank of the USSR. Exports and imports are listed as f.o.b.

For HPEs in Eastern Europe, the CIA handbook also relies on official statistics. Trade with HPEs was derived by converting the value of the trade expressed in the currency of each Eastern European country in rubles and then to dollars at the prevailing foreign exchange rate. Exports are on an f.o.b. basis, as are imports, except for Hungary, which is on c.i.f. basis. The trade data includes trade with HPEs other than the USSR and Eastern Europe.

For Cuba, exports are on f.o.b. basis; imports, c.i.f. Cuban trade with non-HPEs is based on hard currency world prices while its HPE trade uses soft currency negotiated prices that were frequently subsidized in Cuba's favor (notably by the USSR) and do not reflect real market values. The result is a more favorable global trade balance than if Cuba conducted all of its trade at world market prices.

Trade unit values and terms of trade

Trade unit values and terms of trade are shown in detail for the authors' series and, in summary, for ECE data. Some gap-filling draws from the IFS. These indexes may not be fully comparable, and special attention should be paid to the Country Footnotes. Of particular interest are how trade prices are initially derived and in what currency; and how the totals combine trade valued in national currency, dollars, and TRs.

Authors' implicit unit values

The authors derived an implicit unit value series from nationally reported trade in current prices, converted these to dollars (see authors' series trade data in dollars), and divided this by the same series deflated by nationally reported volume indexes, as available from the ECE. The resulting indexes are trade prices in dollars that eliminate the effects on prices in national currency terms of HPE exchange rate depreciations. The general, declining price of ruble trade results in part from the ruble's depreciation against the dollar in recent years. Statistical discrepancies from rescaling were eliminated by reconstructing the aggregate unit value indexes from the annual weighted average of trade in current dollars. The volume indexes used by the authors are nationally reported and may have been explicit originally or implicit. If they are implicit, national assumptions about ruble prices may be asymmetric with the authors' assumptions about them in converting the indexes to dollar terms.

Because index number problems arise in the derivation of price indexes from volume indexes and current price series, the price indexes for highly-aggregated socialist and non-socialist country groups have been calculated as a weighted average of their disaggregated component groups, when available, rather than directly from the aggregate volume index and value series. For example, the "world" index would be an average of the "socialist" and "non-socialist" indexes in each year, if the latter were available. The weights used are the current price dollar value of exports or imports in each year. This method has the effect of placing the discrepancy arising from the index number problem in the index of the more highly aggregated group.

ECE implicit unit values

The ECE series is also adjusted to dollar terms, and ruble trade is converted to U.S. dollars by a single cross-rate series (Hungary's). An advantage of the ECE series over the authors' series may be that the implicit ECE volume indexes are their own, derived from constant price series (from its CPE3 file) based on ECE's assumptions about trade prices (mainly Hungary's) and on the dollar value of the transferable ruble trade (for details see *Economic Bulletin for Europe*, 37, 4, 1985). A disadvantage may be that Hungary's ruble/dollar cross-rate series fluctuates more and depreciates faster than the authors' series, exaggerating the speed with which the ruble

depreciated in the eyes of the CMEA community that used it.

Balance of payments (BoP) and external debt

Balance of payments

The ECE's Common Data Base is the source for the USSR and some Central and East European countries. ECE trade balances for the German Democratic Republic and the USSR reflect trade with all developed and developing market economies (non-socialist countries *plus* Yugoslavia), based on national foreign trade statistics. National statistics are the source for Bulgaria, Czechoslovakia, Hungary (whose data for 1982–90 is revised; see IMF BoP statistics for 1971-81), Poland, and Romania.

External debt

Data on external debt are obtained from several sources, according to availability for each country. Where more than one source provided data, the list below shows the order of preference given:

- World Bank Debtor Reporting System (DRS): China, Hungary, Lao PDR, Nicaragua, Poland, Romania, Yugoslavia, Bulgaria, Czechoslovakia;
- OECD Creditor Reporting System (CRS): Cuba, Cambodia, People's Democractic Republic of Korea, Viet Nam;
- IMF: Mongolia;
- IMF, IBRD, OECD, EBRD: USSR;
- ECE: German Democratic Republic.

No data were available for Albania. Data for all other low- and middle-income countries are from the World Bank's DRS. Some sources cited obtain data from the BIS, though BIS is not used directly as a source for debt data in the Guide. Brief descriptions are given below for the different sources:

The **World Bank DRS** is a debtor-reporting system supplemented by World Bank estimates, except for multilateral loans, which are provided by the multilateral organizations. These data are accessible in a fixed form from the *World Debt Tables*, produced by the World Bank's International Economics Department, Debt and International Finance Division. All creditors are covered for the reporting debtor countries. The DRS is concerned only with economies that borrow from the World Bank Group (IBRD or IDA). Figures on debt refer to amounts disbursed and outstanding, expressed in U.S. dollars converted at official exchange rates.

Total repayments are also reported as separate items of the balance of payments.

OECD's CRS is a creditor reporting system of OECD members supplemented by data from other sources, notably the DRS (non-member creditors, multilateral creditors, and data on bonds) and BIS (non-member country banks). There is some double counting of trade credits by combining the different systems although efforts are made to mitigate this. BIS is a reporting system covering commercial banks in major financial centers only. In any country, some banks are members and others are not. World Bank country reports and IMF occasional papers use national sources where available, supplemented by staff estimates and calculations.

ECE: The data include indebtedness to countries reporting to BIS and OECD. **IMF/balance of payments data** are based on national currency valuations, converted to dollars at official exchange rates. Total external debt has been calculated from BoP stock figures as the sum of all external liabilities reported in the capital account, but excluding foreign direct investment and portfolio investment in corporate equities (BoP lines 54, 55, 56, 57, 58, 65–68, 80–83, 86-88, 90–92, 96, 97, and 110).

Significant differences exist in definitions and coverage among these sources. The differences include such factors as exchange rate assumptions, treatment of arrears and debt reorganization, as well as differences in creditors or debtors included. Therefore, comparisons among countries should be made with caution. Differences between the OECD, BIS, IMF, and World Bank published data are explained at length in *External Debt: Definition, Statistical Coverage and Methodology*, OECD 1988 and OECD's *Financing and External Debt of Developing Countries—1989 Survey*, Chapter VI, Technical Notes. Of particular note are large differences in debt service data for Mongolia between OECD and IMF.

CMEA debt

Since the stock of debt and the debt service of the CMEA countries can be denominated in convertible currencies as well as nonconvertible currencies, CMEA countries' debt is not the residual of its total and convertible debt except where its CMEA debt is denominated wholly in non-convertible currencies. Likewise, convertible debt and debt service cannot be derived from total and CMEA debt and debt service data.

Reserves

The data on reserves and gold holdings are from IFS where possible (China, Czechoslovakia, Hungary, Lao PDR, Nicaragua, Poland, Romania, Viet Nam, and Yugoslavia). Total reserves are the sum of the U.S. dollar value of monetary authorities' holdings of SDRs, the reserve position in the IMF, foreign exchange, and gold reserves. Foreign exchange includes monetary authority claims on nonresidents in the form of bank deposits, treasury bills, short- and long-term government securities, and other claims usable in the event of balance of payments need, including nonmarketable claims arising from intercentral bank and intergovernmental arrangements, without regard as to whether the claims are denominated in the currency of the debtors or the creditors. IFS reports the national valuation of gold reserves for most countries. Market valuation of gold reserves is obtained by multiplying the endyear London gold price in the IFS by the number of troy ounces of gold reserves for each country, as reported on its IFS country page.

Bulgarian reserve data came from the Bulgarian foreign trade bank, as quoted in a World Bank country report. Reserve data for the Soviet Union came from an IMF, IBRD, OECD, and EBRD joint study of the Soviet economy which quotes the Ministry of Finance, Vneshekonombank, BIS, and other estimates. Data for Mongolia are from an IMF occasional paper that quotes the Mongolian State Bank as source. No reliable data were available for Albania, Cuba, German Democratic Republic, Cambodia, and Korea People's Democratic Republic

Employment

The primary source of employment data is the International Labour Organisation. Some demographic and labor force indicators are based on census or household surveys, which occur infrequently. Thus some reported figures are interpolated or extrapolated estimates.

Total labor force defines the "economically active" population. It includes the armed forces and the unemployed, but excludes homemakers and other unpaid caregivers. **Labor in agriculture** covers farming, forestry, hunting, and fishing. **Labor in industry** comprises the mining; manufacturing; construction; and electricity, water, and gas sectors. **Labor in services** includes all other sectors. Differences in employment and labor force approximate unemployment but this implicit relationship may not be a reliable indicator because of statistical discrepancies and differences in vintage of the data.

Domestic finance

Data on monetary aggregates come primarily from the IFS.

For most countries, the **money supply broadly defined** comprises money (IFS line 34) and quasi-money (IFS line 35), the normal forms of financial liquidity that economic transactors hold in the monetary system. By definition, holdings of non-residents and the central government are excluded.

In some countries, other (nonmonetary) financial institutions also incur quasi-monetary liabilities, that is, they issue financial instruments on terms similar to those for quasi-money. Where these are significant, money supply broadly defined is a measure of liquid liabilities comprising the monetary and quasi-monetary liabilities of both monetary and nonmonetary financial institutions. For details of concepts and definitions see IMF, *A Guide to Money and Banking Statistics in IFS*.

The primary source for government finance series is the IMF's *Government Finance Statistics Yearbook* (GFSY). GFSY data are reported by countries using the system of common definitions and classifications found in the IMF *Manual on Government Finance Statistics (1986)*.

The inadequate statistical coverage of state, provincial, and local governments has dictated the use of central government data only. This may seriously understate or distort the role of government, especially in large countries where lower levels of government are important.

Expenditures on defense are provided by **GFS** in national currency units. They are comprised of:

- Military and civil defense administration and operation;
- Foreign military aid;
- Defense-related applied research and experiment development; and
- Defense affairs not elsewhere classified.

Military expenditures in U.S. dollars are from ACDA. Data on Soviet military expenditures are based on CIA estimates of what it would cost in the United States in dollars to develop, procure, staff, and operate a military force similar to that of the Soviet Union. The CIA dollar estimates as shown in this source have been updated and augmented by estimated retirement pay at U.S. rates to improve comparability with expenditures with NATO countries, which include retirement pay.

Estimates of this type—that is, those based entirely on one country's price pattern—generally overstate the relative size of the second country's expenditures in intercountry comparisons. Also, such estimates are not consistent with the methods used here for converting other countries' expenditures into dollars. Nevertheless, the basic CIA estimates are the best available for present purposes.

For "Warsaw Pact" countries other than the Soviet Union, the estimates of military expenditures are from Thad Alton et al. The military expenditures shown here refer only to officially announced state budget expenditures on national defense. These figures understate total military expenditures in view of defense outlays by non-defense agencies of the central government, local governments, and economic enterprises. Subsidization of military procurement may also cause understatement. The dollar estimates were derived by calculating pay and allowances at the current U.S. average rates for officers and lower ranks. After subtraction of pay and allowances, the remainder of the official defense budgets in national currencies was converted into dollars at overall rates based on comparisons of the country GNPs expressed in dollars and national currencies. The rates are based in part on the purchasing power parities estimated by the UN International Comparison Project including the latest Phase V versions. These conversion rates are not as specific as might be desired. Another omission in the Warsaw Pact data is that the nonpersonnel component of military assistance is not covered.

Data used for China are based on U.S. Government estimates of the yuan costs of Chinese forces, weapons, programs, and activities. Costs in yuan are converted to dollars using the estimated conversion rate used for GNP. Due to exceptional difficulties in both estimating yuan costs and converting them to dollars, comparisons of Chinese military spending with other data should be treated as having a wide margin of error.

Land and forests

The data in this section of the Basic Tables are primarily from the Food and Agriculture Organization (FAO). Other data, mainly environmental indicators, are shown in the topical tables and are explained in that section.

Population density: agricultural. Land measures population per square kilometer of agricultural land. **Deforestation rate (net)** is the annual rate of change of forests and woodland area. A positive sign indicates an increase in the forested area. **Total land area** is the surface in square kilometers of land and inland bodies of water.

Social indicators

The primary sources of social indicators are the data files and publications of specialized international agencies, such as FAO (food and natural resource data), International Labour Organisation (labor force data), United Nations Educational, Scientific, and Cultural Organization (education data), the UN Statistical Office (population and food data), and the World Health Organization (medical care data). Supplementary sources are the Population Council, UN Research Institute for Social Development, and World Bank staff estimates.

Population density measures population per square kilometer of land area. The series on **primary school enrollment** are estimates of children of all ages enrolled in primary school. Figures are expressed as the ratio of pupils to the population of children in the country's school age group. While many countries consider primary school age to be six to eleven years, others do not. For some countries with universal primary education, the gross enrollment ratios may exceed 100 percent because some pupils are younger or older than the country's standard primary school age.

The data on **secondary school enrollment** are calculated in the same manner, and the definition of secondary school age also differs among countries. It is most commonly considered to be twelve to seventeen years.

The **tertiary enrollment** ratio is calculated by dividing the number of students enrolled in all post-secondary schools and universities by the population in the twenty to twenty-four year age group. Pupils attending vocational schools, adult education programs, two-year colleges, and distance education centers are included.

The index of **food production per capita** shows the average annual quantity of food produced per capita. For this index, food is defined as nuts, fruits, pulses, cereals, vegetables, starchy roots, sugar beet, sugar cane, edible oils, livestock, and livestock products. Quantities of food are measured net of animal feed, seeds for use in agriculture, and food lost in processing and distribution.

Energy consumption per capita refers to apparent consumption of commercial forms of primary energy—petroleum and natural gas liquids, natural gas, solid fuels (coal, lignite, etc.), and primary electricity (nuclear, geothermal, and hydroelectric power), all converted into oil equivalents. For converting primary electricity into oil equivalents, a notional thermal efficiency of 34 percent has been assumed. The use of firewood and other traditional fuels is not taken into account, as reliable data are not available.

Daily calorie supply per capita is the energy equivalent of net food supplies in a country, per capita, per day. Available supplies comprise domestic production, imports less exports, and changes in stock. Net supplies exclude animal feed, seeds for use in agriculture, and food lost in processing. The **daily protein supply per capita** is calculated from the net supply of food available. Requirements for all countries, established by the United States Department of Agriculture, provide for minimum allowances of 60 grams of total protein per day of which 20 grams of animal or pulse protein.

Population per hospital bed/nurse/physician: calculated from total population estimates and the number of hospital beds available in public and private, general and specialized hospitals, and rehabilitation centers. Hospitals are establishments permanently staffed by at least one physician. Nurses include graduate, practical, assistant, and auxiliary nurses as well as paraprofessional personnel such as health workers, first-aid workers, traditional birth attendants, etc. Physicians includes registered practitioners in the country and medical assistants whose medical training is less than that of qualified physicians, but who dispense similar medical services, including simple operations. Note that the definition of recognized medical practitioners differs among countries.

Female participation in the labor force is based on ILO data. It comprises the "economically active" population, which excludes homemakers and other unpaid caregivers.

Total fertility rate is the average number of children that would be born alive to a woman during her lifetime, if she were to bear children at each age in accordance with prevailing age-specific fertility rates. The data are a combination of observed values and interpolated and projected estimates. **Infant mortality rate** is the number of deaths of infants under one year of age per 1,000 live births in a given year. Some countries, such as the USSR, employed an atypical definition of live births that reduced the reported infant mortality rates relative to the standard WHO definition.

Urban population estimates are based on different national definitions of what is urban, so cross-country comparisons should be made with caution.

Population per passenger car refers to the total population divided by the number of private motor cars seating nine people or less. The figures for population per telephone relate to the number of public and private telephones installed that can be connected to a central exchange. The data are generally those published by the International Telecommunications Union.

Statistical background for the estimates is available in the UN annual *Population and Vital Statistics Report* and the World Bank's annual *World Population Projections.*

General Notes

To facilitate mapping of the numerous and at times complex links between the tables and the technical notes in the Guide, common notations (footnote calls) are used for Global, Comparator, and Basic Tables. These notations signal to the reader where and how to consult the appropriate technical documentation. Country-specific notes are denoted by an "f". General notes are denoted by capital letters A–Z and are explained in the list below.

General notes identify exceptions to standard sources and methods that occur frequently, for more than one country or source. Country notes occur less frequently and pertain to unique issues, a particular country, data series, or time period. At the endo of each country note is a description of country practices in implementing recommendations of the MPS and SNA beyond those discussed in chapter 11. Since these are pervasive, they are not signalled by special footnote calls in the tables.

Country notes signalled by a small "f" are organized by an indicator type and presented in bold typeface in the pages following.

Code letters (A–Z) in the "Notes" column of the tables refer to the following general notes

A   Source: ACDA

B   Basic prices

C   Source: CIA or LWI

D   GDP

E   Authors' series

f   See Country notes.

F   f.o.b.

G   Source: GATT

H   GDP by industrial origin data for at least some years are in purchaser values, not factor cost

I   Index derived from constant price series in original base year and rescaled.

J   Source: IMF balance of payments data.

K   Source: World Bank data.

L   Source: ECE

M   Source: UN Monthly Bulletin of Statistics

N   Source: UNCTAD

O   Source: OECD, *Financing and external debt of developing countries, 1989 survey.*

P   GNP

Q   MPS definition

R   Source: World Bank, Debtor Reporting System

S   Based on national trade statistics covering trade with market economies and Yugoslavia.

T   c.i.f.

U   Military and central government expenditure are converted to dollars in different ways; therefore, their relative sizes in dollars differ from what they would be in national currency terms. See *Sources and methods,* chapter 11.

V   Source: CMEA Statistical Yearbook.

W   Source: IMF, Direction of Trade Statistics

X   Excludes construction

Y   Includes change in stocks

Z   Indexes from original ECE trade prices in national currency units adjusted to remove exchange rate effects. See *Sources and Methods,* chapter 11.

Country Notes

These notes, where printed in boldface, are signalled by "f" in the tables and represent deviations from standard sources and methods. The discussions by country of MPS and SNA practices takes up differences among countries in implementing the standard recommendations of the two national accounting systems.

Albania

SNA accounts
Constant prices: Base year does not correspond to current price data for prices since different price series are used in calculating current versus constant prices.

MPS accounts
Resource balance (current and constant prices): Excludes losses on fixed capital and stocks. 1970 data derived as residual.
Net capital formation (current and constant prices and volume index): Includes losses on fixed capital and stocks.
Final consumption and personal consumption definition: Includes statistical discrepancy.
Other services in NMP definition: Includes domestic and foreign trade.

Exchange and conversion rates
Commercial exchange rate source: For 1975, for 1980–82, Statistik des Auslandes, 1983.

Trade price indexes
Definition: Official data in national currency terms, not adjusted for exchange rate effects.

Balance of payments
BoP indicators source: National statistical authorities.

Bulgaria

SNA accounts
Gross output agriculture: Source, FAO, rescaled from 1979–81 base.

MPS accounts
NMP (constant prices): Derived from official NMP volume indexes.
Services: Delivered as residual.

Exchange and conversion rates
Official rate (per US dollar) source: Official reports to World Bank or ECE.
Commercial rate (per US dollar) source: National authorities.
Definition: Unpublished commercial/premium rate from national authorities.
Non-commercial rate (per US dollar) source: National authorities.
Commercial rate (per ruble) source: National authorities.
Definition: Unpublished commercial/premium rate. Rate varies with trade partner.

Commercial price index source: "Official" as published by CIA, rescaled from 1978 base year.

BoP and external debt
Current balance: Errors may occur due to rounding of original export and import data in billions.
Debt service: As a share of total debt service, debt service to CMEA was 5.9 percent in 1990.

Country practices: SNA and MPS
Bulgaria follows the recommendations of MPS in compiling its macroeconomic aggregates. Relatively little information in absolute value terms is published in the national Statistical Yearbook or in UN sources. While current price values of global NMP are available for all years of the previous four decades, only volume indexes and distribution percentages are available for the origin of NMP by sectors and end-use categories. Bulgaria submitted unadjusted MPS type data for the CMEA Statistical Yearbook.

A considerable amount of household manufacturing activity is recorded as productive activity and included in NMP, e.g., primary processing of agricultural products, spinning and sewing, including goods produced for individual consumption.

Data for "other branches of the material sphere" deviate in some cases from the standard CMEA classification.

In 1990, the level and growth rate of NMP and its main components were revised. The corresponding indicators of the Basic Tables reflect the revised data.

In constant price compilations, the base year was changed at 5–8 year intervals. Only one overlapping year was revalued for the purpose of linking volume indexes.

SNA accounts
The Statistical Office estimated the country's GDP at current prices, showing both the origin of GDP by producing sectors and by end-use categories. The estimates cover the years 1979–89. As described in a previous section of the Guide, the staff and consultants of the World Bank estimated the constant price values for all years of the 1980s and for 1970 and 1975, based on these data and the official volume indexes for the components of NMP.

Cambodia

SNA accounts
Gross output–agriculture: Source is FAO; rescaled from index, 1979–81=100.

Partner trade
Source is UNSO, Comtrade database, Geneva.

BoP and external debt
Debt service: As a share of total external debt service, debt service to CMEA countries was 42.9 percent in 1985.

China

SNA accounts
National accounts data: For 1960–77, estimated based on China Statistical Yearbook.

MPS accounts
NMP produced and components (current and constant prices and volume index): Source for 1970–84 is Statistical Yearbook of China, 1989; for 1984–89, Statistical Abstract of China, 1990. Data rescaled from original base year.
Personal consumption (current and constant prices): Data are, in fact, for personal consumption rather than consumption of the population as with most HPEs.
Services: Derived as residual.

Country practices: SNA and MPS
The national accounts system in China has historically been geared to centrally planned economic management and is patterned on the MPS with its emphasis on gathering output data in physical terms. With the introduction of economic reforms and restructuring of the economy in the late 1970s, efforts began in earnest to strengthen the data-gathering apparatus to enhance its technical expertise and to gradually introduce conceptual changes that would result in information more suitable for managing an economy in which central planning was being complemented by the use of markets. Regular publications began with the release of the first Statistical Yearbook in 1981.

China's present national accounts are a hybrid system that has expanded the MPS production boundary to include the nonmaterial sectors and a more explicit treatment of financial flows. MPS features are retained to satisfy the remaining central planning requirements. The introduction of the SNA, at least in part, is being pursued to provide both a tool for measuring and monitoring the progress of market-oriented reforms and information for international comparison. While the system is intended to derivate both NMP and GDP estimates, it retains MPS as its core.

Current national accounts practices
The main reason advanced by the State Statistical Bureau of China (SSB), for adopting this hybrid system, is that, during a period of transition the economy will change, but even in the evolved state, central planning will coexist with a market-oriented segment, and MPS will continue to provide the means of maintaining the balance of material, financial, and human resources. At the same time the SNA has the advantage of capturing activities not covered by the MPS, and furthermore provides a wide set of useful indicators for purposes of economic management.

GDP estimates, using the MPS as an organizing framework, continue to suffer flaws both because of conceptual or accounting features of the MPS (which, by extension, lead to weaknesses in coverage or computation for the purposes of the SNA), as well as systematic or valuation characteristics that largely have to do with the price system in China.

In deriving the GDP estimates, the SSB attempts to use a definition of the service sector that corresponds closely to the SNA definition. Nevertheless, the scope of the SSB's definition is narrower, mainly because statistics for certain subsectors are lacking. New activities such as domestic service, rural transport, urban informal activities, and business services (accounting, legal, laundry shops) are excluded. The rapid growth of such service activities suggests limited coverage of the services sector.

GDP estimates raise valuation issues due to the pricing system. The absence of market-determined values (e.g. in housing services for determining imputed rents/incomes) and the continued use of price controls (e.g., of grain, in the valuation of agricultural output) impinge on the accuracy of estimates of sectoral shares.

China operates a multiple-tier pricing system-statutory official administered prices, negotiated prices, market prices. Thus, there is little evidence to indicate that market prices in the Chinese context refers to what Western economists would call "market prices", even during the period of economic reforms. Most "market prices" in China are to some degree government-managed prices. All these reduce the accuracy of constant price GDP estimates and, therefore, cause distortions in the measurement of inflation as well as real growth of GDP and its sectoral components. For more information see the Bibliography, World Bank.

Cuba

MPS accounts
NMP produced and sectoral breakdown (current and constant prices): Source is Meza-Lao, C. and Perez-Lopez, Jorge, "Cuban economic growth in current and constant prices, 1975–1988."
Personal consumption (current and constant prices): Data are, in fact, personal consumption rather than consumption of the populations, as for most HPEs.

BoP and external debt
Debt service: As a share of total external debt service, debt service to CMEA countries was 20 percent in 1985.

Dometic finance
Military expenditure: Series likely omits most arms acquisitions.

Czechoslovakia

MPS accounts
Services in NMP (constant prices): Derived as a residual from other sectoral components.

Resource balance (current and constant prices): Includes losses on fixed capital and stocks.

Exchange and conversion rates

Official rate (per U.S. dollar): Sources are national authorities or ECE.

Commercial rate (per ruble): Rate varies with trading partner as of 1989.

Non-commercial rate (per U.S. dollar): Unified with commercial rate January 8, 1990.

Non-commercial rate (per ruble): Applies to interstate settlements and varies with trading partner. Rates shown are for the USSR.

International trade

Total price indexes (authors' series): Derived as average of socialist and non-socialist indexes, weighted annually by the current dollar value of exports or imports.

BoP and external debt

Current Balance: Errors may occur due to rounding of original export and import data in billions.

Debt service: As a share of total external debt service, debt service to CMEA countries was 1.2 percent in 1990.

Country practices: SNA and MPS

The Statistical Yearbook issued by the Federal Statistical Office (FSO) provides considerable information on macroeconomic aggregates compiled according to the national version of MPS; some SNA-type accounts are also given in recent FSO releases (see below). Similarly, detailed and complete data are submitted to the UNSO for the Yearbook of National Accounts Statistics.

The national version of MPS deviates in some respects from the CMEA model. The most important deviation is the exclusion of passenger transport and personal communication. For CMEA comparisons these activities are added to NMP. "Addition" of these items, would tend to reduce the growth rate since price increases have generally been lower for output (e.g., fares) than intermediate inputs; and net value added for these NMP branches may well be negative. The concept of investment is different in the national and CMEA versions of MPS. For example, the national version includes patents and designs.

An unusually large value is assigned to nonmaterial services purchased for production purposes in both material and nonmaterial branches. The reason is unclear, however, as documentation is lacking. While these kinds of costs vary between 3–5 percent of NMP in Bulgaria and Hungary, this ratio for Czechoslovakia is 7 percent in the material sphere (NMP), and approximately 25 percent in the nonmaterial sphere.

Both current and constant price values of the aggregates are published for long periods. However, when changing the base year for constant price compilations (1960, 1967, 1977, 1984) only one year is repriced for linking the different periods, in order to preserve the originally published volume indexes.

Unsuccessful geological exploration is considered as intermediate consumption of material production. Cost of forest plantings is not recorded as output and capital formation; it is included in current input of forestry.

Monetary gold is treated as a material good and is included in exports or imports, or in changes in stocks, depending on the type of transaction.

SNA accounts

The Federal Statistical Office presented a first estimate of the GDP of Czechoslovakia for 1987 at a CMEA seminar held in Spring 1989. In the 1990 Statistical Yearbook a relatively detailed set of data on GDP at current prices was published for 1980 and each year from 1985–89. In addition, additional data were submitted to the World Bank, which enabled the staff and consultants of the Bank to extend these estimates to other years. Constant price values published in the Basic Tables are entirely staff estimates, following the basic method described earlier in the Guide.

German Democratic Republic

SNA accounts

GDP by sector (volume index): For 1970 only, estimated by authors. See *Sources and Methods*, chapter 11.

Exchange and conversion rates

Commercial rate (per U.S. dollar): Source is IIC (Geneva) database.

Commercial rate (ruble per U.S. dollar): After 1985, commercial rate was divided by official rate as reported by IIC.

International trade

Exports, imports, and trade balance (ECE).

BoP and debt

Current balance: Errors may occur due to rounding of original export and import data in billions.

Country practices: SNA and MPS

Official data are presented in the Statistical Yearbook of the German Democratic Republic. Despite considerable deviations from the agreed MPS methodology, the same data are submitted for the CMEA Statistical Yearbook.

Data on gross output and NMP are published in constant price values and in volume indexes. In the 1990 Statistical Yearbook, data are expressed in 1985 constant prices, and all aggregates are shown for all years 1960 to 1989. The data are highly aggregated: branches are shown at the one digit level of the classification.

The constant price value of NMP produced, shown in the Basic Tables, does not include the contribution of foreign trade. No data are published on net exports. However, the total of NMP used in the domestic economy is listed, representing the sum of final material consumption and net accumulation.

The NMP presented is approximately 4 percent less than the sum of net value created by the material branches. This discrepancy can be attributed to statistical adjustment for subsidies provided to enterprises for certain intermediate consumption materials. At the national level, these subsidized goods are valued at full price when sold but at a lower price when consumed. This difference is not attributed to the individual sectors, but subtracted globally from the total net value added of material branches.

Branches of the economy are defined on an "enterprise" basis, i.e., all activities of a state or cooperative enterprise are classified under a specific branch representative of enterprise's activity.

Several kinds of activities with relatively minor weights are classified differently from the CMEA standard classification of economic activities, (e.g., timbering and deep-sea fishing).

Unsuccessful geological exploration is included in intermediate consumption of material production.

Investments in the nonmaterial sphere are not depreciated and their full value is recorded as "accumulation."

SNA accounts

Early in 1990, the State Statistical Office estimated and published (in a weekly magazine) a complete set of GDP data for 1980–90 according to the definitions of the SNA. The global value of GDP, both at current and constant prices, is subdivided according to the main producing branches and the SNA-type categories of end uses. Extensions of this data for the year 1970 were carried out by the authors and are presented in the Basic Tables. As a result of unification, all German Democratic Republic macroeconomic data is currently being merged with the Federal Republic of Germany data, both for current and constant prices. Similar statistical efforts will lead to revisions of the earlier published data for German Democratic Republic. At the time of this report, however, corresponding revised data are not yet available.

The GDP data compiled by German Democratic Republic do not cover the value added of foreign trade. The adjustment item for subsidies deducted from sum of value added of material branches is shown as a distinct item.

Hungary

SNA accounts

GDP by sector of origin (current and constant prices): Value added of services is overstated, while agriculture and industry are understated, because commodity taxes are combined with services as a residual.

MPS accounts

NMP and sectoral breakdown (current and constant prices): Components of NMP may not add to total because of rescaling discrepancies. See UN Yearbook of National Accounts Statistics.

International trade

Exports and imports (national currency): Break in comparability of data: trade values converted at devisa rate through 1975, at commercial rate after 1975.
Total price indexes (author's series): Derived as average of socialist and non-socialist indexes, weighted annually by the current-dollar value of exports or imports.
Non-socialist countries (author's series): Derived as average of developed and developing indexes, weighted annually by the current dollar values of exports or imports.

BoP and external debt

Exports, imports, trade and current account balances (U.S. dollars): Source for 1983–90 is World Bank staff reports. Data for 1989–90 are preliminary. Errors in current account balance may occur due to rounding of original export and import data in billions.
Debt service: As a share of total external debt service, debt service to CMEA countries has decreased from 0.5 percent in 1980 to 0.3 percent in 1985 to 0.2 percent in 1990.

Country practices: SNA and MPS

In 1970 Hungary introduced a national accounting system that integrates the main aggregates of MPS and SNA. The fundamental aim was to construct the system to compile MPS measures as a subset of SNA data. This was achieved within the framework of an input-output table covering all economic activities and dividing them horizontally and vertically between the material and nonmaterial spheres. Accordingly, all incidental, technical, and classification differences between the two systems were removed, making deviations from both MPS and SNA inevitable. The basic concepts of the Hungarian NMP and GDP statistics are, however, in accordance with corresponding international recommendations.

MPS measures like NMP by producing sectors and end-use categories, are regularly published in the Statistical Yearbook. Such data are available in more detail in specialized publications on national accounts. Until 1990, Hungary reported its national accounts data to UNSO for the Yearbook of National Accounts Statistics according to the questionnaire based upon the MPS concept. Since 1990 the SNA questionnaire has been employed for reporting to UNSO. In national and UNSO publications, national accounts data are provided in substantial detail. For the CMEA Statistical Yearbook, MPS aggregates and corresponding indexes were submitted.

In NMP, the branches of the material sphere are shown in a "pure" activity classification, in accordance with the recommendation of the original MPS. End-use categories corresponding to MPS, however, are published in highly aggregated form; detailed data on consumption and investment are shown in the SNA accounts and tables.

Gross output and net value added of individual branches are compiled and published at basic values, i.e. net of commodity taxes and subsidies. The market value of "National Income" is derived by adding the sum of commodity taxes (less subsidies) to the total value created in the material sphere (or to NMP). Therefore, the share of an individual material sector can be determined only by relating the basic value of this sector to NMP measured at basic value prices.

The main components of NMP are published in long time series, in absolute values both at current and constant prices. In introducing a new base year for constant price compilations (1968, 1976, 1981) the earlier constant price values were revalued back to the previous benchmark year, and the previously published "official" volume indexes were replaced by new "official" indexes.

In order to circumvent internal conflicts between MPS and SNA type aggregates, the following main deviations from MPS were introduced:

- Intermediate consumption of the material branches also includes the costs of nonmaterial services purchased (accordingly, the value added of a given sector is the same for MPS and SNA). The total of this amount is "given back" at the end of the compilation of NMP, so its content corresponds to the original definition.
- Compensation for travel expenses is partially included in intermediate consumption (transport, hotel), and partially in wages (per diem used for food, drinks).
- Expenditures on military goods are recorded in collective material consumption.
- Depreciation of housing is included in material consumption of services, not in personal consumption.
- No losses are shown in final use of NMP; losses are disregarded in output, recorded as a cost of production, or outside the NMP account, as a change in the capital stock.
- Uncompleted investments are shown as a separate item of capital formation and not as part of changes in stocks.
- Since 1988 consumption of the population is shown on a "national" basis, i.e., the purchases of foreigners in the domestic market are deducted from this figure, while the value of commodities purchased by residents abroad are added to it.

SNA accounts

Since 1970 Hungary has compiled and published major macroeconomic aggregates according to the definitions of the SNA, with coverage back to 1960. Detailed data are published in the Statistical Yearbook of the CSO and in specialized publications. These official data are reported by Hungarian authorities to the World Bank and IMF.

Aggregated and Basic Tables for gross output and gross and net value added are compiled on the basis of "enterprise" reports. The primary classification of branches is predicated on the allocation of enterprises according to their main activity. In national publications, however, "pure" kind-of-activity classifications are also given for gross and net output. In the present Guide, GDP data according to sector of origin are shown as reported by enterprises in their main activity. Accordingly, these data make international and time-series comparisons and juxtapositions of NMP and GDP growth rates (as is done in the Isomorph table) particularly difficult. For example, the volume index (1980 base=100) of GDP for agriculture in 1988

is 125.6 on the enterprise based (main activity) classification, but is only 112 on a kind-of-activity basis. The latter figure should be used for a correct comparison with the NMP-based index (109) and with the "Building Block" approach index (110). For industry and services, the differences between the two types of classification are considerably smaller.

All individual producing sectors, whether within NMP or GDP, are valued at "basic value prices", i.e. excluding commodity taxes and including commodity subsidies. The sum of the basic values of the industries can serve as a basis for measuring shares of sectors. GDP expressed in market prices is derived by adding the total sum of commodity taxes (less subsidies) at the end of the table. In the Hungarian Basic Tables, the shares of agriculture and industry are understated, while services are shown at a higher level because all commodity taxes are included in services. It should be noted as in the tables in chapter 9, the shares of material and nonmaterial activities are calculated from basic values. Compared to other countries in which market prices are used for calculating shares of services, Hungary's level is upward biased. Because all countries levy commodity taxes primarily on industrial products, the ratio of industry to services is higher at market prices than at basic values.

In estimating changes in stocks at current prices, (following for several years the bookkeeping practice of the enterprises) a considerable part of "pure" price increase is included, thus inflating the current value of GDP. These distortions do not appear in constant price estimates.

Korea, Democratic People's Republic

SNA accounts
Gross output–agriculture: Source: FAO database, 1979–81=100.
GNP (U.S. dollars, current prices): Source is Yoon, Suk Bum, "A trial estimation of an econometric model of North Korea," *Asian Economic Journal*, March 1989.

BoP and external debt
Debt service: As a share of total external debt service, debt service to CMEA countries was 34.7 percent in 1985.

Lao PDR

International Trade
Value of exports and imports (ECE series) (US dollars, current prices): Source is Asian Development Bank, Statistical Yearbook 1980–90.

BoP and external debt
Debt service: As a share of total external debt service, debt service to CMEA countries has decreased from 38.2 percent in 1985 to 15.8 percent in 1990.

Mongolia

MPS accounts
NMP produced and sectoral breakdown (current

prices): Source is Milne, et al.

Trade in NMP (current prices): Distribution and warehousing only.

Exchange and conversion rates

All exchange rates except the informal rate are from Milne, et al. Data for 1990 are through July only.

International trade

Value of exports and imports, trade balance (national currency, current prices): Converted from ruble series at commercial tugrik/transferable ruble rate.

Value of exports and imports, trade balance (U.S. dollars, current prices): Converted from ruble series using commercial tugrik/transferable ruble and U.S. dollar/tugrik exchange rates, obtained from Milne, et al.

BoP and external debt

Total external debt, debt service, and reserves: Source is Milne, Elizabeth, et. al. As a share of total external debt service, debt service to CMEA countries was 33 percent in 1985.

MPS accounts

National income data are compiled on the basis of material balances. Gross material product (GMP) is calculated using an input/output formulation for goods and those services (e.g., utilities, publishing) that are directly required for the production and distribution of goods in the material sector. Inputs of nonmaterial services (e.g., finance, insurance, housing, defense, education, welfare) are excluded. Total GMP is the sum of the gross output of industry, constructions, and other branches of the material product valued at (for the most part) producer prices inclusive of turnover taxes. Net material product (NMP) is calculated by subtracting intermediate consumption of material goods and services, including capital depreciation, from GMP.

Data on physical output appears to be most reliable, reflecting actual and not targeted output, whereas national income accounts data on an expenditure basis are less reliable. Nominal investment flows, which include current spending for ongoing projects, are based on, until 1988, rigid price structure. Data on additions to inventory are partial and depreciation of fixed capital and use of inventories are estimated. National account deflators and official retail price indices appear to underestimate underlying inflation rates, causing an underestimation of nominal rates of growth of NMP, as well as an overestimation of real rates of growth.

Classification and statistical methods used by the Mongolian State Statistical Office (MSSO) were those promulgated by the CMEA. Mongolia treated most statistical information as warranting with minimal publication.

GDP growth in both real and nominal terms, during 1980–88, paralleled that of NMP, although at a slightly higher level. In 1989, however, the trends of GDP and NMP diverged. The slower growth of GDP relative to NMP reflected a slower growth in nonmaterial services, owing mainly to the scaling back of civil service employment.

SNA accounts

The MSSO has taken steps to reorient its work toward Western-style accounting. With the growth of new enterprises, small businesses in particular, and the planned privatization of state-owned enterprises, MSSO recognizes that it will have to organize surveys. It has taken the first step in this direction by establishing a business register. The register contains information of assets, employment, and revenue generated. The register should help in valuation of enterprises and be an important data source in the privatization process. MSSO has identified key prices and is beginning the collection of prices that will be used in the computation of retail price indices. With the reform of the trading system, external trade data will be compiled by the customs rather than by the trading corporations. Work on adaptation of international classifications and standards is proceeding.

During 1991, MSSO made estimates of the GDP. These estimates make some adjustments for coverage of the extended service sectors but do not make adjustments for valuation. Consequently, the GDP estimates in national currency are an underestimate. In the short run, because of the unavailability of adequate price series, little can be done to make major adjustments.

Until more information is available on cross parities with the ruble and the currencies of other trading partners, and trade data by origin destination, little can be done to estimate the US dollar GDP.

Nicaragua

SNA accounts

GDP by sector of origin (current and constant prices): At factor cost through 1987, at market prices after 1987.

International trade

Exports, imports, and trade balance (U.S. dollars): Source is IMF, IFS.

Partner trade

Source is IMF, Direction of Trade Statistics Yearbook, 1990; includes partner trade data as reported by all partners, which may include non-convertible flows.

BoP and external debt

BoP data are consolidated figures, including convertible and non-convertible flows.

Debt service: As a share of total external debt service, debt service to CMEA countries has increased from 1.2 percent in 1985 to 35.7 percent in 1989.

Poland

MPS accounts

NMP produced (current prices): Source for 1970–88 is ECE; for 1988–89, Statistical Yearbook of Poland, 1990.
NMP produced (constant prices): Source for 1985–90 is Statistical Yearbook of Poland, 1990.
Agriculture in NMP (constant prices): For 1970–84,

derived from volume indexes.

Services in NMP (constant prices): Includes statistical discrepancy.

Final consumption NMP (constant prices): Derived as a residual from NMP used and net capital formation.

Exchange and conversion rates

Official rate (per U.S. dollar and per ruble): Rate was discontinued January 1, 1982.

Commercial rate (per U.S. dollar): For 1971–78, parametric internal exchange rate, source is Plan Econ Report, December 16, 1985. For 1979–90, IFS line wf.

Commercial rate (per ruble): Source for 1970–81 is Plan Econ Report, December 16, 1985; for 1882–90, ECE based on official reports.

Non-commercial rate (per U.S. dollar): Source for 1970–81 is national authorities.

International trade

Exports, imports, and trade balance (national currency): Break in comparability of data: trade values converted at devisa rate through 1982, at commercial rate after 1982.

Total price indexes (author's series): Derived as average of socialist and non-socialist indexes, weighted annually by the current dollar value of exports or imports.

BoP and external debt

Current balance: Errors may occur due to rounding of original export and import data in billions.

Debt service: As a share of total external debt service, debt service to CMEA countries increased from 2.1 percent in 1980 to 6.3 percent in 1985, to 23.1 percent in 1990.

Country practices: SNA and MPS

Poland regularly publishes a complete set of macroeconomic aggregates according to MPS, at current and constant prices, in its National Statistical Yearbook and also in the UN Yearbook of National Accounts Statistics. The same data were reported to the CMEA Secretariat. Constant price values in the 1990 Statistical Yearbook are published only for the years after 1984 when the 1984 prices were introduced as constant prices. For international publications the constant price values are given for longer periods. These periods, however, are divided into several subperiods with a different set of constant prices used for each.

Several years ago, in addition to traditional MPS aggregates, Poland introduced the concept of Gross Material Product (GMP). This figure includes, in addition to NMP, the value of depreciation of fixed capital used in the material production. Accordingly, these accounts show the gross value added of the material branches, and, in addition to final material consumption, the gross value of capital formation.

Since 1984, in the classification of branches and compilation of their production, the "enterprise" type unit has been used instead of the "pure" kind-of-activities.

Constant price data are compiled on a given base year for 5–8 years before shifting to a new base year. Only one overlapping year is expressed at two sets of constant prices for the purposes of linking the volume indexes; in this case the previously published "official" indexes are preserved unchanged. Since 1970, prices of 1971, 1977, and 1984 have been used as base years for constant prices.

Expenditures of enterprises for the social, cultural, and welfare services provided to employees are considered as intermediate consumption. Therefore, these figures are not included in final consumption of the population.

Cost of unsuccessful geological exploration is included in final material consumption for collective needs.

SNA accounts

Poland officially reports important macroeconomic aggregates to the World Bank and IMF, compiled according to SNA. These estimates cover 1980–90 and show, at current and constant prices, the origin of GDP by producing sectors and by end-use categories. The staff and consultants of the World Bank estimated the corresponding aggregates for 1970 and 1975, relying mainly on information for NMP.

In its 1990 Statistical Yearbook, the CSO of Poland introduced a new set of national accounts statistics for official estimates of Gross Domestic Product and its components as determined in SNA. GDP data were shown for 1985, 1986, and 1987 only. Volume indexes were published for all components and all years from 1980–89.

Due to hyperinflation in 1989 and 1990, the current price values of GDP and all its components may be uncertain.

It seems most likely that the SNA-type aggregates are derived from MPS-type data, especially the gross value added data of producing branches. For end-use components of GDP, Poland has accumulated considerable experience through participation in the ICP program. Accordingly, GDP for the benchmark years (1975, 1980, 1985) was constructed from very detailed expenditures data.

No methodological description to date captures the detailed treatment of prices and values of goods sold on parallel (black) markets. There has been a substantial increase in the direct export and import of goods (sold and purchased by the population abroad) in recent years; while some steps are being taken to collect information about these transactions, better data seem necessary to properly evaluate current developments. At the same time, variable and often rapid inflation (since the mid-1980s has distorted the current price data to such an extent that it is extremely difficult to measure the domestic effects of such flows.

In 1991, the Polish Statistical Office conducted a study of GDP estimation that suggests significantly different volume indexes for the 1980s than the official series. The study's alternative series differed mostly owing to the choice of base year but also to other adjustments. Since Poland began major price reforms in 1989, the shift to a 1989 base year dramatically alters

Volume indexes of GDP of Poland compiled at different base year prices

Base year	1980	1985	1986	1987	1988	1989	1990
1980 (revised)	100.0	105.0	108.9	106.8	109.6	107.3	100.0
1984 (official)	100.0	99.0	103.1	105.2	109.5	109.2	..
1989 (revised)	100.0	101.8	104.5	102.9	105.3	102.8	..

weights of component growth rates. The table above highlights these differences.

Romania

SNA accounts
Gross output–agriculture: Source is FAO database, 1979–81=100.

MPS accounts
NMP produced (current prices): Source for 1970–79 is ECE; for 1980–90, World Bank.

Trade in NMP (current prices): Includes all other services not specified separately in sectoral breakdown.

NMP produced (constant prices): Source for 1970–80 is CMEA Yearbook, derived from volume indexes; for 1980–90, from World Bank staff reports.

NMP used and resource balance (current prices): Source for 1980–90 is World Bank.

Exchange and conversion rates
Official rate (per U.S. dollar and per ruble): Rate was discontinued January 1, 1981.

Commercial rate (per U.S. dollar): For 1970–72, foreign trade multiplier, source is Plan Econ Report, December 16, 1985. For 1973–90, IFS line wf.

Non-commercial rate (per U.S. dollar): Source for 1970–72 is national authorities; for 1973–90, IFS line xf, secondary rate.

International trade
Exports, imports, and trade balance (national currency): Break in comparability of data: trade values converted at devisa rate through 1980, at commercial rate after 1980.

Total price indexes (author's series): Derived as average of socialist and and non-socialist indexes, weighted annually by the current dollar value of exports or imports.

BoP and external debt
Current balance: Errors may occur due to rounding of original export and import data in billions.

Country practices: SNA and MPS
Until 1990 Romania used the MPS accounting system. However, few value figures were published in the national, UN, or CMEA statistical yearbooks. Although Romania is a member of the World Bank and the IMF, only a small and incomplete set of data was transmitted to these organizations, primarily volume indexes and selected aggregates.

This situation changed at the beginning of 1991 when the 1990 national Statistical Yearbook was published. Covering a period of more than four decades, (with 1989 as the closing year), all fundamental aggregates of NMP at current prices for 1938, 1950, 1960, 1970, 1980, and all years between 1985–89 were published in value terms. In addition, volume indexes of these aggregates are shown for the entire period.

In this latest official publication, previously compiled data up to 1980, including growth rates, are preserved unchanged. However, absolute current value figures for the components of NMP are now available.

In the 1990 Statistical Yearbook, previously published global NMP current values and volume indexes are revised for the period 1980–89. For example, where the unrevised current value of NMP for 1988 was reported as exceeding 850 billion lei, the revised NMP value stands at 697.4 billion lei. GDP was also revised downward by about the same magnitude. Growth rates have also been sharply reassessed: according to the unrevised official publication, the volume index of NMP for the period between 1980 and 1988 was 144 percent, while the 1990 yearbook shows a volume index of 108. The present databook shows the NMP data for the whole period of 1970–89 according to the revised 1990 Statistical Yearbook. However, when comparing the two sets of data for the two decades, it should be noted that growth rates of NMP for the 1970s (nearly 250 percent as measured by volume indexes) are not as reliable for those of the 1980s.

Romania's national accounting system has diverged from the standard MPS in several areas and the nominal value reported to CMEA was slightly (3–4 percent) different from that published in the national statistical yearbook. Some major deviations are:

- Scientific research; certain activities connected with technological development; tourism services are classified as productive activities and included in NMP.
- Processing of agricultural products and some other manufacturing activities carried out in households are included in NMP.
- Expenditures of enterprises for social-cultural and welfare services are considered as intermediate inputs and are not included in final consumption of the population.
- Consumption of the population is defined on a "national" basis, i.e. the purchases of foreigners in the domestic market are deducted from the purchases of residents abroad are added to the domestic turnover.

Romania regularly reports data on GNP and some of its components, which are published in the IFS. The World Bank has not used these data for analysis or publication. The 1990 Statistical Yearbook provides a full set of aggregates for the GDP and its components at current prices for 1980s. It also lists volume indexes for these aggregates based on 1980. These data are shown in the Country Table.

World Bank and IMF staff have prepared constant price values for the 1980s. Toward this end, current price values for 1980 are extrapolated based on the officially published volume indexes.

World Bank staff also estimated GDP at current and constant prices for 1970 and 1975, for which the "official" growth rates of NMP for the 1970s were the primary basis.

USSR

SNA accounts

All indicators are authors' series rescaled to 1987 base from original 1980 base year.

GNP (U.S. dollars, current prices): For 1980–89, official data in local currency converted at exchange rate in box 1b.

GNP by sectoral of origin (current prices): Extrapolated from published benchmark estimates (1980, 1985, 1989) using NMP/GDP ratios and detailed depreciation data.

GNP (national currency, constant prices): Derived from official GDP volume indexes and benchmark estimates.

GNP and components (volume indexes): 1985 data extrapolated on the basis of given growth rates.

MPS accounts

NMP produced (current prices): For 1970–80, source is ECE; for 1980–89, Statistical Yearbook of USSR, 1990.

Exchange and conversion rates

Commercial rate (U.S. dollar): No commercial rate before November 1990. For discussion of proxy rate, see table 11.2.

Trade price indexes

Total price indexes (author's series): Derived as average of socialist and non-socialist indexes, weighted annually by the current dollar value of exports or imports.

Non-socialist countries (author's series): Derived as average of developed and developing indexes, weighted annually by the current dollar value of exports or imports.

Government finance and money

Central government expenditure: Part of estimated total military expenditure may be omitted.

BoP and external debt

Total external debt, debt service, and reserves: Source is IMF, World Bank, OECD, and EBRD, "Study of the Soviet Economy," February 1991.

Country practices: SNA and MPS

MPS macroeconomic data are published annually in the Soviet Statistical Yearbook "The National Economy of the USSR" (Narodnoe Khozyastvo). Despite some deviation from CMEA standards, identical data are submitted for publication in the CMEA Statistical Yearbook.

Gross output, material inputs, and net material product are published exclusively in current prices. NMP is disaggregated into producing branches and end-use categories. Longer periods of time are represented only by volume indexes. The base year used for calculating constant price values is not indicated. Gross fixed capital formation is shown in constant price values for several years.

NMP is published solely for highly aggregated branches (one digit level of classification); end-use categories are also shown in highly aggregated forms within the balance of NMP. More detailed data, differing somewhat in content, are published in "branch statistics" of the Statistical Yearbook. Only data for the socialist sectors are further disaggregated.

Passenger transport and communication of the population and nonmaterial organizations are excluded from NMP.

In accordance with MPS, but deviating from the practice of other HPEs, extraction of timber is classified as industry rather than forestry. Some other deviations from CMEA classifications are evident, but they are of minor importance.

The value added of foreign trade activity and the surplus of exports over imports as an end-use item of NMP is compiled on the basis of domestic prices of commodities traded, excluding the value of trade in foreign currency. As such, no direct link is established between NMP and balance of payments data for traded goods and services. NMP does not include private sector handicraft production.

Expenditures for military durables are most likely recorded under "changes in stocks", but this is not clearly indicated in methodological documentation. Depreciation of the main road network is included in inputs of material production; depreciation of roads within settlements is considered as final consumption. Volume indexes for gross and net output of agriculture for years preceding 1980 were published solely in relation to five-year averages. NMP used in the domestic economy differs from NMP produced by the value of net export and losses. These two items are merged in most official publications. Losses include costs of unsuccessful geological exploration and the value of perished dairy cattle and breeding stocks. Capital repair, in line with MPS, but deviating from the practice of other HPEs, is recorded as capital formation. Changes in the stock of monetary gold is included in material circulating assets, and when used for payment, it is itemized as exports. Alcohol consumption between 1985–89 is probably included in current price values of consumption. Volume indexes of consumption do not reflect the declining effect of alcohol consumption.

SNA accounts

Official GDP estimates at current prices were first published in the National Economy of the USSR 1987, which was issued in 1988. Only global values are shown for years after 1980; however, volume indexes are published for the entire period after 1966. For the period between 1966–80, average growth rates of five-year subperiods are listed. In the 1989 Statistical Yearbook (issued in 1990), in addition to listing global GNP at current prices for all years between 1980–89, the following data are also published:

- Final use of GNP according to main end-use categories for all years between 1985–89 in absolute figures at current prices.
- Percentage shares of the individual branches (six major groups of activities) in GNP for 1980, 1985, and 1988.

Based on these "cornerstones," other data shown in the Basic Tables are derived and estimated by the authors.

The term GNP is used, but according to the methods applied, the published data express GDP.

No methodological information or source of data is available on how the original NMP data were adjusted to arrive at GNP. GNP levels at current prices and GNP volume indexes appear to be overestimated when compared to similar HPE compilations or Western estimates.

Viet Nam

SNA accounts

Gross output–agriculture: Source is Viet Nam General Statistical Office, "Statistical Data of the Socialist Republic of Viet Nam," Hanoi, 1991.

MPS accounts

NMP produced (current prices): Source for 1984–89 is World Bank, country report, 1990.

Resource balance (current prices): 1980 data derived as residual.

International trade

Value of exports and imports, trade balance (authors' series, U.S. dollars, current prices): Source is IFS.

Trade price indexes

Source is Viet Nam General Statistics Office, "Statistical Data of the Socialist Republic of Viet Nam, Hanoi, 1991.

BoP and external debt

Debt service: As a share of total external debt service, debt service to CMEA countries has increased from 55 percent in 1985.

Yugoslavia

MPS accounts

NMP produced and sectoral breakdown (current and constant prices): Data are gross material product. Source is Statistical Yearbook of Yugoslavia.

Exchange and conversion rates

Commercial rate (U.S. dollars): Source is IFS, line rf.

Trade price indexes

Source is IMF, IFS.

BoP and external debt

Debt service: As a share of total external debt service, debt service to CMEA countries increased from 1.5 percent in 1980 to 2.7 percent in 1985 and fell to 0.4 percent in 1990.

Government finance and money

Central government expenditure: Break in comparability of data; see IMF, Government Financial Statistics Yearbook.

Country practices: SNA and MPS

Until recently, the Federal Statistical Office (FSO) of Yugoslavia strictly adhered to the MPS definitions for productive activity and the scope and content of NMP. However, in presenting the main macroeconomic aggregates, the concept of "Social Product" (Drustveni Proizvod) is preferred to National Income (NMP), although the latter is regularly listed in national accounts. In the publication of the national accounts, Yugoslavia applies the double entry recording of the main economic flows in T-accounts, similar to the consolidated accounts of the SNA. "Social Product" is analogous to GDP, but is confined solely to the material sphere. Therefore, in this databook, the term "Gross Material Product" (GMP) is used for this indicator. Its value is larger than NMP by the value of depreciation of fixed capital used in material production. Concurrent with "Social Product" (GMP), the Yugoslavian accounting system also lists the "Gross Social Product" (Drustveni Bruto Proizvod), equivalent to "Global Social Product" as defined in MPS.

The Federal Statistical Office publishes extensive time series of detailed data at both current and constant prices. For example, the 1990 Statistical Yearbook covers the period 1952–89, showing GMP disaggregated by more than fifty producing sectors. The constant price values are shown for the whole period at 1972 prices.

In the UN Yearbook of National Accounts Statistics Yugoslavia reports its data in a questionnaire adopted for the collection of MPS type data. However, under the headings of NMP, Yugoslavia reports the global value and the components of Gross Material Product. (The difference in content is mentioned in footnotes.)

In this Guide, MPS accounts for Yugoslavia reflect GMP rather than NMP. The growth rates of NMP and GMP are similar, with GMP growing somewhat faster than NMP. Shares of the three large sectors presented in the Country Tables are similar for NMP and GMP. However, for end-use categories, the ratio of consumption and accumulation differs: although the consumption component is the same in both aggregates, contrary to the net concept of NMP, GMP covers a gross concept of capital formation.

There are several deviations in the classification of branches of the economy both from the standards adopted by the CMEA and the UN Statistical Commission. These differences do not greatly restrict comparisons of the producing sectors at the highly aggregated level shown in the Basic Tables.

SNA accounts

Yugoslavia regularly compiles and submits comprehensive data on GDP at the request of international organizations. Data regarding the origin and use of GDP are available beginning with 1970. These data are shown in the corresponding sections of the Country Tables.

It is most likely that the SNA-type aggregates compiled by the FSO of Yugoslavia were derived from the original MPS-type aggregates. Until 1990, no SNA-type data are to be published in the Statistical Yearbook of Yugoslavia.

Base Years for National Accounts

Base years for national accounts and material product series

	SNA	MPS
Albania	1986	1986
Bulgaria	1982	1982
Cambodia	1960	
China		1980
Cuba		1981
Czechoslovakia	1984	1984
German Dem. Rep.	1985	1985
Hungary	1981	1981
Korea, Dem. Peoples Rep.	1980	
Lao PDR	1988	1986
Mongolia	1990	1986
Nicaragua	1980	
Poland	1984	1984
Romania	1980	1981
USSR	1980	1980
Viet Nam	1982	1982
Yugoslavia	1972	1972

Bibliography

Abram Bergson, "The USSR Before the Fall: How Poor and Why," *Journal of Economic Perspectives*, Volume 5, Number 4 - Fall 1991, pp. 29–44.

Ackerman, Richard. "Environment in Eastern Europe: Despair or Hope?" *Transition*, Vol. 2, No. 4, April, 1991.

Alexeev, M. V., and C. G. Gaddy. "Trends in Wage and Income Distribution under Gorbachev. Analysis of New Soviet Data." *Berkeley-Duke Occasional Papers on the Second Economy in the USSR*, Paper 25, 1991.

Alexeev, M., and L. Walker, eds. *Estimating the Size of the Soviet Economy*. Washington, D.C.: National Academy Press, 1991.

Alton, Thad P., and others. "Selected Charts of Economic Performance in Eastern Europe." Occasional Paper 114. Washington, D.C.: L.W. International Financial Research, Inc., 1990.

———, and others. "Eastern Europe: Domestic Final Uses of Gross Product 1975–1989." Occasional Paper 112. Washington, D.C.: L.W. International Financial Research, Inc., 1990.

———, and others. "Economic Growth in Eastern Europe, 1975–1989." Occasional Paper 110. Washington, D.C.: L.W. International Financial Research, Inc., 1990.

———, and others. "Money Income of the Population and Standard of Living in Eastern Europe 1970–1989." Occasional Paper 113. Washington, D.C.: L.W. International Financial Research, Inc., 1990.

———, and others. "Agricultural Output, Expenses and Depreciation, Gross Product, and Net Product in Eastern Europe, 1975–1989." Occasional Paper 111. Washington, D.C.: L.W. International Financial Research, Inc., 1990.

Arvay, Janos. *National Product-National Income-National Wealth, the National Accounting System of Hungary*. Kozgazdasagi es Jogi Kiado, Budapest, 1973.

Austrian Central Statistical Office, Vienna; Central Laboratory of Social and Economic Measurement, Moscow; and Research Centre for Statistical and Economic Analysis, Warsaw. *Comparative Analysis of Social Expenditure and Its Finance; Austria, Poland and USSR*. Moscow, Vienna, and Warsaw, 1989.

Azam, Jean-Paul, Patrick and Sylviane Guillaumont. "Methodological Problems in Cross-Country Analysis of Economic Growth," World Bank PRE Working Paper, Series 22. Washington, D.C.: World Bank, 1988.

Bergson, Abram. *The Real National Income of Soviet Russia since 1928*. Cambridge, Mass.: Harvard University Press, 1961.

———. *Planning and Performance in Socialist Economies—The USSR and Eastern Europe*. Boston: Unwin Hyman, 1989.

———. "Real National Income Measurement: In Soviet Perspective." Cambridge, Mass.: Harvard University, Littauer Center, 1991.

Bhagwati, J. "On the Underinvoicing of Imports." *Bulletin of the Oxford University Institute of Economics and Statistics*, Vol. 26, No. 1, 1964.

Blades, D. "The Statistical Revolution in Central and Eastern Europe." *The OECD Observer*, No. 170, June/July 1991.

Blades, D., ed. *Statistics For a Market Economy*. Paris: OECD, 1991.

Boote, Anthony R. "Planned Economies: Statistical, Institutional and Policy Framework." 1990.

Boretsky, Mitchael. "CIA's Queries About Boretsky's Criticism of its Estimates of Soviet Economic Growth: Reply." *Journal of Comparative Economics*, Vol. 14, No. 2, June 1990, pp. 315–326.

Brabant, Josef M. van. *East European Cooperation: The Role of Money and Finance*. New York: Praeger, 1977.

———. *Essays on Planning, Trade and Integration in Eastern Europe*. Rotterdam: Rotterdam University Press, 1974.

———. *Adjustment, Structural Change, and Economic Efficieny—Aspects of Monetary Cooperation in Eastern Europe*. New York: Cambridge University Press, 1987.

———. *Socialist Economic Integration—Aspects of Contemporary Economic Problems in Eastern Europe*. Cambridge: Cambridge University Press, 1980.

Brown, Alan A. and Egon Neuberger, eds. *International Trade and Central Planning*. Berkeley: University of California Press, 1968.

Campbell, Robert W. "The Conversion of National Income Data of the U.S.S.R. to Concepts of the System of National Accounts in Dollars and Estimation of Growth Rate." World Bank Staff Working Paper No. 777. Washington, D.C.: World Bank, 1985.

———. *The Socialist Economies in Transition*. Bloomington: Indiana University Press, 1991.

Cassel, P. "Phenomenon and Effects of Inflation in Centrally Planned Socialist Economies." *Journal of Economic Studies*, Vol. 32, Spring 1990.

Chandler, William, Alexei Makaror and Dadi Zhou. "Energy for the Soviet Union, Eastern Europe and China." *Scientific American*, September 1990, pp. 121–127.

Central Intelligence Agency. *USSR: Measures of Economic Growth and Development, 1950–80*. Washington, D.C., 1982.

———. *The Impact of Gorbachev's Policies on Soviet Economic Statistics*. Washington, D.C., July 1988.

———. *Revisiting Soviet Economic Performance Under Glasnost: Implications for CIA Estimates*. Washington, D.C., 1988.

———. *Selected Countries' Trade With the USSR and Eastern Europe*. Washington, D.C., 1990.

———. *USSR: Demographic Trends and Ethnic Balance in the Non-Russian Republics*, Washington, D.C., 1990.

———. *The Chinese Economy in 1989 and 1990: Trying to Revive Growth While Maintaining Social Stability*. Washington, D.C., 1990.

———. *Soviet Energy Data Resource Handbook*. Washington, D.C., 1990.

———. Directorate of Intelligence. *Handbook of Economic Statistics*. Washington, D.C., 1990 (Annual).

———. *Measuring Soviet GNP: Problems and Solutions*. Washington, D.C., 1990.

———. *Measures of Soviet Gross National Product*. Washington, D.C., 1990.

Commander, Simon. *Managing Inflation in Socialist Economies in Transition*. Washington, D.C.: World Bank, 1991.

———, "Inflation and the Transition to a Market Economy: Overview." *World Bank Economic Review* (International), Vol. 6, January 1992.

Council for Mutual Economic Assistance, Standing Statistical Commission. *Basic Principles of the System of Balances of the National Economy*. Moscow, 1969. (In Russian).

Crane, Keith. *The Creditworthiness of Eastern Europe in the 1980s*. Santa Monica: Rand, 1985.

Dallago, Bruno. "The Non-Socialized Sector in Hungary: An Attempt at Estimating its Importance." *Yearbook of East European Economies*, Vol. 13, No. 2, 1989.

———. "Second and Irregular Economy in Eastern Europe: Its Consequences for Economic Transition." Trento, Italy: Dept. of Economics, University of Trento, 1991.

Economic Commission for Europe. *Economic Bulletin for Europe*. New York, Vol. 37, No. 4, 1985 (Semi-annual).

———. *Economic Bulletin for Europe*. Report prepared by the Secretariat of the Economic Commission for Europe, Geneva. Vol. 42, November 1990 (Semi-annual).

———. *Economic Bulletin for Europe*. New York, 1991.

Ehrlich, Eva. "Contest Between Countries: 1937–1986." *Soviet Studies*, Vol. 43, No. 5, 1991, pp. 875–896.

———. *Orszagok versenye, 1937–1986*. Kozgazdasagi es Jogi Kiado, Budapest, 1991.

———. "Decade of Backwardness": *Invest in Hungary*, (Monthly, Budapest), No. 6, 1991.

Ehrlich, Eva and Revesz, Gabor, "Collapse and Systematic Change in East and Central Europe", *Europe in 1990*, Torino, Italy: EUNANDI, 1992.

Ely, J.E. "Variations Between U.S. and Its Trading Partner Import Statistics." *The American Statistician*, April 1961.

Fallenbuchl, Zbigniew M. "National Income Statistics for Poland, 1970–1980." World Bank Staff Working Paper No. 776. Washington, D.C.: World Bank, 1985.

Franz, A. "East-West Comparison on Basis of PPP." Paper presented at the International Forum Economies in Transition: Statistical Measures Now and in the Future, Sochi, USSR, October 15–17, 1990.

Gaddy, C.G. "The Labor Market and the Second Economy in the Soviet Union." *Berkeley-Duke Occasional Papers on the Second Economy in the USSR*, Paper 24, 1991.

Gallo, D.T. *Reconciliation of Soviet and Western Foreign Trade Statistics*. Washington, D.C.: U.S. Central Intelligence Agency, 1977.

General Accounting Office. "Soviet Economy: Assessment of How Well the CIA has Estimated the Size of the Economy." Washington, D.C., September 1991.

Gardner, H. Stephen. "Product Quality and Price Inflation in Transitional Economies." Waco, Texas: Baylor University, 1991.

Gerschenkron, Alexander. "The Soviet Indexes of Industrial Production." *Review of Economics and Statistics*, Vol. 29, No. 4, 1947.

Grossman, Gregory. "The Second Economy in the USSR and Eastern Europe: A Bibliography." *Berkeley-Duke Occasional Papers on the Second Economy in the USSR*, Paper 21, 1990.

Havlik, Peter, and Friedrich Levcik. "The Gross Domestic Product of Czechoslovakia, 1970–1980." World Bank Staff Working Paper No. 772. Washington, D.C.: World Bank, 1985.

Hee, Michael. "Conversion Factors: A Discussion of Alternate Rates and Corresponding Weights." Policy Research Working Paper No. 479. Washington, D.C.: World Bank, 1990.

Hewett, Edward. *Foreign Trade Prices in the Council for Mutual Economic Assistance*. London: Cambridge University Press, 1974.

———. "The Gross National Product of Hungary: Important Issues for Comparative Research." World Bank Staff Working Paper No. 775. Washington, D.C.: World Bank, 1985.

Hill, T. P. *The Measurement of Real Product*. Paris: OECD, 1971.

Holzman, F. *Foreign Trade Under Central Planning*. Cambridge, Mass.: Harvard University Press, 1974.

———. *International Trade Under Communism Politics and Economics*. New York: Basic Books, 1976.

Ilieva, J., and S. Varjonen. "Comparison of the Balance Sheets of Bulgaria and the National Accounts of Finland." *Statistical Journal of the United Nations Economic Commission for Europe*, Vol. 4, 1974, pp. 395–410.

International Monetary Fund, International Bank for Reconstruction and Development/World Bank, OECD and European Bank for Reconstruction and Development. *The Economy of the USSR: Summary and Recommendations*. 1990.

International Monetary Fund, World Bank, OECD and European Bank for Reconstruction and Development. *A Study of the Soviet Economy*, (3 Vols.). Washington, D.C.: World Bank, 1991. (See also *The Economy of the USSR: Summary and Recommendations*).

Ishihara, Kyoichi. "Inflation and Economic Reform in China." *The Developing Economies*, Vol. 28, No. 2, 1990.

Jackson, Marvin R. "National Accounts and the Estimation of Gross Domestic Product and Its Growth Rates of Romania. A Background Study for Dollar GNPs of the USSR and Eastern Europe." World Bank Staff Working Paper No. 774. Washington, D.C.: World Bank, 1985.

Kaser, Michael. *Comecon: Integration Problems of the Planned Economies*. London: Oxford University Press, 1967.

———— and E. A. Radice, eds. *The Economic History of Eastern Europe 1919–1975*.

Vols. I–III. Oxford: Clarendon Press, 1986.

Kendrick, John W. "Output and Growth Rates." Paper presented at the International Forum, Economies in Transition: Statistical Measures Now and in the Future, Sochi, USSR, October 15–17, 1990.

Kenen, P. "Transitional Arrangements for Trade and Payments among the CMEA Countries." IMF Discussion paper presented at OECD-World Bank Conference on the Transition to a Market Economy in Central and Eastern Europe, Paris, November 28–30, 1990.

Kirenchenko, Vladim. "Return Credibility to Statistics." *Business Economist*, October 1991.

Kravis, I., A. Heston, and R. Summers. *International Comparisons of Real Product and Purchasing Power*. Baltimore: Johns Hopkins University Press, 1978.

————. *World Product and Income*. Baltimore: Johns Hopkins University Press, 1982.

Kravis, I., Z. Kenessey, A. Heston, A. and R. Summers. *A System of International Comparisons of Gross Product and Purchasing Power*. Baltimore: Johns Hopkins University Press, 1975.

Kushnirsky, F.I. *Growth and Inflation in the Soviet Economy*. Boulder, Colo.: Westview Press, 1989.

Marer, Paul. *Postwar Pricing and Price Patterns in Socialist Foreign Trade (1946–71)*. International Development Research Center Report 1. Bloomington: Indiana University Press, 1972.

————. *Soviet and East European Foreign Trade, 1946–1969, Statistical Compedium and Guide*. Bloomington: Indiana University Press, 1972.

————. "Toward a Solution of the Mirror Statistics Puzzle in East-West Commerce". *International Economics-Comparisons and Interdependencies*. Ed. F. Levick. Vienna: Springer-Verlag, 1978.

————. "The Political Economy of Soviet Relations with Eastern Europe." *Soviet Policy in Eastern Europe*. New Haven: Yale University Press, 1984.

———— and World Bank. *Dollar GNPs of the U.S.S.R. and Eastern Europe*. Baltimore: The Johns Hopkins University Press, 1985.

———— and Wlodzimierz Siwinski, eds. *Creditworthiness and Reform in Poland*. Bloomington: Indiana University Press, 1988.

————. "Report on Planning Conference on the Measurement and Evaluation of the Macroeconomic Performance of Selected Centrally Planned Economies and Yugoslavia." World Bank Working Paper. Washington, D.C.: World Bank, May 16–17, 1989.

———— and Andras Koves, eds. *Foreign Economic Liberalization: Transformations in Socialist and Market Economies*. Boulder: Westview Press, 1991.

———— and Salvatore Zecchini, eds. *The Transition to a Market Economy - Vol. I: The Broad Issues, Vol. II: Special Issues*. Paris: OECD, 1991.

Marrese, M., and J. Vanous. *Soviet Subsidization of CMEA Trade with Eastern Europe*. Berkeley: University of California Press, 1983.

———— and L. Wittenberg. "Implicit Trade Subsidies Within the CMEA: A Hungarian Perspective." Northwestern University.

Milanovic, Branko. *Liberalization and Entrepreneurship: Dynamics of Reform in Socialism and Capitalism*. New York: M.E. Sharpe, 1989.

Milne, Elizabeth, and others. "Mongolian People's Republic Toward a Market Economy." IMF Occasional Paper No. 79. Washington, D.C.: IMF, 1991.

Morgenstern, O. *On the Accuracy of Economic Observations*. Princeton: Princeton University Press, 1965.

National Research Council, *Estimating the Size of the Soviet Economy*, Washington, D.C. 1991.

Naya, S., and T. Morgan. "The Accuracy of International Trade Data: The Case of South-East Asian Countries." *Journal of the American Statistical Association*, Vol. 64, No. 326, June 1969, pp. 452–467.

Noren, James H. "The Soviet Economic Crisis: Another Perspective." *Soviet Economy*, January–March 1990, pp. 3–56.

Organization for Economic Co-operation and Development. *Purchasing Power Parities and Real Expenditures*. Paris, 1985.

Pathirane, L., and D.W. Blades. "Defining and Measuring the Public Sector." *Review of Income and Wealth*, September 1982, pp. 261–289.

Pitzer, John S. "The Tenability of the CIA Estimates of Soviet Economic Growth: A Comment." *Journal of Comparative Economics*, Vol. 14, No. 2, 1990, pp. 301–314.

———— and A.P. Baukol. "Recent [Soviet] GNP and Productivity Trends." *Soviet Economy*, Vol. 7, No. 1, 1991.

PlanEcon report, vol. VII, No. 37–38, October 24, 1991.

Pryor, Frederic L. *The Communist Foreign Trade System*. Cambridge: The M.I.T. Press, 1963.

Rangelova, R., and M. Rainova. "Comparability of the Gross Domestic Product in International Comparisons." *Economic Thought*, Vol. 6, 1990.

Renaud, Berrand. *Housing Reform in Socialist Economies*. Washington, D.C.: The World Bank, 1991.

Research Institute for Foreign Economic Relations. *CSFR in International Economy Quarterly*, Prague, Czechoslovakia, March 1991.

Richter, H. V. "Problems of Assessing Unrecorded Trade." *Bulletin of Indonesia Economic Studies*, Vol. 6, March 1970.

Ryan, Michael. *Contemporary Societ Society, A Statistical Handbook*. Brookfield, VT.: Aldershot, Hants, England, 1990.

Schrenk, Martin. *The CMEA System of Trade and Payments—the Legacy and the Aftermath of Its Termination*. Washington, D.C.: The World Bank, 1991.

Schonfelder, B. "Reflections on Inflationary Dynamics in Yugoslavia." *Comparative Economic Studies*, Vol. 32, No. 4, 1990, pp. 85–106.

Schroeder, Gertrude E. "'Crisis' in the Consumer Sector: A Comment." *Soviet Economy*, Vol. 4, January–March 1990, pp. 56–65.

Stankovsky, Jan. "East-West Trade 1988–90: Favourable Conditions for Further Growth (Developments in 1988 and Prospects for 1989/90)." The Vienna Institute for Comparative Economic Studies. 159. Vienna, Austria, 1989.

United Nations. *A System of National Accounts: Studies in Methods*. Series F, No. 2, Rev. 3. New York, 1968.

———. *Basic Principles of the System of Balances of the National Economy:*

Studies in Methods. Series F, No. 17. Statistical Commission and Economic Commission for Europe, New York, 1971.

———. *World Comparisons of Purchasing Power and Real Product for 1980*. Commission of the European Communities, New York, 1986.

———. "International Comparison of Gross Domestic Product in Europe." Report on the European Comparison Programme, 1985. Presented at the Conference of European Statisticians, Statistical Standards and Studies - No. 41. United Nations, New York, 1988.

———. *Statistical Survey of Recent Trends in Foreign Investment in East European Countries*. New York, 1989.

U.S. Department of Commerce, Bureau of the Census, and Statistics Canada. *The Reconciliation of U.S.—Canada Trade Statistics, 1970: A Report*.

Vanous, Jan. "How Big are the Soviet and East European Economies?" *PlanEcon Report*, Vol. 6, No. 52, 1990.

Vienna Institute for Comparative Economic Studies. *Comecon Foreign Trade Data 1985*. Westport, Conn.: Greenwood Press, 1986.

———. *Comecon Foreign Trade Data 1986*. Westport, Conn.: Greenwood Press, 1988.

———. "Comparative Analysis of Social Expenditure and its Finance: Austria, Poland and USSR." No. 125, 1990.

———. *Comecon Data* (Bi-Annual), Vienna, Austria, 1991.

Viet Nam General Statistical Office. "Statistical Data of the Socialist Republic of Viet Nam". Hanoi, 1991.

Wienert, H., and J. Slater. *East-West Technology Transfer: The Trade and Economic Aspects*. Paris: OECD, 1986.

Wiles, P. J. D. *Communist International Economics*. New York: Frederick A. Praguer, 1969.

Wolf, T. *Foreign Trade in the Centrally Planned Economy*. New York: Harwood Academic Publishers, 1988.

World Bank. "The Demise of the CMEA: Implications for Hungary." World Bank Staff Working Paper No. 9074-HU. Washington, D.C.: October 19, 1990.

———. "Lessons of Experience in the Reform of Socialist Economies in Central and Eastern Europe." Washington, D.C.: World Bank, 1991.

Yi, G. 1990. "The Price Reform and Inflation in China, 1979–1988." *Comparative Economic Studies*, Vol. 32, No. 4, 1990, pp. 20–61.

Yoon, Suk Bum. "A Trial Estimation of an Econometric Model of North Korea." *Asian Economic Journal*, March, 1989.

Zoteev, Gennadij N. "The National Product and Income in the Soviet Economic System." *Economic Journal on Eastern Europe and the USSR*, January 1991.